'I would strongly recommend this book to anyone who is interested in shipping or taking a course where shipping is an important element, for example, chartering and broking, maritime transport, exporting and importing, ship management, and international trade. Using an approach of simple analysis and pragmatism, the book provides clear explanations of the basic elements of ship operations and commercial, legal, economic, technical, managerial, logistical, and financial aspects of shipping.'

Dr Jiangang Fei, National Centre for Ports & Shipping, Australian Maritime College, University of Tasmania, Australia

'*Branch's Elements of Shipping* provides the reader with the best all-round examination of the many elements of the international shipping industry. This edition serves as a fitting tribute to Alan Branch and is an essential text for anyone with an interest in global shipping.'

David Adkins, Lecturer in International Procurement and Supply Chain Management, Plymouth Graduate School of Management, Plymouth University

'Combining the traditional with the modern is as much a challenge as illuminating operations without getting lost in the fascination of the technical detail. This is particularly true for the world of shipping! *Branch's Elements of Shipping* is an ongoing example for mastering these challenges. With its clear maritime focus it provides a very comprehensive knowledge base for relevant terms and details and it is a useful source of expertise for students and practitioners in the field.'

Günter Prockl, Associate Professor, Copenhagen Business School, Denmark

Branch's Elements of Shipping

Since it was first published in 1964, *Elements of Shipping* has become established as a market leader. Now in its ninth edition, *Branch's Elements of Shipping,* renamed in memory of Alan Branch, has been updated throughout and revised to take in the many changes that have occurred in the shipping industry in recent years, including the impact of the economic crisis, the Panama Canal expansion and new legislation. All tables and data have been brought up-to-date and many new illustrations have been added.

The book explains in a lucid, professional manner the basic elements of shipping, including operational, commercial, legal, economic, technical, managerial, logistical and financial considerations. It also explores how shipping markets behave and provides an overview of the international shipping industry and seaports. Filling a gap for the discerning reader who wishes to have a complete understanding of all the elements of the global shipping scene together with the interface with seaports, international trade and logistics, it remains essential reading for shipping executives along with students and academics with an interest in the shipping industry.

Alan E. Branch was International Business/Shipping Consultant, Examiner in Shipping, Export Practice and International Marketing and Visiting Lecturer at Cardiff University, Reading University, Plymouth University, Leicester University, London City College and the Rennes International School of Business, France.

Michael Robarts, Master Mariner, is a Member of the Institute of Chartered Shipbrokers and a Fellow of the Institute of Commercial Management (ICM) and an examiner for their Maritime Management programme.

Shipping

Also available from Routledge:

Maritime Economics Management and Marketing
Alan Branch

Global Supply Chain Management and International Logistics
Alan Branch

Books by Alan Branch:

Export Practice and Management

Maritime Economics Management and Marketing

Shipping and Air Freight Documentation for Importers and Exporters

International Purchasing and Management

Global Supply Chain Management and International Logistics

Elements of Port Operation and Management

Dictionary of Shipping International Business Trade Terms and Abbreviations

Dictionary of Commercial Terms and Abbreviations

Dictionary of English–Arabic Shipping/International Trade/Shipping Terms and Abbreviations

Dictionary of Multilingual Commercial/International Trade/Shipping Terms in English French German Spanish

Branch's Elements of Shipping

Ninth edition

Alan E. Branch and
Michael Robarts

Routledge
Taylor & Francis Group

LONDON AND NEW YORK

First published 2014
by Routledge
2 Park Square, Milton Park, Abingdon, Oxon OX14 4RN

and by Routledge
711 Third Avenue, New York, NY 10017

Routledge is an imprint of the Taylor & Francis Group, an informa business

© 2014 Alan E. Branch and Michael Robarts

The right of Alan E. Branch and Michael Robarts to be identified as
author of this work has been asserted by him in accordance with the
Copyright, Designs and Patent Act 1988.

All rights reserved. No part of this book may be reprinted or
reproduced or utilised in any form or by any electronic, mechanical,
or other means, now known or hereafter invented, including
photocopying and recording, or in any information storage or retrieval
system, without permission in writing from the publishers.

Trademark notice: Product or corporate names may be trademarks or
registered trademarks, and are used only for identification and
explanation without intent to infringe.

British Library Cataloguing in Publication Data
A catalogue record for this book is available from the British Library

Library of Congress Cataloging in Publication Data
Branch, Alan E.
  [Elements of shipping]
  Branch's elements of shipping/Alan E. Branch and Michael Robarts.
  – 9th edition.
  pages cm
  1. Shipping. I. Robarts, Michael. II. Title.
  HE571.B67 2014
  387.5′44--dc23
  2014012184

ISBN: 978-1-138-78667-7 (hbk)
ISBN: 978-1-138-78668-4 (pbk)
ISBN: 978-1-315-76715-4 (ebk)

Typeset in Times New Roman
by Florence Production Ltd, Stoodleigh, Devon, UK

Printed and bound by CPI Group (UK) Ltd, Croydon, CR0 4YY

To my wife Kerry Elisabeth

Contents

Figures

Tables

Preface to the ninth edition

Alan Branch first published *Elements of Shipping* in 1964, since when it has become a market leader. As an established international business and shipping consultant who published many books on shipping and logistics practices, he dedicated a career of over fifty years to shipping. His research and publications have proved of immense benefit to maritime students. For his rich contribution to the development of marine studies, through lecturing and training, with a focus on the complexities of shipping, in 1997 he received a Worldaware Business Award – part of the United Nations Organization. At his death in 2009 Alan Branch had an unrivalled reputation among those involved in the maritime industry. He has left this book as an invaluable legacy, which widens general understanding of shipping. Acknowledgement of the debt to Alan Branch includes thanks to his wife Kathleen and daughter Anna, who kindly permitted this revision.

Michael Robarts, Master Mariner and Member of the Institute of Chartered Shipbrokers by examination, has served as a deck officer on VLCC, Product and Gas tankers in foreign trades. In his seagoing career he has been a member of a new-build team standing by and commissioning a number of new passenger and ro/ro vessels. He has worked on the busy European trade, and has served as Master on tugs and dredgers. He is now a Marine Pilot at a major UK port, continues to research and act as a consultant in shipping, and is an examiner for a maritime postgraduate diploma programme. He is a Freeman of the Honourable Company of Master Mariners.

This ninth edition is a light revision. It contains the same divisions as in the first edition, namely, sections on new ship design, amendments to the IMO conventions, ship productivity, (third party) ship management, seaport privatization, documentation, customs, logistics, e-commerce, changing patterns of world trade/ship ownership, containerization, multi-modalism, INCO terms 2010, chartering, dangerous cargo, ships agents, international agencies, freight rates, cruises and ship operation. Some updating has entailed minimal enlarging of chapters, so that this revision preserves much of Branch's simple analysis and pragmatism apparent in his approach to the subject. No material has been reorganized, though this ninth revision incorporates views of future trends, supplementing Branch's narrative with numerous tables, diagrams and case studies. For example, new emphasis is given to the economic trends since the early 2000s and the requisite knowledge for understanding the place of the latest technology and professions operating shipping.

Branch's Elements of Shipping is designed to show in simple terms how the maritime industry in recent years has adapted to a fast-changing, complex maritime environment reacting to global recession. The nature of shipping has always changed to meet economic and technological challenges, and this book analyses many of these changes in shipping operations from the experience both of original author and of reviser. The authors show how, in reacting to the international economic crisis, shipping, with its high-tech management and operations, maintains a high profile in global business. Trade grows in Asian countries, a region now owning a high proportion of world tonnage. Asian countries now account for about half of ships' crews, two-thirds of global port operators, 83% of container ship building, and 99% of demolition or recycling. Twenty-eight of the world's fifty largest liner companies are based in Asia. Over 70% of the top twenty container seaports are based in the Asian region. Shipping has become more competitive and is much more complex. Consequently, all concerned in shipping need comprehensive understanding of the conduct and mechanisms of the maritime industry, which conveys over 99% of world trade, in volume terms.

The readership of *Branch's Elements of Shipping* includes students, professionals in shipping and maritime entrepreneurs. Students in over two hundred countries will be assisted in their studies by the book's clear explanations of the basic elements of ship operations, e-commerce (shipboard/ trade), commercial, legal, economic, technical, managerial, logistics and financial considerations. This book explains details of operational procedures while at the same time offering general information within a broad maritime context about many aspects of global shipping and seaports. For students revising for examinations or researching it provides examples of how shipping markets have behaved in the past and a basic understanding and knowledge of the international shipping industry. It emphasizes salient economic, political, commercial, operating, management, logistic and e-commerce/computerized applications of the subject. Full cognizance is taken throughout the book of the e-commerce and logistic environment and of strategies that respond to events by being effective and which add value at all times.

Branch's Elements of Shipping is suitable for students taking shipping, international trade, shipbroking, maritime transport, international distribution, export, import, chartering, ship management, transport, seaports, logistics, containerization and international management examinations and research or training courses/seminars at degree/diploma level at universities and colleges. Such colleges and universities are situated not only in the UK but also in Hong Kong, Malaysia, Singapore, Scandinavia, China, India, the United

States, Sri Lanka, South Africa, Pakistan, Jamaica, Jordan, Malta, Cyprus, Dubai, Brazil, Australia, New Zealand, Canada, the Middle East, Europe, the Pacific Rim nations and many less developed countries. The book is popular with undergraduates taking Maritime Transport, International Logistics, International Physical Distribution, International Marketing and International Business courses. *Branch's Elements of Shipping* has been popular with a wide range of professional institutes, embracing the Chartered Institute of Logistics and Transport, Institute of Commercial Management, British International Freight Association, Institute of Chartered Shipbrokers, Institute of Export, Institute of Marine Engineers, and the Institute of Purchasing and Supply.

Branch's Elements of Shipping is also intended to be relevant to those working in shipping, ports, agencies, shipbrokers' offices and its general maritime information should prove useful to colleges and universities throughout the world. It includes information and guidance from many international agencies and shipping, port authorities, and companies around the world, reflecting good practice and current and future developments. This outside expertise enhances the book's utility by enabling readers to understand world cultures and industrial and political strategies better. The scope of such contributions is exemplified in the increasing number of organizations helping each new edition, as acknowledged in the main text. Many colleges and universities have also shown interest in this book.

Readers who want to know more about export or import practice should consult companion volumes by Alan Branch: *Export Practice and Management* (fifth edition, 2006) and *International Purchasing and Management* (2000); for more about ship management, marketing, and logistics, *Maritime Economics: Management and Marketing* (third edition, 1997; fourth edition 2010); for logistics *Global Supply Chain Management and International Logistics* (forthcoming); and for documentation, *Shipping and Air Freight Documentation for Importers and Exporters* (second edition, 2000). Students of shipping should also consult the *Dictionary of Shipping International Business Trade Terms and Abbreviations*, published in 2005. As with any textbook, *Branch's Elements of Shipping* cannot provide specialized information for those seeking commercial, technical or historical detail. Those investigating in depth are advised to consult technical manuals or professional brokers.

Updating all aspects covered in the book would have entailed re-writing the whole text. Since this would not be a light revision not all statistics come from the past year or so. Current regulations, however, are covered. Between 1965 and 2005 world seaborne trade increased by over 450%, from 6,000 to 28,000 billion ton miles. Change has since been fast moving and is being driven by many factors. The years 2000 to 2010 saw shipping expand more than at any time during the previous hundred years. But 2009 brought a global recession on a scale not seen since the 1940s, presenting shipping with new challenges. Global shipping and trade are inextricably linked, and recession brought low freight rates, high fuel prices and a new focus on ship productivity, particularly its interface with other transport modes: overland, inland waterways and air.

Branch's Elements of Shipping deals with economic, political, commercial, logistics, operating, information technology, finance and legal aspects of shipping. It continues to feature multi-modalism, logistics and containerization, role of e-commerce, Bolero, development of logistics, growth of globalization, updates of the IMO regulations, changes in ship design, survey methods and cargo vessels, chartering documents and the role of shipbrokers, the Baltic Exchange, increasing role of BIMCO, Intertanko and other international agencies, structure of shipping companies, third party ship management and changing role of politics. It also focuses on current challenges facing the industry. The content also considers the broader picture of factors driving its development. This embraces trading blocs, the WTO and EU. Overall, it features a strategic role.

Branch's Elements of Shipping is well placed to provide background information and knowledge for those students studying courses in maritime management. In the writing of his book Alan Branch involved overseas governments and multinational industries, and infused his writing with knowledge gleaned from many conferences and seminars at which he contributed papers on several maritime subjects. This edition preserves his viewpoint that shipping today is a complex operation, to understand which requires greater knowledge of how the business can be conducted efficiently and profitably. The 'value added benefit' concept remains important, whereby the shipper chooses the maritime service that yields the highest benefit both to exporter and to importer.

The main abbreviations readers will find are IT (information technology), UK (United Kingdom of Great Britain and Northern Ireland), US (the United States of America), and the EU (European Union). All industry-specific terms are explained in the text.

Michael Robarts
Colchester, 2014

Acknowledgements

The author wishes to acknowledge the generous assistance provided by the following companies and institutions:

Alfsen og Gunderson AS
Baltic and International Maritime Council
Baltic Exchange
Bolero Net
British Columbia Ferry Service Inc.
British Shipbuilders Ltd
Bureau Veritas
Chamber of Shipping Club
Clarkson's
Club Méditerranée
Containerization International
COSCO
Denholm Ship Management (Holdings) Ltd
Drewry
Eidesvik Offshore ASA
Exportmaster Ltd
Freight Transport Association
GE Seale Services Ltd
Hanjen Shipping Intercargo
International Association of Classification Societies Ltd
International Association of Independent Tanker Owners
International Cargo Handling Co-ordination Association
International Chamber of Commerce
International Chamber Shipping
International Federation of Freight Forwarders Association
International Maritime Organization
International Maritime Satellite Organization
International Organization for Standardization
International Petroleum Exchange
International Ship Managers Association

International Maritime Industries Forum
International Maritime Pilots Association
International Shipping Federation
International Tanker Owners Pollution Federation Ltd
Intertanko
Kiel Canal
Linde Material Handlling (UK) Ltd
Lloyd's Register of Shipping
LRQA
MacGregor (SWE) AB
Malta Maritime Authority
Maersk Line (A P Møller)
Maritime and Coastguard Agency
MAT Shipping
Multiport Ship Agencies Ltd
Nautical Institute
Norwegian International Ship Register
Norwegian Shipowners' Association
OECD
Oil Companies International Marine Forum
Organization of Petroleum Exporting Countries
Panama Canal Commission
Passenger Shipping Association
Peninsular & Oriental Steam Navigation Company
P&O Ferries
P&O NedLloyd
Port of Rotterdam Authority
SITPRO
St Lawrence Seaway Management Corporation
Suez Canal Authority
United Nations Conference on Trade and Development (UNCTAD)
V Ships
Worldscale
WTO

1 Introduction

1.1 Function of shipping

The function of shipping is the conveyance of goods from where their utility is low to a place where it is higher. Goods may consist of raw materials conveyed in bulk cargo shipments or purpose-built containers, equipment components or parts for assembly at an industrial plant or on-site capital project, like a power station, or the whole range of consumer products, many of which are durable and may be shipped in containers, on swap bodies or by an international trucking operation. A growth area in recent years is outsourcing. This involves manufacturers relocating their industrial plant from a high labour cost economy, such as Germany or the UK, to a low labour cost environment as found in many Far East countries. Components are sourced locally or from neighbouring countries to the industrial assembly plant. Subsequently the products are marketed locally to the major trading centres, such as Europe and North America. Outsourcing is logistically driven and relies primarily on containerized shipment. It exemplifies how shipping is contributing to the growing volume of international trade, the relocation of industry from the developed to the developing economies, as well as to the changing pattern of international trade.

The factors influencing the shipper's choice of transport mode has changed dramatically since the 1980s. Today it is based on the total product concept embracing all the constituents of distribution logistically driven. These include reliability, frequency, cost, transit time, capital tied up in transport, quality of service, packaging, import duty, insurance, and so on. It favours more strongly multi-modalism, with sea transport undertaking the major leg of the overall transit. Logistics, just-in-time delivery, supply chain management and distribution centres or 'distriparks' play a major role in decision-making. All these aspects will be re-examined later as the basis of how the shipowner can best meet the needs of the shipper in the foreseeable future. The paramount consideration is for the shipowner to empathize with the shipper and strive to become flexible and responsive to the shipper's needs on an innovative value-added basis in a competitive logistic global environment. The freight rate is not the only paramount factor, it is the value-added benefit the shipper gains from the service, which is usually a combined transport operation of road, sea and rail.

1.2 **World seaborne trade and world fleet**

(a) World seaborne trade (Tables 1.1 and 1.2) during 1990–2010 expanded at an average of 6.5% each year. This figure was reached despite shipping and many other industries during 2008 and 2009 experiencing global recession. For example, during this period oil trade productivity was down 7.7% and in the dry sectors down 10%. These weaker figures reflected the downturn in overall global wealth and demand. Bucking this downward trend, the dry bulk sector continued to expand, though at a reduced rate of 1.8%. Overall the downturn in world seaborne trade was 6%. Yet in 2010 world seaborne trade expanded to reach a peak of 40,891 billion ton-miles, including a strong increase of 10.7% between 2009 and 2010. The average transport distance also increased, thereby improving ship productivity. Demand for haulage of crude oil and oil products at this time rose by 5.7%. This figure indicates crude oils being moved longer distances – for example, moving from wells in North and West Africa, Barents, Baltic and Black seas to destinations in Europe and North America.

All five main dry bulk cargoes' ton-miles increased by 12.4%, mainly because of rising and continued Chinese industrial demand. The remaining dry cargoes of minor bulks and extended liner cargo supply lines increased by 12.3%. These signs of greater activity can be attributed to demand by developed countries for merchandise, to the lasting effect of relocated industries in the Far East, and to the longer distances between cargo origins and destinations. However, predictions show a slowing of growth, and figures available for 2010–11 estimate a rise at only 4.7%, while 4.1% is predicted for 2011–12.

(b) International seaborne trade (Table 1.3) rose by 7% to 8.4 billion tons of loaded goods in 2010. In 2011 the total of loaded goods is estimated to be 8.74 billion tons, and the growth rate is likely to slacken in subsequent

Table 1.1 World seaborne trade, selected years (billions of ton miles)

Year	Crude	Oil Pro-ducts	Crude plus pro-ducts	Iron ore	Coal	Grain[a]	Five main dry bulks	Other dry cargoes	World total
1970	5,597	890	6,487	1,093	481	475	2,049	2,118	10,654
1975	8,882	845	9,727	1,471	621	734	2,826	2,810	15,363
1980	8,385	1,020	9,405	1,613	952	1,087	3,652	3,720	16,777
1985	4,007	1,150	5,157	1,675	1,479	1,004	4,480	3,428	13,065
1990	6,261	1,560	7,821	1,978	1,849	1,073	5,259	4,041	17,121

Source: Fearnleys, *Review 2004*.

Note: [a] Includes wheat, maize, barley, oats, rye, sorghum and soya beans.

Reproduced with the kind permission of UNCTAD Secretariat.

Table 1.2 World seaborne trade, 1999–2012

Year	Crude	Products	Oil trade	LPG	LNG	Gas trade	Iron ore	Coal	Grain[a]	Five main dry bulks[b]	Other dry cargoes	All cargoes
1999	7,761	1,488	9,249	188	267	456	2,338	2,196	1,122	6,046	11,191	26,942
2000	8,014	1,487	9,500	199	317	516	2,620	2,420	1,224	6,649	12,058	28,723
2001	7,778	1,598	9,376	182	341	523	2,698	2,564	1,293	6,922	12,347	29,168
2002	7,553	1,594	9,146	192	360	552	2,956	2,577	1,295	7,212	12,587	29,497
2003	8,025	1,697	9,723	187	399	586	3,148	2,771	1,382	7,710	13,072	31,091
2004	8,550	1,836	10,386	192	429	621	3,667	2,901	1,397	8,424	13,975	33,407
2005	8,643	2,057	10,701	187	444	631	3,900	2,984	1,459	8,819	14,570	34,720
2006	8,875	2,192	11,067	195	537	732	4,413	3,103	1,496	9,508	15,759	37,065
2007	8,836	2,223	11,060	198	614	812	4,773	3,177	1,610	10,090	16,390	38,351
2008	8,965	2,277	11,241	205	660	865	5,000	3,260	1,721	10,523	16,646	39,276
2009	8,138	2,233	10,371	193	668	862	5,569	3,060	1,693	10,715	14,988	36,936
2010	8,688	2,272	10,960	198	861	1,059	6,121	3,540	1,948	12,042	16,829	40,891
2011[c]	8,762	2,351	11,112	201	955	1,155	6,608	3,664	1,920	12,666	17,861	42,794
2012[d]	8,918	2,449	11,367	213	1,065	1,278	6,948	3,763	1,940	13,141	18,754	44,540

Source: Based on data from Clarkson Research Services' *Shipping Review & Outlook*, Spring 2012. Reproduced with the kind permission of UNCTAD Secretariat.

Notes: [a] Includes soybean. [b] Includes iron ore, coal, grain bauxite/alumina and rock phosphate. [c] Estimated. [d] Forecast.

years owing to the slow-down in the Far East economies, especially in China. This decline can be illustrated by tanker shipments of oil and gas, which rose in 2010 by 4.9% to 2.7 billion tons, whereas estimates of growth in 2011 are for only 0.9%. In 2011 it was estimated that Africa's share of world exports was 9%, America's 23%, Asia's 39%, Europe's 18% and Oceania's by 11%. In 2004 the main producers of oil and gas were the Russian Federation at 578.6 bcm, United States 549.5 bcm, Canada 180.5 bcm, UK 102.7 bcm, Algeria 82.8 bcm, Iran 70 bcm and Indonesia 72.6 bcm. Other producers are located in the Middle East, Latin America and Asia – often obtaining natural gas as a result of oil production. About 20% of natural gas is exported, mainly by pipelines, which carry 75% of all exports. Many LNG tankers are now in the range of 150,000 m³ instead of the traditional 125,000 m³. Designs for a new type of vessel, the compressed natural gas carrier (CNG), were under inspection in North America and Norway. This carrier would provide a cost-effective solution for supplying gas from remote locations too small to warrant full-scale LNG projects. Oil pipeline construction continues in many oil-producing countries. An example is the 1,770 km pipeline from Baku (Azerbaijan) to Ceyhan (Turkey) on the Mediterranean Sea, which reduces the transit of tankers through the Dardanelles Straits.

In 2011 dry cargo shipments recorded an increase of 5.6% to reach 5.95 billion tons. The five dry bulk trades of iron ore, coal, grains, bauxite/

Table 1.3 Development in international seaborne trade, selected years (millions of tons loaded)

Year	Oil and gas	Main bulks[a]	Other dry cargo	Total (all cargoes)
1970	1,440	448	717	2,605
1980	1,871	608	1,225	3,704
1990	1,755	988	1,265	4,008
2000	2,163	1,295	2,526	5,984
2005	2,422	1,709	2,978	7,109
2006	2,698	1,814	3,188	7,700
2007	2,747	1,953	3,334	8,034
2008	2,742	2,065	3,422	8,229
2009	2,642	2,085	3,131	7,858
2010	2,772	2,335	3,302	8,409
2011	2,796	2,477	3,475	8,748

Sources: Compiled by the UNCTAD secretariat on the basis of data supplied by reporting countries and as published on the relevant government and port industry website, and by specialist sources. The data for 2006 onwards have been revised and upated to reflect improved reporting, including more recent figures and better information regarding the breakdown by cargo type. Figures for 2011 are estimated based on preliminary data or on the last year for which data were available.

Note: [a] Iron ore, grain, coal, bauxite/alumina and phosphate. The data for 2006 onwards are based on various issues of the Dry Bulk Trade Outlook, produced by Clarkson Research Services.

Reproduced with the kind permission of UNCTAD Secretariat.

alumina and rock phosphate attained an increase of 6.1% and reached 2.4 billion tons. The remaining dry cargo trades, minor bulks and liner cargoes, increased at a rate of 5.2% to 3.4 billion tons. The share of dry cargo shipments in world seaborne trade was 68% of total goods loaded during the year.

As an example, dry cargo shipments in 2004 of world crude steel production rose by 8.8% to 1,054.6 million tons, world pig iron production rose by 10.8% to 753.9 million, steel consumption rose by 6.1% to 918 million tons, iron ore shipments reflecting steel production rose by 12.6% to 590 million tons, with Australia and Brazil accounting for 70% of world exports; coal shipments rose by 5% to a record of 650 million tons, with thermal coal representing 70% of shipments; grain shipments rose by 4.2% to 250 million tons, split equally between wheat and coarse grain, such as maize, barley, soya beans, sorghum, oats and rye; and shipments of bauxite and alumina – primary inputs for the aluminium industry – rose by 6.3% to 67 million tons. Containerized shipments totalled 1.94 million tons, embracing the east–west (trans-Pacific, Europe–Far East and Transatlantic), north–south and regional routes.

(c) Referring to Table 1.4, world output grew steadily from 2001 to 2008. But in 2009 the global economy experienced a deep recession, though world economic growth revived slowly in 2010. In 2011 growth was recorded at 2.7%. Overall, this figure reflects the fact that virtually all regions of the world recorded some positive economic growth at differing paces. Some countries such as Japan, the United Kingdom and France continued to experience contraction. Tables 1.1, 1.2 and 1.3 give an analysis of the impact of this world growth in the maritime industry, particularly in developing countries. Future growth depends on many factors, especially inflationary oil prices and trade deficits in major developed economies, which long-term are unlikely to be sustainable.

(d) Analysis of the structure of the world fleet (Table 1.5) indicates that it reached 1,534 million deadweight tons (dwt) on 1 January 2012, showing an increase of 9.9% over 2011. Ship-building (Table 1.6) deliveries represented 101.4 million dwt, while 26.5 million dwt were broken up and lost, resulting in a nett gain of 74.9 million dwt over 2011. Oil tanker tonnage in 2011 and 2012 rose by 6.9% and that of bulk carriers by 17%. These two types of ships represented 73.7% of total world tonnage. The world fleet of fully cellular container ships continued to expand substantially in 2011, both in number of ships and in TEU capacity. In January 2012 the total number of container ships was 5,012, with a total capacity of 15,406,610 TEU – an increase of 2.6% in ships and 9.4% in TEU capacity. Average carrying capacity per ship is 3,074. The size of fully cellular container ships continues to increase and reports indicate that the average size of container ship ordered in 2011 will be over 30% larger than ships ordered in the previous year.

Table 1.4 World economic growth, 1991–2012[a] (annual % change)

Region/country	1991–2004 average[a]	2008	2009	2010	2011	2012[b]
WORLD	2.9	1.5	−2.3	4.1	2.7	2.3
Developed economies	2.6	0.0	−3.9	2.8	1.4	1.1
of which:						
United States	3.4	−0.4	−3.5	3.0	1.7	2.0
Japan	1.0	−1.0	−5.5	4.4	−0.7	2.2
European Union (27)	2.3	0.3	−4.4	2.1	1.5	−0.3
of which:						
Germany	1.5	1.1	−5.1	3.7	3.0	0.9
France	2.0	−0.1	−3.1	1.7	1.7	0.3
Italy	1.6	−1.2	−5.5	1.8	0.4	−1.9
United Kingdom	3.1	−1.1	−4.4	2.1	0.7	−0.6
Developing economies	4.7	5.3	2.4	7.5	5.9	4.9
of which:						
Africa	3.2	4.8	0.9	4.5	2.5	4.1
South Africa	2.5	3.6	−1.7	2.8	3.1	2.7
Asia	5.9	5.9	4.1	8.4	6.8	5.5
Association of Southeast Asian Nations	4.9	4.0	1.3	8.0	4.5	4.9
China	9.9	9.6	9.2	10.4	9.2	7.9
India	5.9	7.5	7.0	9.0	7.0	6.0
Republic of Korea	5.0	2.3	0.3	6.2	3.6	3.3
Latin America and the Caribbean	2.7	4.0	−2.0	6.0	4.3	3.4
Brazil	2.6	5.2	−0.3	7.5	2.7	2.0
Least Developed Countries (LDCs)	5.2	7.7	5.0	5.8	4.0	4.1
Transition economies	..	5.2	−6.5	4.2	4.5	4.3
of which:						
Russian Federation	..	5.2	−7.8	4.0	4.3	4.7

Source: UNCTAD *Trade and Development Report, 2012*, table 1.1. World Output Growth, 2004–2012.

Notes: [a] Average % change. [b] Forecasts.

Reproduced with the kind permission of UNCTAD Secretariat.

Table 1.5 World fleet by principal vessel types, 2011–12ᵃ (beginning-of-year figures, thousands of dwt)

% change *Principal types*	*2011*	*2012*	*2012/11*
Oil tankers	474,846	507,454	6.9
	34.0	*33.1*	*–0.9*
Bulk carriers	532,039	622,536	17.0
	38.1	*40.6*	*2.5*
General cargo ships	108,971	106,385	–2.4
	7.8	*6.9*	*–0.9*
Container ships	183,859	198,002	7.7
	13.2	*12.9*	*–0.3*
Other types of ships	96,028	99,642	3.8
	6.9	*6.5*	*–0.4*
Liquefied gas carriers	43,339	44,622	3.0
	3.1	*2.9*	*–0.2*
Offshore supply	33,227	37,468	12.8
	2.4	*2.4*	*0.1*
Ferries and passenger ships	6,164	6,224	1.0
	0.4	*0.4*	*0.0*
Other/ n.a.	13,299	11,328	–14.8
	1.0	*0.7*	*–0.2*
World total	1,395,743	1,534,019	9.9
	100.0	*100.0*	

Source: Compiled by the UNCTAD secretariat, on the basis of data supplied by *IHS Fairplay*.

Note: ᵃ Seagoing propelled merchant ships of 100 GT and above; % shares are shown in italics.

1.3 Challenges facing the shipping industry in the twenty-first century

This section focuses on the major challenges facing the shipping industry. It allows readers to reconcile them with their knowledge of current practice, and makes it possible to identify future trends:

(a) The growing development of a global logistic environment, thereby moving away from the port-to-port operation to the combined transport supply chain embracing road/sea/road, rail/sea/rail, rail/sea/canal.
(b) The continuing liberalization of trade through the GATT/WTO global agreements, thereby providing more trading opportunities.
(c) The changing political scene through the emerging markets' influence in global trade negotiations.
(d) The growth of the Chinese, Indian and Brazilian economies, especially the former, and the extensive programme in China of infrastructure

Table 1.6 World fleet new buildings and demolitions

Deliveries of new buildings, major vessel types and countries where built (2011, thousands of GT)

	China	Korea, Republic of	Japan	Philippines	Rest of world	World total
Tankers	7,613	11,370	4,764	–	617	24,365
Bulk carriers	26,719	11,678	11,656	1,658	1,290	53,001
Container and other passenger	4,291	11,794	2,921	3	2,418	21,427
Offshore and other work vessels	986	1,008	26	0	1,032	3,052
Total	**39,609**	**35,850**	**19,367**	**1,661**	**5,357**	**101,845**

Source Compiled by the UNCTAD secretariat, on the basis of data from *IHS Fairplay.*

Tonnage reported sold for demolition, major vessel types and country of demolition (2011, thousands of GT)

	India	China	Bangladesh	Pakistan	Turkey	Rest of world	World total
Tankers	1,811	610	830	1,485	98	157	4,992
Bulk carriers	3,215	4,367	4,527	1,240	205	114	13,668
Container and other passenger	3,370	1,318	464	176	830	353	6,511
Offshore and other work vessels	366	59	136	548	18	260	1,388
Total	**8,762**	**6,354**	**5,957**	**3,449**	**1,152**	**884**	**26,558**

Source: Compiled by the UNCTAD secretariat, on the basis of data from *IHS Fairplay.*

Reproduced with the kind permission of the UNCTAD Secretariat.

development, especially container ports. India is likewise developing its container ports.

(e) The changing trade flow emerging from the Far East as consumer/ industrial plant is relocated, with Europe and North America the prime consumers. This is the result of outsourcing manufacturing and consumer industries from the developed economies of Europe and North America to developing countries of the Far East, many involving joint ventures.

(f) The growing importance of energy as the vehicle for consumer/industrial demand expansion, especially oil and gas. Gas will grow at double the rate of oil.

(g) The need to improve ship productivity. This is being realized through third party ship management; development of the hub and spoke system, especially through containerization; port modernization and/or privatization; the tendency to build larger vessels such as in container vessels and cruise tonnage; auto carriers and LNG carriers to exploit economies of scale; continuous improvement in ship management; development of longer voyages; continuing improvement in marine engineering, especially in propulsion, shipboard management and longer voyages. Fleet planning and computer technology play a major role in improving ship productivity.

(h) The continuing expansion and increasing influence of economic blocs and customs unions in opening up markets and trading opportunities.

(i) A key factor is for the shipowner to develop strategies to continuously 'add value' to the shipping service provided. This embraces the total product, including all the ingredients featuring ancillary activities. It is driven by the shipper, and a synergy must be developed between the shipper and shipowner in a market research-driven environment.

(j) The changing pattern of the world's mercantile fleet, embracing type of tonnage, the diminishing age of many sectors, and ownership. The trade expansion in the Far East has caused ship ownership to move from Europe to the Far East, a trend which continues, especially in China.

(k) Another key factor is for the shipowner and port operators to adopt strategies which are innovative and flexible in responding to the changing market environment and the challenges it offers.

2   The ship

2.1 Main features of hull and machinery

There are two main parts to a ship: the hull and the machinery. The hull is the actual shell of the ship and includes the superstructure, while the machinery includes not only the engines required to drive it but also the ancillary equipment serving the electrical installations, winches and refrigerated accommodation.

The hull is the shell of the ship and is usually designed for a particular trade in accordance with a shipowner's specification. A vessel is constructed of a series of transverse frames, which extend from the fore to aft of the vessel, rising at right angles to the keel. These frames form the ribs of the ship. Statutory regulations exist regarding the distance between each frame. Each vessel, depending on its classification – passenger, container, tanker, or bulk carrier – must have a number of bulkheads, which are steel walls isolating various parts of the vessel. These are necessary in the interests of containing a fire or flooding following a collision. Ocean-going vessels must have at the fore end a collision bulkhead installed at a distance of not less than 5% of the ship's length from its bow. The obligatory after-peak bulkhead function is to seal off the stern tubes through which runs the tailshaft driving the propeller.

The rear portion of the ship is termed the after end or stern. When moving stern first, the vessel is said to be moving astern. The front portion of the ship is termed the fore end, whilst the extreme forward end is called the bows. When moving bow first, the vessel is said to be moving ahead. Fore and aft are generally used for directional purposes. The area between the forward and aft portions of the vessel is called amidships. The maximum breadth of the vessel, which is found in the amidships body, is known as the beam. The draft of the ship is measured from the waterline to the keel, i.e. using the draft marks found at the fore and aft ends and midships of the ship. The draft is used to calculate how much cargo the ship has loaded and in navigation to calculate the underkeel clearance. The airdraft of the ship in the building dimensions is measured from the keel of the vessel to the uppermost point of the vessel, commonly the mast (or aerials). When used in calculations for voyages it is measured from the waterline to the uppermost point of the vessel.

The engine room houses the machinery required to drive the vessel as well as the generators required for lighting, refrigeration and other auxiliary loads. Engines are usually situated aft, thus releasing the amidships space – at the broadest part of the vessel – for cargo and passenger accommodation. Today a new era of the electric ship is being developed. The ship's funnel, painted in the shipping line colours, is situated above the engine room. In modern passenger liners, this is to keep fumes and smuts clear of the passenger accommodation. The propeller shaft, linking the propeller with the engines, passes through a shaft tunnel and is usually a single controllable or fixed pitch specification. The ship's anchors and the windlasses used to lower and raise them are found in the bow section. On a large ship additional anchors might also be provided. All tankers and bulk carriers are constructed to a double hull formation and carry emergency towing arrangements.

Modern tonnage, particularly tankers, container ships and passenger liners, have transverse propulsion units in the bows, and these are termed bow thrusters. A number of vessels have side thrusters situated at the stern of the ship. Both bow and side thrusters are situated on the port and starboard sides. Their purpose is to give greater manoeuvrability in confined waters, e.g. ports, to reduce or eliminate the need for tugs. The rudder which enables the vessel to maintain its course is situated aft. Some ships have an additional rudder in the bows for easier manoeuvrability in port and these are generally found on ferries. A modern development is the Azipull or Azipod propulsion system. Stabilizers are in appearance similar to the fins of a fish, and are fitted to modern passenger liners and container ships to reduce rolling in heavy seas. They are fitted in pairs, and when in use protrude at right angles from the hull, deep below the water line. Their number depends on the size of the vessel. The provision of a bulbous bow can also improve passenger comfort, as it can reduce pitching in heavy seas and has also been provided in tankers, bulk carriers and modern cargo liners to increase speed when in ballast.

The modern tendency is to have large unobstructed holds with electrically or hydraulic-operated hatch covers, for the speedy handling of cargo, and to reduce turn-round time to a minimum.

A ship's design and its number of decks will depend on the trade in which it plies. A vessel comprises various decks, with the upper-most decks being called the navigational, boat and promenade decks. A continuous deck in a ship would run throughout the length of the vessel from fore to aft.

The transverse bulkheads run from the tank tops or floors of the hold to the deck. The longitudinal framing consists of steel sections running the length of the ship into which are fixed the skin plates forming the hull. Nowadays, with the development of the welded construction, vessels are constructed on the combined system, which uses the longitudinal system in the double bottom, and at deck level uses transverse framing for the sides. Basically the combined system is better for welded construction.

Scantlings are the dimensions of the structural parts of the ship which embrace size of frames, beams, steel plating, bulkheads and decks. A vessel built to the full scantlings would have the maximum draught when the freeboard measured from the loadline to the deckline (the upper side of the continuous main deck or freeboard deck which is equipped with permanent means of closing all openings to the elements) is at its minimum.

Single-deck vessels fall within this category, such as an ore carrier which needs the strongest type of ship construction to convey such heavy deadweight cargoes requiring low stowage factors. Such vessels are built to the highest specification of the classification societies, such as Lloyd's Register of Shipping, American Bureau of Shipping, Bureau Veritas, etc., as regards strength of the component parts of the structure.

To give access to cargo holds, openings are cut into the deck of the vessel and are termed hatchways and are surrounded by coamings, which are like steel walls rising from the deck. The height of these coamings is regulated by statute or classification society regulations.

Each mercantile type vessel has a certain number of various types of tanks for a variety of purposes and the following are the more salient ones:

(a) The fore peak tank is situated in the bows of the vessel between the bows and the collision bulkhead.
(b) Conversely the aft peak tank is situated in the stern of the vessel. It forms the aftermost watertight bulkhead.
(c) The wing tank is located at the side of the holds designed for carrying water ballast. These are found particularly in specialized bulk carriers.
(d) The deep tanks are situated one in each of the holds at the two ends of the ship. Such tanks are used for carrying water ballast and can be used to carry dry cargo. In modern vessels they are constructed to convey oil, either as bunkers, or wood or palm oil.

A tramp, carrying shipments of coal or ore, will be a single-deck vessel with large unobstructed hatches to facilitate loading and discharge. Smaller vessels of this type employed on the coastal trade are sometimes fitted with moveable bulkheads to allow cargo segregation.

The handling of cargo will be mechanized as far as possible with the use of conveyor belts, pallets and containers. The holds of a modern cargo liner are designed to facilitate dealing with such modern methods of cargo handling. Cargo ships used to be fitted with derricks, but modern ships' cranes electrically operated have replaced these. Their lifting capacity can vary from 3 to 50 tons. If heavy items such as locomotives or boilers are commonly carried, jumbo derricks capable of lifting up to 120 tons are provided (see Figure 4.5). The decks are strengthened to accommodate such heavy lift cargoes. A modern vessel called a Combi carrier (see Figure 4.5) has superseded the 'tween-deck tonnage in trades unable to invest in container tonnage and its infrastructure of port facilities and distribution overland network.

The bridge of a vessel is the navigating centre of the ship where its course is determined. The bridge is in direct communication with all parts of the vessel. Most modern tonnage today has the navigating bridge and machinery situated aft thereby facilitating maximum cargo capacity. However, the accommodation and navigation bridge on some modern large container ships have been moved further forward to make room for more containers on deck. The engines are bridge controlled and the navigating officer on watch makes use of a bridge computer to steer the vessel, to work out its course, and give position reports, etc. In an era of high technology it is mandatory for all vessels to have Global Navigation Satellite system (GNSS) receivers, Automatic Identification System (AIS) transponders, voyage data recorders (VDRs) and operational Electronic Chart Display Information Systems (ECDIS). It is also mandatory under the ISPS code for a continuous synopsis record to be provided on board of the history of the ship, together with a ship security alert system. In regard to radio communication, as from February 1999 the SOLAS Chapter IV 1974 was revised in 1988 to embrace amendments to introduce the GMDSS, which became operative from February 1999. A key obligation was for all passenger and cargo ships of 300 gross tonnage and upwards on international voyages to carry equipment designed to improve chances of rescue following an accident, including satellite emergency position indicating radio beacons (EPIRBs) and search and rescue transponders (SARTs) for the location of the ship or survival craft.

Many vessels today, to plan and monitor their voyages, have an Integrated Bridge System (IBS)/Integrated Navigational System (INS) and an Electronic Chart Display Information System (ECDIS). The system is distinct from a manual updating, because it is electronic and suppliers are able to offer a real time updating service that embraces official ENC via Internet or e-mail.

Crew accommodation on modern cargo ships and tankers is situated aft in close proximity to the machinery. Standards of accommodation are high, and are controlled by various statutory regulations, especially since the introduction of the Maritime Labour Convention (MLC).

In the late 1960s the development of the container ship became evident in many cargo liner trades. Such vessels are usually free of cranes or cargo rigging, the newest generation having a capacity in excess of 14,000 high capacity ISO container TEUs (Twenty-foot Equivalent Units). Their speed is between 16 and 22 knots and the more sophisticated type of container vessel is called a cellular ship. Such a vessel is built in the form of a series of cells into which the containers are placed, usually by sophisticated shore-based cranes. Some container vessels have been built to be multi-purpose in design with ramp facilities for transhipping vehicle cargo. This improves the general cargo mix flexibility of the vessel (see Figure 3.4).

Passenger ships classified under the SOLAS regulations have different grades of cabin comfort, as on a hotel basis. This ensures that the most economical use is made of the cubic capacity of the ship. On a cruise passenger liner, it is common to find a swimming pool, cinema, shops, hospital, nursery and numerous other amenities and recreational facilities (see Figure 4.9).

There are various statutory provisions concerning the quantity and type of life-saving apparatus carried on a vessel. Broadly, it is determined by the type of vessel, crew establishment and the passenger certificate (authorized number of passengers permitted to be carried). Life-saving apparatus includes lifeboats, inflatable liferafts, lifebuoys and individual lifejackets.

Freeboard is the distance measured amidships from the waterline to the main deck of the vessel. This is normally the uppermost continuous deck in a ship with one or more decks. However, in a shelter dock vessel it would be the deck below.

The draught of a vessel is the vertical distance from the keel to the waterline.

The maximum permitted draught varies according to the seasons and waters in which she plies. The markings are given in Figure 2.1 and all ships must be loaded so that the loadline corresponding to the zone in which they are steaming must not be submerged. The seasons to which the markings apply are Tropical (T), Summer (S), Winter (W) and Winter North Atlantic (WNA). The world has been mapped off into sections showing where those sections apply.

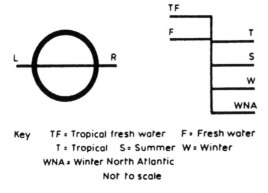

Key   TF = Tropical fresh water   F = Fresh water
        T = Tropical   S = Summer   W = Winter
     WNA = Winter North Atlantic
              Not to scale

Figure 2.1   International load line of cargo vessel. Passenger and timber vessels have additional lines.

2.2 International navigation limits

On 1 November 2003 the Institute Warranty Limits – the former trading limits – were amended and renamed the International Navigation Limits (INL). Details are given below of the INL. When consulting the navigation limits readers should refer to the load line map (Figure 2.2).

Navigation limits

Unless and to the extent otherwise agreed by the underwriters in accordance with, the vessel shall not enter, navigate or remain in the areas specified below at any time or, where applicable, between the dates specified below (both days inclusive).

Area 1 – Arctic

(a) North of 70° N. lat. (b) Barents Sea.

Except for calls at Kola Bay, Murmansk or any port or place in Norway, provided that the vessel does not enter, navigate or remain north of 30° N. lat. or east of 35° E. long.

Area 2 – Northern seas

(a) White Sea. (b) Chukchi Sea.

Area 3 – Baltic

(a) Gulf of Bothnia north of a line between Umea (63° 50° N. lat.) and Vasa (63° 06° N. lat.) between 10 December and 25 May.
(b) Where the vessel is equal to or less than 90,000 dwt, Gulf of Finland east of 28° 45° E. long. between 15 December and 15 May.
(c) Vessels greater than 90,000 dwt may not enter, navigate or remain in the Gulf of Finland east of 28° 45° E. long. at any time.
(d) Gulf of Bothnia, Gulf of Finland and adjacent waters north of 59° 24° N. lat. between 8 January and 5 May, except for calls at Stockholm, Tallinn or Helsinki.
(e) Gulf of Riga and adjacent waters east of 22° E. long. and south of 59° N. lat. between 28 December and 5 May.

Area 4 – Greenland

Greenland territorial waters.

Area 5 – North America (east)

(a) North of 52° 10° N. lat. and between 50° W. long. and 100° W. long.
(b) Gulf of St Lawrence, St Lawrence River and its tributaries (east of Les Escoumins), Strait of Belle Isle (west of Belle Isle), Cabot Strait (west of a line between Cape Ray and Cape North) and Strait of Canso (north of the Canso Causeway) between 21 December and 30 April.
(c) St Lawrence River and its tributaries (west of Les Escoumins) between 1 December and 30 April.
(d) St Lawrence Seaway.
(e) Great Lakes.

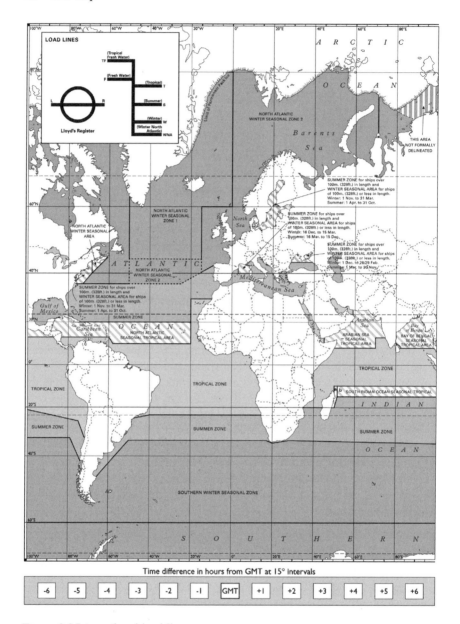

Figure 2.2 International load line zones.

Source: *Lloyd's Maritime Atlas*, 28th edn, 2014. © Informa UK Ltd 2014. Reproduced with permission of Informa UK Ltd.

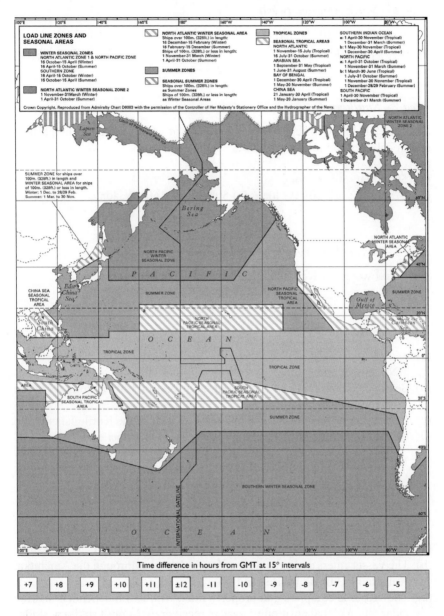

Figure 2.2 continued

Area 6 – North America (west)

(a) North of 54° 30° N. lat. and between 100° W. long. and 170° W. long.
(b) Any port or place in the Queen Charlotte Islands or the Aleutian Islands.

Area 7 – Southern Ocean

South of 50° S. lat. except within the triangular area formed by rhumb lines drawn between the following points:

(a) 50° S. lat; 50° W. long.
(b) 57° S. lat.; 67° 30° W. long. (c) 50° S. lat.; 160° W. long.

Area 8 – Kerguelen/Crozet

Territorial waters of Kerguelen Islands and Crozet Islands.

Area 9 – East Asia

(a) Sea of Okhotsk north of 55° N. lat. and east of 140° E. long. between 1 November and 1 June.
(b) Sea of Okhotsk north of 53° N. lat. and west of 140° E. long. between 1 November and 1 June.
(c) East Asian waters north of 46° N. lat. and west of the Kurile Islands and west of the Kamchatka Peninsula between 1 December and 1 May.

Area 10 – Bering Sea

Bering Sea, except on through voyages and provided that:

(a) Vessel does not enter, navigate or remain north of 54° 30° N. lat.; and
(b) The vessel enters and exits west of Buldir Island or through the Amchitka, Amukta or Unimak passes; and
(c) The vessel is equipped and properly fitted with two independent marine radar sets, a global positioning system receiver (or Loran-C radio positioning receiver), a radio transceiver and GMDSS, a weather facsimile recorder (or alternative equipment for the receipt of weather and routing information) and a gyro-compass, in each case to be fully operational and manned by qualified personnel; and
(d) The vessel is in possession of appropriate navigational charts, corrected up-to-date sailing directions and pilot books.

2.3 International Convention on Load Lines 1966

The first International Convention on Load Lines, adopted in 1930, was based on the principle of reserve buoyancy, although it was recognized then that the freeboard should also ensure adequate stability and avoid excessive stress on the ship's hull as a result of overloading.

In the 1966 Load Lines Convention, adopted by the IMO, provisions are made determining the freeboard of tankers by subdivision and damage stability calculations. The Convention includes Annex I, divided into four chapters: Chapter I, General; Chapter II, Conditions of assignment of freeboard; Chapter III, Freeboards; Chapter IV, Special requirements for ships assigned timber freeboards. Annex II covers zones, areas and seasonal periods, and Annex III contains certificates, including the International Load Line Certificate. The 1966 Convention provided for amendments to be made by positive acceptance. Amendments could be considered by the Maritime Safety Committee, the IMO Assembly or by a conference of governments.

The 1988 Protocol was primarily adopted in order to harmonize the Convention's survey and certification requirement with those contained in SOLAS and MARPOL 73/78. All three instruments require the issuing of certificates to show that requirements have been met and this has to be done by means of a survey, which can involve the ship being out of service for several days. The harmonized system alleviates the problems caused by survey dates and intervals between surveys that do not coincide, so that a ship should no longer have to go into port or repair yard for a survey required by one Convention shortly after doing the same thing in connection with another instrument.

The 1988 Load Lines Protocol provides for amendments to the Convention to be considered either by the Maritime Safety Committee or by a conference of Parties and to be adopted by a two-thirds majority of Parties to the Convention present and voting. Amendments enter into force six months after the deemed date of acceptance – which must be at least a year after the date of communication of adoption of amendments unless they are rejected by one-third of Parties. Usually, the date from adoption to deemed acceptance is two years.

The 1995 amendments concern the southern tropical zone off the coast of Australia and have been incorporated in the 2003 amendments. The amendments adopted in June 2003 and entered into force on 1 January 2005 (under tacit acceptance) to Annex B to the 1988 Load Lines Protocol (i.e. the International Convention on Load Lines, 1966, as modified by the Protocol of 1988 relating thereto) include a number of important revisions, in particular to regulations concerning: strength and intact stability of ships; definitions; superstructure and bulkheads; doors; position of hatchways, doorways and ventilators; hatchway coamings; hatch covers; machinery space opening; miscellaneous openings in freeboard and superstructure decks; cargo ports and other similar openings; spurling pipes and cable lockers; side scuttles; windows and skylights; calculation of freeing ports; protection of the crew and means of safe passage for crew; calculation of freeboard; sheer; minimum bow height and reserve buoyancy; and others.

The amendments, which amount to comprehensive revision of the technical regulations of the original Load Lines Convention, will not affect the 1966 Load Line Convention and will only apply to those ships flying the flags of States party to the 1988 Load Line Protocol.

2.4 Types of propulsion and future trends

Today the world's mercantile fleet is powered primarily by diesel engines. They have low fuel consumption, giving them added deadweight and cubic capacity for cargo. Factors influencing choice of propulsion unit embrace initial cost, required speed, cost and availability of fuel on the route used, cargo carrying capacity required, length of duration of voyage, and operational expenses. The tendency for higher capacity ships, longer hauls, rising bunker costs, need for improved ship productivity, a surge in new builds and the need to make better and more productive use of available shipboard cargo and passenger space, has presented an opportunity for innovative use of ship space and operational cost productivity.

The twenty-first century has therefore brought a new resurgence of interest in marine propulsion. This has been created by demand for the environmental friendliness and cost-effectiveness of marine transport. Hence there is a focus on the development of ships that can offer larger carrying capacities and higher speeds, lower capital and operating costs, increased manoeuvrability, reliability and safety and reduced environmental impact. Developments in technology in ships' power, propulsion and motion control systems are essential to meet many of these objectives. Details are given below of recent developments to achieve these, which were initially driven by a growth in cruise tonnage.

Responding to a need to make better utilization of ship capacity is the idea of an electric ship, which offers Integrated Full Electric Propulsion (IFEP), lower running costs and sometimes reduced capital investment. The IFEP system involves the ship's propulsors being driven by electric motors alone. Power for the electric motors is drawn from a unified electrical power system that also provides all the ship's electrical services. The power and propulsion systems are therefore integrated, because there is only one electrical power system where more conventionally there might have been two.

A major benefit of the IFEP is the layout flexibility offered by the elimination of the shaft tunnel housing the conventional propulsion unit (Figure 2.3), because the prime mover is no longer coupled to the propulsors. Absence of a shaft tunnel housing also provides more freedom for the prime mover location and thereby more effective use of available space. Further benefits of electrical propulsion – both in terms of internal layout and vessel manoeuvrability – can be realized through the use of podded propulsion, in which an electric motor driving a propeller is mounted in a 'pod' beneath the ship. An example of such an arrangement is the Mermaid pod.

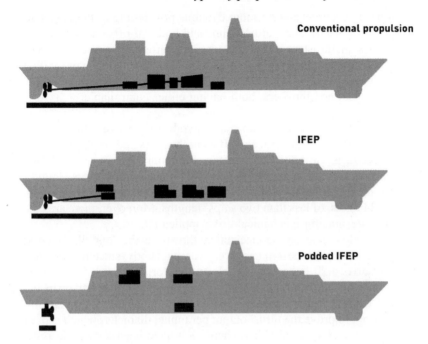

Figure 2.3 Layout of mechanical and electric propulsion systems.

A further benefit of the IFEP system is reduced fuel consumption, because the base load of the ship's service power demand can be used to ensure that the load on the prime movers never falls to inefficient levels. Cruise liners with relatively high service loads and operational profiles that frequently leave the propulsion system operating at fractional loads offer an example of an IFEP system that generates fuel savings.

The next generation of marine prime movers is found in the advanced marine gas turbine. It incorporates both intercooler and recuperator heat exchangers, the combined effect of which is to allow 'waste' heat to be recovered from the gas turbine exhaust and provides significant fuel savings across the entire power range. These complex cycles have been adopted by Celebrity Cruises' Millennium class ships, which have a combined gas turbine and steam turbine electric drive system (COGES). In this situation a steam bottoming cycle, rather than intercooling and recuperation, has been chosen as an alternative solution, to reduce fuel consumption through recovery of exhaust heat.

LNG tonnage prime mover technology is changing, embracing duel fuel diesel engines (natural gas and MDO), heavy fuel diesel engines with a re-liquefaction plant, gas turbines – either single or combined cycle – and a combination of these systems.

Manoeuvrability is a basic safety requirement for all vessels, as well as being an intrinsic element of the operational capability in some applications.

The thruster system enables a more dynamic positioning of the vessel and is widely used in ro/ro ships, cruise ships and types of offshore support ships. Three types of thrusters exist. The azimuth thruster provides the main or auxiliary inboard or outboard propulsion and manoeuvring with 360° turn, using controllable or fixed pitch propeller. The bow and stern thrusters are conventional turned thrusters, both having either controllable or fixed pitch propellers.

A recent development in ship manoeuvrability, realized through a combination of compact, powerful and efficient thrusters and control systems that manage them, is the podded propulsor, commonly known as an AZIPOD. These propulsors provide a high level of manoeuvrability, as found, for example, on the Millennium Ship, which has a tactical diameter, from an initial speed of 24 knots, of less than two ships' lengths. Moreover, there are equally innovative designs for mechanical drive applications.

An example of a steerable mechanical thruster is the Azipull, which has a pulling propeller. This design has a very compact body, since it contains only gears and driveshaft rather than an electric motor. It is ideal for the smaller ferries where electric propulsion is not an economic alternative. In tunnel thrusters, designs with two contra-rotating propellers, one on each side of the gear housing, improve the thrust output per tunnel diameter, which is of great importance for high-speed ships where they have been applied in order to decrease drag.

Noise and vibration are key areas of ongoing research. The major technical areas being addressed include: reduction of propulsor noise at source; isolation of propulsion machinery noise; and control of intake and exhaust noise. These are focused on developing new comfort class requirements for cruise ships and fast ferries.

2.5 Types and methods of tonnage measurement

There are five main kinds of tonnage in use in the shipping business. These are deadweight, cargo, displacement, gross and nett tonnages, the last two of which are now measured according to the International Convention on Tonnage Measurement of Ships 1969 (explained in 2.6 below). Deadweight tonnage (dwt) expresses the number of tons (of 2,240 lb) a vessel can transport of cargo, stores and bunker fuel. It is the difference between the number of tons of water a vessel displaces 'light' and the number of tons of water a vessel displaces when submerged to her loadline. Deadweight tonnage is used interchangeably with deadweight carrying capacity. A vessel's capacity for weight cargo is less than its total deadweight tonnage.

Cargo tonnage is expressed in terms of a weight or measurement. The weight ton in the United States and sometimes in the UK is the American short ton of 2,000 lb, or the British long ton of 2,240 lb. A measurement ton is usually 40 ft^3, but in some instances a larger number of cubic feet is taken for a ton. Most ocean package freight is taken at weight or measurement (W/M) ship's option. With the growth in use of the metric system the metric tonne of 1,000 kg or cubic metre is becoming more widely used. The freight ton is a mixture of weight and measurement tons and can lead to confusion in the collection and analysis of statistics.

Displacement of a vessel is the weight in tons, each of 2,240 lb, of the ship and its contents. It is the weight of water the ship displaces. Displacement light is the weight of the vessel without stores, bunker fuel or cargo. Displacement loaded is the weight of the vessel plus cargo, passengers, fuel and stores.

Gross tonnage applies to vessels, not to cargo. It is determined by dividing by 100 the volume in cubic feet of the vessel's closed-in spaces, and is usually referred to as the gross registered tonnage (GRT). The spaces exempt from the measurement include: light and air spaces; wheelhouse; galley; lavatories; stairways; houses enclosing deck machinery; hatchways to a maximum of 0.5% of the gross tonnage; and open shelter deck. A vessel ton is 100 ft^3. It is used as a basis for pilotage and dry-dock dues, and sometimes tonnage dues. Additionally, it is employed for official statistical purposes, when comparing ships' sizes, and as a basis for Protection and Indemnity Club entries.

Nett tonnage is a vessel's gross tonnage after deducting space occupied by crew accommodation, including facilities for the Master and officers; spaces used for navigation; boatswain's store room; water ballast and fresh water spaces, including forward and aft peak tanks, deep tanks that are provided fitted with manholds and which are not employable for carriage of liquid cargo; and propelling and machinery space which does not represent earning capacity of the ship. A vessel's nett tonnage expresses the space available for the accommodation of passengers and stowage of cargo, and is usually referred to as nett registered tonnage (NRT). A ton of cargo in most instances occupies less than 100 ft^3: hence the vessel's cargo tonnage may exceed its nett tonnage, and indeed the tonnage of cargo carried is almost always greater than the gross tonnage. It is the cubic capacity of all earning space, and it is on this tonnage figure that most harbour dues and other charges are calculated. The aim of the average shipowner is to achieve a low nett tonnage consistent with a maximum cubic capacity for cargo and/or passengers.

The Suez and Panama tonnage regulations make it obligatory for vessels to be measured for tonnage if they are to use these canals.

2.6 International Convention on Tonnage Measurement of Ships 1969

The Convention, adopted by the IMO in 1969, was the first successful attempt to introduce a universal tonnage measurement system. Previously, various systems were used to calculate the tonnage of merchant ships. Although all went back to the method devised by George Moorsom of the British Board of Trade in 1854, there were considerable differences between them and it was recognized that there was a great need for one single international system.

The Convention provides for gross and nett tonnages, both of which are calculated independently. The rules apply to all ships built on or after 18 July 1982 – the date of entry into force – while ships built before that date were allowed to retain their existing tonnage for 12 years after entry into force or until 18 July 1994.

This phase-in period was intended to ensure that ships were given reasonable economic safeguards, since port and other dues are charged according to ship tonnage. At the same time, and as far as possible, the Convention was drafted to ensure that gross and nett tonnages calculated under the new system did not differ too greatly from those calculated under previous methods. The Convention meant a transition from the traditionally used terms gross register tons (grt) and nett register tons (nrt) to gross tons (GT) and nett tons (NT). Gross tonnage forms the basis for manning regulations, safety rules and registration fees. Both gross and nett tonnages are used to calculate port dues. The gross tonnage is a function of the moulded volume of all enclosed spaces of the ship. The nett tonnage is produced by a formula which is a function of the moulded volume of all cargo spaces of the ship. The nett tonnage shall not be taken as less than 30% of the gross tonnage.

Today tonnage measurement methods are under continuous review as vessel design changes to suit numerous trades. In 2006 the IMO sub-committee agreed to amend the provisional formulas for reduced gross tonnage (GT) for open-top container ships prescribed in TM5/circ. 4. This ruling, issued in 1993, gives preliminary the IMO formula for the calculation of gross tonnage for open-top container ships of up to 30,000 gross tonnage under the International Convention on Tonnage Measurement of Ships 1969.

3 Ship design and construction

3.1 Ship design and future trends

The twenty-first century is generating a period of change and opportunity. There is growth in new building and more emphasis on ship productivity. There is renewed pressure on driving down both ship operating and ship building costs. Ship specification is highly regulated by the IMO regulations endorsed by maritime governments. Likewise the operation and maintenance survey of ships are highly regulated, as found in the ISM code. The concept behind such a highly regulated environment is ship safety, which extends to the environment and to the cargoes conveyed.

There are three main factors affecting the technical feasibility and profitability of a ship. The deadweight/displacement ratio indicates the carrying capacity in relation to the total displacement. The deadweight is low for ferries with extensive passenger facilities. Container vessels have much higher deadweight/displacement ratios. Tankers and bulk carriers have the highest values. For all vessel types the deadweight/displacement ratio improves with size. Speed and power should be judged in relation to the displacement. For speeds below 20 knots, power demand increases very slowly with increasing displacement. But at 35 or 40 knots, common with fast ferries, the power curves become very steep. The third factor to observe is the lightweight density, which is an easy way to a first weight-estimate for different ship types.

Ship functions can be divided into two main categories, payload function and ship function. In a cargo vessel the payload function consists of cargo spaces, cargo handling equipment and spaces needed for cargo treatment on board, such as the refrigeration equipment found in reefers and gas ships and the heating coils and cargo pumps found in tankers. The ship functions are related to carrying the payload safely from port to port. The areas and volume demanded in the ship to accommodate all systems are then calculated. The result is a complete system description for the new ship, which includes the volumes and areas needed onboard to fulfil the mission. Total volume of the vessel and the gross tonnage can then be calculated. Based on these data, a first estimate of weight and building costs can be made. The next step in the design process is to select main dimensions and define the form. By variation of the main dimensions the space and weight in the selected design is matched to the system description. Based on the performance and operation economies the best dimensions are then selected. Given below are the salient features in ship design.

(a) The salient factor is the broad specification outlined by the shipping company to the naval architect and shipbuilder, usually following a critical evaluation. It will feature the capital investment parameters, the return on capital, with special emphasis on revenue (cargo/passenger) production and related operating costs, trade forecast and the level of competition. Innovation is a key factor in ship design. The international entrepreneur is very conscious that ship investment is a risk business and the operational life of a ship may be beyond 25 years, during which period trade and market conditions may change. Moreover, the older the vessel becomes the more costly it is to maintain. This is due to the regulatory ship survey and maintenance code, which becomes more severe beyond the fifth survey or subsequent surveys at five-year intervals.

(b) Market conditions and how best to respond to the needs of the shipper will be major factors in ship design. Design will focus on raising standards for the merchant shipper in faster transits and the continuing expansion of multi-modalism. The interface between the ship and berthing operations will be much improved, thereby speeding up ship turn-round time. This involves quicker and more efficient transhipment techniques, both for containerized traffic and for the bulk carrier market. An example of the lengthened container ship technology demonstrating this point is found in Figure 3.4.

(c) The shipowner will continue to extend shipboard efficiency with the aid of continuously improving onboard technology in all areas of operation. The continuing expansion of the INMARSAT shipboard navigation/ communication technology is bringing in a new era of information technology and communications involving EDI (see Chapter 20) in the global maritime field.

(d) Ship safety remains paramount, consistent with efficiency and the application of modern technology. The IMO is continuing to persuade member states of the need to adopt conventions to raise the safety of ships at sea. This involves particularly ship design and specification.

(e) Ships are now subject to inspection by Port State Control Inspectors of the registered state maritime agency whilst in port, usually by accredited classification society surveyors or other designated surveyors, to ensure they are seaworthy. Member states subscribing to the IMO Convention have legal powers to detain tonnage failing to conform to the prescribed standards as found, for example, under MARPOL 90.

(f) Shipowners, as trade increases, are tending to replace tonnage by larger vessels rather than provide additional sailings. This lowers nautical tonne per mile costs, but places more stress on planning and the total logistics operation at the berth. Accordingly, container tonnage has now reached

14,000 TEUs and can attain 18,000 TEUs. Likewise ferries operating in the cross-Channel and Baltic trades have much increased their lane-metre capacity for a combination of cars and road haulage vehicles. This is because vessels are being built with a wider beam, increased length overall, but more especially more decks which increase the ship freeboard. Such developments require extensive research to evolve/design such tonnage to comply with strict IMO safety standards.

(g) More automation is now emerging in transhipment and docking arrangement.

(h) The development of the floating terminal and floating production, storage and offloading vessel is another example of innovation in ship design.

(i) Market research is used extensively to influence the interior design of cruise tonnage, both new build and refurbishment. Focus groups are employed from loyal and potential cruise customers.

(j) Design of the ferry must focus on turn-round time, speed, and passenger interior décor. In order to attract passengers, a ferry must offer a service that the passenger perceives as 'value added'. Passengers will determine their acceptance of the ferry based on a variety of factors relating to comfort. In particular where passengers sit, dine, congregate and recreate will influence their passenger comfort and overall sense of well-being. The levels of vibration, noise, interior environment and lighting that passengers experience will have either a positive or negative effect on design decisions. A second group of passengers will be influenced by vessel design, layout and seakeeping qualities. Factors such as pitching, rolling, slamming, excessive vibration and noise are not conducive to favourable ambient environmental conditions for discerning passengers.

3.2 Ship productivity

Ship productivity is a key factor in ship design and its impact on ship operation. We have already identified the new generation of electrical propulsion systems which will lower operation costs and provide more shipboard cargo and passenger capacity through the elimination of the shaft tunnel. More automation in cargo transhipment and docking arrangements impact on ship design and quicker port turn-round times.

Operational productivity of the world fleet is an analysis of the balance between supply and demand for tonnage. Key indicators are the comparison of cargo generation and fleet ownership, tons of cargo carried, ton miles performed per deadweight ton, and an analysis of tonnage over supply in the main shipping market sectors.

An analysis of Table 3.1 provides indicative data on ton miles performed by oil tankers, dry bulk carriers, combined carriers and the residual world mercantile fleet. As an example, the thousands of ton miles per dwt of oil tankers increased in 2004 by less than 1% to 32.4, while the ton miles per deadweight ton of dry bulk carriers and combined carriers increased by 2.8%

Table 3.1 Estimated productivity of tankers, bulk carriers, combined carriers and the residual fleet, selected years (thousand of ton miles performed per dwt)

Year	Ton miles of oil carried by tankers (thousand of million)	Ton miles per dwt tankers	Ton miles of dry cargo carried by dry bulk carriers (thousand of bulk million)	Ton miles per dwt carriers	Ton miles of oil and dry bulk cargo by combined carriers (thousand million)	Ton miles per dwt of combined carriers	Ton miles of the residual fleet (thousand combined million)	Ton miles per dwt of the residual fleet
1970	6,039	43.8	1,891	39.4	745	52.5	1,979	15.7
1980	9,007	27.6	2,009	14.5	1,569	32.4	4,192	24.8
1990	7,376	30.8	3,804	18.8	1,164	36.0	4,777	26.0
2000	9,840	34.5	6,470	23.9	593	38.5	6,837	28.3
2003	10,210	32.2	7,357	24.9	467	38.6	7,823	33.6
2004	10,898	32.4	7,984	25.7	418	43.1	8,349	34.9

Sources: Compiled by the UNCTAD Secretariat on the basis of data from *Fearnleys Review*, various issues; *World Bulk Trades* and *World Bulk Fleet*, various issues; and other specialist sources.

and 11.6% to 25.7 and 43.1 respectively. The residual fleet increased its productivity by 3.9% to 34.9 ton miles per deadweight ton.

A financier in the building cost analysis may use the cost of the dwt related to the cargo earning potential. The iron ore carrier building cost per dwt is much lower than the high-tech LNG tonnage. The container analysis would relate the TEU capacity to the building cost, which for a cruise liner would relate to the number of berths. The mega container vessel and cruise liner exploit the economies of scale: as the building cost per TEU and per cabin falls the larger the tonnage.

Ship productivity is realized through an efficient cargo flow from ship to shore and vice versa. This ensures a quick turn-round time at the port. Terminal layout is the key factor. Likewise a passenger car/vehicular ferry (Figures 3.1a, 3.1b and 4.9) must be customized in design to the trade and terminals. It illustrates the bow and stern loading arrangement.

3.3 General principles and factors influencing design, type and size of ship

In the choice of a type of ship to be built, the shipowner must consider primarily the trade in which it is to operate. His decision as to size and propelling machinery will be governed by the factors involved in his particular trade, such as the nature of the cargo mix to be moved, the cost and availability of fuel, the minimum carrying capacity required, the length and duration of the voyages and the required speed. Economic, technical, statutory and safety considerations will all influence his choice.

So far as the building and operating costs are concerned, within certain limits, the larger ship is a cheaper proposition. For example, the cost of the propelling machinery for a 100,000 tonner is less than the cost for two 50,000 tonners developing the same power. The larger ship costs less to crew than two smaller ships and its operating costs per ton are lower. In the bulk trades, where the nature of the cargo calls for large roomy holds, the economics of size alone favour the employment of large ships. However, increased size implies deeper draught, and if a general trader is to be operated economically, she must be able to proceed anywhere where cargo is offered. On one voyage she may be going to Mumbai, which permits vessels with a maximum draught of 16 m, while its next employment may be in the River Plate where the draught is limited to about 9 m. She may have to load from an ore jetty off the coast of Chile where safety considerations prohibit the large ship. All these considerations have to be balanced, and today the modern tramp has developed into a handy-sized vessel for dry bulk cargo: Handysize 20,000–35,000 dwt, Handymax 35,000–50,000 dwt, Panamax 50,000–80,000 dwt and Capesize 80,000–150,000 dwt. The speed is 14–16 knots and all are capable of passing through the Panama Canal except the Capesize. The Handymax operates in the Far East and Pacific regions carrying timber and many are family-owned. The Panamax conveys coal or grain between North America to the Far East and Middle East. The Capesize, the most economical per dwt, conveys iron ore and coal between Australia to Japan, China and Brazil to Europe/Far East.

Recently the cellular container ship has featured more prominently in cargo liner trades. Additionally, more purpose-built tonnage is becoming available for carrying such products as liquefied methane, trade cars, etc. Such ships – often owned or on charter to industrial users – are designed for a particular cargo and are frequently involved in ballast runs for part of the round voyage. Purpose-built tonnage requires special terminals – often situated away from the general port area – frequently involving expensive equipment to ensure quick transhipment. As we progress through the early years of the twenty-first century we are experiencing a growth in container tonnage which is driving a logistic environment, causing many shippers, especially fruit and cement carriers, to review their break-bulk and bulk cargo shipments. This has been facilitated by 'ongoing' modernization of container terminals. Moreover, the demise of the mammoth oil tanker of 500,000 dwt – the ultra-large crude carrier of 29 m draught – is due to the very limited number of ports of call it may operate to, owing to its size, when its draught is too deep for some shipping lanes. A further factor is the diminishing number of trades able to support a vessel of such size, other than on a multi-port operation, which is uneconomical. The ore/bulk/oil OBO continues to fall, representing less than 1% of the world fleet. This is due to the high maintenance cost and absence of trades to support such tonnage. No new builds are expected, mainly because

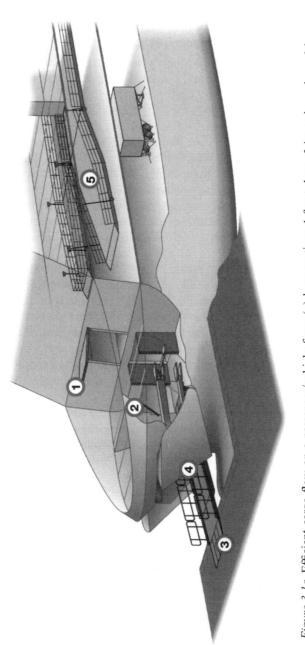

Figure 3.1a Efficient cargo flow on a passenger/vehicle ferry (*a*) bow section: *1* front door, *2* inner bow door, *3* bow ramp/door, *4* bow doors, *5* hoistable car deck.

Source: Reproduced by courtesy of MacGregor Group AB, Stockholm.

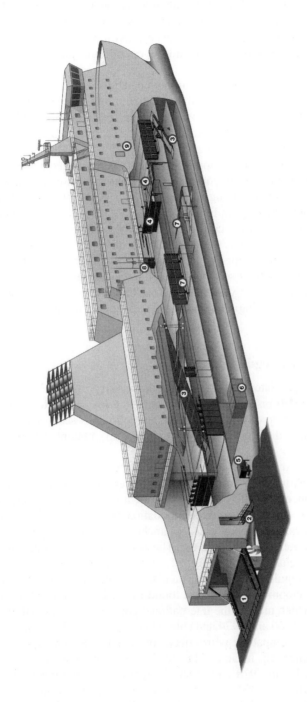

Figure 3.1b Efficient cargo flow on a passenger/vehicle ferry (*b*) stern view: *1* straight stem ramp/door, *2* side ramp/door, *3* hoistable ramps, *4* flood control doors, *5* hydraulic power pack, *6* provision stores, *7* ramp cover, *8* elevators, *9* side doors.

Source: Reproduced by courtesy of MacGregor Group AB, Stockholm.

of high capital costs. The student must study closely the world merchant fleet composition profile and factors driving change. The changing pattern of trade and emerging trends plays a significant role in new investment and employment of tonnage. Where trade situations demand the era of multi-purpose tonnage remains.

Where the vessel to be constructed is intended for long-term charter to industrial users, as in the case of many oil tankers, ore carriers and other specialized cargo ships, the limits of size are dictated by terminal facilities or by obstacles of the voyage – such as arise, for example, in the Panama Canal or St Lawrence Seaway.

Much of the foregoing analysis applies equally to cargo liners, except that flexibility of operation is not so important. A factor tending more to limit their size is the importance of providing frequent sailings which the market can support. The overseas buyer pays for his goods when the seller can produce bills of loading showing that the consignment has been shipped. Under such conditions the merchant demands frequent sailings, and if the shipowner does not provide them his competitors will! Today the container line operator is continuously remodelling their services through larger vessels on core routes to serve hub ports and feeder vessels operating the hub and spoke system. This operation is driven by logistics and ongoing container terminal modernization.

3.4 Safety and other regulations

Associated with the provision of new tonnage, there is an obligation to comply with statutory regulations, classification society rules and international agreements affecting ship design, and this obligation varies according to the requirements of the different flags, particularly in matters relating to accommodation.

Vessels registered in the UK have to be built to the statutory requirements imposed by the Department of Transport, Local Government and the Regions. The regulations concern all life-saving apparatus, navigational aids, the hull and machinery, crew and passenger accommodation, water-tight and fireproof bulkheads, gangways, emergency escapes, anchor cable and hawsers, shell plating, ship inspection at the seaport, etc. The basis of these requirements is included in the Merchant Shipping Act of 1995. Various amendments and additions to these regulations have reached the statute book to meet new conditions and developments. These are found in the IMO Conventions on Maritime Safety, which include the international convention on the safety of life at sea (SOLAS) 1960 and 1974 and entered into force in 1980. It specifies minimum standards, compatible with safety, for the construction, equipment and operation of ships. By means of Protocol it has been amended several times, including twice in 1978 and 1988. A significant amendment, which entered into force in July 2004, was measures to enhance maritime security embracing the International Ship and Port Facility Security Code. Also mandatory provision is made from December 2004 for installation of automatic information, systems and continuous synopsis records to provide 'on board' records of the history of the ship. Other IMO conventions are the International Convention on Load Lines 1966, the Special Trade Passenger Ship Agreement 1973, the Convention on the International Maritime Satellite Organization (INMARSAT) 1976, the International Convention on Standards of Training, Certification and Watchkeeping for Seafarers (STCW) 1978 including the 1995 and 2010 amendments and the International Convention on Maritime Search and Research (SAR) 1979.

All the foregoing have been subject to amendment and protocol as recorded.

3.5 Statutory regulations

International conventions, codes and protocols concerning ship safety and marine pollution are agreed by the member states of the United Nations Agency, the International Maritime Organization. The IMO has promoted the adoption of some 35 conventions and protocols and adopted numerous codes and recommendations. The conventions and codes usually stipulate inspection and the issuance of certificates as part of enforcement. Most member countries and/or their registered shipowners authorize classification societies to undertake the inspection and certification on their behalf. For example, more than 100 member states have authorized Lloyd's Register to undertake such inspection and certification. The IMO conventions define minimum standards, though member states can instigate national regulations which incorporate the IMO standards and apply equally well to their own fleets and visiting foreign ships. Classification societies participate in the work of the IMO as technical advisers to various delegations. Their key function is to provide inspection and certification for compliance and advice on these complex regulations. Various aspects of the IMO conventions are dealt with elsewhere in the book.

Given below is a selection of statutory marine surveys:

(a) *Load Line Certificate.* An international load line certificate is required by any vessel engaged in international voyages, except warships, ships of less than 24 m in length, pleasure yachts not engaged in trade and fishing vessels. It is valid for five years, subject to an annual survey.

(b) *Cargo Ship Safety Construction Certificate.* This is required by any ship engaged in international voyages, with the exception of passenger ships, warships and troop ships, cargo ships of less than 500 gross tonnage, ships not propelled by mechanical means, wooden ships of primitive build, pleasure yachts not engaged in trade, and fishing vessels. Survey classification ensures the SOLAS 1974 convention is complied with in the areas of hull, machinery and other relevant equipment. For vessels of 100 m length and over, compliance with damage stability requirements is also required. It is valid for five years, with an annual survey.

(c) *Cargo Ship Safety Equipment Certificate.* This is required by any ship engaged on international voyages, except for ship types detailed in item (b). Survey classification ensures the SOLAS 1974 convention Chapters II–1, II–2, III and IV are complied with along with other relevant requirements. It is valid from two to five years, with an annual survey.

(d) *Cargo Ship Safety Radio Certificate.* This is required by all cargo ships of 300 gross tonnage and upwards on international voyages, which are required to carry equipment designed to improve the chances of rescue following an accident, including for the location of the ship or survival craft satellite emergency position-indicating radio beacons (EPIRBS) and search and rescue transponders (SARTS). It features under the current SOLAS Convention Chapter IV, Radio Communications, which was completely revised in 1988 and amendments were introduced from February 1999 and which embraced the GMDSS. By that date the Morse Code was phased out. Chapter IV is closely linked with the Radio Regulations of the International Telecommunications Union.

(e) *Passenger Ship Safety Certificate.* This is required by any passenger ship under SOLAS Regulation 12(a)(vii) engaged on international voyages, except troop ships. A passenger ship is a vessel which carries more than 12 passengers. Pleasure yachts not engaged in trade do not require a Passenger Ship Safety Certificate, following compliance with the requirements of the 1974 SOLAS Convention. This includes the survey arrangements for subdivision, damage stability, fire safety, life-saving appliances, radio equipment and navigational aids. It is reviewed annually following:

(f) *International Oil Pollution Prevention Certificate* (IOPPC). It is valid for five years with an annual survey.

(g) *International Air Pollution Prevention Certificate* (IAPPC). This is valid for five years with an annual survey.

(h) *International Sewage Pollution Prevention Certificate* (ISPPC). This is valid for five years with an annual survey.

(i) *Document of compliance* (DOC). Mandatory under the ISM code and is valid for five years with intermediate surveys.

(j) *Carriage of dangerous goods.* SOLAS 1974, as amended, featured 12 chapters in an annex embracing Chapter VII, termed Carriage of Dangerous Goods. It features three parts: Part A, Carriage of dangerous goods in packaged form or in solid form or in bulk. It embraces the International Maritime Dangerous Goods (IMDG) code. A new code was adopted in May 2002 and was mandatory from 1 January 2004. Part B, Construction and Equipment of Ships carrying Dangerous Liquid Chemicals in bulk, requires chemical tankers built after July 1986 to comply with the International Bulk Chemical code (IBC Code). Part C concerns the construction and equipment of those ships carrying liquefied gases in bulk and gas carriers, which were constructed after July 1986 and comply with the requirements of the International Gas Carrier Code (IGC Code).

Two examples are found in the IBC and IGC codes. The IMO international code for the construction and equipment of ships carrying dangerous chemicals in bulk (IBC code) provides safety standards for their design, construction, equipment and operation. An additional code – the BCH – is applicable to ships built before 1 July 1986. A document termed a Certificate of Fitness is issued by the classification society in accordance with the provisions of the IBC or BCM code and is mandatory under the terms of either the 1983 amendments to SOLAS 1974 or MARPOL 73/78. For national flag administrations not signatory to SOLAS 1974, a statement of compliance is issued by the classification society in accordance with a shipowner's request.

The other example is found in the IMO international code for the construction and equipment of ships carrying liquefied gases in bulk (IGC code). This requires that the design, constructional features and equipment of new ships minimize the risk to the ship, its crew and the environment. There are additional gas carrier codes applicable to existing ships built before 1 July 1986. A Certificate of Fitness is mandatory under the terms of the 1983 amendments to SOLAS. For national flag administrations not signatory to SOLAS 1974 a statement of compliance is issued by the classification society in accordance with a shipowner's request.

(a) International Safety Management Code

In 1993 the IMO issued the International Safety Management (ISM) Code. The objectives of the code are to ensure safety at sea, the prevention of human injury or loss of life, and the avoidance of damage to the environment (in particular the marine environment) and property. The functional requirements for a safety management system to achieve these objectives are as follows:

(a) a safety and environmental protection policy;
(b) instructions and procedures to ensure safe operation of ships and protection of the environment;
(c) defined levels of authority and lines of communication between and amongst shore and shipboard personnel;
(d) procedures for reporting accidents and non-conformities within the provisions of the code;
(e) emergency response procedures;
(f) procedures for internal audits and management reviews.

The code effectively supersedes those guidelines in Management for the Safe Operation of Ships and for Pollution Prevention adopted by the IMO Assembly in 1991. The new Chapter IX makes the ISM code mandatory and was adopted by the IMO assembly in November 1993 (Assembly resolution A.741(18)). Until 2002 the ISM was mandatory under SOLAS for passenger ships (including high speed craft), oil tankers, chemical tankers, gas carriers, bulk carriers and cargo high speed craft of 500 gross tonnage and upwards. From

July 2002 it was mandatory for other cargo ships and mobile offshore drilling units of 500 gross tonnage and upwards. To coincide with the extension of the range of ships to which the application of the ISM Code is mandatory, it was necessary to amend Chapter IX of SOLAS 1974 and the ISM code. These amendments resulted in Revised Guidelines on the implementation of the code. The code establishes the following safety management objectives: (a) to provide for safe practices in ships' operation and a safe working environment; (b) to establish safeguards against all identified risks; and (c) to continuously improve safety management skills of personnel, including preparation for emergencies.

The code requires a safety management system (SMS) to be established by 'the Company', which is defined as the shipowner or any person, such as the manager or bareboat charterer, who has assumed responsibility for operating the ship. The Company is then required to establish and implement a policy for achieving these objectives. This policy includes provision of necessary resources and shore based support. Every Company is expected to 'designate a person or persons ashore having direct access to the highest level of management'. The procedures required by the code must be documented and compiled in a Safety Management Manual, a copy of which should be kept on board. The scheme for certification to the International Safety Management Code (ISM Code) is a means to demonstrate a shipping company's commitment to the safety of its vessels, cargo, passengers and crew, and to the protection of the environment, and to compliance with the ISM Code. Overall it provides for the assessment of a company's safety management systems on board vessels, and when appropriate in shore-based offices. It requires each ship in a company fleet and the company's shore-based management systems to be separately certificated. The scheme lays down the assessment procedures to be followed when either the shipboard systems or the shore-based systems or both are assessed for certification, which is usually undertaken by an accredited classification society, such as Lloyd's Register. The assessment confirms company policy and central measures in accordance with the ISM Code.

Certification in accordance with the requirements of this scheme should not be taken as an indication that the company or its vessels comply with international or national statutory requirements other than the ISM Code and it does not endorse the technical adequacy of individual operating procedures or of the vessels managed by the company. Overall the certificate will confirm the following:

(a) An appropriate management system has been defined by the company for dealing with safety and pollution prevention on board.
(b) The system is understood and implemented by those responsible for various functions.
(c) As far as periodic assessments can determine, the key actions indicated in the system are being carried out.
(d) The records are available to demonstrate the effective implementation of the system.

The scheme does not in any way replace or substitute class surveys of any kind whatsoever.

(b) Application for certification

The company's application for certification to the IACS Society and the relevant information must include the size and total number of each ship type covered by the Safety Management System (SMS) and any other documentation considered necessary.

Initial verification

The initial verification for issuing a DOC to a company consists of the following steps:

(i) *Document review.* In order to verify that the SMS and any relevant documentation comply with the requirements of ISM Code, the auditor is to review the safety management manual. If this review reveals that the system is not adequate, the audit may have to be delayed until the company undertakes corrective action. Amendments made to the system documentation to correct deficiencies identified during this review may be verified remotely or during the subsequent implementation audit described in (ii) below.

(ii) *Company audit.* In order to verify the effective functioning of the SMS, including objective evidence that the Company's SMS has been in operation for at least three months, and at least three months on board at least one ship of each type operated by the Company. The objective evidence is, among other things, to include records from the internal audits performed by the Company, ashore and onboard, examining and verifying the correctness of the statutory and classification records for at least one ship of each type of operation by the Company.

The initial verification for issuing a SMC to a ship consists of the following steps:

(i) Verification that the Company DOC is valid and relevant to that type of ship, and that the other provisions are complied with. Only after onboard confirmation of the existence of a valid DOC can the verification process proceed; and

(ii) Verification of the effective functioning of the SMS, including objective evidence that the SMS has been in operation for at least three months onboard the ship. The objective evidence should also include records from the internal audits performed by the company.

If the company already has a valid DOC issued by another IACS Society, that DOC shall be accepted as evidence of compliance with the ISM Code, unless there is evidence indicating otherwise.

Periodic verification

Periodical safety management audits are to be carried out to maintain the validity of the DOC and/or SMC. The purpose of these audits is, among other things, to verify: (i) the effective functioning of the SMS; (ii) that possible modifications of the SMS comply with the requirements of the ISM Code; (iii) that corrective action has been implemented; and (iv) that statutory and classification certificates are valid, and that no surveys are overdue.

Verification of the statutory and classification certificates is to be carried out on at least one ship of each type identified on the DOC. Periodical verification is to be carried out within three months before and after the anniversary date of the DOC. Intermediate verification is to take place between the second and third anniversary date of the SMC.

Renewal verification

A DOC and/or SMC renewal verification shall be carried out from six months before the expiry date of the certificate and shall be completed before the expiry date. DOC and/or SMC renewal verification shall be carried out according to the same principles detailed above for the initial verification, including all elements of the SMS and the effectiveness of the SMS in meeting the requirements of the ISM Code. If modifications to the Company and/or shipboard SMS have taken place, document review shall be part of the renewal verification.

Two key documents exist with the ISM Code – the Safety Management Certificate (SMC) and the Document of Compliance (DOC). The DOC is issued by IACS and is valid for five years, subject to annual verification that the Safety Management System complies with the ISM code. The SMS is issued by another accredited Ship Classification Society that it complies with the ISM code following the annual periodical review inherent in the DOC annual renewal, maintenance compliance with the IMO resolution A739(18) and all statutory certificates are valid.

Associated with the ISPS code: vessels must carry the International Ship Security Certificate to confirm full compliance with the code.

Maritime Labour Convention

The International Labour Organizations Maritime Labour Convention (MLC) came into force in August 2013. The MLC covers a range of obligations the ship operator must comply with, including seafarers' contractual arrangements, oversight of manning agencies, working hours, health and safety, crew accommodation, catering standards and seafarers' welfare. Certification procedure starts when the ship operator applies for a MLC certificate from the flag state of the vessel. A declaration is then issued in two parts by the flag state. The first part covers items the ship operator must comply with, after which the ship operator returns the second part to show that the vessel complies. The flag state then inspects the vessel.

3.6 Survey methods

The traditional way of surveying a vessel was to bring it to a shipyard where items to be surveyed were opened up, cleaned, inspected and reassembled. This method is both time consuming and expensive, but is still practised widely for a variety of reasons. However, a number of alternative survey methods exist today which have been developed by the classification societies and are now very popular. Details are given below:

(a) Voyage survey

The surveyor is in attendance during the ship's voyage and carries out the required surveys. If requested, he prepares specifications in co-operation with the owner of items to be repaired.

(b) BIS notation

Although docking a vessel is still necessary for a number of reasons, the interval between dockings has been increased considerably. Extended intervals may conflict with 'normal' class rules. However, by arranging minor modifications to the hull and its appendages, a notation 'bis' (built for in-water surveys) may be obtained, allowing a docking interval of five years.

(c) Continuous survey

Classification Rules require that surveys of hull and machinery are carried out every four years. Alternatively, continuous survey systems are carried out, whereby the surveys are divided into separate items for inspection during a five-year cycle. For the machinery survey the rules provide that the chief engineer may survey certain of these items. Furthermore, for vessels carrying out machinery maintenance in accordance with a fixed maintenance schedule, this system may replace the continuous machinery survey system, thereby reducing the class survey to an annual survey.

(d) Planned maintenance system

This is subject to a form of approval and may after approval be used as a basis for a special survey arrangement for individual ships at the owner's request.

Today, most cost-conscious shipowners operate advanced planning systems and maintenance procedures in order to meet increasing demand for cost-effective operation.

To avoid unnecessary opening up of machinery and duplication of work, many classification societies have introduced an alternative survey arrangement for the machinery. The arrangement is based on the owner's planned maintenance system already in operation 'on board'. It involves the following sequence of survey programme:

(a) classification society approves the owner's maintenance programme;
(b) initial survey on board by classification society surveyor;
(c) continuous machinery survey to be in operation; and
(d) chief engineer to be approved by classification society.

The annual survey inspections carried out by the chief engineer are accepted as class surveys. However, the annual audit survey must be carried out in conjunction with the ordinary annual general survey (AGS). The audit survey is to verify that the arrangement meets agreed procedures. At the annual audit survey, the surveyor reports the class items requested by the owner.

A summary of the business benefits embraces (a) builds on a shipowner investment budget in planned maintenance; (b) contributes to reduced risk in ship operation through breakdown, etc.; (c) enables the shipowner to demonstrate through the ISM code total commitment to quality ship management; (d) contributes to the shipowner objective to maximize revenue potential through ship availability and productivity; and (e) contributes to reduction in operation costs. Overall, (a) to (e) help to avoid unnecessary off-hire time, chartering needs/costs, and duplication of ship inspection, thereby contributing to improved revenue production/profit potential, less risk of disruption of service and much improved ship management.

3.7 Harmonization of surveys

The conventions require an initial survey before a vessel is put in service for the first time. The vessel then receives its first certificate, and certificate renewal surveys are carried out at one, two or five year intervals thereafter, depending on the certificate and type of ship. In addition, for those certificates valid for more than one year, surveys at annual intervals are required, one of which, at approximately half way and termed 'intermediate', may be of greater extent than an ordinary 'annual'. In February 2000, under amendments to SOLAS 1974 through the 1988 Protocol, a new harmonized system of surveys and certification was introduced which will harmonize with load lines and MARPOL 73/74. The 'Harmonized System of Survey and Certification' (HSSC), implemented by many administrations under the IMO resolutions A.746(18) and A.882(21), brings all SOLAS (except for passenger ships),

MARPOL and Load Line Convention surveys into a five-year cycle. With respect to safety equipment surveys, HSSC uses the term 'periodical' instead of renewal surveys held under the shorter certificate renewal cycles.

The scope of surveys can generally be harmonized with the extents of the classification surveys detailed above and, as far as possible, are held concurrently with them.

The scope of surveys, which does not necessarily encompass 100% of the structure, equipment, etc., of the ship, is laid down in the IMO resolutions and generally increases with the vessel's age. This scope includes sufficient extensive examinations and checks to show that the structures, main and essential auxiliary machinery, systems and equipment of the ship are in a satisfactory condition and are fit for the service for which the ship is intended, in so far as the requirements concerned are met.

Between surveys, the conventions require the flag administration to make it compulsory for the owner to maintain the ship according to the regulations to ensure that the ship will in all respects remain fit to proceed to sea without danger to the ship or persons on board and without unreasonable threat of harm to the marine environment.

The core objective in regular survey programmes is to realize the highest standards of ship safety. The IMO are very conscious of this objective and through their committee mechanism – primarily Maritime Safety Committee – regularly review ship safety, especially with new marine engineering technology on board; GMDSS; ISM code; accidents and the latest generation of new build. Examples emerging from SOLAS 1974 include new provisions emerging from the *Herald of Free Enterprise* disaster featuring ship stability, Chapter II–1, entry into force 1990; grain shipments, Chapter VI; cargo stowage, entry into force January 1994; sinking of *Estonia* featuring new stability for ro/ro passenger ships, Chapters II–1, III, IV, V, VI, entry into force July 1997; high speed craft code 2000, entry into force July 2002; a new generation of high speed craft; Chapters II–1 and XII, embracing new safety measures for construction; and safety focus on bulk carriers, entry into force July 2004.

Finally, with reference to Figure 3.2, focus now moves to some of the various types of survey: (a) the class renewal surveys and/or special surveys are carried out at five-year intervals – these include extensive examination to check that the hull structures, main and essential auxiliary machinery, systems and equipment of the ship remain in a condition which satisfy ship classification rules; (b) the annual survey must be carried out from three months before to three months after each anniversary date – the ship undergoes inspection of the hull, equipment and machinery; (c) an intermediate survey must be carried out within the period from three months before the second to three months after the third anniversary date; (d) bottom/docking survey is the examination of the outside of the ship's hull and related items; (e) the tail shaft survey is the survey of screw shafts and tube shafts; (f) a partial survey allows a postponement of the complete survey, having a periodicity of five years for two and a half years; (g) and non-periodical surveys are carried out at a time of port state control inspections, to update classification documents following change of owner, flag, name of ship, or to deal with damage, repair/renewal, conversion or postponement of surveys.

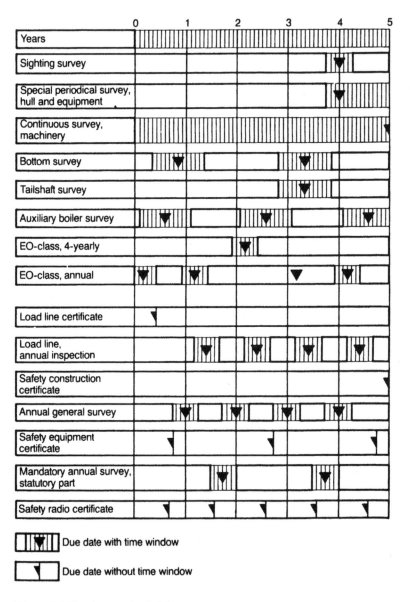

Figure 3.2 Non-harmonized ship survey programme.

Source: Reproduced by courtesy of Det Norske Veritas.

3.8 Vessel lengthening

The operational life cycle of a vessel will vary by ship type and throughout this period the economics of the investment changes. Vessels are tending to be of higher capacity and are increasingly high-tech. These developments involve a refit, maybe an engine transplant, refurbishment, new technology. In some cases a ship is lengthened to take advantage of deeper draught and/or increase its maximum permitted length for using the Panama Canal. An example of increasing ship capacity has arisen in the cruising fleet of Royal Caribbean; for example, the *Song of Norway* was lengthened in 1978, the *Nordic Prince* in 1980 and the *Enchantment* in 2005.

The *Enchantment* was lengthened 22 m to give an overall length of 301–4 m and now provides 151 additional cabins, increasing the passenger certificate to 2,730. Lengthening results in a marginal increase in crew and in fuel consumption. The vessel now offers new public spaces, such as a speciality restaurant, fitness rooms, conference room, a coffee shop and ice cream parlour. On deck various luxurious jacuzzis have been constructed, together with a row of trampolines.

The specialist shipyard in The Netherlands, Keppel Verolme, cut the vessel in two and inserted a mid-section between the two halves of the vessel. It took five weeks to undertake this phase of the work in dry dock at Botlekhaven. The task demanded high engineering skills and involved 1,100 cables, 120 pipes and 60 air ducts to cut, together with 600 m of heavy steel plate. Two days after this operation the new mid-section was positioned. It was constructed at the Keppel Verolme shipyard where the *Enchantment* was launched in 1997. The new mid-section was moved to Rotterdam on a special transport pontoon of sea towage company Smit and positioned, using eight hydraulic hoists, next to the dry docked ship. A specially developed skid system – a form of slide – was used to insert the new mid-section. The ship itself was placed on a similar facility. Following completion of the cutting, the bow segment could be slid forward. Powerful screw jacks were used to move this part of the ship that weighed in excess of 10,000 tonnes. After the new section had been correctly placed – an operation taking two hours – screw jacks were used to push the parts back together until they touched again.

Tensions in the hull of the ship caused a deviation of about 6 cm at the top of the different segments. Work then progressed to weld together the parts from the bottom. In this way the top parts became neatly pressed together again. The welding together of the bow part and afterdeck of the mid-section proved an intensive operation: the welders worked day and night for the twenty-four hour periods to reassemble the ship's hull.

The benefits of having a mid-section installed in a vessel include: prolonged life of the vessel; increased capacity, exploitation of economies of scale through crew complement, bunker and increased freight/passenger revenue; increases in voyage profitability, more competitive tonnage, less capital expenditure to lengthen vessel than build a replacement; timescale much quicker, as vessel conversion takes weeks and not two or three years for new tonnage; vessel pay-back much earlier, as ship starts to earn revenue following conversion; ship capacity can take advantage of enlarged facilities, such as Panamax tonnage; new technology decreases vessel turn-round time in port; and a brand image of converted tonnage strengthens the market appeal of new business. Study Figure 3.5.

3.9 Cruise vessels

Growth in the cruise market since the 1990s has been dramatic and in 2004 carried 10.5 million people. This growth has been due to a number of factors: the decline in the package holiday market; the enormous growth in new cruise tonnage, especially vessels above 2,000 passenger capacity, permitting economies of scale; a new era of cruise ship design, with focus on all age groups, especially younger people and families; development of the fly-cruise market; increasing consumer wealth, especially in developed countries, which stimulates global travel; and a continuous expansion of cruise itineraries.

The cruise market falls into the following divisions: Mediterranean, Caribbean, Atlantic Isles, Scandinavia/Baltic; North America, round the world cruises, and river cruises, especially in Europe. Over 40 cruise lines exist, embracing Carnival Cruise Line, Cunard Line, Mediterranean Shipping Cruises, Royal Caribbean International, P&O Cruises and Swan Hellenic. The North American and Mediterranean markets are the largest.

Carnival Cruise Line in 2005 launched *Carnival Liberty*. This 110,000 GT vessel was built in 24 months and is 290 m long and 38 m wide and has 2,121 cabins with a passenger capacity of 3,710 served by a crew of 1,182. It has a cruising speed of 20 knots and has a 1,500 seat theatre, five swimming pools, four restaurants and 22 bars. A post-Panamax ship has been constructed for Celebrity Cruises. It is 117,000 GT and has a passenger capacity of 2,850 passengers. The cost is US$640 million, involving a berth price of US$225,000. The width of the ship is 36.8 m and length 315 m. It is the first wide body construction ship for Celebrity Cruises and 90% of the outside cabins have balconies. The ship is equipped with pod propulsion and diesel engines, having a combined output of 91,400 hp.

Cruise operators are very conscious of keeping pace with the new generation of cruise tonnage. They tend to replace the main engines with more efficient propulsion and completely refurbish passenger shipboard facilities to meet twenty-first century passenger expectations. An example is the cruise ship *Albatross* of 28,518 GT which is fitted with four Wärtilä main engines, displacing the old Sulzer 9ZH40/48 engines. The ship was built in 1973 and the engine transplant was undertaken in 2005 in Hamburg's Blohm & Voss repair yard.

Many maritime economists think that there will be two prime divisions in the foreseeable future. These are mega-cruise tonnage of 2,000 passenger capacity and above and smaller cruise vessels operating in niche markets.

The cruise business continues to change as new tonnage is launched. In 2005 Stelios Haji-Ioannou inaugurated the ship *easyCruise One*. It was focused on younger passengers. Overall it provided a holiday price that was affordable for many, so the vessel has very few amenities. The vessel has 74 double cabins and seven four-berth cabins, all of which are internal. All cabins have bathroom facilities. Four suites are on the top deck. The cabin accommodation is spread over five decks. A sports bar provides food, a cocktail bar has an outside whirlpool, and there is a Caffe Ritazza for coffee. Prices in 2005 for one night were US$56 for a two berth cabin with a minimum stay of two nights. Once on the ship it cost passengers US$20 each time they wanted their cabin serviced.

3.10 General structure of cargo vessels

Cargo vessels can be classified according to their hull design and construction. Single-deck vessels have one deck, on top of which are often superimposed three 'islands': forecastle, bridge and poop. Such vessels are commonly referred to as the 'three-island type'. This type of vessel is suited to the carriage of heavy cargoes in bulk, because easy access to the holds (with only one hatch to pass through) means that they are cheap to load and discharge. The most suitable cargoes for single-deck vessels are heavy cargoes carried in bulk, such as coal, grain and iron ore. However, these vessels also customarily carry such light cargoes as timber and esparto grass, which are stowed on deck as well as below, the large clear holds making for easy stowage and the three islands affording protection for the deck cargo. This type of vessel is not suitable for general cargo, as there are no means of adequately separating the various items of cargo.

There are a number of variations in the single-deck type of vessel. Some vessels, for example, may be provided with a short bridge while others have a longer bridge.

The 'tween-deck type of vessel has other decks below the main deck, and all run the full length of the vessel. These additional decks below the main deck are known as the 'tween decks; some vessels in the liner trades often have more than one 'tween deck, and they are then known as the upper and lower 'tween decks. 'Tween-deck tonnage is now much in demise, because containerization is superseding it.

An example of a products carrier is found in Figure 3.3. It has an overall length of 182.5 m and a draught of 11.0 m. The service speed is 14 knots. The vessel has a twin-skin double bottom hull structure to give clean, smooth cargo tanks which permit easy and rapid cleaning from one cargo to another and offer reduced heating and coating maintenance costs; individual tank-mounted cargo pumps which strip the tanks efficiently, without problematic long suction lines that obviate the need to have a shipboard pump room; deck-mounted heat exchangers for efficient control of cargo temperature; and versatility of cargoes embracing all of the common oil products and a range

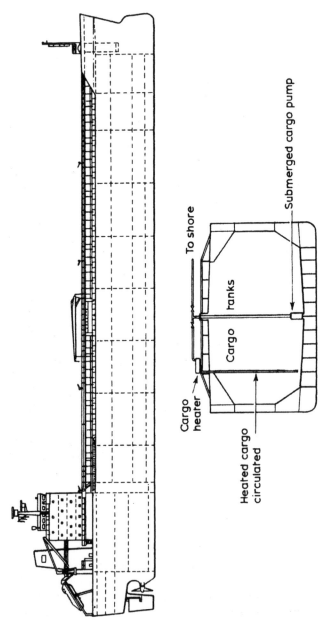

Figure 3.3 Tango products carrier, 47,300 dwt, ideal for bulk shipment of gasoline, aviation gasoline, jet fuel, naphtha diesel fuel, fuel oil, caustic soda, ethanol, BTX, molasses and vegetable oil.

Source: Reproduced by kind permission of British Shipbuilders Ltd.

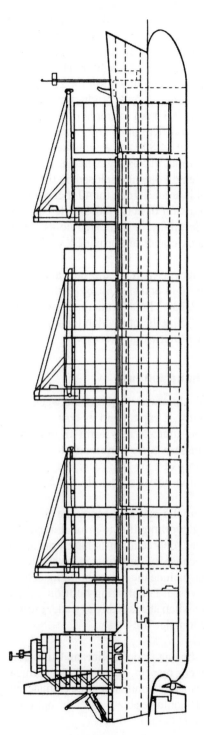
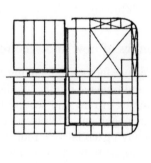

Figure 3.4 Compact container ship of 21,800 dwt and capacity of 1,739 TEU. The crucial feature is its flexibility and fuel economy, as it can hold both 20 ft and 40 ft containers, plus the maximum earning capacity with higher container numbers for the hull envelope. It is ideal for worldwide container trading.

Source: Reproduced by kind permission of British Shipbuilders Ltd.

of easy chemicals including gasoline, aviation gasoline, jet fuel, naphtha, diesel fuel, fuel oil, caustic soda, ethanol, BTX, vegetable oil and molasses. A products carrier has a total deadweight tonnage of 47,300 and a cargo capacity of 50,000 m³ which, for example, would be sufficient for a 30,000 tonne cargo of naphtha. The vessel has 9 tanks and crew accommodation for 25 persons.

This vessel is suitable for worldwide trading in bulk product markets. (It is called the Tango products carrier: Figure 3.3.) An example of a container vessel is found in Figure 3.4. It has an overall length of 162 m and draught of 9.75 m. It has a total deadweight tonnage of 21,800 and a container capacity of 1,739 TEUs. The service speed is 18 knots. It has eight hatches. All are unobstructed and provide full width 40 ft length openings closed by lift on/lift off pontoon-type hatch covers. All the holds are designed for 40 ft containers; 20 ft boxes can be stowed using a combination of cell guides, side bars and stacking cones without the use of portable guides or dedicated holds. Three electro-hydraulically operated slimline deck cranes are provided, each of 36 tonnes capacity.

The vessel is suitable for feeder services as part of the hub and spoke network. It is called a Compact container ship and is built by British Ship-builders Ltd in a size range from 600 to 2,100 TEUs. Sometimes, when the holds have been designed to form a series of cells into which the containers are placed, such tonnage is described as cellular cargo vessels.

3.11 Economics of new and second-hand tonnage

The most decisive factors influencing the shipowner's choice between new and second-hand tonnage are the availability of capital and its cost.

The economics of new and second-hand tonnage now form an important part of ship management. Moreover, with ship costs continuing to rise, the economics of buying a relatively modern ship of up to five years in age proves an attractive proposition, despite conversion costs, especially for countries experiencing hard currency problems.

Among the disadvantages inherent in buying new tonnage is the adequate depreciation of the vessel during its normal working life, to provide funds for replacement. At present, in some countries, depreciation is based on initial and not on replacement cost, which because of inflation is likely to be considerably higher. Further disadvantages include the risk of building delays; uncertain costs at time of delivery if the vessel is not being built on a fixed price; and possible recession in the market when she is ready to trade. Further advantages/disadvantages of buying new tonnage are these:

(a) The vessel is usually built for a particular trade/service and therefore should prove ideal for the route in every respect, i.e. speed, economical crewing, ship specification, optimum capacity, modern marine engineering technology, ship design, etc. In short, it should be able to offer the optimum service at the lowest economical price.

(b) It usually raises service quality and such an image should generate additional traffic.
(c) It facilitates optimum ship operation, particularly if there is a fleet of sister ships aiding minimum stocking of ship spares/ replacement equipment.
(d) Service reliability should be high.
(e) Maintenance and survey costs should be lower than older second-hand tonnage, particularly in a vessel's early years.
(f) New tonnage presents the opportunity to modernize terminal arrangements, particularly cargo transhipment, cargo collection and distribution arrangements, etc. Overall it should improve the speed of cargo transhipment arrangements and reduce ship port turn-round time to a minimum. This all helps to make the fleet more productive.
(g) A significant disadvantage is the timescale of the new tonnage project which can extend up to three years from the time the proposal is first originated in the shipping company to when the vessel is accepted by the shipowner from the shipyard following successful completion of trials. During this period the character and level of traffic forecast could have changed dramatically and/or adversely. In such circumstances it may prove difficult to find suitable employment for the vessel elsewhere.
(h) Annual ship depreciation is substantially higher than the vessel displaced, whilst crew complement is generally much lower.

With second-hand tonnage, a shipowner has the advantage of obtaining the vessel at a fixed price, which may be considerably lower per deadweight ton in comparison with a new vessel. Furthermore, the vessel is available for service immediately the sale is concluded. Conversely, the shipowner will have to face higher maintenance costs for his vessel, lower reliability, generally higher operating costs and its quicker obsolescence, creating a poor image of the service. He is also unlikely to benefit from any building subsidies or cheap loans – available for the new tonnage in certain countries – despite the fact that the shipowner may be involved in a conversion of second-hand tonnage.

Other significant advantages and disadvantages of second-hand tonnage are detailed below:

(a) On completion of the purchase the vessel is generally available for service commencement. However, sometimes the new owner may wish to have the ship painted to his own house flag colours and undertake any alterations to facilitate the economic deployment of the vessel. For example, a new section could be inserted in the vessel to lengthen it and increase cargo accommodation. The extent of such alterations will depend on the trade, age and condition of the vessel and capital availability. The owner's paramount consideration will be the economics of the alterations and the capital return on his investment.
(b) Second-hand tonnage is ideal to start a new service, enabling the operator to test the market in a low-risk capital situation. In the event of the service

proving successful, new tonnage can be introduced subsequently. Likewise, to meet a short-term traffic increase extending over 18/24 months, it may prove more economic to buy second-hand tonnage rather than charter. The advantage of a charter is that the vessel is ultimately returned to the owner to find employment elsewhere, although with some charters there is an option to purchase on completion of the charter term.

(c) Second-hand tonnage tends to be costly to operate in crewing and does not usually have the ideal ship specification, i.e. slow speed, limited cargo capacity, poor cargo transhipment facilities. Such shortcomings can be overcome by ship modification, but this is unlikely to produce an optimum vessel for the service. Ship insurance premium is likely to be high with older vessels, particularly for those over 15 years.

(d) The vessel is likely to have a relatively short life and maintenance/survey/operating costs are likely to be high. If the ship registration is to be transferred from one national flag to another, this can prove costly because standards differ. Moreover, it is not always possible to assess accurately the cost involved until conversion work is in progress. Conversely depreciation is likely to be low.

(e) Service quality could be rather indifferent whilst reliability, i.e. schedule punctuality, could be at risk. For example, the engines may be prone to breakdown and additional crew personnel may be required to keep them maintained to a high reliable standard.

An example of a lengthened third-generation ro/ro container ship is provided in Figure 3.5. It has a draught of 9.75 m, a speed of 20.4 knots and 51,477 dwt.

Finally the ship operator, when conducting the feasibility study of whether to opt for new or second-hand tonnage, must also consider chartered or leased tonnage. Advantages include: no long-term commitment or disposal problems but merely its economical operation for the duration of the charter; almost immediate access to the ship to commence operation; the prospect of a wider range of vessels available for fixture; and the possibility of a more economical modern-type vessel being available. Many shipowners tend to introduce new services or supplement existing services through chartered tonnage.

Market forecasts represent an important aspect both in the acquisition of second-hand ships and in the interface between potential freight and operating/capital costs. Hence the entrepreneur buying second-hand tonnage must formulate an action plan embracing all the ingredients of the project and place a project manager in sole charge. A key factor is the vetting of the ship, involving a physical examination and ideally in a dry dock that has independent surveyor evaluation. All the ship's documents must be thoroughly examined and checked to establish the history of the vessel. The experienced surveyor will be familiar with future regulations involving the IMO conventions and the operational/financial compliance with such obligations. The interface between the ship specification and the ports of call must be examined. Any

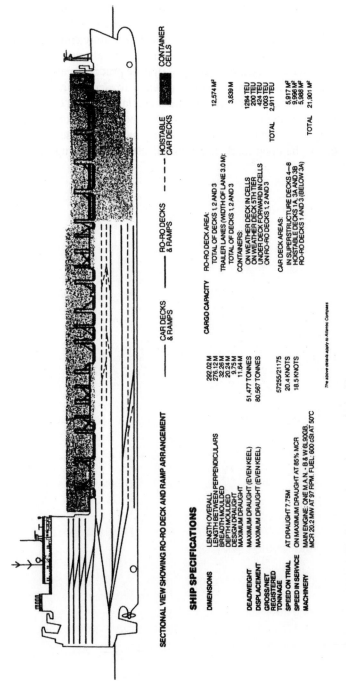

Figure 3.5 Lengthened third generation ro/ro container ship.

Source: Reproduced by kind permission of Atlantic Container Line.

ship modification embracing lengthening, engine transplant, hold modification or refurbishing, such as cruise tonnage and cargo transhipment equipment, must be examined. A financial appraisal is required embracing income/freight, operating cost, crew, fuel, port charges, expenditure embracing survey, insurance and capital investment involving ship alterations and legal compliance with SOLAS, etc., provisions. It may be prudent to examine several vessels and conduct a feasibility study of each to decide the best one. A memorandum featuring all these points and financial appraisal over a five year cycle. A key factor is the method of funding the second-hand tonnage, including return on capital, cost of commercial loans, sale of displaced tonnage, or raising capital on the open market. The implications of gearing must also be considered.

4 Ships, their cargoes, trades and future trends

4.1 Types of ships

The type of merchant vessel employed on a trade route is mainly determined by the traffic carried. There are roughly three main divisions: liners, tramps and specialized vessels, such as tankers.

On occasion, and in particular when merchant vessels in one division are underemployed, a ship may be transferred to another division. For example, a tramp may be put on a liner berth to compete for liner cargoes. Conversely, liners may at times carry tramp cargoes, either as full or part cargoes.

Since the 1990s there has been a trend towards the development of the multi-purpose vessel and the combined transport system. Need for the multi-purpose vessel has arisen to combat trade fluctuations and to enable the vessel to be more flexible in operation. Not only can the vessel vary the cargo mixture capacity on a particular voyage, but also she can switch from one trade to another. Such tonnage, although more expensive to build, should decrease the volume of laid-up tonnage. Examples of multi-purpose tonnage are found particularly in the vehicular ferry and container vessel and an increasing number of combination bulk cargo vessels, including tramp vessels.

A further significant factor is the growing emphasis on quick port turn-round time, the development of logistics and rising standards in ship management and a range of the IMO regulatory measures. This has been manifest in tankers, LNG, container tonnage and a whole range of types of ships. An example of a new range of vessels is the fast ferry. A description of each division follows.

Today, developing countries are taking an increasing share of the world's manufacturing output consequent on the accelerating trend for relocation from high cost to low cost countries. This in turn has lengthened average transport distances for many manufactured articles; and since most of this international transport of raw materials and manufactured goods is by ship, some of it 'added value', demand for shipping services has increased (Tables 1.1 and 1.2). Hence there is a growing shift from European tonnage ownership to Asian countries (Tables 1.4 and 1.5).

4.2 Liners

These are vessels that ply on a regular scheduled service between groups of ports. Readers should note that it is this function, and not the size or speed, which defines the liner. Liner services offer cargo space to all shippers who require them. They sail on scheduled dates, irrespective of whether they are full or not. Hence in liner operation the regular scheduled service is the basis of this particular division, and it is vitally important to the shipowner that everything is done to ensure punctual sailing and arrival dates, otherwise company prestige quickly declines. Liner operation involves an adequately sized fleet and a fairly large shore establishment. Today the modern liner cargo service is multi-modal and is sophisticated in terms of its logistics and computerized operations. Liner companies are continuously striving to improve efficiency and reduce overall transit times to stimulate trade development and improvement in market share. The liner company therefore tends to be a large concern and in more recent years it operates its container tonnage on a consortia basis. However, there still remains in service a very small volume of 'tween-deck break-bulk cargo vessels, particularly in the subcontinent, Orient area, the developing countries and Eastern bloc markets. These vessels are being phased out and displaced by container tonnage, a growing proportion of which is multi-purpose.

The cargo liner operation today falls into several distinct divisions. It is characterized by a regular all year round service operating on a fixed route to ports situated in different countries. It conveys general cargo in a container or trailer/truck or as break bulk (loose cargo). The vessel sails whether she is full or not. The development of combined transport also involves inland distribution by road/rail through the use of a combined transport bill of lading involving a through-rate door-to-door from warehouse to warehouse. Each type is designed to achieve fast turn-round times and a high level of ship management efficiency. Vessels are completely integrated into the seaport operation which involves purpose-built berths and extensive port and inland infrastructure (see Chapter 17), and include container tonnage, ro/ro passenger (road haulage unit/motorist/passenger), ro/ro container, ro/ro other cargo, general cargo/passenger, general cargo single-deck, general cargo multi-deck, and general cargo/container. The container and ro/ro tonnage make up the prime growth sectors as countries worldwide develop their seaports and land freight links to accept this efficient and reliable unitized method of global distribution. Much of the container tonnage is integrated into the seaport's overland rail distribution network. Increasing amounts of liner cargo in all categories of tonnage are being customs cleared inland and away from the former traditional seaport area, and greater proportions of a port's infrastructure operation is now computerized. The era of the global logistics supply chain is fast developing, involving the hub and spoke system. Moreover, decline of the liner conference network has resulted in a new breed of liner management which focuses on door-to-door transit, the supplier to consumer, embracing combined transport, and not as hitherto seaport to seaport transit. Overall the operation is high-tech, with continuous monitoring/tracking of the container throughout its transit.

4.3 Tramps

The tramp, or general trader as she is often called, does not operate on a fixed sailing schedule, but merely trades in all parts of the world in search of cargo, primarily bulk cargo. Such cargoes include steel, coal, grain, timber, sugar, ores, fertilizers, copra, etc., which are carried in complete shiploads. Many of the cargoes are seasonal. The tramp companies are much smaller than their liner cargo counterparts, and their business demands an intimate knowledge of market conditions. In recent years the family tramp business has merged with like-minded family tramp businesses to raise capital for new/second-hand tonnage and because of this have become more efficient in operation and in ship management. Many tramp businesses are adopting a third party ship management strategy, especially in manning, ship survey, bunkering and insurance.

Tramps are an unspecialized type of vessel, with two to six holds, each having large unobstructed hatches. They are primarily designed for the conveyance of bulk cargoes. Some ships are built with special facilities particularly suitable to the five main tramp trades: grain, coal, bauxite, phosphates and iron ore. The modern tramp vessel has a speed of 14/15 knots. The bulk carrier (Figure 4.1) is designed with a single-deck hull which includes an arrangement of topside ballast tanks and holds specially designed for the bulk carriage of various types of loose dry cargo of a homogeneous nature. This includes grain, coal and iron ore. The cargo handling mode may be lift on or lift off to and from the holds by way of weather deck hatches, or alternatively by use of specialized shore-based equipment. Various features may include (a) hopper tanks – which may be combined with topside tanks, (b) strengthening for the carriage of heavy cargo (including ore), (c) holds equipped for the carriage of containers – container securing arrangements – or for the carriage of vehicles – hoistable vehicle decks accessed by way of sheet side doors, (d) weather deck equipped with stanchions for the carriage of logs, (e) self-discharging apparatus, including hopper-shaped holds and in-hold conveyer belts, (f) and design restraints and service restrictions pertaining to operations on the Great Lakes of North America.

An analysis of the bulk carrier world fleet and new building orders comparison is given in Table 4.1. The family tramp operator tends to manage the smaller capacity vessel and, with a limited range of multipurpose shipboard facilities, concentrates on the five bulk homogeneous tramp trades.

To raise safety standards in the bulk carrier tonnage and take advantage of new technology, the IMO revised SOLAS Chapter XII adopted by the MSC79 in December 2004 and which became mandatory in July 2006. This revision concerned those damage stability requirements applicable to bulk carriers,

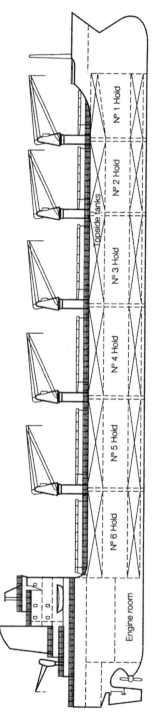

Figure 4.1 Bulk carrier, a ship designed with a single-deck hull, which includes an arrangement of topside ballast tanks and holds specifically designed for the bulk carriage of various types of loose dry cargo of a homogeneous nature. The cargo handling mode may be lift on/lift off to and from the holds by way of weather deck hatches or, alternatively, by way of specialized shore-based equipment. Various features may include: hopper side tanks (which may be combined with the topside tanks); strengthening for the carriage of heavy cargo (including ore); holds equipped for the carriage of containers (container securing arrangements) or for the carriage of vehicles (hoistable vehicle decks, accessed by way of shell side doors); weather deck equipped with stanchions for the carriage of logs; self-discharging apparatus, including hopper-shaped holds, in-hold conveyor belts and a self-unloading boom; design restraints and service restrictions pertaining to operation on the Great Lakes of North America. Related types include: wood chip carrier; cement carrier, with no weather deck hatches, but pumping; piping arrangements for the loading and unloading of cement; ore carrier, two longitudinal bulkheads, side tanks, ore carried in centre holds only; Ore/Bulk/Oil carrier (OBO), a bulk carrier with the additional facilities for the alternative (but not simultaneous) bulk carriage of oil; ore/oil carrier, an ore carrier with additional facilities for alternative (but not simultaneous) bulk carriage of oil.

Table 4.1 Bulk carrier fleet (world tonnage on order, 2000–11)

Beginning of month	Thousands of dwt	Ships	Average vessel size (dwt)[a]
December 2000	31,208	486	64,214
December 2001	22,184	353	62,845
December 2002	28,641	391	73,251
December 2003	46,732	640	73,019
December 2004	62,051	796	77,953
December 2005	66,614	805	82,750
December 2006	79,364	988	80,328
December 2007	221,808	2,573	86,206
March 2008	243,600	2,804	86,876
June 2008	262,452	3,009	87,222
September 2008	288,959	3,316	87,141
December 2008	292,837	3,347	87,492
March 2009	289,763	3,303	87,727
June 2009	280,102	3,194	87,696
September 2009	269,558	3,050	88,380
December 2009	258,343	2,918	88,534
March 2010	250,383	2,890	86,638
June 2010	257,229	2,951	87,167
September 2010	252,924	2,887	87,608
December 2010	239,898	2,823	84,980
March 2011	236,431	2,786	84,864
June 2011	218,453	2,601	83,988
September 2011	204,580	2,470	82,826
December 2011	184,353	2,268	81,284
% of total, December 2011	55.4	33.1	

Source: Compiled by the UNCTAD Secretariat, on the basis of data supplied by *IHS Fairplay*. Reproduced with the kind permission of UNCTAD Secretariat.

Note: [a] Seagoing propelled merchant ships of 100 GT and above.

especially concerning their structural strength. It also included an enhanced programme of inspections of bulk carriers which came into force in January 2007.

Further types of bulk carrier include the cement carrier without weather deck hatches but which has pumping and piping arrangements for the loading and unloading of cement. Numbers of this type of vessel are in decline because of displacement by containerized shipment. The ore carrier has two longitudinal bulkheads, and side tanks, one of which is carried in the centre holds only.

An example of a modern flexible container/bulk carrier ship is found in Figure 4.2. It has eight holds and a deadweight tonnage of 45,500 with a

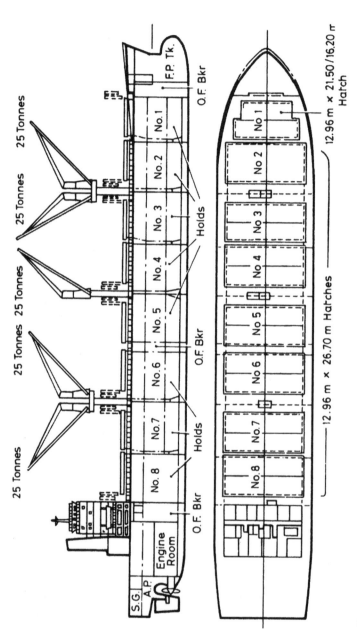

Figure 4.2 Combi King 45 flexible container/bulk carrier. This vessel, of 45,000 dwt, has a grain capacity of 58,700 m³ or a container capacity of 2,127 TEU. It is suitable for worldwide trading in the bulk carriage of grain, coal, ore, bauxite, phosphates, packaged timber, standard pipe lengths and containers.

Source: Reproduced by kind permission of British Shipbuilders Ltd.

draught of 12.2 m. The service speed is 14 knots and the ship's overall length is 194.30 m. The cargo hold grain capacity is 58,700 m³. Container capacity totals 2,127 TEUs of which 1,069 TEUs are above deck. It has one single 25 tons and two twin 25 tons electro-hydraulic deck cranes all fitted with grabs. The crew accommodation complement is 25, of which 9 are officers. The vessel is suitable for worldwide trading in the bulk carriage of grain, coal, ore, bauxite, phosphates, packaged timber, standard pipe lengths and containers. The vessel is called the Combi King 45 flexible container/bulk carrier.

Tramp vessels are engaged under a document called a charter party, on a time or voyage basis. The role of the tramp vessel market continues to change. The tramp operator tends to buy second-hand tonnage and the Greeks remain strong in the market. The trend to have long-term time charters of five to 10 years' duration is becoming more popular.

4.4 Specialized vessels and their trades

A number of cargo ships are designed for carrying a particular commodity, or group of commodities. Such specialization is the result of demand, but its provision may also create a new demand depending on the extent of the market. Examples of such specialized vessels are ore carriers and sugar carriers. A description follows of the more usual types of ship, and, in view of the preponderance of tankers in this group, these will be examined first.

(a) Oil tanker tonnage

The growth of oil tanker tonnage continues to increase annually. In 2011/12 the percentage rise was 6.9%. Overall, this represents 33.1%, or 507,454 dwt, of the world's fleet. The world tanker fleet is one of the most modern. This is due to the mandatory requirement of all 'Category 1' tankers to be double hull structured, to displace single hull tonnage. The phasing out of single hull oil tankers, after the banning of the carriage of heavy grade oil in such tonnage, was adopted in December 2003 as amendments to Annex I of the MARPOL Convention followed the November 2002 sinking of the oil tanker *Prestige* off the Spanish coast. Category 2 and 3 oil tankers were phased out in 2010. The double hull requirements for oil tankers are principally designed to reduce the risk of oil spills from tankers involved in low energy collisions or groundings. Category 1 oil tankers – commonly known as PREMARPOL tankers – include oil tankers of 20,000 dwt and above carrying crude oil, fuel oil, heavy diesel oil or lubricating oil as cargo and tankers of 30,000 dwt and those carrying other oils that do not comply with the requirements of protectively located segregated ballast tanks.

Category 2 oil tankers – commonly known as MARPOL tankers – feature oil tankers of 20,000 dwt and above that carry crude oil, fuel oil, heavy diesel oil or lubricating oil as cargo and those oil tankers of 30,000 dwt and above which carry other oils that comply with the protectively located segregated ballast tank requirement.

Finally, Category 3 tankers are oil tankers of 5,000 dwt and above, but less than category 1 and 2 tankers. Exemptions are permitted for categories 2 and 3 under special circumstances, subject to a condition assessment scheme, but the phase-out date must not go beyond 2015 or the date on which the ship reaches 25 years of age. Hence the average age of the world tanker tonnage will soon be the lowest on record, modern and increasingly productive. Throughout this period many shipyards have had full order books.

In more recent years the oil-producing countries have tended both to own and to operate their own tanker fleet and have as a result achieved complete control over distribution arrangements and costs. Moreover, they are shipping oil as refined oil and thus are not, as previously, allowing major importing industrial nations to refine it and re-export it. Their income is thus improved. A significant proportion of the world tanker fleet is under charter, often on a long-term charter to oil companies. Hitherto oil companies owned and managed tankers, but that era has passed.

Crude oil is transported from oil fields to refineries and petroleum and fuel oil is transported from refineries to distribution centres and bunkering ports. There is now a worldwide network of tanker routes. Investment in pipeline distribution continues globally, resulting in a reduction in short haul business. This strategy, together with other considerations, has resulted in increased productivity, as measured in ton-miles per deadweight ton, from an increase in the long haul business, notably from crude oil. Productivity in terms of tons carried per deadweight ton for oil tanker was 6.7 in 2003 compared with 4.8 in 1980. This improvement continued as the double hull tonnage investment programme neared completion in 2010. There now follows an examination of the range of oil tankers (see Figure 4.3).

(b) Ultra Large Crude Carriers (ULCC)

Vessels in this category range from 300,000 dwt to 500,000 dwt. This category is being phased out. Replacement tonnage is almost nil. The reason for this is the inflexibility of the tonnage, as few ports could accommodate them and because some operators adopted a multi-port operation by calling/discharging at two ports.

(c) Very Large Crude Carriers (VLCC)

Tankers in this category range from 150,000 dwt to 299,999 dwt capacity. The tanker size exploits economies of scale and new build programmes are very buoyant. The vessel is popular in the Arabian Gulf export trade, which represents 80% of demand, and West African crude trade to Asia.

The future of Arabian Gulf exports and VLCC prospects lies in Asia. The bulk of Asian incremental oil needs will be met by imports from the Arabian Gulf or from West Africa. Long-term demand risks include the deepening and widening of the Suez Canal to accommodate fully loaded VLCCs and the

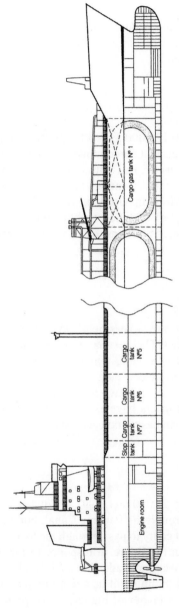

Figure 4.3 Tanker, a category of ship designed with a single deck hull which includes an arrangement of intergral or independent tanks specifically for the bulk carriage of cargo in liquid form. Cargo handling to and from the tanks is by way of shore- and/or ship-based pumping and piping equipment. Tanker types include: oil tanker; chemical tanker; liquefied gas tanker (for LPG and/or LNG), with mainly independent tanks; liquefied gas/chemical tanker; other tankers, e.g. asphalt tanker, fruit juice tanker, with refrigerated holds), wine tanker; water tanker. Various features may include: a double bottom structure, double skin sides and double deck; a particular tank structure/tank coating, or other structural features, which reflect the nature and hazard of the cargo carried; the additional carriage of liquid cargo in independent tanks situated on the weather deck; an additional forward hold for the carriage of dry cargo.

construction of an Iraq–Syria pipeline to the Mediterranean. Most Middle East crude arrives in the Mediterranean via the Sumed pipeline that runs parallel to the Canal. Hence fully loaded VLCC transiting the Suez Canal are likely to put pressure on Sumed rates rather than adversely affect VLCC owners. Of greater concern could be the construction of pipelines that permit export of Iraqi crude through Syrian ports. This would eliminate crude shipments on the far longer sea route around the Cape of Good Hope, which would create a serious reduction in VLCC demand.

(d) Suezmax tanker

This embraces a capacity range from 120,000 dwt to 149,999 dwt. Historically, the name applied to the largest vessels that could transit the Suez Canal. Today the Suezmax vessels are primarily associated with crude exports from West Africa. Other markets that favour this tonnage are the North Sea and Mediterranean trades for local distribution. Growing Black Sea exports from pipelines being built to the Caspian Sea oil fields, together with growing trade from the Caribbean basin to the United States as the berths are improved, will benefit from this tonnage.

(e) Aframax tanker

Aframax means 'average freight rate assessment'. Aframax tankers are between 80,000 dwt and 119,999 dwt. The fleet has expanded dramatically in recent years in response to growing demand, which includes clean product trading. Clean products are refined products, such as aviation spirit and motor spirit. Dirty products are crude oils, such as heavy fuel oils. With the exception of the North Sea, Aframax crude carriers have exhibited growth on all their trade routes, especially the Caribbean basin and east coast of North America.

(f) Panamax tanker

Tankers in this category range from 50,000 dwt to 80,000 dwt. These tankers are presumed to be able to pass through the Panama Canal, but a number of vessels in this size category are too beamy to pass through the locks. However, the term 'Panamax' may change in the future in response to the expansion programme of the Canal. Panamax tanker trades are mainly identified with fuel oil cargoes. Long-term fuel oil trading will be under pressure as refinery upgrades cut the yield on fuel oil in favour of higher-valued products, such as gasoline, gas oil and natural gas. The Panamax fleet remains small and is likely to remain so. Tanker profitability depends on the volatility in natural gas prices.

(g) Product carrier

Product carriers can be segregated into four major divisions: Aframax, Panamax, 'Handy' and small. Aframaxes primarily carry naphtha cargoes between Arabian Gulf and Japan. Both Aframax and Panamax product carriers often require improvements in port and terminals in order to utilize their larger size. The traditional classes of product carriers are medium-sized or handy product carriers of between 30,000 dwt and 50,000 dwt (see Figure 3.3) and small sized product carriers of between 10,000 dwt and 30,000 dwt. Prospects for small sized product carriers are restricted to intra-regional markets. While intra-regional trading is a sizeable business, small sized product carriers are vulnerable to improvements in port and terminal facilities. The prospects for medium-size products are rather better in that these vessels are properly sized to take advantage of future increases in intra-regional movements of clean products, but these vessels are also vulnerable to improvements in ports and terminals that allow access to Panamax and Aframax product carriers.

(h) Parcel tanker

Parcel tankers are designed to carry chemicals, petroleum products, edible oils and molasses. Vessels of this range vary in size, but have a capacity range between 30,000 dwt and 80,000 dwt. The parcel tanker would have a double hull structure embracing double bottom, double skin sides and other structural features which reflect the nature and hazard of the cargo carried.

(i) FPSO and FSU

A growth development in recent years is the provision of offshore floating production, storage and offloading facilities (FPSOs) and floating storage units (FSUs). Such facilities are for bulk liquids and gases. The FSU is a vessel of hull form structure similar to the FPSO, but without any oil processing capacity. Processing is accomplished at nearby platforms. MARPOL Annex 1 regulations were introduced in January 2007 and deal with the prevention of pollution by oil. Both FPSO and FSU have been developed to reduce oil production costs.

(j) Bulk carrier types

The bulk carrier and oil tanker world fleets represent over 73% of the dwt tonnage, the tanker fleet having about 33% of the tonnage and the dry bulk 40%. It is a growth market and represents single commodity shipments usually under charter. It represents a leading industry in the world. The shuttle oil tanker is subject to continuous change and potential innovation. The four main commodities carried are steel, iron ore, coal and grain (see Figure 4.4).

Figure 4.4 Bulk carrier, Handysize (*Castlegate*).

Source: Photo supplied and reproduced by the kind permission of Zodiac Maritime.

(i)   The *Panamax* tonnage range is between 50,000 dwt and 79,999 dwt. These vessels are deployed on several routes, from east North America, Canada, South Africa, China, India, Sweden and Indonesia. They convey primarily coal and iron ore.

(ii) The *Capesize* dry bulk carrier has a carrying capacity between 80,000 dwt to 170,000 dwt. Such vessels are too large for the Panama Canal and fertilizer/grain berths. The Capesize vessels convey coal and iron ore, and are not economical for fertilizer and grain shipments. Many of the ships were built in Japan and China and their average age is 15 years. World average size is 169,000 dwt. Tonnage is becoming uneconomic, due to the vessels' draught and length size, but still remains cheaper and more economical than two Handymax tonnage. Freight rates in 2008 made Chinamax VLOC viable, ships being built at 400,000 dwt.

(iii) The *Handymax* ship has a capacity range from 35,000 dwt to 49,999 dwt. The world fleet average age is nine years. The vessels are popular with smaller shipments and ideal for smaller ports such as those in Brazil that have restrictions on draught, length and storage. Cargoes include coal, iron ore, fertilizer grain, steel slabs, bauxite, alumina, rock-phosphate and grain. The major routes are Black Sea to the Far East, the US Gulf to Ncsa/Skaw Passero, the Far East to the Atlantic and Australia to India.

(iv) The *Handysize* bulk carrier has a capacity range from 20,000 dwt to 34,999 dwt. It is ideal for smaller shipments of a range of bulk cargo types and for serving ports with limited draught and berth length. An example is grain shipments through the Black Sea from the Ukraine and Russia to the Middle East countries.

To focus on seaborne trade volume/analysis in dry bulk in 2011: world seaborne trade in ton miles totalled 42,000 billion, oil cargoes 11,100 billion ton miles, and the five main bulk cargoes 12,500 billion ton miles. Grain shipments totalled 1,920 billion ton miles, coal 3,600 billion ton miles, and iron ore 6,600 billion ton miles. Brazil and Australia account for nearly 73% of world iron ore exports. China and Japan are the biggest iron ore consumers. Other importers include Middle East countries, America, Africa and EU countries – the EU represents 25% of world iron ore products.

Steel production and consumption continues to increase globally, both industrially and in consumer products. This increase is likely to continue as global industrial/infrastructure develops and consumer demand rises. China and the United States have a high steel consumption. The volume of steel scrap is estimated at 400 million tons, and is rising annually. China is a leading importer of steel.

Coal remains a significant energy source in some markets, especially China. In 1970 the world seaborne trade in billions of ton miles was 481 and by 2011 it had risen to 3,600. Estimates suggest that thermal coal makes up 70% of world coal trade. Indonesia has overtaken Australia as the largest exporter of coal and accounts for 34% of world shipment. The United States and Canada are coking coal exporters. Coking coal is used in steel production. China, Indonesia and South Africa are exporters of thermal coal. Main importers are the EU and Japan – 28% each. The Republic of Korea, Taiwan and Province of China are also importers. The trade depends on thermal coal. Prices are affected by deregulation of the energy market. Coal makes up about 75% of China's electricity generation. Grain shipments, wheat, maize, barley, oats, rye, sorghum and soya beans, are subject to seasonal developments. In 1970 world seaborne trade in ton miles of grain was 475 that by 2011 had risen to 2,920. The largest grain exporter is the United States, at 36%, followed by the EU, Argentina, Australia and east coast of South America.

(k) Coaster

These are all-purpose cargo carriers, operating around coasts. They are normally provided with two holds, each supplied with derricks to handle a variety of cargoes, machinery and crew accommodation are aft. Coasters are subject to severe competition from inland transport.

(l) Combi carrier

To cater for the need to improve ship turn-round time, to increase the versatility of vessel employment and to contain operating cost, an increasing number of vessels are now being introduced. These are called Combi carriers, as illustrated in Figure 4.5. Such vessels are a unitized type of cargo carrier, combining container and vehicular shipments, including ro/ro.

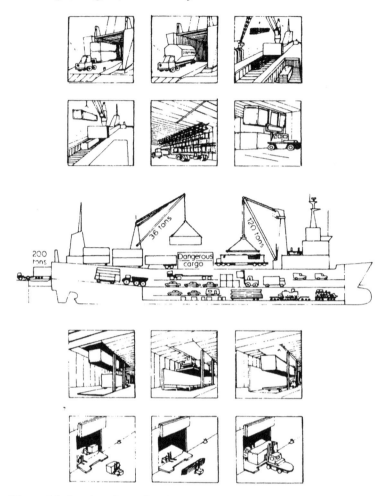

Figure 4.5 Omni carrier, roll on/roll off, lift on/lift off and side loading Combi carrier.

The Combi vessel in Figure 4.5 has an overall length of 135 m and beam of 25 m, with an NRT of 1,714 and GRT of 4,496. Her draught is 6.68 m and dwt (metric) 8,000. The vessel has a container capacity of 516 TEUs with 264 TEUs on the upper deck, 216 TEUs on the main deck and 36 TEUs on the lower deck. The ship has a lane capacity of 563 m on the upper deck, 603 m on the main deck, and 250 m on the lower hold. The car deck area totals 212 m^2 on the main deck and 293 m^2 in the lower hold. The cargo conveyed varies by individual sailing and can be a mixture of containers and vehicle traffic, as illustrated in the figure. This flexibility of ship operation ensures that best use is made of the available vessel capacity and that it responds to market demand.

The vessel is equipped with two derricks of 36 tons and 120 tons, thereby aiding the transhipment of heavy indivisible loads, products much on the increase. By using a medium/heavy duty mobile crane on the quay it is possible to load and discharge at the same time, the vessel using its own gear for loading/discharging through the lift hatch. Loading of containers or other cargo is through the aft hatch. A high capacity fork lift is available for stowing on the main deck. The vessel has a crew of 30.

The stern ramp is 14 m long and has a flap of 4.2 m. The width of the ramp is 8.5 m at the shore-based end. It can be used for fast loading/discharging of containers on trailers or by heavy fork lifts operating with 20 ft containers athwartships.

The spacious main deck may be used for awkward shaped goods, e.g. building cranes, offshore and refinery equipment, prefab building components, etc. The clear height of 6.3 m on the main deck allows double stacking of containers each up to 9 ft 6 in high.

Special suspension hooks underneath the lift provide an additional lifting facility of 60 tons for the transfer of units onto trailers. Containers are placed on trailers for transfer by lift to the lower hold. The lift hatch when required serves as a third point of access for loading/discharging cargo using the shore crane.

A side door of 7.5 × 4.0 m width is provided, allowing simultaneous operation by two fork lifts handling palletized cargo. The wide side door also permits truck loading and the discharge of large items. Containers of 20 ft length can also be handled through the side door.

Advantages of the Combi carrier can be summarized as follows:

(a) It has a versatile cargo mixture, permitting a variation of unitized cargo and awkwardly shaped cargo to be conveyed. This is a major advantage of the cargo liner market, where more consignments are indivisible loads.

(b) The range of cargo transhipment facilities on the vessel, i.e. derricks, stern ramp, side doors, etc., aid quick transhipment and are almost independent of quay transhipment facilities. This independence improves the ship's versatility, particularly in ports where cargo transhipment facilities are poor. It also reduces the cost of using port equipment.

(c) Good shipboard cargo transhipment facilities quicken the ship turn-round time and improve ship utilization/efficiency.

(d) The vessel specification, i.e. draught, beam, length, is an optimum ideal for a wide range of ports, thereby generating versatility of ship employment and worldwide operation.

(e) The vessel is able to convey a wide variety of cargo at economical cost, especially ease of handling.

(f) The ship's specification facilities reduce port congestion because the vessel with its own handling equipment is independent. Furthermore, for example, the 200 ton capacity stern ramp requires only 30 m of quay space.

The foregoing explanation of the Combi carrier specification as illustrated in Figure 4.5 demonstrates the versatility of the vessel. This tonnage is expensive to maintain and is operational in the liner cargo deep sea trades involving less developed nations' seaboards and is being displaced by container and ro/ro tonnage.

(m) Container vessel

These are becoming increasingly predominant in many cargo liner trades (see Figure 4.6). Such tonnage has been described in Chapter 4 and in Figure 3.4. The merits of containerization are described in Chapter 16.

Figure 4.6 Ultra large container ship, 13,000 TEU.

Source: Photo supplied and reproduced by the kind permission of Zodiac Maritime.

(n) Fruit carrier

These are similar in design to refrigerated vessels. Cool air systems are installed in the holds to keep the fruit from over-ripening. Such vessels convey apples, oranges and bananas, and may be owned by the cargo owners. Fast voyage times are essential, otherwise the fruit over-ripens and deteriorates. This type of vessel is in decline now that many shipments are containerized.

(o) Gas tanker

In 2012 the world fleet of liquefied gas carriers was 42,000 million deadweight tons, representing 2.9% of the world fleet. This proportion is likely to increase because of North American growth. The first liquefied gas carrier was built in 1959 and today gas carrying is a growth area. World demand for this energy source is likely to grow annually by 2.75% for the next 20 years. Moreover, production and transport costs have reduced by half since the 1990s, and the cost of sea transport and re-gasification plant has dropped by a third and a quarter respectively. Major gas producers are the United States, Russia Federation, Canada, UK, Algeria and Indonesia. Smaller producers are in the Middle East, Latin America and Asia, often obtaining their natural gas as a result of oil production. Over 20% of natural gas production is exported, mainly through pipelines, which carry 75% of all exports.

An example of a gas tanker, illustrated in Figure 4.7, is the LPG/C *Hans Maersk* of 23,257 dwt and built in 1993. This tanker's overall length is 159.98 m, a beam of 25.6 m and a draught of 8.78/10.90 m, depending on cargo type. The vessel has four bilobe tanks under deck and a pipeline system connected so that two different grades can be cooled simultaneously with two different uncooled grades. The tanks are constructed for loading and carrying cargoes with a temperature down to –48°C. A cargo heater/vaporizer is provided. Cargo can be heated by means of a heat exchanger that uses sea water. The vessel is equipped with a fixed methanol washing system and a methanol storage tank with a capacity of 40 m^3. The tanker can carry anhydrous acids, ammonia, butane, propane, butadiene, propylene, isoprene, monomer propylene oxide, vinyl chloride monomer, methyl chloride and others.

Today, the industry is poised to see a new generation of liquefied natural gas (LNG) ship designs. These include: larger LNG ships; evolution of new tank and hull designs; new approaches to LNG ship boil-off and propulsion; new concepts for offshore floating LNG production; and storage terminals that will necessitate innovative shiploading and discharge facilities. Today's typical deep-water large LNG carriers are 125,000 m^3 to 138,000 m^3 capacity. Smaller tonnage are of 19,000 m^3 to 100,000 m^3 estimated to account for 24% of the fleet and 12% total cargo capacity. These vessels serve trans-Mediterranean markets and buyers in Japan. New build vessels are usually up to 145,000 m^3 capacity.

There are three categories of cargo tank design. Two are based on independent tank design and the other of membrane design utilizing the ship's hull to support the shape of the cargo tank. A feature of the LNG is that the cargo is very cold, –163°C.

The cargo is kept cold in the ship tanks by auto-refrigeration. This involves boiling the cargo. This boil-off gas must be handled safely. The technique is to burn it in the ship's boilers and produce steam for propulsion and electricity generation. As a result all LNG ships today are powered by steam turbine engines using dual-fuel boilers that fire heavy fuel oil and the boil-off gas from the cargo tanks.

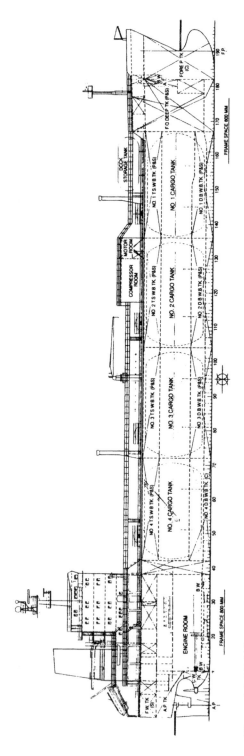

Figure 4.7 LPG/C gas tanker *Hans Maersk*, built 1993, 23,257 dwt, length 159.98 m, beam 25.6 m, draught 8.78/10.90 m depending on cargo type; four bilobe tanks under deck connected by a pipeline system so that two different grades can be cooled simultaneously.

The new generation of LNG feature improvements in tank design, hull design and propulsion type, which will lead to increased cargo-carrying capability, improved efficiency and lower cost for LNG shipments. Ship capacity could rise to 200,000 m³ resulting in changes in berth design, shore storage tank capacity, harbour design featuring channel depth, and turning basin and harbour traffic control. These developments favour long haul trades. Other major innovations are found in the engine room: (a) dual-fuel diesel engines (natural gas and MDO); (b) heavy fuel diesel engines with a re-liquefaction plant; (c) gas turbines – either single or combined cycle; and (d) a combination of these ideas.

Gasfield discoveries located many miles offshore have created an impetus to examine floating production and storage units to serve these remote fields. The design embraces a floating production storage and offloading vessel that incorporates an LNG manufacturing module. Additional modules include a processing facility for dehydration of the gas and extracting liquid petroleum gas, plus a pre-treatment package for removing carbon dioxide, mercury and other contaminants. The whole processing package is designed to fit into the deck of a 312 m long vessel and be capable of delivering 1.5 tons per year of LNG. The vessel is designed to store the LNG until a gas carrier is available for loading, so with six tanks the vessel has a storage capacity of 200,000 m³ – four for LNG and two for LPG (liquid petroleum gas).

(p) General cargo ship

The general cargo ship represents 7% (estimated figures for 2012) of the world fleet size and is designed with a single-deck hull and which has a single holder arrangement of holds and 'tween decks, specially for the carriage of diverse forms of dry cargo. The cargo handling mode is lift on/lift off to and from the holds (and 'tween decks) by way of weather deck (and 'tween-deck) hatches.

Various features may include (a) a single deck, double skin sides and wide deck openings (box shape holds). Vessels of this type may be intended specifically for the carriage of forest products cargo handling which may need use of a gantry crane, (b) strengthening for the carriage of heavy cargoes (including ore), (c) certain holds equipped with container securing arrange-ments, hoistable or movable vehicle decks, or other facilities pertaining to the carriage of a particular type of cargo, (d) the weather deck equipped with container securing arrangements, or arrangements for the shipment of timber, (e) carriage of liquid cargo in specially designed tanks, (f) a refrigerated cargo space for the carriage of perishable cargoes, (g) additional cargo handling to and from the cargo spaces by way of a slide-loading/unloading system (for the carriage of cargo in pallet form and other unitized cargo), and (h) addi-tional cargo handling to and from a 'tween deck by way of a stern, side, or bow door/ramp situated below the weather deck, or where additional cargo segregation is provided by hinged 'tween-deck openings or a hinged mov-able bulk head. The average age of the world general cargo fleet in 2004 was

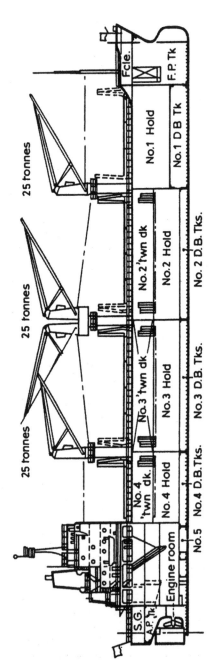

Figure 4.8 Multi King 22 multi-purpose general cargo vessel, 21,500 dwt, grain capacity of cargo hold 30,340 m³, bale capacity 27,950 m³ or container capacity 746 TEU. The vessel is suitable for worldwide trading in general cargoes, dry bulk, long steel products, grain cargoes and containers.

17.5 years. As port modernizations develop more container berths and related infrastructure, container vessels are displacing this type of tonnage.

An example of a multi-purpose general cargo ship is shown in Figure 4.8. It has four holds and a deadweight tonnage of 21,500 with a draught of 10.75 m. The vessel's overall length is 155.5 m and the service speed is 15.3 knots. The cargo hold grain capacity is 30,340 m³ and bale capacity 27,950 m³. The container capacity is 746 TEU, of which some 408 TEU are above deck. The crew complement is 25, nine of whom are officers. The vessel has two single 25 tons and one twin 25 tons electro-hydraulic deck cranes. The vessel is suitable for worldwide trading in general cargoes, dry bulk, long steel products, grain cargoes and containers. The vessel is called the Multi King 22 multi-purpose general cargo ship.

(q) OBO

Ore/bulk/oil ships are multi-purpose bulk carriers designed for switching between bulk shipments of oil, bulk grain, fertilizer and ore trades. A typical vessel would have an overall length of 280 m, draught of 17 m and 270,000 dwt. Its dry cargo capacity would be 170,000 m³ whilst its oil capacity would total 224,000 m³. Cargo space is provided in 11 holds to carry oil of which seven can ship dry cargo or ore as an alternative shipment. Crew accommodation and machinery – much of which is automated – is situated aft. Such vessels, although of high initial cost, are very flexible in their use, keeping ballast voyages to a minimum and are well suited to modern-day requirements in international trade, which demand high capacity (optimum-sized) vessels to move world bulk shipments at a very low cost per ton.

Overall, OBO tonnage represents less than 1% of the world fleet and is in decline, with virtually no new build. The reason for this is a need to find a balanced or triangle trade, coupled with the cost of time consuming cleaning of the vessel's holds/tank structures. Also maintenance costs are high and new tonnage expensive to build.

(r) Passenger vessel

These fall into two distinct divisions. There are those operating in the short sea trade and which have limited cabin accommodation. They also convey motorist and ro/ro (roll-on/roll-off) units. The passenger ship is designed with a multi-deck hull and superstructure specifically for the carriage of passengers in cabin accommodation provided for 12 or more. The trade may be that of cruising or excursions. Additional features may include forward hold or holds for the carriage of cargo, access to which is by lift on/lift off.

Related types include the ferry, a vessel designed to carry passengers. The passenger/ro-ro cargo vessel has passenger facilities and has additional decks in the hull for the carriage of laden vehicles, access to which is by stern or bow door/ramps (Figure 4.9). The passenger/ro-ro cargo/ferry has a passenger certificate awarded under SOLAS regulations.

Figure 4.9 P&O passenger ferry ship *Pride of Kent*, built Bremerhaven 1991–92 as
European Highway, converted 2003: 5,100 dwt, length 179.7 m, beam 28.3
m, displacement 17,894 tonnes, speed 21 knots, capacity 115,15 m units
or 520 cars and 2,000 passengers plus 200 crew.

Source: By courtesy of P&O Ferries.

(s) Platform supply vessels

The A. P. Møller Group, including the Maersk Shipping Company, is a market
leader in the provision of platform supply vessels for the offshore oil and gas
industry. Their fleet exceeds 40 vessels of different types. Platform supply
vessels handle the transportation of all necessary equipment, such as pipes,
cement, tools and provisions, to destinations which include North Sea platforms and drilling rigs. Other tonnage includes multi-purpose anchor handling
tug supply vessels, and advanced multi-purpose offshore support ships. The
total support vessels tow drilling rigs, handle anchors, work as fire-fighting
vessels and are equipped to assist in restraining oil pollution. The world fleet
of offshore support vessels in 2012 was 37.4 million tons dwt, 2.4% of the
world's total fleet.

In 2004 it was estimated that there were 79 drilling rigs for offshore oil
and gas. The largest concentration is in the US 35%; Europe 18%; South East
Asia 18% and the remainder in Africa, Caribbean, Latin America, Far East,
South Pacific and the Mediterranean.

An example of an advanced multi-purpose offshore support vessel is shown
in Figure 4.10, featuring the MS *Maersk Pacer*. It was built in 1991 and has
a speed of 16.6 knots. The overall length is 73.6 m, beam 16.4 m and draught
6.85 m. The vessel has extensive versatile equipment, including a continuous
bollard pull of 180 tons, and towage and very extensive anchor-handling
equipment, including stoppers, shackles, chaser, grapnel, hydraulic guide pins

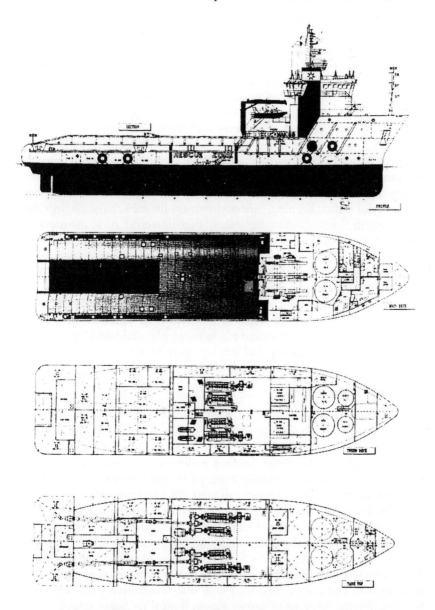

Figure 4.10 Advanced multi-purpose offshore support vessel MS *Maersk Pacer*,
built 1991, 2,651 dwt, overall length 73.6 m, beam 16.4 m, draught
6.55 m, speed 16.6 knots.

of triangular type, winch, triplex shark jaws and rig chain lockers. The bridge equipment/manoeuvring facilities include joystick control, autopilot, gyro compass, repeaters, radars, speed log, Decca and Satnav Shipmates, echo sounder, rapid direction finder facsimile, Navtex and VHF direction finder. Cabin accommodation is provided for six officers and six ratings and there are 12 berths for passengers. A hospital is provided and is equipped to British and Norwegian stand-by rules. The vessel is also equipped for safety/standby duties for 200 survivors, in accordance with Norwegian rules.

The MS *Maersk Pacer* is low on consumption of heavy fuel and is able to carry deck cargo. For towing/anchor handling, she has a high-speed four-drum winch and deep-water anchoring capability, as well as an emergency helicopter landing area, oil recovery capacity, high bow and high freeboard, dry cargo hold, superior station keeping, safe environment for crew, large aft deck, high deck strength, high discharging rates, two powerful bow thrusters and standby/rescue facilities.

The offshore industry continues to grow as maritime oil exploration focuses to meet overall energy global market growth. New technology is being continuously introduced. A market leader is Eidesvck Offshore ASA. This company provides ships and integrated services to oil and gas related activities worldwide. The company operates in the following segments: seismic and survey work; logistics support and platform supply; and stand-by/rescue, oil recovery and anchor handling and sub-sea operations.

(t) Product/chemical carrier

The MT *Rasmine Maersk* featured in Figure 4.11 was built in 1986 and is 27,350 dwt with a US barrel capacity of 195,000. Its gross tonnage is 16,282 and length overall 170 m with a beam of 23.10 m and draught of 11.41 m. Special features of the vessel include a double hull, bow thruster, stern thruster, a hydraulic hose handling crane of 10-ton capacity, an aft crane for stores/provisions of 5-ton capacity, an inert gas generator, nitrogen topping-up, a closed loading system with vapour return, stern discharge, crude oil washing and protective location ballast tanks. This carrier has seven twin cargo tanks situated on port and starboard side and one twin slop tank. It is equipped to convey all petroleum products, crude oil, vegetable oils, molasses, etc., as well as selected IMO class 2 and 3 cargoes. Overall up to eight grades of oil are acceptable and each is provided with true line/double valve separation. The versatility of this type of carrier makes it ideal for many trades.

Cargo and equipment are particularly vulnerable to damage from moisture. For example, when shipping newsprint from cold to warm climates, cargo temperatures can 'lag behind' and humid air from outside can cause condensation, in cargo holds, that damages the cargo. Alfsen & Gunderson AS have designed a cargo hold dehumidifier system. It features a sorption dehumidifier, a circulating air fan and a control/monitoring system that ensures that the cargo arrives dry and undamaged.

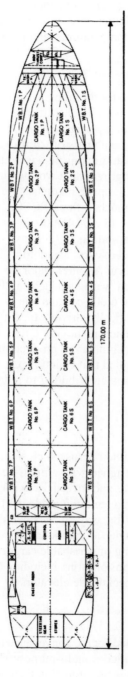

Figure 4.11 Product/chemical carrier MT *Rasmine Maersk*, built 1986, overall length 170 m, beam 23.10 m, draught 11.41 m, 14 tanks.

AG-AS tank dryers are designed for installation on chemical tankers for efficient drying of tanks after cleaning, a method which results in reduced lay time. AG-S maritime dehumidifiers are based on the Recusorb principle: efficient drying at all relevant temperatures, and below 0°C.

(u) Pure Car and Truck Carrier (PCTC)

This type of tonnage is designed for the conveyance of cars, lorries/trucks and other wheeled units. A modern PCTC has thirteen decks and can convey between 5,500 and 5,800 cars or a permutation of 3,200 cars and 600 trucks. Such tonnage can also convey containers on 20 ft (6.10 m) or 40 ft (12.2 m) long Mafi trailers. A major operator in this field is Wallenius Lines Ltd, which has a 19 vessel fleet of PCTCs providing a worldwide service embracing the Far East, North America and European markets.

In 2005 Wallenius Lines launched three PCTCs, each of 5,000 ceu (car equivalent units), and a further five of 4,000 ceu capacity followed shortly after. Additionally, five vessels built in 1978/9 have undergone a conversion in 2004/05 to enable each vessel to carry an additional 1,300 ceu, giving each ship a capacity of over 7,000 ceu. Another major operator, NYK, has a fleet of 93 car carriers, ten of which were launched in 2005 with another six in 2006/7. New builds include two 6,000 ceu and one at 5,000 ceu. This tonnage is a growth area and is logistically driven. In 2003 8 million cars were transported by sea. Car production is moving out of Europe to the Far East. By 2009 it was estimated that Chinese car production would reach 7 million vehicles, which would have tripled that country's car production in a decade. The new generation of PCTCs is contributing to reducing the cost of global car distribution.

(v) Refrigerated vessel

This type of tonnage is in decline because such shipments are containerized in many trades. The ship is designed with a multi-deck hull that includes an arrangement of refrigerated holds and 'tween decks specifically for the carriage of perishable cargoes. The cargo handling mode is lift on/lift off to and from the holds (and 'tween decks) by way of weather deck (and 'tween-deck) hatches. Various features include (a) additional side loading by way of side elevators for the specific loading of perishable cargoes on pallets, and (b) the alternative carriage of other forms of cargo, including facilities for the carriage of road vehicles (by way of special side elevators or side doors).

(w) Ro/ro vessel

A ro/ro type of vessel is designed for the conveyance of road haulage vehicles and private cars. It is often called a multi-purpose ship, and can be seen in Figure 3.1. Ro/ro combination is now found in the container vessel category, as shown in Figure 3.5.

Another example of a ro/ro (roll on/roll off)–lo/lo (lift on/lift off) vessel is one of 17,000 dwt, with an overall length of 140 m. The moulded breadth is 23 m and she has a speed of 16 knots. The ship has a ro/ro lane capacity of 1,300 m and 600 TEUs container capacity. Hold capacity totals 27,000 m³. The vessel has a stern ramp, internal fixed ramps, electro-hydraulic cranes, and hydraulically operated hatch covers. Liquid cargoes (latex or similar) can be conveyed in the foretanks. Such a vessel offers high cargo mix versatility. Hence such a cargo combination could include general break bulk cargo (which could be palletized), bulk cargo, containers, trailers, cars and ro/ro cargo.

The future of ro/ro tonnage lies in short sea trade markets. It is unlikely that any further deep sea ro/ro tonnage will be built as a new generation of PCTC develops.

(x) Timber carrier

These are provided with large unobstructed holds and large hatches to facilitate cargo handling. They are frequently called three-island vessels. They incorporate a raised forecastle, bridge and poop, thereby facilitating stowage of deck cargo, which is now packaged.

(y) Ferry fleet

The ferry non cargo fleet had a steady growth until 2000. A slowdown was forecast, though with a modest fleet growth: 101 were recycled.

About a quarter of the ferry fleet is high speed – 30 knots and above – whereas over 50% are multi-hauled. All fast ferry types depend upon the reduction of surface tension and resistance by either reducing hull drag or by creating dynamic lift. There are four main types of fast ferries: mono-hull, catamarans, hydrofoils and hovercraft.

Fast ferry investment involves high initial cost, high annual cost and short economic life. To be successful, over a short period high income must be generated from high fares and high utilization. Advantages over competing conventional ferries (Figure 4.9) are good sea-keeping, quick embarkation/disembarkation, low noise levels and high quality shipboard facilities. The major advantage is voyage time reduction compared with conventional ferries. This generates a new market, as found on the Italian–Greek passenger trade. Overall, a fast ferry costs more to operate than conventional ferries. This is due to high fuel consumption from operating at 40 knots and more stringent maintenance costs. Fast ferries are licensed to sail with a crew of 23 while conventional ships have a crew of 34. However, costs increase due to overtime and premium pay rates. Fast ferries seldom operate on routes longer than 150 nautical miles, because up to that distance frequent each way trips per day are possible so that the ferry's revenue-generating potential is increased. This need for the vessels to keep active demands fast port turn-round time, dedicated passenger terminals and good operational planning. It is forecast that improved hull design may generate a new build of high-speed ferries capable of more than 50 knots. Conventional ships will rise to 33 knots. High-speed ferries have a relatively short operational life and rapid depreciation compared with a conventional ferry of above 30 years. The era of the hovercraft, hydrofoil and jetfoil is passing.

(z) Heavy lift shipping

The progress of heavy lift shipping has been outstanding since the 1990s and has been driven by offshore opportunities and the transportation of indivisible loads, such as fully erected cranes, yachts and project cargo embracing fabrication industries. An example in 2004 was a 60,000 ton Thunder Horse floating production platform transported from South Korea to the Gulf of Mexico.

These vessels operate in a risk market, the spot market providing a reasonable return. Long-term contracts are found in major oil contractors, fabricators and conversion yards. However, the key to success is through continuous operation. Lay-up is not an option. A leading heavy lift ship operator, Dockwise, has developed new markets in the transport of fully erected container cranes of 1,000 tons. Heavy lift shipping provides the crane builder with an opportunity to erect a crane fully at its own site, transport it to its working location where it can become fully operational and, within days, prove highly beneficial both to builder and to operator. The crane builder can control costs, while the container terminal does not have its operations disrupted.

Coming from the merger of Wijsmuller/Dock Express in 1997, the company acquired two recently built semi-submersibles, the *Blue Marlin* and *Black Marlin*. More recently the *Mighty Servant* was jumbo-ized, the beam being widened by 10 m to 50 m and length to 190 m and the deadweight increased from 27,720 to 45,000 tons. In 2004 it transported what was then the largest cargo ever carried on a ship. It did this by involving an ultra-deep-water semi-submersible Thunder Horse rig from the Daewoo fabrication yard in South Korea over to the Gulf of Mexico. The 60,000 ton rig is designed to operate in 6,000 ft water depth at the Thunder Horse field in the Gulf of Mexico.

In 2003 two Chinese-built semi-submersible vessels, ordered by COSCO, entered service.

5   Manning of vessels

5.1 Introduction

The manning of vessels is an extensive subject, and this chapter is intended only to cover its most important aspects. Ship manning today forms a very important part of the shipping industry and is made complex by an increasingly competitive cost-conscious situation. New technology is being introduced during continuous economic change. Moreover, seafarers' standards, both in ship accommodation and navigation/engineering/catering techniques, are rising. Overall, seafarers' shipboard living standards are improving, a situation further improved by the introduction of the Maritime Labour Convention (MLC). Basically there are important costs which can vary between maritime nations: the effective cost of capital, the flag state's regulating requirements (the country to which the vessel is registered), and crew cost, which we will now examine.

A major factor influencing crew cost is the change in the disposition of the world mercantile fleet. An analysis from 2012 confirms that Greece, Japan, Germany, China, Republic of Korea and the United States are the leading maritime countries (see Table 5.1). Greece has 16% and Japan 15.6%, with the other four nations attracting 26% of the world fleet. China is the fastest-growing maritime fleet nation. Overall, some 35 countries controlled 95% of the world mercantile fleet. In this context, two tables (Tables 17.1 and 17.2), warrant analysis relative to the top 20 container service operators and container terminal operators. An analysis of these Tables shows that Asian countries are the leading container port operators and that they are fast becoming the world's leading container service operators. China in particular has a large new building programme under way. It is therefore not surprising that a large percentage of the world mercantile fleet crew is from Asia and the Indian subcontinent, especially Filipino ratings.

The share of the world merchant fleet in the ten major open registries in 2012 is estimated to be 56.4%. Maritime statistics show growth in fleet sizes. This rise may reflect the increased competitiveness of these registries given the attractive fiscal regimes for shipowners in some developed market-economy countries.

Table 5.1 The 35 countries and territories with the largest owned fleets, as of 1 January 2012[a] (dwt)

Country or territory of ownership[b]	Number of vessels			Deadweight tonnage			Foreign flag as a % of total	Estimated market share 1 January 2012
	National flag[c]	Foreign flag	Total	National flag[c]	Foreign flag	Total		
Greece	738	2,583	3,321	64,921,486	159,130,395	224,051,881	71.02	16.10
Japan	717	3,243	3,960	20,452,832	197,210,070	217,662,902	90.60	15.64
Germany	422	3,567	3,989	17,296,198	108,330,510	125,626,708	86.23	9.03
China	2,060	1,569	3,629	51,716,318	72,285,422	124,001,740	58.29	8.91
Korea, Republic of	740	496	1,236	17,102,300	39,083,270	56,185,570	69.56	4.04
United States	741	1,314	2,055	7,162,685	47,460,048	54,622,733	86.89	3.92
China, Hong Kong SAR	470	383	853	28,884,470	16,601,518	45,485,988	36.50	3.27
Norway	851	1,141	1,992	15,772,288	27,327,579	43,099,867	63.41	3.10
Denmark	394	649	1,043	13,463,727	26,527,607	39,991,334	66.33	2.87
China, Taiwan Province of	102	601	703	4,076,815	34,968,474	39,045,289	89.56	2.81
Singapore	712	398	1,110	22,082,648	16,480,079	38,562,727	42.74	2.77
Bermuda	17	251	268	2,297,441	27,698,605	29,996,046	92.34	2.16
Italy	608	226	834	18,113,984	6,874,748	24,988,732	27.51	1.80
Turkey	527	647	1,174	8,554,745	14,925,883	23,480,628	63.57	1.69
Canada	205	251	456	2,489,989	19,360,007	21,849,996	88.60	1.57
India	455	105	560	15,276,544	6,086,410	21,362,954	28.49	1.53
Russian Federation	1,336	451	1,787	5,410,608	14,957,599	20,368,207	73.44	1.46
United Kingdom	230	480	710	2,034,570	16,395,185	18,429,755	88.96	1.32
Belgium	97	180	277	6,319,103	8,202,208	14,521,311	56.48	1.04
Malaysia	432	107	539	9,710,922	4,734,174	14,445,096	32.77	1.04
Brazil	113	59	172	2,279,733	11,481,795	13,761,528	83.43	0.99

Saudi Arabia	75	117	192	1,852,378	10,887,737	12,740,115	85.46	0.92
Netherlands	576	386	962	4,901,301	6,799,943	11,701,244	58.11	0.84
Indonesia	951	91	1,042	9,300,711	2,292,255	11,592,966	19.77	0.83
Iran	67	71	138	829,704	10,634,685	11,464,389	92.76	0.82
France	188	297	485	3,430,417	7,740,496	11,170,913	69.29	0.80
United Arab Emirates	65	365	430	609,032	8,187,103	8,796,135	93.08	0.63
Cyprus	62	152	214	2,044,256	5,092,849	7,137,105	71.36	0.51
Viet Nam	477	79	556	4,706,563	1,988,446	6,695,009	29.70	0.48
Kuwait	44	42	86	3,956,910	2,735,309	6,692,219	40.87	0.48
Sweden	99	208	307	1,070,563	5,325,853	6,396,416	83.26	0.46
Isle of Man	6	38	44	226,810	6,131,401	6,358,211	96.43	0.46
Thailand	277	67	344	3,610,570	1,542,980	5,153,550	29.94	0.37
Switzerland	39	142	181	1,189,376	3,700,886	4,890,262	75.68	0.35
Qatar	48	37	85	881,688	3,745,663	4,627,351	80.95	0.33
Total top 35 economies	14,941	20,793	35,734	374,029,685	952,927,192	1,326,956,877	71.81	95.34
Other owners	2,172	1,816	3,988	22,491,261	42,344,181	64,835,442	65.31	4.66
Total of known economy of ownership	17,113	22,609	39,722	396,520,946	995,271,373	1,391,792,319	71.51	100.00
Others, unknown economy of ownership			7,179			126,317,184		
World total			46,901			1,518,109,503		

Source: Compiled by the UNCTAD secretariat, on the basis of data supplied by *IHS Fairplay*.

Notes:

[a] Vessels of 1000 GT and above, ranked by deadweight tonnage – excluding the United States Reserve Fleet and the United States and Canadian Great Lakes fleets (which have a combined tonnage of 5.3 million dwt).

[b] The country of ownership indicates where the true controlling interest (that is, the parent company) of the fleet is located. In several cases, determining this has required making certain judgements. Thus, for example, Greece is shown as the country of ownership for vessels owned by a Greek national with representative offices in New York, London and Piraeus, although the owner may be domiciled in the United States.

[c] Includes vessels flying the national flag but registered in second registries such as the Danish International Ship Register (DIS), the Norwegian International Ship Register (NIS) or the French International Ship Register (FIS).

Table 5.2 Comparison of crew costs, based on all UK crew of officers and ratings being 100 index of a bulk carrier

Crew description	Annual crew cost index	Daily crew cost index
UK officers: UK ratings	100	100
UK officers (offshore rates): Filipino ratings	65	65
UK/Indian officers: Filipino ratings	54	54
UK/Indian officers: Hong Kong/ China ratings	53	53
Filipino officers: Filipino ratings	42	42
Indian officers: Indian ratings	50	50

The 35 flags of registration with the largest registered deadweight tonnage shows that in 2012 Panama remained a market leader with 328 million dwt, followed by Liberia with 189 million dwt, and the Marshall Islands at 122 million dwt (see Table 22.1).

A major problem internationally is the differing wage scales offered to seafarers worldwide which make it difficult for owners to compete on equal crew cost terms. An example is given in Table 5.2, which is based on an all-UK crew of officers and ratings for a bulk carrier.

The cost of employing seafarers of a particular nationality is in the first instance related to the general level of wages and cost of living in that country. Accordingly, as Table 5.2 demonstrates, the Far East nationals' skilled seafarers have lower salary levels, giving shipowners clear advantages in their crewing costs when compared with crews of European origin, such as from the UK, Germany or Holland. Moreover, European seafarers are offered more favourable leave facilities. This means that a larger crew complement is required to crew a vessel to cover the more generous leave arrangements. In turn this increases costs. In consequence the crew complement may rise from 1.1 or 1.2 to 1.9, reflecting more generous leave arrangements for crew. The leave provision is more favourable for officers than other crew; also the crew complement for Asian officers compared with a European crew may be 1.5/1.8 to 2.2. Moreover, such reduced crew costs enables some shipowners to offer lower rates and so develop their markets.

To counter this an increasing number of shipowners from developed countries are flagging out their fleets, that is, they are transferring the flag to a national register which has lower crew cost and fringe benefits, as well as overall tax benefits to shipping companies. This tends to counter the very high competitive crew cost in high labour cost maritime fleets. A number of developed countries have introduced measures to reduce the cost of employing national seafarers by granting relief on personal taxation and social security. These remove some or all of the burden of substantial 'on cost' for the employer, reducing the gap between Western and third-world crew costs.

Some governments have also established 'international' or 'second' ship registers that either incorporate tax exemptions for national seafarers or allow employment of foreign seafarers at third-world pay levels.

The UK government, to counter the decline in the UK registered fleet, included in the Finance Act 2000, schedule 22, a legal framework for a 'tonnage tax'. This new form of taxation for shipping is based not on actual profits but on the size of a company's fleet. A notional level of profit is calculated according to an agreed formula based on the nett tonnage of its individual ships. It is then subjected to the standard rate of corporation tax. Overall, the tonnage tax has the following features:

(a) It may apply to seagoing merchant ships above 100 gross tonnes, except for a few specialist categories.
(b) Companies must be operators of ships and have their strategic and commercial management in the UK.
(c) The regime is optional, but existing UK companies must have elected for it by 27 July 2001 and remain in the scheme for at least 10 years.
(d) Flexibility may be allowed in the timing of implementation, depending on company's circumstances.
(e) Groups must elect the same way for all of their qualifying ship companies.
(f) Tonnage tax profits are strictly ring-fenced from non-shipping profits or losses, particularly finance costs.
(g) Capital allowances and capital gains tax are not relevant within the tonnage tax regime, but there are transitional arrangements for companies already in the conventional UK tax regime.
(h) Special rules apply to capital allowances for leasing companies which own ships and lease them to tonnage tax companies.
(i) Qualifying profits may include taxed dividends remitted from overseas shipping subsidiaries.
(j) A pre-clearance facility is available for companies. Companies must accept a minimum training obligation.

Norway is a long established maritime nation and has been concerned in the decline of the Norwegian-controlled International Ship Register (NIS). Following the example of the Netherlands and Greece, the Norwegian government decided to change from 1996 the basis on which shipowners were taxed. Briefly, taxation would be calculated by weight instead of income. Shipping companies were exempt from corporate tax and income tax based on the cargo carried by their vessels. A significant condition was that profits must be reinvested and not distributed as dividends. The impact was that over the next two years several hundred ships were added to the Norwegian fleet and the number of Norwegian seafarers rose by 3,500, and another 4,000 had trained for maritime careers. Despite such measures, the Norwegian fleet fell from third place to sixth by 1 January 2005.

Today an increasing number of shipowners, in order to become more competitive, opt for third party ship management and 'flag out' to reduce cost, including crew cost.

A further partial solution is sought by some industrial nations through reduced manning levels, but the scope for this is limited, considering the continually rising standards in seamanship competence certification. This attempt to cut crew costs is governed by agreement reached by the IMO to raise the number of certificated crew personnel. An example occurred in 1978 when the IMO adopted the Convention on Standards of Training, Certification and Watch-keeping for seafarers. Such international regulations ensure crew on a ship meet the standards required of them. The Convention received worldwide support and is further evidence of measures designed to raise seafaring navigation standards. Staffing levels and duties for UK registered tonnage are contained in the Merchant Shipping Acts 1970 and 1979.

In attaining such crew complement reductions, one must also remember that vessels have tended to increase in size/capacity and resources. Today, there are computerized engine room/navigation aids. These factors have tended to favour maritime nations able to finance new tonnage, because such crew reductions can only be attained without impairing safety standards. Moreover, studies of some industrial maritime nations' fleets are being conducted into ship maintenance, with a view to transferring ship maintenance functions, previously done ashore, to an onboard activity. Onboard maintenance aids improved ship utilization, less time spent in port, more productive use of the crew and overall lower cost to the shipowner. Additionally the need to encourage more crew diversification continues. This has tended to eliminate traditional demarcation lines found in engineering, catering and deck departments, something common in modern container tonnage and foreign-going tankers. Ship productivity is a key factor in crew management.

Many more operators now have up to three crews assigned to a vessel and fly out and back to all ports of the world their crew personnel to ensure their ships are in continuous operation. Modern ships have accommodation for wives to accompany their officer husbands. All these factors add to crew cost when living standards are rising.

In an era when shipowners are endeavouring to reduce their crew costs the following options exist, other than flagging out as earlier described:

(a) Reduction of crew to the minimum number required under legislation. This increases the workload on remaining crew personnel, and ship maintenance and operation may suffer as a result. Further training to familiarize the crew with automation can be undertaken with a possibility to reduce crew numbers.

(b) Increased ship utilization involves shorter turn-round time in port and shorter leave periods, both of which can improve crew utilization. This is particularly relevant to Westernized tonnage crews. It can also extend to lower fringe benefits, leaving it to seafarers to make their own arrangements for medical insurance and pension contributions.

(c) An increasing number of shipowners are employing more low cost non-domiciled seafarers alongside their European crews. Often the officers are European and the ratings Filipinos or North Koreans. Hence a vessel may have a ratings crew of 1.1 or 1.2 compared with an officer crew of 1.5 to 1.8, enabling favourable cost reductions to be achieved.

(d) The process of greater integration of crew personnel duties is likely to accelerate in the twenty-first century as the need to reduce crew cost becomes more significant and shipboard automation increases. The duties of the ship Master and first mate, and chief engineer and second engineer, could be integrated on tonnage where circumstances allow.

In conclusion, one must bear in mind the lower the crew complement and number of crews per ship, plus the longer the voyage length, the greater the cost savings. This applies to fringe benefits especially.

In studying this chapter, one must bear in mind the foregoing arises at a time when, to aid international trade development, it is vital for shipping costs to remain competitive: crew cost has a vital role to play in this situation.

5.2 Duties and responsibilities of the Master

The ship's Master is the person in absolute charge of the vessel, and is commonly referred to as 'Captain'. The term Master is a legal one and this term is referred to under maritime law. It applies whether the ship may be a large passenger liner like the *Queen Elizabeth II* or a relatively small cargo ship engaged in coastal trade.

The Master's duties and responsibilities are varied and extensive. He is the owner's personal representative, and bears the ultimate responsibility for the safe navigation of his vessel and for the efficient loading, stowage and discharge of cargo. Furthermore, he has the power to act as a lawyer, a doctor and may bury the dead. The Master may arrest members of the crew or passengers, if they constitute a nuisance during the voyage. In certain circumstances, particularly if a person is dangerous to other members of the ship, the Master may place the individual under restraint. In the event of any mutiny, any act of the Master is regarded as one entirely of self-defence, and he has the power to call on persons on board to render assistance. Similarly, if the ship is imperilled in any way, the Master may call upon all persons on board to give assistance.

Wide authority is vested in the Master and, under maritime law, acts done within the scope of his authority are binding on his owners. Under very rare circumstances, he is empowered by a 'bottomry bond' to pledge the vessel, and by a 'respondentia bond' its cargo, so that funds may be secured to permit the voyage to proceed.

It is therefore readily apparent that the Master's responsibilities and duties are very diverse. To hold the position of a Master, especially on a large passenger liner, is a much coveted appointment, and is the culmination of years of sea experience. The Master is required to hold a Master's Certificate of Competency, which is obtained by examination and issued by the maritime authority of the flag state. Furthermore, in common with the deck officers, from which department he is promoted, he must be thoroughly competent in navigation matters including the use of such navigational aids as the gyrocompass, radar, direction finder, echo-sounding device, and position-fixing device, together with other instruments.

Modern tonnage provides automation in the engine room, extensive computerization, and minimum crew complement. These reduce crew costs, especially in engineer and deck departments. A further significant aspect is that the departmental system of deck and engineers has become more integrated and more productive in manpower, especially in deep-sea tonnage. SOLAS 1974 Chapter VIII introduced new measures for watch-keeping personnel to prevent fatigue. Masters are required to establish and enforce rest periods for watch-keeping personnel and to ensure that watch systems are so arranged that the efficiency of watch-keeping personnel is not impaired by fatigue. It is featured in the STCW code (1995) and also the revisions contained in the STCW Manila Amendments (2010).

A further aspect of the mandatory STCW code Part A was the minimum standards of competence required by seagoing personnel in Chapter II of the code regarding standards relating to the Master and deck department, as detailed in Table 5.3. The code featured an additional regulation V/3 in Chapter V, which adopted a mandatory minimum requirement from 1999 for the training and qualification of masters, officers, ratings and other personnel on passenger ships other than ro/ro passenger ships. This covered crowd management training, familiarization training, safety training for personnel providing direct service to passengers in passenger spaces, passenger safety, crisis management and human behaviour training. Another amendment to the STCW code, came into force from January 2003 (under tacit acceptance), was focused on minimum standards of crew competence, in particular relating to cargo securing, loading and unloading on bulk carriers, since these procedures could put undue stresses on a ship's structure.

An addition to Chapter VII of SOLAS 1974 was regulations regarding alternative certification known as the 'functional approach'. This process enables crews to gain training and certification in various departments of seafaring rather than their being confined to one branch (such as deck or engine room) for their entire career. At the same time the new Chapter seeks to ensure that safety and the environment are not threatened in any way and that the use of equivalent educational and training arrangements are permitted under article IX. Such a development also reflects the changing approach of entry routes and career progression in the merchant navy. It features marine

Table 5.3 Specification of minimum standards of competence for Masters and chief mates of ships of 500 tons gross tonnage or more

Competence	Knowledge, understanding and proficiency	Methods for demonstrating competence	Criteria for evaluating competence
Establish watchkeeping arrangements and procedures	Thorough knowledge of content, application and intent of the International Regulations for Preventing Collisions at Sea Thorough knowledge of the content, application and intent of the Principles to be observed in Keeping a Navigational Watch. Effective bridge teamwork procedures	Examination and assessment of evidence obtained from one or more of the following: (1) Approved in-service experience (2) Approved simulator training, where appropriate	Watchkeeping arrangements and procedures are established and maintained in compliance with international regulations and guidelines so as to ensure the safety of navigation, protection of the marine environment and the safety of the ship and persons on board

traineeship, marine apprenticeship, officer cadet, undergraduate, graduate and pre-qualified. In 2010 the Manila Amendments for STCW and Flag states must introduce each amendment within a specified deadline. These new regulations include: deck officer training for operating electronic chart display information systems (ECDIS); engineering officer training in high voltage systems; and all seafarers' refresher training in fire-fighting, survival craft, fast rescue boats and security. There are also leadership and management course requirements for officers, and revalidation requirements for tanker endorsements.

An example of an integrated crew manning system is given below and involves the 14-man complement of a RoRo/LoLo vessel of 8,000 dwt:

Master
Chief Officer
Second Officer
Third Officer
Chief Engineer
Second Engineer
Third Engineer
Electrician
Cook
Bosun
Four Ratings

The ship has a total container capacity of 516 TEUs and vehicular deck space of 1,416 m^2; heavy lifting gear for loads up to 120 tonnes is also provided. An integrated crew is especially common with Scandinavian and German-registered tonnage crews.

A brief description of the departments, responsibilities and composition follows, but note that this manning system is becoming much less common now that integration takes place to attain more productive use of the crew.

5.3 Ship's officers and crew manning

(a) Deck department

The running of this department is the responsibility of the chief officer, who supervises the handling of cargo and is responsible for the upkeep of the ship and its equipment, but not the engine room and auxiliary power gear. In addition, he also acts as deputy to the Master. On larger vessels a second and a third officer assist him. There are three certificates of competence for deck officers. After passing examinations and with appropriate qualifying sea time, all deck officers have to be certified by the flag state. It is sometimes the practice for both the chief and second officers to hold Master's Certificate of Competence.

The deck department also includes a Bosun (chief petty officer), including Able Seaman and Ordinary Seaman. The duties of the Bosun are such that he acts as foreman of the ratings. In common with the officers, the Able and Ordinary Seaman are watch keepers, taking their turn at steering and look-out duties, while the remaining deck hands are day workers employed at sea in general duties. The deck department in port usually works cargo watches in 4 or 6 hour stretches.

In the case of a large passenger liner, it is frequent practice to have a Staff Captain whose primary responsibility is as deputy to the Master, with a key role in running a ship with a large complement of crew. Deck officers are now required to hold a GMDSS certificate. This certificate replaced the need for a radio officer. Since the automation of equipment on ships' bridges GMDSS duties are now included in watch-keeping responsibilities. Chapter IV of SOLAS 1974, entitled 'Radio Communications', was revised in 1988 to reflect GMDSS. Hitherto, it was titled 'radio telegraphy' and 'radio telephony', reflecting the forms of radio communication available prior to the introduction of satellites. These amendments became mandatory from February 1999, from which date all passenger and cargo ships of 300 gross tonnage and upwards on international voyages are required to carry equipment designed to improve the chances of rescue following an accident involving EPIRBs and SARTS for the location of the ship or survival craft.

(c) Engine room department

The engine room is the charge of the Chief Engineer, who is responsible to the Master, both for the main propulsion machinery and for auxiliaries comprising electrical plant, cargo winches, refrigerating machinery, steering gear, ventilating system, etc. He is also responsible for fuel, maintenance and repairs. According to the size of the vessel he is assisted by a number of engineer officers. The ratings of the engine room department of a modern cargo ship comprise a fitter (a chief petty officer) and a motorman (engine room rating). The complicated machinery of the modern ship has made the engine room department important. A growing proportion of modern ship propulsion is now electronic.

(d) Catering department

This department role has changed dramatically with the development of the mega cruise tonnage and focus on passenger needs in terms of catering, retail outlets, live and passive entertainment, bars and cabins. The staffing structure is often based on a hotel management style, with personnel in charge of catering, cabins and the range of shipboard facilities. Some shipping lines rely on the purser or hotel services manager to be in overall charge of hotel facilities onboard reporting to the Master. In their catering department most modern cargo ships will carry one cook and one or two stewards.

(e) Manning

'Manning scales' are laid down for vessels flying the British flag, and every vessel must carry a minimum number of duly certificated deck officers and engineers, and ratings as stipulated in the ship's Safe Manning Document.

The number of personnel in each of the various departments depends on the type and size of vessel, and the trade in which she is engaged. For instance, a cargo vessel of 10,000 dwt would have a very small catering department compared with a vessel engaged in deep-sea cruising carrying 750 passengers.

The Merchant Shipping Act 1970 introduced new regulations regarding the certification of deck officers and marine engineer officers. These regulations are contained in the Merchant Shipping (Certification of Deck and Marine Engineer Officers) Regulations 1977, operative from 1 September 1981.

This legislation requires UK-registered ships of 80 gross register tonnage or over and passenger ships to carry a specified number of deck officers, that number determined according to the tonnage of the ship and the voyage to, from or between locations in specified trading areas in which it will be engaged. Similar requirements are prescribed for ships registered outside the UK carrying passengers between places in the UK, between the UK and the Channel Islands or Isle of Man, or voyages which begin or end at the same place in the UK and call at no place outside the UK. Provision is made for the exceptional circumstance when one deck officer cannot be carried because of illness. Special requirements are prescribed for tugs and sail training ships. Certificates of competence will be issued to deck officers who satisfy the requisite standards of competence as determined by the Department of Transport. Additional training is required for certain deck officers in ships carrying bulk cargoes of specified dangerous chemicals or gases. The same applies to certain marine engineer officers. Overall the new standards of certification reflect broadly the outcome of discussions at the IMO.

The minimum number of deck officers to be carried is prescribed in the Merchant Shipping (Certification of Deck Officers) Regulations 1977. These must be regarded as the minimum manning scales and applies equally to marine engineer officers.

Differing scales apply to passenger vessels, and are much higher.

The regulations specify trading limits. The 'Near Continental' is any location within the area bounded by a line from a point on the Norwegian coast in latitude 62° N to a point 62° N 02° W; thence to a point 51° N 12° W; thence to Brest, but excluding all waters which lie to the east of a line drawn between Kristiansand, Norway and Hanstholm lighthouse on the north Danish coast.

The 'Middle Trade' is any location not within the Near Continental trading area but within an area (which includes places in the Baltic Sea) bounded by the northern shore of Vest Fjord (Norway) and a line joining Skemvaer lighthouse to a point 62° N 02° W; thence to a point 58° N 10° W; thence to a point 51° N 12° W; thence to a point 41° 9 N 10° W; thence to Oporto. Basically the unlimited trading area is any location not within the Middle Trade or Near Continental trading areas.

The classes of Certificate of Competence for deck officers are described in the STCW95 amendments. The Master Unlimited certificate is equivalent to the former Master Mariner and is equivalent to the Master Foreign Going Certificate, as prescribed under the Merchant Shipping Act 1894. Likewise, a First Mate Foreign-going Certificate and a Second Mate Foreign-going Certificate are equivalent to the Chief Mate Unlimited and Officer of the Watch Unlimited certificates respectively.

Differing Certificates of Competence exist for tugs and vessels under 3,000GT and 500GT. With regard to the regulations of marine engineer officers these involve UK-registered ships having registered power of 350 kW or more, including all sail-training ships with a propulsion engine. It embraces the voyage to, from or between locations in specified training areas. Similar requirements are prescribed for a specified number of engineer officers for ships registered outside the UK, which carry passengers between places in the UK or between the UK and the Channel Islands or Isle of Man or on voyages which begin and end at the same place in the UK and call at no place outside the UK. Provision is made for the exceptional circumstance when one engineer officer cannot be carried because of illness or incapacity. Special requirements are prescribed for sail-training ships.

Overall there are three classes of Certificate of Competence which are related to the First Class Engineer Certificate as prescribed under the Merchant Shipping Act 1894. Under STCW95 these classes are to be described as the Chief Engineer, Second Engineer and Officer of the Watch (Engineer) Certificates.

In an attempt to raise the status of ratings in deck and engineer departments, plus the need to facilitate the productivity and diversification of rating workload on UK vessels, a new structure has been introduced to a number of posts. Brief details are given below of the new structure:

Deck department	*Engine room department*
Trainee Rating	Trainee Rating
Deck Rating Grade II	Engine Room Rating
(Ordinary Seaman)	(Wiper)
Deck Rating Grade I (Able Seaman)	Motorman
Chief Petty Officer (Bosun)	Chief Petty Officer (Fitter)

Similar restructuring has taken place for catering staff. Further provisions relating to the levels of competence have been adopted in the STCW code and amendments.

5.4 The IMO Convention on Standards of Training, Certification and Watchkeeping (STCW) adopted in 1984

A two-week long conference to amend the most important treaty dealing with the standards of training, certification and watchkeeping of the world's seafarers was successfully concluded on 7 July 1995 at the International Maritime Organization. The treaty is the International Convention on Standards of Training, Certification and Watchkeeping for Seafarers (STCW), 1978. Today, this has been amended under the STCW 1995, which came into force in February 2002, and by the Manila amendments 2010, which came into force in January 2012. The STCW 1995 amendments arose through the ISPS code. Hence there is a significant interface between the two codes. The treaty arising from the International Convention on Standards of Training Certification and Watchkeeping for Seafarers (STCW) 1978 was adopted in July 1995. However, the emergence of the ISPS code (2006) has had an important impact on the STCW (1978) code because of its wide-ranging amendments. There is now a strong interface between the two codes, as will now be explained.

The adoption of the International Ship and Port Facility Security Code (ISPS) at the IMO conference in December 2002 had a profound impact on the STCW code (1978). In June 2003 the Maritime Security Working Group focused on the Safety, Training and Watchkeeping regarding training and security officers. It was agreed that training requirements for ship security officers (SSO) would form part of the STCW 1995 and feature in the 2006 convention. Moreover, it includes company security officers (CSO). By early 2005,114 participants had accepted the STCW (1978) as amended.

The aim of the ISPS is to establish an international framework for co-operation between contracting governments, government agencies, local administrations and the shipping and port industries: to detect security threats and to take preventive measures against security incidents affecting ships or port facilities used in international trade, and to establish relevant roles and responsibilities at national and international levels. The main intention was to enhance maritime security on board ships and at ship/port interface areas. These objectives are to be achieved by the designation of appropriate personnel on each ship, in each port facility and each shipowning company to make assessments, and by putting into effect the security plan approved for each ship and port facility. The conference also adopted several related resolutions and amendments to Chapters V and XI (now divided into Chapters XI–1 and XI–2), which provide the umbrella regulations. The ISPS Code became mandatory on 1 July 2004. This code is divided into two parts: Part A presents mandatory requirements, Part B recommendatory guidance regarding the provisions of Chapter XI–2 of the convention and Part A of the code. It is the first internationally agreed regulatory framework addressing the issue of maritime security.

Chapter XI–2 entitled special measures to enhance maritime security, and applies to passenger ships and cargo ships of 500 gross tonnage and above, including high speed craft, mobile offshore drilling units and port facilities serving such ships engaged in international voyages. The code requires a ship security plan to be drawn up for all SOLAS vessels, and for the plan to be approved by the state administration. Each vessel must also have an approved security plan and must appoint a designated ship security officer (SSO). Additionally, each company must appoint a company security officer (CSO). Minimum mandatory training and certification for SSO have been laid down and feature in Chapter VI of the STCW Convention. Additionally, revised training schedules relating to the use of lifeboats – embracing lifeboat drills – have been adopted and involve an amendment to Table A–V1/2–1 of the STCW code. Particular focus is on the release mechanism. A further revision was on watch keeping and for masters on the requirements of safe anchorage. This features in STCW Code Section A–V11/2. A further item was the training for Automatic Information Systems (AISs) – navigation radar aide. The AIS was mandatory on ships from 31 December 2004.

The ISPS Code identifies details of measures and covers both shipboard and port security plans at each of three increasing levels of security. National administrations are required to set these security levels and to ensure that security level information is provided to ships entitled to fly their flag. Prior to entering a port, or whilst in a port within the territory of the contracting government to the SOLAS Convention, a ship shall comply with the requirements for the security level set by that contracting government, assuming that security level is higher than the security level set by the administration for that ship.

The new Chapter confirms the role of the Master in exercising his professional judgement over decisions necessary to maintain the security of the ship. The Master shall not be constrained by the company, charterer or any other person in this respect.

It is mandatory for all vessels to be fitted with a ship security alert system (SSAS). It will initiate and transmit a ship to shore security alert to a competent authority designated by the administration, identifying the ship, its location and indicating that the security of the ship is under threat or has been compromised. It must be capable of being activated on the bridge and one other location.

Other measures under the code in this Chapter cover the information to the IMO, the specific responsibilities of shipping companies, and control of ships in port, including measures relating to the delay, detention or restriction of operations including movement within the port or expulsion of a ship from port. To improve traceability of vessels a ship's identification number (SIN) must be permanently marked in a visible place, either on the hull or superstructure. Passenger ships must carry the marking on a horizontal surface visible from the air. All vessels must be fitted with a Continuous Synopsis Record (CRS) to provide the 'on board' history of the ship.

Vessels in full mandatory compliance with the ISPS code are issued with the International Ship Security Certificate (ISSC) given to the vessel owning/operating company by the administration of the flag state or recognized security organization. In order to obtain the ISSC under SOLAS Chapters V, X–1 and X–2, the following compliance must obtain: AIS, SIN, SSAS and SCR. Ports are likewise required to have in place within the territory of the contracting government to the ISPS convention, an approved Port Facility Security Plan. This specifies a designated Port Facility Security Officer and control and compliance measures.

Finally, it is important to record that not only is there strong interface between the ISPS and the STCW codes, particularly modification to the STCW 1997 amendments in Part A and Part B but also with the ISM code concerning the issue of the DOC and SMS documents. A 'white list', detailing countries giving full and complete effect to the revised STCW Convention (STCW 1995), was published by the IMO in December 2000. The revised STCW code came into force in February 2002, and further amendments in 2010 are commonly known as the Manila Amendments concerning seafarer training.

5.5 Engagement and discharge of the crew

It has already been established that the person in sole charge of the vessel is the Master. The conditions of employment of seamen are the subject of statutory legislation and regulations under the Merchant Shipping Act 1970.

A voyage is still a venture subject to many hazards and difficulties. To complete the venture successfully, relative rights, duties and restraints must be enforced on all who share the venture. These special circumstances have given rise to legislation in most countries to restrict and protect seamen in their employment.

The Merchant Shipping Act 1970 brought into effect the first major change for many years in the legislation relating to the employment of seamen. It repealed parts of the 1894 and 1906 Merchant Shipping Acts. The 1970 Act deals with crew agreements; crew lists; engagement and discharge of crew; seamen's documents; discipline; wages and accounts; seamen left behind abroad; deceased seamen; and medical treatment and expenses. The more salient aspects are now examined.

A contract of employment is made between the shipowner and the crew. It is called a crew agreement, in which a number of clauses are taken directly from the Merchant Shipping Act 1970 whilst others derive from National Maritime Board agreements. The shipowner is the contracting party, and seamen must sign the crew agreement prior to the intended voyage. It is not necessary for the superintendent or proper officer to be present during the signing on or discharge but in some Commonwealth countries this practice is obligatory under their legislation involving shipping masters/superintendents. The crew agreement contains a voyage clause giving the geographical limits of the voyage, and notice/termination clauses which vary by the trade in which vessel engaged, i.e. foreign-going voyage or home trade. If a seaman wishes to terminate his employment in contemplation of furtherance of an industrial dispute, 48 hours' notice must be given to the Master when the vessel is securely moored at a safe berth in the UK.

It will be recalled that in many maritime countries the employment agreement between the seamen and shipowner is called the articles of agreement. Indeed it is still referred to as such in UK tonnage rather than the 'crew agreement' and applies to individual crew members.

The ship's Master is required to maintain a crew list that must be produced on demand to the Registry of Shipping and Seamen as required under the Merchant Shipping Act 1970 and the Merchant Shipping (Registration etc.) Act 1993. The crew list embraces reference; name of seaman; discharge book number or date/place of birth; mercantile marine office where registered; name of ship in which last employed – if more than 12 months since last ship, actual year of discharge; address of seaman; name of next of kin; relationship of next of kin; capacity in which employed; grade and number of certificate of competence; date of commencement of employment on board; date of leaving ship; place of leaving ship; rate of wages; if discharged – reason for discharge; signature of seaman on engagement; and signature of seaman on discharge.

The crew list remains in being until all the persons employed under the crew agreement have been discharged/expired. A copy must be kept by the UK shipowner of all the changes. Any change in the crew list must be notified to a superintendent or proper officer within two days of the change. Before seamen are engaged on a new crew agreement and before they are added to an agreement which is already current, at least 24 hours' notice must be given to the appropriate superintendent or proper officer. The notice of engagement must include name of ship; port of registry; official number; whether a new crew agreement is to be made or whether a person(s) is to be added; and the capacity in which each person to be engaged is to be employed.

When a seaman is present at his discharge it must be before (a) the Master, or (b) the seaman's employer, or (c) a person so authorized by the Master or employer. The person before whom the seaman is discharged must enter in the official log book the place, date and time of the seaman's discharge and in the crew list the place, date and reason for the discharge. The seaman must sign the entry in the crew list. In the event of the seaman not being present at the time of discharge, similar entries must be made in the official log and in the crew list. All entries in the official log must be signed by the person making the entry and by a member of the crew. The seaman can request a certificate either stating the quality of his work or indicating whether he has fulfilled his obligations under the agreement.

The detailed requirements of seamen's documents are contained in the Merchant Shipping (Seamen's Documents) Regulations (Statutory Instrument 1972 No. 1295). This covers a British seaman card valid for five years, and a discharge book.

The Act also deals with discipline and concerns stowaways and their prosecution, aiding and abetting stowaways, and the Master's power of arrest. This indicates that where the Master considers it necessary for any person on board to be placed under restraint in the interest of safety or for the preservation of good order or discipline on board the ship, the Master is empowered to do so.

The Act makes provision for payment of seamen's wages, including at the time of discharge. Additionally, provision is made for an allocation of his wages to up to two persons and not more than 50% of his income, both of which may be varied only in exceptional circumstances. This arrangement is concluded at the time when the crew agreement is signed.

The Act also places on the employer the primary responsibility and the cost of providing for the relief and repatriation of seaman left behind. This covers the following and relates to the responsibilities of the employer or his agent to the seaman:

(a) Maintenance and cost of repatriating seamen who are left behind.
(b) Provision of their surgical, medical, dental and optical treatment.
(c) Provision of their accommodation.
(d) Making arrangements for their repatriation.
(e) Applying, if necessary, to the proper officer for the issue of a conveyance order.

Basically the regulations relating to the relief and repatriation of seamen are found in the Merchant Shipping (Repatriation) Regulations 1979 (SI 1977

No. 97). Shipboard disciplinary procedures (ss. 23–5) are contained in the Merchant Shipping Act 1979 but have not yet been introduced, except for s. 23.7. This regulation repealed the disciplinary arrangements in the Merchant Shipping Act 1970 and was enforced by statutory instrument SI 1985 No.1827.

The Merchant Shipping Act 1988 amended the law relating to crew agreements and brought the payment of seamen into line with that for other categories of employee.

6 Customs house and ship's papers

6.1 Introduction

It is important to remember that Customs entries are necessary for these reasons:

(a) To provide a record of exports and imports, and so enable the government to assess and thereby control the balance of trade.
(b) To ensure that no dutiable goods enter the country without paying duty.
(c) To bring all imports 'to account' by perfected entries prepared by importers or their agents.
(d) In so far as dutiable cargo is concerned, to provide a valuable form of revenue through the imposition by the government and European Union of certain duties and levies on certain goods imported into a country.

This chapter examines the customs procedures adopted in the United Kingdom as laid down by HM government. The UK is a member of the European Union (EU) and accordingly goods are in 'free circulation' for those commodities which originate and are manufactured in any of the 28 states forming the single market. Goods exported or imported from a third country which is outside the single market, such as the United States, the Far East, Switzerland, etc., are subject to rigorous customs procedures.

Customs procedures and legislation are subject to government policies and the political climate, both nationally and internationally. The Revenue and Customs is the government department responsible for customs and excise and embraces five main areas: landing and shipping, warehousing, excise, value added tax, and preventive duties. Customs procedures and legislation continue to change, much influenced by the World Customs Organization (WCO), which studies questions of co-operation in customs matters to obtain harmony and uniformity. Governments of most countries are members of WCO. Further factors driving change are the globalization of markets and new technology. Details of the areas of accelerating change are these:

(a) Globalization of markets and product/manufacturing outsourcing.
(b) New markets created by improved distribution networks as a result of multi-modalism.

(c) World liberalization realized by WTO initiatives and strategies, particularly market access and elimination of trade barriers.

(d) Decline in tariff barriers through WTO initiatives in an attempt to liberalize trade and open up markets.

(e) More multilateral and bilateral trade agreements to stimulate trade and reduce trade barriers through less severe customs tariffs. These include regional trade agreements.

(f) Simplification and rationalization of customs procedures and documentation as found in SAD.

(g) Growth of multinationals through mergers and acquisition, thereby exploiting economies of scale.

(h) Continuous merger and formulation of operating alliances of major container operators, thereby contributing to the development of more efficient distribution/ship productivity and an accelerating expansion of the global logistic high-tech environment.

(i) Rapid development of technology and development in electronic commerce, including the development of electronic commerce to produce 'seamless' international trade transactions.

(j) Measures to combat terrorism.

(k) The internationalization of criminal activity.

(l) The privatization of seaports, particularly container terminals, creating a new kind of management attitude that extols 'high-tech' good practice, efficiency and logistics.

(m) Continuous expansion of free trade zones and inland clearance depots.

(n) Growth and dominance of containerization.

(o) Growth and enlargement of trading/economic blocs stimulating trade across international borders with few constraints, lower tariffs or free circulation within member states.

(p) Encouragement of customs examination at traders, ICD, free zone location.

6.2 E-commerce; customs

The UK has been a market leader in the development and operation of e-commerce in the conduct of Export and Import customs declarations/ procedures and aligned customs derivatives, such as Excise, IPR, OPR, etc. The system has been developed in close association with the WCO and EU member states to promote freedom of movement of goods within a disciplined environment.

The core of e-commerce strategy is to present to Customs necessary documentation electronically and get it cleared electronically, the whole procedure safeguarded by in-built security and stringent audit checks. This has resulted in speeding up goods clearance dramatically and there is now a strategy of moving away from customs clearance at the seaport either to accredited traders premises or inland at an ICD, free zone, dry port customs warehouse, etc. Transit times are much reduced and trade potential developed. Manual systems have been almost eliminated in UK, and importers/exporters/ agents/carriers/seaports/airports communicate with Customs 'on line'. A constant concern is fraud in e-commerce and having effective measures of detection and prohibition to combat it. The trader today ideally has adequate computer resources and software to handle customs e-commerce. This facility involves an adequate IT software system that maximizes those benefits emerging from electronic documentation, not only in customs but also in processing export consignments.

An analysis of the various aspects of customs follows.

6.3 Value added tax

Consequent on the single market emerging in 1993, throughout the European Community a new system of charging VAT was introduced on goods traded between EU member states. VAT was levied previously by collection at the frontier on importation. Instead, goods supplied between VAT registered traders are zero rated on despatch and any VAT due is payable on acquisition of the goods by the customer. The customer accounts for any VAT due on their normal VAT return at the rate in force in the country of destination of the goods.

There are also special rates for freight transport and associated services. This applies to ancillary transport services and intermediaries arranging freight transport. When the services are supplied to customers registered for VAT in EU member states, the place of supply is the suppliers' member state when the suppliers belong in the member state of the customer. The supplier will charge and account for VAT on the supply at the domestic rate. The customer will be able to recover import tax, subject to the normal rules. Conversely, when the supplier is not from the member state of the customer, the customer gives the supplier a valid VAT registration number.

For VAT purposes, when goods are imported from outside the EU, they are treated as imported into the UK as follows: (a) they arrive directly from outside the EU and the trader enters them for home use in the UK, otherwise customs duty becomes payable on them; (b) they have been placed in another EU country or in the UK under a duty (for removal for home use in the UK, or customs duty becomes payable); (1) temporary storage, (2) free zones, (3) customs warehousing, (4) IPR, (5) temporary importation, (6) external community transit, (7) goods admitted to territorial waters, and (8) excise warehousing.

6.4 Intrastat

Intrastat is the system for collecting statistics on the trade in goods between member states within the EU. The supply of services is excluded from

Intrastat, except for related charges, such as freight and insurance and which form part of the contract to supply goods.

6.5 Export controls

There are three main reasons for controlling the export of goods from the UK. These are as follows.

(a) Revenue interest

These interests (and the economy) may suffer if the following types of transactions are not controlled:

(a) Transhipment goods – should these goods not be transhipped, there is the possibility of loss of revenue.
(b) Goods for re-export after temporary importation.
(c) Goods exported from a bonded warehouse.
(d) Goods exported from an excise factory.
(e) Goods exported on drawback.
(f) Cars supplied free of VAT to overseas residents.
(g) Goods exported for processing and subsequent re-importation.

Should these types of transactions not be controlled, there is a likely loss of revenue through dishonest traders claiming that goods had been exported, etc., when in fact these goods had found their way onto the home market. The insistence on proper documentation for these transactions ensures that revenue is safeguarded.

(b) Prohibitions and restrictions

The regulations regarding prohibitions and restrictions change periodically. This involves export licences, the Intervention Board for Agricultural Produce (IBAP) and prohibitions on the export of certain animals and drugs.

(c) Trade statistics

The introduction of the Intrastat system has important implications for the publication of trade statistics (see section 6.4 above).

6.6 Customs tariff

All products exported must be identified with the current correct class or commodity code. The rationale of such classification is to ensure the trader pays the correct amount of duty and VAT, that the trader receives any export refund due on some agricultural goods provided all other conditions are satisfied, and that the trader contributes to the accuracy of import and export trade statistics and ascertains if an export or import licence is required.

The basis of the integrated tariff of the UK is found in the Combined Nomenclature (CN) of the European Community. The CN is published annually and is based on the Harmonized Commodity Description and Coding System used worldwide. The tariff also includes TARIC requirements, which are integrated tariff classification guides for the EU.

The tariff is in three volumes: Volume I features general information about import/export matters, Volume II contains the schedule of duty and trade statistical description codes and rates, and Volume III outlines information about customs freight procedures, including directions for completing the Single Administrative Document.

The tariff is published annually by the *Official Journal* of the European Communities (OJ). A feature of the tariff is the Binding Tariff Information (BTI) decision, given on request to a trader and which is legally binding on all customs administrations within the European Community for up to six years from the date of issue. Advantages of the BTI include: (a) the correct commodity code is given to the traders for the goods on the customs entry and does not vary throughout the six years of its validity, (b) facilitates the trader to meet legal obligations under the correct tariff classification, (c) identifies any import/export licensing requirement or quota or other quantitative restriction, and (d) contributes to the quality of the overseas trade statistics which form the basis of UK balance of payments and any analysis of market trends.

Governing the interpretation of the nomenclature procedure are six general rules that must be applied to the traders' goods and placed in sequential order. The trader, having correctly determined the commodity code from the tariff, must clarify the following: any licensing requirements; any fiscal measures such as excise or anti-dumping duties; a temporary suspension of duty; a preferential rate of duty, the rate of duty and import VAT applicable to goods.

6.7 Customs Freight Simplified Procedures (CFSP)

HM Revenue and Customs has formulated a range of procedures and authorization conditions involving paperless trading. It embraces CHIEF, and the handling of CFSP declarations is featured in the tariff Volume 3, Part 5. The main principles of the CFSP are authorization; accelerated removal/release of goods; and electronic reporting and audit. Advantages of the CFSP include: earlier release of goods from Customs at the (air) port or an inland clearance depot, subject to anti-smuggling checks; use of one or more of the simplified procedures in combination with normal entry and warehouse procedures; and improved cash flow benefits to the trader as found, for example in LCP, before release to a Customs procedure or use.

Traders using CFSP must maintain a regular pattern of third-country declarations against the Trader Unique Reference Number (TURN), hold authorizations for the other customs procedures to which the trader wishes to enter, using simplified procedures; notify Customs of any change in the computer hardware or software; calculate revenues due, e.g. OPR, report any errors after the final supplementary period, hold and maintain a set of commercial records and declarations; maintain a system in support of the records maintained; keep an archive of all declarations up to four years after date of submission; permit Customs to audit system; and comply with all relevant provisions of EU and UK customs legislation. See HM Customs Notice No. 2005.

6.8 New Export System (NES)

The New Export System (NES) was introduced by HM Revenue and Customs throughout the UK in 2003. It applies to exports to non-EU countries and does not apply to goods removed to destinations in other member states, as these are categorized as removals or despatches. There are three key messages to be submitted to the Customs CHIEF – Customs Handling of Import and Export Freight – computer: pre-shipment advice – export declaration; goods arrived at port – arrival; and goods loaded aboard ship – departure. The NES enables goods to be declared electronically and likewise cleared electronically in the UK. The exporter or their representative must declare all goods for export completed. This involves a full pre-shipment declaration.

The NES provides for the electronic declaration of goods for export using the following: Simplified Declaration Procedure (SDP), Local Clearance Procedures (LCP); the full declaration procedure; and the low value and non-statistical procedure used with either SDP or LCP. A brief commentary on each follows:

(i) *Standard full pre-shipment declaration.* A full pre-shipment declaration submitted electronically at an airport, seaport, inland clearance depot or designated place approved by Customs.

(ii) *Simplified declaration procedure.* A two-part electronic submission. The first part requires the exporter to submit to Customs brief details of the export consignment. When CHIEF has accepted the declaration, the goods may be loaded for export shipment. The second declaration must be undertaken within 14 days of CHIEF acceptance or date of export, whichever is earlier. The pre-shipment declaration compels the trader to use the Unique Consignment Reference based on the WCO standard for each export consignment to enable Customs to trade the consignment through the trader's records. Additionally, the exporter must make a simplified electronic pre-shipment declaration to CHIEF either directly or via a Local Clearance Procedure with the requisite information. SDP is widely used for imported cargo.

(iii) *Local Clearance Procedure* (LCP). This facility is a simplified procedure where goods for export may be declared at the trader's own premises – approved by Customs – or other nominated inland premises. The facility is also available for imported cargo and widely used. For exports of excise goods only, a warehouse keeper may be approved to operate a LCP. When CHIEF has accepted the electronic declaration, the goods may be moved to the frontier. On arrival at the UK port of export a 'goods arrival message' is entered to CHIEF by the port inventory system, or the loader/carrier at a non-inventory linked location. The second part of the declaration – the supplementary declaration – must be made within 14 days of the acceptance by CHIEF of the 'goods departed message' or date of export, whichever is earlier.

When goods arrive at the UK port of export, CHIEF is notified by the port inventory system, or the loader/carrier at a non-inventory linked location with a 'goods arrival message'. Subsequently a 'goods departed message' is issued by CHIEF. See HM Customs Notice No. 760.

(iv) *Designated Export Place* (DEP). The designated export place permits an approved operator, such as consolidator, exporter, forwarder or airline, to present and submit declarations for export to Customs or Customs-approved inland premises. Excise goods, however, cannot be exported from DEP. It also permits goods to be presented to Customs which have been declared to CHIEF under NES by an exporter or third party. The electronic in-house inventory system is formulated by the trader and approved by Customs. The procedures which can be used at a DEP cover full pre-shipment declaration, low value declaration, non-statistical declaration and SDP. All declarations must be made electronically.

6.9 Unique Consignment Reference (UCR)

A Unique Consignment Reference is a reference allocated by the authorized trader to each export consignment. This number can be used by HM Revenue and Customs during an audit to trace that consignment in the trader's records. Additionally, there is the Declaration Unique Consignment Reference (DUCR) which is mandatory for traders authorized for simplified procedures; the Master Unique Consignment Reference (MUCR), normally used to associate or link several DUCRs; and the Bulk Consignment Reference (BUCR), whereby under the NES an approved agent or representative can submit one declaration for consignments from up to 99 exporters.

(v) *Low-value and non-statistical exports*. This is a NES facility for low-value goods. It permits an input of reduced information for all goods, except those that are dutiable or restricted. No supplementary declaration is required for low-value goods exported under the normal procedure. A supplementary declaration is required if the goods are exported under LCP or SDP. See HM Customs Notices Nos 2002 and 2005.

6.10 Customs reliefs

There is a range of customs reliefs:

Inward Processing Relief (IPR)

A system of duty relief applicable to goods imported from non-EU countries for process and re-export. Duty is relieved on imports of non-EU goods processed in the EU and re-exported, provided the trade does not harm the essential interest of community producers of similar goods. Processing can range from repacking or sorting goods to the most complicated manufacturing. IPR provides relief from customs duty, anti-dumping duty and countervailing duty. There are two methods of duty relief suspension or drawback. In either case there must be an intention to re-export from the EU, and authorization to enter goods to IPR is required. Customs duties are suspended when the goods are first entered to IPR in the EU. Drawback arises when the trader can claim duty back if the goods or products are exported and transferred to an IPR suspension authorization holder or disposed in a method approved by Customs. See HM Customs Notice No. 2003.

Processing under Customs Control (PCC)

Traders may obtain customs duty relief if the duty on the raw materials used in the manufacturing process is greater than it would have been in the event of importing the finished product. The goods may be declared for free circulation at the lower rate applicable to the finished product rather than at the rate that applies to raw materials. See HM Customs Notice No. 237.

End Use Relief

End Use provides duty relief on imported goods in order to promote certain EU industries and trades. To qualify, the goods and/or processes must be eligible for end use relief, approved by Customs, and goods must be put to their prescribed end use within agreed time limits. End Use relief applies to customs duty only. See HM Customs Notice No. 770.

Outward Processing Relief, Standard Exchange System and Returned Goods Relief

Outward Processing Relief provides duty on imports from third countries of goods that have been produced from previously exported Community goods. It enables businesses to take advantage of cheaper labour outside the EU while encouraging the use of EU-produced raw material to manufacture the finished products. Goods may be also temporarily exported to undergo processes not available within the Community.

The standard exchange system permits traders to import replacements for faulty goods exported from the EU when it is not practicable to have them repaired. The replacement goods must be of equivalent commercial condition and value.

The returned goods relief permits traders to re-import goods in the same state as they were exported, or they have had unforeseen minor treatment outside the Community, for example, to keep them in working order. See HM Customs Notice No. 235.

ATA and CPD carnets

The ATA carnet is an international document presented to Customs each time goods enter or leave a country. It permits goods to be temporarily imported without payment of customs charges for up to one year and can cover one or more different types of goods. The ATA advantages are that it: avoids need to complete national customs declaration and avoids a need to provide fresh security for customs charges potentially due in each country visited; simplifies Customs clearance of goods in each country visited; can be used in different countries around the world; can help to overcome problems arising from language barriers and having to complete unfamiliar customs forms. The ATA carnet, issued by the chamber of commerce and industry, is valid in 58 countries and valid for one year. It is used extensively by sales departments at trade fairs and exhibitions and by sales executives.

The CPD carnet is an international customs document for temporary import and export of road motor vehicles regulated under the ATA to Istanbul Convention. It is administered by Alliance Internationale de Tourisme (AIT) and Federation Internationale de l'Automobile (FIA) and is not required for use within the EU or other European countries. Its main use is in Africa, Asia, the Middle East, Oceania (Pacific) and South America. See HM Customs Notice No. 2003.

The TIR procedure

The TIR procedure allows goods in road vehicles and containers sealed by Customs, to cross one or more countries en route to their destination, ensuring minimum customs interference. TIR carnets are used for this purpose. Traders cannot use the TIR procedure for transit movements from the UK solely to EU states: CT procedures must be used for these movements. See HM Customs Notice No. 104.

Customs warehousing, free zones, ICDs and ERTS

A customs warehouse is a storage facility. It permits payment of import duties and/or VAT to be suspended or delayed when non-community goods are stored in premises under an inventory system authorized as a customs warehouse. Overall, it is a storage place, premises or an inventory system authorized by Customs for storing non-Community goods that are chargeable with import duty and/or VAT, or otherwise not in free circulation. Customs warehouses may be publicly or privately owned. There are six different types, A–F.

A free zone is a designated area in which non-Community goods are treated as outside the customs territory of the Community for the purpose of import duties. Hence import duties (including agricultural charges) are not due, provided the goods are not released for free circulation. See HM Customs Notices Nos 2004 and 334.

An Inland Clearance Depot (ICD) is a Customs-approved facility where goods can be cleared through customs. Normally only goods in sealed containers, sealed rail freight wagons, and sealed road vehicles may be removed for clearance inland. Enhanced Remote Transit Sheds (ERTS) are usually run by freight agents and approved by Customs. The ERTS accepts non-EU goods from the airport or seaport accepted for temporary storage. The goods are subsequently cleared by customs when an entry has been made at the entry-processing unit (EPU). See HM Customs Notice No. 2002.

Globally there are some 750 free zones and 300 ICDs.

6.11 Importation and exportation of goods

Commercial importations

Customs procedures for commercial imports vary according to the type of traffic involved, though the principles remain broadly the same:

(a) Goods may be imported legally only through places approved by Customs.
(b) Ships and aircraft must lodge a report, including a cargo list, with Customs on arrival (usually before unloading begins).
(c) All goods must be properly 'entered' and any duty or levies on goods subject to the Common Agricultural Policy (CAP) and other charges due must normally be paid before they are released from Customs control; this usually takes place at an airport, seaport, inland clearance depot, ERTS customs warehouse or traders' premises approved by customs under DEP. In the UK and many other countries, this involves an electronic declaration through a Customs approved trade or agent.
(d) Customs officers have the right to examine all goods, to confirm that the goods correspond with the 'entry' made for them.

Import entry procedure

The importer is responsible for preparing an 'entry' for all the goods he is importing. The 'entry' is a document on which he declares the description, value, quantity, rate of duty and various other details about the goods. When presented to customs the 'entry' is normally accompanied by supporting documents, such as copies of commercial invoices and packing lists, to provide evidence of the nature and value of the goods. Frequently the 'entry' is also accompanied by an official document that proves, for duty purposes, the goods' status; this involves the appropriate customs declaration document. In the case of goods imported only under a licence issued by a government department (e.g. the Department of Trade and Industry), the licence must normally accompany the entry. Detailed descriptions of goods for duty and statistical purposes necessary for the preparation of an entry are shown in HM Customs Tariff. The importer or his agent presents to the appropriate customs office the completed entry and supporting documents. In all UK seaports the system is fully computerized and many major importers and agents have on-line access to the customs network CHIEF. Access is undertaken electronically and involves a customs declaration entry on Form C88 – the Single Administrative Document. The agent or trader may process the input entry data by using the computerized entry processing system called the Direct Trade Input (DTI). The entry is checked electronically for accuracy and any duty is then raised for payment by the importer. Many imported consignments are processed under the CFSP, embracing LCP, SDP, ICD or ERTS. All documents are presented and processed electronically.

Variations in entry procedure are explained under items 6.6–9.

Export entry procedure

The range of options to export cargo is fully explained under the New Export System. This involves CHIEF and form C88 SAD. The New Export System is an electronic process.

Report (or entering in) and inland clearance

All vessels arriving at a UK seaport from outside the EU must report their arrival, which is be 'entered in' with Customs in accordance with the Customs and Excise Management Act (CEMA) 1979 Sections 35, 53 and 54, embracing Ship's Report, Importation and Exportation by Sea Regulations 1981 (as amended 1 December 1986 and 11 August 2003) and passenger information (18 October 2001). This Act also incorporates the Community Customs Code EC 2913/92 (as amended) Articles 37–47 and articles 183–9 of the implementation Regulation EC 2454/93 (as amended) specifying the requirements for reporting third-country cargo carried on board ships arriving in the EU.

The Master of the vessel, or a person authorized by him, is responsible for making the report. A shipping agent usually lodges the report on the Master's behalf. Vessels arriving within the EU do not have to report if they are an 'authorized regular shipping service' vessel, such as vessels operating ferry services between UK and Continental seaboard. An 'authorized regular shipping service' is a vessel that only operates between EU (other than free port/free zones) ports on a regular, previously authorized, scheduled service. All customs authorities in each EU port of call are required to approve the service and vessels must carry a valid certificate from the customs authority. All other vessels arriving at a UK port from a port in another EU country must report their arrival.

The report must be made at a designated place of the customs office within three hours of the ship reaching the berth and if that office is closed within one hour of its opening. An agent may apply for an extension if circumstances warrant it, such as adverse weather or when requested by a customs officer visiting the vessel. All vessels required to report must use the following forms:

(a) The IMO FAL form I (C94) *General declaration*. This will feature information relating to the vessel on its arrival and departure from the UK, and a description of cargo as found in a cargo manifest. The form must be signed by the Master or authorized agent.

(b) The IMO FAL form 3 (C95) *Ship stores declaration*. This document provides information relating to ship's stores on arrival. A separate declaration must be provided for each location within the vessel used to store ship's stores. It must be signed by the Master or an officer authorized by the Master and who has personal knowledge of the stores.

(c) The IMO FAL form 4 (C96) *Crew effects declaration*. This form is used to provide information relating to crew's effects. It must be completed by each crew member only when they are in excess of their travellers' allowance or subject to prohibitions or restrictions. The goods cannot be landed in the UK unless duty is paid and any licensing requirements are fulfilled. If a crew member is being paid off or going on leave, goods in excess of their allowance must be produced to a customs officer. When all the individual crew declarations are complete the form must be signed by the Master or authorized ship's officer.

(d) The IMO FAL form 5 (C97) *Crew list*. This provides information relating to the number and composition of the crew on arrival. Customs requires this form to be completed as part of the ship's reporting formalities.

(e) The IMO FAL form 6 (C98) *Passenger list*. This form provides information relating to passengers on vessels that are certified to carry 12 passengers or fewer. The form can be used on arrival and departure. Some ports may accept a dual-purpose declaration for arrival and departure if the passengers are identical and the vessel is in port for only a short stay. Passengers who are not EEA citizens must get an immigration officer's permission to enter the UK.

Declaration of cargo

The cargo declaration normally consists of the manifest, but other commercial or administrative documents relating to the goods and containing the necessary particulars of each consignment may be accepted, including the following:

(a) maritime document, e.g. bill of lading,
(b) container identification/vehicle registration number,
(c) the number, kind, marks and number of packages,
(d) description and gross weight/volume of the goods,
(e) port or place where the goods were loaded into the vessel, and
(f) the original port or place of shipment for goods on a through maritime transport.

Safety certificates are now part of the port state control checks to which all vessels must comply. These include International load line certificate, cargo ship safety construction certificate and cargo ship safety equipment certificate.

Entry outwards and outward clearance

All vessels leaving a UK port for a destination outside the EU, or for a free zone within the EU, must obtain Customs clearance outwards. Vessels destined for another UK port or for other EU ports are not required to obtain Customs clearance. Whether or not a vessel requires Customs outward clearance prior to departure, Masters must ensure compliance with international standards of safety.

The following forms must be completed: The IMO FAL form I (C94) in duplicate, the IMO FAL form 5 (C97), the IMO FAL form 6 (C98), and if the vessel is carrying 12 passengers or fewer a copy of the cargo declaration is required. The IMO FAL form 3 (C95) will be required on departure if stores have been loaded in the UK. Simplified reporting arrangements are available for a particular vessel with predictable sailing patterns, such as ferries, dredgers, rig supply and safety vessels. Facilities are available for an omnibus clearance – covering a fixed time period and specified voyages, or advanced clearance – where details of the next voyages are already known.

6.12 Ship's papers

It must be stressed the inward clearance procedure is customs focused, and mention was made earlier of compliance with appropriate international regulations. These international regulations in particular concern the ISPS Code and interface with port state control, embracing ship inspections and examination of ships papers. These focus on the ISPS code and port state control. All certificates carried on board must be originals.

UK registered ships, where so required, should carry the following documents, including those required by international regulations. It is obligatory for the Master to produce them to any person who has authority to inspect them.

Commercial documents

1 *Charter party* or *bills of lading.*
2 *Cargo manifest.* This contains an inventory of cargo carried on board the vessel giving details of cargo description, consignee/consignor, destination port, container number, etc. The data are despatched, by using courier/air mail/fax/e-mail to the ship/port agent, by the shipowner to give details to port authority importers, customs, etc. Details of cargo for discharge at the next port are usually despatched electronically. It enables the agent to prepare for the ship's arrival.
3 *List of dutiable stores.*

Certificates and documents required to be carried on board all ships

4 *International Tonnage Certificate* (1969). An International Tonnage Certificate (1969) shall be issued to every ship, the gross and nett tonnage of which have been determined in accordance with the Convention. Tonnage Convention, article 7.
5 *International Load Line Certificate.* An International Load Line Certificate shall be issued under the provisions of the International Convention on Load Lines, 1966, to every ship which has been surveyed and marked in accordance with the Convention or the Convention as modified by the 1988 LL Protocol, as appropriate. LL Convention, article 16, 1988 LL Protocol, article 18.
6 An *International Load Line Exemption Certificate* shall be issued to any ship to which an exemption has been granted under and in accordance with article 6 of the Load Line Convention or the Convention as modified by the 1988 LL Protocol, as appropriate. LL Convention, article 6, 1988 LL Protocol article 18.
7 *Intact Stability Booklet.* Every passenger ship, regardless of size and every cargo ship of 24 m in length and over, shall be inclined on completion and the elements of their stability determined. The Master shall be supplied with a Stability Booklet containing such information as is necessary to enable him, by rapid and simple procedures, to obtain accurate guidance as to the stability of the ship under varying conditions of loading. For bulk carriers, the information required in a bulk carrier booklet may be contained in the stability booklet. SOLAS 1974, regulation 11–1/22, and 11–1/25–8; 1988 LL Protocol, regulation 10.
8 *Damage Control booklets.* On passenger and cargo ships, plans shall be permanently exhibited showing clearly for each deck and hold the boundaries of the watertight compartments, the openings therein with the means of closure and position of any controls thereof, and the arrangements for the correction of any list due to flooding. Booklets containing the aforementioned information shall be made available to the officers of the ship. SOLAS 1974, regulations 11–1/23, 23–1, 25–8.

9 *Minimum Safe Manning Document.* Every ship to which Chapter I of the Convention applies shall be provided with an appropriate Safe Manning Document or equivalent issued by the Administration as evidence of the minimum safe manning. SOLAS 1974 (1989 amdts), regulation V/13(b).

10 *Certificates for masters, officers or ratings.* Certificates for masters, officers or ratings shall be issued to those candidates who, to the satisfaction of the Administration, meet the requirements for service, age, medical fitness, training, qualifications, and examinations in accordance with the provisions of STCW Code annexed to the Convention on Standards of Training, Certification and Watchkeeping for Seafarers, 1978. Formats of certificates are given in section A–1/2 of the STCW Code. Certificates must be kept available in their original form on board the ships on which the holder is serving. STCW 1978,1995, 2010 (amdts.) article VI, regulation 1/2, STCW Code, section A–1/2.

11 *International Oil Pollution Prevention Certificate.* An International oil pollution prevention certificate shall be issued after survey in accordance with regulation 4 of annex I of MARPOL 73/78, to any oil tanker of 150 gross tonnage and above and any other ships of 400 gross tonnage and above which are engaged in voyages to ports of offshore terminals under the jurisdiction of other Parties to MARPOL 73/78. The certificate is supplemented by a Record of Construction and Equipment for Ships other than Oil Tankers (Form A) or a Record of Construction and Equipment of Oil Tankers (Form B), as appropriate. MARPOL 73/78, Annex I, regulation 5.

12 *Oil Record Book.* Every oil tanker of 150 gross tonnage and above and every ship of 400 gross tonnage and above other than an oil tanker shall be provided with an Oil Record Book, Part 1 (Machinery space operations). Every oil tanker of 150 gross tonnage and above shall also be provided with an Oil Record Book, Part II (Cargo/ballast operations). MARPOL 73/78, Annex I, regulation 20.

13 *Shipboard Oil Pollution Emergency Plan.* Every oil tanker of 150 gross tonnage and above and every ship other than an oil tanker of 400 gross tonnage and above shall carry on board a Shipboard Oil Pollution Emergency Plan approved by the Administration. MARPOL 73/78, Annex I, regulation 26.

14 *Garbage Management Plan.* Every ship of 400 gross tonnage and above and every ship which is certified to carry 15 persons or more shall carry a Garbage Management Plan which the crew shall follow. MARPOL 73/78, Annex V, regulation 9.

15 *Garbage Record Book.* Every ship of 400 gross tonnage and above and every ship which is certified to carry 15 persons or more engaged in voyages to ports or offshore terminals under the jurisdiction of other parties to the convention and every fixed and floating platform engaged in exploration and exploitation of the sea bed shall be provided with a Garbage Record Book. MARPOL 73/78, Annex V, regulation 9.

16 *Cargo Securing Manual.* Cargo units, including containers, shall be located, stowed and secured throughout the voyage in accordance with the Cargo Securing Manual approved by the administration. The Cargo Securing Manual is required on all types of ships engaged in the carriage of all cargoes other than solid and liquid bulk cargoes, which shall be drawn up to a standard at least equivalent to the guidelines developed by the Organization. SOLAS 19754, regulations VI/5, VII6, MSC/Circ. 745.

17 *Document of Compliance.* A Document of Compliance shall be issued to every company which complies with the requirements of the ISM Code. A copy of the document shall be kept on board. SOLAS 1974, regulation IX/4, ISM Code, paragraph 13.

18 *Safety Management Certificate.* A Safety Management Certificate shall be issued to every ship by the Administration or an organization recognized by the administration. The administration or an organization recognized by it shall, before issuing the Safety Management Certificate, verify that the company and its shipboard management operate in accordance with the approved safety management system. SOLAS 1974, regulation IX/4, ISM Code, paragraph 13.

19 *International Ship Security Certificate.* SOLAS 1974, Chapter XI–2.

20 *International Air Pollution Prevention Certificate.* MARPOL 73/78, Annex VI, regulation VI/6.

21 *Engine International Air Pollution Prevention Certificate.* MARPOL 73/78, Annex VI, paragraph 2.3.6 of NOX Technical Code.

22 *International Sewage Pollution Prevention Certificate.* MARPOL 73/78, Annex IV, regulation 10

23 *Ship Sanitation Control or Ship Sanitation Control Exemption Certificate.* International Health Regulations 2005.

In addition to the certificates listed in 4–23, passenger ships shall carry:

24 *Passenger Ship Safety Certificate.* A Passenger Ship Safety Certificate shall be issued after inspection and survey to a passenger ship which complies with the requirements of Chapters II–1, II–2, III and IV and any other relevant requirements of SOLAS 1974. A record of Equipment for Passenger Ships Safety Certificate (Form P) shall be permanently attached. SOLAS 1974 regulation I/12, as amended by the GMDSS amendments, 1988 SOLAS Protocol, regulation I/12.

25 *Exemption Certificate.* When an exemption is granted to a ship under and in accordance with the provisions of SOLAS 1974, an Exemption Certificate shall be issued in addition to the certificates listed above. SOLAS 1974 regulation I/12, 1988 SOLAS Protocol, regulation I/12.

26 *Special trade passenger ships.* This is a form of safety certificate for special trade passenger ships, issued under the provisions of the Special Trade Passenger Ship Agreement, 1971. STP Agreement, rule 6.

27 *Special Trade Passenger Ships Space Certificate*. This is issued under the provisions of the Protocol on Space Requirements for Special Trade Passenger Ships, 1973. SSTP 73, rule 5.

28 *Search and rescue co-operation plan*. Passenger ships to which Chapter I of the Convention applies, trading on fixed routes, shall have on board a plan for co-operation with appropriate search and rescue services in event of an emergency. SOLAS 1974, (1995 Conference amendments), regulation V/15(c).

29 *List of operational limitations*. Passenger ships, to which Chapter I of the Convention applies, shall keep on board a list of all limitations on the operation of the ship, including exemptions from any of the SOLAS regulations, restrictions in operating areas, weather restrictions, sea state restrictions, restrictions in permissible loads, trim, speed and any other limitations, whether imposed by the administration or established during the design or the building stages. SOLAS 1974, (1995 Conference amendments), regulation V/23.

30 *Decision support system for masters*. In all passenger ships, a decision support system for emergency management shall be provided on the navigation bridge. SOLAS 1974 regulation III 24–4.

In addition to the certificates listed in 4–23, cargo ships shall carry:

31 *Cargo Ship Safety Construction Certificate*. A Cargo Ship Safety Construction Certificate shall be issued after survey to a cargo ship of 500 gross tonnage and over which satisfies the requirements for cargo ships on survey, set out in regulations I/10 of SOLAS 1974, and complies with the applicable requirements of Chapters II–1 and II–2, other than those relating to fire-extinguishing appliances and fire control plans. SOLAS 1974, regulation I/12, as amended by the GMDSS amendments; 1988 SOLAS Protocol, regulation I/12.

32 *Cargo Ship Safety Equipment Certificate*. A Cargo Ship Safety Equipment Certificate shall be issued after survey to a cargo ship of 500 gross tonnage and over which complies with the relevant requirements of Chapters II–1, II–2 and III and any other relevant requirements of SOLAS 1974. A record of equipment for the Cargo Ship Safety Equipment certificate (Form E) shall be permanently attached. SOLAS 1974, regulation I/12, as amended by the GMDSS amendments; 1988 SOLAS Protocol, regulation I/12.

33 *Cargo Ship Safety Radio Certificate*. A Cargo Ship Safety Radio Certificate shall be issued after survey to a cargo ship of 300 gross tonnage and over, fitted with a radio installation, including those used in life-saving appliances, which complies with the requirements of Chapters III and IV and any other relevant requirements of SOLAS 1974. A record of equipment for Cargo Ship Safety Radio Certificate (Form R) shall be permanently attached. SOLAS 1974 regulation, I/12, as amended by the GMDSS amendments; 1988 SOLAS Protocol, regulation I/12.

34 *Cargo Ship Safety Certificate*. A Cargo Ship Safety Certificate may be issued after survey to a cargo ship which complies with the relevant requirements of Chapters II–1, II–2, III, IV and V and other relevant requirements of SOLAS 1974 as modified by the 1988 SOLAS Protocol, as an alternative to the above cargo ship safety certificates. 1988 SOLAS Protocol, regulation I/12.

35 *Exemption Certificate*. When an exemption is granted to a ship under and in accordance with the provisions of SOLAS 1974, an Exemption Certificate shall be issued in addition to the certificate listed above. SOLAS 1974, regulation I/12; 1988 SOLAS Protocol, regulation I/12.

36 *Document of compliance with the special requirements for ships carrying dangerous goods*. This is the appropriate document which gives evidence of compliance with the construction and equipment requirements of that regulation. SOLAS 1974, regulation II–2/54.3.

37 *Dangerous goods manifest or stowage plan*. Each ship carrying dangerous goods shall have a special list or manifest setting forth, in accordance with the classes set out in regulation VII/12, the dangerous goods on board and the location thereof. A detailed stowage plan which identifies by class, and sets out the location of all dangerous goods on board, may be used in place of such special list or manifest. A copy of one of these documents shall be made available before departure to the person or organization, designated by the port State authority. SOLAS 1974, regulation VII5(5); MARPOL 73/78, Annex III, regulation 4.

38 *Document of authorization for the carriage of grain*. A document of authorization shall be issued for every ship loaded in accordance with the regulations of the International Code for the Safe Carriage of Grain in Bulk either by the administration or an organization recognized by it or by a contracting government on behalf of the administration. The document shall accompany or be incorporated into the grain loading manual provided to enable the Master to meet the stability requirements of the code. SOLAS 1974, regulation VI/9; International Code for the Safe Carriage of Grain in Bulk, section 3.

39 *Certificate of insurance or other financial security in respect of civil liability for oil pollution damage*. A certificate attesting that insurance or other financial security is in force shall be issued to each ship carrying more than 2,000 tons of oil in bulk as cargo. It shall be issued or certified by the appropriate authority of the State of the ship's registry after determining that the requirements of article VII, paragraph 1, of the CLC Convention have been complied with. CLC 69, article VII.

40 *Enhanced survey report file*. Bulk carriers and oil tankers shall have a survey report file and supporting documents complying with paragraphs 6.2 and 6.3 of Annex A and Annex B of resolution A.744(18), Guidelines on enhanced programme of inspection during survey of bulk carriers and oil tankers. MARPOL 73/78, Annex I, regulation 13G; SOLAS 1974, regulation XI/2.

41 *Record of oil discharge monitoring and control system for last ballast voyage*. Subject to provisions of paragraphs (4), (5), (6) and (7) of regulation 15 of Annex I of MARPOL 73/78, every oil tanker of 150 gross tonnage and above shall be fitted with an oil discharge monitoring and control system approved by the administration. The system shall be fitted with a recording device to provide a continuous record of the discharge in litres per nautical mile and total quality discharged, or the oil content and rate of discharge. This record shall be identifiable as to time and date and shall be kept for at least three years. MARPOL 73/78, Annex I, regulation 15(3)(a).

42 *Bulk Carrier Booklet*. To enable the Master to prevent excessive stress in the ship's structure, the ship loading and unloading of solid bulk cargoes shall be provided with a booklet referred to in SOLAS regulation VI/7.2. As an alternative to a separate booklet, the required information may be contained in the intact stability booklet. SOLAS 1974 (1996 amdts), regulation VI/7; the Code of Practice for the Safe Loading and Unloading of Bulk Carriers (BLU Code).

In addition to the certificates listed in sections 4–21 and 29–42, where appropriate, any ship carrying noxious liquid chemical substances in bulk shall carry:

43 *International Pollution Prevention Certificate for the Carriage of Noxious Liquid Substances in Bulk* (NLS Certificate). An International Pollution Prevention Certificate for the Carriage of Noxious Liquid Substances in Bulk (NLS Certificate) shall be issued, after survey in accordance with the provisions of regulation 10 of Annex II of MARPOL 73/78, to any ship carrying noxious liquid substances in bulk and which is engaged in voyages to ports or terminals under the jurisdiction of other Parties to MARPOL 73/78. In respect of chemical tankers, the Certificate of Fitness for the Carriage of Dangerous Chemicals in Bulk and the International Certificate of Fitness for the Carriage of Dangerous Chemicals in Bulk issued under the provisions of the Bulk Chemical Code and International Bulk Chemical Code, respectively, shall have the same force and receive the same recognition as the NLS Certificate. MARPOL 73/78, Annex II, regulation 12 and 12a.

44 *Cargo Record Book*. Every ship to which annex II of MARPOL 73/78 applies shall be provided with a Cargo Record Book, whether as part of the ship's official log book or otherwise, in the form specified in appendix IV to the Annex. MARPOL 73/78, Annex II, regulation 9.

45 *Procedures and Arrangements Manual (P&A Manual)*. Every ship certified to carry noxious liquid substances in bulk shall have on board a Procedures and Arrangements Manual approved by the Administration. Resolution MEPC.18(22), Chapter 2; MARPOL 73/78, Annex II, regulations 5, 5A and 8.

46 *Shipboard Marine Pollution Emergency Plan for Noxious Liquid Substances.* Every ship of 150 gross tonnage and above certified to carry noxious liquid substances in bulk shall carry on board a shipboard marine pollution emergency plan for noxious liquid substances approved by the administration. MARPOL 73/78, Annex II, regulation 16.

In addition to the certificates listed in section 4–23 and 29–42, where applicable, any chemical tanker shall carry:

47(a) *Certificate of Fitness for the Carriage of Dangerous Chemicals in Bulk.* A Certificate of Fitness for the Carriage of Dangerous Chemicals in Bulk, the model form of which is set out in the appendix to the Bulk Chemical Code, should be issued after an initial or periodical survey to a chemical tanker engaged in international voyages which complies with the relevant requirements of the Code. BCH Code, section 1.6, BCH Code as modified by resolution MSC.18(58) section 1.6. Note. The code is mandatory under Annex II of MARPOL 73/78 for chemical tankers constructed before 1 July 1986.

47(b) *International Certificate of Fitness for the Carriage of Dangerous Chemicals in Bulk.* An International Certificate of Fitness for the Carriage of Dangerous Chemicals in Bulk, the model form of which is set out in the appendix to the International Bulk Chemical Code, should be issued after an initial or periodical survey to a chemical tanker engaged in international voyages which complies with the relevant requirements of the Code. Note: The code is mandatory under both Chapter VII of SOLAS 1974 and Annex II of MARPOL 73/78 for chemical tankers constructed on or after 1 July 1986. IBC Code, section 1.5; IBC Code as modified by resolutions MSC.16(58) and MEPC.40(29), section 1.5.

In addition to the certificates listed in sections 4–23 and 29–42 where applicable, any gas carrier shall carry:

48(a) *Certificate of Fitness for the Carriage of Liquefied Gases in Bulk.* A Certificate of Fitness for the Carriage of Liquefied Gases in Bulk, the model form of which is set out in the appendix to the Gas Carrier Code, should be issued after an initial or periodical survey to a gas carrier which complies with the relevant requirements of the code. GC Code, section 1.6.

48(b) *International Certificate of Fitness for the Carriage of Liquefied Gases in Bulk.* An International Certificate of Fitness for the Carriage of Liquefied Gases in Bulk, the model form of which is set out in the appendix to the International Gas Carrier Code, should be issued after an initial or periodical survey to a gas carrier which complies with the relevant requirements of the code: Note. The code is mandatory under Chapter VII of SOLAS 1974 for gas carriers constructed on or after 1 July 1986. IGC Code, section 1.5, ICG Code, as modified by resolution MSC.17(58), section 1.5.

In addition to the certificates listed on sections 4–23 and 29–42, where applicable, high-speed craft shall carry:

49 *High-speed Craft Safety Certificate.* A High-speed Craft Safety Certificate should be issued after completion of an initial or renewal survey to a craft which complies with the requirements of the High Speed Craft (HSC) Code in its entirety. SOLAS 1974 regulation X/3; HSC Code, paragraph 1.8.

50 *Permit to Operate High-speed Craft Certificate.* A Permit to Operate High-speed Craft should be issued to a craft which complies with the requirements as set out in paragraphs 1.2.2 to 1.2.7 and 1.8 of the HSC Code. HSC Code, paragraph 1.9.

In addition to the certificates listed on sections 4–23 and 29–42, where applicable, any ship carrying INF cargo shall carry:

51 *International Certificate of Fitness for the Carriage of INF Cargo.* A ship carrying INF cargo shall comply with the requirements of the International Code for the Safe Carriage of Packaged Irradiated Nuclear Fuel, Plutonium and High-level Radioactive Wastes on Board Ships (INF Code) in addition to any other applicable requirements of the SOLAS regulations and shall be surveyed and be provided with the International Certificate of Fitness for the Carriage of INF Cargo. SOLAS 1974 (1999 amdts), regulation 16; INF Code (resolution MSC.88(71), paragraph 1.3.

Other miscellaneous certificates

52 *Special Purpose Ship's Safety Certificate.* In addition to SOLAS certificates as specified in paragraph 7 of the Preamble of the Code of Safety for Special Purpose Ships, a Special Purpose Ship Safety Certificate shall be issued after survey in accordance with the provisions of paragraph 1.6 of the Code of Safety for Special Purpose Ships. The duration and validity of the certificate should be governed by the respective provisions for cargo ships in SOLAS 1974. If a certificate should be issued for a purpose ship of less than 500 gross tonnage, this certificate should indicate to what extent relaxations in accordance with 1.2 were accepted. Resolution A.534(13), as amended by MSC/Circ.739; SOLAS 1974, regulation I/12; 1988 SOLAS Protocol, regulation I/12.

53 *Certificate of Fitness for Offshore Support Vessels.* When carrying such cargoes, offshore support vessels should carry a Certificate of Fitness

issued under the provisions of the 'Guidelines for the Transportation and Handling of Limited amounts of Hazardous Noxious Liquid Substances in Bulk on offshore support vessels'. If an offshore support vessel carries only noxious liquid substances, a suitable endorsed International Pollution Prevention Certificate for the Carriage of Noxious Liquid Substances in Bulk may be issued instead of the above Certificate of Fitness. Resolution A.673(16); MARPOL 73/78, Annex II, regulation 13(4).

54 *Diving System Safety Certificate.* A certificate should be issued either by the administration or any person or organization duly authorized by it after survey or inspection to a diving system which complies with the requirements of the Code of Safety for Diving Systems. In every case, the administration should assume full responsibility for the certificate. Resolution A.536(13), section 1.6.

55 *Dynamically Supported Craft Construction and Equipment Certificate.* To be issued after survey carried out in accordance with paragraph 1.5.1(a) of the Code of Safety for Dynamically Supported Craft. Resolution A.373(x), section 1.6.

56 *Mobile Offshore Drilling Unit Safety Certificate.* To be issued after survey carried out in accordance with the provisions of the Code for the Construction and Equipment of Mobile Offshore Drilling Units, 1979, or, for units constructed on or after 1 May 1991, the Code for the Construction and Equipment of Mobile Offshore Drilling Units, 1989. Resolution A.414(XI), section 1.6; Resolution A.649(16), section 1.6; Resolution A.649(16) as modified by Resolution MSC.38(63), section 1.6.

57 *Noise Survey Report.* A noise survey report should be made for each ship in accordance with the Code on Noise Levels on Board Ships. Resolution A.468(XII), section 4.3.

58 *Ship's Register or Certificate of Registry.* This is the ship's official Certificate of Registration and is issued by the authorities of the country in which the ship is registered. It gives the registration number, name of vessel, port of registry, details of the ship and particulars of ownership. The UK body responsible is called the Registry of Shipping and Seamen (RSS) and is based in Cardiff. Legislation is found in the Merchant Shipping (Registration, etc.) Act 1993.

6.13 Ship's protest

The Master, on arrival at the port, may decide to make a protest before a consul or notary public, declaring that he and his officers have exercised all reasonable care and skill during the voyage to avoid damage to ship and cargo, and that any actual loss is due to extraordinary circumstances beyond their control. Protest is a formality, but in cases where damage or loss has occurred, extending protest can be made within six months of noting, and sworn declaration may be supported by members of the ship's crew. In the UK there is no legal necessity to note protest, but noting of protest assists the defence against claims by consignees. In other countries protest is necessary before certain legal remedies can be obtained.

In the event of any casualty to the ship, the Master and/or his officers would be required to give depositions under oath before a receiver of wrecks, who is a senior customs officer.

7 Maritime canals and inland waterways

7.1 Introduction

All in the shipping industry must consider the geographical position and economic importance of artificial waterways. The development of multi-modalism has made this a subject of growing importance to the shipping industry.

The true economic importance of maritime international canals has, however, changed in recent years, mainly due to the introduction of larger capacity vessels with deeper draught, such as mammoth oil tankers and container ships. Maritime canals must therefore keep pace with new tonnage developments, otherwise ships will follow alternative routes because of the incapability of the canal to accommodate their draught, beam and length. Individual maritime canals should be judged according to their economic importance and their physical ability to accept modern tonnage currently or potentially available, such as in the Suez and Panama canals.

A study of international trade patterns and the disposition of the world maritime fleet shows radical changes since the 1990s. The growth in containerization is driven by logistics and facilitated by new technology in the ports and their environment. Container operators are remodelling their service on the basis of the hub and spoke system. More emphasis is on the multi-modal system, especially in Europe, North America, the subcontinent, Australia and the Far East. The St Lawrence Seaway is playing a greater role in development in North America. Similar remarks apply to the Kiel Canal. Growth in Asian trade, especially China's, has stimulated continuous modernization of the Suez and Panama canals to attract the latest generation of larger Panamax and Suezmax tonnage. Such important trade routes encourage lower freight distribution cost, quicker transits and much improved ship utilization productivity. There is no doubt that such major waterways improve ship productivity, particularly in respect to bunker charges which account for a high voyage cost element.

The key to ship management is flexibility and the presence of major waterways' voyage-route options.

7.2 European inland waterways

Inland waterway networks play a major role in the economic development of Europe. The Maritime Euro Region is focused particularly on the ports of Rotterdam, Hamburg, Antwerp and Dunkerque and their connecting inland waterway systems which penetrate southwards. Such ports have up to 30% of their transhipment cargoes conveyed on the inland waterway network and this market is growing fast, extending not only to bulk commodities, but also to an increasing volume of containerized goods and vehicular merchandise. A major development occurred in 1992 with the opening of the Rhine–Main–Danube (RMD) canal. Its length is 3,500 km between the North Sea and the Black Sea and serves nine East and West European countries. The RMD route runs through the Netherlands and Germany to Mainz and to Bamberg, its northern canal entrance. On the other side of the Franconian Jura, the canal joins the Danube at Kelheim. That river flows through Austria, clips the former Czechoslovakia and continues south through Hungary and the former Yugoslavia. Turning east again, it forms the border between Bulgaria and Romania before turning north to touch on Romania, the southern tip of the CIS, emptying into the Black Sea.

Inland waterways are developing throughout Europe at a time of intermodal development driven by a logistic environment. Europe is experiencing increased road congestion, which, coupled with the introduction of tolls on major highways and cleaner environment, is encouraging the pro-canal and inland waterways political lobby. With its ease of intermodal transfer the growth of containerization is contributing. Hence the strategy to modernize the network continuously and those vessels/barges embracing both bulk cargo and containerized transhipments.

Rotterdam is a key hub in the barge network and is served by 25,000 km of navigable inland waterways. Additionally, Rotterdam is served by over 30 inland waterway operators, running over 120 scheduled container services to 70 industrial centres spread over the entire heartland of Europe (see Table 7.1). Moreover, the growth of inland container shipping is a notable modal shift, as demonstrated in Table 7.2.

Table 7.1 European inland container terminals, 2003

Country	No. of inland container terminals
Germany	29
Netherlands	26
Hungary	1
Slovakia	1
Austria	4
Switzerland	2
France	5
Belgium	8

Table 7.2 Modal split containers

	2012	%	2011	%	2010	%	2009	%
Barge	2,613	35.3	2,393	33.4	2,351	32.8	2,200	33.4
Rail	794	10.7	818	11.4	755	10.5	735	11.2
Road	3,998	54.0	3,951	55.2	4,057	56.6	3,644	55.4
Total	**7,405**	**100.0**	**7,162**	**100.0**	**7,163**	**100.0**	**6,579**	**100.0**
From/to Hinterland	7,405	63.5	7,162	61.1	7,163	65.3	6,579	68.6
Feeder throughput	4,265	36.5	4,556	38.9	3,809	34.7	3,014	31.4
Total	**11,670**	**100.0**	**11,718**	**100.0**	**10,972**	**100.0**	**9,593**	**100.0**
To/from Depot	192		160		176		175	
Total	**11,862**		**11,878**		**11,148**		**9,768**	

Unit: Number of TEU ("moves") × 1,000

Source: Port of Rotterdam Authority / CBL.

It is estimated that traffic volume between northern Germany and Rotterdam is about 25 million tons of cargo travelling by barge annually. This compares with 90 million tons over the north–south axis: the Netherlands (including Rotterdam), Belgium (including Antwerp), and France. Some 80% of this volume is connected with Belgium. Traffic volume between the Netherlands and France totals 8 million tons compared with 17 million tons on the Mosel and Saar. Heavy industry around Thionville, Metz and Nancy in the French district of Lorraine accounts for much of this volume, but there is also cargo that goes to destinations further to the south, past Nancy. Navigating the smaller canals in navigable France, ships sail into what could be called 'capillaries', which constitute one of the most important forms of waterway in this part of the world. Of the twenty million tons of inland cargo transported on the north–south axis (Rhine–Schelde–Gent–Lille) about 10 million tons are connected with Rotterdam. A similar volume applies to transport over the Maas. Together with the Schelde, this river constitutes an equally important connection, drawing cargo to Liège. From this river a great deal of cargo wends its way through to the capillaries of northern, eastern and even southern France. The estimated 17 million tons of inland cargo mentioned above in the area to the south of the German city of Trier is seen as the 'roundabout category' in the north–south navigation, because this volume first avoids the Rhine. Ships travel up the Mosel past the city of Koblenz, situated at the confluence of three rivers. Overall, 95% of inland navigation in Saarland and Lorraine is connected with Rotterdam.

In 2002 the Netherlands' share of north–south traffic totalled 45% on the Rotterdam–Antwerp line, 80% of which was containerized and totalled 850,000 TEUs. The remaining 55% was conveyed in Belgium and French vessels. The most important varieties of cargo for the north–south trade are coal and building materials – especially sand and gravel, petroleum, chemicals, fertilizers, grain (import and export), rolled steel and iron ore. Additionally, there is mixed cargo to bulk liquids by small tanker tonnage.

All of industrial Belgium is accessible by Kempenaar inland barges with a length of 63 m, a 7 m beam and capacity of 550 tons. However, vessels of 110 m length with 2,000 tons capacity operate to Brussels, Gent and Liège on the Maas. The largest vessel between Netherlands and France on the Canal du Nord has a maximum capacity of 800 tons. The Kempenaar vessels have a 32 TEUs capacity or 48 TEUs when stacked three-high. A recent development to counter overland competition has been the provision of the pallet ship. Similar in size to the Kempenaar tonnage, the pallet ship has automatic self-loading and unloading and a capacity of 650 euro-pallets. Overall, between France and the Netherlands (Rotterdam) one million tons of cargo travel on the east–west route. As has already been demonstrated, the Rhine waterway between Rotterdam, Antwerp and on to Germany and France remains Europe's busiest network.

The push barge sector is a major feature of the barge industry in the port of Rotterdam. As an example, in 2012, 32.7 million tons of iron ore and scrap along with 25.3 million tons of coal was moved by the port, representing 13.1% of the total cargo handled in Rotterdam. A leading German operator, Veerhaven, has a fleet of five big push tugs and 53 tug-pushed dumb barges. Six fully loaded barges lashed together with a pusher behind can move 16,500 ton bulk cargoes in a single transport movement. Duisburg is Europe's largest inland port, handling 37 million tons annually. It represents a major hinterland hub. In 2003 a modern intermodal terminal was opened, with direct access to Antwerp and Rotterdam, and a new Rhine–Ruhr shuttle connects to Dortmund and the eastern part of the Ruhr region and northern seaports.

An example of canal design innovation arose in 1969. A plane incline-water slope was installed between Saint-Louis and Arzviller in the Zorn valley between the Vosges mountains and Alsace on the Moselle in France. The construction replaced a chain of 17 locks extending over 4 km which previously took a day to navigate. The plan incline takes 45 minutes and involves a total drop of 44.55 m. The length of the plane incline is 108.65 m with an overall length of 128.65 m. The boat lift overall length is 43 m, the width 5.20 m and boat draught 3.20 m. The weight of the boat lift full of water is 900 tons.

This is the only transverse system in Europe, whereas two longitudinal systems of this type exist: Krasnorkjask on the river Yenisey in Russia and Ronquières on the Charleroi–Brussels canal in Belgium. The foregoing three systems demonstrate the growing importance of the inland canal networks. More focus is now being placed on developing inland waterway infrastructure.

7.3 The Suez Canal Authority

The Suez Canal links the Mediterranean Sea to the Red Sea and was opened for international navigation in 1869. The Suez Canal is a level canal, though the height of the tide differs slightly, being 50 cm in the north and 2 m in the south. The Canal's overall length is 195 km from Port Said to Ismailia to Port Tewfik. The maximum permitted draught of ships is 58 ft. It is the longest canal without locks in the world and is navigable both day and night. The Canal is run on a convoy system: to transit at a fixed speed and a fixed separation distance between two passing ships. Three convoys pass through the Canal daily, two southbound and one northbound. Pilotage is compulsory and speed limits vary from 13 kmh to 14 kmh according to the category and tonnage of ships. It takes a ship 12 to 15 hours to transit the Canal, permitting about 76 ships per day to pass through. The width of the Canal has been doubled in four passing loops, involving a total distance of 78 km out of 195 km of the Canal's length. These are located at Port Said bypass, Ballah bypass, Timsah bypass and finally Deversoir bypass and the Bitter Lanes area. The Canal operates an electronic vessel traffic management system using a radar network to ensure safety of transit for vessels. There are 11 signal stations situated on the western bank of the Canal, each of which is about 10 km apart. These signal stations control traffic and facilitate pilotage operations. The maximum size of vessel able to go through the Canal is called a 'Suezmax', with a permitted draught of 62 ft. The Canal can accommodate all mammoth tankers in service on their ballast trips. Maximum permitted tonnage is 210,000 dwt.

The geographical position of the Suez Canal has made it the shortest navigable route between the east and west as compared with the route round the Cape of Good Hope. It shortens the distance between countries situated to the north of the Canal and those situated to the south, thus offering considerable savings in operating costs, voyage time and bunkers. Details of the distance variations are given in Table 7.3.

Traffic numbers and volumes for ships making full transits through the Canal in both directions in 2012 were 17,225 vessels, with a nett tonnage of 928.5 million tons. The daily average number of ship transits in 2012 was 47,

Table 7.3 Saving in distance, Suez Canal and Cape

| From | To | Distance (nautical miles) | | Saving (%) |
		Suez	Cape	
Ras Tanura	Constantza	4,144	12,094	66
	Lavera	4,684	10,783	57
	Rotterdam	6,436	11,169	42
	New York	8,281	11,794	30
Jeddah	Piraeus	1,320	11,207	88
Mumbai	Rotterdam	6,337	10,743	41

Table 7.4 Origins of main northbound
cargo by region, 2012
(thousands of tons)

Red Sea	59,075
East Africa and Aden	132
Arabian Gulf	105,291
South Asia	37,201
South East Asia	121,177
Far East	28,598
Australia	2,015
Other	52
Total	**353,541**

Source: Suez Canal Authority.

Table 7.5 Origins of main southbound
cargo by region, 2012
(thousands of tons)

East and SE Mediterranean	58,323
North Mediterranean	73,538
W & SW Mediterranean	48,214
Black Sea	64,143
North, West Europe	98,572
Baltic Sea	7,552
America	25,223
Others	10,805
Totals	**386,370**

Source: Suez Canal Authority.

Table 7.6 Cargo ton (exports and imports) for the first ten countries, 2011

No.	Country	Cargo ton (thousands)	%
North the canal			
1	Italy	79,115	10.7
2	Netherlands	77,629	10.5
3	Spain	66,328	9.0
4	Egypt	54,464	7.4
5	UK	52,551	7.1
6	Ukraine	47,401	6.4
7	U.S.A	40,744	5.5
8	France	39,103	5.3
9	Turkey	37,475	5.1
10	Belgium	31,690	4.3
	Others	213,411	28.8
	Total	**739,911**	**100.0**
South the canal			
1	Saudi Arabia	157,473	21.3
2	Singapore	131,860	17.8
3	Malaysia	79,120	10.7
4	China	59,119	8.0
5	India	46,432	6.3
6	UAE	46,178	6.2
7	Oman	34,727	4.7
8	Qatar	26,491	3.6
9	Sri Lanka	22,627	3.1
10	Iraq	17,853	2.4
	Others	118,031	16.0
	Total	**739,911**	**100.0**

Source: Suez Canal Port Authority.

which represents a reduction in the number transiting the Canal. Total nett tonnage passing through in 2012 decreased, attributable mainly to LNG tankers, which were down 27.2% and container carriers 2.3%. These significant reductions in transits explain the decrease in total nett tonnage. However, for some ship types nett tonnage increased because of greater demand for cargo movement. For example, in 2012 tanker nett tonnage increased by 22.3%, bulk carriers 18.4%, general cargo 0.5%, car carriers 4.0%, and passenger ships 15.3%. Figures are shown in nett tonnage to demonstrate the overall flow of cargo capacity.

Tables 7.4 and 7.5 feature north and southbound cargo, whilst Table 7.6 identifies the top 10 countries north and southbound. The Suez Canal Authority, as part of its continuous modernization plan, increased the permitted draught to 66 ft. This enabled the Canal to accept fully loaded tonnages of 58% of the world fleet of crude oil tankers, 99% of bulk carriers and all other types of vessels. Ultimately, it is proposed to increase the draught to 72 ft to accommodate VLCCs and increase the number of passing loops to lengthen the doubled parts of the Canal. Two shipyards exist on the Canal, at Port Said and Port Tawfit.

7.4 The Kiel Canal

The Kiel Canal connects the river Elbe at Brunsbüttel with Kiel Fjord at Kiel-Holtenau – a total distance of 100 km involving a passage time of six and a half to eight and a half hours, depending on ship size and traffic density. Ships travelling through this canal achieve an average saving of about 250 nautical miles compared with the Skaw route.

A continuous modernization programme has been executed, spanning 40 years, resulting in canal widening and lock replacement. Locks are provided at each end of the Canal. Vessels of up to 9.5 m draught are permitted, with a length of 160 m and beam of 27 m or 193 m length and 20 m beam. The Canal is open 24 hours per day. Two traffic control centres exist at Brunsbüttel and Kiel-Holtenau.

Annual traffic growth is continuous and totalled 40,000 vessels in 2003, involving 111 million GRT. It is the most widely used maritime canal in the world, with an average of 105 vessels per day. Parity exists between east and westbound vessel density. An increasing volume of business through the Kiel Canal is feeder container vessels from the ports of Hamburg and Bremerhaven to smaller Baltic ports. Such feeder tonnage benefits from the voyage time advantage the Canal affords over the Skagen route in Denmark. Overall, growth markets are Russian, Finnish and Baltic seaports. The largest vessel transiting the canal in 2003 was MS *Norwegian Dream,* 50,000 GRT, 230 m length and 33–20 m beam.

7.5 The Panama Canal

A world class waterway, the Panama Canal is managed by the Panama Canal Authority (PCA), an autonomous entity of the government of Panama. Prior to the transfer of this canal from the United States' stewardship on 31 December 1999, in accordance with the Panama Canal Treaty of 1977, various improvements were undertaken to replace ageing plant and equipment and to apply the latest technology. These improvements reflect the profound changes in global shipping and transport global industries. They have permitted longer vessels and specialized tonnage, generating a major growth in Canal traffic passing through.

The PCA embarked on a modernization programme in 2000 to increase capacity within five years by 20%. A major feature of the programme was the widening of the Gaillard Cut, the narrowest stretch of the Canal, and beyond, allowing two-way Panamax traffic for the first time. It involved widening the cut from 500 ft to 630 ft and deepening the lake to provide more water storage capacity by an additional 300 million gallons of water per year – a 25% increase of usable storage volume. Additionally, lock machinery was upgraded to a hydraulic system and lock machinery control was automated, rail track renewed, additional locomotives used to maintain transiting vessels in position while in the locks, and seven tugboats were added.

A new traffic management system has been introduced throughout the 51 mile length of the Panama Canal alongside a complex land-based industrial environment that embraces rapidly changing factors ranging from technical to climatic. The Canal has an enhanced vessel traffic management system (EVMS), which is a modern system that tracks vessels and other transit resources, prepares schedules efficiently, and makes all operation-related information available to anyone requiring it. The system is designed to achieve maximum safety and efficiency during Canal transits and provides a method for the integrated management of traffic and resources.

The system has the latest technological advancements in information systems, differential global positioning systems (DGPS) and telecommunications, and integrates under a single Y2K-compliant policy. This includes automatic tracking of vessels and other operation resources; collection of operation-related information; access to information on the characteristics and conditions of vessels and resources; automatic support for traffic and resources scheduling; monitoring of established schedules in 'real time' access by authorized parties to consolidated operational reports; and provision of early warning and alarms in case of emergencies. Benefits include the maximization of Canal traffic, a reduction in the Canal-waters time – the time between a ship's arrival at one side of the Canal and its departure at the other end; an increase in transit safety; retention of all specialized Canal operational knowledge into an intelligent, single electronic system; and optimization of the Canal's transit resources. Customers may also access the EVTMS for certain key data.

The EVTMS consists of two main integrated components, one is based on information systems and computer programming. The other creates an electronic 'life' map of the Canal and distributes this information to all interested parties and is known as the Communications Traffic Administration and Navigation (CTAN). CTAN uses GPS technology to track vessels and resources and displays information on computer screens.

The system provides access to external vessel databases. Data is automatically incorporated into the EVTMS as a 'life' map or graphic screen of the Canal and shows all vessels on screens to visualize details such as characteristics, conditions, Canal pilots and support units. These personnel may select any vessel on screen to see characteristics, conditions, position, direction, speed and cargo details. This technology assists the vessel's Master and Canal pilot by providing data on their vessel to give a complete view of Canal traffic, which improves safety during transits.

The system assists the transit scheduler by integrating all necessary information to generate the schedule and provide multiple optional schedules by means of a graphic interface. It also updates schedules automatically. The EVTMS assists in programming operational resources and assists establishment of priorities, which in turn permits including capacity or water limitations into the calculations, as well as better understanding operational and safety restrictions. In case of emergency or problem, it provides early warning to the marine traffic control centre and involved units. The EVTMS also permits electronic data interchange (EDI) – a standard for exchanging information between dissimilar systems – which in a safe and efficient manner permits an exchange of data with the PCA customers' systems.

Water is the key natural element that allows vessels to be raised from sea level over a mountain range and then lowered back to sea level at the other end of a canal. As traffic levels have risen over the years the demands placed on existing resources have also increased. When a ship is ready to transit the Panama Canal, one or more PCA pilots and a contingent of line-handlers board the vessel. From the Atlantic entrance the ship heads for Gatún Locks, where it is lifted 85 ft in three stages, taking about an hour. The chambers are filled with water from Gatún Lake, a vast reservoir created by damming the Chargres river. At 164 square miles, the reservoir was the largest man-made lake in the world when it was created. There are no pumps, water rushing into the chambers by force of gravity. Once through this first set of locks the ship navigates 23 miles across Gatún Lake. At the other end of the cut, there are two more sets of locks to lower the ship to sea level at Pedro Miguel. Plans are in hand to increase alternative water resources as traffic growth continues. It is important to note that as larger vessels use the Canal, water storage use increases.

The Panama Canal, linking the Atlantic and Pacific Oceans, is a relatively inexpensive passageway and has greatly influenced world trade patterns, spurred growth in developed countries, and has been the primary impetus for economic expansion in many remote parts of the world. For example, a vessel laden with coal sailing from the east coast of the United States to Japan via the Panama Canal saves about 3,000 miles in comparison to the shortest alternative all-sea route, and for a vessel laden with bananas sailing from Ecuador to Europe the distance saved is about 5,000 miles.

The Panama Canal serves a number of important world trades, including east coast US–Asia, Europe–west coast US–Canada, east coast US–west coast South America, Europe–west coast South America, and east coast US–west coast Central America. Cargo moving on these routes includes important shipments of grain, coal, phosphates, containerized cargo, chemicals and petroleum products from the US to Asia; manufactures of iron and steel, automobiles, and containerized cargo from Asia to the US; timber and products, coal and petroleum coke from the US and Canada to Europe; and containerized cargo and manufactures of iron and steel from Europe to North America. Leading exports from west coast South America to the US include petroleum and petroleum products, refrigerated foods, ores and metals, minerals and agricultural commodities. Important commodities from Europe destined for west coast South America include containerized cargo and fertilizers. The principal cargo moving from the US to west coast Central America consisted of grain, petroleum and products, and phosphates, and from Central America to the US agricultural products and minerals.

By far most of the traffic through the Canal moves between the east coast of the United States and the Far East, while movements between Europe and the west coast of the United States and Canada comprise the second major trade route at the waterway. Overall, 141 trade routes converge at the Panama Canal, serving 50 countries.

The PCA continues to attract major investment, including at the two key entrance ports to the Canal, which now has privatized container terminals, making it the fifteenth most important transhipment centre in the world. About 6,000 container vessels call at the entrance ports, 3,331 of which transited the Canal in 2012. A major cruise terminal, with hotels, is available at the Atlantic entrance to the Canal. Over 211 cruise vessels transited in 2012, out of a total of over 12,862 transits by oceangoing ships in that year. The road superhighway continues to be improved/developed and an intermodal link between major Canal area ports, embracing the Isthmian railroad, is now available. A wide range of ship types uses the Canal, including car carriers – PCTC; cargo vessels, containers, dry bulk, general cargo; cruise tonnage, reefer tonnage and oil tankers.

The PCA's future is one of growth and continuous investment in its infrastructure, including port terminals. The PCA is undergoing expansion and it is building new locks at both the Atlantic and Pacific sides of the Canal. These new locks will each have three chambers with a water reutilization basin. It is planned that the new locks will also involve widening the channel at Gatun Lake and deepening the channel at Culebra cut. These enlargements will allow modern-sized container ships to access the Canal.

7.6 The St Lawrence Seaway

Opened in 1959, the St Lawrence Seaway is formed by a natural waterway along the St Lawrence river and into the Great Lakes and their connecting channels, stretching more than 3,700 km from the Atlantic Ocean to the heartland of North America. The system consists of the five Great Lakes; the Seaway and the St Lawrence river from the Atlantic Ocean to the port of Montreal. The five great lakes are Ontario, Erie, Huron, Michigan and Superior. There are 15 twin locks between Montreal and Lake Erie accommodating vessels of a beam of 23.8 m, length 225.5 m, permissible draught 8.0 m and height above water level 35.5 m.

Six short canals account for less than 60 nautical miles. The South Shore Canal has two locks and runs 14 nautical miles from the port of Montreal to Lake St Louis. The Beauharnois Canal is 11.3 nautical miles long and includes two locks and links Lake St Louis to Lake St Francis. The Wiley–Dondero Canal is eight nautical miles long. It includes two US locks and provides access to Lake St Lawrence. The Iroquois Canal is only 0.3 nautical miles long, and has one lock and a water level control facility. The Welland Canal links Lake Ontario to Lake Erie. Seven of its eight locks are located at its northern extremity and three of these locks are twinned and contiguous. The eighth lock, located near the southern end of the 23.5 nautical mile canal, is a control lock. The St Mary Falls Canal, at Sault Ste Marie, consists of four parallel locks of varying dimensions. It links Lake Huron to Lake Superior.

Seaway locks are filled or emptied by gravity. Each lockage takes 45 minutes from the time the bow passes the approach wall until the stern clears the lock area. Safety features are built into the lock area. The signal light systems guiding ships into lock chambers are designed to eliminate unnecessary delays.

The five Great Lakes offer access to world-class ports. The routing system is made up of separate shipping lanes adopted by the Canadian and US inland fleets. These upbound and downbound lanes are shown on the general charts of the Great Lakes.

Ships sailing beyond Lake Erie should respect the St Clair and Detroit River Navigation Safety regulations which contain speed limits, traffic calls and reports, as well as navigation and anchorage rules. Ships enter Lake Superior, the largest of the Great Lakes, through the Sault Ste Marie locks, operated by the US Army Corps of Engineers. Facilities include four parallel locks of varying dimensions.

Ship operators planning a Seaway voyage must have a copy of the Seaway handbook, featuring Canadian and US regulations. Prior to the first transit of the Seaway, ships are inspected for automatic identification system requirements: alarms, anchors, draught markings, fenders, landing booms, masts, mooring lines, radio telephone equipment and sewage disposal.

The Great Lakes St Lawrence Seaway System serves the heartland of North America, involving a system of lakes and waterways capable of moving hundreds of millions of tonnes of cargo per annum. This involves the Great Lakes and St Lawrence Waterway. More than 40 provincial and interstate highways and nearly 30 rail lines link the major and regional ports of the system carrying consumer products and industries all over North America. Overall, the St Lawrence Seaway and Great Lakes, which run between Canada and the United States, serve over 100 million people. The Canadian provinces of Ontario and Quebec represent two-thirds of the gross domestic product and on the American side the Great Lakes States generate 40% of the United States manufacturing base. Overall, there are 41 ports provided with on/off ramps that connect to an extensive network of roadways and rail lines, all providing complete door-to-door service. This network includes over 40 provincial and interstate highways and 30 rail lines linking the major and regional ports of the system with consumers, products and industries all over North America.

Traffic growth has been considerable in recent years. It is estimated that the core of the business is about 90%, of which grain on commodity markets accounts for 24%, coal 10%, iron ore 26%, general 6% and other bulk cargo, e.g. chemicals, oil, etc., 34%. Future emphasis is being placed on containers from China transhipped at the port of Halifax and coke transhipment at the port of Quebec for Great Lakes steel mills. Coke will be carried to its destination by lake vessels. A further activity is the cruise business.

The economic vibrancy of the Seaway arises from its continuous improvement, and market forecasts indicate that as global trade continually increases marine traffic volume will triple by 2025.

The St Lawrence Seaway Management Corporation, established in 1998, is a not for profit corporation by Seaway users and other interested parties. The SLSMC manages and operates the Canadian assets of the St Lawrence Seaway for the federal government under a long-term agreement with Transport Canada, as governed by the Canada Marine Act.

7.7 The influence of canals on ship design

The construction of artificial waterways, and any necessary locks, is very costly and therefore the size of ships able to use them is often restricted. Bearing such limitations in mind, the ship designer limits the dimensions of the vessels so that they can navigate those waterways ships are likely to use. Such limitations affect the draught in many canals, and length and beam of ships in respect of locks. To deal with overhead obstructions, retractable top masts and removable funnel tops may be needed.

The development in recent years of inland waterways in certain European countries has fostered the development of major ports such as Antwerp, Rotterdam, Hamburg, Dunkerque and Calais. To get the longest possible sized vessel through various locks designers may choose a compromise whereby vessels suited to canals have inferior sea-keeping qualities and added cost per deadweight tonne.

Canal authorities charge dues on the tonnage of vessels using their waterways; major canals such as Suez and Panama have their own system of tonnage measurement.

7.8 Canal areas as points of economic growth

Not all ships pass directly through canals; through regular services traversing the waterway ports at their entrances become important transhipment ports. Other activities concerned with shipping, such as bunkering, also develop. These entrance ports may offer flat land and excellent facilities for private quays and a location on ocean trade routes. All these are very important factors in siting modern large-scale industry.

This aspect of choice of site is observed more in artificial waterways not mentioned in any detail – those leading to an important trade centre or industrial area. Ports like Dunkerque and Rotterdam can only be reached through their own canals by ocean vessels, and it is on the banks of these canals that modern industrial installations are found, flourishing because of deep-water quays on their sites. Refineries, iron and steel works, paper mills and chemical installations all are in this category.

7.9 Inland waterways

Shipping is becoming more integrated with inland waterways as the concept of the combined transport system develops. The provision of LASH, BACO and Seabee liner concepts are facilitating such developments, primarily in African markets. This tonnage is in decline as containerization develops and port facilities expand to accommodate containers. Combi carriers, train ferries and ro/ro vessels rely primarily on rail and road as a distributor.

Inland waterways have a useful role to play in many less developed and developing countries. The infrastructure in such countries tends to be inadequate in quality transport and distribution to and from ports. Acting as a port feeder service, inland waterway barge distribution is long established in many developing and less developed countries. Examples can be found in the markets of Africa, the subcontinent and the Far East and in the ports of Bangkok, Klang and Dar-es-Salaam, where overside loading is permitted to speed up the turn-round of vessels.

For all these reasons lighterage remains an important distributor of primary products in particular and of other non-containerized cargoes. Lighterage is economical and aids the quicker port turn-round of vessels. Moreover, it reduces the level of congestion in the port and at the quayside.

7.10 The Channel Tunnel

In 1994 the Channel Tunnel opened, linking the British rail network with Europe's 150,000 miles of rail system. The Channel Tunnel is a 31 mile subterranean rail tunnel between Folkestone (UK) and Frèthun, near Calais (France). It is built below the sea bed in the English Channel and comprises three tunnels, two of which are 7.6 m diameter, to convey trains, and one of 3.3 m, which is a service tunnel. Terminals with road and rail access are provided at both portals (Ashford and Calais). This Tunnel competes with ferries and other shipping for vehicular, freight and passenger traffic.

7.11 The Scanlink projects

The Oresund fixed transport link between Denmark and Sweden was completed in the year 2000. It involves a 16 km long tunnel and bridge link between Malmö and Copenhagen. Four contracts were involved – a tunnel, two artificial islands and other bridges that link the new structure with the Swedish mainland. The link also includes a tunnel and bridge link across Denmark's Great Belt between Zeeland and Funen. These two main links provide a permanent and fixed connection between western Denmark (Jutland) and Sweden. It has reduced journey times between Öresund and Malmö to ten minutes and has created a region of 3.2 million people, including Copenhagen and Malmö. Overall, the region has the eighth largest gross national product in Europe.

7.12 The Ghan (Melbourne–Darwin rail route)

In 2004 the Australian north–south railway link between Adelaide and the deep-water port of Darwin opened. With a distance of 3,000 km its transit time is 43 hours. It will further stimulate the Australian economy and provide easier access to Asian markets. Moreover, northern hemisphere trades will benefit from shorter voyage times to Darwin's deep-water port, rather than having to take a longer voyage round to south-eastern Australia seaports. It will favour not only containerized traffic, but also dry bulk cargo such as iron ore. Overall, the transit time to/from Singapore to/from Adelaide/Melbourne via Darwin will be four days quicker. Darwin has become the regional deep-sea port and gateway to/from South East Asia in Australia.

8 Services performed by principal shipping organizations

8.1 Introduction

This chapter focuses attention on a wide range of national and international shipping and trade organizations which exist to develop international shipping and promote professionalism at all levels and activities in shipping. Understandably the number of organizations annually tends to increase, and existing ones change their focus to respond to changing international shipping and trade embracing aspects of technology, politics, economics and commerce. Safety remains paramount in the conduct and operation of maritime fleets and their interface operations.

Since the 1990s the United Nations has taken on a significant role in the development of multilaterism among member nations to achieve unilateralism in shipping and trade regulations. This organization's contribution has helped create greater uniformity in the development of trade and transport of goods between nations. In particular, WTO, IMO, ILO, UNCTAD, UNCITRAL, together with numerous international organizations, such as IACS, BIMCO, ICC, OPEC, ITOPF and Intertanko work, with the UN.

These organizations regulate the industry and today there is a strong interface between trade and shipping. They facilitate trade development by encouraging adoption of a common code of practices. Many of these trade bodies work within the United Nations organization, examples being the IMO, ILO, UNCTAD, WTO, whilst others, such as BIMCO, ICC, Intertanko and IACS, act as consultants to the United Nations. United Nations organizations operate through specialist committees reflecting a whole range of issues. These committees submit recommendations to, for example the IMO, and these are discussed/evaluated by member state government representatives. Ultimately, a recommendation is made that member state governments then ratify through their state legislatures. When the requisite number of governments has approved the recommendation, a convention is adopted and it becomes mandatory for all signatories. To seek the most recent information, readers should visit individual web sites of those organizations examined in this chapter.

Since the 1990s the pattern and development of world trade has changed and trade and shipping organizations have responded so as to maintain and develop high professional standards and good practice.

8.2 International Association of Classification Societies

The International Association of Classification Societies (IACS) founded in London in 1968 is an association representing the world's major classification societies. Its main objectives are to promote the highest standards in ship safety and to prevent marine pollution. Over 90% of the world's merchant fleet in terms of tonnage is covered by the standards of IACS's 13 members. Members include the American Bureau of Shipping (ABS), Bureau Veritas (BV), the China Classification Society (CSS), Det Norske Veritas (DNV), Germanischer Lloyd (GL), the Korean Register of Shipping (KR), Lloyd's Register (LR), Nippon Kaiji Kyokai (NK), Registro Italiano Navale (RINA), the Russian Maritime Register of Shipping (RS), the Indian Register of Shipping (IRS), the Croatian Register of Shipping (CRS), and the Polish Register of Shipping (PRS). IACS works closely with the IMO and with the world's maritime industries and international organizations.

Compliance with the various IMO international conventions on safety is mandatory for the issue of statutory safety certificates by any of the states that have signed the conventions. Without such certificates ships cannot legally operate internationally. Statutory safety certification under these conventions is conditional on a ship's hull structure and essential shipboard engineering systems being satisfactory in all respects. The only recognized authoritative rules for these conventions are set by the major classification societies.

Compliance with the rules of the major classification societies is therefore the only practical basis for essential statutory certification. To ensure adequate implementation worldwide, over one hundred IMO member states have delegated statutory surveys to the IACS member societies.

Compliance with the IACS Quality System Certification Scheme (QSCS) and observance of the IACS code of ethics is mandatory for IACS members and associates. The bedrock of the IACS members' work code is ethics, for classification societies live on their reputation. Acceptance of their technical work can only be maintained by continuous proof of integrity and competence. Competition between societies therefore should be on the quality of services (technical and field) rendered to the marine industry. There must be no compromises in safety of life and property at sea or to the lowering of technical standards.

IACS has held consultative status with the IMO since 1969. It is the only non-governmental organization possessing this status at the IMO when the IMO is formulating/developing rules/regulations in consultation with other interested parties. The maritime industry accepts these rules, implemented by its member societies, as its technical standards. In areas where the IMO intends to establish detailed technical and procedural requirements, the expertise of IACS endeavours to ensure that these requirements are easily applicable and as clear and unambiguous as possible.

The IMO representatives routinely attend IACS Council meetings and IACS representatives participate as observers at the meetings of the Assembly of the Maritime Safety Committee, the Marine Environment Protection Committee, and many sub-committees and working groups of the IMO. IACS also liaises with international organizations to exchange views and information on matters of mutual interest. This ensures that the views of the industry are taken into consideration in the work of IACS. Examples of such organizations are international marine insurers, the International Chamber of Shipping, the Oil Companies International Marine Forum, the Society of International Gas Tanker and Terminal Operators Ltd, the International Standarization Organization, CIMAC and Intertanko.

Role of classification societies

These are organizations that establish and apply technical standards in relation to the design, construction and survey of marine related facilities, including ships and offshore structures. Most ships are built and surveyed to the standards laid down by classification societies. These standards are issued by the classification society as published rules. A vessel that has been designed and built to the appropriate rules of a society may apply for a certificate of classification from that society. The society issues this certificate upon completion of relevant classification surveys. Such a certificate does not imply fitness for purpose of seaworthiness of a ship and should not be construed as an express warranty of safety. It only attests that the vessel complies with the standards developed and published by the society that issues the classification certificate. More than 50 organizations worldwide define their activities as providing marine classification. Ten of these organizations form the International Association of Classification Societies (IACS). Classification is but one element within a network of maritime safety partners. Other elements are parties, such as the shipowner, the shipbuilder, the flag state, port states, underwriters, shipping financiers and charterers, among others.

The role of classification and classification societies has been recognized in the International Convention for the Safety of Life at Sea (SOLAS), and in the 1988 Protocol to the International Convention on Load Lines. As an independent, self-regulating, externally audited body, a classification society has no commercial interests related to ship design, ship building, ship ownership, ship operation, ship management, ship maintenance or repairs, insurance, or chartering. In establishing its rules, each classification society may consult members of the industry considered expert in their field. Classification rules are developed to assess the structural strength and integrity of essential parts of the ship's hull and its appendages, and the reliability and the function of the propulsion and steering systems, power generation and those other features and auxiliary systems which have been built into the ship in order to maintain essential services on board. Classification rules are not intended as a design code and cannot be used as such. A ship built in accordance with an IACS member's rules will be assigned a class designation by the society on satisfactory completion of the relevant surveys. For ships in service, the society carries out surveys to ascertain that the ship remains in compliance with those rules. Should any defects that may affect class become apparent, or damages be sustained between the relevant surveys, the ship owner and operator are required to inform the society concerned without delay. A ship is maintained in class provided that the relevant rules have, in the opinion of the society concerned, been complied with and surveys carried out in accordance with its rules. Classification societies also maintain significant research departments that contribute towards continuous development of appropriate and advanced technical standards.

Implementing the published rules, the classification process consists of:

(a) a technical review of the design plans and related documents for a new vessel to verify compliance with the applicable rules;
(b) attendance at the construction of the vessel in the shipyard by a classification society surveyor(s), and at the relevant production facilities that provide key components, such as the steel, engine, generators and castings, to verify that the vessel is constructed in accordance with the classification rules;
(c) upon satisfactory completion of the above, the shipowner's request for the issuance of a class certificate will be considered by the relevant classification society and, if deemed satisfactory, the assignment of class will be approved and a certificate of classification issued; and,
(d) once in service, the vessel's owner must submit the ship to a clearly specified programme of periodical class surveys, carried out on board the vessel, to verify that the ship continues to meet the relevant rule conditions for continuation of class.

Class rules do not cover every piece of structure or item of equipment on board a vessel, nor do they cover operational elements. Activities which generally fall outside the scope of classification include such items as: design and manufacturing processes, choice of type and power of machinery and certain equipment (e.g. winches), number of qualified new crew or operating personnel, form and cargo carrying capacity of the ship and manoeuvring performance; hull vibrations; spare parts; life-saving appliances and maintenance equipment. These matters may however be given consideration for classification according to the type of ship or class notation(s) assigned.

It should be emphasized that the shipowner has total control over a vessel, including the manner in which it is operated and maintained. Classification is voluntary and its effectiveness depends upon the shipowner, and other interests, operating in good faith by disclosing to the class society any damage or deterioration that may affect the vessel's classification status. If there is the least question, the owner should notify class and then schedule a survey to determine if the vessel is in compliance with the relevant class standard.

A class surveyor may only go on board a vessel once in a 12 month period. At that time it is neither possible, nor expected that the surveyor scrutinize the entire structure of the vessel or its machinery. The survey involves a sampling, for which guidelines exist based upon empirical experience which may indicate those parts of the vessel or its machinery that may be subject to corrosion, or are exposed to the highest incidence of stress, or may be likely to exhibit signs of fatigue or damage.

A classification survey is a visual process that normally consists of an overall examination of the items for survey; detailed checks of selected parts and witnessing tests, measurements and trials where applicable.

The United Nations Convention on the Law of the Sea (UNCLOS) is an umbrella convention concerned with many aspects of the sea and its uses, including the granting a ship's registration by a state. Once a ship is registered, the flag state has certain duties laid out in UNCLOS. In particular, under Article 94, the flag state must 'effectively exercise its jurisdiction and control in administrative, technical and social matters over ships flying its flag' and take 'such measures for ships flying its flag as are necessary to ensure safety at sea'. International conventions have been agreed, setting out uniform standards that facilitate acceptance of a ship registered in one country in the waters and ports of another and in the general furtherance of safety at sea and protection of the environment. These standards are commonly referred to as 'statutory' requirements. Broadly, they cover three distinct areas:

(a) aspects of the ship's design and its structural integrity – load line and stability in intact but damaged condition, essential propulsion, steering equipment, etc.;
(b) accident prevention, including navigational aids and pollution and fire prevention;
(c) the situation after an accident (fire, flooding), including containment and escape.

Some or all of these may also be reproduced in a particular class society's rules.

Undoubtedly IACS will continue to make a major impact in raising ship safety and reducing marine pollution.

8.3 International Association of Dry Cargo Shipowners (Intercargo)

Intercargo's objective is to provide a safe, efficient and environmentally friendly dry cargo maritime industry whose members' ships serve world trade, operating competitively, safely and profitably. The Association is located in London and represents the interest of its full and associate members who collectively own or operate about 800 dry cargo ships. It promotes the interest of its member companies in regulatory forums, such as the IMO and IACS. It also works closely with BIMCO, ICS, Intertanko and the IMO to achieve its objectives.

Intercargo members assisted the IMO to gain agreement in principle for comprehensive measures that address bulk carrier safety. New bulk carriers will be constructed with double hulls and free-fall lifeboats. Existing vessels will have to comply with measures designed to counter known problems. Additional measures include the strengthening of the side frame structure and hatchcover securing arrangements and banning of alternate hold loading. All bulk carriers are expected to have water ingress alarms in their holds.

8.4 International Chamber of Shipping (ICS)

The International Chamber of Shipping is based in London and shares a secretariat with the ISF. ICS is the international trade association for international shipowners and operators. It represents the collective views of the international maritime industry. Membership comprises national shipowners' associations representing over half of the world's fleet. It is engaged in a wide variety of areas including all technical, legal and operational matters affecting merchant ships, and is unique in that it represents the global interest of all different trades in the industry, particularly through its consultative status with the IMO and other international organizations.

Recent discussions embrace the implementation of the Maritime Labour Convention, low sulphur fuel, ship recycling, e-navigation, Arctic navigation, ballast water management, double hulls, piracy and armed robbery at sea, including hostage taking, performance of flag states, threat to international law and promoting the sound reputation of the industry. Over the years the ICS has developed and published best practices and guidelines for operations and for the implementation of conventions. The ICS is represented on the IMO and on other governmental and non-governmental regulatory bodies.

8.5 International Association of Independent Tanker Owners (Intertanko)

Intertanko was formed in 1970, is based in Oslo, and has offices in London, Arlington and Brussels. It represents the tanker industry, embracing the transport of liquid energy and chemicals. Overall, the aim is to foster a safe, reliable, competitive and responsible tanker industry. Membership is open to independent (i.e. not oil company and not state-controlled) tanker owners and operators. Overall, there are 219 members and 320 associate members with interests in tanker shipping. Intertanko has members in 37 countries, with 3,250 tankers of 284 million dwt. It is a forum where the tanker industry meets and is a valuable source of information, opinions and guidance for its membership. Its structure of secretariat, committees and regional panels, and the strong support it gains from its membership and from the tanker and shipping industries, allows it to contribute authoritatively and proactively at international, national, regional and local levels of the tanker community. In total, there are 14 committees, 4 regional forums or panels supported by teams of 21 secretariats.

Intertanko has a strong working relationship with many international agencies, especially with the IMO, BIMCO, OCIMF, ITOPF, UNCTAD, IACS, ICS, Intercargo and IMPA, and classification societies; the Shipbuilders' Associations of China, Japan and South Korea, and the Chemical Carriers Association.

The Committees of Intertanko cover the following:

(a) Safety, Technical and Environmental Committee.
(b) Insurance and Legal Committee.
(c) Human Element in Shipping Committee.
(d) Offshore Tanker Committee.
(e) Worldscale and Market Committee.
(f) Vetting Committee.
(g) Short Sea Tanker Group.
(h) Associate Members Committee.
(i) Bunker Sub-committee.
(j) Environmental Committee.
(k) Chemical Tanker Sub-Committee Americas.
(l) Chemical Tanker Committee.
(m) Council.
(n) Documentary Committee.
(o) *Asian Regional Panel* provides a forum for the Asian membership and to enhance their participation in the Association's activities.
(p) *North American Panel* promotes the activities and priorities of North American members in relation to Intertanko governing bodies and committees.
(q) *Latin American Panel* acts as a resource group for the Intertanko bodies establishing priorities and raising matters of concern to the Latin American tanker industry.
(r) *Hellenic Forum* creates a forum for members in South East Europe and Mediterranean region to facilitate better communication and to share experience.

Intertanko provides a Port Information website and a range of tanker-focused publications. In its annual report it also provides market reports and analysis, together with analysis of the world tanker fleet.

8.6 International Federation of Freight Forwarders Associations (FIATA)

The International Federation of Freight Forwarders Associations (FIATA) was founded in 1926 and represents 40,000 freight forwarders in 150 countries.

It is the global representative of freight logistics with the objective to accelerate the growth of the forwarding industry worldwide. It is one of the largest transport related nongovernment organizations in the world and currently holds consultative status with UNCTAD, ECOSOC, UNECE, UNICITRAL and UNESCAP.

FIATA has created several trade documents, such as FIATA Multimodal Consignment Note, and encourages document/form standardization to facilitate trade. It has a major world role in electronic commerce and international trade logistics embracing supply chain management. Most freight forwarders today are logistic operators in computer-driven international trade. FIATA strongly emphasizes training and professional development across all transport distribution modes. More recently it has focused its attention on marketing, arbitration and security.

8.7 International Energy Agency

The International Energy Agency was founded in the oil crisis of 1973–74 and its initial role was to co-ordinate measures in times of oil supply emergencies. Today, the IEA's focus goes well beyond oil crisis management and extends to broader energy issues. These issues include climate change policies, market reform, energy technology collaboration and aspects of the global economy.

The IEA has 26 member countries and a staff of 150 of primarily energy experts and statisticians. It conducts a broad programme of energy research, data compilation, publications and public dissemination of the latest energy policy analysis and makes recommendations on good practices.

As the projections indicate, because of increases in oil consumption globally, especially in Asian countries, it is vital that IEA co-ordinate with non-member countries. The IEA's adopted goals include: diversity, efficiency and flexibility within the energy sector; quick response to energy emergencies; achievement of an environmentally sustainable provision and use of energy; development of more environmentally acceptable energy sources; improved energy efficiency globally; through market research and market development to encourage new and improved energy technologies; generate undistorted energy prices; encouragement of free and open trade; and promotion of co-operation among all energy market participants.

The IEA's emergency response mechanisms were set up as part of an International Energy programme in 1974 which requires IEA countries to hold oil stocks equivalent to at least 90 days of nett oil imports and to release stocks, switch to other fuels, increase domestic production and to share available oil, if necessary, in the event of a major oil supply disruption.

Today the IEA member countries represent half of the world's energy consumption. In the long term, the IEA's influence will intensify as the growth of oil production continues.

8.8 International Maritime Industries Forum (IMIF)

The International Maritime Industries Forum is based in London and comprises shipowners, shipbuilders, flag registers, ship breakers, ancillary service suppliers, class societies, P&I clubs, insurers, underwriters, shipping banks, maritime lawyers and accountants drawn from 25 countries.

Governments recognize the growing influence of the Forum in the maritime world, and its opinion on various topics is regularly sought by major inter-governmental bodies such as UNCTAD, the OECD and the EU, as well as by individual governments.

IMIF was founded during the 1973 tanker crisis, following the publication of a report on the problems of the tanker industry commissioned by tanker owners, banks, shipbuilders, and oil companies who were all concerned at the disturbing effects of the crisis on a surplus of tanker capacity. In subsequent years IMIF expanded its area of concern beyond the tanker industry to include all aspects of maritime industries, not least government-related activities. It is still the only nongovernmental body – perhaps with the sole exception of the International Chamber of Commerce – affording shipowners, shipbuilders, bankers, cargo owners – indeed, all components of maritime industries – the opportunity to meet regularly at the highest level for discussions on the many problems faced by their separate industries, their prosperity being inextricably linked.

An IMIF objective embraces future finance for the world's fleet. In particular it focuses on the mass obsolescence consequent on the huge new building programme of the mid–1970s, the need for a revival and modernizing of ship breaking, the posture of governments, the role of classification societies and insurers, the need to improve operating and safety standards, and the reinforcement of port state control.

8.9 International Maritime Organization

The International Maritime Organization (IMO) is a specialized agency of the United Nations and is concerned solely with maritime affairs. Its interest lies mainly in ships used in international services.

What it is

In the 1940s it had long been recognized that action to improve safety in maritime operations would be more effective if carried out at an international level rather than by individual countries acting unilaterally and without co-ordination with others.

It was against this background that a conference held by the United Nations in 1948 adopted a convention establishing the International Maritime Organization (IMO) as the first international body devoted exclusively to maritime matters.

In the ten-year period between the adoption of the convention and its entry into force in 1958, other problems related to safety but requiring slightly different emphases attracted international attention. One of the most important of these was the threat of marine pollution from ships, particularly pollution by oil carried in tankers. An international agreement on this subject was adopted in 1954, and responsibility for administering and promoting it was assumed by the IMO in January 1959. From the beginning, improvement of maritime safety and prevention of marine pollution have been the IMO's most important objectives.

The organization is the only United Nations specialized agency to have its headquarters in the United Kingdom. It consists of 170 member states and three associate members. Its governing body, the Assembly, meets once every two years. Between sessions, the Council, consisting of 32 member governments elected by the Assembly, acts as the IMO's governing body.

The IMO is a technical organization and most of its work is carried out in a number of committees and sub-committees. The Maritime Safety Committee (MSC) is the most senior of these.

The Marine Environment Protection Committee (MEPC) is responsible for co-ordinating the Organization's activities in the prevention and control of pollution of the marine environment from ships.

There are a number of sub-committees whose titles indicate the subjects they deal with: Safety of Navigation (NAV); Radiocommunications and Search and Rescue (COMSAR); Training and Watchkeeping (STW); Carriage of Dangerous Goods, Solid Cargoes and Containers (DSC); Ship Design and Equipment (DE), Fire Protection (FP); Stability and Load Lines and Fishing Vessel Safety (SLF); Flag State Implementation (FSI); and Bulk Liquids and Gases (BLG).

The Legal Committee dealt with legal problems arising from the *Torrey Canyon* accident of 1967 and today has responsibility for considering legal matters within the scope of the Organization. The technical Co-operation Committee is responsible for co-ordinating the organization's provision of technical assistance in maritime issues, particularly those in developing countries. The Facilitation Committee is responsible for the IMO's activities and functions relating to the facilitation of international maritime traffic. These are aimed at reducing the formalities and simplifying the documentation required of ships when entering or leaving ports or other terminals. All the committees of the IMO are open to participation on an equal basis by all Member Governments.

The Technical Co-operation committee considers matters within the IMO that require implementation and are a technical co-operation project.

The IMO Secretariat is headed by the Secretary General, who is assisted by a staff of some 300 international civil servants. The Secretary General is appointed by the Council, with the approval of the Assembly. The IMO has promoted some 40 conventions and protocols and has adopted well over 800 codes and recommendations concerning maritime safety, the prevention of pollution and related matters.

Safety

The first conference organized by the IMO was in 1960 and was concerned with maritime safety. That conference adopted the International Convention on Safety of Life at Sea (SOLAS), which came into force in 1965, replacing a version adopted in 1948. The 1960 SOLAS Convention covered a wide range of measures designed to improve the safety of shipping. They included subdivision and stability; machinery and electrical installations; fire protection, detection and extinction; life-saving appliances; radiotelegraphy and radiotelephony; safety of navigation; carriage of grain; carriage of dangerous goods; and nuclear ships.

The IMO adopted a new version of SOLAS in 1974. This incorporated amendments adopted to the 1960 Convention as well as other changes, including an improved amendment procedure under which amendments adopted by the MSC would enter into force on a predetermined date unless they were objected to by a specified number of states. The 1974 SOLAS Convention entered into force on 25 May 1980 and has since been modified on a number of occasions, to take account of technical advances and changes in the industry. Other safety-related conventions adopted by the IMO include: the International Convention on Load Lines, 1966 (an update of previous, 1930, Convention); the International Convention on Tonnage Measurement of Ships, 1969; the Convention on International Regulations for Preventing Collisions at Sea (COLREG), 1972, which made traffic separation schemes adopted by the IMO mandatory and considerably reduced the number of collisions in many areas; and the International Convention on Maritime Search and Rescue, 1979.

In 1976, the IMO adopted the Convention on the International Maritime Satellite Organization (INMARSAT) and its Operating Agreement. The Convention came into force in July 1979 and resulted in the establishment of the INMARSAT, which is based in London.

Fishing is different from other forms of maritime activity and few conventions of the IMO could be made directly applicable to fishing vessels. The 1977 Torremolinos International Convention on the Safety of Fishing Vessels was intended to remedy some of these problems, but technical difficulties meant that the Convention never entered into force. It was modified by a protocol in 1993.

The IMO has always attached great importance to the training of ships' personnel. In 1978 the Organization convened a conference which adopted the first ever International Convention on Standards of Training, Certification and Watchkeeping for Seafarers. The Convention entered into force in April 1984. It established, for the first time, internationally accepted minimum standards for crews. It was revised in 1995, giving the IMO the power to audit the administrative, training and certification procedures of Parties to the Convention. The amendments entered into force in 1997. Further amendments were agreed in 2010. The amendments in 2010 are commonly known as the STCW Manila amendments and came into force in January 2012. These cover seafarer medical fitness, revised hours of rest, refresher training, and ECDIS for deck officers.

Preventing pollution, providing compensation

Although the 1954 Oil Pollution Convention was amended in 1962, the wreck of the *Torrey Canyon* in 1967 resulted in a series of conventions and other instruments, including further amendments to the 1954 Convention, adopted in 1969.

The International Convention relating to Intervention on the High Seas in Cases of Oil Pollution Casualties, 1969, which established the right of coastal states to intervene in incidents on the high seas which are likely to result in oil pollution, entered into force in 1975. The International Convention on Civil Liability for Oil Pollution Damage, 1969, and the International Convention on the Establishment of an International Fund for Compensation for Oil Pollution Damage, 1971, jointly established a regime to provide compensation to victims of oil pollution. In 1971 the 1954 Oil Pollution Convention was amended again because a completely new instrument was required to control pollution of the seas from ships, and in 1973 the IMO convened a major conference. This resulted in the adoption of the first comprehensive antipollution convention, the International Convention for the Prevention of Pollution from Ships (MARPOL). The MARPOL Convention deals not only with pollution by oil, but also pollution from chemicals, other harmful substances, garbage and sewage. It greatly reduces the amount of oil which may be discharged into the sea by ships, and in certain areas bans such discharges completely.

In 1978, the IMO convened the Conference on Tanker Safety and Pollution Prevention, which adopted a protocol to the 1973 MARPOL Convention introducing further measures, including requirements for certain operational techniques and a number of modified constructional requirements. The Protocol of 1978 relating to the 1973 MARPOL Convention in effect absorbs the parent Convention with modifications. This combined instrument is commonly referred to as MARPOL 73/78 and entered into force in October 1983. The Convention has been amended on several occasions since then. In 1990 the IMO adopted the International Convention on Oil Pollution Preparedness, Response and Co-operation (OPRC). It is designed to improve the ability of nations to cope with a sudden emergency. It entered into force in May 1995.

In 1996 the IMO adopted the International Convention on Liability and Compensation for Damage in Connection with the Carriage of Hazardous and Noxious Substances by Sea. The Convention establishes a two-tier system for providing compensation up to a total of around £250 million. It covers not only pollution aspects but other risks, such as fire and explosion.

The IMO carries out Secretariat functions in connection with the Convention on the Prevention of Marine Pollution by Dumping of Wastes and Other Matter, 1972 (London Convention). It entered into force in 1975. The

Convention prohibits the disposal of certain substances known to be particularly harmful. It contains specific regulations concerning the dumping of several other materials presenting a risk to the marine environment and to human health.

Other matters

In 1965 the IMO adopted the Convention on Facilitation of International Maritime Traffic. Its primary objectives are to prevent unnecessary delays in maritime traffic, to aid co-operation between governments, and to secure the highest practicable degree of uniformity in formalities and procedures in connection with the arrival, stay and departure of ships at ports. The Convention came into force in 1967.

In 1971 the IMO, in association with the International Atomic Energy Agency and the European Nuclear Agency of the Organization for Economic Co-operation and Development, convened a conference to adopt the Convention relating to Civil Liability in the Field of Maritime Carriage of Nuclear Material.

In 1974 the IMO adopted the Athens Convention relating to the Carriage of Passengers and their Luggage by Sea, which established a regime of liability for damage suffered by passengers carried on seagoing vessels.

The general question of the liability of owners of ships was dealt with in a convention adopted in 1957. In 1976 the IMO adopted a new Convention on Limitation of Liability for Maritime Claims, which raised the limits, in some cases by 300%. Limits are specified for two types of claim – those for loss of life or personal injury and property claims, such as damage to ships, property or harbour works.

In 1988 the Convention for the Suppression of Unlawful Acts against the Safety of Maritime Navigation was adopted. It is intended to improve measures for dealing with incidents, such as terrorist attacks, on commercial shipping. It entered into force in March 1992.

For most of the century, salvage at sea has been based on a formula known as 'no cure, no pay'. While it has been successful in most cases, the formula does not take pollution into account: a salvor who prevents massive pollution damage but does not save the ship and its cargo can expect no compensation. The 1989 International Convention on Salvage was adopted to remedy this defect. It entered into force in July 1996.

The IMO's codes and recommendations

In addition to conventions and other formal treaty instruments, the IMO has adopted several hundred recommendations dealing with a wide range of subjects.

Some of these constitute codes, guidelines or recommended practices on important matters not considered suitable for regulation by formal treaty instruments. Although recommendations – whether in the form of codes or otherwise – are not usually binding on governments, they provide guidance in framing national regulations and requirements. Many governments apply the provisions of the recommendations by incorporating them, in whole or in part, into national legislation or regulations. In some cases, by including appropriate references in a convention important codes have been made mandatory.

In appropriate cases, recommendations may incorporate further requirements which have been found to be useful or necessary in the light of experience gained in the application of previous provisions. In other cases the recommendations clarify various questions arising in connection with specific measures and thereby ensure their uniform interpretation and application in all countries.

Examples of the principal recommendations, codes, etc., adopted over the years are: International Maritime Dangerous Goods Code (IMDG Code, first adopted in 1965); Code of Safe Practice for Solid Bulk Cargoes (BC Code, 1965); International Code of Signals (all functions in respect of the code were assumed by the Organization in 1965); Code for the Construction and Equipment of Ships Carrying Dangerous Chemicals in Bulk (BCH Code, 1971); Code of Safe Practice for Ships Carrying Timber Deck Cargoes (1973); Code of Safety for Fishermen and Fishing Vessels (1974); Code for the Construction and Equipment of Ships Carrying Liquefied Gases in Bulk (1975); Code of Safety for Dynamically Supported Craft (1977); Code for the Construction and Equipment of Mobile Offshore Drilling Units (MODU Code, 1979); Code on Noise Levels on Board Ships (1981); Code of Safety for Nuclear Merchant Ships (1981); Code of Safety for Special Purpose Ships (1983); International Gas Carrier Code (IGC Code, 1983); International Bulk Chemicals Code (IBC Code, 1983); Code of Safety for Diving Systems (1983); International Code for the Safe Carriage of Grain in Bulk (International Grain Code, 1991); International Safety Management Code (ISM Code, 1993); International Code of Safety for High Speed Craft (HSC Code, 1994 and 2000); International Life-saving Appliance Code (LSA Code, 1996); International Code for Application of Fire Test Procedures (FTP Code, 1996); Technical Code on Control of Emission of Nitrogen Oxides from Marine Diesel Engines (NOx Technical Code, 1997).

Other important recommendations have dealt with such matters as traffic separation schemes (which separate ships moving in opposite directions by creating a central prohibited area); the adoption of technical manuals such as the Standard Marine Navigational Vocabulary, the International Aero-nautical and Maritime Search and Rescue Manual (jointly with the Inter-national Civil Aviation Organization), and the Manual on Oil Pollution; crew training; performance standards for ship-borne equipment; and many other matters. These are guidelines to help implementation of particular conventions and instruments.

Summary of the IMO conventions, January 2005

International conventions: adoption, entry into force, amendment and enforcement.

Maritime safety

- International Convention for the Safety of Life at Sea (SOLAS), 1960 and 1974.
- International Convention on Load Lines (LL), 1966.
- Special Trade Passenger Ships Agreement (STP), 1971.
- Protocol on Space Requirements for Special Trade Passenger Ships, 1973.
- Convention on the International Regulations for Preventing Collisions at Sea (COLREG), 1972.
- International Convention for Safe Containers (CSC), 1972.
- Convention on the International Maritime Satellite Organization (INMARSAT), 1976.
- Torremolinos International Convention for the Safety of Fishing Vessels (SFV), 1977.
- International Convention on Standards of Training, Certification and Watchkeeping for Seafarers (STCW), 1978.
- International Convention on Standards of Training, Certification and Watchkeeping for Fishing Vessel Personnel (STCW-F), 1995.
- International Convention on Maritime Search and Rescue (SAR), 1979.

Maritime pollution

- International Convention for the Prevention of Pollution from Ships, 1973, as modified by the Protocol of 1978 relating thereto (MARPOL 73/78).
- International Convention Relating to Intervention on the High Seas in Cases of Oil Pollution Casualties (INTERVENTION), 1969.
- Convention of the Prevention of Marine Pollution by Dumping of Wastes and Other Matter (LDC), 1972.
- International Convention on Oil Pollution Preparedness, Response and Co-operation (OPRC), 1990.
- Protocol on Preparedness, Response and Co-operation to Pollution Incidents by Hazardous and Noxious Substances, 2000 (HNS Protocol).
- International Convention on the Control of Harmful Anti-fouling Systems on Ships, 2001.
- International Convention for the Control and Management of Ships' Ballast Water and Sediments, 2004.

Liability and compensation

- International Convention on Civil Liability for Oil Pollution Damage (CLC), 1969.
- International Convention on the Establishment of an International Fund for Compensation for Oil Pollution Damage (FUND), 1971.
- Convention relating to Civil Liability in the Field of Maritime Carriage of Nuclear Material (NUCLEAR), 1971.
- Athens Convention relating to the Carriage of Passengers and their Luggage by Sea (PAL), 1974.
- Convention on Limitation of Liability for Maritime Claims (LLMC), 1976.
- International Convention on Liability and Compensation for Damage in Connection with the Carriage of Hazardous and Noxious Substances by Sea (HNS), 1996.
- International Convention on Civil Liability for Bunker Oil Pollution Damage, 2001.
- Adoption of amendments of the limitation amounts in the protocol of 1996 to the convention on limitation of liability for maritime claims 1976, 2012

Other subjects

- Convention on Facilitation of International Maritime Traffic, 1965.
- International Convention on Tonnage Measurement of Ships, 1969.
- Convention for the Suppression of Unlawful Acts against the Safety of Maritime Navigation, 1988.
- Protocol for the Suppression of Unlawful Acts against the Safety of Fixed Platforms Located on the Continental Shelf, 1988.
- International Convention on Salvage, 1989.
- International Convention on Maritime Liens and Mortgages, 1993.
- International Convention on Arrest of Ships, 1999.

Technical assistance

The purpose of the technical assistance programme is to help nation states, many of them developing countries, to ratify the IMO conventions and to reach the standards contained in the SOLAS Convention and other instruments. As part of this programme, a number of advisers and consultants are employed by the IMO to give advice to Governments.

In 1977, recognizing how important it was to secure better implementation of the instruments it adopted, the organization took steps to institutionalize its Technical Co-operation Committee – the first United Nations body to do so.

A key element of the technical assistance programme is training. The IMO measures can only be implemented effectively if those responsible are fully trained, and the IMO has helped to develop or improve maritime training academies in many countries around the world.

While the IMO supplies the expertise for these projects, funding comes from various sources. The United Nations Development Programme (UNDP) is the most important of these, with other international bodies such as the United Nations Environment Programme (UNEP) contributing in some cases. Individual countries also provide generous funds or help in other ways.

The most ambitious of all the IMO's technical assistance projects is the World Maritime University in Malmö, Sweden, which opened in 1983. The other maritime training centres associated with the organization's technical assistance programme are the IMO Maritime Law Institute, in Malta, and the International Maritime Academy, in Italy.

How it works

The IMO works through a number of specialist committees and sub-committees. All of these bodies are composed of representatives of member states. Formal arrangements for co-operation have been established with more than 30 intergovernmental organizations, while nearly 50 non-governmental international organizations have been granted consultative status to participate in the work of various bodies in an observer capacity. These organizations represent a wide spectrum of maritime, legal and environmental interests and they contribute to the work of the various agencies and committees through the provision of information, documentation and expert advice. However, none of these organizations has a vote.

The initial work on a convention is normally done by a committee or sub-committee; a draft instrument is produced which is submitted to a conference to which delegations from all states within the United Nations system – including states which may not be the IMO Members – are invited. The conference adopts a final text, which is then submitted to governments for ratification.

An instrument so adopted comes into force after fulfilling certain requirements, which always include ratification by a specified number of countries. Generally, the more important the convention the more stringent are the requirements for entry into force. Implementation of the requirements of a convention is mandatory on countries party to it. Codes and recommendations adopted by the IMO Assembly are not binding on governments; however, their contents can be just as important, and in many cases they are implemented by governments through incorporation into domestic legislation. See the IMO web site (www.imo.org) for details of the IMO conventions.

8.10 International Organization for Standardization (ISO)

The International Organization for Standard (ISO) is a United Nations organization based in Geneva. It is the world's leading developer of international standards. The global network identifies what international standards are required by business, government and society. ISO develops them, in partnership with the sectors that will put them to use, adopts them by transparent procedures based on national input and they are then implemented worldwide. The ISO standards have an international consensus with the broadest possible base of stakeholder groups. Expert input comes from those closest to the needs for the standards and also to the results of implementing them. In this way, although voluntary, ISO standards are widely respected and accepted by the public and private sectors internationally.

The ISO – a non-governmental organization – is a federation of the national standards bodies of 149 countries, one per country, from all regions of the world, including developed, developing and transitional economies. Each ISO member is the principal standards organization in its country. The members propose the new standards, participate in their development and provide support in collaboration with ISO Central Secretariat for the 3,000 technical groups that actually develop the standards. ISO members appoint national delegations to standards committees. In all, there are some 50,000 experts contributing annually to the work of the organization. When their work is published as an ISO international standard, that standard may be adopted as a national standard by the ISO members and translated.

The ISO has a current portfolio (2005) of 15,036 standards that provide practical solutions and benefit almost every sector of business, industry and technology. They make up a complete offering for all three dimensions of sustainable development – economic, environmental and social. ISO's work programme ranges from standards for traditional activities, such as agriculture and construction, through to mechanical engineering, manufacturing and distribution, to transport, medical services, the latest in information and communication technology developments, and to standards for services.

The ISO 9000 and ISO 14000 families of management systems standards have spearheaded a widening of ISO's scope to include managerial and organizational practice. The ISO does not carry out certification to these or any other of its standards, nor does it control the certification business. The ISO works closely with its partners in national standards, particularly IEC, ITU-T, WSC and WTO.

The ISO has a strong maritime, seaport, trade, e-commerce, supply chain and container focus. Details are these:

(a) ISO guidelines to assist industry for maritime port security reflecting the ISPS code; effective from 1 July 2004. It has been adopted by 100 countries of the IMO code and features detailed related requirements for governments, port authorities and shipping companies. It is intended to enable better monitoring of freight flows to combat smuggling and to respond to the threat of terrorist attacks. Overall, it provides a framework to assist marine port facilities in port assessment, personnel assessment, and security planning to protect people, ships and cargo.

(b) Continuing focus on applying the ISO standards to containers and working with industry in the development of new container types reflecting new technology.

(c) The development of ISO standards in dangerous cargo shipment undertaken in consultation with specialized agencies. A recent example of new provisions is found in UN recommendations *Orange Book*, fourteenth edition.
(d) Developing a code of practice in supply chain operation. This embraces 'Best Practice for Custody in Supply Chain Security' and 'Security Management Systems for the Supply Chain' publications.

ISO is also renowned for its ISO 9000 and ISO 14000 management standards globally. It devised a strategic plan 2005–10 covering seven key objectives: facilitation of global trade; improvement of quality; safety security, environmental and consumer protection; rational use of natural resources; and global dissemination of technologies and good practices. The ISO website gives up to date information on latest developments (www.iso.org).

8.11 International Ship Managers' Association (ISMA)

ISMA was formed in 1991 and is based in Horsham, Sussex. Its mission statement contains four objectives: to maintain the ISMA code as the leading quality standard in the ship and crew management industries; to discuss matters of common interest to the ship and crew management industries; to promote the interests of the ship and crew management industries in general; to encourage the highest standards in ship management and crew management through innovation, creativity; and the sharing of knowledge amongst members.

ISMA has a strong input from underwriters, P&I clubs, bankers and charterers. It also co-operates with other bodies such as the IMO, BIMCO, ILO and EU. It also has a major focus on the application of ISO 9001:2000 code of accreditation as applied to ship and crew managers. ISMA has published guidelines on the interpretation of the ISO 9001:2000 code. ISMA publishes regularly a newsletter, *Focus*, to keep members up to date on current issues facing the ship management industry.

The role of ship management has changed dramatically during the past ten years and the ISMA has been at the forefront of change. Ship managers today focus on cadet/crew/officer training, development and implementation of IT systems and introducing safe working practices. ISMA initiated the drive for quality assurance in shipping, a focus which resulted in various classification Quality Assurance systems. It joined with the IMO to tackle ISM requirements.

The stringent ISMA Code of Ship Management Standards underwent its second five-year revision in 2000. That revision incorporated new ISO standard ISO 9002:2000. The reconstructed code is in two parts. Part 1 contains general matters, shoreside management, crew management and all elements common to both crew and ship managers, while Part 2 is specific to ship management.

ISMA, through its consultative status at the IMO, continues to influence discussion of core issues of management of ship and crew.

8.12 International Tanker Owners Pollution Federation (ITOPF)

The International Tanker Owners Pollution Federation was established in 1968 as a non-profit-making service organization. It provides a broad range of technical services in marine pollution for its shipowner members and associates, their P&I insurers and other groups, such as the International Oil Pollution Compensation Fund.

ITOPF priority service is to respond to accidental spills of oil and chemicals. It assesses the damage caused by the spills to the environment and economic resources; provides advice on the technical merits of claims for compensation; conducts contingency planning and training arrangements; produces a wide range of publications; and maintains various databases, including a web site. Membership comprises over 6,300 tanker owners and bareboat charters who operate over 11,000 tankers, barges, and combination carriers involving a gross tonnage of 338 million GT. This embraces virtually all the world's bulk oil, chemical and gas carrier tonnage. The main properties affecting the behaviour of spilled oil at sea are specific gravity (its density relative to pure water, often expressed as API); distillation characteristics (its volatility); viscosity (its resistance to flow); and pour point (the temperature below which it will not flow).

Since the interactions between the various weathering processes are not well understood, reliance is often placed on empirical models based upon the properties of different oil types. For this purpose, it is convenient to classify the most commonly transported oils into four main groups, roughly according to their specific gravity. After classifying the oils, expected rates of dissipation can be predicted.

OPA90, HNS Convention and OPRC Convention

Three pieces of legislation relative to oil pollution are: OPA90, HNS Convention and OPRC Convention.

In the wake of the *Exxon Valdez* oil spill in March 1989, the US Congress passed the Oil Pollution Act of 1990 (OPA90). It is a comprehensive piece of legislation. Only those sections of OPA90 that relate to liability and compensation for clean-up and damage and to prevention and preparedness are briefly summarized here. More detailed information, including a complete copy of the Act and associated regulations, can be accessed via the US Coast Guard's web site at www.uscg.mil.

A wide range of damages are specifically covered by OPA90. They include: real or personal property; damage, loss of profits or earning capacity; loss of subsistence; use of natural resources; loss of government revenues from taxes, royalties, rents, fees, etc.; cost of increased public services; natural resource damage; and the costs of assessing such damage.

Any person or government who incurs an allowable cost, damage or loss as a result of an oil pollution incident may submit claims against the responsible party or its guarantor. The International Convention on Liability and Compensation for Damage in Connection with the Carriage of Hazardous and Noxious Substances by Sea (HNS Convention) was adopted by the IMO in May 1996. It aims to ensure adequate, prompt and effective compensation for damage that may result from shipping accidents involving hazardous and noxious substances.

The convention entitles claimants to compensation for loss or damage to persons, property and the environment caused by incidents involving cargoes of oil, gases and chemicals, plus other substances hazardous when in packaged form. Pollution damage caused by persistent oils already covered by the CLC and Fund Convention is excluded, as is damage caused by radioactive materials and coal.

The International Convention on Oil Pollution Preparedness, Response and Co-operation (OPRC) was adopted by an IMO Diplomatic conference in November 1990. It entered into force in May 1995. In March 2000 it was extended by way of a protocol to cover pollution incidents by hazardous and noxious substances. This protocol has not yet entered into force.

The primary objectives of OPRC 1990 are to facilitate international co-operation and mutual assistance between States and regions when preparing for and responding to major oil pollution incidents, and to encourage States to develop and maintain adequate capability to deal with such emergences. OPRC 1990 covers oil spills from offshore oil exploration and production (E&P) platforms, ports, oil handling facilities and ships.

By ratifying OPRC a state commits itself to establish a national system for responding promptly and effectively to oil pollution incidents. This should include, as a basic minimum, a national contingency plan; designated national authorities and focal points responsible for oil pollution preparedness and response; oil pollution reporting procedures, and arrangements for handling requests for assistance. In addition, each party to the Convention, either individually or through bi- or multilateral co-operation and in co-operation with the oil and shipping industries, port authorities and other relevant entities, is required to ensure: a minimum level of pre-positioned oil spill combating equipment; a programme of exercises for oil pollution response organizations; a training programme for relevant personnel; mechanisms or arrangements to co-ordinate the response to an oil pollution incident, and capabilities to mobilize resources.

The operators of ships, E&P facilities, ports and oil terminals are also required to prepare oil pollution emergency plans. In the case of ships, this is the same plan that is required under MARPOL – the Shipboard Oil Pollution Emergency Plan, or SOPEP.

The OPRC Convention benefits shipowners because it results in more effective oil spill response around the world. For this reason ITOPF, together with other industry associations, has been co-operating with the IMO to assist states to meet the various requirements of the Convention.

8.13 Lloyd's Register of Shipping

Lloyd's Register was founded in London in 1760 to examine merchant ships and 'classify' them according to their condition. In the 1990s Lloyd's Register brought its expertise to bear on other industries, in particular the energy sector. It also widened its services to include management systems certification. In recent years the Lloyd's Register Group has expanded its services to the wider transport industry, beginning with rail. Lloyd's Register develops products and services through three business streams: Marine, Energy and Transportation, and Management Systems – Lloyd's Register Quality Assurance (LRQA). These products and services reach clients worldwide through a network of agencies, including Lloyd's Register Asia, Lloyd's Register EMEA (Europe the Middle East and Africa), Lloyd's Register North America and Lloyd's Register Central and South America.

The Lloyd's Register Group has over 200 offices worldwide, served by some 5,000 employees. Lloyd's Register operates independently of any government or other body and can assure absolute commercial impartiality. A General Committee, comprising representatives of the main industry sectors that Lloyd's Register works for, oversees the organization.

A significant amount of the profit the organization generates is used in the support of the industries they serve. This support can be seen in the funding of research and development and the education and training of those either seeking or furthering a career in these industries. These support activities are separate from the normal course of business within the Lloyd's Register Group.

The marine business work involves classification, which sets standards of quality and reliability that must be maintained if a ship is to remain in 'class'. The ship's hull and machinery must meet the requirements of the *Rules*, and Lloyd's Register carries out periodic surveys throughout the life of a ship to help ensure this.

The *Rules* for ship construction and maintenance are constantly revised and updated in line with changes and developments in shipbuilding and current research. The Lloyd's Register Group also carries out statutory inspections in conformity with international conventions for various national administrations.

A large proportion of the marine business concerns tankers and bulk carriers, but the Lloyd's Register Group is also a world leader in some of the most technologically advanced vessels: cruise and ro/ro ships, LNG (liquefied natural gas) carriers and naval vessels.

Beyond classification and statutory activities, the Lloyd's Register Group helps ship operators understand risks and reduce business losses through a number of services such as:

(a) Shore-based technical emergency support, available 24 hours a day, for ships in the event of a casualty.
(b) Fuels and lubricant analysis and advice to help manage the risks of using below-specification products.

(c) Technical investigation services which can quickly find the causes of problems and minimize losses due to unscheduled maintenance.

(d) A comprehensive environmental protection analysis package.

The Lloyd's Register Group's information service provides answers to shipping enquiries and a historical research service. Also, Lloyd's Register–Fairplay (a joint venture between Lloyd's Register and Fairplay Publications) is the world's largest independent supplier of maritime data.

The Lloyd's Register Group provides independent risk management solutions that add value in various industry and service sectors: oil and gas; road and rail; utilities; general engineering and manufacturing; and insurance and project finance.

A wide range of independent verification, certification and advisory services is available to meet client needs at any stage of a project, process or asset life cycle – from feasibility to decommissioning – including:

(a) independent monitoring, evaluation and verification of major capital projects;

(b) verification of asset management systems;

(c) systems and safety engineering, including quantitative and qualitative risk assessment, and preparation and assessment of safety cases;

(d) design appraisal, inspection and certification of pressure vessels and other industrial equipment to recognized codes, standards and regulations including ASME and PED;

(e) RAMS (reliability, availability, maintainability and safety) assessments;

(f) asset integrity services including risk-based inspection, corrosion, engineering, etc.;

(g) global vendor inspection and expediting services;

(h) training and workshops in relation to quality, safety and environmental risk management, asset management and special training programmes on all the services listed above.

The management systems business is provided under the brand Lloyd's Register Quality Assurance (LRQA). LRQA's services have grown over recent decades to make it one of the world's largest international certification bodies. The aim is to provide certification of compliance with international management system standards, thereby helping clients use management systems to reduce risks and improve their business.

The certification market is global and LRQA certificates have been issued in almost every country. Offering a consistent service worldwide enables clients to benefit from Lloyd's Register's local knowledge and language capability. LRQA services span a complete range of businesses, from manufacturing, including food, and all transport sectors, to most of the service sectors, including telecommunications, design services, IT, finance and distribution. Assessment criteria cover certification to national, international and industry sector management systems standards in quality, environment and occupational safety management.

Some members of the Lloyd's Register Group, including LRQA, are 'notified bodies' providing services to support EC product directives that ensure consistency of essential product safety requirements across the European Union. This growing activity already encompasses pressure equipment, lifts, railway interoperability and medical devices, bringing together the management systems assessment capability and design appraisal available within the Lloyd's Register Group.

The following section examines two examples or case studies of Lloyd's Register of Shipping relative to LNG tonnage.

The birth of the large LNG carrier

LNG carriers are now sometimes larger than 200,000 m³. There are several primary technical factors involved in making this capacity feasible. Qatargas's 209,000 m³ and 216,000 m³ LNG carriers from three Korean yards are gas ships that represent a major increase in size. The increasing demand for LNG, especially in the United States and Europe, and the need to reduce long haul transport costs from the Middle East to the United States, is driving this increase in ship size, although it is uncertain whether this trend to ever larger ships for general trades is sustainable, because LNG carriers are restricted by existing port facilities to an upper limit of around 155,000 m³. The bigger sizes are therefore limited to specific projects involving either the construction of new terminals specially designed to handle these carriers or construction of cargo tanks for LNG offshore floating units.

Tank size and configuration

There are several technical factors to be considered during the design, construction and operation of large LNG carriers, primarily determining tank size and configuration and propulsion.

Tank size becomes important when the beam for larger ships increases. Calculation of overall tank length has to take into account pressure loads from fluid motion in a laden tank.

There are two options for a larger ship – five tanks of conventional size, or four larger tanks. The five-tank configuration is inherently less 'risky', as knowledge of the ability of a containment membrane to withstand sloshing loads is based on tanks of conventional size. Furthermore, model testing demonstrates that the highest fluid pressures are associated with diagonal tank motion: lengthening the tank and the diagonal could result in more pressure on the tank membrane.

However, for a number of years shipyards have been investigating tank configuration in anticipation of ordering large LNG carriers. Daewoo

Shipbuilding & Marine Engineering (DSME), for instance, has carried out a number of studies to validate bigger tanks, including:

(a) LNG tank sloshing studies at MARINTEK in Norway as part of a joint development project with Lloyd's Register.
(b) Cargo containment system capability testing by dry-drop tests carried out at the Korea Institute of Metals and Machinery.
(c) Dynamic hydro-elasticity properties of cargo containment systems by both numerical analysis and experiments at the University of Illinois in the United States.

New propulsion options

For the larger ship sizes, propulsion is a major issue. The large size of some vessels has led to development of a twin-skeg, twin-screw arrangement as a means of maintaining normal trading speeds. Further, the draught limitation imposed on the new generation of LNG tankers makes it difficult to design an efficient propeller or hull form for a single-screw vessel.

This in turn has prompted the industry to turn away from the traditional steam turbine propulsion utilized by the vast majority of the world's LNG fleet. The overall complexity and cost of a twin-screw steam turbine arrangement would involve a multi-input gearbox and very large steam-raising plants, making twin-screw steam turbine propulsion cumbersome and expensive. The industry has therefore turned to a number of new propulsion options: (a) dual-fuel diesel electric; (b) twin slow-speed diesel with relique-faction; (c) gas turbine. The Qatargas ships, for instance, use slow-speed diesel propulsion with reliquefaction.

These advances in propulsion have implications for conventional-size ships as well, as all the new options provide the main advantages of a shorter engine room and therefore more cargo carrying capacity. The 155,000 m^3 LNG carriers ordered by BP Shipping, for instance, achieved this capacity increase by opting for dual-fuel diesel electric propulsion.

As with any new technology, the risks need to be assessed. Lloyd's Register, in its work with DSME during the process of the yard's development of a workable large LNG carrier design, carried out a number of assessments using a typical 'safety case' methodology. This method involves two key elements: a hazard identification study (HAZID), which identifies critical issues and looks at engine room arrangements and layout; and a hazard operability study (HAZOP), which looks at detailed piping and instrumentation diagrams from a safety and operability point of view.

Lloyd's Register Asia's Busan office facilitated a number of safety cases for DSME, with input from other Lloyd's Register Group offices around the world. 'Both types of studies were carried out using a prescribed format of capturing data in a workshop environment with the designers, engine manu-facturers, component suppliers, classification and the intended operator,' says

Thanos Koliopulos, Special Projects Manager for Lloyd's Register's Oil and Gas Division. 'The key benefits of this approach are that it gives the necessary confidence to all parties involved and deals with all the technical issues on the table.'

One of the first HAZIDs Lloyd's Register Asia carried out for DSME assessed the safety, operability and maintainability of dual-fuel propulsion. A key output of this first HAZID was the adoption of double-wall gas supply pipework instead of the conventional single-wall arrangement. This finding made dual-fuel a more viable arrangement from the safety and operability point of view and enormously improved engine room layout.

Innovations in LNG propulsion

Dual-fuel engines are beginning to make inroads in the LNG sector. The following paragraphs mention some advantages of this system over the traditional steam turbine and also some safety concerns.

Market developments and the introduction of large LNG carriers mean that propulsion is being reassessed. Traditionally, LNG carriers have utilized steam boilers and geared steam turbine plants, but now reciprocating engines are emerging as a viable alternative for the next generation of LNG carriers, for both the new +200,000 m^3 ships and for conventional-size vessels.

Conventional LNG carrier propulsion plant involves the use of boil-off gas in steam boilers to drive the turbines. The advantages of the steam turbine include its simple energy conversion, high reliability and relatively low maintenance cost. Initial capital investment, however, is high and steam turbines have a relatively low efficiency. As a result, in most marine applications they have been replaced by other means of propulsion, although not in the LNG sector, because until recently there have been no other suitable prime movers capable of using boil-off gases.

Dual-fuel engines

One of these new options is the dual-fuel engine, which is capable of burning both conventional or heavy fuel or oil gas fuel with oil fuel pilot injection. It is capable of operating on either of the two modes when required.

During the gas operation mode, gas is introduced into the engine cylinder either during the air suction cycle at low pressure or injected directly into the cylinder at high pressure during the compression cycle. The gas injection subsystem is normally located directly on the engine and its basic function is to provide timely and accurate delivery of the gas fuel into the cylinder. In the low-pressure system, gas is delivered through an electronically actuated control valve to the engine air inlet ducting. In the high-pressure system, gas is injected directly into the combustion chamber, usually through an electro-hydraulically controlled injection valve.

Dual-fuel has become attractive and viable due to the concurrent development of electronically controlled combustion. The dual-fuel options currently being adopted utilize electric power generation to drive electric propulsion systems, such as conventional propellers driven by electric motors.

Diesel electric propulsion systems are considered attractive because they command higher power density than steam turbines and as a result provide more flexibility in terms of machinery arrangements, allowing designers to obtain more overall cargo capacity. The high efficiency of dual-fuel, combined with its low fuel consumption, reduces owners' and operators' operating costs and increases their earnings.

Dual-fuel engines incorporating electronically controlled combustion give low Nox and CO_2 emissions, claimed to be equal or lower than steam turbine plant, potentially making them a more environmentally friendly choice. An ability of dual-fuel engines to operate on gas or on liquid fuel provides increased operational flexibility and supports the varying demands of ship's operating schedule.

System safety

The transition of dual-fuel engines into the maritime environment presents a number of design challenges primarily related to aspects of the safe handling of gas in ship spaces. The primary function of these systems is to deliver gas at the required operating pressure prior to its injection into the cylinder.

The low-pressure gas delivery system consists of filters and control valves. The design of the valve arrangement must ensure that the gas supply can be shut off by predefined abnormalities detected by the engine safety monitoring system and that they can also be shut off manually by the ship's staff.

The high-pressure gas delivery system is similar, but also contains a compression module consisting of a compressor, pressure vessels and heat exchangers. Gas is compressed to the required pressure and delivered to the common rail system through gas accumulators, thus reducing the risk of pressure cyclic loading on the gas pipes and its connections.

Any leaks from the gas injection system and its associated piping need to be detected and dealt with in a safe manner. 'Machinery spaces must be monitored by a suitable number of gas detectors and have mechanical ventilation installed to prevent the formation of gas pockets. In practice, constructing a ventilated hood above the engine often fulfils this requirement.'

The safety requirements governing the construction and operation of gas-fuelled propulsion plants are detailed in the International Code for the Construction and Equipment of Ships Carrying Liquefied Gases in Bulk (IGC Code) and the Rules of classification societies.

Lloyd's Register's involvement

Since 2000 Lloyd's Register has provided certification for a number of dual-fuel engine designs intended for offshore and land-based power generation applications. Design approvals in principle for marine applications have been given for both low and high gas pressure dual-fuel systems. Although duel-fuel is now increasing in the LNG sector, already the industry is looking at future propulsion options. In the medium term, gas turbines may become a viable propulsion option for LNG carriers. Gas ships may benefit from the additional power generation capacity provided by gas turbines operating alongside diesel generators in 'combination of diesel and gas' or 'combination of diesel or gas' configurations. However, as gas turbine efficiency is relatively low at partial loads, its use would most likely be limited to peak power demands.

The operation of gas turbines utilizing boil-off gases is well understood and has been successfully used for many years for power generation both in offshore as well as land-based applications.

Services for shipowners

Strategic planning

* *Risk management studies.* Services helping shipowners to assess and manage risk; including: due diligence; port risk assessment; company risk management strategy; major disaster planning; reliability, availability and maintainability (RAM) studies; security assessment; and dependable system review.
* *Technical investigations.* Identifying and evaluating technical risks, and providing solutions to help shipowners manage the impact on their business.
* *Integrated management systems.* Helping shipowners to develop an integrated management system incorporating the international safety management (ISM) code, ISO 9001 and ISO 14001.
* *Ship life extension studies.* Evaluating the feasibility of ship life extension and associated risks.
* *Design and regulatory advice.* Advice on design and statutory trends, including: current design trends; impact of regulatory requirements; and forthcoming regulations.

Ship design

* *Design appraisal services.* Providing a design appraisal service using skilled and experienced personnel, including: assessing ship design (hull and machinery) concordance with Lloyd's Register's benchmark Rules and statutory codes; providing design advice; identifying critical areas; improving detail design; problem solving, assisted by Lloyd's Register of Shipping tailored software solutions, including: RulesCalc – an integrated Rule calculation package; ShipRight procedures and software – for advanced structural and fatigue analysis; and Rulefinder – consolidated Rule and statutory requirements.

- *Risk management studies.* Services helping shipowners to assess and manage risk, including: risk management – design evaluation; hazard identification; risk assessment (design, operations, management); reliability, availability and maintainability (RAM) studies; identification of risk reduction measures; and fire and evacuation analysis.
- *Technical investigations.* Identifying and evaluating technical risks including: noise prediction and analysis; passenger and crew accommodation comfort; design assessment, ship hydrodynamics, machinery dynamics, computational fluid dynamics; finite element and stress analysis; concept design and vibration studies.
- *Environmental services.* Helping shipowners to manage environmental risks with: environmental protection notation; and environmental risk assessment.

Shipbuilding

- *Construction survey.* Managing the technical risks associated with new ships' construction. Lloyd's Register of Shipping's unique knowledge and experience of design and construction helps ensure that their specialist surveyors offer practical solutions during construction through: on-site survey; construction monitoring, and focusing on critical areas identified at the design stage.
- *Materials and equipment procurement.* Services helping shipowners to ensure the quality of materials and equipment, including: works approval; quality assurance scheme; and type approval.
- *Technical investigations.* Identifying and evaluation of technical risks, including: commissioning and sea trials; noise prediction and analysis; passenger and crew accommodation comfort; dynamic testing (structure and machinery); materials investigation and laboratory services; specialist consultancy and problem solving.
- *Shipowners' project management and superintendent.* Providing project management and superintendent services around the globe.

Operations

- *Periodical survey.* Maintaining shipowners' vessel to Lloyd's Register class – helping shipowners to manage their assets to the maximum, maintain operational effectiveness and minimize risk to life, property and the environment.
- *Class Direct Live.* The web-based information service providing shipowners with on-line access to the latest classification details for their ships and a wide range of invaluable supporting information.
- *Maintenance management.* Aligns the classification process with shipowners' existing maintenance and inspection regime – reducing costs and risk using: hull condition monitoring; machinery condition monitoring;

screwshaft condition monitoring; turbine condition monitoring; planned maintenance; lubricant quality scan and machinery reliability software (Wave(r)).

- *Risk management studies*. Services helping shipowners to assess and manage risk, including: risk identification; risk assessment (design, operations, management); maintenance strategy optimization; reliability, availability and maintainability (RAM) studies; evaluation of risk mitigation measures, fire and evacuation analysis, and safety case.
- *Technical investigations*. Identifying and evaluating technical risks, including: failure investigation and fault diagnosis; hydrodynamic performance and seakeeping analysis and problem solving; noise and vibration analysis; passenger and crew accommodation comfort; structural and machinery condition monitoring; dynamic testing; materials investigation and laboratory services and specialist consultancy.
- *ISM and ISPS Code certification*. Helping shipowners to develop their safety and security management systems to comply with the ISM and ISPS Codes.
- *Integrated management systems*. Helping shipowners save time through an integrated management system audit incorporating the ISM and ISPS Codes, ISO 9001 and ISO 14001.
- *Ship emergency response service*. Helping shipowners to manage the impact of unexpected events such as collisions and grounding.
- *Environmental services*. Services helping shipowners to manage environmental risk, including: environmental protection notation; ballast water management; and environmental risk assessment.
- *Fluids analysis*. Services helping shipowners to reduce risk associated with onboard fluids, including: fuel oil bunker analysis; bunker quantity survey; and lubricant quality scan.
- *Ship life extension studies*. Evaluating the feasibility of ship life extension and associated risks.
- *Owner's superintendent*. Providing superintendent services globally.
- *Condition assessment programme* (CAP). Providing an independent evaluation of ship condition.
- *Sale and purchase*. Services to help shipowners manage the risk associated with sale and purchase, including: condition survey; owner's superintendent and records review.
- *Marine training*. Helping shipowners companies evolve through training and their staff to develop their skills.

8.14 Malta Maritime Authority

The Malta Maritime Authority was established by law in 1991 as a government agency and so vested with detailed regulatory powers. Its role is to enable ports, merchant shipping and yachting centres to operate with centralized supervision.

The objectives of the Authority is to market Malta as a world maritime centre; to facilitate foreign trade; to render the administration, services and operations of ports and yachting centres more efficient and cost effective; to provide a sound financial basis for the Authority and achieve target return on investment; to standardize practices in line with the EU; to attract cruise liner traffic; to market the Malta flag abroad; and to further complement maritime business activity.

A key area of the MMA is registration of ships under the Maltese flag. Vessel registration under the Malta flag and the operation of Maltese ships are regulated by the Merchant Shipping Act of 1973, a law based mainly on UK legislation, but subsequently revised and amended in 1986, 1988, 1990 and 2000. The main legislation is supplemented by a comprehensive set of rules and regulations.

All types of vessels, from pleasure yachts to oil rigs, including vessels under construction, may be registered, provided that they are wholly owned by legally constituted corporate bodies or entities, irrespective of nationality or by EU citizens. Generally, trading vessels of over 25 years are not registered. There are low company formation, ship registration and tonnage tax costs, progressive reductions in registration and tonnage tax cost for younger ships. There are no restrictions on the nationality of the Master, crew and officers, the sale or transfer of shares of a company owning Maltese ships, the sale and mortgaging of Maltese ships and trading restrictions. Preferential treatment is granted to Maltese ships in certain ports.

The following documents are to be submitted during provisional registration: previous ownership featuring bill of sale or any other document by which the vessel was transferred to the applicant registry including builder's certificate; any cancellation of registry certificate issued by the administration where the vessel was last documented; for SOLAS vessels the last updated Continuous Synopsis Record issued by the administration where the ship was last documented; certificate of survey and copy of the International Tonnage Certificate; evidence that the vessel has been marked in accordance with law; and where valid appropriate convention certificates are not in place, the ship will be issued with a non-operational certificate of registry. A certificate of Malta registry is subject to renewal on the anniversary of the Maltese registration.

Malta has adopted all the major international maritime conventions. Survey, tonnage and convention certificates may be issued on behalf of the Malta government by the following organizations: American Bureau of Shipping; Bureau Veritas; China Classification Society; Class NK; Det Norske Veritas; Germanischer Lloyd; Hellenic Register of Shipping; Korean Register of Shipping; Lloyd's Register of Shipping; Registro Italiano Navale; and Russian Maritime Register of Shipping.

In 2004 the number of vessels registered under the Maltese flag was 3,660, involving a gross tonnage of 24 million. It puts Malta as the second largest register in Europe and one of the largest in the world.

8.15 International Maritime Pilots' Association

The International Maritime Pilots' Association was formed in 1970 and is based in London and has nongovernmental organization status at the IMO. Its membership is of over 7,600 Marine Pilots serving worldwide and who have national membership of pilots' associations in their own country. IMPA's object is to promote safe and sound pilotage worldwide. Marine Pilots are professionals employed around the world to navigate and manoeuvre vessels in ports and congested waterways. Their role requires considerable expertise in knowledge of ships, navigation and the control of vessels in all weathers and in confined waters and locations within their area of official competence. IMPA in its council meetings and bi-annual congresses brings together pilots from across the world.

8.16 Nautical Institute

The Nautical Institute, founded in 1972, aims to promote and enhance nautical studies worldwide by promoting high standards of qualification, competence and knowledge among those on, or concerned with, the sea. It has 6,500 members in over 110 countries. The Nautical Institute provides a wide range of services to enhance the professional standing and knowledge of members, who are drawn from all sectors of the maritime world. *Seaways* is the International Journal of the Nautical Institute.

8.17 Norwegian International Ship Register

The Norwegian International Ship Register (NIS) was established in 1987. Its purpose is twofold: to offer a flexible and commercially attractive alternative to open registers while retaining the essential features of quality registers, i.e. effective procedures for ensuring full compliance with all international conventions and treaties which Norway is party to.

In several areas the administrative procedures were simplified compared with those governing the ordinary Norwegian Register (NOR), but the provisions relating to mortgages, guarantees and other securities are subject to the same control and enforcement by Norwegian authorities.

NIS and NOR are different in two major areas: (a) NIS enables direct registration by foreign shipowning companies, and (b) the NIS legislation allows employment of foreign seafarers on local/national wages (above the ILO levels) established through collective wage agreements between an employers' federation, i.e. Norwegian Shipowners' Association, and an independent union which organizes the seafarers in question.

Formal registration of ships is recorded in a register, located in an independent office and filled in under Ministry of Trade and Industry rules. The office was the first centralized registration of ships in Norway and does today also perform NOR registrations. The regulations containing the conditions for registration of ships are formulated and administered by the Ministry of Trade and Industry. The Maritime Directorate is the enforcement agency for all matters relating to the seaworthiness of the ships (NOR and NIS) and to the safety and qualifications of seafarers. The Norwegian Shipowners' Association may also be consulted on NIS matters.

The International Transport Workers' Federation (ITF) has not added NIS to its list of registers what it considers 'flags of convenience'. Norwegian owned and controlled NIS-registered vessels are considered wholly national, and NIS vessels beneficially controlled by non-Norwegian owners may be classified as FOC, unless covered by an ITF-approved collective agreement. The Norwegian seamen's unions, which are entitled to participate in all wage negotiations for NIS vessels, are affiliated to the ITF.

8.18 Norwegian Shipowners' Association

Norwegian shipowners have been world leaders in the maritime business for more than a century. The country has the fifth largest commercial trade fleet in the world. Overall, there are 200 Norwegian shipping companies with over 1,600 ships in foreign trade.

The Norwegian Shipowners' Association is a special interest organization serving Norwegian shipping businesses and the offshore contracting sector. The Association's mission is to protect, serve and promote the interests of member companies and owners within the Norwegian shipping and offshore industry in relation to matters where collective representation is more likely to succeed than companies acting individually or through intermediaries. The Shipowners' Association conducts its activities in close liaison with the industry. The management is through member-elected boards and councils. An important part of the NSA activities is handled by groups and committees with board member company representation. An annual report is published.

8.19 Oil Companies' International Marine Forum (OCIMF)

The OCIMF, based in London, was formed initially as the oil industry's response to increasing public awareness of marine pollution, particularly oil after the *Torrey Canyon* incident. Governments had reacted to this incident by debating the development of international conventions and national legislation, and the oil industry sought to play its part by making its professional expertise available and its views known to government and inter-governmental bodies. OCIMF was granted consultative status in 1971 at the IMO and is organized to co-ordinate oil industry views at the IMO meetings, to review technical proposals circulated by the IMO and to advise its membership on international and regional legislative activities as they develop. OCIMF also has consultative status with the UN Economic and Social Council, the International Oil Pollution Compensation Fund (IOPC Fund) and the ISO.

As well as participating actively in the work of the IMO and the IOPC Fund, OCIMF presents its members' views before regional and individual national governmental authorities and maintains a close liaison with other industry bodies and associations. An important contribution to the overall safety of the industry is the role that OCIMF plays in producing technical and operational guidelines, either by itself or in co-operation with other industry associations or with its development and management of the Ship Inspection and Reporting (SIRE) database.

Overall, the OCIMF has six objectives:

(a) *Standards*. To identify safety and environmental issues facing the oil tanker and terminal industries and develop and publish recommended standards that will serve as technical benchmarks.

(b) *Regulatory*. To contribute to the development of the international conventions and regulations that enhance the safe construction and operation of oil tankers and terminals, working with the IMO and other regulatory bodies, both regional and national.

(c) *Enforcement*. To encourage flag states, port states and classification societies in their enforcement of international conventions and regulations.

(d) *Promulgation*. To facilitate access by charterers and authorities to data on tankers relating to safety and pollution prevention, through SIRE.

(e) *Consultation*. To promote notification and implementation of international compensation conventions.

(f) *Promotion*. To actively promote OCIMF's role in the development of safety and environmental guidelines and recommendations, harnessing the skills and experience of OCIMF members and holding industry events addressing the issues.

The OCIMF conducts its business through four committees: Executive; Legal; General Purpose; and Ports and Terminals, together with a number of sub-committees.

A key area of OCIMF activity is the SIRE programme introduced in 1993. Its five aims are: (a) make available to OCIMF members and others who share OCIMF's concern for safety, details relating to the condition and operational standards of tankers; (b) increase the number of vessels that could be considered for charter; (c) utilize ship inspectors more efficiently; (d) increase the number of vessels inspected; and (e) reduce the number of repeat inspections on the same vessels and thereby reduce the burden on vessels' personnel. An enhancement of the SIRE programme emerged in 2004 with inspection of barges, tugs and vessels carrying road tankers and packaged cargoes.

8.20 Organization for Economic Co-operation and Development (OECD)

The OECD emerged from the Organization for European Economic Co-operation which was set up in 1947 with support from the United States and Canada to co-ordinate the Marshall Plan for the reconstruction of Europe after the Second World War. Created as an economic counterpart to NATO, the OECD took over from the OEEC in 1961 and is based in Paris. Today the OECD is a forum where the governments of 34 market democracies work together to address the economic, social, environmental and governance challenges of the globalizing world economy, as well as to exploit its opportunities.

The organization provides a setting where governments compare policy experiences, seek answers to common problems, identify good practice and work to co-ordinate domestic and international policies. It is a forum where peer pressure can act as a powerful incentive to improve policies and implement 'soft law' – non-binding instruments such as its Guidelines for Multinational Enterprises – and can on accession lead to formal agreements or treaties.

Exchanges between OECD governments use information and analysis provided by a secretariat in Paris. The secretariat collects data, monitors trends and analyses and forecasts economic developments. It also researches social changes or evolving patterns in trade, environment, agriculture, technology/taxation and more.

The OECD helps governments to foster prosperity and fight poverty through economic growth, financial stability, trade and investment, technology, innovation, entrepreneurship and development co-operation. It is helping to ensure that economic and social development are not achieved at the expense of rampant environmental degradation. Other aims include job creation, social equity and clean and effective governance.

The OECD is at the forefront of efforts to understand and helps governments respond to new developments and concerns such as corporate governance, the abuse of the international financial system by terrorists and other criminals, managing new technologies and the challenges related to an ageing population. The OECD is long established as the world's largest and most reliable source of comparable statistical, economic and social data. OECD databases span areas as diverse as national accounts, economic indicators, the labour force, trade, employment, migration, education, energy, health, industry, taxation, tourism and the environment. Much of the research and analysis is published.

Since the 1990s, the OECD has tackled a range of economic, social and environmental issues, while broadening and deepening its engagement with business, trade unions and other representatives of civil society. Negotiations at the OECD on taxation and transfer pricing have resulted in bilateral tax treaties around the world.

OECD membership is limited only by a country's commitment to a market economy and a pluralistic democracy. It is rich in that its 34 members produce

60% of the world's goods and services, but it is by no means exclusive. Non-members are invited to subscribe to OECD agreements and treaties, and the OECD shares expertise and exchanges views on topics of mutual concern with more than 100 countries worldwide from Brazil, China and Russia to least developed countries in Africa.

The OECD has some 200 committees, working groups and expert groups embracing a whole range of policy areas and topics. One of these is the Maritime Transport Committee, which discusses a whole range of current issues/problems. More recently this includes marine insurance, safety, the environment, container transport security, terrorism, ownership and control of ships.

8.21 Organization of Petroleum Exporting Countries (OPEC)

The Organization of Petroleum Exporting Countries was initiated in 1949 when Venezuela approached Iran, Iraq, Kuwait and Saudi Arabia to suggest an exchange of views and encouragement of regular and closer communication between them. The need for closer co-operation in 1959 unilaterally reduced the posted price of Venezuelan crude by 5¢ and 25¢ per barrel and that for the Middle East by 18¢ per barrel. Subsequently, the first Arab Petroleum Congress in Cairo adopted a resolution calling on oil companies to consult with the governments of the producing countries before unilaterally taking any decision on oil prices and set up the general agreement on the establishment of an 'Oil Consultation Commission'. In the following year, oil companies further reduced Middle East posted prices. This resulted in a conference in Baghdad involving all five governments and the establishment of OPEC as a permanent intergovernmental organization. In 1965 it was decided to locate the OPEC headquarters in Vienna.

The supreme authority of OPEC consists of heads of delegation – normally the Ministers of Oil, Mines and Energy – of member countries. The conference meets twice per year and operates on the principle of unanimity. The board of governors – with one governor nominated by each country – directs the management of the organization, implements resolutions of the conference, draws up the annual budget and submits to the conference for approval. The secretariat structure under a Secretary General embraces divisions on research, energy, petroleum market analysis, data services, administration/human resources, economics and public relations and information.

In 2013 OPEC has 13 member countries, embracing the five founder member countries of 1960, plus the full members of Qatar, Indonesia, Libya, United Arab Emirates, Algeria and Nigeria. OPEC operates in strict observance of the UN principles and purposes and works closely with IMF and UNCTAD. OPEC world oil production in 2006 was approximately 30 mb/d, rising to nearly 60 mb/d by 2025 thereby obtaining parity with non-OPEC producers. In contrast the natural gas production by OPEC members rose from 336,365 million standard m^3 in 1997 to 431,809 million m^3 in 2003. Growth continues in crude oil, gas, and refined product pipelines, with lengths up to 1,349 miles and the diameter ranging from 8 in. to 36 in. The continuing growth in pipelines in both OPEC and non OPEC producing countries is having a distinct impact on maritime distribution.

The primary objective of OPEC is to work with other market participants to maintain stability and ensure a timely response to global oil supply needs. OPEC continues to strengthen dialogue and co-operation between OPEC and non OPEC producers by hosting and participating in numerous workshops and seminars held in and outside the secretariat, in particular to those which foster and enhance mutual understanding and dialogue amongst energy-producing and energy consuming nations.

The next decades may see increases in energy demand met predominantly by fossil fuels, with oil sustaining its major role. There is a clear expectation that the oil resource base is sufficiently abundant to satisfy this demand growth. Moreover, although non OPEC production is seen as continuing its recent expansion over the medium term, it is generally agreed that OPEC will increasingly be relied upon to supply the incremental barrel. Global oil demand rose from 12 million barrels per day near to 89 mb/d from 2002 to 2010, an average annual growth rate of 1.5 mb/d or 1.8% per annum over that period. The demand may grow by another 9 mb/d to 115 mb/d by 2025. Almost three-quarters of the increase in demand over the period 2002–25 comes from developing countries. Gas demand in contrast is expected to rise from 2,101 mtoe in 2000 to 4,453 in 2025 – an annual growth of 2.9%–3.2%. Solid fuels demand will rise more slowly, from 2,101 mtoe to 4,452 in 2025 – an annual growth rate of 1.1 to 0.8%. Maritime fleet growth/investment should be considered when looking at this forecast analysis.

The uncertainties over future economic growth focus on government policies, and the rate of development and diffusion of newer technologies. Government policies raise the question of the future scale of investment required. Such uncertainties, coupled with long lead times, inevitably complicate the task of maintaining market stability. Moreover, medium-term prospects suggest a need to ensure that spare capacity is consistent with such stability.

8.22 Passenger Shipping Association (PSA)

The Passenger Shipping Association was founded in 1976. It was called the Ocean Travel Development in 1958, until its transmission to the PSA. In 1987 the PSA formed a subsidiary company, the Passenger Shipping Association Retail Agents (PSARA) to focus on education and training for travel agents. Overall, the prime objective of the PSA is to promote travel by sea. The PSA membership is divided into two sections: cruise and ferry. Overall, it is a UK focused organization. In recent years there has been an enormous growth in the cruise business and the ferry market has undergone radical change. This is because of the Channel Tunnel, the development of low cost airlines, the abolition of intra-EU duty free goods and expansion of fast ferry tonnage offering greater added value to markets.

8.23 World Trade Organization (WTO)

The WTO's creation on 1 January 1995 marked the biggest reform of international trade since the end of the Second World War. It also brought to reality – in an updated form – the failed attempt in 1948 to create an International Trade Organization.

Much of the history of those 47 years was written in Geneva, but it also has spanned continents from that hesitant start in 1948 in 'trade rounds' in Havana (Cuba), followed by Annecy (France), Torquay (UK), Tokyo (Japan), Punta del Este (Uruguay), Montreal (Canada), Brussels (Belgium), and then to Marrakech (Morocco) in 1994. During that period the trading system came under GATT, salvaged from the abortive attempt to create the ITO. GATT helped to establish a strong and prosperous multilateral trading system that became more and more liberal through rounds of trade negotiations. But, by the 1980s the system needed a thorough overhaul. This led to the Uruguay round and ultimately WTO.

From 1948 to 1994 the General Agreement on Tariffs and Trade (GATT) provided the rules for much of world trade and presided over periods that saw some of the highest growth rates in international commerce. It seemed well established, but throughout those years, it was a provisional agreement and organization.

The original intention was to create a third institution to handle trade arising from international economic co-operation, joining the two 'Bretton Woods' institutions, the World Bank and the International Monetary Fund. Over 50 countries participated in negotiations to create an International Trade Organization as a specialized Agency of the United Nations. The draft ITO charter is ambitious. It extends beyond world trade disciplines to include rules on employment, commodity agreements, restrictive business practices, international investment and services.

In the early years, the GATT trade rounds concentrated on further reducing tariffs. The Kennedy round in the mid–1960s brought about a GATT Anti-dumping Agreement and a section on development. The Tokyo round during the 1970s was the first major attempt to tackle trade barriers that do not take the form of tariffs, and to improve the system. The eighth, the Uruguay round of 1986–94, was the last and most extensive of all. It led to the WTO and a new set of agreements. Details of the GATT trade rounds are given in Table 8.1.

The trade rounds are often lengthy – the Uruguay round took seven and a half years – but can have advantages. Moreover, the size of the package can mean more benefits, because participants can seek and secure advantages across many issues.

Table 8.1 The GATT trade rounds

Year	Place/Name	Subjects covered	Countries
1947	Geneva	Tariffs	23
1949	Annecy	Tariffs	13
1951	Torquay	Tariffs	38
1956	Geneva	Tariffs	26
1960–1961	Geneva (Dillon round)	Tariffs	26
1964–1967	Geneva (Kennedy round)	Tariffs and anti-dumping measures	62
1973–1979	Geneva (Tokyo round)	Tariffs, non-tariff measures, 'framework' agreements	102
1986–1994	Geneva (Uruguay round)	Tariffs, non-tariff measures, rules, services, intellectual property, dispute settlement, textiles, agriculture, creation of WTO, etc.	123

Agreements can be easier to reach through 'trade-offs' – somewhere in the package there should be something for everyone. This has political as well as economic implications. A government may want to make a concession, perhaps in one sector, because of the economic benefits. But, politically, it could find the concession difficult to defend. A package may contain politically and economically attractive benefits for other sectors that could be used as compensation.

Developing countries and other less powerful participants have a greater chance of influencing the multilateral system in a trade round than in bilateral relationships with major trade nations. Overall, the size of the trade round can be both a strength and weakness.

The formation of the WTO is 'member-driven', with decisions taken by consensus among all members. Today, membership consists of 159 countries and recent members include China in 2001 and UAE in 2005.

All major decisions are made by the membership as a whole, either by ministers (who meet at least once every two years) or by their ambassadors or delegates (who meet regularly in Geneva). Decisions are normally taken by consensus. In this respect, the WTO is different from other international organizations such as the World Bank and International Monetary Fund. In the WTO, power is not delegated to a board of directors, or the organization's head.

The WTO is rules based; its rules are negotiated agreements. The WTO agreements cover goods, services and intellectual property. They outline the principles of liberalization and the permitted exceptions. They include individual countries commitments to lower customs tariffs and other trade barriers, and to open and keep open services markets. They set procedures for settling disputes and prescribe special treatment for developing countries. Moreover the WTO requires governments to make their trade policies transparent by notifying the WTO about laws in force and measures adopted and through regular reports by the secretariat on countries' trade policies.

At the fourth Ministerial Conference in Doha, Qatar, in November 2001, WTO member governments agreed to launch new negotiations. They also agreed to work on other issues, in particular the implementation of the present agreements. The entire package is called the Doha Development Agenda. There are 19–21 subjects listed in the Doha Declaration, depending on whether you count the 'rules' subjects as one or three. Most of them involve negotiations: other work includes under 'implementation' analysis and monitoring. The fifth Ministerial Conference was conducted in Cancun and focused on taking stock of progress in the negotiations, providing any necessary political guidance and taking decisions as necessary. However, the outcome was more work in some key areas would enable them to conclude negotiations and fulfil commitments taken at Doha. Subsequent negotiations focused on agriculture, cotton, non-agricultural market access and the Singapore issues. Later the Trade Negotiations Committee (TNC) was reactivated to carry out the Doha mandate to supervise the progress and overall conduct of the negotiations.

It will be appreciated the WTO has an immense task to realize consensus on a whole range of trade issues involving some 150 countries, each involving differing interests, culture and economic structures.

The WTO annual report features leading exporters and importers in world merchandise trade and leading exporters and importers in world trade in commercial services.

8.24 Baltic Exchange

The Baltic Exchange is the only international shipping exchange in the world and is a major earner of foreign currency for Britain. Its origins can be traced to the seventeenth century, when shipowners and merchants met in London coffee houses. Foremost among these were the Jerusalem Coffee House and the Virginia and Maryland Coffee House (known from 1744 as the Virginia and Baltic, as the cargoes dealt with came from the American colonies or from the countries on the Baltic seaboard). The proprietors provided newspapers and commercial information for their customers as well as refreshments, and cargoes were auctioned there.

In 1810 larger premises were acquired at the Antwerp Tavern in Threadneedle Street and were renamed the Baltic. Membership of the 'Baltic Club' was limited to 300, and in 1823 a committee was set up to control its affairs. From that moment onwards the importance and membership of the Baltic increased.

In 1900 the Baltic amalgamated with the London Shipping Exchange and became the Baltic Mercantile and Shipping Exchange. Shortly afterwards, in April 1903, a site was purchased in St Mary Axe. After the Second World War an adjoining site was acquired. In 1994 the Baltic Exchange celebrated 250 years (1744–1994) of serving world shipping and relocated to 38 St Mary

Axe, London. The Baltic Exchange has increased its activities, especially in the hybrid areas, to keep pace with expansion of the market for global shipping centred on London. Today it is the world's largest shipbroking market place, with a freight value annually in excess of £1 billion.

The matching of ships and cargoes remains the core of the exchange's business today. Digital services provide on-line access to impartial freight market data in real time and are based on a digital trading floor which supplies data on thousands of ships and ports.

The Baltic Exchange is at the heart of the global shipping industry and plays a vital role in the transport of world trade. Each year over 6 billion tonnes of commodities are transported by sea. Basic foodstuffs (grain, sugar and rice), fuel (oil, coal and coke), materials (steel, iron ore and cement) and luxury goods are exported around the globe in bulk carriers, tankers and container vessels.

Shipowners and charterers rely upon the professional services of shipbrokers to identify opportunities for their ships and cargoes, provide market advice and to negotiate favourable deals. Each year, more than 30% of the world's dry cargo fixtures are negotiated by Baltic Exchange brokers, together with 50% of the tanker fixtures and 50% of the vessels that are bought and sold. The Baltic Exchange provides an independent market place for shipbrokers worldwide – producing the daily freight market information that brokers rely upon and demanding that members work to an ethical code expressed in the well-known maxim, 'My word is my bond'.

The Baltic Exchange is a self-regulated market. Membership is open to shipbrokers, shipowners and charterers worldwide, as well as an increasing number of related maritime service and commodity companies. Members are able to call upon the Baltic's experience and expertise in resolving commercial disputes. This embraces unpaid commissions, demurrage claims and arbitration awards that have not been honoured. The service is free of charge to all members.

Membership of the Baltic Exchange enables members to keep abreast of market and industry developments through Baltic Briefing and the Baltic Exchange, such as member news, a searchable membership database for networking contacts, market guides, daily shipping news, daily bunker prices, weekly container reports and piracy reports.

Overall, the Baltic is the world's only provider of high quality, independent freight market information covering the dry and wet markets. It offers: (a) 47 separate route assessments, (b) settlement prices, (c) market-to-market information, (d) four dry cargo reports, (e) Baltic Ship Valuation Assessments, (f) daily dry cargo fixture list, (g) searchable fixture database, (h) LPG route assessments, (i) historical index and route rate database, (j) charting facilities, and (k) downloadable raw data.

The Baltic records in *Lloyd's List and Shipping Gazette* six daily wet and dry bulk cargo indices:

Dry market

(a) Baltic Exchange Dry Index.
(b) Baltic Exchange Capesize Index – 10 routes.
(c) Baltic Exchange Panamax Index – 7 routes.
(d) Baltic Exchange Supramax Index – 5 routes.
(e) Baltic Exchange International Tanker Index – 18 oil routes.
(f) Baltic Exchange Liquefied Petroleum Gas Route – stand-alone daily assessment.

A daily fixture list of dry bulk fixtures is published in London. The sale and purchase market is covered in the Baltic Sale and Purchase assessment (BSPA). This provides a weekly independent assessment on the market value of six ship types – VLCC, Aframax, medium-range products tanker, Capesize, Panamax and Supramax. The Baltic demolition assessment is covered on a weekly benchmark price on the demolition values of bulk carriers and tankers.

The freight derivatives market is covered by the Baltic forward assessment, which features mid prices available two years forward for dry Baltic Exchange routes and time charter averages. In regard to the settlement data average prices for the purposes of settling forward freight agreements, these are published for all Baltic routes.

The forerunner to the foregoing was BIFFEX, which was launched in 1985 – the world's first freight futures exchange. It performed well up to 1989/90, when volumes started to drop. Subsequently the market shifted to trading in forward freight agreements, a more flexible product with a direct correlation to a principal's underlying risk. FFAs have now rocketed in popularity and the market in 2004, for example, had a value of over US$30 billion. BIFFEX moved off the Baltic Exchange floor to the London Futures and Options Exchange (London Fox) and then to London International Financial Futures and Options Exchange (LIFFE), but ceased trading in 2001.

Today Baltic freight market information continues to grow in range and sophistication. The core of its exchange business remains the matching of ships and cargoes in chartering environment time or voyage.

8.25 Baltic and International Maritime Council (BIMCO)

The Baltic and International Maritime Council (BIMCO) was founded in 1905. It is a leading force in international shipping, representing shipowners, shipbrokers, agents, P&I clubs, and associate members across the globe. Today in an era of e-commerce BIMCO employs the most up-to-date technology to keep members informed of matters affecting their businesses. It is located in Bagsvaerd, Denmark, and has ongoing dialogue/consultation with international agencies such as the IMO, UNCTAD, ILO, OPEC, WTO and Intertanko. BIMCO also intervenes effectively on its members' behalf with intergovernmental organizations, regional and national authorities. It works closely with the EU. BIMCO's strategy is to continue to improve and expand its services to assist members in their activities. It is a strong advocate of international rather than regional or national regulations, implemented on equal basis in all states. BIMCO's objectives are:

(a) To be the leading interest group and membership organization providing practicable and tangible services to shipowners, brokers, agents, operators, associations and other entities connected with the international shipping industry.

(b) To develop free trade, access to markets, trade facilitation and harmonization, promotion of quality and safety including security.

(c) To promote high shipping standards, and support of existing measures to ensure quality shipping as well as the standardization of regulations and implementation on a worldwide basis.

(d) To consolidate its position as the recognized leader in the production of standard documents for the maritime industry thus providing a tangible contribution to trade facilitation and harmonization of the shipping industry.

(e) To provide core services such as intervention, charter party advice, IT products, training courses as well as maritime, port-related and company information.

(f) To encourage action against those engaged in the breach of ship and crew security, piracy, armed robbery, smuggling, refugee transportation and terrorism.

(g) To remain as a private, independent, non-political organization and be thus recognized by governments, intergovernmental and non-governmental organizations.

(h) To support issues affecting members and shipping industry through dialogue, consultation and media presentation.

(i) To ensure the industry's position and pragmatic solutions are brought to the attention of the US, EU and other global maritime authorities.

(j) To focus on key areas which yield the most benefits to its members.

(k) To maintain contact with other maritime organizations, associations and interest groups in order to seek when necessary, mutual understanding and co-operation on industry matters.

BIMCO represents more than 65% of the world's oceangoing dry cargo and tanker fleet and in some segments 80% of the cargo carrying capacity of specific ship types.

One of BIMCO's core activities for the past 100 years has been the production of standard forms. BIMCO Documentary Committee meets twice per year to discuss a wide range of documentary to keep up to date with market conditions. In autumn 2004 it approved one new agreement, two updated standard forms of contract and two standard clauses as detailed below:

(a) *Boxtime container vessel charter.* A new Boxtime time charter named Boxtime 2004. It took three years to update and features a number of BIMCO standard clauses such as war risk, dispute resolution, ISPS and fuel sulphur content.

(b) *Boxchange.* The Boxchange container interchange agreement enables container operators to exchange owned containers or containers leased from third party lessors to meet demand for boxes.

(c) *Projection.* A new charter designed for the barge and tug sector.

(d) *Supplytime.* An offshore service vessel time charter party introduced in 1989 and revised in 2005.

(e) *Gencoa.* A new standard contract of affreightment featuring the terms and conditions to govern the transportation of an agreed volume of dry bulk cargo or an agreed number of shipments in a voyage charter. It displaced Volcoa developed in 1982.

(f) *Conwartime and voywar.* The revision of two war risk clauses which were first introduced in 1993. The new clauses will feature in new/revised BIMCO approved charter parties.

(g) *General average.* The new set of York–Antwerp rules 2004 are under review for inclusion in BIMCO approved documents.

BIMCO is renowned for innovation in documentation and is consulted widely. Its Internet document editing application is widely used to edit a wide variety of BIMCO documents from any computer and then exchange them using e-mail. A summary of other BIMCO activities is given below:

(a) It has a membership in 123 countries and is able to draw on local experience and know-how embracing technical, legal, commercial and documentary expertise.

(b) A member owed money such as an owner having problems getting payment for freight or demurrage or an agent having difficulties in recovering his outlays or commissions can ask BIMCO to intervene on his behalf with a view to retrieving the outstanding balance, provided that the amount owing is undisputed.

(c) The Security and International Affairs Department handles matters relating to security, such as piracy, armed robbery, stowaways, drug smuggling, terrorism, fraud and extortion, in addition to co-ordinating BIMCO's involvement on issues of importance to the shipping industry that arise in Brussels, the US Congress and elsewhere. BIMCO has formally endorsed Anti-drug Smuggling agreements with many customs authorities to reduce smuggling on board merchant ships, thereby committing members to greater on-board security and matters concerning stowaways and port security.

(d) A close watch is focused on the security of ships and BIMCO receives reports of incidents from members and others.

(e) Continuous dialogue is maintained on enforcing safety at sea. Close co-operation is maintained with international shipping organizations, the shipbuilding industry and P&I clubs. A partnership agreement exists with the US Coast Guard to find non-regulatory approaches to enhance safety.

(f) BIMCO's website is one of the most extensive shipping information sites. Information on-line contains databases, access to which is required in the fixture stage, for voyage planning, preparation of port calls, post fixture work, as well as data of a marine technical nature.

(g) A wide range of publications is available from BIMCO on Shipping Documents, check before fixing, Shipmasters Security Manual, Freight Taxes and the annual review.

8.26 Freight Transport Association, incorporating the British Shippers' Council

The Freight Transport Association is the only UK trade association that exists to safeguard the interests of and provide services for trade and industry as operators and users of all forms of freight transport. It is accordingly recognized in this capacity by both central and local government and by other public bodies. This recognition extends worldwide and involves international agencies.

Full FTA membership is open to all companies concerned with the movement of goods as an ancillary part of their main trade or business, whether as operators of their own goods vehicles or as users of services provided by others such as road hauliers and railway authorities.

Overall the Association has two main functions. The prime function is to represent members' interest as operators and users of freight transport and to provide services for the benefit of members and associate members alike. The second function is to represent British shippers through the British Shippers' Council.

8.27 United Nations Conference on Trade and Development (UNCTAD)

UNCTAD was established in 1964 to affirm United Nations General Assembly's conviction that international co-operation in trade and development is vital for world economic growth and the economic development of developing countries.

With a membership of 187 states, UNCTAD, based in Geneva, is a permanent intergovernmental body and a principal organ of the General Assembly. The intergovernmental machinery comprises the Conference, the Trade and Development Board (TDB), and its subsidiary bodies serviced by a permanent secretariat. It is committed to accelerating international trade and development through co-operation, negotiation and partnership. It is distinctive not only for what it has achieved, but also because it is the only United Nations body dealing with economic issues in holistic terms, going beyond sectional interests to include how sectors interact and interlink. Its special quality is its view that change is the hallmark of development.

UNCTAD's objectives are:

(a) To encourage consensus in favour of changes in the world trade system to foster economic development.
(b) To formulate pragmatic principles and policies on international trade and development and facilitate their application.
(c) To promote the international trade and economic development of developing countries.
(d) To introduce a development dimension into international economic policies.
(e) To promote appropriate natural policies, particularly in developing countries, supporting market orientation, entrepreneurship, transparent decision-making, efficient practices and good economic management.
(f) To promote trade and economic co-operation among developing countries whatever their stage of development or economic and social systems.
(g) To provide special help for the poorest developing countries, often the least able to take advantage of the benefits of trade for their economic development.

The UNCTAD secretariat publishes an annual maritime review.

9 Passenger fares and freight rates

9.1 Theory of passenger fares

Passenger fares are usually dictated by the nature of the voyage, the class of ship and the accommodation offered. The docking expenses of the passenger vessel on an international voyage involving the disembarkation of passengers are costly and many cruise operators rely on passenger tenders (launches) to convey passengers to and from the vessel situated in outer harbour. Shipboard operating costs are high, since food and service must be provided. Product differentiation is an outstanding factor, since the service and comfort of different cruise lines and vessels by class of cabin accommodation vary greatly.

Generally speaking, the cruise shipowner will charge a fixed rate per day depending on the accommodation offered. But market pricing exists in both passenger ferry and cruise markets. For example, in the short sea trade the peak season passenger tariffs are much higher than the shoulder/off peak period reflecting a lower market demand for passenger shipping space. Group travel is also available for 10 passengers or more and shipowners offer discounted tariffs. Hence the peak passenger fare may be, for example, €100, off peak €75, and group travel with 10% off the published tariffs.

The cruise market entered a new phase of accommodation to gain wider market appeal. There are now mega cruise vessels of 2,500/3,000 passenger capacity and massive growth in new tonnage since the turn of the century. This new tonnage caters to all age groups: the youth market, young families, couples and the older generation. Hitherto it concentrated on passengers over 50 years old. The tariff is based on a fixed rate per day, reflecting the type of accommodation offered, the cruise itinerary and the season. The range of shipboard facilities in mega tonnage is extensive, offering a range of restaurants and a variety of passive and active entertainment. Cruise line operators generate substantial revenue from a range of shipboard facilities, particularly in retail outlets such as shops, hairdressers, tailors, etc. A substantial volume of cruise business is 'fly cruise' for which passengers travel by airline to join the vessel.

9.2 Theory of freight rates and effect of air competition on cargo traffic

Freight is the reward payable to the carrier for the carriage and arrival of goods in a mercantile or recognized condition, ready to be delivered to the merchant.

The pricing of cargo ships' services, like all pricing, is dependent on the forces of supply and demand, but the factors affecting both supply and demand are perhaps more complicated than in the case of most other industries and services. As with all forms of transport, the demand for shipping is derived from the demand for the commodities carried, and is, therefore, affected by the elasticity of demand for these commodities.

The demand for sea transport is affected both by direct competition between carriers and also, because it is a derived demand, by the competition of sub-stitutes or alternatives for the particular commodity carried. On any particular route, the shipowner is subject to competition from carriers on the same route, and also from carriers operating from alternative supply areas. The com-modities carried by the latter may be competitive with the commodities from his own supply area and, to that extent, may affect the demand for his services. On some routes there is also competition from air transport for high value to low weight ratio consignments, and in the coasting trade there is also competition from inland transport.

A growth market is the sea/air market, particularly when flights carry one-way freight only or have limited cargo demand for the return. Entrepreneurs have opportunities to generate maritime business on a combined sea/air basis.

The elasticity of demand for shipping services varies from one commodity to another. In normal times, an important factor affecting elasticity of demand for sea transport services is the cost of transport in relation to the market price of the goods carried. The cost of sea transport and associated expenses is often a considerable element in the final market price of many commodities. It may be between 8 and 15%.

The price eventually reached depends largely on the relationship between buyers and sellers. Where both groups are numerous with equal bargaining power, and where demand is fairly elastic, conditions of relatively perfect competition prevail. Under these circumstances, prices are fixed by the 'haggling of the market' and are known as contract prices. The market for tramp charters operates under such conditions, and the contract is drawn up as an agreement known as a charter party.

The contract may be for a single voyage at so much per tonne of the commodity carried, or it may be for a period at a stipulated rate of hire, usually so much per tonne of the ship's deadweight carrying capacity. Charter rates are quoted on a competitive basis in various exchanges throughout the world. Foodstuffs and raw materials in particular are traded in a highly competitive world market, and their movement is irregular, depending upon demand and supply conditions. It is usual for cargoes of these commodities to be loaded and marketed during transit, the charterers, while the ship is en route, instructing the ship to proceed to a certain range of ports and determining the port of discharge. For long-term charters, tankers or ore carriers, the rate of hire is fixed to give the owner a reasonable return on his investment.

Under these conditions, the rate structure for tramps is an uncomplicated product, emerging from competitive interplay of supply and demand. From an economist's point of view, rates made in this way represent the most efficient methods of pricing, for where price is determined under conditions of perfect competition, production is encouraged to follow consumers' wishes, and price itself does not deviate to any great extent from average total cost. In this way the customer is satisfied and production capacity most usefully employed. Detailed below are the factors influencing the formulation of a fixture rate:

(a) Ship specification, which would also embrace the type of vessel, i.e. bulk carrier, containership, oil tanker.
(b) The types of traffic to be conveyed.
(c) General market conditions. This is a major factor and generally an abundance of available ships for charter tends to depress the rate particularly for voyage and short-term charters.
(d) The daily cost to be borne by the charterer. This basically depends on the charter party terms. In a favourable shipowners' market situation the shipowner would endeavour to negotiate a rate to cover not only direct cost, which, depending on the charter party terms, covers fuel, crew, etc., but also contributions to indirect cost, such as depreciation and mortgage repayments. In so doing the shipowner strives to conclude a profitable fixture rate. Some shipowners under demise time charter terms insist on retaining their own Master for various reasons, a cost borne by the charterer. This could be extended to include chief engineer.
(e) The duration of the charter. Generally speaking the longer the charter, the less it is influenced by the market situation relative to the availability of ships and the demand for them.
(f) The terms of the charter. It must be remembered that the shipowner and charterer are free to conclude a charter party of any terms. Usually, however, a charter party bearing one of the code names for a particular trade, e.g. Boxtime for containers, is used when practicable. It is frequently necessary in such circumstances to vary the terms of the charter party by the deletion or addition of clauses to meet individual needs.
(g) The identity of cost to be borne by the charterer and shipowner must be clearly established. For example, it may be a gross form charter or FIO charter or nett form.
(h) Responsibility for the survey costs of the vessel must be clearly defined as to whether they are for the charterer's or shipowner's account.
(i) The urgency of the charter. If a charterer requires a vessel almost immediately there tends to be less haggling on fixture rates and this favours the shipowner.

(j) The convenience of the charter to the shipowner. If the broker negotiates a charter which terminates and places the vessel in a maritime area where demand for tonnage is strong, his decision will tend to depress the rate. In such circumstances the shipowner will have a good chance to secure another fixture at a favourable rate and with no long ballast voyage.

(k) The research data from the Worldscale and market research data available from leading brokers and research establishments specializing in various trades.

(l) The OPEC strategies influence the level of oil production amongst its members and the pressures on seaborne demand for tanker shipping capacity.

(m) The new build and recycling programme will forecast over a two to three-year period whether particular elements of tramp fleet are in decline or growth, thereby determining the available ship capacity. This must be related to market forecast (item n).

(n) Market forecasts such as OPEC, IEA and WTO will focus on individual markets and the shipping economist must correlate such data with the tramp fleet forecast. This embraces the trade cycle.

(o) The development of the global infrastructure, port privatization/ modernization, decline of particular types of cargo tonnage – fruit carriers/ reefer tonnage/ULCC/OBOs and impact it has on other tonnage categories. This can include pipeline development. Overall, in regard to (m), (n) and (o), it will impact on the changing pattern of world trade routes and the tramp markets.

(p) Any change in global financial market, especially the exchange rate movement and its impact on international trade confidence.

(q) A number of indices demonstrate fixture rate movement from which subsequent trends can be devised. These feature in *Lloyd's List and Shipping Gazette* and include the J. E. Hyde shipping index, J. E. Ryde Handymax, Axsmarine Capesize coal index, Axsmarine Capesize iron ore index, MGN on-line tanker industry index, Baltic Dry Bulk indices and Baltic Tanker indices – the latter two indices are produced by the Baltic Exchange.

(r) Each month the Institute of Shipping Economics and Logistics publishes the dry cargo tramp time charter and dry cargo trip charter.

(s) Table 9.1 features a history of container ship time charter rates. It reflects charter rates for all types of container ships. It is important to indicate that the impact of containerization on both the tramp and liner trades is greater than that implied by the size of growth of the fleet.

(t) Market reports are published in *Lloyd's List and Shipping Gazette* and are also available from leading shipbrokers.

(u) The CE Futures produces a range of statistics, including futures in oil and gas production industry prices. These include gas oil futures, natural gas futures volume, Brent crude futures volume, and Brent crude options volume. Such data measures the volume sold on a monthly basis and

Table 9.1 Container ship time charter rates (dollars per 14-ton slot per day)

Ship type and sailing speed (TEUs)	Yearly averages									
	2002	2003	2004	2005	2006	2007	2008	2009	2010	2011
Gearless										
200–299 (min 14 kn)	16.9	19.6	25.0	31.7	26.7	27.2	26.0	12.5	12.4	12.4
300–500 (min 15 kn)	15.1	17.5	21.7	28.3	21.7	22.3	20.0	8.8	9.9	12.8
Geared/gearless										
2,000–2,299 (min 22 kn)	4.9	9.8	13.8	16.4	10.5	11.7	10.0	2.7	4.8	6.3
2,300–3,400 (min 22.5 kn)	6.0	9.3	13.2	13.0	10.2	10.7	10.7	4.9	4.7	6.2
Geared										
200–299 (min 14 kn)	17.0	18.9	27.0	35.4	28.0	29.8	32.1	16.7	18.3	22.1
300–500 (min 15 kn)	13.4	15.6	22.2	28.8	22.0	21.3	21.4	9.8	11.7	15.4
600–799 (min 17–17.9 kn)	9.3	12.3	19.6	23.7	16.6	16.1	15.6	6.6	8.4	11.2
700–999 (min 18 kn)	9.1	12.1	18.4	22.0	16.7	16.9	15.4	6.0	8.5	11.5
800–999 (min 18 kn)	n.a.	n.a.	n.a.	n.a.	n.a.	n.a.	n.a.	4.9	7.8	10.8
1,000–1,260 (min 18 kn)	6.9	11.6	19.1	22.6	14.3	13.7	12.2	4.0	5.9	8.7
1,261–1,350 (min 19 kn)	n.a.	n.a.	n.a.	n.a.	n.a.	n.a.	n.a.	3.7	4.9	8.1
1,600–1,999 (min 20 kn)	5.7	10.0	16.1	15.8	11.8	12.8	10.8	3.5	5.0	6.8

Source: Reproduced with the kind permission of the UNCTAD secretariat.

reflects market pricing movement embracing the US dollar per barrel of oil and US dollar per tonne of gas oil.

The importance of each of the points will vary according to the circumstances. In considering the previous analysis, it is important to note that there are two tramp markets. The 'spot charter' is usually at a discounted price below the market norm of the current fixture rate. This is an open market transaction whereby a charter is traded 'on the spot' at current market rates or discount rate. The other market conditions are usually negotiated over a longer period, 'the period charter market', and is subject to 'haggling'/negotiation – often reflecting many of the items identified above, items (a) to (u).

The tramp industry can be regarded as a pool of shipping, from which vessels move in accordance with world demand to the employment in which they are most valued by the consumer. Freight fixtures for tramp charters are recorded daily in such shipping publications as *Lloyd's List,* which students are recommended to study. The liner trade is dominated by the top 20 liner operators, who have 67% of the world's total container carrying capacity (TEUs). Moreover, a very large proportion of the containerized shipments emerge from multinational business. This trend is likely to continue as the global trading pattern changes and more industries are relocated in the Far East. An example of freight rates on the three major liner trade routes (2003–05) is found in Table 9.2.

The container rate structure falls into two divisions. The rate per container, TEU (Table 9.2), which is usually negotiated between the shipper and container operator and reflects the trade, type of container, origin and destination, nature of cargo and any volume discounts on the basis the shipper guarantees a particular volume during a specified period. Additional charges per container may be raised for CAF, BAF, port congestion charge, handling cost, terminal security fees, etc. This is categorized as the FCL.

The other market is where the agent negotiates a rate with a container operator and despatches groupage consignments. Alternatively, the container operator may offer such a service direct to the market under the LCL arrangement. Liner conferences do not feature extensively in the container business and are in decline; the tables/schedules are remodelled with emphasis on the hub and spoke and transhipment markets. The LCL market is based on a W/M ship option.

Liner rates are based partly on cost, and partly on value. Many freight rates are quoted on a basis of weight or measurement at ship's option. This means that the rate quoted will be applied either per metric ton of 1,000 kg (2,205 lb) or per tonne of 1.133 m³, whichever will produce the greater revenue. The reason for this method of charging is that heavy cargo will bring a vessel to its loadline before its space is full, while light cargo will fill its space without bringing it down to its maximum draught. To produce the highest revenue a vessel must be loaded to its full internal capacity, and immersed to its maximum permitted depth. Therefore charging by weight or measurement is

Table 9.2 Freight rates (market averages) on the three major liner trade routes, 2003–05 (US$ per TEU)

	TransPacific		Europe–Asia		Transatlantic	
Quarter (% change)	Asia– US	US– Asia	Europe– Asia	Asia– Europe	US– Europe	Europe– US
2003						
First quarter	1,529	826	704	1,432	899	1,269
Change (%)	0	1.1	−1.1	9.8	6.6	4.4
Second quarter	1,717	861	762	1,570	924	1,400
Change (%)	12.3	4.2	8.2	9.6	2.8	10.3
Third quarter	1,968	834	777	1,629	817	1,426
Change (%)	14.6	−3.1	2	3.8	−11.6	1.9
Fourth quarter	1,892	810	754	1,662	834	1,469
Change (%)	−3.9	−2.9	−3	2	2	3
2004						
First quarter	1,850	802	733	1,686	778	1,437
Change (%)	−2.2	−1	−2.8	1.4	−6.7	−2.2
Second quarter	1,863	819	731	1,738	788	1,425
Change (%)	0.7	2.1	−0.3	3.1	1.3	−0.8
Third quarter	1,946	838	735	1,826	810	1,436
Change (%)	4.6	2.3	0.5	5.1	2.8	0.8
Fourth quarter	1,923	806	769	1,838	829	1,471
Change		−3.8	4.6	0.6	2.3	2.4
2005						
First quarter	186.7	800	801	1,795	854	1,514
Change (%)	−2.9	−0.7	4.2	−2.3	3	2.9

Notes: Information from six of the trades' major liner companies. All rates are all-in, including the inland intermodal portion, if relevant. All rates are average rates of all commodities carried by major carriers. Rates to and from the United States refer to the average for all three coasts. Rates to and from Europe refer to the average for northern and Mediterranean Europe. Rates to and from Asia refer to the whole of South East Asia, East Asia and Japan/Republic of Korea.

a cost question. In most trades, cargo measuring under 1.133 m³ per tonne weight is charged on a weight basis, whilst cargo measuring 1.133 m³ or more per ton is charged on a measurement basis. With the spread of the metric system, most freight rates are quoted per 1,000 kg or m³ (35.33 ft³).

Liner tariffs cite rates for many commodities that move regularly. These rates are based on the stowage factor (rate of bulk to weight), on the value of the cargo and on the competitive situation. Many tariffs publish class rates for general cargo not otherwise specified. Some tariffs publish class rates whereby commodities are grouped for charging into several classes. On commodities of very high value *ad valorem* rates are charged at so much % of the declared value. When commodities move in large quantities, and are susceptible to tramp competition, tariffs often employ 'open rates', i.e. the rate is left open, so that the shipping line can quote whatever rate is appropriate. To illustrate the calculation of the freight rate an example is given below.

It involves the conveyance of electrical goods from Birmingham to Bilbao, involving a maritime movement and alternative road vehicle transit throughout – all items are packed in wooden cases.

16 cartons:	120 × 80 × 60 cm
Weight of each carton:	75 kg

Freight rates by sea/road
(assume US$1.5 = £1):
- Sea: US$175 per tonne W/M
- Road: US$350 per 1,000 chargeable kg

Chargeable weight/volume
ratios for each mode
(CBM = cubic metre):
- Sea: 1 CBM = 1,000 kg
- Road: 3 CBM = 1,000 kg

Sea rate per tonne (1,000 kg):
US$175

Rate sterling per tonne:	US$175 ÷ 1.5 = 116.66
Rate sterling per kg:	£116.66 ÷ 1,000 = £0.11

Volumetric rate:

$$1 \text{ carton} = \frac{120 \times 80 \times 60}{1,000} \text{ kg}$$

$$16 \text{ cartons} = \frac{16 \times 120 \times 80 \times 60}{1,000} \text{ kg}$$

$$= 9,216 \text{ kg}$$

Sea freight rate:
$$= £0.11 \text{ per kg}$$
$$= £0.11 \times 9216$$
$$= £1,013.76$$

Rate by weight:
1 carton	= 75 kg
16 cartons	= 16 × 75 kg
	= 1,200 kg

Sea freight rate:	= £0.11 per kg
Total sea freight rate:	= 1,200 kg × £0.11 per kg
	= £132

In some trades the rate would be based on the nearest tonne in which case the volumetric rate would rise from 9,216 kg to 10,000 kg and yield £1,166.60, and the weight from 1,200 kg to 2,000 kg to produce £220.

Road rate per chargeable
1,000 kg: US$350
        Rate sterling per
        chargeable 1,000 kg: US$350 ÷ 1.5 = £233.33

Rate sterling per kg: £233.33 ÷ 1,000 = £0.23

Volumetric rate:

$$1 \text{ carton} = \frac{120 \times 80 \times 60}{3,000} \text{ kg}$$

$$16 \text{ cartons} = \frac{16 \times 120 \times 80 \times 60}{3,000} \text{ kg}$$
$$= 3,072 \text{ kg}$$

Road freight rate: = £0.23
Total road freight rate: = 3,072 × £0.23
     = £706.56

Rate by weight:
    1 carton   = 75 kg
    16 cartons   = 16 × 75 kg
     = 1,200 kg

Road freight rate: = £0.23

Total road freight rate: = 1,200 × £0.23
     = £276

In some trades the rate would be based on the nearest tonne, in which case the volumetric rate would rise from 3,072 kg to 4,000 kg and yield £933.32, and the weight from 1,200 kg to 2,000 kg to produce £466.66.

Accordingly the carrier would charge the volumetric or weight rate that will yield the highest income:

Sea volumetric: £1,166.60
Road volumetric: £933.32

In recent years there has been a tendency in an increasing number of liner cargo trades to impose a surcharge on the basic rate and examples are given below of the types which emerge:

(a) *Bunkering or fuel surcharge.* In an era when fuel costs now represent a substantial proportion of total direct voyage cost – a situation which has arisen from the very substantial increase in bunkering expenses from 2005 to 2007 – shipowners are not prepared to absorb the variation in fuel prices. They take the view that price variation of bunker fuel tends to be unpredictable and that it is usually based on the variable dollar rate of exchange and that is difficult to budget realistically for this cost to make it reflect adequately in their rate formulation. Moreover, an increase in the bunkering price erodes the shipowner's voyage profitability.

(b) *Congestion charge.* This arises when a vessel may have to wait several days outside a seaport waiting for a berth due to an increase in traffic volume and the facilities cannot cope with the situation. Examples are found in container terminals and a surcharge is raised on a landed container basis.

(c) *Currency surcharge* (currency adjustment factor, CAF) arises when the freight rate is related to a floating currency, such as sterling. For example, if the rate were based on euros, which both operate fixed rates of currency, then the sterling rate of exchange in January would probably be different from the situation in the following July. For example, when sterling is depressed, it would probably earn more euros per £1 sterling in January than in the following July. Accordingly, a currency surcharge is imposed to minimize losses that the shipowner would incur, bearing in mind the shipowner obtains less sterling equivalent in euro-rated traffic whilst, at the same time, port expenses in euros would be greater due to the depressed sterling rate of exchange.

An example of a currency surcharge scale involving the Anglo-Euro trade is given in Table 9.3. The freight tariff is sterling based on €1.40 to £1, and the rate per tonne is £20 or €28.

(i) Payment in sterling – exchange rate €1.350 to £1

10 tonnes at £20 per tonne	£200
4% surcharge based on exchange rate of €1.350	8
Total	£208

(ii) Payment in euros – exchange rate €1.428 to £1

10 tonnes at €28 per tonne	€280
5% surcharge based on exchange rate of €1.482	14
Total	€294

(d) Surcharges are usually raised for heavy lifts such as indivisible consignments and on excessive height or length of ro/ro rated traffic, together with any other traffic where special facilities are required.

(e) Consequent on the introduction of the ISPS code reflecting mandatory security measures on ships and ports as adopted by the IMO, seaports have introduced a terminal security fee to recover security cost. Moreover, container lines likewise to recover security cost on ships have introduced a carrier security fee payable by the shippers/consignees.

Table 9.3 Example of a currency surcharge scale involving the Anglo-Euro trade

When charges are to be paid in euros to £1	*Surcharge in euros (%)*
1.466 to 1.484	5
1.51 to 1.465	4
1.436 to 1.450	3
1.421 to 1.435	2
1.396 to 1.420	1
No surcharge 1.315 to 1.395 (void area)	nil (no surcharge)
When charges are to be paid in sterling to euros to £1	*Surcharge in sterling (%)*
1.381 to 1.404	1
1.366 to 1.380	2
1.351 to 1.365	3
1.336 to 1.350	4
1.316 to 1.335	5

Note: The percentage of surcharge will be determined each week by reference to the average rate as published in *Le Monde* and the *Financial Times* on Saturdays (i.e. Friday's closing prices).

Special rates apply to for livestock and dangerous classified cargo, reflecting the additional facilities the shipowner provides to convey this traffic. Dangerous cargo classified traffic usually attracts a 50% surcharge above general rated traffic and requires extensive pre-booking arrangements and a declaration signed by the shipper of the cargo contents.

It is important to note that a substantial volume of general merchandise cargo now moves under groupage or consolidation arrangements. This involves the freight forwarder who originates the traffic from a number of consignors to a number of consignees and despatches the compatible cargo in a container or international road haulage vehicle. The freight forwarder, in consultation with another freight forwarder in the destination country, operates on a reciprocal basis. The rate includes the collection and delivery charges, usually undertaken by road transport. The freight forwarders operate from a warehouse which may form part of some leased accommodation at a container base with inland clearance depot facilities. The latter will permit the cargo to move under bond to and from the port. The rates are based on a weight/ measurement (W/M) basis, whichever produces the greater revenue to the freight forwarder. A cargo manifest accompanies the consolidated consignment throughout the transit. It is usual for the freight forwarder to pre-book shipping space for the container or road vehicle on specific sailings, and so offer a regular assured service to the shipper.

Rate making is affected by such factors as susceptibility of a cargo to damage or pilferage, nature of packaging, competition, transit cost and convenience of handling. A properly compiled tariff should encourage the movement of all classes of cargo, to ensure the best balance between revenue production and the full utilization of vessels.

There follows an examination of factors in the formulation of freight rates.

1 Competition. Keen competition on rates exists among various modes of transport. For example, in the UK–Europe trade, competition exists amongst air freight agents offering consolidated services, Le Shuttle (EuroTunnel), ISO containerization in the Asia/Europe, Asia/North America and Europe/North America trades and international road haulage.
2 The nature of the commodity, its quantity, period of shipment(s) and overall cubic measurements/dimensions/value.
3 The origin and destination of the cargo.
4 The overall transit cost.
5 The nature of packaging and convenience of handling.
6 The susceptibility of the cargo to damage and pilferage.
7 The general loadability of the transport unit.
8 Provision of additional facilities to accommodate the cargo, such as heavy lifts, strong room, livestock facilities, etc.
9 The mode(s) of transport.
10 Actual routing of cargo consignment. Alternative routes tend to exist in some trades – particularly with multi-modalism/containerization – with a differing rate structure and overall transport cost.
11 Logistics – the supply chain 'value added benefit'.
12 Security cost. This embraces ISPS Code.

The factor that has come to prominence in rate assessments in recent years – particularly through containerization – is 'value added benefit' that a shipper derives from the mode(s) of distribution used. The overall rate may be high, but it enables cost savings to be realized in lower inventory cost, improved service to the importers' clients, much reduced down time on unserviceable machinery undergoing repair, replenishment of stocks to meet consumer demand, assembly of component parts in low labour-cost markets with suppliers sourced worldwide, and benefits derived by the shipper from a high profile quality distribution network. Reliability, frequency, and transit time and the overall quality of the service involving the 'total product' concept embracing all distribution elements, are major and decisive factors. Today, liner cargo rates are calculated within a logistic driven global market.

Today, all mega ports both 'hub and feeder' and operating containerized networks, undertake customs examination/clearance outside the port environs at ICD free zones /importers/exporters premises or dry port. Hence the freight tariff will cover not only the port-to-port rate but also charges relating to overland transport, handling, customs, security tariff, etc. The forwarding agent/container operator may raise this tariff at the time of shipment or on arrival at destination. Likewise, at the commencement of the transit the collection/haulage/handling/customs tariff will be raised as an inclusive rate to the destination or raised separately. The Incoterm 2010 selected is crucial to allocation of payment arrangements. Less cargo is now being despatched under FOB, CIF, CFR terms but more CPT, CCP, DAF, FCA as combined transport develops. The foregoing applies both to FCL and to LCL containerized shipments.

In regard to break bulk cargo services, the cargo may be delivered and cleared into transit sheds or onto the quay so that loading and discharging expenses are met by the shipowner and covered by the freight rate quoted.

However, this method of shipment is fast declining as these cargoes are consolidated into containers and cleared outside port environs. This decline is due to port privatization and a drive to raise port productivity.

A market developed extensively in recent years is that of project forwarding. It involves the despatch/conveyance arrangements stemming from a contract award, such as for a power station project. The contract is usually awarded to a consortium and the freight forwarder undertakes all the despatch/conveyance arrangements. This process involves the freight forwarder negotiating with the shipowner special rates for the merchandise conveyed and the associated pre-booking and shipment arrangements. Often such shipments require special arrangements and purpose-built equipment for which a comprehensive rate is charged, usually on a cost plus profit basis. This applies to indivisible loads and heavy lifts.

Another market is antiques, such as valuable paintings and a collection of furniture. Such goods require specialized packing by professional packers. Pre-shipment arrangements are extensive and include security and documentation. Two types of antiques market exist: one the very valuable art treasures with national prestige, and the other the much larger market of less valuable antiques. The rates of the former market are negotiated with the shipowner and have regard to various provisions including security and the cost thereof. Much of this traffic travels as airfreight. The latter market of less valuable antiques is usually containerized and can be found in British–North American trade. For the many kinds of antiques there are standard rates according to strict conditions of shipment, such as packing by specialized agents.

An additional method of freight rate assessment applies to ro/ro services. It is based on the area occupied by the vehicle on the ship's deck or alternatively by length at a given charge per foot/metre, depending on the overall length of the road vehicle. The rate usually remains unchanged, irrespective of type of cargo shipped in the road vehicle. Rates vary if the vehicle/trailer is empty or loaded, accompanied or unaccompanied. When the vehicle uses the same route for the return load concessionary rates sometimes apply for particular trades. Generally speaking, air competition has made no serious inroads in carriage of cargo – certainly not to the extent experienced in the passenger trade. Nevertheless, the tendency has been for certain types of traffic having a relatively high value and low weight ratio or demand a fast service, due to the nature of the cargo or urgency of the consignment, to be conveyed by air. Such competition has had little effect on tramping, but air has had a more significant effect on liner cargo services: in some markets sea/air bridges have been developed.

Most of the world's principal liner cargo routes are now containerized and intermodal (see Chapter 16), offering much faster services by providing faster ships and rationalized ports of call. Rates are often from an inland terminal, such as a container base, to a similar facility in the destination country. Many container shipments for the general cargo-covered type of container are mixed cargoes, each individually rated by commodity classification. The more specialized form of container has individual rates formulated by classified container type.

Continuous expansion of maritime containerization has adversely tempered the further growth of airfreight. However, the world's airlines are beginning to increase airfreight capacity, by deploying wide-bodied aircraft, and greater marketing effort, including developing sea/air bridges. Such developments have only marginally abstracted traffic from the consolidated ISO container market of high value to low weight ratio high cube commodities in distance markets. Examples include fresh flowers from Kenya and Tanzania to Europe and urgent medical supplies and spare parts. Currently some 10% of the world's trade by value is conveyed by air transport.

In recent years the CABAF technique has been introduced: a currency and bunkering adjustment. When shipping companies calculate their freight rates, they take account of the exchange rate level and fuel costs. In so doing they use rates applicable at the time the freight rate is compiled or the market forecasts of currency exchange rates and bunker costs operative at the time the new freight rate is introduced on the service/trade. For example, if the shipowner is calculating his rate in US dollars, and an exporter is paying for freight in sterling, in the event of the US dollar rate rising the shipowner will want more sterling for the freight so he adds an adjustment factor to the freight invoice. If the price of bunker fuel is also likely to vary a surcharge relative to the increased cost may be imposed. In some trades these are called simply currency and fuel surcharges and their application varies. The bunker surcharge is usually consolidated into the rate as soon as new rate levels are introduced, which in many trades is every 6 or 12 months, depending on current levels of inflation.

9.3 Relation between liner and tramp rates

In general, liner and tramp rates fluctuate in similar ways. Liner rates, however, are more stable than tramp rates, which are particularly sensitive to short-term supply and demand conditions. Comparisons are not easy because published data on liner rates are fragmentary and no index of liner rates is available to set against the quarterly issued tramp rate indices. Nevertheless, although tramps provide liners with only limited competition, the world tramp fleet remains a factor in the market. When tramp rates fall liner rates fall similarly for fear of tramp competition. Conversely, when tramp rates rise, liner operators feel able to increase rates, particularly when costs rise. Generally speaking, liner rates are less sensitive to changes in market demand and more sensitive to changes in cost than are tramp rates. Readers should note that increasing specialization in container types may eliminate tramp competition for some commodities and routes, so that rates for these kinds of commodities may remain uninfluenced by competition. In the next decades correlation between liner and tramp rates may decline further, especially as multi-modalism increases.

9.4 Relation between voyage and time charter rates

A voyage charter is a contract for a specific voyage, while a time charter is a contract for a period of time covering perhaps several voyages. Therefore, the voyage charter rate is a short-term rate, while the time charter rate is often a long-term rate. When trade is buoyant and voyage rates are rising, charterers, in anticipation of further rises, tend to charter for longer periods to cover their commitments; when rates are expected to fall, they tend to contract for shorter periods. Therefore, the current time charter rate tends to reflect the expected trend of future voyage rates. If rates are expected to rise, time charter rates will tend to be above the current voyage rates; if they are expected to fall, time charter rates will tend to be below current voyage rates. Generally, the two rates move in the same direction, but because time charter rates depend on market expectations they tend to fluctuate more widely than voyage rates. When conditions are improving, long-term rates tend to rise more rapidly than voyage rates; when conditions are deteriorating, voyage rates tend to fall more rapidly. Readers should study tramp rate indices and those market conditions which determine variations.

9.5 Types of freight

Study of freight rates needs an examination of the types available. The true test of a shipowner's right to freight is whether the service in respect of which the freight is contracted to be paid has been substantially performed, or, if not, whether its performance has been prevented by any act of the cargo owner. Freight is normally payable 'ship lost or not lost'. Details of the various types are these:

(a) *Advance freight* is payable in advance, before delivery of the actual goods. This is generally regarded as the most important type of freight and is extensively used in liner cargo trades and tramping. It should not be confused with 'advance of freight' which may be a payment on account of disbursements or an advance to the Master, in which case the charterer would be entitled to a return of money advanced. Such a payment is a kind of loan.

(b) *Lump sum freight* is the amount payable for the use of the whole or portion of a ship. This form of freight is calculated on the actual cubic capacity of the ship offered, and has no direct relation to the cargo to be carried. Lump sum freight is payable irrespective of the actual quantity delivered.

(c) *Dead freight* is the name given to a damage claim for breach of contract by, for example, the charterer to furnish a full cargo to a ship. Such a situation arises when the charterer undertook to provide 500 tonnes of cargo but only supplied 400 tonnes. The shipowner is, under such circumstances, entitled to claim dead freight for the unoccupied space. Alternatively, a shipper may fail to provide all the cargo promised and for which space has been reserved on a particular sailing, in which case the shipowner may claim dead freight for the unoccupied space. The amount of dead freight chargeable is the equivalent of the freight which would have been earned, less all charges which would have been incurred in the loading, carriage and discharge of the goods. It can be understood as a form of compensation, the shipowner not being entitled to make more profit by dead freight than he would by actual carriage of the goods. He must make an allowance for all expenses not incurred. There is no lien on dead freight, but by express agreement in the contract a lien may be extended to other cargo for the payment of dead freight.

(d) *Back freight* arises when goods have been despatched to a certain port, and on arrival are refused. The freight charged for the return of the goods constitutes back freight.

(e) *Pro-rata freight* arises when the cargo has been carried only part of the way and circumstances make it impossible to continue the voyage further. For example, ice formation at the original port of delivery may entail the owner deciding to accept delivery of the cargo at an intermediate port. The point then arises whether the freight is payable *pro rata* for the portion of the voyage actually accomplished. This will happen when there is clear agreement by the cargo owner to pay.

(f) *Ad valorem freight* arises when a cargo is assessed for rate purposes on a percentage of its value. For example a 2% *ad valorem* rate on a consignment value at £10,000 would raise £200.

10 Liner conferences

10.1 Introduction

The liner conference was first conceived in 1875. It is perhaps failing to meet the many challenges facing the maritime industry.

10.2 Liner conference system

The liner conference is an organization whereby a number of shipowners offer their services on a given sea route on conditions agreed by conference members. Conferences are semi-monopolistic associations of shipping lines formed for the purpose of restricting competition between their members and protecting them from outside competition. Conference agreements may also regulate sailings and ports of call, and in some cases pooling of nett earnings is arranged. Conferences achieve their object by controlling prices and by limiting entry to trade. They seek to establish a common tariff of freight rates and passenger fares for a trade, conference members being free to compete for traffic on the basis of the quality and efficiency of the service they offer. The organization of a conference varies from one trade to another. It may consist of informal and regular meetings of shipowners at which rates and other matters of policy are discussed, or it may involve a formal organization with a permanent secretariat and prescribed rules for membership, together with stipulated penalties for violations of agreement. Members are often required to deposit a cash bond to cover fines in respect of non-compliance with their obligations.

In some conferences there exists a pooling agreement whereby traffic or gross or nett earnings in the trade are pooled, members receiving agreed percentages of that pool. Under the gross earnings arrangements, each shipowner bears all his operating/investment costs and pools the gross revenue. If the arrangement is based on nett earnings each operator pools his nett earnings only, meaning a more efficient low-cost shipowner to operate within the pool can be undercut by a more expensive and less efficient operator. Each operator has no control on other operators' expenditure, tending thereby to favour the less efficient shipowner because there is no real incentive for him to contain his costs: these will be borne by other members of the pool. The object of such an arrangement is to guarantee to members a certain share of the trade, and to limit competition. It leads to the regulation of sailings and may in some circumstances enable the trade to be rationalized. An excess of tonnage in a particular trade is likely to lead to an agreed reduction in the number of sailings and pooling of receipts. When the conferences perform special services, such as lifting unprofitable cargo or resorting to chartering to cover temporary shortages of tonnage, they often pool the losses or profits.

A further example of a liner conference agreement is where each member agrees to operate a percentage of the sailings and thereby have an identical percentage of the total pooled income. Hence there may be four operators two of these operators each undertaking 20% of the sailings and receiving 20% of the pooled revenue. The other two may provide 30% of the sailings and likewise receive 30% of the pooled receipts. Each operator is in this instance responsible for his costs.

The objects of the liner conference are to provide a service adequate to meet the trade requirements; by regulating loading to avoid wasteful competition among members; to organize themselves so that the conference can collectively combat competition from others; and to maintain a tariff by mutual agreement as stable as conditions will permit.

10.3 Deferred rebate and contract systems

Associated with liner conferences are the deferred rebate and contract systems. The deferred rebate is a device to ensure that shippers continue to support a conference. A shipper who ships exclusively by conference vessels can, at the end of a certain period (usually six months), claim a rebate, usually 10% of the freight money paid by him during the period. Hence the shipper has an inducement to remain loyal to the conference in so far as he stands to lose a rebate by employing a non-conference vessel. In recent years the deferred rebate system has tended to become less popular in some trades due to the high cost of clerical administration. Accordingly, it has been substituted – under the same code of loyalty conditions – by the immediate rebate system. This has a somewhat lower rebate – maybe 9.5% – but granted at the time freight payment is made and not some six months later, as with the deferred rebate system. Such a lower deferred rate is termed a nett rate. The level of deferred rebate varies by individual conference.

A further way of retaining the shipper's support for a conference is by the contract or special contract agreement systems. The contract system is when a shipper signs a contract to forward all his goods by conference line vessels, either in the general course of business or perhaps associated with a special project over a certain period. The kind of contract may, for example, concern a large hydroelectric scheme, goods for which special equipment would be likely. Under this contract system the shipper would be granted a cheaper freight rate than a non-contract shipper. There are also special commodity agreements, specially negotiated between the trade and conference, covering goods shipped in large quantities and often for short duration. The shipper may be forwarding a commodity, such as copper, tea, rubber, foodstuffs or cotton, in considerable quantities.

Shippers' criticism of the deferred rebate system is that it enables conferences to create monopolies and thereby keep rates at a higher level. A shipper can be reluctant to use outside tonnage for fear of loss of rebate, the system restricting his freedom of action. Another criticism is that a record must be kept of all freight paid subject to rebate to enable claims. This involves clerical expenses, and also a shipper argues he is losing money from loss of interest on the rebate while it remains with the carrier. The carrier may maintain that retention of this rebate for an appropriate period is a disincentive to shippers' use of non-conference vessels. Retention of rebate is a bargaining device, carrier being sole arbiter in deciding whether or not any shipper's rebate should be forfeited. Carriers also have little difficulty in keeping rebate records in their manifest freight databases and, because of the amount of work involved, justify having small rebate departments. They explain it is not compulsory for shippers to remain with the conference, but should they choose to ship outside it, these shippers will forfeit their rebates. Shippers who forfeit their rebates have, after all, enjoyed the benefits of conference shipments, which later they are free to discard for something better.

10.4 Harmonization conferences

A development in recent years has been the formulation of harmonization conferences amongst liner cargo operators, some of which may be members of a number of different conferences.

A situation may emerge in a particular trade whereby the majority of cargo operators are anxious to avoid rate wars and are keen to provide a quality service for a reasonable and competitive tariff. This service is likely to be indirectly in competition with other cargo operators at different ports, each operator offering a variable voyage time and distance. Individual rates would be different.

The object of the harmonization conference is to regulate any rate increases and reach agreement on rebate levels and a code of application. Other matters of mutual concern are documentation, the basis of the constituents of the freight rate, currency/fuel surcharges, etc. Harmonization conferences are voluntary and often involve shipowners of many nationalities. These conferences are likely to broaden their range of influence.

10.5 The future of the liner conference system in the twenty-first century

The future of the liner conference system looks unpromising. Factors responsible are these:

(a) The inflexibility of the system strongly favours shipowners in matters of rates, localized conference contracts (as distinct from a global contract) covering all the conferences, and the tendency for shippers to despatch cargo under CPT, CIP and FCA using combined transport rather than port-to-port FOB, CIF, CFR, over which the shipowner has complete control in terms of cost and service, something he does not have over combined transport operating under CPT, CIP, FCA.

(b) The system is tightly regulated, tying a shipper to the conference without redress should the client wish to use non-conference ships – the latter use has severe penalties.

(c) Changing rates is a tedious process, requiring consensus from liner conference members.

(d) The deferred rate system is an anachronism.

(e) Parity exists on rates amongst conference members. This immunity from competitive legislation favours the shipowner, because competitive rates bring cheaper prices and focus on the 'value added concept'. In 2006 the EU repealed regulation 4056/86 which spared the maritime industry from competition law. Shipowners who offer competitive rates encourage volume shipments. Through continuous investment and positive cash flow they improve service quality, which benefits shippers through new facilities in overseas markets.

(f) Containerization is a growth market. It is opening up new markets by developing and managing global logistic supply chains. It extols combined transport road/sea/road, rail/sea/rail because it offers door to door rates and develops the hub and spoke system. The liner conference system tends to restrict port-to-port operation, not usually focusing on contracts with railborne container trains to the ICD.

(g) The continuous merger and acquisition of container operators to provide a gross TEU capacity of over 250,000 TEU is resulting in fewer but larger container businesses. This growth is resulting in larger container tonnage (10,000–14,000 TEU), continuous remodelling of container services, continuous development of port modernization, increasing investment in containerized railborne services, e.g. Darwin–Adelaide, and more ICD FTZ Distriparks. The liner conference does not feature in these developments, because mega container operators can negotiate a global rate across all services/trades, something not possible with the (fragmented) liner conference.

(h) The United States has outlawed the liner conference. Today less than 10% of liner cargo trade is conveyed under liner conference conditions, an inexorable decline resulting from new container tonnage worldwide.

11 Ship operation

11.1 Factors to consider in planning sailing schedules

When planning a vessel's sailing schedule it is important to ensure its full available employment. A shipowner derives no income when a ship is laid up – whether for survey, general maintenance or due to lack of traffic – so periods of a ship's inactivity must be minimized. This is important because of the large capital invested in a ship and heavy annual depreciation charges. A ship, having a limited existence, when ultimately withdrawn from service, raises the question of what profit it has earned when in service. An owner who has secured full employment for the vessel is more likely to realize a larger profit than one who has been content to operate the vessel during peak periods only, and who has made no effort to find additional employment at other times. When a vessel might have a few months' uneconomic service a year it might be worthwhile for the shipowner to reduce the size of his fleet to allow him to utilize it better.

Eventually, however, the cost of increasing the size of a fleet exceeds the additional revenue gained, the operator sustaining a consequent loss. In this instance, the project should be abandoned unless there are compelling reasons, e.g. social, political, or even commercial, not to do so. The optimum size of fleet is when the minimum number of vessels earns the maximum revenue. An owner does not always have a standby vessel available, because of the considerable amount of capital tied up in each vessel.

Today an increasing number of vessels are multi-purpose, permitting flexibility of operation, something advantageous during international trade depressions. Multi-purpose operation enables a vessel to switch from one trade to another, or carry a variety of cargoes rather than a specialized cargo. Some multi-purpose container ships carry containers as well as vehicles; the ro/ro vessel is capable of shipping all types of vehicular traffic. Such tonnage is better able to combat economically unequal trading.

There are basically two types of service: the regular and those operated according to a particular demand. The first type of vessel is primarily associated with liner cargo trades, whilst the latter is mostly confined to tramps.

Liner cargo vessels may be cellular container ships, dual-purpose vessels with accommodation both for container and conventional cargo, ro/ro vessels, and conventional break bulk ships. The tramp vessel may vary from the general cargo vessel to modern bulk carriers of 90,000 tonnes. The latter may involve bulk dry or wet cargoes. Additionally there exists a significant volume of world trade moved by specialized – often purpose-built – bulk cargo tonnage on charter to industrial companies conveying raw material for industrial processing. This movement of cargo embraces oil tankers, LNGs, PCTCs, ro/ro vessels and bulk carriers of coking coal, iron ore and scrap metal, chemical carriers, bauxite vessels and timber carriers. Such services are often scheduled to meet an industrial production programme and operate from special purpose-built berths.

Growth in cruise markets has been considerable since 1995, especially with mega tonnage operating all year round to deep sea schedules. Each sailing schedule is prepared months in advance for each itinerary. Moreover, itineraries are continuously extended as cruise passengers' preferences change and ports invest in modern cruise liner berths to encourage passengers to spend time ashore. An increasing number of itineraries are 'round the world'. Many are linked to the fly–cruise concept, whereby passengers are flown to the port to join their cruise liner. The passenger ferry business remains formidable in services in the UK/Europe, including Scandinavia; Irish channel; the Baltic Sea and in the Mediterranean. Extensive services are found in British Columbia and in the Far East between the seaboards. Some more modern cruisers are also fast ferries. The larger cruise vessels are designed as multi-purpose tonnage with a speed of 24–6 knots, as compared with the fast ferry with a speed of up to 50 knots. The multi-purpose tonnage is often refurbished and a typical vessel was the *Pride of Kent*, operative on the Dover–Calais P&O Ferries route (Fig. 4.9), specification: built 1991, refurbished 2003, dwt 5,100, GT 30,635, passengers 2,000, crew 200, classification Lloyd's, machinery Sulzer diesel, bow thrusts/bladed propellers/flap rudders, cargo load 115 ro/ro units each of 15 m units or passenger cars, speed 21 knots, length 179.7 m, breadth 28.3 m, two cargo decks with ramps on upper deck, and bow door/inner bow door/ bridge front door, stern door.

With the cargo liner, the frequency of sailings is predetermined. Cargo traffic attracted to a liner service includes a wide variety of commodities and consumer goods, such as machinery, chemicals, foodstuffs, motor vehicles, etc. At certain times and in various trades, there is need for increased sailings to cater to seasonal traffic variations, and these are sometimes obtained by chartering additional tonnage. Chartering has the advantage of ensuring that the additional tonnage required is available only in peak periods and not throughout the year, when traffic considerations could not justify it. Surveys and overhauls are undertaken when practicable outside peak periods. In many container liner trades, vessels are on continuous survey to ensure the frequency and time spent in dry dock is minimized, a survey also applying to modern specialized bulk carriers.

A variety of specialized bulk carrier tonnage now exists. This tonnage includes oil tankers and ore carriers, very large crude carriers, liquefied natural gas carriers, bulk carriers, car carriers, etc. Such tonnage, sometimes under charter, requires extensive planning of schedules that maximize ship utilization. Schedules have to be integrated with production/supply areas at the point of cargo despatch and dovetailed in with industrial processes and/or storage capacity at destination ports. Many terminals are situated offshore to meet the excessive draught of these vessels, some of which exceed 65 m. The schedules and type of ship may permit cargo to be conveyed only in one direction, such as with crude carriers, entailing a return voyage in ballast perhaps at faster speed.

The tramp vessel has no regular sailing schedule, but plies between ports throughout the world, anywhere cargo is offered. The extent of advanced sailing schedules varies from months, weeks, days, or in extreme cases to a matter of hours. The spot market, depending on market and trading conditions, governs schedules.

These are various factors in formulation of sailing schedules:

1 The overall number of ships and their availability.
2 The volume, type and any special characteristics of the traffic.
3 Traffic fluctuations such as peak demands.
4 Maintenance of time margins where services connect. For example, with multi-modalism involving container tonnage and the dry port concept involving dedicated rail networks port turn-round time is crucial. This involves the containerized 'hub and spoke' system.
5 Availability of crew and cost, with reference to STCW applicable from Feb. 1997 and Jan. 2010.
6 Arrangements for relief measure in cases of emergency.
7 Climatic conditions. Some ports are ice-bound throughout certain periods of the year, which prevents any shipping calling at these particular ports.
8 Competition. This arises when conference and non-conference tonnage, for example, operate schedules alongside each other and compete in the same market place. This gives emphasis to the 'value added' benefit derived from the service provided to the shipper.
9 Time necessary for terminal duties at the port. This will include loading and/or discharging, customs procedure, bunkering, victualling, etc.
10 Voyage time.
11 The actual types of ship available and their size, incorporating the length, beam and draught, together with any special characteristics. For instance, some may be suitable for cruising. Other vessels, by virtue of their size, can only operate between ports that have deep-water berth facilities. Hence a large fleet of small vessels has more operating flexibility than a small fleet of large vessels restricted to a limited number of ports with adequate facilities to accommodate them. Another vessel may require special equipment for loading and discharging its cargo.
12 Any hostile activities taking place or envisaged in any particular waters.
13 Location of canals, such as the Suez and Panama as alternative routes.

14 Actual estimated voyage cost and expected traffic receipts.
15 Political actions such as flag discrimination, bilateral trade agreements causing unbalanced trading conditions.
16 General availability of port facilities and dock labour, and any tidal restrictions affecting times of access and departure.
17 Plying limits of individual ships, and for liner tonnage, any condition imposed by liner conference agreements.
18 With multi-purpose vessels conveying road haulage vehicles, passengers and accompanied cars, the number of cars and road haulage vehicles shipped can vary according to the time of year and/or period of the day.

A schedule in liner cargo trades should help the operator to increase his market share, having regard to the need to operate a profitable service. To the container operator the number of containers available for shipment, their type (40 ft reefer or 20 ft steel flat rack), have to be predetermined coupled with the number of containers and their specification to be discharged at a particular port. This data has to be reconciled with the ship specification. Variations in demand on trade vehicle or ferry operators can be made by using vehicle decks controlled by means of hydraulically operated ramps. Thus a vessel, which for one sailing may accommodate 50 cars and 30 large road haulage vehicles, can on another occasion carry as many as 300 cars exclusively.

Sailing schedules are based primarily on commercial considerations. Political, economic, operating and, to some extent, the technical issues all play a role as contributory factors. Container operation is multi-modal.

11.2 Problems presented to shipowners by fluctuations in trade and unequal balance of trade

Unused capacity in ocean transport is largely caused by secular or long-term fluctuations in world trade. This is further aggravated by the fact that shipping capacity, in common with all forms of transport, cannot be stored and is consumed immediately it is produced.

Unequal balance and fluctuation in trade are common to all forms of transport, and in shipping is particularly difficult to overcome. It is caused by economic, social or political factors. In all, there are nine main sets of circumstances in which unbalanced trading arises in shipping:

1 One of the largest streams of unbalanced trading is found in the shipment of the world's oil. Tankers convey the oil outwards from the port serving the oilfield, whilst the return voyage is in ballast.
2 An abnormal amount of cargo in a particular area can give rise to unequal trading. Such a glut tends to attract vessels to the area for freight, the majority of which often arrives in ballast. The situation may arise due to an abnormally heavy harvest. Conversely, a country may be in a state of famine or short of a particular commodity or foodstuff. This tends to attract

fully loaded vessels inward to the area, whilst on the outward voyage the ship is in ballast.

3   Government restrictions might be imposed on the import and/or export of certain goods. This may be necessary to protect home industries, restricting certain imports to help maintain full employment. Additionally, this restriction may be introduced due to an adverse balance of trade caused by a persistent excess of imports over exports. Such restrictions may be short term or permanent, depending on the circumstances in which they were introduced.

4   Climatic conditions such as ice formation restrict the safe navigation of rivers, canals and ports to certain periods of the year.

5   Passenger trades have seasonal fluctuations, which presents to the shipowner the problem of how to fill unused capacity during off-peak seasons.

6   Political influence can cause imbalance of trade. This can result from flag discrimination which in effect is pressure exerted by governments who wish to divert cargoes to ships of the national flag, regardless of those commercial considerations that normally govern routing of cargo. Flag discrimination can be exercised in a number of ways, including bilateral trade treaties, import licences and exchange control. Bilateral trade treaties include shipping clauses reserving either the whole of the trade between the two countries, or as much of it as possible, to the ships of the two flags. Brazil, Chile and India have all used the granting of import licences to ensure carriage of cargoes in ships of the national flag. Exchange control also offers endless means of making shipment in national vessels either obligatory or so commercially attractive that it has the same effect. In the interests of their national fleets Brazil, Colombia and India have used this method of control.

7   A number of countries, to sustain and develop their maritime fleet, legislate to influence cargoes towards their national flag fleet. Such fleets have low-cost crews and charge rates up to 30% below those of established liner cargo services. This circumstance particularly applies to imported goods operating through an agent who buys goods under EXW terms to obviate any payment to a foreign flag operator.

8   A major problem in fluctuations in trade arises in the container business involving the redistribution/repositioning of containers. This is examined in Chapter 16.

To counteract unequal trading, liner and tramp operators strive to get the maximum loaded capacity of the vessel and avoid ballast runs. A growing number of multi-purpose vessels permit operating flexibility and counter trade imbalance in liner trades.

The larger the fleet the better it is able to combat problems of unequal trading. The operator of a large fleet is generally in a number of different trades and is able to switch his vessels to trades where demand is greatest. Hence in particular trade 'A', due to seasonal variations, demand for shipping may be light, whilst in another trade 'B' the demand may be exceptionally heavy. The prudent operator would accordingly arrange to transfer some of his vessels from trade 'A' to trade 'B'.

A further method of combating unequal trading is to have dual-purpose vessels. A ship may be equipped to carry either oil or ore, or another vessel can convey either refrigerated or general cargo. Ships of this type, which are more expensive to build, are flexible to operate because the shipowner can vary the trades in which they ply.

The liner cargo containerized market is sensitive to the imbalance of trade and the need to reposition containers to meet market needs. Container operators are giving greater attention to designing/ developing container types that cope with unequal trading patterns. Sea Containers is a market leader in this area and has developed successfully the platform flats, flat-rack, Stakbed, Sea Cell and Sea Deck Sea Vent container types. Major container operators are under heavy pressure to continue to enhance services through quality and improved transit operations. Imbalance of trade remains a problem and any solution may lie with marshalling of containers. However, the current trend is to rationalize long-haul services and to develop the hub port concept, entailing fewer direct calls, and increased regional or inter-regional transhipment services. This 'hub and spoke' system should improve ship capacity utilization and reduce the impact of imbalance of trade.

The tramp operator obtains much of this trade through a shipbroker. His vessel is chartered by the shipper, who is responsible for providing the cargo on a voyage or time-charter basis. When the charter has been fixed, the prudent operator endeavours to obtain a further fixture. By adopting these tactics, coupled with the most favourable rate offered, the operator plans movement of his vessels as far in advance as possible and reduces ballast hauls to a minimum.

Since the 1980s, modern technology has developed various techniques – in particular modern processing and storage plant have permitted the seasonal nature of international bulk foodstuff distribution in certain trades to be spread over a longer period. This has helped counter the problem of unequal trading by extending the period over which such shipments are made, and has largely been facilitated by the range of hardware available in the international distribution system. This includes an ever-increasing range of container types, the computerized temperature controlled warehouses found at major trading ports such as Rotterdam, Singapore and Hong Kong, and major technical developments in the agricultural industry in all areas of their business.

Greater co-operation amongst carriers, consolidators, distributors, importers, exporters, railway operators, customs, road hauliers, governments, seaports and airports is developing international trade. It has facilitated the growing international network of multi-modalism and has encouraged forward planning amongst shippers and carriers to make the best use of available carrier capacity. This aids efficiency and reduces costs to acceptable market levels.

A major development is the expansion of the sea/air/ land bridge concept. Examples are to be found from Singapore and Dubai to Europe and the United States. Such development stimulates trade and brings markets closer together.

On the passenger side, however, the problem of unused capacity during off-seasons is largely solved by the organization of cruises, but in many markets such an opportunity does not exist. Cruising is now confined to purpose-built tonnage operating all the year round schedules.

11.3 Fleet planning

Fleet planning is an important area in ship operation and embraces the effective management of the fleet to produce optimum results, in particular with regard to markets and levels of profitability. It reflects the business plan objective strategy. Fleet planning embraces the effective use of company resources and is market driven. Budgeting features strongly.

The key to fleet planning is a market forecast that identifies the ship capacity required per port, cargo mix, throughout the 12 months, on a daily basis per month. A market forecast is likely to vary throughout the year and by direction: north–south traffic flows, for example. Problems may arise when the volume of imports or exports varies by port and cargo equipment/container type needs. In some trades in periods of recession, the voyage times may be extended and thereby need a smaller fleet to meet the trade on offer and likewise save on cost: smaller crews/lower bunker through slower speeds, and opportunity to re-engage the displaced tonnage on other routes and intensify the survey programme. In periods of acute depression, an opportunity arises to dispose of tonnage approaching its fifth survey, as the low freight yield would not produce this tonnage in a profitable operation. This situation arises in the tramp market of bulk cargo commodities. Voyage cost and the interface with revenue production indicate a profit/loss situation.

Fleet planning is usually programmed over two years, but sometimes five, and accords with the company business plan. It embraces the following areas: mission statement, trades/operational alliances, market forecast, ship investment – method of funding, voyage/time charter demise or non-demise, voyage planning, operation schedules, third party/outsourcing, and operating costs. Overall, the fleet planning budget will identify the income – freight/ passenger tariffs, the cost – voyage cost/port charges/capital cost and the profit/ loss. Budget performance reflects trading conditions and seasonal variations.

A number of factors significantly influence decision-making in operational fleet planning:

(a) Larger vessels tend to be more economical, but can be severely constrained by the availability of deep-water berths, such as VLCC and mega cruise liner.
(b) The tendency in container fleet development/operation is to build larger vessels 10,000/14,000 TEUs to keep pace with trade growth rather than opt for smaller tonnage and increase the sailing schedule frequency. Larger

vessels maintain existing schedules relative to the ships they displace and in so doing provide increased capacity in line with market demand.

(c) Sister vessels – built to the same specification – are easier to manage, having regard to speed, capacity, layout, age and flag. This is particularly relevant when a service disruption arises and vessels have to be rescheduled, because each vessel has similar capacity and speed.

(d) Smaller vessels give more operational flexibility. Not only do they have a wider range of port/berth/channel access but also the market can more easily fill a smaller vessel than a larger one, especially in times of economic depression.

(e) Schedules must be devised to make the best use of existing fleet loadability, noting particularly that costs are incurred whether the vessel is working or not.

(f) Management must decide whether to plan the fleet needs for peak, average, or trough demands.

(g) Management must evaluate whether to plan for annual growth of demand. The method of providing increased capacity must be decided: it may involve larger capacity vessels, chartering in new tonnage or faster schedules and/or quicker port turn-round time. In the liner cargo trade it may involve remodelling the service to involve fewer ports of call and/or developing the hub and spoke system. It could embrace an operating alliance whereby two container operators are allocated a number of slots on each sailing. For example, company A may allocate 15% of the container capacity to company B and company B allocate 25% of the capacity to company A.

(h) The growth in the hub and spoke system has brought a new era to containerized fleet management and its associated trades and its interface with port modernization. The hub port success is determined by the range of feeder services provided, particularly in the frequency of such services. The fleet planning management needs minimum 'down time' of the container from the time it is discharged from the hub vessel to the time it is loaded onto the feeder ship and vice versa. This ensures quick transits and no delay in the transhipment process at the hub port. There is a need for frequent services at the hub port and to operate dedicated schedules that link the hub and feeder networks and vice versa.

(i) The changing pattern of world trade is evident on the Suez and Panama Canal trade routes. At the entrances to the Panama, both from the Atlantic and Pacific, modern container terminals form hub ports where containers are transhipped to vessels about to transit the canal, or for 'onward shipment' for containers which have just transited the Panama Canal. A similar operation obtains in the new container terminal at Port Said at the northern end of the Suez Canal entrance.

(j) The oil tanker trades feature increasingly the shuttle service. The mega-tanker tonnage VLCC serve the oil terminals; in some trades oil is distributed to other maritime oil terminals in smaller tanker vessels.

(k) When fleet planning the introduction of the ISPS code and Maritime Labour Convention must be taken into consideration.

Fleet planning is focused on ship management's control of costs and then to align them to market demand.

11.4 Interface between fleet planning and ship survey programme

A tendency recently has been the minimizing of the time vessels spend in shipyards undergoing their ship survey. The IMO's recognition of the harmonization of ship survey programmes has contributed to improved ship productivity. Moreover, the trend towards having an increasing volume of pre-survey work undertaken while the vessel is operational is both economical and less disruptive, as it results in a shorter period during which the vessel is withdrawn from service.

An increase in third party ship management has enabled shipowners to have more competitive shipyard survey tenders well in advance of survey dates, facilitating sailing programme preparation. Fleet manager work closely with the marine engineer department/third party ship managers to realize the most acceptable survey programme compatible with market forecast/trading conditions and ship specification. Any need to 'charter in' tonnage should be kept to a minimum.

11.5 Relative importance of speed, frequency, reliability, cost and quality of sea transport

There are five factors that influence the nature of a shipping service: speed, frequency, reliability, cost and quality.

Speed is important to the shipper who desires to market his goods against an accurate arrival date and eliminate banking charges for opening credits. Selecting the fastest service available and obtaining minimum intervals between ordered and despatch of goods and delivery at their destination can reduce these charges. Speed is particularly important to manufacturers of consumer goods: it avoids expense and the risk of obsolescence to a retailer ordering large stocks. In the case of certain commodities, especially fresh fruit and semi-frozen products and fashionable goods, a regular and fast delivery is vital to successful trading. The need for speed is perhaps most felt in long-distance trades where voyage times may be appreciably reduced and the shipper given the benefit of an early delivery and frequent stock replenishment. These various needs are fully recognized by the liner operator, to whom speed is expensive, both in terms of initial expenditure on marine engines and actual fuel cost. His aim is to provide a vessel of the maximum speed and at minimum cost which will fulfil the shipper's requirements. These aspects have been the major driving force in logistic container services operating within global supply chain management.

Speed is not so important in the world tramp trades where generally lower-value cargoes are being carried and where many trades are moving under programmed stockpile arrangements. This category includes coal, mineral ores, timber, bulk grain, and other cargoes normally in shiploads and having a relatively low value: these demand a low transport cost. An example is iron ore from Australia to China for its steel industry.

Frequency of service is most important when goods can only be sold in small quantities at frequent intervals. Here the liner operator will phase his sailings to meet shippers' requirements, whilst the vessels must be suitable in size, speed and equipment for the cargoes offered. The shipper of perishable fruit and vegetables also relies on frequent, fast ships to obtain maximum benefit from seasonal crops. Fashionable goods and replacement spares also benefit from frequent service. Again, it is logistically focused on 'value added'.

To the tramp charterer, frequency of sailings is not of paramount importance, he must not allow his stocks to run down but have a margin within which to operate safely and buy and ship when conditions suit his business.

Reliability is an essential requirement to the shipper engaged in the usually multi-modal liner service, in which goods are sold against expiry dates on letters of credit and import licences. Furthermore, the liner shipper relies upon the operator to deliver his traffic in good condition. To the shipper, therefore, reliability means the vessel sailing and arriving at the advertised time; the shipowner will look after the cargo during pre-shipment, throughout the voyage and after discharge on carriage; and, finally, the operator can be relied upon to give adequate facilities at the terminal, usually inland (ICD/ CFS) and at his offices to enable satisfactory completion of appropriate documents and other formalities. Prestige in the liner trade goes with the reliance the shipper can place on any particular multi-modal service. The mega container service has online cargo tracking for the shipper to identify the location of his cargo during the voyage.

The tramp shipper marketing goods of relatively low value must seek the lowest possible transport *cost*, as the freight percentage of the total value may have a direct bearing on the saleability of the commodity. He has therefore a prime interest in the availability of tramp shipping space at any particular time by reason of the fact that freight and chartering rates reflect variations in supply and demand. In markets with plenty of vessels the shipper is able to charter at a rate only marginally above the operating costs of the vessel. Conversely, he may be forced to pay more, though there is a limiting factor in the price of the commodity at the point of sale and the rate the shipowner may receive. In these conditions operators of the most efficient ships earn premium returns. In weak market conditions their relative efficiency ensures a small profit; others just break even. Where the market is strong, proven reliability can ensure that the services of such vessels are sought before other opportunities present themselves.

In the liner trades freight costs are more stable and controlled; the shipowner is able to hold the rate at a fair level to show a profit margin, but must be careful not to hold rates so high that they price the goods out of the market; at this point there is need for joint consultation between shipper and carrier and other parties to the multi-modal operator. It can be argued that the liner shipper should pay a higher transport charge to compensate for expensive-to-run liner services.

Quality of service is especially important in the competitive world of shipping and international trade. The service provided must be customer-oriented, emphasis being placed on providing a reliable service and handling goods and documentation efficiently.

The foregoing five factors reflect also the increasingly discerning needs of the shipper. Today all these factors are essential for international trade to operate under conditions of business confidence, competition and market/product development. Liner cargo services must be competitive in all areas of the business, a situation stimulated by the development of logistics in multi-modalism. Many companies operate on the 'just in time' concept and review regularly their international distribution network on the basis of the value added concept: the value added to a product by using a particular distribution network against the total cost of the service.

11.6 Indivisible loads

A growing market recently is movement of indivisible loads, e.g. a transformer or engineering plant with a total weight of up to 250 tonnes.

Such a product requires special arrangements. The freight forwarder specializing in such work usually has a project-forwarding department to handle these transits. Points relevant to the international movement of indivisible loads are:

(a) The ports of departure, destination and any transhipment areas need to be checked out to ensure they can handle such a shipment, especially regarding the availability of heavy lift equipment.
(b) The shipowner needs to have a plan and specification of the shipment, to evaluate the stowage and handling arrangments, as well as to identify the weight distribution.
(c) The transport of indivisible loads to and from the ports requires special planning of route and timescale. Usually such goods may only move at night subject to police permission and escort.
(d) The rates are usually assessed on a cost plus profit basis. The cost can be heavy for any heavy-lift equipment and for special arrangements to transport the goods overland to and from the ports. Freight forwarders work closely with the correspondent agent in the destination country. Transhipment costs can be much reduced if a MAFI type six-axle trailer is used, as in the ro/ro tonnage.

The advantages of the indivisible load shipment to the shipper/ buyer/importer include: lower overall transport cost; quicker transit; much reduced site assembly cost; less risk of damage in transit; lower insurance premium; less technical aid, i.e. staff resources, required by the buyer, because there is no extensive site assembly work; equipment tested and fully tested operationally in the factory before despatch; no costly site assembly work; less risk of malfunctioning equipment arising; and earlier commissioning of the equipment which in turn results in the quicker productive use of the equipment with profitable benefits to the buyer overall.

11.7 Ship and port security: ISPS Code and port state control

Internationally, one of the most important developments in maritime security was the 1 July 2004 International Ship and Port Facility Security Code (ISPS Code). In December 2002 the IMO adopted the ISPS Code as part of an additional chapter to the 1974 Safety of Life at Sea Convention (SOLAS). The new code enhances maritime security on board ships and at ship/port interfaces. It is mandatory for ships to comply with the ISPS Code. The code contains detailed security-related requirements for governments, port authorities and shipping companies (Part A), together with a series of guidelines, about how to meet these requirements, in a second, non-mandatory section (Part B). The IMO conference resolved to add weight to these amendments by encouraging application of the measures to ships and port facilities not covered by the code.

The new security regime imposes a wide range of responsibilities on governments, port facilities and shipowning and operating companies. These are the main obligations in the three sectors:

(a) *Responsibilities of contracting governments.* The principal responsibility of the contracting states under SOLAS Chapter XI–2 and Part A of the code is to determine and set security levels. These include (a) approval of Ship Security Plans, (b) issuance of International Ship Security Certificates (ISSC) after verification, (c) carrying out and approval of Port Facility Security Assessments, (d) approval of Port Facility Security plans, (e) determination of port facilities which need to designate a Port Facility Security Officer, and (f) an exercise of control and compliance measures including procedures for port state control procedures. Governments may delegate certain responsibilities to Recognized Security Organizations (RSO) outside government.

(b) *Responsibilities of vessel owning and/or operating companies.* Vessel-owning and/or operating companies have a range of responsibilities, the key one being to ensure that each of its vessels obtains an International Ship Security Certificate (ISSC) from a flag state or an appropriate RSO, such as a classification society, e.g. Lloyd's Register of Shipping. To obtain an ISSC the following measures must be taken: (i) designation of a Company Security Officer (CSO), (ii) carrying out Ship Security Assessments (SSA) and development of Ship Security Plans (SSP), (iii) designation of a Ship Security Officer (SSO), and (iv) training, drill and exercises.

A number of special mandatory requirements in SOLAS Chapters V, X–1 and X–2 apply to ships and create additional responsibilities for vessel-owning companies and for governments. These specially include (v) Automatic Identification system (AIS), (vi) Ship Identification Number (SIN), (vii) Ship Security Alert System (SSAS), and (viii) Continuous Synopsis Record (CSR).

(c) *Responsibilities of port facilities.* Depending on size, there may be, within the legal and administrative limits of any individual port, several or even a considerable number of port facilities for the purposes of the ISPS code. These include (i) Port Facility Security Plans (PFSP), based on the Port Facility Security Assessment carried out, and upon completion, approved by the relevant national government, a Port Facility Security Plan, (ii) a Port Facility Security Officer (PFSO) – for each port facility, a Security Officer must be designated, and (iii) training drills and exercises.

The ISPS Code affects port state control facilities, e.g. the IMO 1999 resolution A.882(21) and the port facility (item (c) above) embracing the control and compliance, SOLAS Chapter X1–2 and Part A of the ISPS Code. When a ship is at a port or is proceeding to a port of a contracting government, the contracting government has the right, under the provisions of regulation X1–2/9, to exercise various control and compliance measures with respect to that ship. Ships may be subject to port state control inspections, as well as to additional control measures if the contracting government exercising the control and compliance measures has reason to believe that the security of the ship, or the port facilities that have served it, has been compromised.

The relevant authorities may request information regarding the ship, its cargo, passengers and ship's personnel prior to the ship's entry into the port, and there may be circumstances in which the entry into port could be denied. All of this information is part of the inward clearance procedure. The list of documents arising from port state control includes those relating to a vessel inspected by a government agency at a port. It is stressed that all certificates carried 'on board' must be originals. The government agency in the event of regulations being compromised will detain the ship and prevent it from trading.

Port state control arose in 1995. Recognizing a need for a single document to facilitate the work of maritime administrations and Port State Control Offices, the IMO conducted a comprehensive review. This resulted in adoption of resolution A.787(19), which provides guidance to port state control officers on the conduct of inspections, in order to promote consistency worldwide and to harmonize criteria for deciding on deficiencies of a ship, its equipment and its crew, as well as the application of control procedures. Developments in the period since 1995 have prompted proposals for amendments to resolution A.787(19) – for example, to take the ISM Code and 1969 Tonnage Convention into account; to provide for suspension of inspections and to define procedures for the rectification of deficiencies and release. After consideration by the relevant sub-committees of the Maritime Safety Committee and the Marine Environment Protection Committee, the IMO Assembly in 1999 adopted amendments by resolution A.882(21). More recently the Port State Control has established a strong interface with the ISPS Code. It is likely port state controls will become more stringent.

The ISPS Code has an equal responsibility on both the ship and port. The contracting government has to select the port facilities, a Port Facility Security Officer (PFSO) has to be appointed and trained, a Port Facility Security Assessment (PFSA) has to be made and agreed by the contracting government, and a Port Facility Security Plan (PFSP) must be produced based on the recommendations of the PFSA. The plan has then to be implemented and tested by the contracting government, and if all is correct, the port is issued with a certificate of compliance.

As for shipping executives' and Master's obligations, each company must appoint a Company Security Officer (CSO) personally responsible for implementing the code. It is very similar to the designated person required under the International Safety Management (ISM) code. In those companies which own or manage a large number of ships, several CSOs may be appointed for different classes or ships, although there is usually one CSO who, in Orwellian terms, is 'more equal than the others'. This ensures uniformity throughout the fleet. The CSOs must be trained. On each ship there must be a Ship Security Assessment (SSA), carried out by a competent and credible expert – then, based on the SSA, the Ship Security Plan (SSP) is produced and implemented. A designated officer called the Ship Security Officer (SSO) is responsible for implementation of the SSP. The SSO must be trained for specific security responsibilities, as must the rest of the crew. Once the SSP has been in operation for about two months, a surveyor from a Recognized Security Organization (RSO), often a classification society, comes on board, verifies the correctness of the SSA and the implementation of the SSP, and if satisfied issues the International Ship Security Certificate (ISSC). This document confirms the contracting government/flag state's decision and certifies the shipowner's compliance with all mandatory security legislation.

Other documentation to be carried on board a vessel include: a Continuous Synopsis Record giving the history of the ship; a declaration of security to demonstrate port and ship co-operation; certification of training exercises carried out; certification that different categories of security procedures have been carried out if changes in the threat levels have been required; certification of alternative security agreements have been made; certification of audits and reviews; certification of the seafarers' suitability of employment and their biometric identification; certification of the ship's security alert system; and certification concerning the ship's identification and long-term tracking procedures.

In addition, the Master will have another set of papers concerning the security of his cargo. Vessels going to the United States are especially subject to security investigation by the US's customs agencies. This set of papers relates to the Container Security Initiative (CSI), which checks out the integrity of the container from the original point of 'stuffing' through the complex system of transport, including the ship, to its final destination.

The CSI goals establish criteria for identifying high risk containers, to pre-screen containers before they are shipped to the United States, to use non-intrusive technology to pre-screen high-risk containers, and to develop smart and secure containers. It was devised by the US customs service in consultation with a number of major trade partners pending implementation of two schemes: the CSI and the Customs–Trade Partnership Against Terrorism (C–TPAT). The IMO in co-operation with the WCO seeks more security on ships.

The stringent security measures under the ISPS code results in increased paperwork and stringent security searches of cargo, stores, unaccompanied baggage and of people boarding the ship. Sensitive areas, such as the wheelhouse, rear steering gear room, control stations, spaces containing dangerous goods, paint stores, water tanks, cargo pumps, air conditioning systems and crew accommodation, have to be designated 'Restricted Areas' and have to be locked to deny 'unauthorized access'.

There is concern to find the right balance to keep strategically important shipping lanes secure and open to international maritime traffic, thereby ensuring world trade flows are not interrupted. The IMO is seeking ways for authorized agencies to collaborate while observing the sovereign rights of the coastal states concerned.

One of the world's strategic vital shipping channels is the Malacca Strait. It is 800 km long, and in places this narrow link between the Indian Ocean and South China Sea is an artery through which runs a huge proportion of global trade. Tankers and bulk carriers move vast quantities of oil, coal, iron ore and grain to the manufacturing centres of South East and North East Asia, while high value manufactured goods, carried in millions of containers, pour back through the same outlet to serve world consumer markets. Some 50,000 ship movements, carrying as much as one-quarter of the world's commerce and half the world's oil, pass through the Malacca and Singapore straits each year. Any serious disruption to this traffic through this channel would have a widespread and far reaching detrimental effect on world trade. It is a location that is particularly vulnerable to operational and navigational incidents and to external threats posed by pirates and armed robbers. South East Asia has the highest number of pirate attacks globally. There is a possibility that terrorists could resort to pirate-style tactics, or even work in concert with pirates, to harm shipping, crews and trade.

Through co-operation – led by the bilateral states of the Malacca and Singapore straits, and including other user states and stakeholders (such as industry organizations) and by applying various means of state-of-the-art technology (including the utilization of the Marine Electronic Highway project, specially designed by the IMO for the Malacca Strait) – this strategic lane should continue to remain open to international navigation and serve seaborne trade and regional and global economies.

12 Bills of lading

When a shipowner, or other authorized person, e.g. an agent, agrees to carry goods by water, or agrees to furnish a ship for the purpose of carrying goods in return for a sum of money, such a contract is called a contract of affreightment and the sum to be paid is called freight. Shipment of the goods is usually evidenced in a document called a bill of lading. Once a 'shipped on board' endorsement has been added (if required), it becomes a receipt for goods shipped on the nominated vessel.

The bill of lading is a receipt for goods shipped on board a ship and is signed by the person (or his agent) who contracts to carry them, and states the terms on which the goods were delivered to and received by the ship. It is not the actual contract, which is inferred from the action of shipper or shipowner in delivering or receiving the cargo, but forms sound evidence of the terms of the contract. In most cases it is the contract. The fact of its not being issued does not mean that no contract exists, as a contract commences at the time of booking and the subsequent issue of the bill merely confirms this and provides evidence of the agreed contract.

12.1 Carriage of Goods by Sea Acts 1971 and 1992

Two Acts have an important part in the role and function of the bill of lading, the Carriage of Goods by Sea Act 1971, which succeeded the Carriage of Goods by Sea Act 1924, and the Carriage of Goods by Sea Act 1992, which repealed the Bills of Lading Act 1855.

The bill of lading provides evidence of a contract of carriage between carrier and shipper, under which carrier and shipper promise that the goods will be carried from the port of loading and safely delivered to the port of discharge. During the voyage ownership of the goods will usually be transferred from the original seller to the ultimate receiver, who will take delivery of the goods from the ship. There may in exceptional cases be 100 or more buyers who (or whose banks) will pay for the goods and then receive payment from the next buyer in the chain. During this process the goods are not in the possession of any of the parties. They are, or should be, safely on board the ship, crossing the ocean. Neither the buyer of an unascertained portion of a bulk nor an endorsee after discharge have rights against the carrier.

The defect at the heart of the Bills of Lading Act 1855 was the link between property in the goods and the right to sue on the bill of lading contract. Under the 1992 Act this was removed.

The 1992 Act provides that any lawful holder of the bill of lading has the right of suit but that *only* he/she has that right (thus preventing more than one claimant for the same breach of contract). If, as can arise, someone other than the holder of the bill of lading has sustained the actual loss, the holder must account for the damages to the person who has suffered the actual loss.

The Act also recognizes the rights of suit of someone who became holder of the bill of lading after discharge of the cargo, provided that he did so under arrangements made before that date (thereby preventing trading in bills relating to goods known to be damaged – in effect, trading in causes of action).

The Act recognizes the rights of parties interested in two forms of shipping documents in common use today but which no longer appear within the 1855 Act. The consignee under a sea waybill and the holder of a ship's delivery order will both have rights to sue on the contract in question. It will affect the P&I clubs who can no longer take unmeritorious defences based on lack of title to sue. Those involved in the bulk commodity trades gained rights they did not previously have, as have consignees named in a waybill. Banks which finance international trade are now able to enforce the bill of lading rights in their own name.

International conventions set out minimum terms and conditions out of which carriers cannot contract to the detriment of merchants. Carriers can accept terms more favourable to merchants. Generally, international conventions aim to regulate international carriage and, in most cases, national carriage is allowed freedom of contract, though in most countries there are standard trading conditions that usually apply.

The Hague Rules were agreed in Brussels in 1924. They govern liability for loss of or damage to goods under a bill of lading and carried by sea. They are officially known as the 'International Convention for the Unification of Certain Rules relating to bills of lading' and were made effective in the UK by the Carriage of Goods by Sea Act 1924.

The Hague Rules apply to all exports from any nation which ratified the Rules. This is an almost universal application wherever they have not been superseded by the Hague–Visby Rules, either by the application of law or by contractual incorporation into the terms and conditions of the relevant bill of lading.

The main features of the Hague Rules are as follows:

1   Minimum terms under which a carrier may offer for the carriage of all goods other than live animals, non-commercial goods including personal and household effects, experimental shipments and goods carried on deck where the bill of lading is claused to indicate such carriage.
2   The carrier has to exercise due diligence to provide a seaworthy vessel at the voyage commencement, and this cannot be delegated. Additionally,

the goods must be cared for adequately during the transit. Provided the carrier complies with these requirements, if loss or damage still occurs, he can rely on a number of stated defences. The majority of these requirements elaborate on the general principle that the carrier is only liable for loss or damage caused by his own negligence, or that of his servants, agents or subcontractors. However, the carrier remains protected in three situations where the loss or damage has been caused by negligence as detailed below:

(a) negligence in navigation;
(b) negligence in the management of the vessel (as opposed to the care of the cargo);
(c) fire, unless the actual fault or privity of the carrier.

Before the Hague–Visby Rules superseded the Hague Rules liability in the UK was £100 per package. Other nations set alternative limits: United States US $500 and Japan Y100,000.

In 1968 an international conference revised the Hague Rules, primarily those relating to limitation. The amended rules, the Brussels Protocol, are more popularly known as the Hague–Visby Rules and are incorporated into the UK Carriage of Goods by Sea Act 1971.

Limitation was amended to provide a weight/package alternative, and originally limits were set in Poincaré francs – a fictitious currency. This proved unacceptable and, accordingly, the 1979 Special Drawing Rights (SDR) Protocol was adopted in 1984. In 2003 there were 30 member countries, primarily European and including the UK. Limitation in terms of SDRs is now the greater of SDR 666.67 per package or unit, or SDR 2 per kilo.

The Brussels Protocol which embraced the Hague–Visby Rules became operative in 1977 and has 38 contracting member states including the UK, Japan and some European countries. The Visby amendment applies to all bills of lading in the following situations:

(a) The port of shipment is in a ratifying nation.
(b) The place of issue of the bill of lading is in a ratifying nation.
(c) The bill of lading applies Hague–Visby Rules contractually.

At a maritime lawyers' international conference in 1990 greater uniformity of the law of carriage of goods by sea was debated and resolved to maintain the Hague–Visby Rules without amendment.

A 1978 international conference in Hamburg adopted a new set of rules, the Hamburg Rules. These radically alter the liability shipowners have to bear for loss or damage to goods in the courts of those nations where the rules apply. The main differences between the new rules and the old Hague–Visby Rules are given below:

1. The carrier will be liable for loss, damage or delay to the goods occurring whilst in his charge unless he proves that he, his servants or agents took all measures that could reasonably be required to avoid the occurrence and its consequences. The detailed list of exceptions set out in the Hague and Hague–Visby Rules is no longer available to the carrier. In particular, the carrier is no longer exonerated from liability arising from errors in navigation, management of the ship or fire.

2. The carrier is liable for delay in delivery if 'the goods have not been delivered at the port of discharge provided for under the contract of carriage within the time expressly agreed upon or in the absence of such agreement within the time which it could be reasonable to require of a diligent carrier having regard to the circumstances of the case'.

3. The dual system for calculating the limit of liability, either by reference to package or weight as found in the Hague–Visby Rules, has been readopted, but the amounts have been increased by 25% to SDR 835 per package and SDR 2.5 per kilo. The liability for delay is limited to an equivalent to two and half times the freight payable for the goods delayed, but not exceeding the total freight payable for the whole contract under which the goods were shipped. In no situation would the aggregate liability for both loss/damage and delay exceed the limit for loss/damage.

4. The Hamburg Rules cover all contracts for the carriage by sea other than charter parties, whereas the Hague/Hague–Visby Rules apply only where a bill of lading is issued. The Hamburg Rules are therefore applicable to waybills, consignment notes, etc.

5. The Hamburg Rules cover shipment of live animals and deck cargo, whereas the Hague/ Hague–Visby Rules may not.

6. The Hamburg Rules apply both to imports and exports to/from a signatory nation, whereas the Hague/Hague–Visbyy Rules apply only to exporters.

The Hamburg Rules became operative in 1992 and involved the requisite minimum 20 nations. In 2005 the total was 30 nations, primarily featuring African nations but only four European states. The convention is the United Nations Convention on the Carriage of Goods by Sea 1978 (Hamburg Rules). The adoption of the Hamburg Rules destroys the uniformity currently obtaining between the Hague and Hague–Visby Rules, thereby creating a third force in the market.

The liability of the carrier under any of the above sea carriage conventions is always subject to the overriding application of the provisions of the Merchant Shipping Acts relating, as well as other things, to limitation of liability. The current UK Act is the Merchant Shipping Act 1995, which implemented the 1976 International Convention on Limitation of Liability for Maritime Claims (LLMC). The 1976 convention has been ratified and acceded to by 38 nations (1 January 2003).

A 1996 Protocol to the 1976 LLMC was agreed in 1996, as part of the HNS diplomatic conference in London, to update liability levels. The new limits are as follows:

(a) In respect of claims for loss of life or personal injury:
  (i)   SDR 1 million for a vessel with tonnage not exceeding 300 tons.
  (ii) SDR 2 million for a vessel with tonnage not exceeding 2,000 tons.
  (iii) For a vessel with tonnage in excess thereof, in addition to that mentioned in (ii): for each ton from 2,001 to 30,000 tons, SDR 800; for each ton from 30,001 to 70,000 tons, SDR 600; for each ton in excess of 70,000 tons, SDR 400.

(b) In respect of any other claims:
  (i)   SDR 500,000 for a vessel with tonnage not exceeding 300 tons.
  (ii) SDR 1 million for a vessel with tonnage not exceeding 2,000 tons.
  (iii) For a vessel with tonnage in excess, therefore, in addition to that mentioned in (ii): for each ton from 2,001 to 30,000 tons, SDR 400; for each ton from 30,001 to 70,000 tons, SDR 300; for each ton in excess of 70,000 tons, SDR 200.

By article 15 of the Convention, contracting states are allowed to make alternative provisions for vessels of under 300 tons. The UK has availed itself of this concession to provide for increased limits instead of the SDR 166,667 for loss of life and personal injury, and SDR 83,333 for other claims under the 1976 Convention. These figures are increased to SDR 1 million and SDR 500,000 respectively under the 1996 protocol. Under the Merchant Shipping (Convention on Limitation of Liability for Maritime Claims) Amendment Order 1998, the protocol limits will replace the Convention limits when the protocol enters into force internationally. By 2003 the 1996 protocol had been ratified or acceded to by 12 nations. Most other nations now apply earlier conventions, with lower levels of limitation and a 'fault and privity' approach to the right limit, whilst others use the basis of the value of the ship plus freight earned at the end of the voyage, as with the United States.

12.2 Salient points of a bill of lading

The salient points incorporated in a bill of lading can be conveniently listed as follows:

1 The name of the shipper (usually the exporter).
2 The name of the carrying vessel.
3 Full description of the cargo (provided it is not bulk cargo) including any shipping marks, individual package numbers in the consignment, contents, cubic measurement, gross weight, etc.

4 The marks and numbers identifying the goods.
5 Port of shipment or dry port/CFS.
6 Port of discharge or dry port/CFS.
7 Full details of freight, including when and where it is to be paid – whether freight paid or payable at destination.
8 Name of consignee or, if the shipper is anxious to withhold the consignee's name, shipper's order.
9 The terms of the contract of carriage.
10 The date the goods were received for shipment and/or loaded on the vessel.
11 The name and address of the notified party (the person to be notified on arrival of the shipment, usually the buyer).
12 Number of bills of lading signed on behalf of the Master or his agent, acknowledging receipt of the goods.
13 The signature of the ship's Master or his agent and the date.

Below are clauses found in a bill of lading for Port to Port, or Combined Transport, or a mix, Port to Port at one end with Combined Transport at the other:

(a) *Shipper*. Name of the party with whom the contract of carriage has been concluded by the carrier. This may be the shipper or shipper's freight forwarder.
(b) *Consignee or order*. Four options:

    (i) With the name of the consignee unqualified.
    (ii) *'to order'*. In this situation the shipper is also the consignee and it is to him that the carrier must look for delivery instructions involving three options – by specific endorsement on the bill of lading; by attaching authorized delivery instructions on the shipper's stationery; or by blank endorsement on the bill of lading and passing the document to the consignee.
    (iii) *'to the order of'* a named party who must give delivery instructions.
    (iv) *'to bearer'*. This is equivalent to an 'order' bill blank endorsed. Bills of lading endorsed 'Order' and a 'Bearer' are bearer documents and the carrier must make delivery to whoever presents them unless he has reason to suspect fraud.

(c) *Notify party/address*. The name of the party to whom the carrier will send the arrival notification. However, the responsibility to monitor the transit and take delivery rests with the merchant.
(d) *Vessel and voyage number/Port of loading/port of discharge*. If the place of receipt/place of delivery are blank, the bill is a Port to Port contract, so the ports of loading and discharge are the points of commencement and termination.
(e) *Place of receipt/Place of delivery*. This is valid for combined transport indicating where contract of carriage commences and terminates.

(f) *Undermentioned particulars as declared by the shipper but not acknow-ledged by the carrier.* The main details shown in the bill of lading are commercial details provided and required by the shipper for commercial purposes, the accuracy of which the shipper warrants and for which the carrier accepts no responsibility.

(g) *Total number or containers/packages received by the carrier.* This is the tally which the carrier acknowledges and for which he accepts responsi-bility. In the case of FCL goods, it will be one or a number of container(s) and, in the case of LCL goods it will be a tally of pieces or packages. In the case of multiple bills of lading FCLS it will be 'one of . . . part cargoes in the container'.

(h) *Movement.* This information is incorporated to provide details of the movement of both ends of the sea transit.

(i) *Freight payable at.* This is an indication of where the shipper has told the carrier that he wishes the freight to be paid. It is not an undertaking by the carrier that freight is only payable at this place and if the carrier is unable to collect freight here, he may exercise his lien for freight to refuse delivery until someone pays the freight or require the shipper to pay it, notwithstanding that delivery has been effected.

(j) *Incorporation clause.* This is the clause on the face of the bill of lading which links the terms and conditions of the reverse of the bill of lading and in the tariff with the details set out on the face into one contract.

(k) *Number of original Bills of Lading.* Bills of lading are usually issued in sets of two or three originals together with a number of non-negotiable copies for office/filing use. As more than one original exists, any one of which carries title to the goods, the only way the buyer can be sure of title is to ensure that he has all the originals – not copies of originals. Hence all bills must indicate how many bills have been issued.

(l) *Place and date of issue.* Place where the bill of lading was issued and date thereof. This date may be any date after the goods have been received for carriage, but not before. This therefore is a cargo receipt.

(m) *Signature clause.* Above the authenticating signature, the provision in the incorporation clause for one original probably needing to be surrendered to secure delivery is reinforced with the provision that after delivery has taken place against one original bill, all other originals of the same tenure become worthless. A full set of originals is not necessary to secure delivery, one only will do.

Electronic trading is now beginning to dominate, as demonstrated by BOLERO, a system of paperless trading using electronic bills of lading. This is explained later in the book.

12.3 Types of bills of lading

There are several types and forms of bills of lading. In combined or multi-modal transport they are called transport documents.

(a) Shipped bill of lading

Under the Carriage of Goods by Sea Act 1971 (Hague–Visby Rules), the shipper can demand that the shipowner supplies bills of lading to prove that the goods have been shipped. For this reason, most bill of lading forms are already printed as shipped bills and commence with the wording: 'Shipped in apparent good order and condition'. It confirms the goods are actually on board the vessel.

This is the most satisfactory type of receipt and the shipper prefers such a bill to remove doubt about the goods being on board and, in consequence, avoid disputes with bankers or consignee. This facilitates earliest financial settlement of the export sale.

(b) Received bill of lading

This arises where the word 'shipped' does not appear on the bill of lading. This received bill of lading confirms that the goods are now in the custody of the shipowner. The cargo may be in his dock, warehouse/transit shed or even inland, such as dry port/CFS/ ICD, etc. The bill has, therefore, not the same meaning as a 'shipped' bill and the buyer under a CIF or CFR contract need not accept such a bill for ultimate financial settlement through the bank unless provision has been made in the contract. Forwarding agents will invariably avoid handling 'received bills' for their clients, except in special circumstances.

(c) Through Transport Document (TTD)

It may be necessary to employ two or more carriers to get goods to its destination. The on-carriage may be either by a second vessel or by a different form of transport (for example, to destinations in the interior of Canada). In such cases it would be complicated and more expensive if the shipper has to arrange on-carriage himself by employing an agent at the point of transhipment. Shipping companies, therefore, issue bills of lading to cover the whole transit, the shipper dealing with the first carrier only. This Through Transport Document enables a through rate to be quoted and with the development of containerization is increasingly popular. The carrier who issues the TTD acts as a principal only during the carriage on his own vessel(s) and solely as an agent at all other times. Therefore, the liabilities and responsibilities are spread over several carriers and the carriage. The fact that a bill of lading bears the wording 'Combined Transport Document/Bill of Lading', is no guarantee that it is so. Hence, it is important that the terms and conditions of the document are examined.

(d) Stale bill of lading

It is advisable for the bill of lading to be available at the port of destination before the goods arrive or, failing this, at the same time. Bills presented to the consignee or his bank after the goods are due at the port are said to be stale. A cargo cannot normally be delivered by the shipowner without the bill of lading, and the late arrival of this obligatory document may have undesirable consequences, such as warehouse rent, etc.

(e) Groupage and house bills of lading

A growth sector of the containerized market is the movement of compatible consignments from individual consignors to various consignees, usually situated in the same destination (country/area), and forwarded as one overall consignment. The goods are consolidated into a full container load and the shipping line issues a groupage bill of lading to the forwarder. This is the ocean bill of lading and shows a number of consignments of groupage of a certain weight and cubic measurement in a cargo manifest form. The forwarder issues a house bill of lading cross-referring to the ocean bill of lading. It is merely a receipt for the cargo and does not have the same status as the bill of lading issued by the shipowner. Shippers choosing to use a house bill of lading should clarify with the bank if it is acceptable for letter of credit purposes, and should ensure it is stipulated as acceptable before the credit is opened. Advantages of groupage include: less packing; lower insurance premiums; usually quicker transits; less risk of damage and pilferage; and lower rates when compared with such cargo being despatched as an individual parcel/consignment.

(f) Transhipment bill of lading

This type is usually issued by shipping companies when there is no direct service between two ports but when the shipowner is prepared to tranship the cargo at an intermediate port at his expense.

(g) Clean bill of lading

Each bill of lading states: 'in apparent good order and condition', which refers to the cargo. If this statement is not modified by the shipowner, the bill of lading is regarded as 'clean' or 'unclaused'. By issuing clean bills of lading, the shipowner admits his full liability under the law and his contract for the cargo described in the bill. This type is much favoured by banks for financial settlement purposes.

(h) Claused bill of lading

If the shipowner does not agree with any of the statements made in the bill of lading he may add a clause to this effect, causing the bill of lading to be termed as 'unclean', 'foul' or 'claused'. There are many recurring types of such clauses including: inadequate packaging; unprotected machinery; second-hand cases; wet or stained cartons; damaged crates; cartons missing, etc. The clause 'shipped on deck at owner's risk' may thus be considered to be claused under this heading. This type of bill of lading is usually unacceptable to a bank.

(i) Negotiable bill of lading

If the words 'or his or their assigns' are contained in the bill of lading, it is negotiable. There are, however, variations in this terminology, for example the word 'bearer' may be inserted or another party stated in the preamble to the phrase. Bills of lading may be negotiable by endorsement or transfer.

(j) Non-negotiable bill of lading

When the words 'or his or their assigns' are deleted from the bills of lading, the bill is regarded as non-negotiable. The effect of this deletion is that the consignee (or other named party) cannot transfer the property or goods by transfer of the bills. This particular type is seldom found and will normally apply when goods are shipped on a non-commercial basis, such as household effects.

(k) Container bill of lading

Containers are now a major factor in international shipping, and container bills of lading are becoming more common. Container bills of lading cover the goods from port to port or from inland point of departure to inland point of destination. It may be an inland clearance depot, dry port or container base. To the shipper, the most useful type of bill of lading is the clean, negotiable 'through bill', because it enables goods to be forwarded to the point of destination under one document, although much international trade is based on free carrier (named place) (FCA), free on board (FOB), cost, insurance, freight (CIF), carriage and insurance paid (to named point of destination) (CIP) and delivered at frontier (named place) (DAF) contracts.

(l) Bill of lading in association with a charter party

With the development of combined transport operations, an increasing volume of liner cargo trade and bulk cargo shipments are carried using bills of lading issued in association with a selected charter party.

The combined transport document rules are found in the ICC Rules for a Combined Transport Document (brochure No. 298) and are widely used by major container operators and reflects the earlier Tokyo–Rome Rules, the Tokyo Rules and TCM Convention.

(m) Straight bill of lading

This is an American term for a non-negotiable bill of lading (i.e. a waybill) and is governed by the US Pomerene Act, known more correctly as the Federal Bills of Lading Act 1916. This 1916 Act has been updated – the 2003 update ref. 49 USC80103, US code. 'Non/Not Negotiable' bills are preferred to the 'Straight' in the original Act. A straight bill is one where the consignee is clearly nominated by name without any qualification ('to the order of . . .', or similar). It is the opposite of an 'order' or 'bearer bill'. The straight bill is not negotiable and cannot be issued to transfer title by endorsement. In the US the Pomerene Acts provide that delivery of goods represented by a 'Straight Bill' can be made to the nominated consignee without surrender of any documentation, but merely upon production of proof of identity. To qualify as a straight bill the relevant US statute requires the bill to be made out direct to a nominated consignee and marked 'Not negotiable'. In 2003, the Act refers to US exports and interstate traffic. Elsewhere in the world the position of the carrier delivering against a 'straight bill' remains unclear.

(n) Combined Transport Document (CTD); Multimodal Transport Document (MTD)

These are two names for the same document. This document is issued by a Combined/Multimodal Transport Operator (CTO/MTO) and covers the multimodal transport door to door in one contract of carriage. The CTO/MTD by issuing the CTD/MTD, undertakes to perform, or in his own name carry out the performance of the Combined/Multimodal Transport. Hence a CTD/MTD is a document issued by a carrier who contracts as a principal with the merchant to effect a Combined/Multimodal Transport. Therefore, the CTO/MTO issuing the CTD/MTD is primarily liable to the merchant under the terms of the CTD/MTD throughout carriage.

(o) Optional Combined Transport or Port to Port bill of lading

Consequent on the development of logistics embracing combined transport, some major container operators offer an optional combined transport or Port to Port bill of lading. According to how the bill of lading is prepared, every variety of carriage can be covered. The tendency is for the shipowner to issue a bill of lading from point 'A' to point 'B' embracing the entire transit, though this restricts application of Combined Transport liability from/to those areas where he has representation and control. However, where there is a requirement to issue bills either from or to an area that does not qualify, a suitable transhipment clause is added to the face of the bill, making the shipowner a through transport operator instead of a CTO for the period whilst the goods are in the hands of a carrier outside a Combined Transport area. Being on the face of the bill and not on the reverse, any stated deviation from the normal pattern of liability is clearly drawn to the attention of the merchant.

(p) Electronic bill of lading

Digital transmission of bills of lading has led to considerably reduced paper documentation in trading. This method of trading is subject to the agreement of both parties under Incoterms 2010 eUCP supplement to the Uniform Customs and Practice for Documentary Credits for Electronic Presentation and UCP 600 (2007) – the successor to eUCP 500. Moreover, the CMI – Comité Maritime International, domiciled in Belgium whose prime aim is the promotion of international uniformity in the law governing maritime matters – has introduced rules about 'Electronic Bills of Lading'. Currently, the bill of lading as the document of title has to be a paper document. However, e-commerce permits all documents of trade to be digital.

(q) Negotiable FIATA combined transport bill

This document is increasingly used in the trade and is a FIATA bill of lading (FBL), employed as a combined transport document with negotiable status. It has been developed by the International Federation of Forwarding Agents Associations and is acceptable under the ICC Rules on the Uniform Customs and Practice for Documentary Credits (ICC publication No. UCP 500-revision 1994). The FIATA bill of lading should be stipulated in letters of credit where the forwarder's container groupage service is to be utilized and a house bill of lading is to be issued.

FIATA states that a forwarder issuing a FIATA bill of lading must comply with the following:

(a) The goods are in apparent good order and condition.
(b) The forwarder has received the consignment and has sole right of disposal.
(c) The details set out on the face of the FBL correspond with the instructions the forwarder has received.
(d) The insurance arrangements have been clarified – the FBL contains a specific delete option box which must be completed.
(e) The FBL clearly indicates whether one or more originals have been issued.

The FIATA FBL terms create more shipper obligations in the areas of packing, general average, payment of charges and description of goods. Additional rights are conferred on the forwarder in the areas of lien, routing of cargo and stowage, handling and transport of consignments. Many commercial systems and procedures have been abandoned recently because they were paper based; they have been replaced by digital communications; these are faster, cheaper and more accurate. One area of commerce is the electronic bill of lading.

12.4 Function of the bill of lading

A bill of lading has four functions. Briefly, it is a receipt for goods shipped, a transferable document of title to the goods enabling the holder to demand the cargo, evidence of the terms of the contract of affreightment but not the actual contract, and a quasi-negotiable instrument.

Once the shipper or his agent becomes aware of the sailing schedules of a particular trade, through database or other form of advertisement, he books cargo space on a vessel or in a container from the shipowner. Most container operators have comprehensive websites, detailing sailing schedules, tariffs, booking arrangements and range of container types, and which have hotlinks to many trades as well as customs documentation and clearance.

Exporters and their agents need accurate documentation issued promptly after receipt of goods into the system. Computers facilitate fast processing of bills of lading, invoices and cargo manifests. It is therefore important that exporters or their agent provide accurate information relative to their consignment(s). Computers process large volumes of data relating to cargo processing, customs, analysis, collection, delivery, voyage, freight payable arrangements, tracking arrangements, etc. They provide consistency of information throughout a documentary chain. They allow production of the bill of lading and invoice immediately goods have been packed into the container, always provided that the shipowner has accurate documentation.

Initially, when a booking is made, whether FCL or LCL, the booking party is allocated a 'unique booking reference' number. To ensure immediate identification of the consignment this must be quoted on all source documents.

The Export Cargo Shipping Instruction (ECSI) provides all relevant data the carrier needs to complete the bill of lading and specifies who is responsible for freight charges. This Instruction includes packing specifications and makes provision for supplementary services, such as customs entries. It applies both to general, LCL and FCL cargo. The ECSI is submitted by post, fax or e-mail. In countries where no such document is used, the bill of lading details and instructions are conveyed in the customary form. A named signatory of the shipper or of his representative must submit written instructions as soon as possible after making a booking, but before the vessel sails.

Hitherto, in the UK, the Standard Shipping Note (SSN) prepared by the shipper has accompanied the delivery of goods to the terminal and a copy of the same has been accepted by the HM Customs as a pre-shipment advice under their Simplified (Export) Clearance Procedure. Under a NES involving electronic customs clearances, the SSN no longer serves the pre-shipment function but must be completed, to reconcile the loaded and booked data upon arrival of the container at the port.

The shipper will, on acceptance of the cargo consignment booking and documentation arrangements, despatch the consignment to the CFS/ICD/seaport/dry port.

The goods are signed for by the vessel's chief officer or ship's agent. If the cargo is in good condition and everything is in order, no endorsement will be made on the document, and it can be termed a clean bill of lading. Conversely, if the goods are damaged or a portion of the consignment is missing, the Master or his agent will endorse the document appropriately, and the bill of lading will be either 'claused' or 'unclean'.

Bills of lading are made out in sets, and the number varies according to the trade. Generally it is three or four – one of which will probably be forwarded immediately, and another by a later mail in case the first is lost or delayed. In some trades, coloured bills of lading are used, to distinguish the original (signed) bills from the copies which are purely for record purposes. Where the shipper has sold goods on letter of credit terms established through a bank, or when he wishes to obtain payment of his invoice before the consignee obtains the goods, he will pass the full set of original bills to his bank, who will then arrange presentation to the consignee against payment.

The shipowner or his agent at the port of destination will require one original bill of lading to be presented to him before the goods are handed over. Furthermore, he will normally require payment of any freight due, should this not have been paid at the port of shipment. When one of a set of bills of lading has been presented to the shipping company, the other bills in the set lose their value.

In the event of the bill of lading being lost or delayed in transit, the shipping company will allow delivery of the goods to the person claiming to be the consignee provided he submits a letter of indemnity; this is normally countersigned by a bank, and relieves the shipping company of any liability should another person eventually come along with the actual bill of lading.

With the advent of combined transport and the enactment of new legislation, there have been many changes to the bill of lading document. Basically, because different carriers' bill of lading terms and conditions vary so much (and are able to do so on account of the absence of mandatory law regarding combined transport in ports), shippers are urged to familiarize themselves with the terms of the contracts of carriage into which they enter.

Hence, although the bill of lading bears the legend 'combined transport', it is no guarantee that the carrier accepts liability for the transit throughout: instead it may be a through or transhipment bill.

The following items are common discrepancies found in bills of lading being processed and all should be avoided:

(a) Document not presented in full sets when requested.
(b) Alterations not authenticated by an official of the shipping company or their agents.
(c) The bill of lading is not clean when presented in that it is endorsed regarding damaged condition of the specified cargo or inadequate packing thereby making it unacceptable to a bank for financial settlement purposes.
(d) The document is not endorsed 'on board' when so required.
(e) The 'on-board' endorsement is not signed or initialled by the carrier or agent and likewise not dated.

(f)   The bill of lading is not 'blank' endorsed if drawn to order.

(g)   The document fails to indicate whether 'freight prepaid' is as stipulated in the credit arrangements, i.e. CFR or CIF contracts.

(h)   The bill of lading is not marked 'freight prepaid' when freight charges are included in the invoice.

(i)   The bill of lading is made out 'to order' when the letter of credit stipulates 'direct to consignee' or vice versa.

(j)   The document is dated later than the latest shipping date specified in the credit.

(k)   It is not presented within 21 days after date of shipment or such lesser time as prescribed in the letter of credit.

(l)   The bill of lading details merchandise other than that prescribed.

(m) The rate at which freight is calculated and the total amount are not shown when credit requires such data to be given.

(n)   Cargo has been shipped 'on deck' and not placed in the ship's hold. Basically 'on-deck' claused bills of lading are not acceptable when clean on-board bills of lading are required.

(o)   Shipment made from a port or to a destination contrary to that stipulated.

(p)   Other types of bills of lading presented although not specifically authorized. For example, charter party to forwarding agent's bills of lading are not accepted unless expressly allowed in the letter of credit.

Additionally, having regard to UCP 515, 600 and eUCP, shippers are urged to pay attention to the following items:

(a)   Use the correct Incoterm 2010.

(b)   Do not prohibit transhipment for combined transport shipments.

(c)   Avoid shipped on board requirements if the exporter wants earlier payment.

(d)   Do not ask for detailed bill of lading descriptions.

(e)   Control the letter of credit details through carefully worded sales contracts.

(f)   If a door-to-door service is required obtain a combined transport document and not a marine ocean bill of lading.

(g)   Avoid calling for clauses or certificates that are not available from the carriers.

(h)   Check the letter of credit to ensure it meets shippers' requirements.

(i)   If the cargo necessitates a temperature clause for refrigerated goods, ensure it is reasonable and feasible. This has arisen through increasingly strict food regulations.

Buyers (importers) who request a shipped on board bill of lading may prefer to consider if they need to include in their instructions the 'shipped on board bill of lading' wording, or whether it might be more appropriate to ask for a combined transport bill of lading and omit all reference to 'on board'. This should not prejudice their interest and would enable the necessary documents

Bill of Lading for Combined Transport shipment or Port to Port shipment

| Shipper | B/L No.: |
| | Reference: |

P&O Nedlloyd

www.ponl.com

| Consignee or Order (for U.S. Trade only: Not Negotiable unless consigned 'To Order') | |

| Notify Party/Address (It is agreed that no responsibility shall attach to the Carrier or his Agents for failure to notify (see clause 20 on reverse)) | Place of Receipt (Applicable only when this document is used as a Combined Transport Bill of Lading) |

| Vessel and Voy. No. | Place of Delivery (Applicable only when this document is used as a Combined Transport Bill of Lading) |

| Port of Loading | Port of Discharge | |

Undermentioned particulars as declared by Shipper, but not acknowledged by the Carrier (see clause 11)

Marks and Nos; Container Nos;	Number and kind of Packages; Description of Goods	Gross Weight (kg)	Measurement (cbm)

| * Total No. of Containers/Packages received by the Carrier | Movement | Freight payable at |

Received by the Carrier from the Shipper in apparent good order and condition (unless otherwise noted herein) the total number or quantity of Containers or other packages or units indicated in the box above entitled "Total No. of Containers/Packages received by the Carrier" for Carriage subject to all the terms and conditions hereof (INCLUDING THE TERMS AND CONDITIONS ON THE REVERSE HEREOF AND THE TERMS AND CONDITIONS OF THE CARRIER'S APPLICABLE TARIFF) from the Place of Receipt or the Port of Loading, whichever is applicable, to the Port of Discharge or the Place of Delivery, whichever is applicable. If the acknowledged tally is of Containers, this indicates that the Container has been packed and sealed by the Merchant at his premises without the Carrier being represented and able to check or verify either the tally of Goods or the stowage, which are consequently unknown to him (See Clause 8). The Merchant accepts that, except by special arrangement or pursuant to Clause 9 hereof, Containers are not weighed by the Carrier at any time. If the Carrier so require, Containers are not weighed by the Carrier at any time. If the Carrier so require, before he arranges delivery of the Goods one original Bill of Lading, duly endorsed, must be surrendered by the Merchant to the Carrier at the Port of Discharge or at some other location acceptable to the Carrier. In accepting this Bill of Lading the Merchant expressly accepts and agrees to all its terms and conditions whether printed, stamped or written, or otherwise incorporated, notwithstanding the non-signing of this Bill of Lading by the Merchant. Without prejudice to the generality of this reference, attention is drawn, inter-alia, to Clauses 12 (Shipper's/Merchant's Responsibility), 19 (Dangerous Goods) and 24 (Law & Jurisdiction).

| Number of Original Bills of Lading | Place and Date of Issue | IN WITNESS of the contract herein contained the number of originals stated opposite has been issued, one of which being accomplished the other(s) to be void |

EXCESS VALUATION: REFER TO CLAUSE 7 (3) ON REVERSE SIDE (U.S. TRADE ONLY)......

1/DRS B/L5 8/00

Figure 12.1 Bill of lading for combined transport.

Source: By courtesy of P&O Nedlloyd.

to be issued more quickly because there would be no delay awaiting confirmation of shipment on board.

An example of a bill of lading for Combined Transport shipment or Port to Port shipment is given in Figure 12.1.

12.5 International Convention concerning the Carriage of Goods by Rail

This section examines CIM and CMR documentation.

The COTIF Convention Concerning International Carriage by Rail, Berne 1980, was given legal effect in the UK by section I of the International Transport Conventions Act 1983, effective from May 1985. COTIF abrogated the existing CIM convention, which did not have the force of law in the UK. An amended draft of CIM was attached to COTIF as Appendix B to govern the carriage of goods. (COTIF has a wider application and covers passengers, baggage, as well as goods.) CIM applies when either the place of loading or the destination of the goods is a COTIF member state. In common with CMR it applies only to international carriage and is not applicable to domestic traffic.

The opening of the Channel Tunnel extended the scope of COTIF/CIM. As a private company Eurotunnel operates an independent contract not subject to any mandatory liability for delay. Limitation of SDR 8.33 is applied in common with CMR. The terms and conditions of COTIF/CIM are similar to CMR, but limitation is substantially higher at SDR 17 per kilo. The carrier may also be liable for delay, fees limited to four times the carriage charges.

12.6 Convention on the Contract for the International Carriage of Goods by Road

The CMR convention governing the International Carriage of Goods by Road, Geneva 1956, became law in the UK with the Carriage of Goods by Road Act 1965. The Convention has been adopted solely by European nations and applies to contracts for the international carriage of goods by road in vehicles over the territories of two different countries, of which at least one is a contracting party to CMR. Hence it only applies to UK imports/exports by ro/ro services or Eurotunnel where goods remain on the same road vehicles throughout their transit. If the same container on the same journey was lifted off the trailer at the Dover ferry port onto a vessel and carried to the continent on any other trailer, there would have been no crossing of a frontier on a road vehicle and therefore the Convention would not apply. Under the Convention the carrier is liable for loss or damage from the time that he takes over the goods until the time that he delivers them to the consignee, unless he can prove that the loss or damage occurred because one of a list of excepted perils. The carrier is entitled to limit his liability to SDR 8.33 per kilo, but cargo shippers are entitled to recover a return of freight and other charges relating to carriage and duty on top of this limitation. The carrier is also liable for delay if the goods have not been delivered within the agreed time limit, or, if there is no such agreement, within a reasonable time. Liability for delay, in addition to the SDR 8.33 per kilo, is up to the amount of the carriage charges.

12.7 Combined transport

After the failure in the 1970s to draft a convention to cover loss or damage to goods carried under a combined transport document, the Tokyo–Rome rules, the Tokyo rules and the TCM convention, the International Chamber of Commerce revised particular elements and published a draft known as the 'ICC rules for a Combined Transport Document'.

However, UNCTAD intervened with an international convention to govern combined transport. It was adopted at an international conference in Geneva in 1980 as the 'United Nations Convention on International Multi-modal Transport of Goods' or as more commonly known the 'UNCTAD MMO Convention'. If widely adopted it is likely to increase carrier insurance costs, probably resulting in increased freight rates without any corresponding reduction in cargo insurance premiums. Some thirty countries need to ratify it before acceptance and by 2003 it had the support of only nine countries.

The UNCTAD MMO owes much in its drafting to the Hamburg Rules. Its approach to limitation of liability may be described as 'a plateau with peaks showing through'. That is to say, the Rules set a limit (about 10% above the Hamburg limit and expressed in SDRs) with a dual weight/package alternative criterion; but where any unimodal conventions apply a higher limit of liability and loss or damage occurs in their period of applicability, their limits applying in preference to the UNCTAD MMO limit.

It has been many years since the MMO convention was adopted. Meanwhile significant advances in technology and communication, together with prolific globalization, have resulted in substantially increased use of multi-modal transport. In the absence of uniform international regulation, national and regional laws are applied, which create further diversity at international level. The UNCTAD United Nations Convention and International Multimodal Transport of Goods 1980, has 10 (2005) contracting states, but requires 30. UNCITRAL, UNCTAD and ICC continue to strive to provide a new international multimodal convention.

12.8 Sea waybill and common short form bill of lading

A sea waybill is a receipt and is evidence of a contract of carriage. It is not a document of title, as is the bill of lading. It is not mandatorily subject to the relevant Carriage of Goods by Sea Act (applying the Hague, or Hague–Visby rules which only apply to bills of lading, but not waybills).

In recent decades carriers have encouraged exporters to use waybills as an alternative to the ubiquitous bill of lading (see Figure 12.2). The waybill's primary advantage is when a document of title is not required, either to facilitate security of payment and delivery in an international transaction or to facilitate negotiation whilst the goods are in transit to enable the goods to be sold and title passed. This may occur when shipment is to an associated company and payment is a book entry or when alternative payment arrangements have been made. Other advantages include the absence of the need to transmit paper documents to destinations to secure delivery, because delivery is made to the nominated consignee against proof of identity – usually a delivery order on consignee's headed stationery. Waybills facilitate paperless transactions.

Recently it seemed there was no way of using waybills involving security of payment/delivery or subsequent sale whilst in transit and would invariably require a bill of lading, which being a document of title must always be a paper document. Hence the use of the waybill has been slow but could be accelerated should waybills be used in documentary credits whilst meeting all the requirements of the parties involved.

The waybill in digital transactions must first identify the parties involved – other than the carrier – and their requirements. If this is possible, in most international trade transactions the waybill can prove an acceptable document where at present the bill of lading is viewed as the only acceptable document. These are the requirements of the parties:

(a) *The shipper*. The shipper's requirement is to be paid and to retain control over his goods until he is paid or has his bill of exchange accepted.
(b) *The consignee*. Conversely, the consignee requires assurance that his seller does not get paid without giving up control of the goods to him or his agent (usually his bank).
(c) *The bank*. In a documentary credit, if a bank is advancing funds against documents, a bank is looking for security for the payment it makes (or promises to make) on behalf of the consignee in case of default by the consignee (e.g. insolvency). A document of title can provide this security.
(d) *The insurer*. The insurer wishes to ensure that, in the event that he has to pay claim, he has adequate recourse under subrogation of the carrier on acceptable terms to minimize his nett exposure.

The waybill is a contract between the shipper (seller) and carrier that was not subject to the 1855 Bill of Lading Act, a consignee acquiring no rights under a waybill. The shipper could vary the identity of the nominated consignee at will at any stage of the transit, so a waybill, in its normal format, represents no security to a consignee (buyer).

However, the Carriage of Goods by Sea Act 1992 repealed the 1855 Bill of Lading Act by providing for consignees under waybills to be in the same position as if they were bill of lading consignees, so far as becoming a party to the contract of carriage and being able to sue and be sued on that contract in their own name, when they approach the carrier to claim delivery. As a

Non-Negotiable Waybill for Combined Transport shipment or Port to Port shipment

Shipper		Waybill No.:
		Reference:

P&O Nedlloyd

www.ponl.com

Consignee	(If the name shown in this space is a Bank, the Bank named is specifically excluded from the list of parties coming within the definition of Merchant in the Carrier's contract of carriage and incurs no liability to the Carrier under said contract unless applying for delivery in its own name.)

Notify Party/Address	(It is agreed that no responsibility shall attach to the Carrier or his Agents for failure to notify)	Place of Receipt	(Applicable only when this document is used as a Combined Transport Waybill)

Vessel and Voy. No.	Place of Delivery	(Applicable only when this document is used as a Combined Transport Waybill)

Port of Loading	Port of Discharge

Undermentioned particulars as declared by Shipper, but not acknowledged by the Carrier

Marks and Nos; Container Nos;	Number and kind of Packages; description of Goods	Gross Weight (kg)	Measurement (cbm)

WAYBILL

* Total No. of Containers/Packages received by the Carrier	Movement	Freight payable at

Received by the Carrier from the Shipper in apparent good order and condition (unless otherwise noted herein) the total number or quantity of Containers or other packages or units indicated in the box above entitled "Total No. of Containers/Packages received by the Carrier" for Carriage from the Place of Receipt or the Port of Loading, whichever applicable, to the Port of Discharge or the Place of Delivery, whichever applicable. SUBJECT TO THE TERMS OF THE CARRIER'S STANDARD BILL OF LADING TERMS AND CONDITIONS AND TARIFF FOR THE RELEVANT TRADE, WHICH ARE MUTATIS MUTANDIS APPLICABLE TO THIS WAYBILL (copies of which may be obtained from the Carrier or his agents). Except for live animals and Goods which are stated herein to be carried on deck and are so carried, these terms and conditions are warranted by the Carrier in respect of the sea portion of the Carriage to apply the Hague Rules or Hague Visby Rules, whichever would have been applicable if this Waybill were a Bill of Lading. In either case the provisions of Article III Rule 4 of the Hague Visby Rules are deemed to be incorporated herein. The contract evidenced by this Waybill is deemed to be a contract of carriage as defined in Article I (b) of the Hague Rules and Hague Visby Rules. However this Waybill is not a document of title to the Goods. Delivery will be made to the Consignee named, or his authorised agent, on production of proof of identity at the Port of Discharge or the Place of Delivery, whichever applicable. Should the Consignee require delivery to a party under premises other than as shown above in the "Consignee" box, then written instructions must be given by the Consignee to the Carrier or his agent. Unless the Shipper expressly waives his right to control the Goods (until delivery by means of a clause on the face hereof, such instructions from the Consignee will be subject to any instruction to the contrary by the Shipper. Unless instructed to the contrary by the Shipper prior to the commencement of Carriage and acted accordingly on the face hereof, the Carrier will, subject to the aforesaid terms and conditions, process cargo claims with the Consignee. Claims settlement, if any, shall be a complete discharge of the Carrier's liability to the Shipper. The Shipper accepts the said standard terms and conditions on his own behalf, on behalf of the Consignee and the Owner of the Goods, and authorises the Consignee to bring suit against the Carrier to his own name but as agent of the Shipper, and warrants that he has authority so to accept and authorise. The Shipper further undertakes that no claim or allegation in respect of the Goods shall be made against the Carrier by any person other than in accordance with the terms and conditions of this Waybill.

This Waybill is issued subject to the CMI Uniform Rules For Sea Waybills	Place and Date of Issue	IN WITNESS whereof this Waybill is signed.
		P&O Nedlloyd

Beagle House, Braham Street, London E1 8EP   3/DRS W/B 3/03

Figure 12.2 Waybill.

Source: By courtesy of P&O Nedlloyd.

waybill does not need to be sent to the destination to be surrendered to obtain delivery, it was not possible to link the acquisition of this right of acceptation of a document as is the case with the bill of lading. There remained a problem of synchronizing the payment to the seller with the passing of control of the goods to the buyer.

As the waybill is not a document of title, it can be either in digital form or paper document. A paper waybill can be used by the shipper to negotiate credit with the bank, thereafter the rest of the transaction can be EDI. Alternatively, no paper need ever be issued. Digital messages can attach waybill messages to the shipper and bank and the shipper then receives digital confirmation from the bank that the waybill has been accepted against the letter of credit.

The waybill is ideal for use in the following circumstances:

(a) House to house shipments, such as shipment between associated companies or branches of multinational companies where no documentary credit transaction is required.
(b) Open account sales which arise where goods are shipped to an agent for sale at destination or 'an account sale basis'.
(c) Transactions between companies where the security of a documentary credit transaction is not required, perhaps because of trust arising from a long trading relationship or an alternative basis of payment being arranged.

Advantages of using sea waybills instead of a bill of lading:

(a) No requirement to send a document of title to destination to secure delivery as is necessary with a bill of lading.
(b) No possibility of a requirement for a letter of indemnity for delivery of cargo without a bill of lading.
(c) In many trades carriers charge for producing bills of lading, but not waybills.
(d) Reduced chance of fraud or problems caused by lost or stolen documents.
(e) A waybill can be a paper document or digital message.
(f) If a waybill – with a control clause – is used for the carriage of goods that the merchant wishes to trade at destination prior to the goods arrival, this can be done using a carrier's delivery order, which the merchant can obtain from the carrier at destination much quicker than a bill of lading through a documentary credit system, which is as valid a document of title as is a bill of lading.

Credit transactions with security for the interest of all parties concerned – seller, buyer, insurer, banker, carrier – must use a waybill embracing:

(a) Incorporate a 'control clause'.
(b) Be issued subject to the CMI Uniform Rules for Sea Waybills.
(c) Show the bank as a consignee in the consignee box on the waybill which would be qualified by the waiver to the bank or bear a banker lien clause.

The common short form bill of lading was introduced in 1979, replacing the traditional shipping company 'long form' bills. It is identical in legal and practical terms to the traditional bills, but is more simple and can be used with any shipping line. This document covers the shipper/forwarder and provides bills from port to port and through-transport, including container bills of lading. It does not cover combined transport bills of lading. It is described as a 'short form' document because of the use of an abridged standard clause on the face of the document which incorporates the conditions of carriage of the contracting carrier. This eliminates the mass of small print on the reverse side of the bills of lading. It is suitable for outward shipments from the UK, involving 'through transit', or port to port carriage of cargo for both 'break bulk,' and 'unit loads' of all types traditionally covered by 'long form' bills of lading.

13 Cargoes

13.1 Cargo stowage/packing overview

Cargo stowage is the process of accommodating an item of merchandise in a transport unit to prepare it in a mercantile condition. It concerns the nature of the transit, any likely hazards and the most economic conveyance of the cargo.

Since the 1980s stowage and packing have grown in international trade, particularly as the pattern of liner trades changes and packaging technology develops. It is an area where cost-effective cargo stowage can aid overseas market growth through lower distribution costs. Influencing these developments and reflecting changing patterns in international trade distribution are:

(a) The development of the LCL and NVOCC transport mode requires more skill in stowage of compatible cargo.
(b) New technology involving computers and packing techniques will add a new dimension to cargo stowage.
(c) More pressure is being placed on shippers to reduce their distribution unit cost. This can be realized through more productive stowage techniques and more sophisticated skills in formulating the stowage plan.
(d) The transport unit, especially in the area of combined transport operation, is tending to become of greater capacity as found in the trailer and high-capacity cube container. This will require more skills for effective stowage.
(e) As world trade develops especially in the growth market of consumer goods, it will intensify the competition in the market place to have/receive quality goods in an undamaged condition. This requires more advanced stowage/packing techniques.
(f) Technology is developing rapidly in international destinations. New equipment is constantly being introduced and existing equipment improved. Moreover, new regulations are being adopted continuously. Furthermore the range of equipment is being designed so as to reduce packing specifications/cost and thereby lower distribution costs. Sea Containers is a market leader in the development of container types. A recent development is Sea Cell, which accommodates palletized cargo, thereby facilitating cargo transhipment.

(g) The development of combined transport operation multi-modalism has encouraged door-to-door transit with no transhipment. Again, packing costs/needs are much reduced.

(h) The producer should ideally design the product to make its transport relatively easy and capable of being lifted and secured safely, clearing factory doors and entrances, and not exceeding the weight or size restriction of transit.

(i) In 2001 European Packaging waste legislation required each Member State to have 50–65% of used packaging to be recovered, 25–45% to be recycled and a minimum of 15% of each main type of packing material to be recycled.

(j) Stringent regulations exist regarding dangerous classified cargo shipments as specified by the IMO.

Notes (a) to (j) above must be reconciled when examining cargo stowage. Future needs involve better co-operation/consultation by all interested parties in the transit, the principal carrier and buyer taking the lead. The exporter must ensure the production process/packing specification is so designed to make the best use of the transport unit capacity available, both in cubic and weight terms. Full use must be made of computers to maximize utilization of cargo space effectively.

13.2 Stowage of cargo

The ultimate responsibility for stowage of cargo rests with the Master. In practice, whilst the Master retains overall responsibility, the supervision of stowage of cargo is usually delegated to the chief officer. His task is to see that neither the ship nor its cargo is damaged. Furthermore, he is responsible for safe handling, loading, stowage and carriage, including custody of the cargo throughout the voyage. Above all, he must ensure that the carriage of goods does not imperil the ship. His aim must be to have the cargo evenly distributed throughout the ship, to ensure its general stability. In regard to container ships shore-based computers are used to formulate the stowage plan. In practice, it is usual for the ship to be loaded a little deeper aft, to improve the vessel's movement through the water. This is called 'trimmed by the stern', the term 'trim' referring to the difference in draught between the stem and stern. A vessel trimmed by the bow refers to the difference in draught between the stern and bow. It is regarded as an unseaworthy vessel. A ship with a centre of gravity too low will be stiff and apt to strain heavily in rough weather. Conversely, a ship with a centre of gravity too high will be tender and inclined to roll, thereby creating instability.

There are two types of cargo: bulk and general cargo. Bulk cargoes present little difficulty in stowage, as they tend to be conveyed in specialized vessels between two ports, and are often loaded and discharged by modern technology. Single commodity shipments, such as iron ore, steel, scrap metal, timber, coal, oil, gas, bauxite, grain and heavy lifts, all require special treatment in stowage. Ship design and the IMO stowage regulations have contributed to the safety of the ship in such bulk cargo shipments. Computers greatly aid stowage and cargo distribution arrangements. Grain, coal, copra and similar cargoes must be adequately ventilated during the voyage, as they are liable to spontaneous combustion. Moreover, a range of bulk cargo shipments can shift during voyage.

With general cargo, the problem is more difficult, and calls for great skill when shipped in a loose condition and conveyed in cargo liners provided with numerous decks, including 'tween decks acting like pigeonholes to facilitate stowage. This represents a very small portion of the market today. Most liner cargoes are conveyed in containers, often in consolidated consignments, whilst in the UK/European trade a substantial volume of traffic is conveyed by international road haulage – again usually under consolidated arrangements involving road trailer movement throughout.

In regard to container tonnage a mammoth task of extensive planning is ensuring up to 8,000–10,000 TEUs are unloaded and loaded from the vessel operating on a quick port turn-round time. Today most containers are cleared outside the port environs involving an ICD, free zones, dry port, shippers' premises and CFS, thereby reducing the prospect of port congestion and enhancing port productivity through substantially increasing throughput per container berth. Less modern ports have containers cleared locally by customs, involving co-ordination with customs, port authorities, rail/road/lighterage operators, stevedoring personnel, agents, etc. Computers aid planning, stowage and operations in modern ports and a shipping company. A similar criterion applies to the consolidated consignment conveyed under international road haulage arrangements.

There are four main factors to consider in the stowage of cargo:

1   Best use should be made of the ship's deadweight and cubic capacity. Broken stowage is space wasted in the ship by cargo of irregular-shaped packages, or irregularity of cargo spaces and should be kept to a minimum consistent with the general stability of the ship. Generally 10% to 15% of the total cubic capacity is allowed for broken stowage. As far as practicable, full use should be made of the cubic capacity of the vessel, with a view to ensuring that the ship is down to its marks when she sails. If there is not an even distribution of cargo when the ship sails, with no compensating ballast, hogging or sagging may arise. Hogging arises when most of the cargo's weight has been stowed in the forward and after holds of the vessel, causing the two ends of the ship to drop lower than the midship portion. Conversely, if most of the cargo is stowed amidship, the two ends of the vessel tend to be higher than the midship portion. This is called sagging. Both hogging and sagging have an adverse effect on the hull and impair the vessel's stability, which can be ameliorated by ballasting the portion of the ship empty of cargo.

2   Associated (to some extent) with the previous factor is the need to prevent damage to the ship. There should be a proper distribution of cargo to ensure adequate stability and trim and properly secured to prevent shifting. If there is movement of the cargo during the voyage the ship may list. This situation can be made serious should the cargoes be dangerous: spontaneous combustion for example could cause a fire or explosion. Shifting of cargo applies primarily to bulk cargoes such as grain, small coal, flint stone or iron ores, and is not usually associated with liner cargo shipments. To reduce movement of cargo, dunnage is provided. This is in the form of foam rubber, polystyrene, inflatable bags, timber boards or mats placed between the cargo to prevent movement during the voyage.

3   Similarly, fragile cargo taints easily, is liable to leakage, scratches easily, has strong odours or is liable to sweat and requires proper segregation; otherwise the shipowner may be faced with heavy claims and possible loss of goodwill amongst shippers.

4   A proper segregation of stowage of different consignments for various ports must be made, to prevent delay in discharging and avoid double handling, which is not only costly and increases the risk of cargo damage and pilferage, but also increases turn-round time. The computerized stowage plan plays a vital role in realizing this objective. This plan applies equally to container vessels which call at fewer ports compared to the 'tween-deck tonnage they displaced.

Study of cargo stowage includes the principles of ISO container stowage, a popular method of international distribution. For container specifications see Figure 16.2. Increasingly exporters use the full container load consignment and undertake their own stowage. The principles of container stowage are as follows. Safe container transport depends primarily on a correct and immovable cargo stow and even weight distribution:

1   The container must be stowed tightly so that lateral and longitudinal movement of the cargo within is impossible. Tight stowage can be optimum module of the container. Alternatively, if a unit load is being used such as a pallet, the base of it must form a module of the container.

2   As an alternative to item 1, the cargo must be effectively restrained within the container. This is necessary for a variety of reasons including: (a) to prevent collapse of the stow while packing, unpacking or during transit, for example rolls of felt on end; (b) to prevent any movement during transit of part-loads or single heavy items, for example large pieces of machinery (the heavier the item the more damage it will do if allowed to move); and (c) to prevent the 'face' of the stow collapsing and leaning against the container doors, that is to prevent it from falling out when the doors are opened at destination or for customs inspection.

3   The consignment must be adequately secured. Details of the various techniques are these:

(i)   *Shoring:* bars, struts and spars located in cargo voids to keep the cargo pressed against the walls or other cargo;

(ii) *Lashing:* rope, wire, chains, strapping or nett secured to proper anchoring points within the container and tensioned against the cargo;

(iii) *Wedging:* wooden distance pieces, pads of synthetic material, inflatable dunnage to fill voids in the cargo and keep it immobile against the container walls;

(iv) *Locking:* cargo built up to give a three-dimensional brick wall effect.

4   The growth of container temperature controlled cargo shipments has been substantial. It embraces frozen meat, poultry, fish, seafood, fruit, vegetables, confectionery, ice-cream, dairy products, chocolate, live plants, flower bulbs, films, pharmaceuticals, hazardous and obnoxious cargoes. This involves temperature controlled cargo shipment arrangements. P&O Nedlloyd (now part of the Maersk Group) are market leaders in this market and recent developments feature the 'snap freeze operation' and the 'bulb mode'. Snap freeze reduces the heat input to the container during the machine defrost cycle, essential for the carriage of sensitive chilled produce. The 'bulb mode' has been developed to stabilize the environment within the container and optimize carriage conditions for bulbs and live plants.

5   Packaging is a fundamental element in the transport of temperature controlled cargoes. It is essential to protect cargoes from damage and contamination. The correct design and highest quality of materials need to be used to ensure it can withstand the refrigeration process and transit. Where appropriate, packaging materials must be able to: protect products from damage as a result of 'crushing'; be able to withstand 'shocks' occurring in inter-modal transport; be shaped to fit on pallets or directly into the container for stowage; prevent dehydration or reduce the water vapour transmission rate; act as an oxygen barrier preventing oxidation; withstand condensation and maintain its wet strength; prevent odour transfer; and withstand temperatures of −30°C or colder.

The wide variety of cargoes coupled with the design and quality requirements of packaging materials listed above are the reasons for many different packaging types and styles. Perishable fruits and vegetables require packaging that allows refrigerated air to circulate around the products to remove the gases and water vapour produced by their respiration.

Often cargoes are carried in cartons: these cartons must be capable of being stacked to the maximum height allowed in the container; this is approximately 2.5 m (9 ft) in a hi-cube integral container. Many packaging types used for other forms of transport, for example, road haulage, may be inadequate for sea transport.

There is no simple method of securing cargo in a container and only experience can aid perfection and solution. Each cargo must be treated on its merits with regard to the type of cargo, the way in which it is stowed, the cargo handling equipment available and the permanent fittings in the container. The built-in securing points, dunnage brackets, etc., should be used extensively. Any timber dunnage used must be dry and comply with any quarantine regulations. Any shoring which presses against the container wall should have extra timber laid longitudinally between the wall and point of support to spread the weight over two or more side posts. Useful filler pieces for wedging or preventing chafe include old tyres, polyurethane slabs, macerated paper pads and, for light packages, rolled-up cardboard. Unless an identical stow is anticipated on the return container journey, it is best that the lashing equipment chosen and considered is expendable. Where synthetic strapping material is used terylene is preferable to nylon for heavy loads because it is less liable to stretch.

Various techniques exist to restrain cargo, depending on the commodity involved. Top-heavy articles should be wedged, shored and lashed to prevent toppling. Heavy weights should be secured to stout ring-bolts (sited in the container floor and side walls) and/or be shored with timber. Chain or wire with bottle screws may be used. Wheeled vehicles should be chocked and lashed with Spanish windlasses, with the chocks chamfered or padded to protect the tyres. If the floor is of extruded aluminium, portable securing devices must be used. Resilient loads can cause lashings to slacken. This may be overcome by introducing elasticity, for example rubber rope, into the lashing pattern. No securing of pallets is necessary, provided the load is properly secured to the pallet, if the distance between pallets and container walls is 100 mm (4 in) or less. Pallets must not be allowed any longitudinal movement. If securing is necessary, stow pallets against container walls and wedge wooden blocks between the pallets. It may be necessary to insert sheets of board between pallet loads to protect against chafe and prevent bags, cartons, etc., interweaving and jamming the stow. Shippers are urged to use the purpose built palletized container such as Sea Cell to realize the best results.

In many instances there is a space 25–152 mm remaining between the face of the cargo and container doors. Cargo must be prevented from collapsing into this space. This can be achieved in a variety of ways as follows:

1   Use of suitably positioned lashing points with wire, rope, strapping, etc., woven across.
2   A simple wooden gate for the wider gaps and heavier cargo.
3   Use of filler pieces, that is macerated paper pads, polystyrene, wood, wool pads, etc., for the narrower gaps and lighter cargoes, for example cartons of biscuits.

Care must be taken to ensure that when the container doors are opened there is no 'fall out'. This is particularly relevant for a container completely packed with cartons or sacks in, for example, interlocking tiers of packages, in which case it is advisable to use any fixing points located in the door posts of the container. Nylon strapping, polypropylene or wire threaded through such points forms an effective barrier. To ensure there is adequate and correct overall distribution of cargo within the covered container, the goods must be secure within their packages. Moreover, the pack itself must be as full as possible so as to resist pressures external to it. Packages must be sufficiently rigid to withstand the weight imposed upon them when stacked, usually to a minimum height of 2.10 m (6.88 ft). If more than one type of cargo is stowed in the container, they must be compatible and not contaminate or be contaminated. Heavy items and liquids should be placed at the bottom with light and dry ones on the top. Within practical physical limitations of handling, the unit package should be as large as possible since this can reduce costs by up to 20% and increase volumetric efficiency by up to 10%. Consult when practicable the consignee about the proposed method of loading and sequence. This will facilitate discharge at the destination. Where relevant, stowing should be carried out in sequence to permit rapid checking and stowage operations during and subsequent to unloading. In the event of the consignment being subject to customs pre-entry procedures, it would facilitate customs examination should this occur and obviate unloading if such cargo was stowed at the door end of the container. Shippers should avoid having a gap in the stow along the centre line of the container or at the sides which could generate cargo movement in the transit and possibly result in damaged cargo.

13.3 Types and characteristics of cargo

The following is a broad selection of the main cargoes carried, together with their characteristics, including stowage factors where appropriate. The stowage factor is the space occupied in cubic metres in the ship's hold by one metric tonne of cargo (1,000 kg). Heavy cargoes shipped in bulk, such as those with a low stowage factor, occupy the smallest space, and are most suitable for single-deck type of ships. Those cargoes of a higher stowage factor, such as garments and machinery, are lighter, occupy more space, and are best suited usually to container vessels. Accordingly, most of the following cargoes are now containerized and the shipper must reconcile the type required and the main areas of shipment.

Apples are packed in cases, boxes, cartons or pallet boxes and stowed at a temperature of about 1°C. If the temperature is too high, the fruit becomes sticky and soft. Apples 'breathe' after being picked, and are individually wrapped in chemically treated paper to help absorb carbon dioxide. Their stowage factor is about 2.266, and they are mainly shipped in containers. The latter involves the Scoresby tray pack carton of either pulp or polystyrene trays accommodated in cartons. Each 20 ft (6.1 m) covered container has a 518 carton capacity. The fruit is packed diagonally allowing more and larger fruit to be packed per layer in the non-pressure tray pack design.

Butter is packed in cases, cartons, boxes or kegs, with a stowage factor varying from 1.558 to 1.699. It is normally conveyed in containers.

Cement. A very large volume of the world's cement is now distributed in purpose-built cement bulk carriers and on liner containerized services in specialized containers. It has a stowage factor of 1.0 to 1.133.

Coal constitutes a dangerous cargo. It is liable to spontaneous combustion, especially on long voyages, and therefore, it is undesirable for it to be shipped with acids or chemicals. The stowage factor varies from 1.0 to 1.416, according to the grade of cargo. Coal (especially small coal) is liable to shift on a long voyage. It therefore must be well trimmed into the sides and ends of the holds if a full cargo is to be loaded, to maintain the ship's stability. The cargo loses its value if broken into small pieces or dust during loading and discharge. Main shipments originate in the UK, Poland, Germany, Holland, Belgium, Australia, South Africa, Canada and the United States. Coal is generally conveyed in vessels with a single deck, large hatches and self-trimming holds.

Coffee is packed in hessian bags. It must be kept dry and taints very easily. With a stowage factor of 1.699, it is normally shipped in ventilated containers.

Confectionery is shipped in many forms of packing, the most common of which are cartons. Shipments originate in many parts of the world and are carried on most liner services much of it being containerized. It has a high stowage factor and must be given cool stowage. The cargo must be kept dry. It is particularly suitable for FCL container shipments.

Copra is usually shipped in bulk, but small shipments may be carried in second-hand (S/H) bags in containers. It has a stowage factor varying from 2.125 to 2.266. This commodity gives off oily odours and should therefore never be shipped with such commodities as tea or sugar. It is liable to heat, and good ventilation is essential. Copra is liable to spontaneous combustion.

Cotton is shipped in pressed bales in containers, and has a stowage factor varying, according to the quality of the cargo, from 1.416 to 2.833. It is highly inflammable, and liable to spontaneous combustion if shipped damp or greasy. Cotton should be kept dry and conveyed in Combi carriers or liner tonnage (containers).

Eggs are conveyed in crates or cases. Raw eggs taint very easily, and can be refrigerated down to about 2°C, but must not be frozen. The stowage factor is somewhat high and varies according to the type of packing. The bulk of the shipments are containerized.

Esparto grass is shipped in bales in containers. It is liable to spontaneous combustion, and must be well ventilated. It has a low stowage factor varying from 2.833 to 4.249.

Fertilizers are shipped in bulk in single-deck vessels or containers. It should be kept dry. Their stowage factor varies according to the variety.

Flour is generally shipped in bulk in containers, and must be kept dry. It taints very easily, and is subject to weevil damage. It has a stowage factor of 1.416.

Grain is usually conveyed in bulk, although a small proportion of it may be shipped in bags to improve the general stability of the vessel. The IMO convention on Safety of Life at Sea includes grain regulations. This emerged in the SOLAS International Convention amendment 1973, Chapter VI. Provision is made for ships constructed specially for the transport of grain and specifies a method for calculating the adverse heeling movement due to a shift of cargo surface in ships carrying bulk grain. It also provides for documents of authorization, grain loading, stability data and associated plans of loading. Copies of all relevant documents must be available on board to enable the Master to meet the IMO requirements.

Grain must be kept dry and requires good ventilation, as it is liable to heat and ferment. Its stowage factor varies according to the type of grain and whether it is shipped in bulk or bags. The heavy grains such as wheat, maize and rye have a stowage factor of approximately 1.416, whilst with the lighter grains, which include barley, oats and linseed, it is about 1.558 to 2.408. If the cargo is shipped in bags, these figures need to be increased by 10%. Grain is most suitably conveyed in single-deck vessels with self-trimming holds, and it forms one of the major tramp cargoes. Main shipments originate in Australia, Canada, the United States, Russia, Romania, Bulgaria and the Argentine.

Jute is usually shipped in bales in containers, and is liable to spontaneous combustion. It has a stowage factor of 1.699.

Meat is shipped frozen in refrigerated holds, at a temperature of −10°C or is chilled at −3°C. It is a worldwide market and shipped in reefer containers.

Motor vehicles are generally shipped unpacked to reduce freight. Each vehicle must be individually secured and stowed on a firm level floor. Space must be left round each vehicle to avoid damage by scratching or rubbing. Cars cannot be over-stowed, and space is lost if other cargo cannot be built up under vehicle stowage. More recently, an increasing number of ships have been adapted by incorporating skeleton decks built into the holds to which the vehicles are secured thus in effect increasing the number of 'tween decks. This has permitted bulk shipments of motor vehicles in vessels called multi-purpose containers ships. The decks can be removed either wholly or partly for the return voyage, thus allowing cargoes of a different nature to be carried. The vehicles are transhipped by means of a ramp. Nowadays, the distribution of motor vehicles – frequently termed as trade cars – is very much a growth sector of international trade development. To meet this expansion, purpose-built pure car and truck carriers with up to 13 decks and capable of conveying 5,800 cars operate, with 'drive on/drive off' facilities at the ports. Main shipments originate in the UK, Sweden, Japan, United States, France, Italy, Malaysia, Korea and Germany. It is a large global market.

Oil cakes are conveyed in bulk or bags in containers. They are liable to sweat damage and spontaneous combustion. Their stowage factor is 1.558.

Oil and petroleum are conveyed in specialized vessels, called tankers, and are dangerous cargoes. Oil, being a liquid, will follow all movement of the ship, and thus have a large free surface, unless some method is employed in breaking up this surface. This is done by the use of longitudinal bulk heads, which divide the vessel into either three or four longitudinal sections. Other bulk heads athwartships divide the longitudinal sections into tanks. The number of tanks depends on the design of the tanker. During the voyage the tanks are never filled to capacity, i.e. there is always a free surface in the tanks of a tanker. Cofferdams are found fore and aft of the tank space as a protection against the serious fire risk inherent with this cargo. Oil is classified as clean or dirty, according to type, and it is usual for vessels to carry the same type on consecutive voyages, as the cost of tank cleaning is high. Dirty oils include fuel oil and crude oil, whereas clean oil covers refined petroleum, lubricating oil, diesel oil and so on. Shipments of oil are mainly from the Persian Gulf, the West Indies, the United States, the Black Sea, Nigeria, Libya, Venezuela and the East Indies.

Oranges are shipped in cartons. They should not be stowed anywhere near cargo liable to taint. They are usually shipped in containers and have a stowage factor of about 1.841 to 2.125.

Ores. There is a great variety of ores, including chrome, manganese, copper, bauxite, iron, zinc and barytes. Ores are essentially bulk cargoes, conveyed in specialized single-deck ore carriers and, depending on the type of cargo, have a stowage factor varying from 0.340 to 0.850. They are therefore very heavy cargoes, and, although the vessel may be fully loaded down to its marks, very little of the actual space in the vessel is utilized. Consequently, the whole weight of the cargo is concentrated in the bottom of the vessel, which tends to make the vessel 'stiff' and causes it to roll heavily in bad weather, with consequent stress and strain. There is very little risk of most types of ores shifting, and in order to raise the height of the cargo so that the ship will ride more easily, the cargo is heaped up in the middle of the holds, and not trimmed into the wings (the sides of the holds). Some ores are, however, shipped wet, and set in stowage to reduce the possibility of the cargo shifting. Ores form one of the major tramp cargoes, and specialized ore carriers are used. Main shipments of iron ore originate in Newfoundland, Brazil, Spain, Australia and North Africa; copper ore from Chile, Spain and East Africa; chrome ore from Turkey and South Africa; bauxite from Malaysia and British Guiana; zinc ore from Chile, Newfoundland and Spain; barytes from Nova Scotia; and manganese ore from Ghana, Sierra Leone and India.

Rice is shipped in bags, and is liable to heat and sweat. Rice bran is generally shipped as a tramp or liner filler cargo. Rice generally is stowed by itself although there can be consignments of polished and brown rice in the same stow. Good ventilation is essential. The stowage factor is 1.416, and main shipments originate in Burma, Italy, Thailand, Egypt and Brazil.

Rubber is conveyed in bags, bales or cases. Its stowage factor varies from 1.481 to 2.125. Latex is shipped in containers.

Salt is shipped in bulk or bags in containers, and must be kept dry because it absorbs moisture very rapidly. Excessive ventilation results in loss of weight in very dry weather. It has a stowage factor of 1.000, and is best shipped in single-deck vessels.

Sugar is usually shipped in bulk (raw), or bags (raw or refined). If it is overheated it sets hard, and if too cold the sugar content diminishes. Sugar must be kept dry, and is liable to taint. Its stowage factor varies from 1.133 to 1.416, and main shipments originate in Australia, Brazil, Cuba, Jamaica, the Philippines, Java and San Domingo. Sugar is shipped in containers.

Tea is shipped in lined cases, and loses its aroma and value if not kept dry. It taints very easily, and has a low stowage factor of about 1.481. Tea is shipped in liner tonnage in containers or Combi carriers.

Timber is carried both under deck and on deck. The stowage of timber varies considerably, according to the type of timber carried. Hardwoods, such as teak and mahogany, have a stowage factor of about 0.708 to 0.850, pit props about 1.699 and DBB (deals, battens and boards) about 2.550. Hardwoods are carried on a metric tonne basis, whilst props and DBB are conveyed on a fathom and standard basis respectively. A large quantity of timber is moved under the Nubaltwood charter party terms which provides the following definitions in regard to the method of shipment:

(a) Battens to be considered 44 mm × 100 mm and up to 75 mm × 175 mm.
(b) Slattings to be considered 25 mm and under in thickness, and 75 mm and under in width.
(c) Packaged goods will have a single length and size in each package, except that where the residue is insufficient for complete package lengths they may be combined provided that one end of each package is squared off.
(d) Truck bundled goods involves goods bundled in mixed lengths of one size provided that one end of each bundle is squared off.
(e) Pre-slung goods involves the owner providing slings to place around the cargo before loading onto the vessel and for these to remain during the voyage until the cargo has been discharged.

The most suitable vessel for bulk shipments is the single-deck three-island type with well decks and a broad beam, which make for easier stowage and a good deck cargo. Considerable quantities of softwoods are also conveyed in tramps, whilst hardwoods are usually shipped in liner tonnage, either in logs or cut. Shipments of softwoods originate in the Baltic and the White Sea, and North and South America, whilst hardwoods originate in southern Europe, Japan and numerous tropical countries. Today, to facilitate speedy transhipment, much of the timber is shipped as packaged unit loads.

Tobacco is packed in hogsheads, bales or cases. Moisture causes mildew, and excessive ventilation reduces the flavour. It is a cargo that taints very easily. This cargo is conveyed in liner cargo tonnage in containers.

Wines are shipped in bulk in containerized glass-lined tanks, but in the European trades small tank vessels are employed. Main shipments originate in South Africa, the United States, Australia, France and Spain.

Wool is shipped in pressed bales or large bags. It is an inflammable cargo, and needs to be kept dry. Its stowage factor varies from 5.099 to 7.932, according to the quality. Wool is shipped in containers in cargo liner tonnage.

A wide range of fruits, vegetables, meat, dairy products and fish now supplied to a global market, involves temperature-controlled containerized shipment. Details are given in the temperature-controlled cargo guide, Appendix 13.1.

13.4 Cargo and container handling equipment

The form of cargo-handling equipment employed is mainly determined by the kind of cargo, the type of packing used and where and how it is stored prior to shipment, such as in a modern computer-controlled warehouse.

Handling facilities now use mechanization and computers. Bulk cargoes such as grain, sugar, coal, ore and oil are suited to high-tech computerized handling, and, provided the equipment is well utilized to cover capital charges and interest, it cheapens and speeds output. Such equipment is normally situated at a special berth. For bulk cargoes handling facilities may use power-propelled conveyor belts, fed at the landward end by a hopper (a very large container on legs) or grabs, which may be magnetic for handling ores, fixed to a high capacity travelling crane or travelling gantries. These gantries move parallel to the quay and can run back for considerable distances, thus serving a large stacking area. They also reach into the ship's hold. These two types of equipment are suitable for handling coal and ores. In the case of bulk sugar, for which a grab is also used, the sugar is discharged into a hopper, feeding by gravity a railway wagon or road vehicle below.

Elevators are usually associated with grain. They may be bucket elevators, or operated by pneumatic suction, sucking grain out of the ship's hold. The Port of London (Tilbury) grain terminal uses both bucket and pneumatic suction. Plastic buckets are faster, although the other type is preferred for a near-empty hold. This latter type is now popular and is designed to weigh the grain at the same time. Elevators may be situated on the quayside or be of a floating type, involving the provision of special pipes. Elevators are connected to the granaries (bulk grain storage warehouse) by power-operated conveyor belts.

Movement of bulk petrol and oils from the tanker is undertaken by means of pipelines connected to the shore-based storage tanks. Pumping equipment is provided in the tanker storage plant or refinery ashore, but not on the quayside. In view of the dangerous nature of such cargo, it is the practice to build the special berths some distance from the main dock system on the seaward side.

General merchandise in almost all liner cargo trades is containerized. Meanwhile dockers' handling of cargo continues, particularly in Third World countries where dock labour costs are more moderate, though there are efforts to expand use of mechanized cargo-handling equipment there. Labour-intensive dock labour cargo handling is declining fast. Containerization is, however, firmly established in the distribution of international trade under liner cargo arrangements: few maritime countries are not be served by container services. Not all liner cargo trade is totally containerized when circumstances dictate otherwise. When the cargo consists of a heterogeneous collection of packages of different sizes, weight and shapes, its loading and unloading, compared with the handling of bulk shipments, presents a different problem, particularly in regard to the use of mechanized equipment.

General loose non-containerized cargo is handled by cranes on the quay, by floating cranes or by the ship's own derricks or cranes. Attached to such lifting gear is a U-shaped shackle linking the crane or derricks to the form of cargo-handling equipment used. The shackle is joined at its open end by means of a loose pin to form a link. For most lifts a hook is used. The volume of loose cargo using 'tween-deck tonnage has diminished since containerization, the Combi carrier, ro/ro, and changing patterns in world trade. Hence, much equipment described in the next paragraph is mainly used in less developed countries and has been displaced elsewhere by the fork-lift truck and other modern methods of cargo-handling equipment/techniques.

There are numerous types of cargo-handling equipment that can be attached to the lifting gear. They include the sling or strop, which is probably the most common form of cargo-handling gear. This kind of equipment, generally made of rope, is ideal for hoisting strong packages, such as wooden cases or bagged cargo, which is not likely to sag or damage when raised. Similarly, snotters or canvas slings are suitable for bagged cargo. Chain slings, however, are used for heavy slender cargoes, such as timber or steel rails. Can or barrel hooks are suitable for hoisting barrels or drums. Cargo nets are suitable for mail bags and similar cargoes that are not liable to be crushed when hoisted. Heavy lifting beams are suitable for heavy and long articles such as locomotives, boilers or railway passenger coaches. Vehicle-lifting gear, consisting of four steel wire legs (with spreaders) attached to one lifting ring, are suitable for hoisting motor vehicles, trays and pallets, the latter being wooden or of steel construction, are ideal for cargo of moderate dimensions, which can be conveniently stacked, such as cartons, bags, or small wooden crates or cases. Additionally, dog or case hooks, and case and plate clamps are suitable for transhipping cargo to railway wagons or road vehicles, but not to or from the ship, except to facilitate transhipping the cargo in the hold to enable suitable cargo-handling gear to be attached. Dog hooks are not suitable for frail cases and should only be used to enable slings to be placed. Plate clamps are used for lifting metal plates.

Dockers working in the ship's hold use pinch- or crow-bars for heavy packages, and hand hooks for manoeuvring packages into position.

Much equipment facilitates movement of the cargo to and from the ship's side and the transit shed, warehouse, barge, railway wagon or road vehicle. These include two-wheeled hand-barrows and four-wheeled trucks, either manually or mechanically propelled, and mechanically or electrically propelled tractors for hauling four-wheeled trailers. There are also conveyor belts mechanically or electrically operated, or rollers, all perhaps extending from the quayside to the transit shed, warehouse, railway wagon or road vehicle. Mechanically powered straddle carriers are designed to straddle their load or set, pick it up and convey it to a convenient point on the quayside, transit shed, or elsewhere in the dock area. In appearance they resemble a farm tractor with a raised chassis, below which are clamps to raise and carry the cargo underneath the 'belly' of the tractor. They are suitable for timber, pipes and long cases. The larger straddle carriers distribute the ISO containers on the quay and stand over 12 m high giving an appearance of an inverted 'U'-shaped structure.

A wide range of cargo-handling equipment exists. The best handling solutions involve the least handling. Handling adds to the cost but not the value of the product. The choice of the right equipment or system to optimize material flow is broadly a definition of materials handling and includes cranes, con-veyors, automated vehicles, tractors, free-ranging forklifts, order pickers, stackers and pallet trucks. The handling method used should be the one which gives the greatest efficiency with economy and which makes full use of any existing facilities and equipment. Products whether they be cartons, bags, cans, bottles, drums or sacks are assembled together to form a unit load. Flat wooden (sometimes plastic) pallets are the commonly used base on which are placed unit loads, ISO containers, roll cages and tote bins. Others are stillages, box and cage pallets, bulk containers, etc. Products are often handled without pallets using specialized attachments in place of forks: bales, white goods, cookers, carpets, tyres, drums, beer kegs, paper rolls, milk crates, etc., are examples of the many products where attachments are utilized.

Fork-lift trucks are battery, electric or powered by internal combustion engine – diesel, petrol, LPG or compressed natural gas – and fitted in front with a platform in the shape of two prongs of a fork or other device. The prongs lift and carry the pallet either by penetrating through specially made apertures, or passing under it. The platform, affixed to a form of mast, can be raised and tilted, and the truck can travel with its load at any height up to its maximum. It is very manoeuvrable and can stack cargo up to a height of 5 m. The lifting capacity varies from 1,000 kg to 3,000 kg, when the trucks are called freight lifters. The majority of trucks in use are limited to 1,000 kg lifting capacity.

Details are given below of the types of fork-lift trucks available:

(a) *Side shift mechanism.* It enables the fork to move laterally either side of centre and thus considerably reduces the necessity to manoeuvre the fork-lift truck in the container or confined space.
(b) *Extension forks.* Ideal for handling awkward loads and to obtain extra reach. Subject to the fork truck being of sufficient capacity for clearing a space equivalent to the depth of two pallets on each side of a trailer-mounted container thus providing easy operation of the pallet. Numerous other examples of its use exist.
(c) *Boom.* Ideal for carpets, pipes, etc.
(d) *Crane jib.* Converts the fork-lift truck into a mobile crane.

(e) *Squeeze clamps.* Suitable for handling unit loads and individual items without the aid of pallets.

(f) *Drum handler.* Handles one or two drums at a time.

(g) *Barrel handler.* Not only does it clamp the barrel with two sets of upper and lower arms, but it also revolves so that the barrel can be picked up and handled on the roll or in the upright position.

(h) *Push-pull attachment.* It is specifically designed for use with slip sheets on containers.

(i) *Lift truck satellite.* A form of powered pallet truck which can be attached to a fork-lift truck carriage and used both to load/unload and also to transport pallet loads down the length of containers under remote control from the fork-lift truck which remains on the ground outside the container. A wide range of attachments are also available for palletless handling and specialized fork options, including:

(j) *Double pallet handler* permits two pallets to be handled side by side.

(k) *Carton clamp* similar to squeeze clamp with integral sideshift.

(l) *Rotating paper roll clamp* handles paper rolls by clamping using articulated contact pads, then rotating them to the vertical position for stacking on end.

(m) *Rotating fork unit* fitted with forks for handling bins, etc., which need to be rotated to discharge the contents

(n) *Load push-pull* enables load to be carried on a slip-sheet instead of a pallet – the push-pull has two broad platens in lieu of forks.

(o) *Load stabilizer* used to stabilize high loads.

(p) *Double deep* is provided with extending forks to enable loads to be stacked two deep in the rack to increase space utilization.

(q) *Fork positioners*, side shift optional.

(r) *Paper roll tippling clamp* (up-ender), rotation optional.

(s) *Brick clamp* for unit packs of bricks.

(t) *Hydraulic scoop.*

(u) *Cask clamp* and stabilizer for handling beer kegs.

A selection of fork-lift trucks is shown in Figure 13.1. Computers make use of fork-lift trucks more efficient in the warehouse. Bar codes identify, route and record stowage location in the warehouse. Nedlloyd Districentres' computers give the shipper on-line access and provide a data integration system between producer and distributor. Each commodity is coded on arrival into the Districentre using the bar code system. This enables orders to be processed automatically and offers a tracking system to check the total flow of goods thereby maintaining accurate stock control.

The latest generation of materials handling equipment is the electric pallet truck, manufactured by Linde Material Handling, which has a rider platform and is ergonomic functional. Locating the operating position at an angle of 45° to the direction of travel minimizes physical body movement when

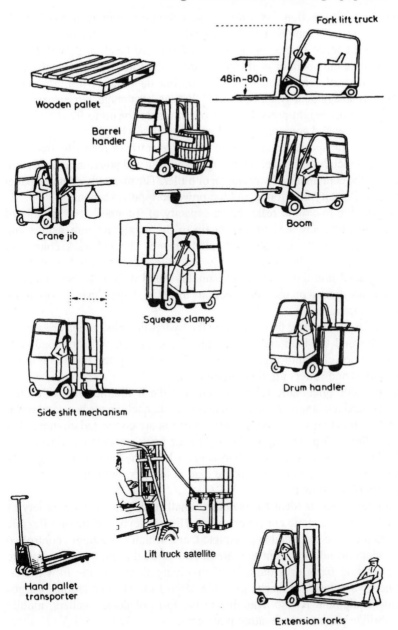

Figure 13.1 Fork lift trucks.

changing travel direction. As a result, the operator maintains a comfortable driving posture with unobstructed all-round visibility. Additionally, the latest technology of reach trucks includes the informative head-up digital display which ensures the operator is always aware of the truck's operational status; data communication available for mobile on-line data transfer for proprietary warehouse management systems; CC-TV for high lift storage, retrieval or stack auditing; and lift height pre-selector programmable for up to 99 shelf levels for safe, precise and economical load handling at any height.

The pallet transporter/truck may be battery, electric or manually operated. It is very manoeuvrable and efficient in transporting and positioning loads into and within the container, railway wagon or trailer. The manually operated pallet truck has a capacity of 1 tonne and the powered type 1.5 tonnes.

The portable hydraulic roller has a capacity of 2 tonnes. It is capable of loading/unloading any size or weight up to the maximum dimensions and weight capacity of the container. Parallel lines of channel track connected together are laid on the container floor and the requisite number of roller sections placed into them. The load, suitably fitted with a flat base or cross bearers, is positioned on the roller sections by crane, large capacity fork truck or other equipment.

The roller sections are then raised by the hydraulic units, which are always exposed beyond the load and pushed into the container with the load. The load is now lowered into prefixed bearers by operating the hydraulic units. The channels and rollers are then withdrawn.

The portable pneumatic roller unit, unlike the hydraulic unit which has separate channels, is integral and consists of a channel, an air hose and roller conveyor. Units to give any desired length of run are connected up in parallel lines and the load placed upon them. The air bags are inflated from an air supply thus raising the roller conveyor and enabling the load to be moved into the container. By releasing the air the load is lowered onto prefixed bearers and the units withdrawn.

A conveyor belt is ideal for handling small packages. A wide variety of powered mobile or static conveyors exist. The conveyor can be of a flexible type which can be extended and retracted, and which has a boom controlled by the operator, adjustable in the lateral and vertical planes. It may operate from a loading bank or ground level involving final stowage in a trailer, container, warehouse, or discharging the cargo from such situations. Cargo-handling equipment is also available in the form of dock levellers, mobile ramps, bridge plates and elevating platforms.

The dock leveller is designed to bridge both the vertical and horizontal gap, for example between a loading bank and a trailer-mounted container. There are two types primarily: those positioned exterior to the loading bank and those made integral with the bank.

The mobile ramp obviates the need for a loading bank. It is ideal for stuffing/unloading a trailer or container affixed to a trailer. The ramp is attached securely to the rear of the container or trailer unit. The height of the operation from ground to the trailer/ container is adjustable.

Bridge plates straddle the gap on a loading bank or at ground level. They are portable and can be moved to different positions as required.

The elevating platform can be either static or mobile and thereby obviate the need for a loading bank. The mobile type can easily be positioned at the doors of a trailer-mounted container adjacent to any vehicle, or any other situation. The platform raises the mechanical handling equipment, load and operator from the ground, for example to the level of the container floor, onto which it is driven by means of an integral bridge plate. They are powered usually by electro/mechanical or electro/hydraulic packs.

The fork-lift truck, and such equipment as the pallet and pallet truck, operate on the basis that goods at first handling are placed on boards, skids or pallets. The fork-lift truck inserts its forks through or under the pallet, situated in the railway wagon, transit shed or on the quayside, raises the load and carries it to the ship's side. The pallet is then used as a sling and hoisted direct into the ship's hold where the contents are stowed. The fork-lift truck can be used to tier cargo in a shed or on the quay in a well-established system called palletization. It is used in less developed countries and especially in tranship-ment ports involving lighterage serving the warehouse which distributes/ receives the maritime cargo from the deep-sea liner cargo services. It has to some extent changed methods of cargo handling in many liner ports. Both the fork-lift truck and to a lesser extent the pallet truck are used in stuffing and discharging containers on a very wide scale.

Palletization is growing in use, as demonstrated with the range of fork lift trucks available. It provides the following benefits: (a) it is a unitized method of distribution; (b) reduces handling costs and packaging; (c) lower insurance premiums through less damage; (d) more productive use of container space (Sea Cell container) and warehouse space; (e) speeds up handling and transit time; (f) ideal for supply chain management involving multimodalism; (g) develops markets; and (h) provides improved security. With the containerized shipment, particularly the full load, despatched by one shipper as distinct from the consolidated break bulk consignment, the total consignment is sometimes fully palletized. In such circumstances it facilitates container-contents stowage and permits quicker loading/discharging of the contents. The pallet forms an integral part of the packaging and remains with the cargo until it reaches its final destination which may be a lengthy rail or road journey to the importer distribution depot.

More recently the high cube dry container has been introduced of 8 ft (2.44 m) width, 9 ft 6 in. (2.9 m) high and either 40 ft (12.20 m) or 45 ft (13.72 m) long. Such containers are ideal for low weight high cube products such as garments from the Far East markets. Other types of containers and equipment exist – see Chapter 16.

Other containerized handling equipment includes the following:

(a) *Power jacks.* Four jacks which fit into the bottom corner castings of the container and controlled from a console. They lift and lower individually or in unison by selection and are either electro/hydraulic or electro/mechanical. Manually operated versions are also available.

(b) *Mobile gantries.* Electro/hydraulic operated with self-adjusting rams to ensure even lifting. Swivel lock castors permit the gantries when unladen to be manually manoeuvred and towed to different positions but off-balance loads need to be compensated by chain sling adjusters.

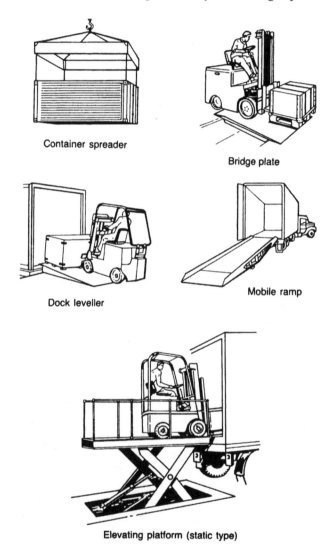

Figure 13.2 Container handling equipment.

Source: By courtesy of P&O Containers.

Containerization is fully examined in Chapter 16 and a selection of container-handling equipment is shown in Figure 13.2. Container terminals are purpose-built.

With the development of the multi-purpose vessel conveying road haulage vehicles and trailers – some of the latter being unaccompanied – the tug Master has emerged as an essential part of port equipment. The tug Master is a motorized unit attached to the unaccompanied trailer enabling that trailer to be driven on or off the vessel.

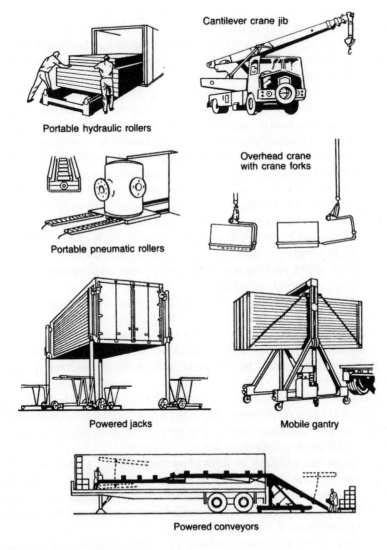

Portable hydraulic rollers

Cantilever crane jib

Portable pneumatic rollers

Overhead crane with crane forks

Powered jacks

Mobile gantry

Powered conveyors

Figure 13.2 continued

13.5 Types of packing

The method of packing depends primarily on the nature of the goods themselves and the method of transit for the anticipated voyage. Further subsidiary factors include the use to which the packing may be put when the goods reach their destination; the value of the goods (low value goods have less packing than those of high value); any customs or statutory requirements that must be complied with; ease of handling (awkward-shaped cargo suitably packed in cartons or cases can facilitate handling); marketing requirements; general fragility; variation in temperature during the voyage; the size of the cargo and its weight, and, in particular, whether elaborate packing is likely to increase the freight to the extent that it might price the goods out of the market; facilities available at the ports (some ports may not have highly mechanized cargo-handling equipment or elaborate storage accommodation); type and size of container; and the desirability of affixing to the packing any suitable advertisement. Overall, the export product price will include packing cost which will have particular regard to transit, packaging design and its cost.

A recent development concerns the packing needs for a consignment found in a distribution warehouse such as a districentre. The goods arrive in an FCL consignment and require distribution in small lots to clients situated in different countries: overall this is a break-bulk consignment, though the goods can also be consolidated with products from other sources. The packing requires consideration of the transport mode to be used for the on-carriage, the culture/language needs as regards labelling/instructions, such as translation into French/Italian/German/Spanish, and the value added concept – if the goods are for a retail outlet, packing is important in the method of selling at the point of sale. Other examples are where goods are received into a warehouse and processed. Such goods may be foodstuffs or require assembly from unit components to form the finished product for the market. The goods are then sold to neighbouring countries, perhaps with differing cultures and languages, which affects the labelling and instructions on the packing. This type of operation is found in many trading ports, such as Singapore, and overall is a growth market.

Packing is a form of protection to reduce the risk of goods being damaged in transit and to prevent pilferage. The right type of packing, its correct quality and the form of container used is important. The most important types of packing and their description are these:

Many goods have little or no form of packing and are *carried loose*. These include iron and steel plates, iron rods, railway sleepers and steel rails. Such cargoes are generally weight cargoes, with a low stowage factor. Heavy vehicles, locomotives and buses are carried loose, because of the impracticability and high cost of packing.

Bailing is a form of packing consisting of a canvas cover often cross-looped by metal or rope binding. It is most suitable for paper, wool, cotton, carpets and rope.

Bags made of jute, cotton, plastic or paper are a cheap form of container. They are suitable for cement, coffee, fertilizers, flour and oil cakes. Their prime disadvantage is that they are subject to damage by water, sweat, hooks or, in the case of paper bags, breakage.

A recent development in packaging technique is the liquid rubber container. It is called a *bulk liquid bag* or container, and can store various kinds of liquid cargo. When not in use the bag can be folded to 2% of its volume, Other cargoes can then be conveyed in the unit on the return trip. The fold-up facility eliminates wasted space in the rigid tank containers and steel drums which otherwise could not carry dry goods on the return journeys. In cost terms the bulk liquid bag is one sixth of the price of a steel drum and one fourth of a tank container. Each bulk liquid bag can carry a volume of liquid cargo equivalent to 210 large capacity steel drums.

Cartons are a common form of packing, and may be constructed of cardboard, strawboard or fibreboard. This form of packing is very much on the increase, as it lends itself to ease of handling, particularly by palletization. The principal disadvantage is its susceptibility to crushing and pilfering. It is a flexible form of packing and therefore prevents the breakages occurring when rigid containers are used. Many kinds of consumer goods are packed inexpensively in cartons, making cartons ideal packaging for container cargo. Polystyrene now aids packing in cartons. The triwall in common with the carton may be palletized with provision for fork-lift handling.

Crates, or skeleton cases, are a form of container, half-way between a bale and a case. They are of wooden construction. Lightweight goods of larger cubic capacity, such as light machinery, domestic appliances like refrigerators, cycles and certain foodstuffs, for instance oranges, are suitable for this form of packing.

Carboys, or glass containers, enclosed in metal baskets have a limited use, and are primarily employed for the carriage of acids and other dangerous liquids transported in small quantities.

Boxes, *cases* and *metal-lined cases* are used extensively. Wooden in construction, they vary in size and capacity, and can be strengthened by battens and metal binding. Many of them, such as tea chests, are lined to create airtight packing so as to overcome difficulties arising when passing through zones of variable temperature. Much machinery and other items of expensive equipment, including cars and parts, are packed in this form.

Barrels, *hogsheads* and *drums* are used for the conveyance of liquid or greasy cargoes. The main problem associated with this form of packing is the likelihood of leakage if the unit is not properly sealed, and the possibility of the drums becoming rusty during transit. Acids can also be carried in plastic drums and bottles. The drum is usually of 45 gallons or 205 litres capacity and may also convey liquid (oil, chemicals) or powder shipments. Drums are usually stowed in a cradle to facilitate mechanical handling stowage and stacking.

Shrink wrapping has arisen through the need to reduce packaging costs particularly with regard to wooden cases and similar relatively high-cost materials. It involves placing the goods to be covered on a base – usually a pallet for ease of handling – and covering them with a film of plastic, which is shrunk to enclose the items by the use of hot-air blowers (thermo-guns). It is a relatively cheap form of packing particularly in comparison with timber and fibreboard cartons. Moreover, it gives a rigid protection and security to the cargo. Its configuration follows the outline of the goods. Packing in shock-absorbent polyurethane foam with a plastic foil in the pallet is in wide use.

Shrink wrapping is used extensively for palletized consignments to secure goods to the pallet unit. This is a more rigid unit and improves the security of the goods throughout the transit. It can facilitate handling of the palletized unit and stacking of the goods in the warehouse. The palletized goods may be in a trailer movement, container (LCL or FCL) or break bulk shipment, as for example in lighterage. Colour films are available to protect light-sensitive cargo, and provide a degree of protection against pilferage.

The *cov pak* is a pal box, a jumbo fibreboard box placed on an independent pallet. Seven sizes are available, including the half Europa (800 mm – 600 mm – 830 mm), the half container (1,100 mm – 900 mm – 710 mm), the ISO No. 2 (1,200 mm – 1,000 mm – 685 mm) and ISO No. 1 (1,200 mm – 1,000 mm – 1,040 mm). The container body is made from twin-wall heavy-duty board. Internal fittings can suit individual needs. A four-way pallet base and self-locking integral construction of the container ensure the pack is unitized throughout the transit. The cov pak is supplied flat with its own patented self-locking timber pallet. It offers multi-stacking, is subject to weight constraints, and the container body can be delivered flat with the pallets inter-nested. The goods are placed into the container body and sealed by means of polypropylene strapping with metal seals for greater protection, or it can be sealed with tape. The cov pak is also termed the mac pak, some having polystyrene legs. Many shippers have smaller boxes inside the container body. Mixed loads are permitted and the cov pak is reusable for several transits.

The *jiffy bag* has 67 different types. These bags are an envelope with bubble-wrap padding inside, making them ideal for small consignments, such as medical samples, promotional items and computer items.

Metal envelope packaging is used in the movement of steel shipments and encapsulates the consignment to make it more secure.

Two recent developments in packaging are these:

(a) Flat wrapping enables furniture such as kitchen and dining room wooden chairs to be flat wrapped. This lets component units lie on top of one another and permits furniture assembly in customers' homes. Furniture manufactured in Malaysia is despatched globally using high cube containers and retailed by Ikea throughout Europe.

(b) A new generation of plastic containers now meets supply chain requirements. The majority have been heavy-duty crates, stackable and nestable boxes, which minimize the cost of moving empty packaging. When used to transport goods from the manufacturer/supplier/exporter, the shipping cube is fully utilized. For other transits in the supply chain the empty fold-down boxes provide a 140% better utilization of transport space compared with nestable containers. Their sizes range from 400 mm by 300 mm up to 1,200 mm by 3,000 mm. This development has arisen by the European Packaging Waste Legislation 2001. The regulations cover one-trip packaging, but importers must absorb the 'rolled up' obligations of their suppliers. Hence a retailer located in an EU state importing a packed product incurs all the obligations of the raw material supplier, packaging, manufacturer and packer. In contrast when a returnable or reusable package enters the system its tonnage becomes obligated, though there is no obligation on subsequent trips, however long it is in the system. There may arise some situations where users of returnable packaging systems have no recycling or recovery obligations.

As containerization develops, packing needs for shipped cargo will change, because containerization requires less packing. Undoubtedly, packing will become less robust.

Associated with types of packing is the marking of cargo. When goods are packed, they are marked on the outside so that the marks remain legible for the whole voyage. First, there is some mark of identification, and then immediately underneath this the port mark is shown. For example, the merchant may be J. Brown Ltd and the goods are being shipped in the SS *Amsterdam* to Rotterdam, in which case the marks will be as in Figure 13.3.

These simple markings are adequate for identification, and are entered on the bill of lading. In the event of there being several cases in one shipment, the number of the case is also entered, in this case No. 2. All goods must be marked with a shipping mark on at least two sides clearly, to include the name of the destination port/depot. These marks on the shipping documents must correspond exactly with those on the goods. The figures below the number are the dimensions of a case in metres, and may be used in assessing the freight. An internationally recognized code sign may also be stencilled on the case to facilitate handling and to indicate the nature of the cargo. Such code signs indicate 'sling here', 'fragile goods' 'keep dry' (as illustrated in Figure 13.3),

J.B. LTD. No. 2
2.5 m x 1.8 m x 1.3 m
Rotterdam

Figure 13.3 Example of the marking of cargo.

Figure 13.4 Recognized international marking symbols.

'do not drop', etc. A selection of the labels used in the international cargo-handling code is found in Figure 13.4.

13.6 Dangerous cargo

Dangerous goods have been defined as substances classified as 'dangerous' in Acts, rules or by-laws or having similar properties or hazards. Legislation applicable to all British-registered tonnage or vessels loading in British ports is contained in the Merchant Shipping (Dangerous Goods and Marine Pollutants) Regulation 1997, as well as the Dangerous Substances in Harbour Areas Regulations 1987, the Health and Safety at Work etc. Act 1974, the Environment Protection Act 1990, and the Carriage of Dangerous Goods (Classification Packaging and Labelling) Regulations 1996 and Management of Health and Safety at Work Regulations 1992 as amended. These require all packaged goods to be:

(a) Classified and declared by the shipper to the Master.
(b) Packaged in a manner to withstand the ordinary risk of handling and transport by sea, having regard to their properties.
(c) Marked with proper shipping name and indication of the danger.
(d) Properly stowed and effectively segregated from others which may dangerously interact.
(e) Listed in a manifest or stowage plan giving stowage details. This must be aboard the ship.

The requirements of the Merchant Shipping (Dangerous Goods and Marine Pollutants) Regulations 1997 reflect the International Maritime Dangerous Goods (IMDG) Code, produced by the International Maritime Organization (IMO); 50 countries, responsible for 85% of world tonnage, have adopted the Code.

The IMDG code was developed as a uniform code for the transport of dangerous goods by sea covering such matters as packing, container traffic, and stowage, with particular reference to the segregation of incompatible substances. Amendments to the IMDG code originate from two sources: proposals submitted directly to the IMO by member states and amendments required to take account of changes to the United Nations Recommendations on the Transport of Dangerous Goods, which sets the basic requirements for all transport modes. Amendments to the provisions of the United Nations recommendations are made on a two yearly cycle, and approximately two years after their adoption the authorities responsible for regulating the various transport modes adopt them. In this way a basic set of requirements applicable to all modes of transport is established and implemented, ensuring no difficulties occur where different modes meet.

The IMDG code, Chapter VII of the IMO SOLAS Convention, was developed as a uniform code for the transport of dangerous goods by sea and is concerned with, for example, such matters as packing, container traffic and stowage, with particular reference to the segregation of incompatible substances. Amendments to SOLAS Chapter VII (Carriage of Dangerous Goods) were adopted in May 2002 to make the IMDG code mandatory from 1 January 2004. The May 2002 IMDG code is known as amendment 31.

The code lays down: basic principles; detailed recommendations for individual substances, material and articles; and a number of recommendations for good operational practice, including advice on terminology, packing, labelling, stowage, segregation and handling and emergency response action. The IMDG code embraces the following. However, the provisions of the following parts of the code will remain recommendatory:

- Chapter 1.3 (Training).
- Chapter 2.1 (Explosives, Introductory Notes 1 to 4 only).
- Chapter 2.3, section 2.3.3 (Determination of flashpoint only).
- Chapter 3.2 (columns 15 and 17 of the Dangerous goods List only).
- Chapter 3.5 (Transport schedule for Class 7 radioactive material only).
- Chapter 5.4, section 5.4.5 (Multi-modal dangerous goods from), in so far as layout of the form is concerned.
- Chapter 7.3 (Special requirements in the event of an incident and fire precautions involving dangerous goods only).

In practice, legally the whole of the IMDG Code is mandatory, but provisions of a recommendatory nature are editorially expressed in the Code (e.g. using the word 'should' instead of 'shall') to clarify their status.

The mandatory IMDG Code incorporates certain changes relating to specific products, as well as relevant elements of the amendments to the UN Recommendations on the Transport of Dangerous Goods, Model Regulations adopted by the UN Committee of Experts on the Transport of Dangerous Goods at its twenty-first session in Geneva from 4 to 13 December 2000.

The two-volume Code is divided in this way:

- *Volume 1* (parts 1, 2 and 4–7 of the Code) contains sections on: (a) general provisions, definitions, training; (b) classification; (c) packing and tank provisions; (d) consignment procedures; (e) construction and testing of packagings, IBCs, large packagings, portable tanks and road tank vehicles; and (f) transport operations.
- *Volume 2* contains: the Dangerous Goods List (equivalent to the schedules in previous editions of the Code), presented in tabular format: (a) limited quantities exceptions; (b) the index; and (c) appendices.
- *The Supplement* contains the following texts related to the IMDG Code: (a) EMS Guide; (b) Medical First Aid Guide; (c) Reporting Procedures; (d) Packing Cargo Transport Units; (e) Safe Use of Pesticides; and (f) INF Code.

It is estimated that more than 50% of the cargoes transported by sea today can be regarded as dangerous, hazardous and/or harmful (marine pollutants) under the IMO classification, designation or identification criteria. Some are dangerous or hazardous to safety and could be harmful to the marine environment; others are harmful to the marine environment alone. These concerned include products transported in bulk, such as solid or liquid chemicals, gases and products for and of the oil refinery industry. Between 10% and 15% of the cargoes transported in packaged form, including shipborne barges on barge-carrying ships, freight containers, bulk packagings, portable tanks, tank-containers, vehicles, intermediate bulk containers (IBCs), unit loads and other cargo transport units, fall under these criteria.

In an increasingly complex industrialized world transport by sea of these cargoes continues to rise and the list of products grows. If shipping is to maintain and improve its safety record, these cargoes must be stored, handled and transported with the greatest care.

Figure 13.5 shows how the nine classes of dangerous goods are identified on the labels, placards, marks and signs.

Classes of dangerous goods from the IMDG Code

Definitions

Substances (including mixtures and solutions), and articles subject to the provisions of this Code, are assigned to one of the classes 1–9 according to the hazard or the most predominant of the hazards they present. Some of these classes are subdivided into divisions. These classes or divisions are as listed below:

Class 1 Explosives

- Division 1.1, substances and articles which have a mass explosion hazard.
- Division 1.2, substances and articles having a projection hazard, but not a mass explosion hazard.
- Division 1.3, substances and articles which have a projection and either a minor blast hazard or a minor projection hazard or both, but not a mass explosion hazard.
- Division 1.4, substances and articles which present no significant hazard.
- Division 1.5, very insensitive substances which have a mass explosion hazard.
- Division 1.6, extremely insensitive articles which do not have a mass explosion hazard.

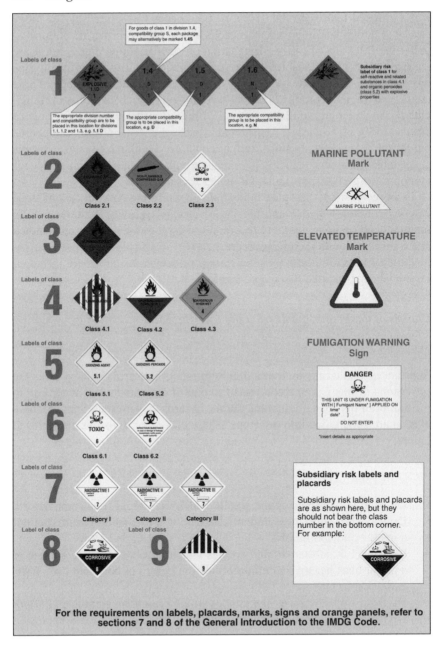

Figure 13.5 Labels, placards and signs warning of dangerous goods carried by sea.

Source: By courtesy of the International Marine Organization.

Class 2 Gases

- Class 2.1, flammable gases.
- Class 2.2, non-flammable, non-toxic gases.
- Class 2.3, toxic gases.

Class 3 Flammable liquids

Class 4 Flammable solids; substances liable to spontaneous combustion; substances which, in contact with water, emit flammable gases

- Class 4.1, flammable solids, self-reactive substances and desensitized explosives.
- Class 4.2, substances liable to spontaneous combustion.
- Class 4.3, substances which, in contact with water, emit flammable gases.

Class 5 Oxidizing substances and organic peroxides

- Class 5.1, oxidizing substances.
- Class 5.2, organic peroxides.

Class 6 Toxic and infectious substances

- Class 6.1, toxic substances.
- Class 6.2, infectious substances.

Class 7 Radioactive material

Class 8 Corrosive substances

Class 9 Miscellaneous dangerous substances and articles

The numerical order of the classes and divisions does not reflect the degree of danger.

The shipowner handles dangerous cargo by prior written arrangement and on the express condition that the shipper provides a full and adequate description of the cargo. If accepted a special stowage order – often referred to as a dangerous goods form – will be issued to indicate to the Master that the cargo conforms to the prescribed code of acceptance laid down by the shipowner. Shipment will not take place until a special stowage order has been issued by the shipowner: the shipowner's special stowage order is the authority to ship. Moreover, the shipper must fully describe the cargo and ensure it is correctly packed, marked and labelled. Often he does this through a freight forwarder.

Before dangerous goods can be authorized for shipment the following information is required:

(a) Name of sender.
(b) Correct technical name of the dangerous goods (the trade name may not be sufficient to identify the hazard) followed by the words 'Marine Pollutant' (if applicable).
(c) Class of dangerous goods.
(d) Flashpoint (where applicable).
(e) UN No. to identify substance.
(f) Details of outer packing.
(g) Details of inner packing.
(h) Quantity to be shipped in individual packages and in total.
(i) Additional information for radioactive materials, explosive and consignments in bulk (e.g. tank containers, road tankers, etc.).

The dangerous goods authority form will bear a reference number and show the sailing details, including port of departure and destination on which consignment is authorized, the hazard class, UN No., labels, key number (for emergency in event of any incident, spillage, etc.), and any special instructions (i.e. special Department for Transport (DFT) approval or restrictions on stowage, i.e. on deck only (passenger ship), freight vessel only, etc.).

On arrival of the goods at the departure port the goods and authority to ship are submitted to the Master of the ship for ultimate approval prior to loading and customs clearance.

The Master of the ship carrying packaged goods shall cause a special list, manifest or stowage plan to be carried in the ship. It will identify where in the ship the goods are stowed. Also it will provide details obtained from the shipping documents submitted by the shipper of the packaged goods on board, including the correct technical name of the goods, their classification in accord with the Regulation 7(2) of the Merchant Shipping (Dangerous Goods and Marine Pollutants) Regulations 1990, and their mass or volume.

Packaged goods shall be stowed, segregated and secured on board the vessel in accordance with the IMDG Code. For container shipments, it is the responsibility of the person loading the vehicle or freight container to ensure that packaged goods are correctly stowed, segregated and secured in accordance with the IMDG Code. No explosives may be carried unless the Master fully complies with the provisions of the Merchant Shipping (Dangerous Goods and Marine Pollutants) Regulations 1990, Part II, Section 13, and the relevant parts of the IMDG Code.

Deep-sea container shipment is ideal for the transport of dangerous cargo, particularly as it avoids multiple handling, protects the goods from interference by unauthorized persons and eliminates the risk of damage from the use of inappropriate methods of slinging. The following information is required at the time of booking the container:

(a) Name of vessel.
(b) Port of loading.
(c) Port of discharge.
(d) Number, kind and size of individual packages (including inner packages if valid) and total quantity, i.e. gross and nett weight in kilos.
(e) Correct technical name of substance, as defined in IMDG Code.
(f) Hazard classification of substance (IMO).
(g) UN number of substance.
(h) Marine pollutant – if applicable.
(i) Packaging group.
(j) Flashpoint – if any.
(k) EmS Number if NOS – Emergency Schedule for Dangerous Goods – not otherwise specified; (as listed in IMDG Code). (l) MFAG table number (as listed in IMDG Code).

With 'tween-deck or bulk cargo shipments the loading of the ship is undertaken by stevedores/dockers, though for containers loading is performed by container packers, who are usually container operators or freight forwarders. Accordingly, a 'packing certificate' must be completed and signed for container operators or freight forwarders which certifies the following:

(a) The container was clean, dry and fit to receive the cargo.
(b) No cargo known to be incompatible has been stowed therein.
(c) All packages have been inspected for damage, and only dry and sound packages loaded.
(d) All packages have been properly stowed and secured and suitable materials used.
(e) The container and goods have been properly labelled and placarded.
(f) A dangerous goods declaration has been received/ completed for each dangerous consignment packed in the container.

The packing certificate must be duly completed and signed by the shipper, to confirm to the shipping line and the Master that packing the container has been properly carried out. The document accompanies the goods throughout the voyage. In regard to FCL containers, the Dangerous Goods Packing Certificate may be incorporated in the IMO Dangerous Goods Note.

Other SOLAS amendments which entered into force in 2004, including these:

• *Updates to Chapter IV, Radiocommunications.* The amendments to this chapter relate to changes following the full implementation of the Global Maritime Distress and Safety System (GMDSS) on 1 February 1999, which renders some of the provisions relating to implementation dates in the current Chapter IV superfluous.
• The amendments also state that a listening watch on VHF channel 16 for distress and safety purposes should be kept.

- *Carriage requirement for IAMSAR Manual*. An amendment to Chapter V, Safety of navigation, requires ships to carry an up-to-date copy of Volume III of the *International Aeronautical and Maritime Search and Rescue* (IAMSAR) *Manual*.
- *Other amendments*. Amendments to the 1988 protocol to SOLAS, 1974, relate to updates to the Record of Equipment for the Passenger Ship Safety Certificate (form P); Record of Equipment for the Cargo Ship Safety Radio Certificate (form R); and Record of Equipment for the Cargo Ship Safety Certificate (form C).

APPENDIX 13.1
Temperature-controlled cargo guide commodity tables (reproduced by courtesy of P&ONedlloyd)

Commodity	Recommended temperature setting (°C)	Recommended temperature setting (°F)	Approximate shelf life (days)	Warmest freezing point (°C)	Warmest freezing point (°F)	Ethylene production rate	Sensitivity to ethylene
Fruit and vegetables							

All the following fruit and vegetable products need fresh air supply during long-distance transport. This fresh air supply is to be expressed in cubic metres per hour (CBM). The older integrals have a fresh air inlet maximum of 90 CBM and the latest new integrals can allow up to 260 CBM. All the recommendations below are general and depend upon the cultivar, growing area, time of the year, and routing. A large number of variations are possible when carrying these cargoes as post-harvest treatments and packaging significantly affect shelf life.

Commodity	Recommended temperature setting (°C)	Recommended temperature setting (°F)	Approximate shelf life (days)	Warmest freezing point (°C)	Warmest freezing point (°F)	Ethylene production rate	Sensitivity to ethylene
Apple	−1 to +4	+30.2 to +30.9	40–240	−1.5	+29.3	Very high	High
Apricot	−0.5	+31.1	7–14	−1.1	+30.0	High	High
Asparagus	+2	+35.6	14–21	−0.6	+30.9	Very low	Medium
Aubergine	+10	+50.0	10–14	−0.8	+30.6	Low	Low
Avocado	+4 to +13	+39.2 to +55.4	14–56	−0.3	+31.5	High	High
Banana	+13.5	+56.3	7–28	−0.8	+30.6	Medium	High
Bean – green	+7	+44.6	10–14	−0.7	+30.7	Low	Medium
Beansprout	0	+32.0	49–63	−0.4	+31.3		
Belgian endive	+2	+35.6	14–28	−0.1	+31.8	Very low	Medium
Black radish	0	+32.0	60–120	−0.7	+30.7	Low	None
Blackberry	−0.5	+31.1	2–3	−0.8	+30.6	Low	Low
Breadfruit	+13	+55.4	14–40			Medium	Medium
Broccoli	0	+32.0	10–14	−0.6	+30.9	Very low	High
Cabbage	0	+32.0	90–180	−0.9	+30.4	Very low	High

Commodity	Recommended temperature setting (°C)	Recommended temperature setting (°F)	Approximate shelf life (days)	Warmest freezing point (°C)	Warmest freezing point (°F)	Ethylene production rate	Sensitivity to ethylene
Cantaloupe	+4	+39.2	10–14	−1.2	+29.8	High	Medium
Carambola	+8	+46.4	21–28			Low	Low
Casaba melon	+10	+50.0	21–28	−1.1	+30.0	Low	Low
Cassava root	0 to +5	+32.0 to +41.0	20–24			Very low	Low
Cauliflower	0	+32.0	20–30	−0.8	+30.6	Very low	High
Celery	0	+32.0	14–28	−0.5	+31.1	Very low	Medium
Cherry – sweet	−1	+30.2	14–21	−1.8	+28.8	Very low	Low
Chicory	0	+32.0	14–28			Very low	High
Chilli pepper	+8	+46.4	14–21	−0.7	+30.7	Low	Low
Chinese cabbage	0	+32.0	60–90			Very low	Medium
Clementine	+4	+39.2	14–28	−0.1	+31.8	Low	None
Coconut	0	+32.0	30–60	−0.9	+30.4	Low	Low
Corn (Sweet-)	0	+32.0	4–6	−0.6	+30.9	Very low	Low
Courgette	+7	+44.6	14–21	−0.5	+31.1	Low	Medium
Cranberry	+2	+35.6	60–120	−0.9	+30.4	Low	Low
Crenshaw melon	+10	+50.0	21–28	−1.1	+30.0	Medium	High
Cucumber	+10	+50.0	10–14	−0.5	+31.1	Low	High
Date	0	+32.0	165–365	−15.7	+3.8	Very low	Low
Durian	+4	+39.2	42–56				
Endive	0	+32.0	14–21	−0.1	+31.8	Very low	Medium
Fig	0	+32.0	7–10	−2.4	+27.7	Medium	Low
Garlic	0	+32.0	140–210	−0.8	+30.6	Very low	Low
Ginger	+13	+55.4	90–180			Very low	Low
Grape	0	+32.0	56–180	−2.2	+28.0	Very low	Low
Grapefruit	+13	+55.4	28–42	−1.1	+30.0	Very low	Medium
Haricot vert	+4	+39.2	7–10				
Honeydew melon	+10	+50.0	21–28	−1.0	+30.2	Medium	High
Horseradish	0	+32.0	300–350	−1.8	+28.8	Very low	Low
Kiwano	+10	+50.0	180				
Kiwi	0	+32.0	28–84	−0.9	+30.4	Low	High
Kohlrabi	0	+32.0	25–30	−1.0	+30.2	Very low	Low
Lemon	+12	+53.6	30–180	−1.4	+29.5	Very low	Medium
Lettuce	0	+32.0	8–12	−0.2	+31.6	Low	Medium
Lime	+12	+53.6	21–35	−1.6	+29.1	Very low	Medium
Logan	+1.5	+34.7	21–35	−0.5	+31.1		

Commodity	Recommended temperature setting (°C)	Recommended temperature setting (°F)	Approximate shelf life (days)	Warmest freezing point (°C)	Warmest freezing point (°F)	Ethylene production rate	Sensitivity to ethylene
Loquat	0	+32.0	14–21	−0.9	+30.4		
Lychee	+1	+33.8	21–45	−0.5	+31.1	Medium	Medium
Mandarin	+7	+44.6	14–28	−1.1	+30.0	Very low	Medium
Mango	+13	+55.4	14–25	−0.9	+30.4	Medium	High
Mango – sour	+8	+46.4	20–30	−0.6	+30.9	Medium	Medium
Mushroom	0	+32.0	12–17	−0.9	+30.4	Very low	Medium
Nectarine	−0.5	+31.1	14–28	−0.9	+30.4	Medium	Medium
Olive	+7	+44.6	28–42	−1.4	+29.5	Low	Medium
Onion – dry	0	+32.0	30–180	−0.8	+30.6	Very low	Low
Orange – green	+7	+44.6	21–56	−0.8	+30.6	Very low	Medium
Orange – Jaffa	+8	+46.4	56–84	−1.0	+30.2		
Orange – Seville	+10	+50.0	90	−0.7	+30.7	Low	None
Orange – Texas	+2	+35.6	56–84	−0.8	+30.6	Very low	Medium
Papaya	+12	+53.6	7–21	−0.9	+30.4	High	High
Paprika	+8	+46.4	14–20	−0.7	+30.7	Low	Low
Passion fruit	+12	+53.6	14–21			Very high	High
Peach	−0.5	+31.1	14–28	−0.9	+30.4	High	High
Pear	−1	+30.2	60–90	−1.6	+29.1	High	High
Pepper – bell	+8	+46.4/	12–24	−0.7	+30.7	Low	Low
Pepper – chili	+10	+50.0	14–20	−0.7	+30.7	Low	Low
Persian melon	+10	+50.0	14–21	−0.8	+30.6	Medium	High
Persimmon (Kaki)	0	+32.0	60–90	−2.2	+28.0	Low	High
Pineapple – Guatemala	+5	+41.0	14–21	−0.8	+30.6	Medium	Low
Pineapple – Mature	+10	+50.0	14–25	−1.0	+30.2	Low	Low
Pineapple – ripe	+8	+46.4	14–36	−1.1	+30.0	High	Low
Pineapple – unripe	+13	+55.4	14–20	−1.0	+30.2	Low	Low
Plantain	+14	+57.2	10–35	−0.8	+30.6	Low	High
Plum	−0.5	+31.1	14–28	−0.8	+30.6	Medium	High
Pomegranate	+5	+41.0	28–56	−3.0	+26.6	Low	Low
Potato – processing	+10	+50.0	56–175	−0.8	+30.6	Very low	Medium
Potato – seed	+4	+39.2	84–175	−0.8	+30.6	Very low	Medium
Potato – table	+7	+44.6	56–140	−0.8	+30.6	Very low	Medium
Pumpkin	+12	+53.6	84–160	−0.8	+30.6	Low	Low
Radish	0	+32.0	21–28	−0.7	+30.7	Very low	Low

Commodity	Recommended temperature setting (°C)	Recommended temperature setting (°F)	Approximate shelf life (days)	Warmest freezing point (°C)	Warmest freezing point (°F)	Ethylene production rate	Sensitivity to ethylene
Rambutan	+12	+53.6	7–21			High	High
Salsify	0	+32.0	60–120	–1.1	+30.0	Very low	Low
Spinach	0	+32.0	10–14	–0.3	+31.5	Low	Medium
Starfruit	+8	+46.4	21–28			Low	Low
Sugar apple	+7	+44.6	28				Low
Sweet corn	0	+32.0	4–6	–0.6	+30.9	Very low	Low
Tangerine	+7	+44.6	14–28	–1.1	+30.0	Very low	Medium
Tomato – green	+13	+55.4	21–28	–0.5	+31.1	Very low	High
Tomato – orange	+10	+50.0	14–28	–0.5	+31.1	Very low	High
Tomato – pink	+8	+46.4	7–14	–0.5	+31.1	Medium	High
Tomato – red	+6	+42.8	14–26	–0.5	+31.1	Low	Medium
Tree tomato	+4	+39.2	21–70	–0.4	+31.3	High	Medium
Water chestnut	+4	+39.2	100–128				
Watermelon	+10	+50.0	14–21	–0.4	+31.3	Low	Low
Yam	+13	+55.4	50–115	–1.1	+30.0	Very low	Low
Zucchini	+7	+44.6	14–21	–0.5	+31.1	None	None

Meat, dairy products, fish and other

Commodity	Recommended temperature setting (°C)	Recommended temperature setting (°F)	Approximate shelf life (days)	Warmest freezing point (°C)	Warmest freezing point (°F)		
Bacon – chilled +28.4/+36.5		30	–1	–2/+2.5	+30.2		
Beef – chilled +29.3/+32.0		70–95	–1.5	–1.5/0	+29.3		
Butter – fresh +30.2/+40.1		30	0	–1/+4.5	+32.0		
Butter – frozen			–14 or colder		+6.8 or colder		
Cheese[a] +32.0/+50.0 Concentrate			+4	0/+10	+39.2		

Notes: Temperature settings and shelf lives are influenced by the quality of the raw materials, the processing and packaging. The above figures can vary significantly depending on the length of the transit. The design and capabilities of refrigerated containers are advancing rapidly with varying control systems between different integral containers as well as with porthole containers. Their specific operating characteristics as well as differing local conditions will influence the temperature settings required for any individual booking.

[a] Temperature may vary with type of cheese, also whether or not it requires ripening during the trip. Some categories may require ventilation during transit. Care must be taken when opening the doors of a reefer container with 'ripening' unventilated cheese, due to possible high carbon dioxide levels, and not enough oxygen left for breathing. Cargo must be 'aired' first.

14 The shipping company

14.1 Size and scope of the undertaking

Changes in the size and scope of shipping companies are based on company business plans formulated by directors. These factors are relevant:

(a) The company will have marketing as a core objective. Marketing is creating new kinds of management culture throughout shipping companies. It is customer focused, embracing and responding to and empathizing with customer needs competitively. Hitherto, company priorities were determined primarily by operating considerations. Marketing, however, now embraces promotion strategies as well as market research, product development, such as new types of container, quicker transit and marketing plans, including budget-driven marketing management.

(b) The IMO codes introduced recently include ISM, STCW, and ISPS codes, which influence company structure, primarily in marine sectors of the business. In particular, the chain of command between ship and shore emphasizes ship management and security.

(c) Logistics is growing in liner cargo companies.

(d) Information technology (see Chapter 20) increases in sophistication, quickening the pace of the decision-making. IT extends to all parts of the shipping company organization and in many companies has resulted in the elimination of layers of management structure – especially in the middle management range. This has shortened the decision management chain and resulted in quicker decisions, making a company more competitive.

(e) Headquarters structure is smaller and authority is devolved to encourage more accountability of personnel at all management levels. The profit centre concept has meant strong budgeting management. Devolution of executive authority has involved cross-border structures that yield tax benefits and lower wage scales. Development of computerized technology is at the root of this change.

(f) Diversification of the business means that while shipping may remain the core of a shipping business, many entrepreneurs pursue other commercial interests, such as property acquisition and construction and ancillary activities of the shipping business, such as road haulage, seaports, warehouse and shipbroking.

(g) Development of third party ship management outsourcing is growing, especially in crew, insurance, ship survey and bunker management.

(h) There are operating alliances among shipping companies.

(i) There are mergers and acquisitions among an increasing number of shipping companies. These exploit economies of scale and raise capital to fund new tonnage and infrastructure, especially IT. An example is the merger of P&O Nedlloyd and Maersk Line, to form the Maersk Line. Shipping is now dominated by fewer but mega-container operators.

These developments have seen the emergence of a new breed of shipping executive, who must be a specialist in his/her shipping business, professionally qualified, market-driven in attitude, assiduous, culture orientated, multilingual, profit motivated and computer literate. Shipping executives receive, or should receive continuous training in technology, market environments, commercial opportunities and business strategies.

The size of a shipping undertaking, its organization and cost structure, and pricing of its sea transport services, are influenced by the type of service operated, and particularly by differences between liner and tramp operation.

There is great variation in size among shipping undertakings, ranging from a single ship company to giant groups. Entrepreneurs try to maximize profits and expand output, as long as an increase in total costs is less than the increase in total revenue. They continue to expand their business to the point where marginal additional cost is equal to marginal additional revenue.

Recent years have seen mergers between liner and tramp shipping companies, the reasons being numerous, but which include: economies realized on administration cost; improved prospects of raising more capital for new tonnage; rationalization of facilities, for example port agents, departments, overseas offices, berths, ports of call, etc.; long-term consideration of likely improvement on tonnage utilization and productivity, with possible limited rationalization of a fleet and centralization of marine department activities, covering manning, management, survey programme and new builds; a larger customer portfolio; a larger trading company with improved competitive ability and the long-term possibility of a more economical service at lower cost with consequently improved tariffs; and generally the larger the company the better it is able to combat the challenges of new investment, which will be vast, and competition, which will intensify.

14.2 Liner organization

The liner company structure features the objectives identified in the company business plan. This plan determines the strategies for all sectors of the company's business.

The fleet is the prime production unit in the liner trade, and operators plan and think in terms of a service rather than a number of self-contained voyages. The liner service implies the operation of a fleet of vessels providing a fixed service at regular advertised intervals between named ports; the owners offer space to cargo destined for the named ports and delivered to the ship by the advertised date. The liner company, unlike the tramp operator, must seek its own cargo, which originates mainly in relatively small consignments from a multitude of shippers. The tramp operator is in primarily a single commodity market embracing bulk dry and wet cargoes. In contrast, the liner operator serves a mass market embracing consumer and industrial shippers, a large proportion of this market originating from multinational companies. Organization must reflect the logistical operation, and this involves an expensive organization ashore at all ports; agents/regional offices are required inland to market the services and process shipments both for import and export. These offices are located near an ICD/CFS linked by computer to the shipping company's database. However, an increasing volume of the liner container business is customs cleared at the shipper's premises.

The liner company – which may contain an element of tonnage on charter or available for charter – tends to have a diverse organization reflecting the complex nature of its business and extent of its trades involving numerous countries/ports.

The shipping company is managed by a general manager responsible to a board of directors and who normally sits on the board. He is responsible for carrying out the board's directions dealing with all major issues of policy, including finance, senior executive appointments, the introduction of new services, and major items of capital expenditure including new tonnage, etc. In some companies, to facilitate prompt decision-making and to streamline administration, the general manager post has been abolished and the day-to-day control and management of the company vested in the managing director. Each board director is usually responsible for certain aspects of the business, such as finance, marketing, passengers, cargo, IT, logistics, marine staff and administration, etc.

The organization may be functional or departmental. The functional system involves direct responsibility for a particular activity of the company business, such as the post of trade or service manager for a particular route, the holder of which would be responsible for its ultimate performance and control embracing all operating/commercial/marketing/financial aspects, etc. The advantage of such a system is that it produces better financial discipline. The departmental system involves the splitting up of all company activities into various departments, i.e. commercial/operating/technical, etc. Both types of organization have merit and each company decides which suits their situation best. Generally the larger the company the greater the advantages of a functional organization, which encourages better financial control by being budget-driven.

The tendency today is to have a 'flat' organization with IT interfaces between various sectors of the business in terms of communication, performance monitoring, business development, on-line access to shippers, port operators, cargo tracking and all sectors of the business.

Organizational structure of a shipping company engaged in the liner business varies in these ways:

(a) Fleet size and overall financial turnover.
(b) The trade(s) in which the company is engaged.
(c) The scale of the business involved. For example, the company may rely on agents to develop the business in terms of canvassing for traffic and thereby need only a few salesmen. Additionally, all new tonnage design may be entrusted to a consultant naval architect, and thereby avoid the need for a full-time naval architect employee with an intermittent workload. And the company may have a shipbroker's department to diversify its business.
(d) It may be a subsidiary company reporting to a parent company with common services, such as a legal department, planning organization, etc.
(e) The company may have offices abroad, rely on agencies, or be part of a consortium.
(f) The company may outsource many of its ship management activities (Chapter 21).

A possible shipping company organizational structure is found in Figure 14.1. Below is a commentary on each of a shipping company's departments, bearing in mind that each company devises its organizational structure to best suit its business. The responsibilities of these departments change over time to reflect changes of situation. Each employee must have a job specification that reflects business-plan objectives. The business plan should be displayed on the company's website.

In the company structure found in Figure 14.1 the policy and control of the company is vested in the chairman and some eight directors, including a managing director. These people constitute the company board which is responsible to shareholders if it leads a public company, or if the company is state owned a government minister.

The categories below assume the company has twenty-five ships engaged in six deep-sea liner cargo services and some passenger business on two short sea trade routes.

(a) Chairman and directors

The chairman's role is ultimate control and management of the company. He is responsible for company policy and development of the business in collaboration with his board of directors, who overall form the senior management team. He works closely with the managing director. In the

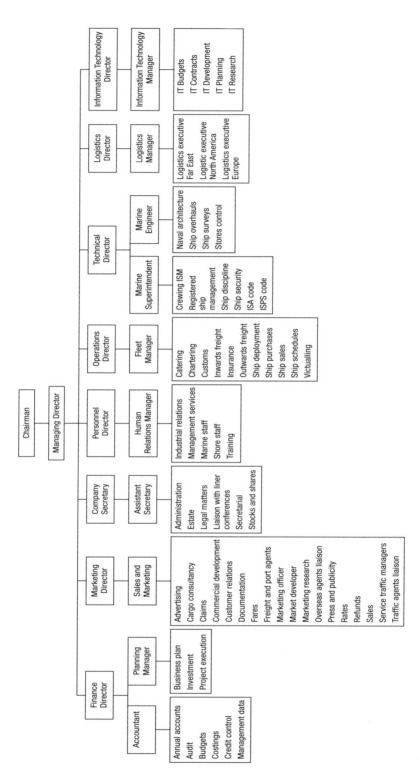

Figure 14.1 A liner company's organization.

American style shipping company structure the chairman is designated chief executive officer (CEO). At the next level is the position of president who is a deputy to the chairman. Executive vice-presidents are the equivalent broadly to the directors found in Figure 14.1.

The managing director's role tends to be the liaison link in general management terms between the board of directors and senior managers. He is essentially concerned with the day-to-day running of the business, particularly its development, and formulating policy in consultation with his directors. It is a key post in the company and a good managing director favourably influences the company's financial results.

(b) Finance director

The finance director has an accountant responsible to him. The accountant's department is responsible for: the annual accounts; budgets covering revenue, expenditure, investment and cash flow forecasts; credit control involving the billing of customers/shippers and payment of accounts; preparation of management data which may cover every month's traffic carryings, revenue and expenditure results against budget; and costing data such as voyage costs and economics of individual traffic flows. It is likely that the accountant's department would have an individual officer responsible for each function, such as audit officer, budgets officer, costing officer, credit controller, etc. All would have supporting staff and be responsible to the accountant and liaise with other departments.

Only large shipping companies have a planning manager. He is under the finance director's control, his department particularly concerned with developing company policy and strategy over a wide range of activities. He looks after the development and implementation of capital projects, formulation of a 5- to 10-year business plan, and liaison with government and other national and international organizations as they relate to shipping. The planning department works liaises with other departments and officers within the company.

(c) Operations director

The operations director is responsible for producing his fleet's optimum performance. He does this by reconciling traffic needs with ship capacity availability, etc., to devise the most viable service meeting both short- and long-term needs. This may also involve reconciling sailing schedules with the obligations of a joint service or liner conference, whereby each operator may be allocated a certain percentage of the sailings. The operations director's policy must be to ensure sailings are profitable. The success of a shipping line depends on the efficient operation of its ships under budgetary control.

The operations department reports to the fleet manager, who is responsible to the operations director for crew cost and IMO codes. The fleet manager covers ship schedules, ship deployment, customs formalities (including the entering and clearance of ships), chartering, insurance, victualling, ship sale and purchase, inwards freight and outwards freight departments.

Ship schedules may be entrusted to the operations officer, which includes customs formalities (including the entering in and clearance of ships), and port operation. The operations officer works closely with the marine superintendent on ship manning/crew costs having regard to the required schedules. He liaises and appoints port agents/loading brokers, etc. He may become involved in negotiating with port authorities the provision of berthing/quay facilities and related equipment/handling equipment, etc. This could embrace rail, road, inland waterway authorities, featuring the combined transport operation incorporating the sea leg–port to port operation. A qualified shipbroker would look after chartering, insurance and ship sale and purchase. In such circumstances the chartering department fixes additional tonnage and secure fixtures for the company's own vessels when offered on the market. In some cases he may act as a shipbroker.

The inward freight department deals with customs clearance of imports and their delivery to consignees. It also deals with the transhipment of such cargo, if necessary. Likewise the outwards freight department processes export cargo and related documentation, and supervises the provision of shipping space for cargo bookings. The processing of an international consignment is an important function, involving close liaison with the ports. Pre-booking of cargo shipping space, with the development of containerization, is fully computerized, extending to the billing of customers, preparation of bills of lading, etc.

(d) Personnel director

The personnel director's responsibilities cover all aspects of staff, including those ashore and afloat. The Human Relations manager is responsible to the personnel director. His/her post covers: training, education, recruitment, career development, appointments, redundancy, shore discipline, wages and salaries negotiation, industrial relations, service conditions, etc. Management services provide a consultancy service within the company. The Human Relations manager's department works closely with other departments. The extent of the management services role will depend on company policy employing such a specialist or engaging outside consultants for specified projects, such as reorganization, recruitment of senior managers, etc.

(e) Technical director

The marine engineer and marine superintendent report to the technical director. The marine engineer's department embraces marine engineering, electrical engineering, naval architecture, ship contracts for new building and surveys. It provides technical advice and service, etc., on new construction design, negotiation and monitoring of shipbuilding contracts and fleet maintenance/

surveys to required statutory/classification society obligations. The annual survey programme of the fleet would be undertaken in this department in consultation with the fleet manager's organization to reflect ship availability and traffic needs. The naval architect is responsible for ship design and providing data on ship stability, etc. In smaller companies a consultant is engaged on ship design when new tonnage is required. The marine workshop and stores control is part of the marine engineer's department, together with bunkering arrangements. All these three activities may be co-ordinated under a marine services officer, responsible to the marine engineer. Also responsible to the technical director is the marine superintendent who is the registered manager. This latter task devolves on the marine superintendent legally responsible for the maintenance and operation of the registered fleet in accordance with the relevant merchant shipping legislation. It could be equally undertaken by the fleet manager but it is usual to entrust the responsibility to someone of wide nautical experience and of high professional calibre. The marine superintendent within the organizational structure of this particular company is responsible for crewing involving the level of manning and appointments of ship officers. Additionally the marine superintendent is very closely involved in ship safety, relevant navigational matters and ship discipline. The marine superintendent is closely concerned with the acceptance and conveyance of dangerous cargo and related procedures/conditions.

The Marine Superintendent's responsibilities are extensive and embrace full compliance in resource and command control/monitoring terms with the STCW, ISM and ISPS. With regard to ISM and ISPS, this embraces specially designated personnel, which in regard to ISPS code, features the appointment of a Company Security Officer (CSO). More than one CSO would be appointed for a large number of ships and/or for different classes of ships. The Marine Superintendent has regard to port state controls.

Both the Marine Superintendent's and Marine Engineer's responsibilities may be reduced with third party ship management in some areas. The recruitment/appointment/certification of seafarers' documents may rest with the Marine Superintendent, but usually the HR department looks after pay and company conditions for seafarers.

(f) Marketing director

The marketing director's responsibilities are extensive and primarily involve development of company business within the freight and passenger markets. In this particular organization the sales and marketing manager is the departmental head but, depending on the size of the business, the job may be split between marketing, passenger and freight managers. The marketing function in the liner shipping company today is an important one. Today the marketing department is a key department, driving the business in revenue generation, value added benefit services, logistics development in consultation with the logistics department, customer liaison, market research and product development. It will have a mission statement and marketing plan to which commitment is paramount throughout the marketing department, including agents, and in other areas of the company organization.

The marketing and sales manager may have a number of officers under him to run the department to aid quick decision-making and maximize market impact within the commercial policy of the board as interpreted by the marketing director.

The marketing manager would be responsible for the annual sales and marketing plan. His job includes responsibilities for sales, including a field salesforce, advertising – particularly promotions – and publicity material, including public relations. Recommended further reading: *Maritime Economics, Management and Marketing* by Alan Branch, Chapters 14–17 (Routledge, www.tandf.co.uk).

(g) Public relations

The public relations/press officer role can include development of the market/business both in passenger and freight sectors in liaison with passenger and freight managers. This role can include market research. The marketing manager would also be responsible for the appointment of the advertising agency.

The freight manager's task includes: dealing with freight rates; freight and customs documentation; liaison with trade associations, chambers of commerce and shippers' councils; liner conferences and cargo claims. Some companies have a cargo consultancy organization to advise on the most ideal methods of transit involving the technique of transport distribution analysis. The freight manager would be responsible for the appointment and liaison with port agents and freight forwarders.

The passenger manager covers fares, refunds, baggage, appointment and liaison with travel agents, passenger complaints and liaison with passenger associations and liner conferences. Passenger, freight and marketing managers must liaise closely to realize the best results.

Some companies have a service, sector or route manager who is responsible for the traffic management of the route(s), covering fares, rates, service pattern and so on. Overall, it is a profit centre and subject to strict budgetary control techniques. Such a company structure ensures the optimization of resources on the route(s) compatible with market demand. It comes under the control of the marketing manager but requires close liaison with the freight and passenger managers and other departments including the fleet manager.

(h) Company secretary

The company secretary is responsible for convening board meetings, preparation and circulation of board minutes, and looking after the shipping company's statutory affairs. In this particular company, the assistant secretary takes charge of the department and reports to the company secretary. The department is likely to be small compared with the marketing manager's organization. It will include: maintaining records of stocks and shares; processing estate matters such as land and property sales and purchases; general administration of the company's affairs; and dealing with legal matters. The larger company would employ a solicitor whilst the smaller company would merely engage a solicitor as required.

The department is responsible for liaising with liner conferences though the marketing manager could undertake this. The assistant secretary's department would be responsible for the retention of any company agreements, such as a revenue pooling agreement with four other operators on a particular service. Negotiations for the renewal of any such agreements or the development of other similar agreements would involve this department's consulting other parts of the organization, particularly fleet and marketing managers.

(i) Information technology director

The information technology director is a specialist and has a high profile in many shipping companies (see Chapter 20). The director would have various managers under him/her to cover budgetary control of all aspects of IT; a contracts manager to negotiate new and existing contracts; a development manager liaising with the computer industry and departments within the shipping company to develop/expand the role/activities of IT within the company; a planning manager to ensure the effective use of IT within the company and to formulate the investment budget; and a research manager to improve end-user and customer satisfaction with the company's IT network. Such a post liaises with the market research manager in the marketing department and also with appointed market research agencies. The IT research manager would be responsible for monitoring and interpreting research data and works closely with the development manager to implement research findings. Training may come under the research manager.

(j) Logistics director

The logistics director is a specialist. The work embraces time-related positioning of resources to ensure that materials, people, operational capacity and information are in the right place at the right time and in the right quantity and at the right quality and cost. Now that the world is a single integrated market place, supply chain efficiency is a competitive necessity. The multinational industry – a high proportion of MNI form part of the container clientele market – is now logistically driven and the MNI manager is logistically focused.

The structure of the department varies by trade, but logistic executives could be appointed for each trade – Europe, North America, Far East, South America.

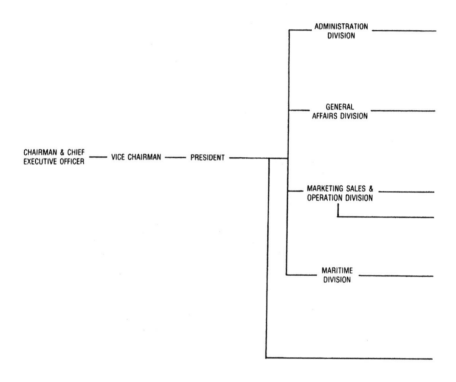

Figure 14.2 Organization chart of the Hanjin Shipping Company.

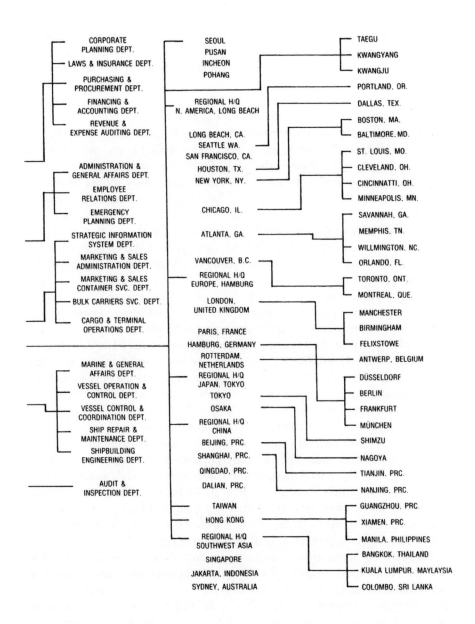

The focus is on supply chain management in all its aspects, with a view to continuous improvement targeting the client needs and added value to the business.

To conclude this examination of a shipping company's possible organization structure, it is important to note that each shipping company devises its organization to best suit its needs to maximize profitability and its long-term future.

The size of each department, and its continued existence in the company, depends on the size of the company and the trades in which it operates. The larger the company the greater is the tendency to have a larger number of departments. Overall there is much merit in reviewing every two years the adequacy of an organization in the light of market considerations.

Shipping companies conduct their business abroad by means of branch offices or agents; these act as the owners' local representatives in the clearance and discharge of the owners' vessels, and they secure cargo for shipment. At head office, departmental managers specialize in the particular duties performed by their departments; but the manager of a branch or agency has a much wider range of duties, and is usually responsible for all aspects of the shipping work of his office.

The Hanjin Group, established in 1937, is a land, sea and air transport conglomerate which includes heavy construction industries, financing and information communications, and marine insurance, education, travel, medical and banking services in its portfolio. Overall it embraces 24 companies. Its total assets were 11 trillion won and gross revenue was 7.5 trillion won. By the year 2000 transport and heavy industry contributed to the development of these global logistics companies. The Hanjin Group has grown into a global technological conglomerate.

Hanjin operates a global shipping line with a turnover of 10 billion dollars and maritime fleet of 300 ships covering the markets of North America, Europe, Africa and Asia. The company provides a total logistics operation embracing shipping, inland transportation, dedicated terminals and warehouse resources. The company operates a total of 14 liner routes, including three routes on the growth market of the Far East–North America; the Far East–Europe route; the Australian route; the Intra-Asia route; the Korea–China route. The Hanjin organization is illustrated in Figure 14.2.

Merger and acquisition strategies continue, as an analysis of Maersk reveals. An increasing number of shipping companies now have a range of subsidiaries in related maritime services. Some have divested themselves of their shipping companies in favour of concentrating and developing their subsidiary in container port terminals. Such policies are largely determined by the need to lessen the impact of trade recessions and low profitability levels and to yield an adequate profitable cash flow.

14.3 Tramp organization

Tramp companies do not have the many specialist departments found in liner companies. The function of the tramp operator is to provide ships for hire or charter. Therefore he must keep in close touch with the tramp ship market. Today, the tramp company makes full use of IT. The organization is small compared with the liner company, though it deals with operations, ship maintenance/survey/stores/victualling, accounts and market intelligence/research. The latter function is important because brokers' clients look for services which add more value. Additionally, the tramp business tends to have perhaps six ships and, to remain competitive, it contracts out some core activities, particularly manning, bunkering, ship survey and insurance. The cost of employing a marine superintendent and marine engineer in shore-based positions can be uneconomic, the small family size dry/wet cargo fleet often working on small profit margins with second-hand tonnage. Hence the tendency in recent years for such companies to merge to raise capital and reduce costs.

The mega tramp operator often tends to be part of the larger shipping company. This could include a fleet of 40 ships with a total dwt of 4 million. The fleet may feature crude carriers, gas carriers, product carriers, chemical carriers and other tonnage. The organization would be departmentalized by the category of the ship product operations, crude operations, handy product tankers, VLCC, LNG, etc.

The shipbroking business is at the forefront of change, examined later in this chapter.

14.4 Holding companies and subsidiaries, including ancillary activities of shipping undertakings

The liner trade, with its greater financial requirements, has grown considerably, with the formation of several large groups of associated and subsidiary companies. Sometimes two companies competing on the same route have found it advantageous to merge or amalgamate. In other cases, companies have retained individual identities and have exchanged shares and have common directorships. Sometimes successful companies have bought out unsuccessful companies, often with a view to securing their goodwill and loading rights in a particular trade.

Many of these groups are controlled by means of holding companies. The term 'holding company' was originally used to describe a company formed with the object of taking shares in two or more operating concerns. But more recently the term has come to include companies which, besides having a controlling interest in others, carry on business themselves. Generally, the associated and subsidiary companies in these groups are run as individual concerns with separate identities, organizations and ships.

With the expansion of containerization in recent years it has stimulated the development of consortiums. The merits of consortiums are these:

(a) It is impracticable for a sole shipowner to raise capital and bear the risk involved of such an assignment.
(b) It facilitates good development/relationships with governments/countries involved through the shipping company resident in the country.
(c) A consortium can counter state-subsidized fleets through concerted action through their governments. A sole operator would not be as effective in dealing with such a situation.
(d) A consortium which is broadly based strengthens the economic ties amongst the countries involved which in turn helps to influence trade to such a service and counter trade depression.
(e) It reflects the shipping corporation formally associated with the trades/markets which in turn reflects much experience. A sole operator could not achieve such expertise/commercial intelligence.
(f) A consortium produces economies of scale particularly in terms of agents and encourages the use of common services.
(g) It involves individual shipping companies of varying nationalities which permit the maritime countries involved to make, if available, any contribution to subsidize new building terms.
(h) A consortium can yield substantial tax benefits, reduced manning costs and new tonnage investment grants/subsidies.
(i) It develops good practice and value added benefit to the shipper and encourages a new vision with a new breed of management to run an enlarged business usually better able to combat the challenges and opportunities of the twenty-first century in the maritime and international trade environment.

14.5 Operational alliances

An operational alliance exists when two or more shipping companies come together through merger, acquisition or by working together and sharing common facilities. Overall, it yields the following results, emerging through the concentration and centralization of the company's facilities: common resources such as berths, ship's agents, computerized network involving information technology, marketing resources, marketing and sales plan, shipbroking, ship management, logistics and training resources. In situations of working together and sharing common facilities, costs are apportioned in accordance with the company schedule, but share capital remains unchanged.

Operational alliances are found in liner cargo services, especially containers, ro/ro operational and the ferry business. It is usual for operators to have an allocation of capacity/number of container slots per sailing on a pre-arranged basis and subject to regular review. Overall, the benefits are economies of scale to the operators, more frequent service offered to the shippers, and improved ship and shipowning productivity.

14.6 Ship management companies

Ship management companies are now common and their expansion can be attributed to the gradual change from the traditional shipping company to two new shipping groups: the developing nation bloc and the large bulk shippers who are seeking greater involvement in shipping operation. Additionally, for many years a number of multinational companies have tended to rely on ship management companies.

Ship management companies primarily become involved in the efficient manning, chartering and maintenance of a vessel for an owner. Ship management involves: the recruitment, training and appointment of both ship- and shore-based personnel; advice on the most suitable type of vessel, method of financing and source of ship supply; advice on the options available of ship registration, manning, trading and maintenance – this situation tends to emerge with companies in developing nations which are required by law to have their ships manned by nationals, whilst the management company has the flexibility to register the vessel elsewhere yet use it as a training ship for national crews for subsequent additions to the fleet. A further area is the ability of the management company to obtain cheaper insurance by inclusion of the vessel(s) on the main owner-fleet cover to take the advantages of sharing in bulk buying of spares, stores, etc., overall. To be effective the shipowner must seek a manager who reflects this philosophy. Those major oil companies operating with mixes of owner/time chartered/spot chartered vessels recognize the ship management company. Accordingly the management company provides the ideal method for ensuring daily operation and maintenance of vessels are correctly superintended; there is no need to set up their own operations department. There is also the advantage of being able to terminate the agreement when the market no longer supports chartered tonnage. The basic aim of ship management is to provide the owner, for a management fee, with vessels with quality high service standards at a reasonable competitive cost.

Some multinational companies have built up their own fleets to carry raw materials or manufactured products to overseas markets. This service offers many benefits to the multinational company, including complete control of the transport distribution system, which can be fully integrated into the manufacturer's distribution programme; it aids competitiveness of the product as the goods are conveyed at relatively low cost and not at the normal market tariffs found on liner cargo services; it permits flexibility of operation inasmuch as when trade is buoyant additional tonnage can be chartered; and it enables the multinational company to exploit economies of scale by permitting various countries to specialize in particular products and avoid duplication of investment plant. This latter arrangement is advantageous in free trade areas. Today multinationals rely on chartered tonnage or they remodel their distribution arrangements by relying on the liner cargo container network.

The ship management company may be a subsidiary of an established liner company and is therefore able to draw on the expertise within the parent shipowning group. In so doing a package deal can be concluded of a comprehensive nature. Today, ship management is integrated with third party ship management, as examined in Chapter 21.

14.7 Ownership of vessels

The Merchant Shipping Act 1988 is relative to registration of British ships:

(a) The exclusion of Commonwealth citizens and companies from those persons qualified to be owners of British ships.
(b) The replacement of the present obligation to register a British ship by an entitlement to register.
(c) The introduction of a requirement to appoint a representative person when a company qualified to own a British ship wishes to register it in the UK, but has its principal place of business outside the UK.
(d) The Secretary of State for Transport to have the power to refuse or terminate the registration of a ship.
(e) Powers to restrict the size and types of ships registered in the British Dependent Territories.

The above represents Part I of the Merchant Shipping Act 1988: Part II deals with the registration of British fishing vessels.

British vessels have to be registered (through the Customs at their local port) with the Registry of Shipping and Seamen, based in Cardiff (postcode CF24,5JW).

14.8 Capitalization and finance of shipping undertakings

In the nineteenth century most British shipping companies grew on the retention of profits earned and short-term finance for expansion, obtained by security on the fleet. The shares of the larger companies were normally quoted on stock exchanges, but large-scale public subscriptions to form new undertakings were rare, as shipping has always been considered a risky undertaking.

Resulting from the vulnerability of freight rates, profits and depreciation, funds have been barely sufficient to allow shipowners to renew their fleets at current shipbuilding prices. In recent years some of the larger Greek shipping companies – especially in the tanker and dry bulk cargo sectors – have amassed considerable liquidity from their listing on the New York Stock Exchange, the National Association of Securities Dealers and the American Stock Exchange. There are basically three most commonly used methods to access the US capital markets: (a) raising equity in the US public markets; (b) raising equity in the US institutional market; and (c) raising debt in the US bond markets. This situation is due to the fact that much of the shipping industry is rated sub-investment grade, which typically means accessing the high-yield bond market.

Ship finance is a specialist sector of banking and has four salient features:

(a) *Capital intensity.* Shipping is one of the world's most capital intensive industries. A ship is likely to have an operational life of up to 15 years but many owners – especially liner cargo operators – renew their fleet every 10–12 years depending on market conditions and ship management efficiency factors.

(b) *Mobility of assets.* The vessel has a global operating potential and its registration may change to put it under the legal jurisdiction of a 'flag of convenience'.

(c) *Volatility of market.* Overall the market is volatile, especially with regard to chartered bulk tonnage, both in the area of ship purchase and the daily earnings of the vessel. The same applies in the deep-sea container market earnings. Study the various freight earning indices as found in *Lloyd's List and Shipping Gazette.*

(d) *Limited information.* Many substantial shipping companies are owned by individuals who prefer not to publish organization structures or audited accounts. This makes it difficult to carry out conventional 'credit analysis' on which most bank lending relies.

Many large international shipping families have established some of the most valuable asset-holding trusts in the world. A trust is created when an individual or corporation holds legal title to certain assets, but is under an obligation to utilize those assets exclusively for the benefit of others, the beneficiaries. The advantages of a trust embrace: (a) families can manage wealth through generations; (b) it permits head of the family to influence the way in which the assets will be managed both during his/her lifetime and following his/her death; and (c) it encourages financial planning and estate planning to provide a structured income for families, charities and other organizations. The taxation structure for trust varies by country.

An area of higher priority in today's business environment is maritime trade credit management. Credit risk is the potential for a company to fail to meet its obligations in accordance with agreed terms. The goal of credit risk management is to maximize the control of the risk of return by maintaining credit risk exposure within acceptable parameters.

Companies giving credit need to manage the credit risk inherent in the entire portfolio as well as the risk in individual credits or transactions. They should also consider the relationship between credit risks and other risks. For most trades, receivables are the largest source of credit risk. Other sources of credit risk exist throughout the activities of a company, including the rental and sales of assets both on and off the balance sheet.

A company needs a credit strategy that outlines the processes, responsibilities and culture governing credit management, even more so if e-commerce is being used as a sales instrument. It embraces six stages: (a) formulating strategy; (b) proactive process; (c) monitoring process; (d) primary action stage; (e) adoption stage; (f) potential crisis. A credit management strategy with a proactive approach is likely to make credit management an extra tool for a company.

Many shipowners finance their new tonnage from three sources: loan capital obtained on the open market, including a bank mortgage or provided by government on very favourable low interest terms; money provided by the shipping company through liquidation of reserve capital; and government grants, which are usually conditional. Few shipping companies today finance their new tonnage from within their own financial resources. This is due to the low level of profitability and return on capital, often between 2% and 3%; depressed trading conditions; and the failure in many trades for rates to keep pace with rising costs.

A further method of financing new tonnage is through a leasing arrangement with a finance company. This enables the maximum benefit to be taken of any available tax advantage, and the quarterly or half-yearly leasing payments reflect this. With these sorts of agreements, however, it is not normal for legal ownership of the vessel to pass to the shipping company, even after the leasing period expires.

There are four main types of financial structures used in ship finance today:

(a) *Equity finance* entitles the investor to share in the risks and rewards of the business, usually without time limit; to liquidate his investment the investor has to sell the shares. Overall, there are four main types of financial structure for raising equity: (i) owner equity; (ii) limited partnership; (iii) ship funds; and (iv) public offerings.

(b) *Debt finance* is a legally enforceable loan agreement in which the lender receives interest at predetermined intervals with the repayment of the principal after a specified period. Overall, there are four main types of financial structure for raising equity: (i) owner equity; (ii) limited partnership; (iii) ship funds; and (iv) public offerings.

(c) *Mezzanine finance* involves an intermediary form of financial structure, which contains elements of debt and of equity. This type of finance is for the middle market or non-investment grade companies. Capital ranks after senior debt, but before ordinary equity. It may take many forms – secured or unsecured loan stock, preferred shares, subordinated notes, second-mortgage loans, junk bonds. In some cases such finance will include the option to convert into ordinary equity. Mezzanine finance is less secure than senior financing and consequently interest costs are higher. Its use in shipping is expected to increase as a means of bridging the gap between first mortgage loans and the owner's equity, but financiers have found it difficult to develop mezzanine instruments suited to the shipping industry.

(d) *Leasing* is a hire-purchase arrangement in which the borrower 'bareboat' charters the vessel from its nominal owner. This is occasionally used as an alternative to debt financing. The two common types of leasing structure embracing the operating lease are used widely for hiring equipment and the finance lease. Under the operating lease, the risk and benefits of ownership are usually the responsibility of the lessor, who is responsible for repairs, maintenance and insurance. It carries the risk of obsolescence and the residual value at the end of the lease is important to the lessor. In contrast the finance lease is a form of lease with an option to purchase the ship. Lease payments may be considered as payment for the cost of the vessel. The lessor, whose main role is as financier, has little involvement with the asset beyond ownership. All operating responsibilities fall on the lessee, who, in the event of early termination, must fully compensate the lessor. Leasing is available for marine and cargo handling equipment.

An increasing number of countries subsidize their fleets in one way another, subsidies including bunker fuel, state aid for social contributions by crew personnel, national flag subsidized port charges, and subsidized national ship insurance.

Debt finance for new building has two aspects that deserve consideration. First, the capital cost is generally too high in relation to its likely spot market earnings to finance the cash flow, especially if the loan is amortized over the short periods of five to eight years favoured by commercial banks. Second, the finance is needed before the ship is built, so there is a period before delivery when part of the loan is drawn but the hull is not available as collateral. Overall, it involves pre-delivery finance, and post delivery finance on delivery of the vessel. The latter may involve a shipyard credit scheme, commercial bank credit or leasing.

The staged loan documentation procedure for ship finance from a bank involves these items: (a) commitment letter sent to the borrower by the bank; (b) loan agreement; (c) bank letter of commitment to the shipbuilder; (d) bank letter of guarantee to the shipyard; (e) promissory note; (f) shipyard performance bond; (g) supporting documents, i.e. collateral security; shipboard documents at time of delivery, project evaluation, legal options, shipyard performance bond, etc.; (h) timescale of the payments featuring a schedule – and credit analysis; (i) and the vessel risk analysis – cash flow; capital contributed by shareholders; collateral. The significance of each item will vary according to circumstances.

The subject is dealt with in greater detail in *Maritime Economics: Management and Marketing*, Alan Branch, Chapter 3, Routledge (www.tandf.co.uk).

14.9 Income and expenditure

Income and expenditure varies according to the type of operations conducted by the shipping organization. With a liner company conveying passengers and cargo, there are many items of income and expenditure. Items of income include revenue from passengers, cargo, catering, postal parcels, letter mails and perhaps chartering. Chartering arises when a liner company releases a vessel on charter to another undertaking. Expenditure items would include crew costs, maintenance of ships, fuel, lubricants, port disbursements (including dues and cargo-handling cost), depreciation, publicity expenses, administration costs, insurance, commission to agents, passenger and cargo claims, interest on capital, compensation for accidents in collisions, and any chartering expenses involving the hire of additional vessels to augment the fleet.

In the case of the tramp undertaking, there is one main source of income and this accrues from chartering. The items of expenditure, however, vary according to the type of charter party. With a 'demise' charter, there are few items of expenditure, and these broadly include ship depreciation, interest on capital and administration costs. The number of expenditure items is, however, increased with non-demise 'time' and 'voyage' charters, and include crew costs, ship maintenance, depreciation, insurance, interest on capital, compensation for accidents in collisions and administration costs. The administration costs form a small portion of the expenditure of a tramp undertaking compared with the liner company.

In view of the large payments incurred when new vessels are purchased. shipping companies as far as possible maintain reserves in easily redeemable securities.

14.10 Statistics

Statistics are important to the successful management of shipping. The shipowner must constantly review the performance of his ships, items of earnings and costs. A careful and detailed analysis has to be made of the revenue and expenditure accounts of each voyage.

Important operational statistics include, for example, voyage distances, fuel consumption, load factors and fleet utilization. The shipowner requires to know voyage distances in relation to fuel consumed per nautical mile. This calculation indicates engine performance. Passengers and/or cargo conveyed are recorded and are related on a voyage basis to the available capacity. This will give the ship's load factor as a percentage, indicating how much of the available revenue earning capacity on a particular voyage has been filled. For example, if a ship with a passenger certificate of 1,000 conveyed 750 passengers, it would have a load factor of 75%. It is necessary to record the number of days a vessel is at sea and the time spent in port loading and/or discharging or alternatively undergoing survey and overhaul. Turn-round time in port is influenced by the cargo handled and port resources, and necessitates compilation of statistics showing average tons loaded or discharged per day in various ports which the ship visits and all related costs. The aim is to keep turnround time to a minimum, because it represents idle time to the shipowner and earns no revenue. Similarly, time spent on surveys and overhauls should be the minimum, and if possible undertaken outside peak traffic times. How successful the shipowner is in achieving these objectives is established by maintaining accurate statistics. These enable him to relate the days a vessel spends at sea with time spent either in port or in a shipyard.

The victualling department of passenger carrying lines requires statistics, such as meals served and cost per meal and profitability per day or per head. Such data, when related to the number of passengers carried, helps to establish the general popularity and profitability of the meals, and enable the victualling results on one ship to be compared with another.

Traffic analysis is important, and statistics must be kept of various commodity movements and average freight earnings. Bills of lading, sea waybills and charter parties must be carefully analysed and data abstracted regarding commodities, ports of loading and discharge, weight and stowage factors, and other features of interest, such as damage or pilferage to cargo. When properly analysed, this data enables the shipowner to estimate in advance his future tonnage requirements throughout the year, and provide valuable information which influences ship design.

In the shipping industry, statistics are now particularly important, because great emphasis is put on improved efficiency and an ever-increasing cost consciousness, which involves development of profit centres in a trade or on a particular area basis. Statistics is a reliable means of measuring the performance and efficiency of an individual ship and of the fleet. Provision of statistics can be costly, however, and the volume of data needs constant review. IT provides essential management information to shipping businesses, and includes traffic analysis, voyage costs, load factors, etc. Such data are produced weekly or monthly and are related to budget predictions.

Most shipowning companies operate on a budget-driven basis, so that income and expenditure are monitored against traffic volume carried. Moreover, in the annual report, efficiency data is featured, such as that for revenue earnings per employee, credit and debt analysis, return on capital, number of employees, traffic volume carried by type, and a range of ship productivity details.

14.11 Freight forwarders

A freight forwarder is a person or company involved in the processing and/or movement of goods, on behalf of another company or person, which crosses international boundaries. The freight forwarder provides two main services: the movement of goods out of a country on behalf of exporters or shippers, in which case the forwarder would be termed an export freight agent; and the bringing of goods into the country on behalf of importers, in which situation the forwarder is called an import freight agent, customs clearance agent or customs broker.

The freight forwarder has four prime activities: to provide a range of independent services such as packing, warehousing, port agency and customs clearance; to provide a range of advice on all the areas relative to international consignment distribution as found in transport distribution analysis; to act as shipper agent processing transport/shipping space on behalf of his principal/shipper and executing his instructions; and to act as a principal, usually as a multi-modal transport operator conveying goods from A to B across international frontiers and involving usually several carriers, often as an NVOCC.

Nearly all large freight forwarders are logistics operators focusing on supply chain management and on-line access to carriers, customs, shippers, etc.

The freight forwarder provides some or all of the following services, depending on the trade in which the company operates and the resources available:

Export

(a) *Transport distribution analysis* – an examination of the options available to the shipper to distribute the goods.
(b) *Transportation arrangements* – a major function involving the booking and despatch of the goods between the consignor's and consignee's premises or other specified points.
(c) *Documentation* – provision of all the prescribed documentation for the goods, having regard to all the statutory requirements and terms of the export sales contract.
(d) *Customs* – all the customs clearance arrangements, including documentation and entry requirements at the time of exportation and importation.
(e) *Payment of freight and other charges* – payment of freight to the prescribed carrier including any handling charges raised by the airport, seaport or elsewhere during the transit.
(f) *Packing and warehousing* – packing of goods for transit and warehousing provision.
(g) *Cargo insurance* – the process of insuring goods during the transit.
(h) *Consolidation, groupage and special services* – many forwarders specialize in consolidation offering major benefits to the shipper.

Import

(a) *Notification of arrival* – the process of informing the importer of the date and location of the goods' arrival and the requisite documents required for customs clearance. The exporter and importer may have different agents and the two agents will liaise to ensure the smooth flow of goods through customs, keeping their principals informed.
(b) *Customs clearance* – presentation and clearance of the cargo through customs. This closely involves all requisite documents. Most major seaports and airports now have IT customs clearance to speed up the process and eliminate risk of errors.

(c) *Payment of VAT, duty, freight and other charges* – the forwarder will co-ordinate and effect payment of all such payments on behalf of his principal at the time of importation. This avoids delay in the despatch of the goods to the importer.

(d) *Delivery to the importer* – the process of delivering the goods to the importer's premises following customs clearance.

(e) *Breaking bulk and distribution* – the agent may be an agent who consolidates his own client's merchandise with those of other agents with whom he has a contractual arrangement. On arrival of the goods in the destination country, the cargo is handed over to the respective agents for process through customs and distributed.

The freight forwarder will despatch cargo by air or surface transport modes. By air it may involve: scheduled passenger aircraft; combi, the modern generation of jets permitting a flexible use of space combining freight and passengers according to market demands; chartered aircraft; and scheduled freighters. For surface distribution it will involve containers, usually multi-modal; international road transport/trucking, using the ro/ro ferry; international rail movement with through trains or wagons, Eurotunnel; and specialized movement involving project forwarding, consolidators, bloodstock, 'out of gauge' loads, household effects, refrigerated goods or bulk liquids. An increasing number of freight forwarders provide services as a NVOCC or NVOC.

The freight forwarder is closely involved in customs clearance/ processing arrangements, both for exports and imports. An increasing number of major forwarders have the facility to undertake on their own premises the clearance of cargo at the time of export and/or their import. This speeds up the operation and avoids delays at sea- or airports. It is a feature of multi-modalism. It is called forwarders' local export control (FLEC), and for import, forwarders' local import control (FLIC). Under FLIC the examination of cargo takes place at the forwarders' premises, while the actual entry may be lodged at the seaport or other entry processing unit (EPU) convenient to the forwarder. Major forwarders have IT communication to deal with customs clearance, in a system called 'designated export place'. Modern freight forwarders are logistically focused on all areas of the business existing between shipper/ agent/carrier(s) and all major parties in the supply chain, thereby permitting on-line consignment tracking.

The British International Freight Association (BIFA) represents the freight forwarding industry and incorporates the Institute of Freight Forwarders. Both organizations are committed to developing the industry and the attainment of quality control in accordance with British Standards in Quality Systems, BS 5750. BIFA has established a Quality Assurance Manual, and lays down trading conditions. Companies which have been engaged in the business of moving freight for a period of not less than three years can apply for registered trading membership, provided they meet the criteria laid down by the Association. Affiliated trading membership is available to those firms not directly involved in the freight moving industry but which have a working relationship with the forwarder.

Circumstances when an exporter/importer employs a freight forwarder include: dealing with an unfamiliar overseas market; endeavouring to sell under CIP, CPT or DDP terms; complex shipping or customs arrangements; the workload of the exporter, subject to significant peaks and troughs; the exporter is a small firm and needs to concentrate on the careful marketing of the product overseas; the freight forwarder can obtain more favourable freight rates especially for groupage shipments; the freight forwarder has access to priority of booking cargo space on transport modes, and the provision of specialist services/resources including groupage/antiques/perishable cargo/livestock/'out of gauge' consignments, etc. An exporter examining the merits of having an 'in house' shipping department in preference to employing a freight forwarder needs to consider: the capital and revenue expenditure in office space and equipment; the volume of overseas business; the number of markets and their degree of similarity; the availability of suitably qualified staff; the pattern of the business and the degree of seasonal variation; and the nature of the business including the degree of specialism. Overall, a financial appraisal is required.

Monitoring the performance of a freight forwarder enables the exporter to ensure the situation remains competitive. This process involves monitoring the budget against actual results in terms of price, transit time, etc.; seeking the buyer/consignee's opinion; undertaking test transits; and the overall quality/reliability of the service and competence/calibre of the management. Shippers, in their evaluation of possible freight forwarders, should check out: the viability of the company; any legal disputes; the trading conditions; the calibre of the management and their qualifications; experiences of other customers; the degree of technology; quality of overall service; the competitiveness of the tariffs; nature of the business and suitability of the equipment/resources; the company position in the market place; and the liability insurance maintained by the firm.

Project forwarding is a main part of freight forwarding and is often allied to turnkey projects. Project forwarding involves the despatch/conveyance arrangements stemming from a contract award. For example, a company in country A has a contract with a consortium in country B to build a factory involving the import of substantial quantities of merchandise, especially technical equipment. This requires acute co-ordination, involving the buyer/seller in terms of despatch arrangements and the site construction programme.

Shippers wishing to use a freight forwarder need to consider the following selection and economic criteria:

(a) Membership of BIFA very desirable and BS 5750 registration.
(b) Profile of freight forwarder and nature of business.
(c) Value added benefit emerging from employing the freight forwarder's operations.

(d) Alternative cost of the shipper doing the work and the requisite organization structure.
(e) Volume of business and any seasonal variation.
(f) Terms of export sales contract.

An increasing number of shippers entrust part of their business to the freight forwarder, especially spasmodic shipments to new markets, while the core of the business is undertaken 'in house' through their own shipping department, direct with a carrier. Smaller companies with limited experience and resources use the freight forwarder. The role and image of the freight forwarder is changing. An increasing number operate as a NVOCC and form part of the multi-modal network, especially through the European trucking/lorry system and global container network.

Most freight forwarders operate as NVOCC and form part of the multi-modal logistic network, especially through European tracking systems and global container networks. The future of freight forwarding rests with its fast growing development as a third party logistic provider.

14.12 Chartered shipbrokers

The basic function of the shipbroker is to bring together ship and cargo owners. Following negotiations between them, a charter party is concluded. The broker's income is derived from commission payable by the shipowner on completion and fulfilment of the contract.

A further role of the shipbroker – other than fixing vessels – is acting as agent for the shipowner. As such he is responsible for everything concerning the vessel whilst it is in port. This embraces: customs formalities; matters concerning the crew; loading/discharge of vessels; bunkering/ victualling, etc.

Duties of the shipbroker are these:

(a) Chartering agent whereby he acts for the cargo merchant seeking a suitable vessel in which to carry the merchandise.
(b) Sale and purchase broker acting on behalf of the buyer or seller of ships and bringing the two parties together.
(c) Owner's broker whereby he acts for the actual shipowner in finding cargo for the vessel.
(d) Tanker broker dealing with oil tanker tonnage.
(e) Coasting broker involving vessels operating around the British coast and/or in the short sea trade, e.g. UK/Continent. Additionally he can at the same time act for the cargo merchant in this trade should circumstances dictate. The deep-sea broker, however, will act for the shipowner or cargo merchant – not both at the same time.
(f) Cabling agent involving the broker communicating with other international markets.

The Institute of Chartered Shipbrokers is the professional body for the shipbrokering industry. It was founded in 1911 and conducts examinations, successful completion enabling membership to be taken. Membership is open to any citizen of any country in the world, and ICS is regarded as the professional body for all engaged in all aspects of shipping.

The shipbroker has many roles, but is mainly the middle person between the two principals concerned in a charter party.

14.13 Future of shipbroking

The role of shipbroking continues to change. Forward-thinking global businesses focus on core competences, striving for greater productivity and effectiveness. In this connection shipbroking is driven by three factors: logistics, value added and technology.

Logistics form a key part of the shippers/shipowners distribution plan, in companies/suppliers becoming more competitive in markets. Under relentless pressure to compete, companies globally work to increase the quality of all their services or goods as well as reducing costs. This is industrial supply chain management, of which the sea leg forms a part. It involves the integrated combined transport operation, ensuring unimpeded flow of cargo during transhipment. The merchant seeking chartered tonnage is keen to secure a fixture offering a cost-effective distribution arrangement which incorporates the voyage plan, from supplier to consumer. It may be an iron ore mine inland to a steel manufacturing plant involving rail–sea–rail transit and the need to have an iron ore carrier equipped to facilitate cost-effective transhipment.

Paramount is the need for the shipbroker to provide a 'value added' service. Brokers' clients increasingly expect investment, statistical analysis and administrative and operational support. From freight futures trading to negotiating charter-back deals, the range of services provided by shipbrokers continues to grow. Shipbrokers who provide their marketing services to the international shipping industry as independent companies, operating as competitive brokers paid on a 'no cure, no pay' basis, are successful for one reason – they provide worldwide marketing services more cost-effectively and more efficiently than owners and charterers do who utilize in-house resources. Brokers can draw upon their intimate knowledge of the market as a whole, specific research undertaken by themselves, and their research colleagues and external independent indicators of the market, such as the Baltic indices and market reports. A shipbroker's research department plays a key role in adding value to services they provide, because they can supply accurate statistics and administrative and operational assistance.

The Internet permits development of personal relationships between shipbrokers and businesses. Shipbrokers operate with up-to-date IT and earn commission only when they conclude business.

14.14 Ship's agent

An agent is a person who acts for, or on behalf of, another (the principal) in a way that maintains that the principal is legally responsible for all acts carried out.

The ship's agent represents the shipowner/Master at a particular seaport, either on a permanent or temporary basis. He deals with: notification of arrival and departure of vessel; acceptance of vessel for loading, discharge, repairs, storing and victualling; arranging berths, tugs, harbour pilots, launches; ordering stevedores, cranes, equipment, etc. 'In port' requirements include: the requirements of the Master, covering bunkers, stores, provisions, crew mail and wages, cash, laundry, engine and deck repairs, and crew repatriation; completion of customs, immigration and port health formalities; hatch and cargo surveys; collection of freight; collection and issuing of bills of lading; completion of manifests; notarial and consular protests, etc. The agent has a marketing and sales role in accord with the guidelines supplied by the principal.

The Federation of National Associations of Shipbrokers and Agents (FONASBA) has now introduced its Standard Liner Agency Agreement, which BIMCO recommends for global use.

A growth market for ship agents is representation of a cruise liner when it calls at a specified port, i.e. as part of the ship's itinerary. Mostly a cruise line berth accommodates the vessel, as in Vancouver, Rotterdam and Singapore, whilst other ports rely on a ferry to convey passengers to and from the ship, a situation persisting in Dubrovnik, Croatia, where up to seven vessels call daily at the port in the summer. The agent not only has responsibility looking after the welfare of the ship and its passengers but must also arrange inland excursions, multilingual tours conducted in the town, and also the passenger ferry to and from the ship. New passengers may be embarking, whilst others may be disembarking at the conclusion of the cruise. In some ports the ship's agent and passenger agent may be separate people, the former dealing with the ship and cruise passenger welfare, the latter generating/marketing the cruise line.

14.15 Lloyd's Register Quality Assurance, ISO 9001:2000

A global market leader in quality assurance is Lloyd's Register Quality Assurance Ltd. A new standard was introduced by the ISO in 2000 – ISO 9001, superseding that of 20 years earlier. The prime focus is 'management of quality'.

The ISO assessment embraces the following: (a) establish the structure, decision-making and reporting lines, the products and the markets being served, to ensure the context of the system is understood and to confirm its aims and objectives are relevant to the business; (b) it gives confidence that the assessor knows and understands what the system is designed to do and understands how this is to be achieved; (c) undertake an 'in-depth' evaluation of what drives the business, and experts carry it out using language and terms the company understands; (d) establish any major issues preventing the system from being effective – problems the company will want to acknowledge and solve; (e) focus on the effectiveness of improvement programmes; (f) includes time to discuss actual and potential problems so that the company understands and deals with them once the assessor leaves; (g) have time to support system management and gain a balanced view of what works and does not work; and (h) provide an honest, impartial and reliable report on the effectiveness of management in achieving its objectives, and include time to present this to those who need to act on it.

The route to ISO 9001:2000 approval includes the following: (a) application form; (b) quotation and contract; (c) scheduling dates; (d) stage I document review and planning visit; (e) stage II initial assessment; (f) positive reporting; (g) approval; (h) surveillance visits; and (i) certificate renewal.

The ISO 9001 has closely connected with the ISM code.

14.16 British Columbia Ferry Service Inc.

BC Ferries is an independent marine transport company operating a complex coastal ferry system providing vehicle and passenger transport. It services British Columbia's coastal waters in Canada. In terms of annual traffic volume and transport infrastructure it is one of the largest ferry operators in the world. With 35 vessels and 47 terminals it provides year round services on 25 routes.

The company is governed by an independent board of directors appointed by the BC Ferry Authority, which owns the single voting common share of BC ferries. The provincial government of British Columbia owns cumulative preferred shares of BC Ferries but has no voting interest in either the BC Ferry Authority or BC Ferries. The company works with the commissioner to ensure compliance with regulatory obligations under the Coastal Ferry Act of Canada and the Coast Ferry Services.

The fleet profile falls into eight classes, as detailed in Table 14.1. The average age of the larger vessels is 29.6 years, that of the intermediate and small vessels 33.8 years, and of the northern vessels 34.0 years. BC Ferries wishes to evolve into an independent, customer-focused entity. It has a clear vision, mission, core values and planning framework for its company ambitions, which include a range of major capital projects, new tonnage and modernization of some existing vessels, terminal modernization, and modernization of ship to shore communication infrastructure.

Table 14.1 BC Ferry Service fleet profile

Class	GRT	Passenger/ Crew capacity	Car capacity	Speed/ knots	Route
S	18,747	2,100	470	19.5	Tsawwassen– Swartz Bay
C	5,863	1,200	295	19	Duke Point– Tsawwassen Bay
V	9,304	1,656	376	19	Vancouver– Vancourer Island, etc.
Burnaby	4,902	684	192	16.5	Comox-Powell river, etc.
Century	2,453	600	100	18	Fulford harbour– Swartz Bay
Cumberland	2,856	462	85	14	Earls Cove–Saltery Bay, etc.
Minor	1,486	408	68	14	Crofton–Vesuvius
Northern Route	5,618	400	115	14	Prince Rupert– Skidegate, etc.

15 Charter parties

A large proportion of the world's trade is carried in tramp vessels. Often one cargo will fill a whole ship, and, in these circumstances, one cargo owner or one charterer enters into a special contract with the shipowner for the hire of his ship, and this contract is known as a charter party. It is not always for a full shipload, though this is usually what happens.

A charter party is a contract whereby a shipowner agrees to place his ship, or part of it, at the disposal of a merchant or other person (known as the charterer), for the carriage of goods from one port to another port on being paid freight; or to let his ship for a specified period, his remuneration being known as hire money. The terms, conditions and exceptions under which the goods are carried are set out in the charter party.

15.1 Demise and non-demise charter parties

There are two main types of charter parties: demise and non-demise.

A demise or 'bareboat' charter party arises when the charterer is responsible for providing the cargo and crew, while the shipowner provides the vessel only. In consequence, the charterer appoints the crew, taking over full responsibility for operation of the vessel and paying all its expenses. A demise charter party is for a period of time, varying from a few weeks to several years.

A non-demise charter arises when the shipowner provides the vessel and its crew, whilst the charterer supplies the cargo only. It may be a voyage charter for a particular voyage, in which instance the shipowner agrees to carry cargo between specified ports for a prearranged freight. The majority of tramp cargo shipments are made on a voyage charter basis. Alternatively, a time charter may be for a stated period or voyage for a remuneration known as hire money. The shipowner continues to manage his own vessel, both under non-demise voyage or time charter parties under the charterer's instructions. With a time charter, it is usual for the charterer to pay port dues and fuel costs and overtime payments incurred in an endeavour to obtain faster turn-rounds. It is quite common for liner companies to supplement their services by taking tramp ships on time charter, but this practice is reduced by containerization.

There are several types of non-demise voyage charters and these are given below. It will be seen that they all deal with the carriage of goods from a certain port or ports to another port or ports, and the differences between them arise mainly out of payment for the cost of loading and discharging, and port expenses.

1   *Gross terms form of charter.* This is probably the most common form of charter used by tramp ships today. In this form, the shipowner pays all the expenses incurred in loading and discharging and also all port charges plus of course voyage costs. It can be varied by having gross terms at the loading port and nett terms at the discharging port in which case it is called gross load, free discharge.
2   *FIO charter.* Under this charter, the charterer pays for the cost of loading and discharging the cargo, hence the expression of FIO (meaning 'free in and out'). The shipowner remains responsible for the payment of all port charges. It can be described as nett terms.
3   *Lump sum charter.* In this case, the charterer pays a lump sum of money for the use of the ship and the shipowner guarantees that a certain amount of space (i.e. bale cubic metres) will be available for cargo, along with the maximum weight of cargo that the vessel will be able to carry. A lump sum charter may be on either a gross basis or an FIO basis. Such a charter is useful when the charterer wishes to load a mixed cargo – the shipowner guarantees that a certain amount of space and weight will be available and it is the charterer's responsibility to use that space to his best advantage.

The above forms of charter are all quite common today, and in each case the shipowner pays the port charges.

4   *Liner terms.* This is an inclusive freight rate more usually found on cargo liner services and covers not only the sea freight but also loading and discharging costs for a particular consignment. Under a voyage charter the shipowner is paid freight which includes the costs of loading, stowing and discharging the cargo. It is most evident in short sea tramp shipping. It is desirable for the shipowner to agree with the shipper or receiver on the appointment of the dockers/stevedores.
5   *Berth terms.* Under this term the shipowner agrees to his vessel's loading or discharging operation to begin, subject to the custom of the port where the cargo handling is taking place; or he may be agreeing that the vessel will load or discharge as fast as possible or under customary despatch or any or all of this type of term. Hence the shipowner is responsible to pay for loading and discharging costs and only indefinite laytime exists.

There are numerous variations that may be made to the above broad divisions and these are a matter for negotiation when the vessel is being 'worked' for future business. For example, the gross and FIO charters may be modified to an FOB charter (free on board), meaning that the charterer pays for the cost of loading and the shipowner pays for the cost of discharge, or alternatively the charter may be arranged on the basis of free discharge, i.e. the charterer pays for the cost of discharging.

The same general terms of contract are found in all the above types of charter.

A significant proportion of the charters are negotiated through a shipbroker on the Baltic Exchange in London.

The following items are included when formulating a remit to a shipbroker to obtain a general cargo vessel on charter.

(a) vessel capacity;
(b) vessel speed;
(c) actual trade/ports of call including cargo specification and volume;
(d) duration of charter;
(e) type of charter, i.e. demise or non-demise, voyage or time;
(f) date of charter commencement and duration – the latter with any options for extensions;
(g) overall dimensions of vessel, draught, length and beam;
(h) any constraints likely to be imposed, e.g. carriage of dangerous cargo;
(i) classification of vessel and any trading limits;
(j) possible band of fixture rate likely to be viable;
(k) any shipboard cargo-handling equipment needs.

The extent to which the above items are needed depends on circumstances. Moreover, the urgency of need of the tonnage is significant as are falling or rising market fixture rates. Given time, the charterer examines the market in depth, having the benefit of securing a more suitable vessel which may not be immediately available. Full use is made of opportunities available using agencies such as Clarkson's, Fairplay, Galbraith and relative market reports.

The Baltic Exchange conducts most of the chartering global market. Other exchanges exist in Piraeus, New York, Hong Kong, Tokyo and Frankfurt.

The Baltic Exchange core business is communication and information. The Exchange has three principal components. First, is digital data – its raw material – that matches ships with cargoes. Subscribers can choose to whom they disseminate their information by selecting any one of several options. For example, brokers can distribute their tonnage lists only to other colleagues within the same company or to a limited number of individuals outside the company; alternatively, the information can be transmitted to all members of the Exchange or all subscribers to the platform. The electronic floor is linked to the Lloyd's Register Fairplay database – which is updated weekly – containing details of more than 40,000 bulk ships and more than 8,500 ports.

The second component is the freight market information section containing a full range of shipping market information, published daily by the Exchange, embracing dry bulk and oil cargoes indices, together with a list of fixtures for which charters have been fixed. The third element is a 'click to trade' facility, enabling on-line trading of forward freight agreements. Brokers operating on the exchange earn a 1.25% commission. As the world economy is increasingly industrialized the oil energy market is changing and gaining some political influence. The price of a barrel of oil may continue to rise in the next decades, which should result in higher fixture rates and improved profit margins for the tanker owner. This will generate more new builds. It should be noticed that the crude oil tanker is less expensive to build than the product carrier. Oil producing countries ship crude oil and consuming countries refine crude oil, as found in the United States, Rotterdam, and Singapore.

A range of selected refined products is this:

US Gulf (cargoes)
 Naphtha
   Premium gasoline (unleaded 93)
   Regular gasoline (unleaded 87)
 Jet/Kerosene
   Gasoil (0.05% S)
   Fuel oil (1.0% S)
   Fuel oil (3.0% S)
Rotterdam (barges fob)
 Naphtha
   Premium gasoline (unleaded 50 ppm)
   Premium gasoline (unleaded 95)
 Jet/Kerosene
   Gasoil/Diesel (50 ppm)
   Fuel oil (1.0% S)
   Fuel oil (3.5% S)
Mediterranean (cargoes)
 Naphtha
   Premium gasoline (unleaded 95)
 Jet/Kerosene
   Gasoil/Diesel (50 ppm)
   Fuel oil (1.0% S)
   Fuel oil (3.5% S)
Singapore (cargoes)
 Naphtha
   Premium gasoline (unleaded 95)
   Regular gasoline (unleaded 92)
 Jet/Kerosene
   Gasoil/Diesel (50 ppm)
   Fuel oil (180 cst 2.0% S)
   Fuel oil (380 cst 3.5% S)

Using BIMCO approved documentation IT enables swift communication in fixture research and negotiation. Dry and wet trade market reports can be found in *Lloyd's List and Shipping Gazette*. The Worldscale indicators are used as are the range of indices produced by the Baltic Exchange and the J. E. Hyde and MGN on-line indices, as recorded in Lloyd's List.

In addition to the trade to and from the UK, many cross voyages, i.e. from one foreign country to another, are fixed on the London market, often to a vessel owned in another country. It is not compulsory to conduct negotiations through a shipbroker on the Baltic Exchange. Many negotiations are conducted direct between charterer and shipowner. It is a matter for the shipowner's judgement whether he engages a shipbroker to conduct his negotiations direct with the charterer. When the shipbroker is negotiating a series of voyage charters for his principal, the shipowner will endeavour to reduce the number of ballast voyages to the minimum. These arise between termination of one voyage charter, for example at Rotterdam, and commencement of the next voyage charter, for example at Southampton, involving a ballast voyage Rotterdam–Southampton. The use of the BIMCO approved documentation on chartering is important when minimizing risk of misinterpretation of the terms.

The report of a vessel's fixture is recorded in the shipping press. Extracts of two fixtures in grain and two time-charter fixtures are given below:

Interpretation of two fixtures in grain and two time charter fixtures

(i) Chicago–Belfast: *Sugar Crystal,* 14,000 HSS $27.50, option Glasgow/Leith $28.00, 3 days/3,000, 2–14 May (Peabody).

Loading Chicago, discharging Belfast: MV *Sugar Crystal;* cargo 14,000 tonnes heavy grains, sorghums or soyabeans at a freight rate of US $27.50 per tonne, with the charterer's option to discharge instead at Glasgow or Leith at the freight rate of US $28.00; 3 days allowed for loading; 3,000 tonnes rate per day allowed for discharging. Vessel to present ready to load between laydays 2 May and the cancelling date of 14 May, charterers being Messrs Peabody.

(ii) US Gulf–Constanza: *Myron,* 19,000/19,800 min/max SBM, $31.50, FIO, 3,000/1,000, option 4,000 load at $31.25, 26 May–15 June (Coprasol).

Loading at a port in the US Gulf, discharging Constanza: MV *Myron;* cargo minimum 19,000 tonnes/maximum 19,800 tonnes soyabean meal, at a freight rate of US $31.50 per tonne; cargo to be loaded and discharged free of expense to the owner (FIO); 3,000 tonnes rate per day for loading, 1,000 tonnes rate per day for discharging, with charterer's option to increase the speed of loading to 4,000 tonnes per day, in turn paying a reduced freight rate of US $31.25 per tonne. Vessel to present ready to load between laydays 26 May and the cancelling date of 15 June, charterers being Messrs Coprasol.

(iii) *Acropolis* (Fortune type): Greek, built 1988, $5,350 daily. Delivery Casablanca trip, redelivery Le Havre. 20–25 April (Dreyfus).

MV *Acropolis* (a Japanese Fortune type of vessel), Greek flag. Built 1988, $5,350 daily hire. Delivery to charterers at Casablanca for a time charter trip, redelivery to owners at Le Havre. Delivery not earlier than 20 April, not later than 25 April, charterers being Messrs Dreyfus.

(iv) *Camara*, 25,689 dwt, 1.2 M ft^3, Danish, built 1989, 15 knots on 37 tonnes, 1500 s. 5 × 15 tonne cranes. $6,250 daily. Delivery Antwerp, trip via north France and Bulgaria, redelivery Gibraltar. Spot (Philipp Bros.).

MV *Camara,* 25689 summer deadweight, 1,200,000 ft^3 capacity, Danish flag, built 1989. 15 knots on 37 tonnes (CS 180) F/O, 5 × 15 tonne cranes, US $6,250 daily hire. Delivery on time charter at Antwerp for a time charter trip via north France and Bulgaria with redelivery to owners upon vessel passing Gibraltar. Vessel available immediately at Antwerp (spot), charterers being Messrs Philipp Bros.

The dry and wet bulk cargo markets continue to change, placing pressure on the shipbroker to offer accurate market research and intelligence data to their clients for business plan formulation and future fixture requirements. China is consuming considerable quantities of iron ore and oil to develop its industries and its export product markets. The US and OECD (the Organization for Economic Co-operation and Development) also demand oil. The tanker broker continues to focus on the range of oil production/demand data merging from EIA Energy Information Administration, IEA, OPEC, Intertanko, OECD and leading tanker brokers, such as Galbraiths. Seaborne tanker trade is switching over to longer haul growth rather than shorter haul, influenced by continuous expansion of pipeline networks. The nature of the tanker fleet is changing, with the near elimination of the ULCC tonnage and a preference for the VLCC when building replacement programmes. As an example, the crude oil dwt tanker demand in market shares 2002 was VLCC 51%, Handymax 8%, Suezmax 18% and Aframax 23%.

15.2 Voyage and time charter parties

No statutory clauses are required to be incorporated in a charter party. The terms and conditions of a charter party represent the wishes of the two parties to the contract. There are some essential clauses necessary to some charter parties, whilst other clauses are optional. For example, an ice clause would be essential if the vessel were trading in the White or Baltic Seas but would not be necessary if the ship was operating in the Tropics. When being formulated the charter party contract must adopt the definition of the terms as set out in 'Voylayrules 93', specified by BIMCO. Given below are the desirable essential clauses found in a voyage charter party, together with possible problem areas. They are not in all charters.

1 *The preamble.* The contracting parties; description of the vessel; position of vessel and expected readiness date to load.

2 *Description of the cargo.* The quantity of cargo is usually stated as a full and complete cargo, with a minimum and a maximum quantity. This means that the ship guarantees to load at least the minimum and the ship may call for any quantity up to the maximum, which the charterer must supply; in other words, the quantity of cargo loaded is any quantity between the minimum and the maximum in the shipowner's option. The normal margin is 5 to 10% more or less than a stated quantity. The cargo must be clearly described in negotiations and in the charter party. If the cargo is liable to occupy a lot of space (or cubic) it is advisable to have the stowage factor stated in the charter. The word 'stemmed' means that the cargo (or bunkers) for the ship have been booked, or reserved.

3 *Loading date and cancelling date.* This is the period of time (anything from a few days to a few weeks) given in the charter during which the vessel may present herself for loading, and is sometimes rather loosely referred to as its laydays, although this is not the correct meaning of laydays. The charterer is not obliged to load the vessel before its loading date, even though the vessel may be ready. If the vessel is not ready to load on or before the cancelling date, the charterer has the option of cancelling the charter with a right of damages against the shipowners. If the vessel looks to miss its cancelling date, she is still legally bound to present for loading, even if it means a long ballast voyage, and it is only then that the charterers need declare whether they will cancel or maintain the vessel. In practice, if the vessel looks like being late the shipowner will approach the charterer to get an extension of the cancelling date or else a definite cancellation before the vessel proceeds to the loading port.

   When stating the layday/cancelling dates these two points must be borne in mind: the contractual position if the vessel presents herself for loading too early; and the position if the vessel cannot meet the cancelling date. (See also item 8.)

4 *Loading port or place.* The loading port or place is always stated in a voyage charter. Sometimes it is a single named port, or one out of a range of picked ports (i.e. several good named ports) or a port to be nominated along a certain stretch of coastline (e.g. 'A/H Range' which means a port between Antwerp and Hamburg inclusive). If the loading port is named, the vessel is under an obligation to get to that port, and if a particular berth or dock in that port is named in the charter, then the vessel is under an obligation to get to that dock or berth. In other words, when fixing his vessel to load at a named port it is up to the owner to make sure that the vessel can both enter and leave the port safely. These remarks also apply if the vessel is to load at one or more named ports out of a selection. If they are named in the charter then the shipowner undertakes to get there, and is excused only if he is frustrated from so doing. Quite often a vessel is fixed to load at any port in the charterer's option out of a range

(i.e. a particular stretch of coastline) in which case the charterer could order the vessel to any port in that range. The shipowner, to protect his interest, should stipulate, when fixing, for a *safe port*. The charterer can then order the vessel only to one which the owner and the Master consider safe for the vessel. A safe port means a port which a vessel may go to and leave safely, without danger from physical or political causes. The port must be safe when the vessel is ordered to it and safe when the vessel arrives at port. If, in the meantime, the port has become unsafe the shipowner may refuse to send his ship there and request the charterer to nominate another port.

5 *Discharging port or place.* The above remarks apply to the discharging port. As soon as a discharging port is ordered (out of, for example, a range of ports) then that port becomes the contract terminus of the voyage.

6 *Alternative ports of discharge; seaworthy trim between ports; geographical rotation.* When there is more than one port of discharge, the shipowner should stipulate that the ports are in geographical rotation, i.e in regular order along the coast, either north to south, east to west, or vice versa, and not jumping about from one to another, backwards and forwards in a haphazard manner.

7 *Payment of freight.* Unless there is a condition to the contrary (e.g. special terms of contract as to 'advance freight' etc.) freight is construed in the ordinary commercial meaning, i.e. the reward payable to the carrier on arrival of the goods, ready to be delivered to the consignee. The true test of the right of freight is whether the service in respect of which freight was contracted has been substantially performed. The following circumstances are relevant:

(a) Ships to deliver cargo on being paid freight. This establishes that freight is payable as the cargo is discharged, i.e. concurrent with discharge. Literally it means that freight is payable as each ton is discharged. In practice, freight is paid so much on account at various stages of the discharge, e.g. day by day on out-turn.

(b) On right and true delivery of the cargo. In this case freight is earned only after delivery of the cargo, but is paid for day by day on out-turn and adjusted on final delivery.

(c) On signing bills of lading. Freight is payable when the ship is loaded and the bills of lading have been signed. This is usually followed by the words 'discountless and non-returnable, ship and/or cargo lost or not lost', i.e. once the shipowner receives his freight he retains it. Payment in this manner is known as advance freight and the bill of lading is endorsed 'freight paid'. (The above is not to be confused with advance of freight which may be issued to the shipowner to cover his disbursements at the loading port. This advance of freight should really be considered as a loan, and the charterer who gives the shipowner this facility usually makes a small charge of, say, 10%.)

(d) The insurance of freight. Irrespective of how the freight is paid, both parties to the contract incur certain expenses in preparation for the voyage, and in the event of the ship being lost do not wish to lose the freight as well, and it is therefore insured. If freight is payable on delivery the shipowner will insure the freight in case the vessel is lost. If freight is paid in advance, then the charterer will insure the freight, because if the ship is lost he will not receive any refund from the shipowner.

Note that the currency of payment is closely evaluated, with particular consideration of exchange rate fluctuations and measures available to counter them; if the freight rate payment and the currency in the country of the recipient are different; and/or if freight is not directly payable to his bank at the place of domicile but is collected by an agent.

8 *Laydays.* This is the rate of discharge per weather working day. Laydays are the number of days permitted in a charter party for loading and discharging the vessel. Alternatively, it may be either applied for loading or discharging a vessel in calculating the implications when the layday period prescribed has been exceeded. In such a situation demurrage arises, the terms of which arise in the following clause. Conversely, despatch arises when the loading and/or discharge is completed sooner than prescribed. Various types of laydays exist, as detailed below:

(a) Running or consecutive days concern consecutive calendar days (midnight to midnight) including Sundays and holidays when laydays count. Once laydays commence this runs continuously unless any holidays arise which specifically exclude laydays.
(b) Reversible laydays confirming all time saved or lost on loading vessel may be added or deducted from the time allowed for discharge.
(c) Weather working days indicate that laydays do not count when adverse weather conditions prevail thereby preventing loading or discharging to take place.
(d) Surf days arise when a heavy swell or surf prevents loading or discharging at ports which are usually roadsteads. Surf days do not count as laydays.
(e) Working days are days when work is normally performed. These exclude Sundays (when recognized) and holidays officially recognized. The number of working daily hours depends on the custom of the port. To lessen such risks brokers are urged to check the BIMCO holiday calendar.

9 *Demurrage and despatch.* If a ship loads and/or discharges in less than the prescribed time, the owners pay despatch money as a reward for time saved; if, on the other hand, the prescribed time is exceeded, then demurrage is payable at an agreed rate to the owner as compensation for delay of the ship. The term 'all time saved' within the context of despatch

money should be used with caution as it can result in a situation in which the number of days on which despatch has to be paid exceeds the number of days agreed as laytime allowed.

10 *Cessor or limitation of liability clause.*

11 *Lien clause.* This gives the shipowners the right to hold cargo against payment of freight or hire. The following checklist is relevant on lien on cargo: (a) the owner's bank must be instructed to reject any late payment on-line; (b) due care must be taken to notify clearly the time charterers of withdrawal and to instruct the Master immediately; (c) withdrawal of vessel with cargo on board is not possible because of owners' responsibility *vis-à-vis* bill of lading holders; (d) consult owners P&I/Defence Club with a view to attempting to place lien on voyage sub-freights or bill of lading (unless pre-paid); (e) act in full co-operation with P&I/Defence Club as soon as hire problems may arise and furnish the club with the requisite documentation; (f) consult owners' P&I/Defence Club with a view to undertaking steps aimed at securing time charterers assets – if any; (g) lien on cargo is possible only in the rare cases when the cargo belongs to the time charterers, i.e. when bill of lading holders and time charterers are identical; and (h) leniency in accepting late hire payments has the effect that before contemplating withdrawal of vessel, owners must place time charterers 'on notice' well in advance that late payment of next hire instalment will not be accepted.

12 *Loading and discharging expenses.*

13 *Appointment of agents and stevedores.*

14 *Lighterage.*

15 *Deviation and salvage clause.*

16 *Bills of lading clause.*

17 *Exemptions from liability clause.*

18 *General average.*

19 *Arbitration.*

20 *Ice clause.* It is important to consider the consequences faced by vessels and their operators when trading in areas affected by ice, particularly important when the Baltic and the Gulf of St Lawrence Seaway are included. Moreover, severe winters cause a number of ports to restrict navigation to having ice class and the icebreakers are on duty later into the spring. The following criteria on ship handling in ice conditions may prove relevant: (a) the Master may wish to engage a pilot; (b) propellers and rudders are the most vulnerable parts of the ship – vessels should go astern in ice with extreme care with rudder amidships; (c) be prepared to go full astern at any time; (d) do not underestimate the hardness of the ice; (e) do not enter ice if an alternative route is available; (f) enter ice at low speed to receive initial impact, and once into the pack increase speed to maintain headway and control of the ship; (g) wherever possible pressure ridges should be avoided and a passage through pack ice under

pressure should not be attempted; (h) all forms of glacial ice (icebergs, bergy bits, growlers) in the pack are current driven and should be given a wide berth, even though the pack as a whole is wind driven; (i) when a ship navigating independently becomes beset, it usually requires icebreaker assistance, and (j) navigation in pack ice after dark should not be attempted without high-power search lights controlled from the bridge.

21 *Strikes and stoppages.*

22 *Overtime.*

23 *Sailing telegram.*

24 *Sub-letting.* This gives or refuses to allow permission of the ship to be sub-let, or sub-chartered under the charter party.

25 *Address commission.* A percentage of commission sometimes specified due to charterers based on the amount of freight.

26 *Brokerage.* Indicates the rate of brokerage that shall be paid.

27 *Penalty for non-performance.*

28 *War clause.*

29 *New Jason clause.*

30 *Both to blame clause.*

31 *Clause paramount.*

32 *ISPS code clause.* The ISPS code outlines requirements shipowners can only meet with co-operation from charterers, such as providing information about the contact details of the charterers and any sub-charterers. Moreover, delays and expenses may be incurred in connection with security measures taken by the local port authorities or other relevant authority according to the ISPS code, the burden of which must be borne by the owners or the charterers or shared between them. It is important the ISPS clause does not conflict with the War Clause. The ISPS code does not stipulate new duties for the port agents, who must be prepared to assist arriving ships and their respective Ship Security Officers raising security-related issues.

33 *US Customs* Trade Partnership Against Terrorism (C-TPAT) clause December 2004, US Security Clauses for Time and Voyage Chartering December 2004. Shipowners wishing to help the charterers comply with their obligations under the C-TPAT Agreement may use the clause, although not legally bound to do so.

Note that it is the shipowner's right to decide who should represent his interests and attend to his vessel at any particular port. In the event the shipowner may need to employ a port agent named or appointed by the charterers. The port agent so appointed should be fully aware that no matter what his connections with the charterers may be, he is the agent of the vessel and his duty is to represent/defend the interests of the shipowner. An example of a voyage charter codenamed 'GENCON' used for general cargo is given in Figure 15.1. and contains 17 clauses. This charter party is widely used.

Adopted by
the Documentary Committee of the General
Council of British Shipping, London
and the Documentary Committee of the Japan
Shipping Exchange, Inc., Tokyo

RECOMMENDED
THE BALTIC AND INTERNATIONAL MARITIME CONFERENCE
UNIFORM GENERAL CHARTER (AS REVISED 1922 and 1976)
INCLUDING "F.I.O." ALTERNATIVE, ETC.
(To be used for trades for which no approved form is in force)
CODE NAME: "GENCON"

Part I

1. Shipbroker

2. Place and date

3. Owners/Place of business (Cl. 1)

4. Charterers/Place of business (Cl. 1)

5. Vessel's name (Cl. 1)

6. GRT/NRT (Cl. 1)

7. Deadweight cargo carrying capacity in tons (abt.) (Cl. 1)

8. Present position (Cl. 1)

9. Expected ready to load (abt.) (Cl. 1)

10. Loading port or place (Cl. 1)

11. Discharging port or place (Cl. 1)

12. Cargo (also state quantity and margin in Owners' option, if agreed; if full and complete cargo not agreed state "part cargo") (Cl. 1)

13. Freight rate (also state if payable on delivered or intaken quantity) (Cl. 1)

14. Freight payment (state currency and method of payment; also beneficiary and bank account) (Cl. 4)

15. Loading and discharging costs (state alternative (a) or (b) of Cl. 5; also indicate if vessel is gearless)

16. Laytime (if separate laytime for load. and disch. is agreed, fill in a) and b). If total laytime for load. and disch., fill in c) only) (Cl. 6)

a) Laytime for loading

b) Laytime for discharging

c) Total laytime for loading and discharging

17. Shippers (state name and address) (Cl. 6)

18. Demurrage rate (loading and discharging) (Cl. 7)

19. Cancelling date (Cl. 10)

20. Brokerage commission and to whom payable (Cl. 14)

21. Additional clauses covering special provisions, if agreed.

Copyright, published by The Baltic
and International Maritime
Conference (BIMCO), Copenhagen

It is mutually agreed that this Contract shall be performed subject to the conditions contained in this Charter which shall include Part I as well as Part II. In the event of a conflict of conditions, the provisions of Part I shall prevail over those of Part II to the extent of such conflict.

Signature (Owners)

Signature (Charterers)

Printed and sold by Fr G Knudtzon Ltd., 55 Toldbodgade, DK-1253 Copenhagen K, Telefax +45 33 93 11 84
by authority of The Baltic and International Maritime Conference (BIMCO), Copenhagen

Figure 15.1 The 'GENCON' BIMCO Uniform General Charter Party.

Source: Reproduced by kind permission of BIMCO.

PART II
"Gencon" Charter (As Revised 1922 and 1976)
Including "F.I.O." Alternative, etc.

It is agreed between the party mentioned in Box 3 as Owners of the 1
steamer or motor-vessel named in Box 5, of the gross/nett Register 2
tons indicated in Box 6 and carrying about the number of tons of 3
deadweight cargo stated in Box 7, now in position as stated in Box 8 4
and expected ready to load under this Charter about the date in- 5
dicated in Box 9, and the party mentioned as Charterers in Box 4 6
that: 7
The said vessel shall proceed to the loading port or place stated 8
in Box 10 or so near thereto as she may safely get and lie always 9
afloat, and there load a full and complete cargo (if shipment of deck 10
cargo agreed same to be at Charterers' risk) as stated in Box 12 11
(Charterers to provide all mats and/or wood for dunnage and any 12
separations required, the Owners allowing the use of any dunnage 13
wood on board if required) which the Charterers bind themselves to 14
ship, and being so loaded the vessel shall proceed to the discharg- 15
ing port or place stated in Box 11 as ordered on signing Bills of 16
Lading or so near thereto as she may safely get and lie always 17
afloat and there deliver the cargo on being paid freight on delivered 18
or intaken quantity as indicated in Box 13 at the rate stated in 19
Box 13. 20

Owners' Responsibility Clause 21
Owners are to be responsible for loss of or damage to the goods 22
or for delay in delivery of the goods only in case the loss, damage 23
or delay has been caused by the improper or negligent stowage of 24
the goods (unless stowage performed by shippers/Charterers or their 25
stevedores or servants) or by personal want of due diligence on the 26
part of the Owners or their Manager to make the vessel in all respects 27
seaworthy and to secure that she is properly manned, equipped and 28
supplied or by the personal act or default of the Owners or their 29
Manager. 30
And the Owners are responsible for no loss or damage or delay 31
arising from any other cause whatsoever, even from the neglect or 32
default of the Captain or crew or some other person employed by the 33
Owners on board or ashore for whose acts they would, but for this 34
clause, be responsible, or from unseaworthiness of the vessel on 35
loading or commencement of the voyage or at any time whatsoever. 36
Damage caused by contact with or leakage, smell or evaporation 37
from other goods or by the inflammable or explosive nature or in- 38
sufficient package of other goods not to be considered as caused 39
by improper or negligent stowage, even if in fact so caused. 40

Deviation Clause 41
The vessel has liberty to call at any port or ports in any order, for 42
any purpose, to sail without pilots, to tow and or assist vessels in 43
all situations, and also to deviate for the purpose of saving life and/ 44
or property. 45

Payment of Freight 46
The freight to be paid in the manner prescribed in Box 14 in cash 47
without discount on delivery of the cargo at mean rate of exchange 48
ruling on day or days of payment, the receivers of the cargo being 49
bound to pay freight on account during delivery, if required by Cap- 50
tain or Owners. 51
Cash for vessel's ordinary disbursements at port of loading to be 52
advanced by Charterers if required at highest current rate of ex- 53
change, subject to two per cent. to cover insurance and other ex- 54
penses. 55

Loading Discharging Costs 56
* (a) Gross Terms 57
The cargo to be brought alongside in such a manner as to enable 58
vessel to take the goods with her own tackle. Charterers to procure 59
and pay the necessary men on shore or on board the lighters to do 60
the work there, vessel only heaving the cargo on board, 61
If the loading takes place by elevator, cargo to be put free in vessel's 62
holds, Owners only paying trimming expenses. 63
Any pieces and/or packages of cargo over two tons weight, shall be 64
loaded, stowed and discharged by Charterers at their risk and expense. 65
The cargo to be received by Merchants at their risk and expense 66
alongside the vessel not beyond the reach of her tackle. 67
* (b) F.i.o. and free stowed.trimmed 68
The cargo shall be brought into the holds, loaded, stowed and/or trim- 69
med and taken from the holds and discharged by the Charterers or 70
their Agents, free of any risk, liability and expense whatsoever to the 71
Owners. 72
The Owners shall provide winches, motive power and winchmen from 73
the Crew if requested and permitted; if not, the Charterers shall 74
provide and pay for winchmen from shore and/or cranes, if any. (This 75
provision shall not apply if vessel is gearless and stated as such in 76
Box 15). 77
* indicate alternative (a) or (b), as agreed, in Box 15. 78

Laytime 79
* (a) Separate laytime for loading and discharging 80
The cargo shall be loaded within the number of running hours as 81
indicated in Box 16. weather permitting, Sundays and holidays ex- 82
cepted, unless used, in which event time actually used shall count. 83
The cargo shall be discharged within the number of running hours 84
as indicated in Box 16, weather permitting, Sundays and holidays ex- 85
cepted, unless used, in which event time actually used shall count. 86
* (b) Total laytime for loading and discharging 87
The cargo shall be loaded and discharged within the number of total 88
running hours as indicated in Box 16, weather permitting, Sundays and 89
holidays excepted, unless used, in which event time actually used 90
shall count. 91
(c) Commencement of laytime (loading and discharging) 92
Laytime for loading and discharging shall commence at 1 p.m. if 93
notice of readiness is given before noon, and at 8 a.m. next working 94
day if notice given during office hours after noon. Notice at loading 95
port to be given to the Shippers named in Box 17. 96
Time actually used before commencement of laytime shall count. 97
Time lost in waiting for berth to count as loading or discharging 98
time, as the case may be. 99
* indicate alternative (a) or (b) as agreed, in Box 16. 100

Demurrage 101
Ten running days on demurrage at the rate stated in Box 18 per 102
day or pro rata for any part of a day, payable day by day, to be 103
allowed Merchants altogether at ports of loading and discharging. 104

8. Lien Clause 105
Owners shall have a lien on the cargo for freight, dead-freight, 106
demurrage and damages for detention. Charterers shall remain re- 107
sponsible for dead-freight and demurrage (including damages for 108
detention), incurred at port of loading. Charterers shall also remain 109
responsible for freight and demurrage (including damages for deten- 110
tion) incurred at port of discharge, but only to such extent as the 111
Owners have been unable to obtain payment thereof by exercising 112
the lien on the cargo. 113

9. Bills of Lading 114
The Captain to sign Bills of Lading at such rate of freight as 115
presented without prejudice to this Charterparty, but should the 116
freight by Bills of Lading amount to less than the total chartered 117
freight the difference to be paid to the Captain in cash on signing 118
Bills of Lading. 119

10. Cancelling Clause 120
Should the vessel not be ready to load (whether in berth or not) on 121
or before the date indicated in Box 19, Charterers have the option 122
of cancelling this contract, such option to be declared, if demanded, 123
at least 48 hours before vessel's expected arrival at port of loading. 124
Should the vessel be delayed on account of average or otherwise, 125
Charterers to be informed as soon as possible, and if the vessel is 126
delayed for more than 10 days after the day she is stated to be 127
expected ready to load, Charterers have the option of cancelling this 128
contract, unless a cancelling date has been agreed upon. 129

11. General Average 130
General average to be settled according to York-Antwerp Rules, 131
1974. Proprietors of cargo to pay the cargo's share in the general 132
expenses even if same have been necessitated through neglect or 133
default of the Owners' servants (see clause 2). 134

12. Indemnity 135
Indemnity for non-performance of this Charterparty, proved damages, 136
not exceeding estimated amount of freight. 137

13. Agency 138
In every case the Owners shall appoint his own Broker or Agent both 139
at the port of loading and the port of discharge. 140

14. Brokerage 141
A brokerage commission at the rate stated in Box 20 on the freight 142
earned is due to the party mentioned in Box 20. 143
In case of non-execution at least ¹⁄₃ of the brokerage on the estimated 144
amount of freight and dead-freight to be paid by the Owners to the 145
Brokers as indemnity for the latter's expenses and work. In case of 146
more voyages the amount of indemnity to be mutually agreed. 147

15. GENERAL STRIKE CLAUSE 148
Neither Charterers nor Owners shall be responsible for the con- 149
sequences of any strikes or lock-outs preventing or delaying the 150
fulfilment of any obligations under this contract. 151
If there is a strike or lock-out affecting the loading of the cargo, 152
or any part of it, when vessel is ready to proceed from her last port 153
or at any time during the voyage to the port or ports of loading or 154
after her arrival there, Captain or Owners may ask Charterers to 155
declare, that they agree to reckon the laydays as if there were no 156
strike or lock-out. Unless Charterers have given such declaration in 157
writing (by telegram, if necessary) within 24 hours, Owners shall 158
have the option of cancelling this contract. If part cargo has already 159
been loaded, Owners must proceed with same, (freight payable on 160
loaded quantity only) having liberty to complete with other cargo 161
on the way for their own account. 162
If there is a strike or lock-out affecting the discharge of the cargo 163
on or after vessel's arrival at or off port of discharge and same has 164
not been settled within 48 hours, Receivers shall have the option of 165
keeping vessel waiting until such strike or lock-out is at an end 166
against paying half demurrage after expiration of the time provided 167
for discharging, or of ordering the vessel to a safe port where she 168
can safely discharge without risk of being detained by strike or lock- 169
out. Such orders to be given within 48 hours after Captain or Owners 170
have given notice to Charterers of the strike or lock-out affecting 171
the discharge. On delivery of the cargo at such port, all conditions 172
of this Charterparty and of the Bill of Lading shall apply and vessel 173
shall receive the same freight as if she had discharged at the 174
original port of destination, except that if the distance of the sub- 175
stituted port exceeds 100 nautical miles, the freight on the cargo 176
delivered at the substituted port to be increased in proportion. 177

16. War Risks ("Voywar 1950") 178
(1) In these clauses "War Risks" shall include any blockade or any 179
action which is announced as a blockade by any Government or by any 180
belligerent or by any organized body, sabotage, piracy, and any actual 181
or threatened war, hostilities, warlike operations, civil war, civil com- 182
motion, or revolution. 183
(2) If at any time before the Vessel commences loading, it appears that 184
performance of the contract will subject the Vessel or her Master and 185
crew or her cargo to war risks at any stage of the adventure, the Owners 186
shall be entitled by letter or telegram despatched to the Charterers, to 187
cancel this Charter. 188
(3) The Master shall not be required to load cargo or to continue 189
loading or to proceed on or to sign Bill(s) of Lading for any adventure 190
on which or any port at which it appears that the Vessel, her Master 191
and crew or her cargo will be subjected to war risks. In the event of 192
the exercise by the Master of his right under this Clause after part or 193
full cargo has been loaded, the Master shall be at liberty either to 194
discharge such cargo at the loading port or to proceed therewith. 195
In the latter case the Vessel shall have liberty to carry other cargo 196
for Owners' benefit and accordingly to proceed to and load or 197
discharge such other cargo at any other port or ports whatsoever, 198
backwards or forwards, although in a contrary direction to or out of or 199
beyond the ordinary route. In the event of the Master electing to 200
proceed with part cargo under this Clause freight shall in any case 201
be payable on the quantity delivered. 202
(4) If at the time the Master elects to proceed with part or full cargo 203
under Clause 3, or after the Vessel has left the loading port, or the 204

Figure 15.1 continued

PART II
"Gencon" Charter (As Revised 1922 and 1976)
Including "F.I.O." Alternative, etc.

last of the loading ports, if more than one, it appears that further 205
performance of the contract will subject the Vessel, her Master and 206
crew or her cargo, to war risks, the cargo shall be discharged, or if 207
the discharge has been commenced shall be completed, at any safe 208
port in vicinity of the port of discharge as may be ordered by the 209
Charterers. If no such orders shall be received from the Charterers 210
within 48 hours after the Owners have despatched a request by 211
telegram to the Charterers for the nomination of a substitute discharg- 212
ing port, the Owners shall be at liberty to discharge the cargo at 213
any safe port which they may, in their discretion, decide on and such 214
discharge shall be deemed to be due fulfilment of the contract of 215
affreightment. In the event of cargo being discharged at any such 216
other port, the Owners shall be entitled to freight as if the discharge 217
had been effected at the port or ports named in the Bill(s) of Lading 218
or to which the Vessel may have been ordered pursuant thereto. 219

(5) (a). The Vessel shall have liberty to comply with any directions 220
or recommendations as to loading, departure, arrival, routes, ports 221
of call, stoppages, destination, zones, waters, discharge, delivery or 222
in any other wise whatsoever (including any direction or recom- 223
mendation not to go to the port of destination or to delay proceeding 224
thereto or to proceed to some other port) given by any Government or 225
by any belligerent or by any organized body engaged in civil war, 226
hostilities or warlike operations or by any person or body acting or 227
purporting to act as or with the authority of any Government or 228
belligerent or of any such organized body or by any committee or 229
person having under the terms of the war risks insurance on the 230
Vessel, the right to give any such directions or recommendations. If, 231
by reason of or in compliance with any such direction or recom- 232
mendation, anything is done or is not done, such shall not be deemed 233
a deviation. 234

(b) If, by reason of or in compliance with any such directions or re- 235
commendations, the Vessel does not proceed to the port or ports 236
named in the Bill(s) of Lading or to which she may have been 237
ordered pursuant thereto, the Vessel may proceed to any port as 238
directed or recommended or to any safe port which the Owners in 239
their discretion may decide on and there discharge the cargo. Such 240
discharge shall be deemed to be due fulfilment of the contract of 241
affreightment and the Owners shall be entitled to freight as if 242
discharge had been effected at the port or ports named in the Bill(s) 243
of Lading or to which the Vessel may have been ordered pursuant 244
thereto. 245

(6) All extra expenses (including insurance costs) involved in discharg- 246
ing cargo at the loading port or in reaching or discharging the cargo 247
at any port as provided in Clauses 4 and 5 (b) hereof shall be paid 248
by the Charterers and/or cargo owners, and the Owners shall have 249
a lien on the cargo for all moneys due under these Clauses. 250

17. GENERAL ICE CLAUSE 2
Port of loading 2

(a) In the event of the loading port being inaccessible by reason of 2
ice when vessel is ready to proceed from her last port or at any 2
time during the voyage or on vessel's arrival or in case frost sets in 2
after vessel's arrival, the Captain for fear of being frozen in is at 2
liberty to leave without cargo, and this Charter shall be null and 2
void 2

(b) If during loading the Captain, for fear of vessel being frozen in, 2
deems it advisable to leave, he has liberty to do so with what cargo 2
he has on board and to proceed to any other port or ports with 2
option of completing cargo for Owners' benefit for any port or ports 2
including port of discharge. Any part cargo thus loaded under this 2
Charter to be forwarded to destination at vessel's expense but 2
against payment of freight, provided that no extra expenses be 2
thereby caused to the Receivers, freight being paid on quantity 2
delivered (in proportion if lumpsum), all other conditions as per 2
Charter. 2

(c) In case of more than one loading port, and if one or more of 2
the ports are closed by ice, the Captain or Owners to be at liberty 2
either to load the part cargo at the open port and fill up elsewhere 2
for their own account as under section (b) or to declare the Charter 2
null and void unless Charterers agree to load full cargo at the open 2
port. 2

(d) This Ice Clause not to apply in the Spring. 2

Port of discharge 2

(a) Should ice (except in the Spring) prevent vessel from reaching 2
port of discharge Receivers shall have the option of keeping vessel 2
waiting until the re-opening of navigation and paying demurrage, or 2
of ordering the vessel to a safe and immediately accessible port 2
where she can safely discharge without risk of detention by ice. 2
Such orders to be given within 48 hours after Captain or Owners 2
have given notice to Charterers of the impossibility of reaching port 2
of destination. 2

(b) If during discharging the Captain for fear of vessel being frozen 2
in deems it advisable to leave, he has liberty to do so with what 2
cargo he has on board and to proceed to the nearest accessible 2
port where she can safely discharge. 2

(c) On delivery of the cargo at such port, all conditions of the Bill 2
of Lading shall apply and vessel shall receive the same freight as 2
if she had discharged at the original port of destination, except that if 2
the distance of the substituted port exceeds 100 nautical miles, the 2
freight on the cargo delivered at the substituted port to be increased 2
in proportion. 2

Figure 15.1 continued

A time charter, as mentioned earlier, is defined as a contract of affreightment under which a charterer agrees to hire, and the shipowner agrees to let, his vessel for a mutually agreed period of time or a specified voyage, the remuneration being known as hire. There are certain advantages and disadvantages to the shipowner and to the charterer in placing a vessel on time charter, as compared with ordinary voyage charter trading.

From the shipowner's standpoint, the ship is employed for a definite period of time, with a regular income to the shipowner and the minimum of risk. Time charter provides the shipowner with a 'good cover' against a decline in freight rates. The shipowner does not have to worry about the day-to-day trading of the vessel so far as bunkers, port charges and cargo expenses are concerned; the vessel will remain on hire even if delayed by port labour troubles. The disadvantages to the shipowner are that to a certain extent he loses control of his vessel, although he still appoints the Master and crew, but subject to the charter limitations he does not control the cargo loaded in the vessel or the voyage. If the freight market should rise the shipowner is unable to take advantage of it, and the charterer gets the benefit instead. The vessel may not be in a convenient position for the owner to perform maintenance work on his vessel, although the disadvantage would apply only in the case of a long-term charter.

1. Shipbroker	THE BALTIC AND INTERNATIONAL MARITIME COUNCIL (BIMCO) UNIFORM TIME CHARTER PARTY FOR CONTAINER VESSELS CODE NAME: "BOXTIME" PART I
	2. Place and Date
3. Owners/Disponent Owners & Place of Business, Telephone, Telex and Telefax Number	4. Charterers & Place of Business, Telephone, Telex and Telefax Number
5. Vessel's Name	6. Call Sign/Telex Number
7. GRT/NRT	8. DWT on Summer Freeboard	9. TEU Capacity (Maximum)
10. Class (Cl. 5)	11. Flag	12. Service Speed (See Part III)	13. Fuel Consumption (See Part III)
14. Type(s) of Fuel(s) (Cl. 12 (d))	15. Maximum Bunker Capacity
16. Bunkers/Price on Delivery (Min.-Max.) (Cl. 12 (a) and (c))	17. Bunkers/Price on Redelivery (Min.-Max.) (Cl. 12 (a) and (c))
18. Place of Delivery (Cl. 1 (b))	19. Earliest Date of Delivery (local time) (Cl. 1 (b))
20. Latest Date of Delivery (local time) (Cl. 1 (b))	21. Place of Redelivery (Cl. 6 (m))
22. Trading Limits (Cl. 3 and Cl. 5 (c))	
23. Period of Charter and Options if any (Cl. 1 (a), Cl. 6 (m) and Cl. 7 (f))	24. State number of Days Options have to be declared after commencement of Charter Period (Cl. 1 (a))
25. Rate of Hire per Day and to whom payable (Cl. 1 (a), Cl. 7 (a) and (b))	26. Quantity of Hazardous Goods allowed (Cl. 4 (b))
27. Insured Value of Vessel (Cl. 18 (a))	28. Daily Rate for Supercargo (Cl. 13 (h))
	29. Victualling Rate per Meal for other Charterers' Servants etc (Cl. 13 (j))
30. Name of Owners' P & I Club (Cl. 18 (b))	31. Name of Charterers' P & I Club (Cl. 18 (b))
32. Charterers' maximum Claim settlement authority (Cl. 18 (h))	33. General Average to be adjusted at (Cl. 14 (c))
34. Law and Arbitration (state a, b, or c of Cl. 20, as agreed; if c agreed also state Place of Arbitration) (Cl. 20)	35. Brokerage Commission and to whom payable (Cl. 21)
36. Number of Additional Clauses covering special Provisions	

It is mutually agreed between the party mentioned in Box 3 (hereinafter referred to as "the Owners") and the Party mentioned in Box 4 (hereinafter referred to as "the Charterers") that this Contract shall be performed in accordance with the conditions contained in Part I including additional clauses, if any agreed and stated in Box 36, and Part II as well as Part III. In the event of a conflict of conditions, the provisions of Part I and Part III shall prevail over those of Part II to the extent of such conflict but no further.

Signature (Owners)	Signature (Charterers)

Printed and sold by Fr. G. Knudtzons Bogtrykkeri A/S, 55 Toldbodgade, DK-1253 Copenhagen K, Telefax +45 33 93 11 84, by authority of The Baltic and International Maritime Council (BIMCO), Copenhagen.

Figure 15.2 The 'Boxtime' BIMCO Uniform Time Charter Party for Container Vessels.

Source: Reproduced by kind permission of BIMCO.

The charterer has the advantage of being able to trade the vessel almost as if it were his own, subject only to the charter party limitations. He can hire the vessel on a long or short-term basis (generally the longer the period the cheaper the rate at which he can secure tonnage), and it provides him with a good cover if the freight markets show any signs of rising. The liner companies can take tonnage on time charter and so supplement their own sailing if the volume of trade is such as to warrant additional tonnage. The disadvantages to the charterer are that he is committed to the payment of hire over a period of time and, should trade diminish, he may have to face a loss. The charterer, by the terms of the charter, may be limited in his range of trading, but he should consider this when negotiating the charter. The charterer is responsible for the ship's bunker supply, port charges and cargo-handling expenses.

There is an increasing tendency for modern bulk purpose-built carriers, including tankers, to be on time charters of seven years duration or longer. Special provision can be made in the charter party for the fixture rate to be reviewed, which at the time of the initial fixture negotiation broadly reflects a modest return to the shipowner on his capital investment throughout the duration of the charter.

When fixing a vessel on time charter, the shipowner should consider the trading limits, or the areas where the vessel will be trading, and also the type of trade in which the vessel will engage.

Many charters stipulate that the vessel shall trade within International Navigation Limits (i.e. the districts considered safe by the insurance authorities). If the vessel is to break these warranty limits the question of who is to pay the extra insurance must be decided. The owner must also consider what trade his vessel is to be employed in. For example, regular employment in the ore trade is likely to cause heavy wear and tear on the vessel; loading and discharging of ore is usually quick and the vessel has little time in port in which to carry out engine maintenance.

The clauses in a time charter are rather different from those found in voyage charters, by reason of the different nature of the trade. A number of clauses are common to both types of charter.

Further BIMCO approved charter party, codename 'Boxtime', is illustrated in Figure 15.2. It is used in the container trade for time charters and has 22 clauses with 844 lines, incorporating Part II featuring the terms of the charter party, and Part III the vessel specification.

15.3 Approved forms of charter parties and related bills of lading

Terms and conditions of a charter party vary according to the wishes of the parties to the contract. Nevertheless the Baltic and International Maritime Council (BIMCO) approved or recommended a number of charter parties – about sixty – for certain commodities in specified trades. Most of these charter parties have been negotiated with organizations representative of charterers. Owners and charterers are recommended to use the printed texts but there is no power of sanction, and amendments are made to suit the requirements of individual fixtures. A selection of the more popular forms is found in Appendix 15.1. Associated with the charter parties listed in the appendix there exist a number of bills of lading with specific code names for use with such charter parties. Their use is purely optional and details of the bills of lading and sundry other forms are also given in Appendix 15.1.

BIMCO is the recognized global authority on chartering and related documents on the chartering business. It has an active documentary committee which in 2002 reviewed the following documents: (a) a new Standard Grain Voyage Charter Party (Graincon); (b) revision of the Orevoy and Gasvoy voyage charters; (c) revision of the Boxtime charter party; (d) revision of the Standard Ship Repair Contract (Repaircon); (e) and provision of a new Standard Service Contract – a volume contract for use in the liner trade. Further documents under review include Volcoa the standard dry cargo volume contract of affreightment, and Bimchemtime, the standard time charter for vessels carrying chemicals in bulk. Following the development of the Cruisevoy voyage charter for cruise vessels in 1999, a time charter version for the industry is being developed. A standard absorption clause is being formulated. The Standard General Average Absorption clause should feature in shipowners' hull and machinery policies.

15.4 Worldscale

The Worldscale (1969) is recognized internationally as the definitive work of reference in the chartering of tankers. Informed by the knowledge and expertise of leading shipbrokers on both sides of the Atlantic it reflects their contact with the international tanker industry. The printed schedule consists of some 500 pages comprising 75,000 rates compiled from a database of more than 350,000 flat rates. Its website shows all 350,000 rates, 24 hours a day, all year round and is accessed regularly by thousands of users, including oil companies, shipowners, tanker operators, oil traders, brokers, insurers, bankers, lawyers and other interest worldwide.

The Worldscale website features a voyage enquiry system that allows button-clicking updates of voyage rates.

New distance tables were introduced in 2005. BP Shipping has always been the supplier of distances to Worldscale for use in calculating rates. The previous edition was 1991, since when much changed concerning traffic separation zones, exclusion zones, environmentally friendly exclusion zones, new oil terminals, wrecks, etc. Remapping of the world's shipping routes was undertaken by AtoBviac on behalf of BP Shipping.

The website holds all rates and circulars are updated daily in real time. The website displays (a) over 350,000 rates; (b) all the alternative routes which have been requested over the past years, not just the most economical route; (c) all the supplementary messages that accompany the rates; (d) all the charterers account items associated with a rate; (e) all fixed and variable differentials associated with a rate; (f) all circulars as soon as they become effective; (g) through rates from the Arabian Gulf, Black Sea, and Lake Maracaibo ports to final destination; and (h) historical rates from 2000 onwards.

The Worldscale is based on an indices of WS 100 for each category and when in decline it will fall to WS 75 and increase to WS 175. All rates are quoted in US dollars.

15.5 Voyage estimates

The aim of a voyage estimate is to provide the shipowner (or charterer) with an estimate of the financial return expected from a prospective voyage. When provided with this information the owner can compare several alternatives and decide upon the most profitable and suitable venture. Although every estimator should aim to be as accurate as is reasonably possible, in modern shipbroking time often does not permit a series of detailed estimates to be undertaken for each and every 'open' vessel. In practice, a 'rough' estimate is usually performed for each alternative, and only when two or three desirable voyages are identified does more 'exact' estimating become necessary, along with the results which should be read with the owner's preferred direction of voyage, etc., borne in mind.

Needless to say, the final objective is for the estimate to compare favourably with the eventual voyage result, and normally reasonable comparisons can be made with experience of both the vessel and its trade, despite the vagaries of wind and tide and any man-made difficulties. Voyage estimating is an art, and an estimator – in order to succeed – should aim to understand all complexities of ship operating and trading, together with the various methods of chartering and analysing voyage returns, in order to perform his duties efficiently. An example is given below.

Open Seville

26,500 tonnes summer deadweight

15 knots (about) on 32 tonnes per day if IF C/S fuel oil and 11½ tonnes marine diesel oil at sea. 1 1⁄2 tonnes MDO in port

Running costs: US$4,000 per day

Cargo estimate: Sailing Philadelphia

Full cargo grain – Philadelphia/Bremen – US$16.50 per tonne –

Fiot – 4 days L/5,000 MT D – per WWDAY – Shex Bends – 2.5% A/C

Chartcon – vessel open Seville

Freight (less commission)

25,000 metric tonnes at $16.50 = $412,500

less 2.5% commission = $402,187 nett freight

Days		Ports	Disbursements		
Steaming	Lay		Port charges	Cargo	Agency fees Despatch Sundries
9		Seville/Philadelphia			
	6	Philadelphia	$20,000	$–	$1,500
11		Philadelphia/Bremen	$15,000	$–	$1,500
	7	Bremen			
20	13				

Fuel consumption:

At sea: 20 days at 32 tonnes p d   = 640 tonnes F/O
In port: 13 days at – tonnes p d   – tonnes F/O
                                                          640 tonnes

At sea: 20 days at 1.5 tonnes p d   = 30 tonnes   D/O
In port: 13 days at 1.5 tonnes p d   = 20 tonnes   D/O
                                              50 tonnes

Bunker oil:

On board: 640 tonnes F/O at $135 = $86,400
                         50 tonnes D/O at $215 = $10,750

Total bunker cost:	$97,150
plus voyage expenses:	$38,000
Total voyage expenses:	$135,150

Nett freight	$402,187
less:	
Total voyage expenses	$135,150
Gross profit	$267,037

Gross profit: $267,037 ÷ 33 days' voyage duration = gross daily profit $8,092. Gross daily profit: $8,092 *less* daily running cost $4,000 per day = $4,092 nett daily profit.

An example of a time sheet and a statement of facts are given in Figures 15.3 and 15.4, based on the following charter party terms.

1   Discharge rate, 5,000 metre tonnes per weather working day of 24 consecutive hours.
2   Sundays and holidays excepted, unless used, when half time actually used in excepted period to count as laytime.
3   Notice of readiness to be tendered in office hours Monday/Friday 0900/1700 h.
4   Time to count from first working period on first working day following acceptance of notice of readiness to discharge.
   continued

1. Agents Johan Smitzen Bremen	STANDARD TIME SHEET (SHORT FORM) RECOMMENDED BY THE BALTIC AND INTERNATIONAL MARITIME CONFERENCE (BIMCO) AND THE FEDERATION OF NATIONAL ASSOCIATIONS OF SHIP BROKERS AND AGENTS (FONASBA)	
2. Vessel's name m.v. Trader	3. Port Bremen	
4. Owners Disponent Owners Trader Shipping Enterprises Monrovia	5. Vessel berthed Thursday 14th June 0600 hrs	
	6. Loading commenced -	7. Loading completed -
8. Cargo 25000 Mtons Grain	9. Discharging commenced 14 June 1300	10. Discharging completed 22 June 1000
	11. Cargo documents on board -	12. Vessel sailed 22 June 1210
13. Charter Party Norgrain 1st May 19	14. Working hours meal hours of the port 0800/1200) 1300/1700) Monday/Friday 1800/2200)	
15. Bill of Lading weight/quantity 25000 MT	16. Outturn weight/quantity 24995 MT	
17. Vessel arrived on roads 13 June 17.00 (Weser Pilot)	18. Time to count from 1st Working Period next working day following acceptance Nor	
19. Notice of readiness tendered 14 June 0900	20. Rate of demurrage ₿ 5000 pd.	21. Rate of despatch money ₿ 2500 pd.
22. Next tide available 13 June 2330	23.	
24. Laytime allowed for loading	25. Laytime allowed for discharging 5 WW Days	26.

LAYTIME COMPUTATION

Date	Day	Time worked		Laytime used			Time saved on demurrage			Remarks
		From	to	days	hours	minutes	days	hours	minutes	
14 June	Thursday	-	-	-	-	-				(NOR tendered and (accepted 0900 hrs
15	Friday				16					Laytime commenced 0800 hrs
16	Saturday	0800	1200		2					Overtime
17	Sunday									Holiday
18	Monday				16					Laytime recommenced 0800 hrs
19	Tuesday	1300	1500	-	2					(Rain 0300/1300
				-	1	30				(" 1500/2230
20	Wednesday			1	0	0				
21	Thursday			1	0	0				
22	Friday				10					Completed discharge 1000 hrs
							1	0	30	
				3	23	30	1	0	30	

General remarks

Place and date
Bremen   23/6/-

Signature

Signature

Signature

Signature

* See Explanatory Notes overleaf for filling in the boxes

Printed and sold by Fr. G. Knudtzon Ltd. 55 Toldbodgade Copenhagen by authority of BIMCO

85-0

Published by The Baltic and International Maritime Conference (BIMCO), Copenhagen

Figure 15.3 Standard time sheet (short form).

Source: Reproduced by kind permission of BIMCO.

1 Agents	STANDARD STATEMENT OF FACTS (SHORT FORM)
Johan Smitzen	RECOMMENDED BY THE BALTIC AND INTERNATIONAL MARITIME CONFERENCE (BIMCO) AND THE FEDERATION OF NATIONAL ASSOCIATIONS OF SHIP BROKERS AND AGENTS (FONASBA)

2 Vessel's name	3 Port
m.v. Trader	Bremen

4 Owners Disponent Owners	5 Vessel berthed
Trader Shipping Enterprises Monrovia	Thursday 14th June 0600 hrs

	6 Loading commenced	7 Loading completed
	—	—

8 Cargo	9 Discharging commenced	10 Discharging completed
25000 Mtons grain	14/6/- 1300	22/6/- 1000
	11 Cargo documents on board	12 Vessel sailed
	—	22/6/- 1210

13 Charter Party	14 Working hours meal hours of the port
Norgrain 1st May 19	0800/1200) 1300/1700 } Monday/Friday 1800/2200)

15 Bill of Lading weight quantity	16 Outturn weight quantity
25000 MT	24995 MT

17 Vessel arrived on roads	18
13 June 1700 (Weser Pilot)	

19 Notice of readiness tendered	20
14 June 0900	

21 Next tide available	22
13 June 2330	

DETAILS OF DAILY WORKING

Date	Day	Hours worked From	to	Hours stopped From	to	No of gangs	Quantity load/disch	Remarks
14 June	Thursday	1300	1700	1700	1800	Two	1800 MT	Commenced
		1800	2200	2200	2400	Two	1698	discharge
15 June	Friday			0001	0800			
		0800	1200	1300	1300	Two	1727	
		1300	1700	1700	1800	Two	1715	
		1800	2200	2200	2400	Two	1720	
16 June	Saturday			0001	0800			
		0800	1200	1200	2400	Two	1637	Overtime
17 June	Sunday			0001	2400			
18 June	Monday			0001	0800			
		0800	1200	1200	1300	Two	1401	
		1300	1700	1700	1800	Two	1224	
		1800	2200	2200	2400	Two	1330	
19 June	Tuesday			0001	1300			} Rain
		1300	1500	1500	2400	Two	601	
20 June	Wednesday			0001	0800			
		0800	1200	1200	1300	Two	1426	
		1300	1700	1700	1800	Two	1630	
		1800	2200	2200	2400	Two	1558	
21 June	Thursday			0001	0800			
		0800	1200	1200	1300	Two	1550	
		1300	1700	1700	1800	Two	1597	
		1800	2200	2200	2400	Two	1525	
22 June	Friday			0001	0800			
		0800	1000			Two	856	Completed discharge

24995 MT

Place and date	Name and signature (Master)
Bremen 23/6/-	
Name and signature Agents	Name and signature (for the Charterers Shippers Receivers)

See Explanatory Notes overleaf for filling in the boxes

Produced and sold by Fr G Knudtzon Ltd 55 Toldbodgade Copenhagen by authority of BIMCO

83 0

Figure 15.4 Standard statement of facts (short form).

Source: Reproduced by kind permission of BIMCO.

5 Time not to count between midnight Friday (or day preceding a holiday) until commencement of first working period Monday (or day following a holiday).
6 Despatch on working time saved.

The time sheet and laytime calculations are based on the MV *Trader* voyage estimate for discharge at Bremen.

Laytime calculation:

Laytime allowed	5 days	0 hours	0 minutes
Laytime used	3 days	23 hours	30 minutes
Laytime saved	1 day	0 hours	30 minutes

1 day 0 hours 30 minutes = 1.02 days

1.02 days at $2,500 per day = $2,550 despatch money

15.6 Sale and purchase of ships

The sale and purchase of vessels is a specialized activity and is undertaken by a sale and purchase broker. This broker usually acts for the buyer or for the seller of a ship, and occasionally acts between buyer's broker and seller's broker, each of which may be in different countries dealing with a foreign ship. The market is international and the ship may be sold for scrap or operational purposes. If the latter, the new owner must change the ship's name and may be forbidden to operate in trades competitive to its former owner. Details are given below of the information circulated of a possible ship sale:

(a) Classification society.
(b) Ship's deadweight, dimensions and draught; year of build, place, shipbuilder; cubic capacities, deck arrangements, water ballast capacities, number of holds and hatches; machinery details and builders, horse power, speed and consumption; bunker capacity, special and classification survey position.
(c) The purpose-built tonnage details of special facilities, i.e. refrigeration plant, tanker capacity, container capacity, passenger accommodation, derricks, car decks, etc.
(d) Light displacement including propeller details, i.e. bronze or iron, and if spare tail shaft on board. Such data only given in event of ship being sold as scrap.
(e) Ship price and position for inspection and delivery.

The brokers' function is not to express an opinion of the vessel's condition, unless there exists a serious defect, but to leave this assessment to the buyer's superintendent or consulting surveyor: the ship's classification records are critical. The ship inspection may take place prior to sale negotiations commencing, or be a condition of the sale offer. A dry dock inspection is usually not necessary. However, if conducted, it is the seller's responsibility and cost to bring the vessel to the dry dock and subsequently from the dry dock to the berth or place of delivery. The buyer bears the expense of putting in and taking out of dry dock the vessel plus the dry dock dues. The seller, however, would meet this expense if the rudder, propeller, bottom, or other underwater part(s) or tailend shaft were defective.

The buyer will make his offer for delivery at a specified port or time, with the option to cancel if the vessel is not delivered by the latest specified date. Moreover, the vessel's classification must not lapse. Additional payment to the seller is involved on delivery for on-board ship stores and bunkers. The vessel's trading certificates must be valid at the time of delivery.

On agreement on the price and conditions of sale, the seller's broker draws up a memorandum of agreement, which operates under the code name 'Saleform 1993'. A specimen is given in Figure 15.5 which contains 16 clauses ranging from the price to arbitration and involving 283 lines, as well as provision for an appendix.

The occasion of a ship sale for scrap is a simpler procedure carried out by the execution and delivery of a bill of sale under seal, a specimen of which is given in Figure 15.6. The bill of sale is handed over on receipt of a letter releasing the deposit and a banker's draft for the balance of the price. Payment, if any, for bunkers and stores is dealt with at the same time.

The broker arranges to provide for the vessel sold for operational purposes the following documents, which must be attached to any insurance cover and handed over at the time of delivery:

(i)   Certificate of registry.
(ii)   International load line certificate.
(iii)   Document of compliance.
(iv)   International Tonnage Certificate.
(v)   Safety Management certificate.
(vi)   International Ship Security certificate.
(vii)   Cargo Ship Safety Equipment certificate – cargo vessels.
(viii) Cargo ship Safety Construction certificate – cargo vessels.
(ix)   Cargo Ship Safety Radio certificate.
(x)   International Certificate of Fitness for the Carriage of Dangerous Chemicals in bulk – chemical carrier.
(xi)   International Certificate of Fitness for the Carriage of Liquefied gases in Bulk – gas carrier.
(xii)   High Speed Craft Safety Certificate – high speed craft.
(xiii) Classification certificates.
(xiv)   Plans.

MEMORANDUM OF AGREEMENT

Norwegian Shipbrokers' Association's Memorandum of Agreement for sale and purchase of ships. Adopted by The Baltic and International Maritime Council (BIMCO) in 1956.
Code-name
SALEFORM 1993
Revised 1966, 1983 and 1986/87.

Dated:

hereinafter called the Sellers, have agreed to sell, and	1
hereinafter called the Buyers, have agreed to buy	2
Name:	3
Classification Society/Class:	4
Built: By:	5
Flag: Place of Registration:	6
Call Sign: Grt/Nrt:	7
Register Number:	8
hereinafter called the Vessel, on the following terms and conditions:	9

Definitions   10

"Banking days" are days on which banks are open both in the country of the currency   11
stipulated for the Purchase Price in Clause 1 and in the place of closing stipulated in Clause 8.   12

"In writing" or "written" means a letter handed over from the Sellers to the Buyers or vice versa,   13
a registered letter, telex, telefax or other modern form of written communication.   14

"Classification Society" or "Class" means the Society referred to in line 4.   15

1.   Purchase Price   16

2.   Deposit   17

As security for the correct fulfilment of this Agreement the Buyers shall pay a deposit of 10 %   18
(ten per cent) of the Purchase Price within   banking days from the date of this   19
Agreement. This deposit shall be placed with   20

and held by them in a joint account for the Sellers and the Buyers, to be released in accordance   21
with joint written instructions of the Sellers and the Buyers. Interest, if any, to be credited to the   22
Buyers. Any fee charged for holding the said deposit shall be borne equally by the Sellers and the   23
Buyers.   24

3.   Payment   25

The said Purchase Price shall be paid in full free of bank charges to   26

on delivery of the Vessel, but not later than 3 banking days after the Vessel is in every respect   27
physically ready for delivery in accordance with the terms and conditions of this Agreement and   28
Notice of Readiness has been given in accordance with Clause 5.   29

Figure 15.5 'Saleform 1993' memorandum of agreement of sale (first page only).

Source: Reproduced by kind permission of the Norwegian Shipbrokers' Association.

RECOMMENDED STANDARD BILL OF SALE – CODE NAME: "BIMCOSALE"

BILL OF SALE

1. Seller(s) (state full name, description and address)		2. Buyer(s) (state full name, description and address)	
3. Name of Vessel	4. Type of Vessel	5. Port of Registry	6. Call Signs
7. Gross Register Tonnage	8. Net Register Tonnage	9. Date of Memorandum of Agreement	
10. Purchase Sum (in figures and in letters)			
11. Details of subsisting or outstanding Mortgage(s) or other encumbrances, if any; also state other details, if any, relevant to the sale and transfer of the Vessel			

The Seller(s), named in Box 1, who is (are) the Owner(s) of the Vessel described in Boxes 3 to 8, both inclusive, hereby confirm(s) having sold and handed over the said Vessel with everything belonging to her to the Buyer(s), named in Box 2, for the Purchase Sum, as stated in Box 10.
Unless otherwise stated in Box 11, the Seller(s) warrant(s) that the Vessel is free from encumbrances, debts and maritime liens of any kind whatsoever and confirm(s) that the sale and transfer of the Vessel is effected in accordance with Memorandum of Agreement dated as indicated in Box 9.
In consideration of the said Purchase Sum, paid to the Seller(s) by the Buyer(s), the Seller(s) hereby transfer(s) the Vessel to the Buyer(s) so that the Vessel shall hereinafter become his (their) legal property.
IN WITNESS whereof this Bill of Sale has been issued and signed at the place and on the date stated in Box 12 in the presence of the Witness(es) as indicated in Box 13 whose signature(s) has (have) been certified (if required) by the person indicated in Box 14.

(* Space for translation of text)

12. Place and date and signature of Seller(s)
13. The undersigned Witness(es) hereby certifies(y) the correctness of the Seller(s)' signature(s) to this Bill of Sale and the date hereof (state full name, title and address of Witness(es))
14. The undersigned Consul (General) hereby certifies the correctness of the Witness(es)' signature(s) as stated in Box 13

Published by The Baltic and International Maritime Conference (BIMCO), Copenhagen

Printed and sold by Fr. G. Knudtzon Ltd., 55, Toldbodgade, Copenhagen, by authority of The Baltic and International Maritime Conference (BIMCO), Copenhagen

Figure 15.6 Bill of sale.

Source: Reproduced by kind permission of BIMCO.

In the event of the broker requiring to register the vessel in the new owner's name, he presents the following documents to the registrar:

(a) Bill of sale.
(b) Declaration of ownership.
(c) Appointment of managing owner or ship's husband.
(d) Articles of association.
(e) Certificates of incorporation.
(f) Appointment of public officer.

Items in (d), (e) and (f) are only presented if the buyer has not previously owned a ship. With regard to foreign buyers, usually the bill of sale must be signed before a notary public and bear the visa of the buyer's consul. The Certificate of British Registry is returned to the registrar at the port of registry. The foreign buyer for his own registration purposes will require a transcript of the cancelled British registry available from the registrar after the ship sale.

Frequently vessels are sold under extended terms of payment in which case a security for the unpaid portion of the purchase price is through a banker's guarantee, otherwise a mortgage has to be given.

Details of vessels available for sale are recorded in the shipping press and examples are given below.

EWL Suriname – container

8020 MTDW on 6.581 m
Built 1982 Rickmers
Classed GL ice strengthened
127.67 m LOA 117.23 m LBP 20.1 m beam
2 decks 2 holds 2 hatches
10060 grain 10010 bale
582 TEU 50 reefer
CR: 2 = 35T
1 = Deutz Köln RSBV12M540,6,000 BHP 1 thruster
15.5K on 23.5 DO (80.5 CAP.) HV (599.5 CAP.) DM 15 million

Port au Prince – tanker

38549 MTDW on 9.722 m
Built 1979 Imabari Marugame
Classed LR SSH + CSM due 5/99 last DD 5/94
184.16 m LOA 172.02 m LBP 30.05 m beam
12 tanks 43200 oil
Pumps 2/3,000 M3 HR centrifugal 2 = stripping
MHI/Sulzer 6RND76,12,000 BHP
13.75K on 30 TS FO + 1.2 DO Zinc silicate coating/uncoiled NO IGS/
    NOW COW

Owners have no official price ideas but are asking for outright offers in line with the market.

Evangelia T – **bulk carrier**

66289 MTDW on 13.691 m Built 1974 Hakodate Hakodate Classed NV
    SS 3/97 DD passed 8/94
219.08 m LOA 208.01 m LBP 32.29 m beam
1 deck 7 holds 7 hatches McGregor covers
63004 grain
CR: 4 = 15T
IHI/Sulzer 6RND90,17400 BHP
13 K ON 38 TS 180
Try US$6 million
(Details without guarantee)

The ship demolition market – more widely known as recycling – grows annually as a consequence of the scrapping of single hull tanker tonnage and buoyant new building programmes, some of which has been driven by new regulations concerning mandatory requirement of a double hull structure for dry bulk cargo ships. There is a correlation of recycling between uneconomic/ low freight rates encouraging owners to recycle tonnage beyond the fifth survey, new mandatory ship construction regulations, and the urgent need to displace/recycle old tonnage in preference to high productive new build.

Major ship breakers are situated in the Indian subcontinent, China, Bangladesh and Pakistan. The fringe areas are Spain, Turkey, Vietnam, the Philippines and Mexico. It is a volatile market.

In contrast, the second-hand market is linked with certain parts of the new build sector. Demand for modern tankers is favourable because volume of seaborne tanker trade rises. The Greeks are usually active in the second and new tanker tonnage market. The market for second-hand bulk carriers tends to be less buoyant, but is related to world steel production and global industrialization. Container new-build tonnage remains buoyant, smaller vessels being displaced and becoming available often for feeder networks and some demolition activity. Reefer vessels are active in the demolition market together with the multi-purpose/general cargo/'tween-deck tonnage, all of which are being displaced because of the expanding container network. Uncertain market prospects and falling freight rates and diminishing profits accelerate the increased scrap market and results in lower demolition prices. For example, in 2004 the year started at US$300 per light displacement ton (ldt) – a historically high level – to climb still higher to US$400 per ldt. By mid-year, prices had collapsed to the initial level, but they then proceeded to increase steadily to reach US$440 by the year end.

APPENDIX 15.1
Examples of standard charter parties, associated bills of lading, waybills/cargo receipts, sundry forms and clauses (reproduced by courtesy of BIMCO)

Code Name/Subject	Code Name/Subject
Agency Agreement, Standard Liner and General	HEAVYCONRECEIPT
Agreement, Sub-	Hydro Bill of Lading
AUSTWHEAT 1990	HYDROCHARTER
AUSTWHEATBILL	INTANKBILL 78
BALTIME 1939	International Broker's Commission Contract
BARGEHIRE 94	LINEWAYBILL
BIMCHEMTIME	MINREPCON
BIMCO AM WELSH 93	MULTIDOC 95
BIMCOSALE	MULTIWAYBILL 95
BOXCHANGE	NANYOZAI 1997
BOXTIME	NAVEXCON
BPTIME 3	NIPPONCOAL
Bunker Contract, Standard	NIPPONGRAIN
CEMENTVOY	NIPPONORE
CEMENTVOYBILL	NORGRAIN 89
CHEMTANKVOY BARECON 2001	NORGRAIN Bill of Lading
CHEMTANKVOYBILL	NUBALTWOOD
CHEMTANKWAYBILL 85	NUBALTWOOD Bill of Lading
COALOREVOY	NYPE 93
COALOREVOYBILL	PANSTONE
COMBICONBILL	POLCOALBILL
COMBICONWAYBILL	POLCOALVOY
CONGENBILL	POLCOALVOY Slip
CONLEASE	PROJECTCON
CONLINEBILL 2000	QAFCOBILL
CONLINEBOOKING 2000	QAFCOCHARTER
CREWMAN A	REPAIRCON
CREWMAN B	RUSWOOD
CRUISEVOY	RUSWOODBILL
Dangerous Goods Declaration	SALEFORM 1993
Dangerous Goods Packing Certificate	SCANCON
DEMOLISHCON	SCANCONBILL
FERTICON	SHIPMAN 98
FERTIVOY 88	SLOTHIRE
GASTANKWAYBILL	Statement of Facts (Short Form)
GASTIME	Statement of Facts (Long Form)
GAS VOY 2005	Statement of Facts (Oil and Chemicals) (Short Form)
GENCOA	Statement of Facts (Oil and Chemicals) (Long Form)
GENCON	SUPPLYTIME 2005
GENTIME	SYNACOMEX 2000
GENWAYBILL	TANKERVOY 87
GRAINCON	TANKWAYBILL81
GRAINCON BILL	Time Sheet (Short Form)
HEAVYCON	
HEAVYCONBILL	

Code Name/Subject	Code Name/Subject
Time Sheet (Long Form)	WORLDFOODRECEIPT 99
TOWCON	WORLDFOODWAYBILL
TOWHIRE	WRECKFIXED 99
VOYLAYRULES 93	WRECKHIRE 99
WORLDFOOD 99	WRECKSTAGE 99

Voyage charter parties	*Code name*

Cement

Standard Voyage Charter Party for the Transportation of Bulk Cement and Cement Clinker in Bulk
(For explanatory notes, see BIMCO Bulletin 5/90, pp. 3–7) — CEMENTVOY

Coal (including Coke and Patent Fuel)
Baltic and International Maritime Conference Coal Voyage Charter 1971 (revised 1976 and 1997)
(For explanatory notes, see BIMCO Bulletin IV–1976, pp. 3767–68 and Bulletin 4–97, pp. 56–7) — POLKCOALVOY

'Polcoalvo' Slip–1995 Loading and Demurrage Scales Japan Shipping Exchange, Coal Charter Party
(For explanatory notes, see BIMCO Bulletin1–1984) — NIPPONCOAL / AMWELSH 93

Americanized Welsh Coal Charter
(For explanatory notes, see BIMCO Bulletin 1/94, pp. 46–50)

BIMCO Standard Coal and Ore Charter Party — COAL-OREVOY

Fertilizers

Chamber of Shipping Fertilizers Charter, 1942 — FERTICON

North American Fertilizer Charter Party 1978 (amended 1988)
(For explanatory notes, see BIMCO Bulletin V1–1978 pp. 4884–91 and Bulletin 2/88, p. 9084) — FERTIVOY 88

Hydrocharter Voyage Charter Party (amended 1975 and 1997)
(For explanatory notes, see BIMCO Bulletin IV–1976, p. 3779 and Bulletin 5–97, pp. 37–9) — HYDROCHARTER

Fertilizer Voyage Charter Party (amended 2001)
(For explanatory notes, see BIMCO Bulletin 5/92, pp. 5–7 and Bulletin 4/2000, pp. 33–5) — QAFCOCHARTER

Gas

Standard Gas Voyage Charter Party for the LPG, Ammonia and Liquefied Petrochemical Gas Trades
(For explanatory notes, see BIMCO Bulletin 111–1972, pp. 1494–6 and Bulletin 4/05 pp. 42–4) — GASVOY 2005

Voyage charter parties	*Code name*
General	
Baltic and International Maritime Council Uniform General Charter (as revised 1922, 1974, 1976 and 1994) *(For explanatory notes, see BIMCO Bulletin 1/95, pp. 6–14)*	GENCON
Baltic and International Maritime Council Scandinavian Voyage Charter 1956 (amended 1962 and 1993) *(For explanatory notes, see BIMCO Bulletin 1/94, pp. 90–1)*	SCANCON
World Food Programme Voyage Charter Party *(For explanatory notes, see BIMCO Bulletin 5/99, pp. 10–13)*	WORLDFOOD 99
Standard Cruise Voyage Charter Party *(For explanatory notes, see BIMCO Bulletin 2/98, pp. 52–5)*	CRUISEVOY
Grain	
Australian Wheat Charter 1990 (amended 1991) *(For explanatory notes, see BIMCO Bulletin 6/90, pp. 33–5 and Bulletin 2/92, p. 15)*	AUSTWHEAT 1990
Continent Grain Charter Party *(For explanatory notes, see BIMCO Bulletin 4/01, pp. 33–9)*	SYNACOMEX 2000
North American Grain Charter Party 1973, issued by the Association of Ship Brokers and Agents (USA) *(For explanatory notes, see BIMCO Bulletin 6/73, pp. 2412–18, Bulletin 1/74, p. 2501 and Bulletin 1/90)*	NORGRAIN 89
Standard Grain Voyage Charter Party 2003	GRAINCON
Nippon Grain Charter Party *(For explanatory notes, see BIMCO Bulletin 4/98, pp. 53–4)*	NIPPONGRAIN
Ore	
Japan Shipping Exchange, Iron Ore Charter Party	NIPPONORE
BIMCO Standard Coal and Ore Charter Party	COAL-OREVOY
Stone	
Chamber of Shipping Stone Charter Party, 1920 (amended 1925, 1959, 1974 and 1995)	PANSTONE
Tank	
International Association of Independent Tanker Owners Tanker Voyage Charter Party	TANKERVOY 87
Standard Voyage Charter Party for the Transportation of Chemicals in Tank Vessels *(For explanatory notes, see BIMCO Bulletin V–1979, pp. 5293–98 and Bulletin 2/92)*	CHEMTANKVOY

Voyage charter parties	Code name
Wood (including Pitwood, Props, Pulpwood, Roundwood and Logs)	
Baltic and International Maritime Council Baltic Wood Charter Party 1973 (revised 1997 and 2002) *(For explanatory notes, see BIMCO Bulletin IIIA–1973, pp. 2047–50 and Bulletin 6–97, pp. 73–5)*	NUBALTWOOD
Russian Wood Charter Party 1961 (as revised 1995 and 2002) *(For explanatory notes, see BIMCO Bulletin 1/95, pp. 31–41)*	RUSWOOD
Japan Shipping Exchange Charter Party for Logs 1997	NANYOZAI 1997

Time charter parties	Code name
Baltic and International Maritime Conference Uniform Time Charter (as revised 2001) *(For explanatory notes, see BIMCO Bulletin 1–2002, p. 33)*	BALTIME 1939
BPTIME 3 Time Charter Party *(For explanatory notes, see BIMCO Bulletin 1–2001, p. 39)*	BPTIME 3
Time Charter Party for Offshore Service Vessels *(For explanatory notes, see BIMCO Bulletin 1/76, p. 3549, Bulletin 6/89, pp. 25–6 and Bulletin 5/05, pp. 35–66)*	SUPPLYTIME 2005
Standard Time Charter Party for Container Vessels *(For explanatory notes, see BIMCO Bulletin 6/90, pp. 7–13 and Bulletin 1/05, pp. 24–45)*	BOXTIME 2004
Baltic and International Maritime Conference Uniform Time Charter Party for Vessels Carrying Liquified Gas *(For explanatory notes, Technical Gas Form and Operational Guide, see BIMCO Bulletin V–1980, pp. 5757–5809)*	GASTIME
Baltic and International Maritime Conference Uniform Time Charter Party for Vessels Carrying Chemicals in Bulk *(For explanatory notes, see BIMCO Bulletin II–1984)*	BIMCHEMTIME
New York Produce Exchange Time Charter *(For explanatory notes, see BIMCO Bulletin 6/93, pp. 17–23)*	NYPE 93
General Time Charter Party *(For explanatory notes, see BIMCO Bulletin 5/99, pp. 38–44)*	GENTIME

Bills of lading	Code name
Combined Transport Bill of Lading 1995 *(For explanatory notes, see BIMCO Bulletin 1/96, pp. 30–7)*	COMBICONBILL
Bill of Lading to be used with Charter Parties (edition 1994)	CONGENBILL
Liner Bill of Lading (Liner Terms approved by BIMCO) 2000 *(For explanatory notes, see BIMCO Bulletin 2/2001, p. 28)*	CONLINEBILL

Bills of lading	*Code name*
For Shipments on the 'Ruswood' Charter Party	RUSWOODBILL
For Shipments on the 'Cementvoy' Charter	CEMENTVOYBILL
For Shipments on the 'Polcoalvoy' Charter (edition 1997)	POLCOALBILL
For Shipments on the 'Hydrocharter': Norsk Hydro Bill of Lading Form	HYDROBILL
For Shipments on the 'Qafcocharter'	QAFCOBILL
For Shipments on the 'Scancon' Charter (edition 1993) *(For explanatory notes, see BIMCO Bulletin 1/94)*	SCANCONBILL
For Shipments on the 'Austwheat' Charter	AUSTWHEATBILL
For Shipments on the 'Norgrain' Charter Party: the North American Grain Bill of Lading Form	NORGRAINBILL
For Shipments on the 'Grainvoy' Charter	GRAINVOYBILL
For Shipments on the 'Orevoy' Charter	OREVOYBILL
For Shipments on the Tanker Voyage Charter Party: the 'Intankbill 78' Bill of Lading	INTANKBILL 78
For Shipments on the 'Chemtankvoy' Charter	CHEMTANKVOY-BILL
For Shipments on the 'Nubaltwood' Charter	NUBALTWOOD
For Shipments on the 'Heavycon' Contract	HEAVYCONBILL
Multimodal Transport Bill of Lading, issued subject to ICC Rules *(For explanatory notes, see BIMCO Bulletin 1/96, pp. 21–9)*	MULTIDOC 95

Non-negotiable waybills/cargo receipts	*Code name*
Non-negotiabie General Sea Waybill for Use in Short-sea Dry Cargo Trade	GENWAYBILL
International Association of Independent Tanker Owners Non-negotiable Tanker Waybill	TANKWAYBILL 81
Non-negotiable Chemical Tank Waybill *(For explanatory notes, see BIMCO Bulletin 5/85, pp. 8183–86)*	CHEMTANKWAY-BILL 85
Non-negotiabIe Gas Tank Waybill for Use in the LPG Trade *(For explanatory notes, see BIMCO Bulletin 2/88, p. 9090)*	GASTANKWAY-BILL
The World Food Programme Non-negotiable Liner Waybill WAYBILL *(For explanatory notes, see BIMCO Bulletin 6/89, pp. 9–10)*	WORLDFOOD-
Non-negotiable Cargo Receipt to be used with 'Worldfood 99' Charter *(For explanatory notes, see BIMCO Bulletin 5/99, pp. 10–13)*	WORLDFOOD-RECEIPT 99
Non-negotiable Cargo Receipt to be used with 'Heavycon' Contract	HEAVYCON-RECEIPT
Combined Transport Sea Waybill *(For explanatory notes, see BIMCO Bulletin 1/96, pp. 30–37)*	COMBICONWAY-BILL

Non-negotiable waybills/cargo receipts	*Code name*
Multimodal Transport Waybill *(For explanatory notes, see BIMCO Bulletin 1/96, pp. 21–9)*	MULTIWAYBILL 95
Non-negotiable Liner Sea Waybill *(For explanatory notes, see BIMCO Bulletin 2/98, pp. 70–3)*	LINEWAYBILL

Sundry other forms	*Code name*
Standard Statement of Facts (Short Form)	–
Standard Statement of Facts (Long Form)	–
Standard Time Sheet (Short Form)	–
Standard Time Sheet (Long Form)	–
Standard Statement of Facts (Oil and Chemical Tank Vessels) (Short Form)	–
Standard Statement of Facts (Oil and Chemical Tank Vessels) (Long Form)	–
Liner Booking Note to be used with 'Conlinebill' Liner Bill of Lading	CONLINE-BOOKING 2000
Voyage Charter Party Laytime Interpretation Rules 1993 *(For explanatory notes, see BIMCO Bulletin 1/94, pp. 23–4)*	VOYLAYRULES 93
Baltic and International Maritime Conference Dangerous Goods Declaration	–
Baltic and International Maritime Conference Dangerous Goods Container/Trailer Packing Certificate *(For explanatory notes, see BIMCO Bulletin 2/85)*	–
Memorandum of Agreement (revised 1983,1986 and 1993) *(For explanatory notes, see BIMCO Bulletin V–1983, pp. 7341–42, Bulletin 2/87, p. 8740, Bulletin 6/87, pp. 8969–70 and Bulletin 2/94, pp. 50–51)*	SALEFORM 1993
Recommended Standard Bill of Sale *(For explanatory notes, see BIMCO Bulletin V–1978, p. 4797)*	BIMCOSALE
Standard Contract for the Sale of Vessels for Demolition and Recycling *(For explanatory notes, see BIMCO Bulletin 4/02, pp. 34–7 and Bulletin 6/04, p. 49)*	DEMOLISHCON
Standard Contract of Affreightment for Dry Bulk Cargoes *(For explanatory notes, see BIMCO Bulletin V–1982, pp. 6827–36 and 2/05, pp. 44–6)*	GENCOA
Special Projects Charter Party *(For explanatory notes, see BIMCO Bulletin 1/06, pp. 37–40)*	PROJECTCON
International Ocean Towage Agreement (Daily Hire)	TOWHIRE
International Ocean Towage Agreement (Lump Sum) *(For explanatory notes, see BIMCO Bulletin 5/85, pp. 8169–82)*	TOWCON

Sundry other form	Code name
Baltic and International Maritime Council Standard Transportation Contract for Heavy and Voluminous Cargoes	HEAVYCON
Standard Ship Management Agreement *(For explanatory notes, see BIMCO Bulletin 4/98, pp. 33–8)*	SHIPMAN 98
Standard Slot Charter Party *(For explanatory notes, see BIMCO Bulletin 6/93, pp. 54–8)*	SLOTHIRE
International Wreck Removal and Marine Services Agreement (Fixed Price – 'no cure, no pay') *(For explanatory notes, see BIMCO Bulletin 6/99, pp. 46–52)*	WRECKFIXED 99
International Wreck Removal and Marine Services Agreement (Daily Hire) *(For explanatory notes, see BIMCO Bulletin 6/99, pp. 46–52)*	WRECKHIRE 99
International Wreck Removal and Marine Services Agreement (Lump Sum – Stage Payments) *(For explanatory notes, see BIMCO Bulletin 6/99, pp. 46–52)*	WRECKSTAGE 99
FONASBA Standard Line and General Agency Agreement *(For explanatory notes, see BIMCO Bulletin 3/02, pp. 36–41)*	–
Standard Crew Management Agreement (Cost Plus Fee) *(For explanatory notes, see BIMCO Bulletin 4/99, pp. 27–33)*	CREWMAN A
Standard Crew Management Agreement (Lump Sum) *(For explanatory notes, see BIMCO Bulletin 4/99, pp. 33–8)*	CREWMAN B
Baltic and International Maritime Council Standard Bareboat Charter *(For explanatory notes, see BIMCO Bulletin 5/74, pp. 2894–2901, Bulletin 1/76, p. 3558, Bulletin 6/89, pp. 14–20 and Bulletin 2/02, pp. 31–40)*	BARECON 2001
Standard Barge Bareboat Charter Party *(For explanatory notes, see BIMCO Bulletin 2/95, pp. 6–10)*	BARGEHIRE 94
BIMCO Standard Bunker Contract *(For explanatory notes, see BIMCO Bulletin 1–02, pp. 60–63)*	–
FONASBA International Broker's Commission Contract	–
Standard Container Lease Agreement *(For explanatory notes, see BIMCO Bulletin 6/97, pp. 67–9)*	CONLEASE
Standard Naval Exercise Contract *(For explanatory notes, see BIMCO Bulletin 4/98, pp. 48–50)*	NAVEXCON
FONASBA Sub-agency Agreement	–
REPAIRCON Standard Ship Repair Contract *(For explanatory notes, see BIMCO Bulletin 4/2003, pp. 34–8)*	REPAIRCON
MINREPCON Standard Minor Repair Work Contract *(For explanatory notes, see BIMCO Bulletin 6/2003, p. 46)*	MINREPCON
Standard Container Interchange Agreement *(For explanatory notes, see BIMCO Bulletin 1/05, pp. 46–55)*	BOXCHANGE

Clauses issued, supported or recommended by BIMCO

Average Bond Clause

BIMCHEMTIME Vetting and Inspection Clause for Chemical Carrier Time Charter Paties

Both-to-Blame Collision Clause

Bulk Carrier Safety Clause

Bulk Shipping Quality Clause for Voyage Charter Parties

Bunker Fuel Sulphur Content Clause for Time Charter Parties 2005

Bunker Quality Control Clause for Time Chartering

Bunker Price Adjustment Clause for Voyage Chartering

Bunker Supply and Payment Clause for Voyage Charters (Tank Vessels) (approved by the Documentary Committee of INTERTANKO)

Cancelling Clause 2002 (code name: CANCELCON 2002)

Cargo Handling Gear Clause

Carriage of Nuclear Materials

Cleaning of Cargo Compartments Clause

Containers Clause 2002

Currency Clause

Delay for Charterers' Purposes Clause

Delivery and Re-delivery Surveys Clause

Dispute Resolution Clauses

Double Banking Clause

ECCTO/EPCA/INTERTANKO/BIMCO's Standard Model Clauses for the Chemical/Parcel Trades General Average

General Average Absorption Clause

Hamburg Rules Charter Party Clause

Himalaya Clauses

Ice Clause for Voyage Charter Parties

Ice Clause for Time Charter Parties

ISM Clause

ISPS/MTSA Clause for Time Charter Parties 2005

ISPS/MTSA Clause for Voyage Charter Parties 2005

Japanese Law and Arbitration Clause

Lay-up Clause

Lien Clause for Time Charters – Recommended Additional

Lien on Vessels (Additional Clause)

Loading and Discharging with Grabs

Mediation Dispute Resolution Clause

New Jason Clause

Non-lien provisions, suggested amplification of Clause 18 of NYPE 1946

Oil Pollution, Financial Responsibility in respect of P&I Bunker Deviation Clause 1948

Clauses issued, supported or recommended by BIMCO
Paramount Clause
Protective Clauses
Putting Back Clause
Requisition Clause
Return of Containers Clause
Scrap Metal Clause
Seaway and Great Lakes Trading Clause
Seaworthy Trim Clause
Shifting and Warping
St Lawrence Seaway Clause
Stevedore Damage Clause for Time Chartering
Stevedore Damage Clause for Voyage Chartering
Stowaways Clause for Time Charters
Strike Clause
Trimming and Grab Clauses for Bulk Cargo Trimming
Unit Limitation Clause
US Anti-drug Abuse Act 1986 Clause for Time Charters
US Customs AMS Clause for Time Charter Parties
US Customs AMS Clause for Voyage Charter Parties
US Customs-Trade Partnership Against Terrorism (C-TPAT) Clause
US Customs 24 Hours Rule for Voyage Charter Parties
US Customs 24 Hours Rule for Time Charter Parties
US Tax Reform 1986 Clause
Waiting for Berth Clause (code name: WAITBERTH 2002)
War Cancellation Clause 2004
War Risks Clause for Time Charters, 2004 (code name: CONWARTIME 2004)
War Risks Clause for Voyage Chartering, 2004 (code/(name: VOYWAR 2004)

Notes:

[a] The clauses are to be considered recommended only.
[b] Parties using one or the other of the recommended clauses must be careful to make sure that they will be compatible with and not conflict with otherwise clear conditions of this charter party.

16 Containerization

16.1 Introduction

Containerization is a method of distributing merchandise in a unitized form thereby promoting an intermodal transport system with possible combinations of rail, road, canal and maritime transport. The system is long established but came more into use in the North American coastal trade in the 1930s, when the vessels were called Van ships. Nowadays, as the benefits of containerization are experienced worldwide generations of container ships have evolved, aiding rising living standards and trade expansion.

The worldwide container business serves over 140 trading nations and 360 ports, generating over 100,000 possible routes. Containerized cargo seaborne trade has averaged annual growths of 10%; in 2005 it was one billion tons. Containerized trade grew twice as fast as world seaborne trade. At the same time the trade matrix widened when many new countries and cargoes entered the trade. As the container fleet was more established, the average size of vessels deployed increased from 21,000 dwt in 1992 to 31,000 dwt in 2005 and has continued to increase ever since. Containerization has increased ship productivity by exploiting economies of scale.

In 2011 the world's ports handled an estimated 570 million TEUs. In 2012 the world fleet of container tonnage was 5,012 cellular container ships generating over 15.4 million TEU slots. In 2012 the global equipment pool totalled 21.1 million TEUs. Containerization has been largely responsible for the globalization of trade.

16.2 Major container trades

Major container trades have undergone continuous remodelling of the container network, which is one of continuous expansion through new tonnage and growth in port modernization and related infrastructure. This expansion extends particularly to the hub and spoke network and has changed shippers' attitudes in favour of container shipment. An example is the South African fruit market, where during the period November 2004 to April 2005 the container reefer market share increased by 65% to 1,800 TEU per week, while

Table 16.1 Growth rates on east–west head haul trades (%)

Trade leg	2000–05[a]	2000–05	2000–06	2005–10[a]
Asia–northern Europe	10.5	10.6	10.4	9.7
Asia–Mediterranean	15.2	23.0	18.1	10.5
Asia–North America	11.8	9.0	8.0	6.8
Asian east–west head haul	11.7	12.1	9.9	8.2
Northern Europe–North America	1.9	4.1	6.2	5.3
Mediterranean–North America	3.8	2.9	4.7	5.1
Atlantic east–west head haul	2.5	3.7	5.7	5.2
Head haul aggregate	10.1	10.9	9.3	7.8

Source: Courtesy of Drewry Consultants.

Note: [a] Average percentage per annum.

the specialist reefer vessel capacity remained static. Structural factors are likely to help carriers balance supply and demand.

These include port congestion consequent on ports failing to keep pace with container growth, trade imbalances and longer trade distances. Increased trade distances and longer vessel round-voyage durations assist in absorbing capacity, such as the greater share of transPacific cargo moving via east coast North America/US Gulf ports rather than overland from west coast North American ports. Increasing trade imbalances occur when there is a more than proportionate increase in capacity for a given two-way cargo volume and head-haul growth continues to outpace back-haul growth. Further factors include continued outsourcing of production, greater stability of east–west flows with lower-value cargo in the supply chain, and continuous merger and acquisition programmes, as found in Maersk Line. Fewer but larger mega-container operators in the global market are increasing their market share and dominance. An examination of growth rates on east–west head-haul trades is found in Table 16.1.

The Asian export trades predicts an annual growth rate of 3%, below the rate of the past few years. In contrast Atlantic trades should produce improved performance, accounting for 15% of aggregate east–west primary head-haul volumes and an even lower share of vessel demand because of their short voyage durations. Significantly they employ smaller ships than the Asian east–west trades and so provide little scope to absorb much of the new post-Panamax tonnage.

The regional and north–south markets and east–west routes employing sub-5,000 vessels are earmarked for ship capacity growth. Since 2012 some major lines have employed vessels with 14,000 TEU capacity. However, growth in the primary east–west trades to North America and Europe remains unpredictable. There is an imbalance between these trades and the rest of the market. This imbalance may result in the cascading of smaller and older tonnage into the secondary east–west markets and primary north–south trades, to spread overcapacity around more equally. Also focus on tonnage-intensive routes to help absorb the excess capacity is encouraged.

A factor helping to resolve any excessive container tonnage growth without a corresponding increase in containerized shipment may be the process of arranging the deployment of an increasingly imbalanced asset pool to cover the global spread of trade requirements.

Major container trade must be reconciled with rising bunker costs, the political situation, the cost pressures, the slow down in primary east–west trades, the continuous merger and acquisition strategy of container operators, influence of WTO, and the economic forecast of Europe, US, and OECD countries, coupled with the economic growth of China and India. A key factor is tonnage supply to meet demands as the container fleet expands by 50%, and this fleet's interface with trade and shipping cycles. Shipping economists monitor economic indicators, including exchange rates and any political tensions. Meanwhile, container operators strive to drive down costs and develop market drive–volume using freight rate marketing strategies.

16.3 Two container operators

Two major container operators are the China Shipping Container Lines (CSCL) and Maersk.

(a) China Shipping Container Lines

In 1997 CSCL had 15 vessels and in 2012, 145 vessels owned or under charter and was in the league of the top ten ocean carriers. A major investor is Hutchison Whampoa, the parent company of Hutchison Port Holdings. Table 16.2 shows as an example CSCL's key business indicators from 2004/5.

The company's objective is to become one of the top ocean carriers. The CSCL policy is twofold, with a combination of owned ships and long-term leases, usually in conjunction with Seaspan. CSCL has the reputation in the maritime industry of being an advanced carrier with a young fleet and capacity in TEU slots to provide a 'world class integrated shipping container logistics enterprise'.

One of CSCL's advantages is a comprehensive network in China, more extensive than any other carrier. CSCL's young fleet has the capability of a service speed of 24 knots. It maintains customer focus and has a range of logistics services providing shipping as well as access to terminals, container storage and transport networks, enabling a 'door to door' service. To give an example, details of the CSCL major services in 2005 are in Table 16.3. CSCL has developed its services further with the following: Asia–US east coast; Asia–Europe; transatlantic; Asia–west coast of South America and Central American feeder network; Asia–Australia; and Asia–West Africa. Long-term CSCL plans to enter the logistics business. Its South East regional headquarters are based in Port Klang, Malaysia.

Table 16.2 CSCL'S key business indicators, 2004/05

Indicator	2004	H1 2004	H1 2005	% change
Revenue (US$)	2.76 bn	1.22 bn	1.67 bn	36.40
Operating profit (US$)	636 m	272 m	324 m	25.30
Return on sales (%)	23.00	22.20	20.40	
TEU carried	3.65 m	1.697 m	2.194 m	29.30
Slot operating capacity (TEU)	254,207	217,300	299,672	37.90
Average freight rate (US$/TEU)ª	981	936	986	5.30
Total operating costs (US$)	2.08 bn	857 m	1.32 bn	41.80

Source: China Shipping Container Lines.

Notes: *bn* billion, *m* million. *H1* first half. ª International business.

(b) Maersk Line

The Maersk Line was founded in 2006 when Maersk Sealand fused with P&O Nedlloyd (PONL). This combination of two companies' container pools made considerable savings on fleet management, maintenance and repair and empty repositioning. The A. P. Møller-Maersk Group previously operated around 2 million TEU, of which one-third was leased, and P&O Nedlloyd had 1 million TEU, 20% of which was leased – very much in line with the normal ratio of two TEU to one TEU of vessel slot capacity. It is likely the group will establish its own container manufacture company in southern China, which will further reduce new equipment costs. Maersk Line has a larger number of the 8,000 TEUs than anyone else in the market and has now introduced the E class Maersk of 14,000 TEU and an even larger EEE Maersk with an estimated 18,000 TEU. The comparable costs of an 8,000 TEU post-Panamax vessel – including crewing, maintenance, insurance and fuel – are at least 13% lower than a 5,000 TEU ship, though these may increase with the larger TEU vessels of the E and EEE classes. This cost-reduction is particularly advantageous to Maersk Line, which operates in the world's two largest deep-sea lanes: the eastbound transPacific and the westbound Asia to Europe routes. Additionally, the A. P. Møller-Maersk Group has a formidable integrated supply chain management while Maersk Logistics provides warehousing and contract logistics and A. P. Møller Terminals container terminal services. Maersk Line also has an impressive IT network that enables vast amounts of data to be transmitted quickly, including booking requests, shipping instructions, status reports, and historical record analysis. The Maersk Line is involved in the Rotterdam-based European Rail Shuttle (ERS). This fast expanding rail specialist for container traffic offers services to near and distant markets, such as Italy and Poland, its volumes totalling 500,000 TEU in 2005.

The Maersk Line headquarters are in Copenhagen and it now possesses a broadly based maritime business and fleet, involving logistics and an extensive range of ship types, which include crude tankers, product carriers, ro/ro vessels, gas carriers, pure car/track carriers, anchor-handling tugs/supply

Table 16.3 CSCL'S major services as of 28 November 2005

Trade route	Service name	Vessels (average TEU)	Comments
Asia/USWC	AAS	5 × 5,688	S/C Zim
	AAC	5 × 4,860	
	AAT	7 × 4,250	Replaced ANW1 in December 2005
	ANW 2	13 × 4,250	Zim/Norasia/CSCL joint service – part of Zim AMP service calling Asia/Med/ Asia/USWC; CSCL provides one 4,250 TEU vessel
	AAN	5 × 4,250	CMA CGM removed three ships in November 2005, being phased out December 2005/January 2006
Asia/USEC	AAE 1	9 × 4,250	CSCL/CMA CGM/PONL joint service
Asia/USGulf/ Carib	PGX (PEX 2)	8 × 4,000	CSCL slot charters on CMA CGM/PONL service
Asia/Europe	AEX 1	9 × 7,190	S/C Zim, CMA CGM
	AEX 2	9 × 5,600	CSCL/Zim joint service
	AEX 3 (FAL)	8 × 6,500	CSCL slot charters on CMA CGM service
	AEX 4 (NCX)	8 × 5,700	CSCL slot charters on CMA CGM service
	AEX 6	12 × 5,652	CSCL slot charters on Evergreen service
Asia/Eur/ Mid-East	AEX 5 (SUNDEX)	7 × 3,000– 4,250	CSCL/CMA CGM joint service
Asia/Med/ USEC	AMAX	10 × 4,200	Launched July 2005
Asia/Med/ USEC	AAE 3 (ZCS)	14 × 4,713	CSCL slot charters on Zim service
Asia/Mid-East/ Ind/Eur/ USEC	Round the World	13 × 2,500	CSCL/Norasia/Gold Star Line joint service; CSCL provides one 2,500 TEU vessel
Asia/Black Sea	AMX 3 (ABX)	4 × 2,500	Fortnightly CSCL/Zim joint service
Asia/Saf/ S America	SEAS	10 × 2,500	CSCL/CMA CGM/Maruba joint service
Asia/Saf/Waf	WAX	Eight ships	Three CSCL vessels being withdrawn from CMA CGM joint service; new service details unknown
China, Japan, SE Asia/Aus	AUS 1, 2, 3	Average 2,450	Three services in partnership with OOCL, ANL, Cosco, Gold Star Line, Hamburg Sud

Sources: China Shipping Container Lines, ci-online.

Notes: FAL service is being upgraded to 8,200 TEU vessels. CSCL planning new Asia to West Africa service, as Delmas is replacing it in joint WAX service. *Aus* Australia, *Med* Mediterranean, *SA* South America, *Saf* South Africa, *S/C* slot charters, *Waf* West Africa, *USEC* US east coast, *USWC* US west coast.

vessels, platform supply vessels, cable-laying vessels, drilling barges and terminals. But its container business provides its major income.

Growth in China Shipping Container Lines and the Maersk Line in the next decades will be a key indicator of the health of global trade.

16.4 Container ships; terminals

(a) Container ships

Examples of container ships are shown in Figure 3.4 and Figure16.1. Both of these vessels were designed to provide flexibility of operation. There is also the cellular vessel, which has larger tonnage. Each hold is fitted with a series of vertical angle guides adequately cross-braced to accept containers. These holds are dedicated either to 20 ft or to 40 ft containers and ensure each succeeding container in a stack rests securely on the weight-bearing corner castings of the one below. The guides facilitate discharging and loading by guiding spreader frames of container cranes onto the corner castings of containers, without the crane driver making fine adjustments to line up the lifting frame. Many of the non-cellular type ships are conversions and operate as feeder services. The modern cellular vessel in the deep-sea trades is free of open deck obstructions – including derricks – to allow unimpeded container handling.

(b) Container terminal

The organization necessary to feed/distribute vessels of 8,000/10,000/14,000 TEU at a specialized berth requires careful planning. IT assists in container control/distribution. Rail is now more prominent in many countries in feeder/distribution arrangements at the container berth, especially in western Europe, the United States and the trans-Siberian rail link.

Container berths are either purpose-built for exclusive container use or are multi-purpose in handling container and other types of cargo vessels. The purpose-built container berth is the most productive container throughput. The most modern is computer-operated and handles double stack container trains. Basically there are three methods of container handling:

(a) Quay portainer crane working in association with van carriers.
(b) Quay portainer crane working in association with tractor/trailer operation.
(c) Quay portainer crane working in conjunction with tractor/trailer operation and container stacking cranes – the latter situated often some distance from the actual berth area.

The actual quay portainer crane may have a long outreach over the water and a short landward reach behind or with long outreach over both water and quay. The latter is preferred as it permits stowage for containers under the crane

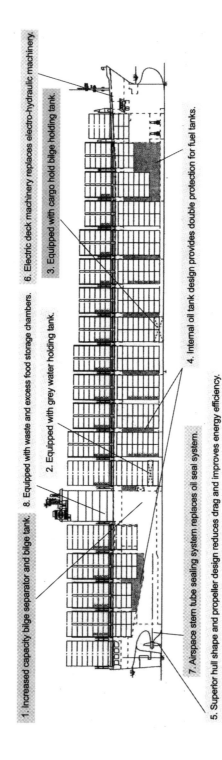

1. Increased capacity bilge separator and bilge tank.

2. Equipped with grey water holding tank.

3. Equipped with cargo hold bilge holding tank.

4. Internal oil tank design provides double protection for fuel tanks.

5. Superior hull shape and propeller design reduces drag and improves energy efficiency.

6. Electric deck machinery replaces electro-hydraulic machinery.

7. Airspace stern tube sealing system replaces oil seal system.

8. Equipped with waste and excess food storage chambers.

Figure 16.1 Side elevation of Evergreen S type container Greenship series.

Source: By courtesy of Evergreen.

structure. All three methods involve the import landed container being moved away from the crane by van carrier/tractor and trailer to a container stacking area.

With increasing emphasis on quicker port turn-round times, the most modern system uses a 336 ft long gantry crane which moves containers overhead to and from the berthed vessel instead of using the traditional straddle carrier. A notable saving is in the straddle carriers. The 500 tonne capacity gantry crane can handle five containers at a time. It functions like a huge cartridge and is fed continuously by rubber-tyred yard cranes. This transfer device enables both the shipside crane and the yard gantry to operate simultaneously but independently with an obvious saving in work time. IT is important to the operation, controlling the delivery and pick-up of containers from the truckers as well as the movement and positioning of all containers in the terminal.

The container is then processed through customs clearance, unless it is destined for an inland clearance depot, in which case the container under bond is transferred to a rail or road vehicle for despatch. In the case of the locally cleared containers it may be despatched by road or rail to importers' premises/inland situated container base/or simply discharged locally through the port/berth container base. The process is reversed with exported containers. Straddle carriers are used extensively to move containers within the berth area.

Container terminal planning requires these considerations:

(a) Does the port have a strategic geographical location and will it become a hub?
(b) Will it be a transhipment port? Terminals located on a small island/small country may be the only option, but a port with a larger hinterland generates more volume but at higher commercial risk.
(c) Can the port generate a larger volume – despite competing nearby ports – through the establishment of FTZ, and connecting railborne container trains?
(d) Would it be a single or multi-user terminal?
(e) Does the terminal have physical or legal constraints?
(f) Does the port have flexibility in terms of development?
(g) Evaluate the size of the container vessel impact on berth lengths, specification of quayside cranes and dredging requirements in terms of access channel to the port/berth, turning basin, and depth of water alongside the berth.
(h) The new berths are often located in greater water depths, the old berths having too many constraints for modern container tonnage.
(i) Increased weight, operating speeds and sophistication of cranes impose a heavier electrical power demand.
(j) Ship/shore cranes continue to become larger/heavier to provide increased reach, lift heights and lifting capacity.
(k) Wider quay aprons are needed for cranes and vehicle circulation.

(l)   High land cost reclamation encourages high-density container stacking to reduce land take.

(m) Uninterrupted open areas are required for terminal operations and future development.

(n)   Container yard equipment must match quay crane productivity.

In regard to the terminal layout, many elements have to be considered including: (a) terminal equipment; (b) stock or yard capacity; (c) use of computerized terminal management; (d) customs procedures; (e) gate capacity; (f) road/rail/inland waterway services; and (g) automation. Quay equipment and procedures include: (a) electronic box tagging and continuous tracking in the terminal; (b) positioning systems for stacking equipment-radio/data radar/GPS; (c) quay and yard gantry cranes – anti-sway and final positioning devices; (d) EDI and use of IT – pre-planning of stacks for in-bound boxes and retrieval boxes for loading; and (e) quay cranes – twin lift (lifting two boxes at once) and double trolley that separates the vessel crane and trailer movements.

These comments so far do not reflect any hydrographic, topographic, wave recording or soil investigations. However, modern container terminals are very high-tech and focused on productivity both for the shipowner and port authority. It involves high capital cost; reliable market forecast and method of funding, including return on capital, are key areas.

Examples of modern container berths are found in the ports of Singapore, Hong Kong, Vancouver, Cherbourg, Felixstowe, Dubai, New York, and Shanghai and are explained in Chapter 17.

The container berth varies greatly in size. Much depends on anticipated annual throughput and vessel capacity. Capacity can vary from 5 ha to 8 ha for the second generation cellular ship, to one of over 30 ha with the fifth generation vessel. Stacking of containers in excess of three high is rarely exceeded because of creating problems. Two high is the most common.

A typical terminal in an upper medium size port would be 8.5 ha, designed to handle 3,000 containers on and off ship within 72 hours. Stacking area would be of 1,800 general cargo and 400 insulated containers – the latter being housed in a specially cladded stack connected to a refrigerated plant. Where double stack container trains serve the container berth, as found in most major ports of the east and west coast of North America, this area is much increased.

The loading of containers on board the vessel can create many problems particularly when a number of different container lengths and port destinations are involved. The vessel has to be properly trimmed by the stern and the loading plan must take into account dangerous cargo and those containers requiring special attention, e.g. an open container with a commercial vehicle in excess of the accepted container height and requiring to be stowed on the upper or open deck. The formulation of the stowage plan uses IT.

Container ships usually carry substantial quantities of containers on the open deck where special equipment/fittings are provided. Stacking up to five high

Table 16.4 Analysis of container size growth (TEU)

Size	4,900	6,200	6,700	12,000
LOA	272.05	299.90	299.90	380
BM	40.00	40.00	42.80	55.00
DM	24.30	23.90	24.40	–
DW	62,700	82,275	88,669	–
Draught	13.5	14.00	14.00	14.5
Speed	24.5	23.00	24.5	–

Source: Korean Maritime Industry.

on open deck is common. Such a practice of open-deck container shipments enhances the productivity of such ships and is particularly ideal for distributing empty containers caused through imbalanced working.

The increased size of container vessels has been notable recently, as demonstrated in Table 16.4. On the basis of dimensional considerations the future optimum Ultra large container vessel (ULCV) will be configured as follows: overall capacity 12,500 TEU, maximum LOA around 380–400 m; ship's maximum breadth 60 m; maximum design draught 14.5; and designed to accommodate slow or economical speeds of 15–18 knots and sea speeds of 23 and 25 knots, depending upon powering considerations. The above allows estimation of scale economies.

A side elevation of the latest fleet of Evergreen S type container green-ships is shown in Figure 16.1. The vessels were designed by Mitsubishi Heavy Industries' Kobe shipyard. The design meets or exceeds the strictest global environment standards. It has received Lloyd's Register environmental protection (LREP) and the equivalent to ES notation with the American Bureau of Shipping (ABS). The vessels use the latest low-sulphur fuel systems, advanced oil–water separators, environmentally friendly Freon (chroro-fluorocarbon), large high-temperature incinerators and dock power systems to protect the purity of the oceans and air quality around the ports.

The port of Dubai has become the container hub of the region and is developing the latest generation of container terminals. In 2004, at Jebel Ali, it handled its largest container ship – the 9,200 TEU MSC *Pamela* at 'quay 4', which has a draught of 17 m. The quay areas for feeder vessels have a draught of 11.5 m. During the period Dubai took delivery of 16 additional super-post-Panamax ship-to-shore gantry cranes and 52 rubber-tyred gantry (RTG) cranes at Jebel Ali. In 2006 six more quayside gantry cranes and 24 RTGs were commissioned to give an annual throughput of 9 million TEU. Dubai is also pressing ahead with the building of 'Jebel Ali 2' on reclaimed land adjacent to existing facilities to provide an additional capacity of 5 million TEU annually. The project allows an additional 2,060 m of berths for container berths with a draught of 18 m and 11 super-post-Panamax gantry cranes and supporting yard equipment which began operation in 2007. The terminals have rail-mounted stacking gantry cranes (RMGs), rather than RTGs, to generate higher levels of automation and efficiency. The role of the port of Dubai is explained in Chapter 17.

The presence of the 9,500 TEU vessel places an enormous pressure on container ports to keep pace with the latest generation of container tonnage, as demonstrated in Dubai. Mega seaports failing to keep up with such development are at commercial risk for failing to attract major container operators. An examination of the possible specification of the Ultra Large Container Vessel (ULCV) of 12,500+ TEU reveals the following:

(a) Two hull structures obtain: (i) the wider beam with containers loaded to nine tiers and 18 stacks in the holds and for the deck seven tiers and 22 stacks or (ii) the narrower beam with containers loaded 20 stacks, and nine tiers in the holds and 22 stacks and seven tiers on deck. The wider beam with the deckhouse above the engine room would have a capacity of 12,100 TEU whilst the narrow beam has a capacity of 13,000 TEU by moving the deckhouse forward.

(b) Most ship designers consider the midship section a critical area because of the stress imposed on these parts such as bending movement – sagging and hogging – and torsion strength. To protect the strength, the midship section scantling specifies HT 36 steel throughout for a frame spacing of 10 ft, 65 mm thick steel is used for hatch-side coming and topside structure 60 mm. Midship section scantlings for the narrow beam option is likewise 65 mm together with the topside structure.

(c) Manoeuvrability is a key factor in confined waters, especially in a port, because the ULCV, like a mega cruise liner, has a high freeboard. The vessel would have three or four bow thruster units operating independently.

(d) The propulsion system, with a service speed of 25 knots, presents a series of options: the single screw; twin engine with twin screw, contra-rotating propellers, and single engine with twin podded units; the latter is still being developed.

The future of the ULCV will be determined by current and forecast development of container port and terminal. The latest generation, the fifth, of 9,500 TEU, presents many challenges. Key areas of the ULCV, excluding economic and technical, are the ability of seaports to accommodate the length, beam and draught (Table 16.4). The capital cost per slot on the ULCV would be 10% lower than the 10,000 TEU, allowing economies of scale.

The time spent in loading and discharging containers varies by port and circumstances. In broad terms, one can attain 25–30 containers per hour for discharging cargo, whilst for cargo exports the figure falls to 20–25 per hour per crane of single container capacity. Many ports now have cranes of two-container capacity offering much improved loading/discharging rates.

A container berth handling third-generation container ships with seven or eight vessels per month is likely to handle 22,000–26,000 containers, more than seven times conventional berth handling capacity.

Examples of transit times from Felixstowe/Southampton/Tilbury involving container vessels are these:

- *Far East and Jeddah*. Jeddah 8 days; Busan 27 days; Yokohama 31 days; Singapore 19 days; Kaohsiung 25 days; Kobe 29 days.
- *Australia and New Zealand*. Adelaide 34 days; Sydney 39 days; Melbourne 36 days; Auckland 44 days; Wellington 47 days.
- *North America and Carribbean*. Long Beach 23 days; Houston 13 days; Port Everglades 10 days; Charleston 9 days; New York 11 days; Boston 9 days.
- *Middle East, Gulf, South Asia, Bay of Bengal*. Mumbai 21 days; Chennai 20 days; Cochin 27 days; Colombo 25 days; Dubai 14 days.

A significant feature of containerization that involves 'through transport' is the domination of IT in all processes. Internet and satellite provide instant communication between container terminals and ships at sea. Complete bills of lading, stowage plans and container terminal layouts can be processed and transmitted swiftly and accurately.

A number of companies, such as Sea Containers, lease containers to shippers. It is a computer-operated/managed system and when on hire features details of the client, the date unit will be off hire, container 'depot out' and container 'depot in' dates, the billing and interchange arrangements. The computer also logs whether containers are available for immediate leasing, any damaged containers, if damaged to what extent and who is responsible, and billing for repair. Basically, when the container leaves the depot, control of the container is transferred to the lessee. All new Sea Container units are fitted with a recess so that a tag can be fitted for automatic container control.

Continuous growth of the double-stack container train is especially significant in North America and Australia. This has resulted in a rationalization of ports of call by container tonnage. A modern double-stack container train of nearly one mile's length is capable of conveying 820 TEUs. The double-stack container trains are integrated with specific container shipping line sailings and are called mini land bridges. In North America these trains travel overland distances of between 2,000 and 3,000 miles. The trains convey 6.10 m or 12.20 m containers of 2.4 m width and 2.6 m height. The flatcars are 60 ft or 80 ft long.

In recent decades ten new waterfront rail transfer facilities for double-stack operations were completed at the west coast ports of Long Beach and Los Angeles. Today over 250 double stack container trains per week are operating from these west coast ports. A further example of an innovative shipping strategy is that adopted by the Maersk Line for its distribution operation in North America. Double-stack container trains operate between the east coast, Gulf and west coasts linking the seaports of Seattle, San Francisco, Halifax, Boston, New York, Charleston and New Orleans.

The completion in 2004 of the Australian north–south railway link between Adelaide and the deep-water port of Darwin, spanning 3,000 km with a transit time of 43 hours, has stimulated the Australian economy and provided easier access to Asian markets. Moreover, northern hemisphere trades will benefit from the shorter voyage times to Darwin deep-water port rather than the longer voyage to south eastern Australia seaports. This development favours not only containerized traffic but also dry bulk cargo such as iron ore. Overall, the transit time to/from Singapore to/from Adelaide/Melbourne via Darwin will be four days quicker. Darwin has become the regional deep sea port as a gateway to/from South East Asia in Australia.

The ro/ro vessel operating in the deep sea trades is capable of conveying a combination of both ISO containers and ro/ro units. The ro/ro units are usually unaccompanied trailers plus trade cars, lorries, etc. Advantages of this type of tonnage include flexibility of ship capacity because of its variable capacity to carry a mixture of ro/ro units and containers. This flexibility facilitates productive use of ship capacity in a variable international market. Moreover, the vehicle traffic driven on and off the ship aids quick port turn-round of the vessel. It also facilitates the shipment of the indivisible load, very much on the increase. Usually, such vessels do not require a portal ramp facility but have their own ramp facility accommodated on the ship and hydraulically operated.

16.5 Container distribution

Modern-day container operations require the skill to ensure the right container is at the right place at the right time to meet the shipper's demands. This involves a logistics operation whose complexity is aided by IT. Overall, for the container operator it means the constant repositioning of containers. This repositioning arises from the imbalance of trade, and perhaps more significantly from a lack of harmonization between those goods imported into a country and those exported. For example, commodities imported may consist of heavy capital goods requiring flat-rack containers whilst those exported may consist of foodstuffs needing high cube reefer containers.

The Far East is an interesting market to examine which leads to the rationale behind the movement of containers. It is the fastest growing region in the world and seven of the top 10 container ports are located there. Asia has become a major supplier of departmental store goods from countries such as China, Japan, Malaysia, Indonesia, Burma, Hong Kong, Taiwan, Korea, Thailand, the Philippines and the subcontinent of India and Pakistan. The container trades involved are Europe/Asia and Asia/America.

Asia receives raw materials and semi-finished goods from Europe. These are generally bulky cargoes and are often heavy. With regard to exports the opposite applies. Consumer goods produced in Asia are relatively light. For a container ship this means that imports into Asia are carried in 20 ft containers whilst exports are shipped in 40 ft containers. This kind of shipment results in an imbalance of containers, almost compelling shipping operators to carry empty containers back to their area of origin.

In addition to these substantial logistics problems, the value of cargo in the containers must also be considered. Basic products have a considerably lower value per unit weight than finished exports. These problems and the characteristics of the goods are reflected in the tariffs of the shipping operators and the freight rates for Asian exports. For sea freight containers, these have to compensate for the low rates for imports.

The round-the-world service concept allows extensive re-use of containers in other imbalanced world trades, considerably helping to reduce cost. The bigger and more diversified the cargo areas, the more successful these measures become. The Far East, with its multi-country structure, offers ideal conditions in this respect.

In the trade between the Far East and the United States the flow of containers is much the same as in the Europe/Asia trade: heavy incoming cargo and light outgoing cargo. The large difference is that in contrast to the trade with Europe, the heavy cargo is also carried in 40 ft containers. In this respect there is a balance between the container types. However, the American market constitutes a special challenge to shipping operators in the Far East.

Because of the geographical situation, all ships coming from the Far East call at American west coast ports. The big shipping companies on the Pacific have established land bridge services involving rail connections between ports, such as San Francisco and New York, in order to bring cargo to the east coast. This means that the round-the-world carrier competes with the relatively cheap east–west rail links of the United States.

Vietnam, Burma, Thailand, Taiwan, Indonesia and Korea are relatively new sources of supply for department stores in Europe and the United States. The port installation infrastructure of most of these countries is not yet adequately developed to handle relatively large container ships. Feeder services have been developed with shipboard crane facilities. The region is covered by an extensive network of feeder services. The European single market, the former Eastern bloc countries and those with Mediterranean seaboards will have a profound impact on the Far East. The enlarged European Union of 28 member states incorporating many former East European countries has an impact on Far East trade. The growth of the Indian market and much improved Japanese trade performance will contribute to a changing trade portfolio in the region. The countries of the Far East will increase their demand for capital goods and basic products, while at the same time export more consumer goods. To conclude, the Far East container trades is subject to continuous change.

16.6 Container types

The range of container types tends to expand annually to meet increasing market demands in this fast-growing international distribution of merchandise. The majority of containers used are built to ISO (International Standards Organization) specification which permits ease of use internationally.

Given below are details of some of the types of containers available and some of their features (see also Figure 16.2). Details of the dimensions of specific containers, pallet-wide intermodal containers and swapbody types are given in Table 16.5.

(a) *Dry freight container.* This container type is ideal for both the FCL and LCL markets. It is designed for all types of general merchandise and with suitable modification for the carriage of bulk cargoes both solid and liquid. It is available in 20 ft, 40 ft and 40 ft hi-cube sizes. Most 20 ft containers have a maximum gross weight of 30,480 kg. Additionally, there is the 45 ft hi-cube container designed to carry similar products as the 40 ft, but with 13% additional volume. It is the world's most widely used container for the movement of general cargo and its most cost-effective means of transporting non-perishable cargoes (Figure 16.2).

(b) *Insulated containers.* These protect against heat loss or gain and are used in conjunction with a blown-air refrigeration system to convey perishable or other cargo requiring to be carried under temperature control. Internally the containers are equipped with an aluminium T-section floor and the inside face of the doors is fitted with moulded vertical battens to permit air flow around the cargo. It is important that when cargo requiring temperature control is loaded in this type of container, an air space of approximately 7.5 mm is left over the top of the cargo to allow free air circulation. Securing points are positioned along each side of the floor, while lashing points to prevent cargo falling out are sited at the door end of the container by the corner posts. This is an ideal container for the movement of foodstuffs.

(c) *Refrigerated containers.* GE SeaCo has the world's largest refrigerated container lessor fleet of over 100,000 TEUs available in 20 ft, 40 ft and 40 ft hi-cube sizes, for shipment of perishable and frozen cargoes. The reefer containers are designed to operate independently of a blown-air refrigerated system, and are filled with their own refrigeration units which require an electrical power supply for operation. Each container is capable of being set at its own individual carriage temperature. It is ideal for meat, dairy products and fruit. An increasing volume of former bulk tonnage reefer cargoes is now being containerized. The containers embrace the latest design and construction methods; hi-grade stainless steel on exterior panels; corrosive resistant hot-zinc-sprayed corten steel frame; and for added resistance, all exterior surfaces are primed and coated with thick gloss top coat (Figure 16.2).

(d) *Bulk containers.* These are designed for the carriage of dry powders and granular substances in bulk. To facilitate top loading three circular hatches (500 mm diameter) are fitted in some containers in the roof structure. The dry freight container is displacing the bulk and ventilated container (see Figure 16.2).

(e) *Ventilated containers.* This type of container is broadly similar to the dry freight container specification, except for the inclusion of full length ventilation galleries sited along the top and bottom side rails, allowing the passive ventilation of the cargo. It is ideal for products such as coffee (see Fig 16.2).

(f) *Flat rack containers and platform flats.* Both these types of containers are primarily designed to facilitate the carriage of cargo of awkward, oversize and project cargoes. These units are also used as temporary ''tween decks' for the carriage of large, indivisible loads. Such containers have a collapsible end. GE SeaCo's fleet includes the innovative Sea Deck and Domino units, both flush-folding flat-racks. These units combine the benefits of a flat-rack and a platform flat in one unit. They have collapsible, spring-assisted end walls, which allow easier operation, enabling both wheeled and crawler equipment to be driven on to the unit during loading. A combination of two or more flat-rack containers can be used to form a temporary break-bulk space for uncontainer-able cargo moved on a Port to Port basis, provided that the total weight and point of loading of the cargo does not exceed the static capabilities of the flat-racks.

Flat-racks are ideal for trades where there is cargo in one direction and nothing in the other. The end walls are folded down and five units can be returned in one stack back to the point where the cargo is loaded. Most flat-racks are 40 ft with a maximum gross weight of 45,000 kg.

(g) *Open top containers.* This type of container is suitable for the carriage of awkwardly shaped indivisible or oversize cargoes which cannot be stowed in the dry freight container. It is available in 20 ft and 40 ft sizes. The units offer increased versatility over standard boxes and are designed for loading through both the top of the container and the doors. It may also be described as an open sided/open top container. Tarpaulin tilts are available to protect the cargo. This container is ideal for sheet glass, timber and machinery (Figure 16.2).

(h) *Tank containers.* Growth in the volume of containerized bulk liquid – hazardous and non-hazardous – shipments is phenomenal and likely to continue. The IMO regulation is severe in terms of the container tank construction and their shipment, especially for dangerous classified cargo. A wide range of dry bulk cargoes is shipped in tank containers. GE SeaCo is a market leader and is one of the world's largest tank container lessors with a modern fleet of tanks ranging from 12,000 to 35,000 litre capacities. Tank containers are ideal for the transport and storage of all types of bulk liquid and can be shipped by rail, road and sea. A range of specialists tanks is available for particular applications, such as units for the transport

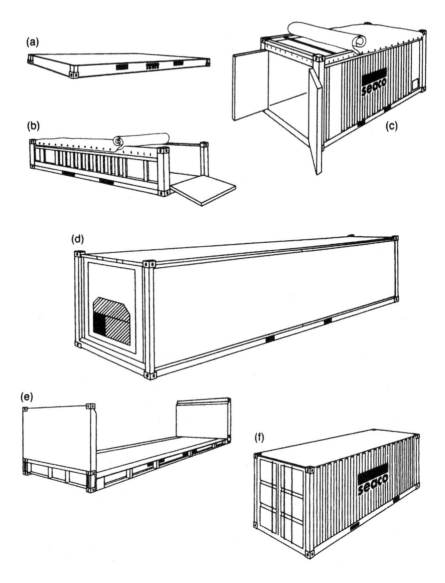

Figure 16.2 Container types: (*a*) 20 ft platform flat, or bolster (40 ft size available) for building materials, vehicles, indivisible loads, lumber, etc. (*b*) 20 ft half-height with ramp end door and tarpaulin roof, for heavy loads, building materials. (*c*) 20 ft open top (40 ft size available) for large awkward items such as machinery, tarpaulin roof for watertight integrity, door header swings to assist loading of high items. (*d*) 40 ft refrigerated container with integral refrigeration machinery for chilled and frozen cargoes. (*e*) 20 ft spring-assisted folding end flat-rack (40 ft size available), can be provided with built-in interlocking mechanism for multiple empty transport (*f*) 20 ft covered container, 8 ft 6 in. high (40 ft available).

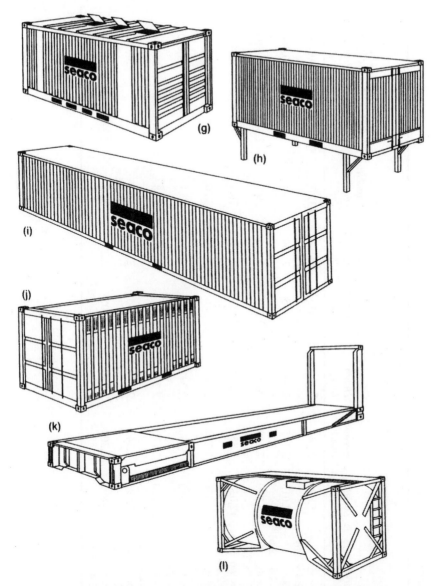

Figure 16.2 (cont.) Container types: (*g*) 20 ft bulk container for grain, powders, etc. (*h*) 7.15 m swapbody with demountable legs, 2.5 m width for two-palletwide European operation. (*i*) 40 ft high cube 9 ft 6 in. high (45 ft also available) for cargoes that cube out. (*j*) 20 ft ventilated container for cargoes such as coffee and cocoa that experience condensation damage. (*k*) 40 ft sea deck-style combined flat-rack and platform flat (20 ft size available) for large items of machinery, construction equipment, etc. (*l*) 20 ft tank container for bulk hazardous and non-hazardous liquids.

Source: Reproduced by kind permission of GE SeaCo.

Table 16.5 ISO container dimensions by type

Container type	Overall dimensions (ft/m)	Interior dimensions (minimum)			Door dimensions		Cubic capacity (minimum) (m³)	Tare weight (maximum) (kg)	Gross weight (maximum) (kg)
		Length (mm)	Breadth (mm)	Height (mm)	Breadth (mm)	Height (mm)			
General purpose	20 × 8 × 8½ (6.1 × 2.4 × 2.6)	5,890	2,345	2,400	2,335	2,290	32.7	2,450	30,480
General purpose	40 × 8 × 8½ (12.2 × 2.4 × 2.6)	12,015	2,345	2,362	2,335	2,260	66.3	3,700–4,380	30,480
Insulated	20 × 8 × 8½ (6.1 × 2.4 × 2.6)	5,760	2,260	2,235	2,260	2,215	29.0	2,413	24,000
General purpose high cube	40 × 8 × 9.6 (12.2 × 2.4 × 2.9)	12,033	2,352	2,694	2,580	2,340	76.4	3,780	30,480
General purpose high cube	45 × 8 × 9.6 (13.7 × 2.4 × 2.9)	13,558	2,354	2,696	2,586	2,340	86.0	4,700	30,480
Refrigerated	20 × 8 × 8½ (6.1 × 2.4 × 2.6)	5,450	2,260	2,247	2,260	2,247	27.7	3,460	24,000
Refrigerated	40 × 8 × 8½ (12.2 × 2.4 × 2.6)	11,550	2,270	2,200	2,270	2,170	57.8	4,670–4,940	30,480
Bulk	20 × 8 × 8½ (6.1 × 2.4 × 2.6)	5,892	2,347	2,379	2,335	2,285	33.1	2,730	24,000
Ventilated	20 × 8 × 8½ (6.1 × 2.4 × 2.6)	5,892	2,303	2,380	2,305	2,273	32.3	2,720	24,000

Table 16.5 continued

Container type	Overall dimensions (ft/m)	Interior dimensions (minimum)			Side openings		Cubic capacity (minimum) (m³)	Tare weight (maximum) (kg)	Gross weight (maximum) (kg)
		Length (mm)	Breadth (mm)	Height (mm)	Breadth (mm)	Height (mm)			
Flat-rack	20 × 8 × 8½ (6.1 × 2.4 × 2.6)	5,940	2,400	2,310	5,576	2,310	31.9	2,610–2,810	30,480
Flat-rack	40 × 8 × 8½ (12.2 × 2.4 × 2.6)	12,066	2,263	2,134	11,662	2,134	58.6	5,960–6,100	45,000

Container type	Overall dimensions (ft/m)	Overall interior dimensions			Door dimensions		Roof aperture		Cubic capacity (min) (m³)	Tare weight (max) (kg)	Gross weight (max) (kg)
		Length (mm)	Breadth (mm)	Height weight (mm)	Breadth weight (mm)	Height (mm)	Length (mm)	Breadth (mm)			
Open top	20 × 8 × 8½ (6.1 × 2.4 × 2.6)	5,890	2,345	2,340	2,335	2,260	5,712	2,175	32.4	2,093–2,513	24,000–30,480
Open top	40 × 8 × 8½ (12.2 × 2.4 × 2.6)	12,025	2,247	2,305	2,235	2,200	11,832	2,150	63.47	3,949–4,650	30,480
Half height	40 × 8 × 4¼ (12.2 × 2.4 × 1.3)	12,010	2,235	940	2,284	980	11,900	2,073	25.2	3,656	30,480

Container type	Overall dimensions (ft/mm)	Total water capacity (litres)	Tank material	Tare weight (maximum) (kg)	Gross weight (maximum) (kg)
Tank	20 × 8 × 8½ (6.1 × 2.4 × 2.6)	24,000	Stainless steel	3,150	30,480

Table 16.5 continued

Container type	Overall dimensions (ft/m)	Interior dimensions			Door opening		Cu. cap. (min) (m³)	Tare weight (max) (kg)	Pay-load (max) (kg)	Gross wt (max) (kg)	Top opening		Side opening	
		Length (mm)	Breadth (mm)	Height (mm)	Breadth (mm)	Height (mm)					Length (mm)	Breadth (mm)	Length (mm)	Breadth (mm)
40 high cube dry container (aluminium container)	40 × 8 × 9½ (12.2 × 2.4 × 3.0)	12,056	2,347	2,684	2,340	2,585	76.0	2,900	29,600	32,500	—	—	—	—

Container type	Overall dimensions	Pallet capacity (per layer)	Capacity (m³)	Maximum payload
Sea Cell (general purpose Palletwide)	20 × 2.4 × 8 ft 6 in.	14	34.2	28,250
Sea Cell (general purpose High Cube Palletwide)	20 × 2.4 × 9 ft 6 in.	14	38.6	27,990
Sea Cell (general purpose Palletwide)	40 × 2.4 × 8 ft 6 in.	30	70.1	29,900
Sea Cell (general purpose High Cube Palletwide)	40 × 2.4 × 9 ft 6 in.	30	79.1	29,850
Sea Cell (general purpose High Cube Palletwide)	45 × 2.4 × 9 ft 6 in.	33	88.4	29,050
Sea Cell (Bulk Palletwide High Cube Palletwide)	20 × 2.4 × 9 ft 6 in.	14	38.6	27,920

Table 16.5 continued

Container type	Overall dimensions (ft/m)	Number that interlock into 8 ft 6 in.	Door openings End door Width (m)	End door Length (m)	Side door Width (m)	Side door Length (m)	Tare weight (maximum) (kg)	Payload (maximum) (kg)	Cubic capacity (minimum) (m³)	Gross weight (maximum) (kg)
Sea containers										
Platform flat	20 × 8 × 8½ (6.1 × 2.4 × 2.6)	7	—	—	—	—	1,500	25,400	—	—
Platform flat	40 × 8 × 8½ (12.2 × 2.4 × 2.6)	4	—	—	—	—	4,200	35,780	—	—
Fixed end flat rack	20 × 8 × 8½ (6.1 × 2.4 × 2.6)	—	—	—	—	—	2,900	20,320	—	—
Collapsible flat rack	20 × 8 × 8½ (6.1 × 2.4 × 2.6)	4	—	—	—	—	2,900	22,100	—	—
Spring-assisted flat rack	20 × 8 × 8½ (6.1 × 2.4 × 2.6)	5	—	—	—	—	2,600	27,400	—	—
Fixed-end flat rack	40 × 8 × 8½ (12.2 × 2.4 × 2.6)	—	—	—	—	—	5,098	25,383	—	—
Spring-assisted flat rack	40 × 8 × 8½ (12.2 × 2.4 × 2.6)	3	—	—	—	—	4,995	30,567	—	—
Sea deck flush deck	20 × 8 × 8½ (6.1 × 2.4 × 2.6)	7	—	—	—	—	2,560	27,920	—	—
Sea deck flush deck folding end	40 × 8 × 8½ (12.2 × 2.4 × 2.6)	4	—	—	—	—	5,300	39,700	—	—
40 ft Palletwide 8 ft 6 in. high unit inter-modal container	(12.19 × 2.5 × 2.59)	—	2.4	2.2	—	—	5,300	39,700	—	—

Table 16.5 continued

Container type	Overall dimensions (ft/m)	Number that inter-lock into 8 ft 6 in.	Door openings				Tare weight (maximum) (kg)	Payload (maximum) (kg)	Cubic capacity (minimum) (m³)	Gross weight (maximum) (kg)
			End door		Side door					
Sea containers			Width (m)	Length (m)	Width (m)	Length (m)				
40 ft Palletwide 8 ft 6 in. side door unit inter-modal container	(12.19 × 2.5 × 2.6)	—	2.4	2.2	2.3	2.2	4,100	26,280	70.8	30,480
40 ft Palletwide 9 ft high unit inter-modal container	(12.19 × 2.5 × 2.74)	—	2.4	2.3	—	—	3,950	26,530	74.6	30,480
40 × Palletwide 9 ft 6 in. cube unit—inter-modal container	(12.19 × 2.5 × 2.89)	—	2.4	2.5	—	—	4,000	26,480	79.1	30,480
7.15 stackable box swapbody	—	—	—	—	—	—	—	—	—	

of food-grade cargo intended for human consumption and for the safe carriage and storage of toxic and hazardous products. Overall there are five types:

(i) The IMO type for chemicals involving hazardous cargo and a capacity ranging from 12,000 litres to 35,000 litres.
(ii) Lightweight tanks offering reduced tare weight for increased payload. Designed for a range of chemical and bulk liquids with a capacity of 21,000 litres.
(iii) Food grade tanks for edible cargo with a gross weight of 34,000 kg and tare weight of 3,300 kg.
(iv) Insulated tanks for liquids which are non-heat-sensitive with a gross weight of 34,000 kg and tare weight of 3,345 kg.
(v) Special tanks for highly hazardous liquids and gases with a capacity ranging from 12,000 litres to 35,000 litres.

The tank container offers a safe and straightforward method of controlling cost while using a recyclable resource. On arrival the tank discharges directly into the production process, saving both time and costly handling and heating charges. Shippers save time and money and the tank unit provides up to 35% additional cargo over drums in each ISO shipment. Wastage from drums through spillage or damage is an estimated 5% per transit. Other cost savings include the drum provision and its disposal in an environmentally conscious world.

The container is protected by an ISO frame and has stainless steel construction to aid cleanliness.

The specialist tanks include units for transport of food grade cargo intended for human consumption and for the safe carriage and storage of toxic and hazardous products.

(i) *Sea Cell containers*, developed by GE SeaCo to meet the growth of market needs of palletized cargo and more recently non-palletized cargo such as break-bulk. A sea cell container provides an increased volume of 3.5% and heavier payload of 34 tons compared to 30 tons in a traditional 40 ft container. This container type is popular with logistic operators globally.

The 6.10 m (20 ft) Sea Cell has 1.5 m and the 12.20 (40 ft) box 3 m extra capacity and both carry 27% more pallets than a standard box container. It is an intermodal extra-width container within a standard ISO frame. With corner castings at the usual locations all types of container handling equipment can lift it. Sea Cell containers may be loaded into both cellular and non-cellular containerships, giving complete intermodal capability. Unlike conventional dry freight boxes, the container's unique sidewall corrugations extend beyond the frame width and are designed to allow Sea Cell pallets to be located side by side with other Sea Cell pallets or standard ISO boxes, even on the tightest 25 mm deck locations. This permits in a 20 ft Sea Cell container 14 (11) pallets, in a 40 ft Sea Cell 30 (25) pallets and in a 45 ft Sea Cell 33 (27) pallets.

Figures in parenthesis represent the conventional dry freight box. Each pallet is 1,200 mm × 800 mm. The advantages of the use of pallets in Sea Cell include: (a) saves time and expense at loading/unloading; (b) less cargo damage; (c) potential of reduced insurance premiums; (d) claims record improves; and (e) easier handling of cargo. Sea Cells are designed for full ISO stacking – 7 high for 40 ft units and 9 high for 20 ft – and in addition to corner castings for spreader lifting in 20 ft units laden-lift fork pockets are provided.

The use of containers has revolutionized the transport of most internationally traded cargoes. Sea Cell takes the container revolution to new levels of productivity and efficiency. It is compatible with ISO container types from boxes to flat-racks and is cellular friendly for use in cellular and non-cellular ships, barges and ro/ro vessels. To the logistics operator, every manufacturer, every shipper and end user, it optimizes capacity utilization, adding value in a highly competitive containerized shipment industry.

(j) *Military containers.* Overseas military forces and peace-keeping missions need out-of-area rapid supply of equipment using an extensive range of specialized containers. Conventional units such as tanks, dry freight and refrigerated containers are used, as also are a wide range of purpose-built units for deployment on land, sea and air. These have been produced by Charleston Marine Containers Inc (CMCI) to the following types: (a) Quadcon – a mini container permitting the interlocking of four containers and integrated storage systems, and (b) Tricon series, permitting the interlocking of three containers permitting a wide range of uses. The 3 Tricon and 4 Quadcon create a 20 ft ISO module. It is intermodal and can be separated into its individual units, which can be delivered using smaller mechanical handling devices and vehicles.

(k) *Hanger containers.* These are used for dry cargo and are equipped with removable beams in the upper part. They are used for the shipment of garments on hangers. They are 12.20 m long, 2.4 m wide, and 3.0 m high, or 6.10 m long, 2.4 m wide and 3.0 m high.

The high cube dry container of 45 ft (13.72 m) or 49 ft (14.94 m) long or 8 ft (2.44 m) width and 9 ft 6 in (2.90 m) high has been developed by many major container operators, including the Maersk Line. The 45 ft container has some 27% larger cubic capacity than the general purpose container, which is 12.20 m long, 2.4 m wide and 2.4 m high. It is ideal for a wide variety of consumer products having a high cube but low weight ratio. These products include garments carried on removable beams in the upper part of the container provided by the Maersk Line, low tech products usually made up of components to be assembled, and a wide variety of other dry cargoes. They are popular in the Far East and North American markets and feature in multi-modal operation on double-stack container trains operating from east and west coast ports in North America (see Figure 16.2).

The swapbody was pioneered largely in Germany to meet domestic transport requirements dictated by use of road vehicles. This is now a fast growing industry. A wide variety of swapbody types exist, including tank, reefer, box side door, tautliner curtain side, tilt, speciality units, i.e. storage modules, and flat bases on to which ISO containers can be locked.

(l) *Swapbodies*. The swapbody market (Figure 16.2) is a growth market. Two types are popular, Class A (13.6 m) and Class C (7.15 m and 7.45 m). The 7.15 m and 7.45 m laden units can be stacked three-high and two-high for 13.6 m units. The 13.6 m curtainside swapbody is stackable and can be top-lifted while laden. Both box and curtainside designs are tailored to meet specific operational requirements for the carriage of palletized cargo in Europe. Both types can be both top and bottom lifted. The swapbody can be easily transferred between rail wagon and truck, and between truck and barge to complete an overland journey. The increased capacity of the 13.6 m units, which carry the same number of pallets as standard European road vehicles, allows pallets to be carried more economically than in standard marine containers.

The units can be utilized in lift on/lift off short sea and barge operations and may be stacked in terminals and yards, saving valuable storage space. Design features, such as demountable legs on 7.15 m and 7.45 m units, allow the tractor unit to be driven away leaving the container in place for loading or unloading. The continuous development of container types reflects the impact major shippers have on the industry. It is driving the globalization of trade and is opening up new markets. Global logistics and international supply chain management are stimulating expansion. Trade is a highly competitive market in which the container provides increased productivity, lower cost and a more competitive shipment.

16.7 Non-containerizable cargo

Non-containerizable cargo can be divided into four categories (see also Table 16.7) as follows:

(a) *Rollable cargo* with its own wheels or trailers that can be driven aboard or towed. Examples are road vehicles and agricultural machinery.
(b) *Cargo that is carried on trailers*. This involves MAFI and heavy-duty trailers for pier-to-pier movements, flatbed trailers for door-to-door transportation, and trailers for the movement of exceptionally large or heavy loads door-to-door.
(c) *Special project cargo* that requires experience and expertise to find a cost-effective solution. This includes, for example, the conveyance of trains in the ro/ro decks by laying rail lines into the ship; purpose-built road bogies to carry subway carriages door-to-door and special extendable flatbed trailers for the carriage of 22 m (72 ft) long aircraft wings.

(d) *Neo-bulk cargo*, a term given to a wide range of staple products that can be efficiently carried in the ro/ro decks as unitized break-bulk (e.g. wood pulp, board, paper, logs and steel). Details of the range of equipment used for non-containerizable cargo are given in Table 16.6 and in Table 16.8.

Ro/ro container vessels are large and flexible and are able to carry a variety of cargo mixes. Ro/ro decks incorporate hoistable car decks which can be raised or lowered according to market demand at the time. Even in the lowered position, the space underneath these car decks allows the blockstowing of a wide range of neo-bulk commodities and the stowage of normal ro/ro cargo. With the car decks raised, the height permits the carriage of out-of-gauge ro/ro cargo, which can be on trailers or wheeled or tracked. Examples include heavy machinery, locomotives, yachts, aircraft, earthmovers, automobiles and caravans. Block stowing in several layers is possible so that high utilization can be achieved in such tonnage.

Table 16.6 Range of equipment for non-containerizable cargo

Capacity (tonne)	Length (mm)	Width (mm)	No. of axles	Commentary
Roll trailers				
20	6,096	2,438	1	Units with capacities of up to 180 t are available for pier-to-pier movements. Operational advantages include low timber surfaced cargo platforms, multi-wheel bogies for extreme manoeuvrability, separate lashing points for cargo and trailer, and a high degree of stability, even when carrying oversize units
30	12,190	2,438	2 bogie	
40	12,190	2,438	2 bogie	
55	12,190	2,438	2 bogie	
60	12,190	2,438	2 bogie	
100	12,190	3,048	4 bogie	
180	12,954	3,454	8	
Flatbed trailers				
20	12,190	2,438	2	Special house-to-house trailers for through transport of machinery and other outsize and/or high cargo units. These are either owned by the shipper or available on lease. Special heavy-lift trailers for house-to-house movement of extra-heavy loads are available from shipowner
Bolsters: flats without hardboards				
20	6,000	2,438		This is a unit constructed with a strengthened floor which can be stowed from either the top, sides or ends

Table 16.7 Categories of non-containerizable cargo

Rollable	Trailer/MAFI	Special projects	Neo-bulk
Tractors	Boats	Subway/underground	Woodpulp
Backhoes	Yachts	carriages and	Linerboard
Trucks	Machinery	rolling stock	Plywood
Cars	Linerboard	Fixed-wing aircraft	Newsprint
Earthmovers	Cotton liner pulp	Aircraft wings	Lumber
Mobile cranes	Flower bulbs	Helicopters	Waferboard
Combine harvesters	Mining shields	Forging machines	Particle board
Buses	Hay balers	and presses	Press board
Bulldozers	Specialized steel	Crankshafts	Iron and steel
Excavators	products	Transformers	products
Wheel loaders	Crane parts	Boilers	Logs
Track loaders	Injection moulds	Pipe mills	
Motorgraders	Compressors	Dryers	
Air compressors	Cranes	Press rolls	
	Alternators	Steel rolls	
	Rotors	Converters	
	Turbines	Military vehicles	
	Constructionals	Streetcars	
		Oil rigs	
		Earthmovers over 55 t	
		Railway locomotives	
		Ballast cleaners	
		Metalworking machinery	
		Large boats and yachts	
		Long and wide loads	

The vessel is fitted with a 'jumbo angled stern ramp' which permits the simultaneous two-way movement of roll trailers and other ro/ro cargo. Loading and discharging of ro/ro or block stowed cargo at the same time as cars is achieved by providing separate ramp systems within the vessel.

16.8 Features of containerization

The advantages and disadvantages of containerization are these:

1 It permits a door-to-door service, maybe from the factory production site to the retail distributor's store – an overall distance of may be 10,000 km.
2 No intermediate handling at terminal (port) transhipment points.
3 The absence of intermediate handling plus quicker transits permits less risk of cargo damage and pilferage.
4 Low risk of cargo damage and pilferage enables more favourable cargo premiums to be obtained compared with conventional cargo shipments, i.e. 'tween-deck tonnage.

Table 16.8 Equipment for non-containerizable cargo

Rollable	Trailer/MAFI	Special projects	Neo-bulk
Maximum weight varies according to machine. Items over 132,275 lb (60 tonne) are considered special projects. Refer to the vessel's cargo specification on weight and dimension. Items may be towed or driven under their own power into the ship. Cargo is normally delivered to the port of loading by and collected at the port of discharge by the consignee or his agent. The normal ship's securing system using chains etc. is employed on board the vessel. Shipowner does not usually supply tarpaulins.	*Road trailers for door-to-door transport* Consignments may be considered 'in gauge' where dimensions do not exceed L 40 ft (12.19 m) × W 8 ft (2.43m) × H 8 ft 6 in. (2.59 m) Maximum payload without additional charges for 'in gauge' cargo is 39,682 lb (18 t). Heavier, indivisible loads can be carried, but prior arrangements and clearance must be obtained. Normal available equipment is the 40 ft (12.19 m) flatbed trailer with side pockets for stanchions. Equipment may be loaded or discharged at the shipper's or consignee's factory, or at the ocean terminal. For inland transport of 'in gauge' cargo normal container rules apply, but 'out of gauge' cargo requires prior clearance. Chains, nylon web lashing and Signode banding may be used to secure the cargo. If required, tarpaulins must be supplied by the shipper or trucker. *MAFI trailers for pier-to-pier transport* *The maximum dimensions of cargo should normally not exceed* L 40 ft (12.19 m) × W 10 ft (3.05 m) × H 10 ft (3.05 m). Normal maximum weight is 121,252 lb (55 t). Cargo in excess of this is considered a special project. Roll trailers are available to carry up to 20 t, 30 t, 40 t, 55 t and 60 t.	The shipowner defines special projects as cargo where any one of the following dimensions is exceeded: L 40 ft (12.19 m) × W 10 ft (3.05 m) × H 10 ft (3.05 m), or where the weight exceeds 121,275 lb (55 t) Rollable cargo is classed as a special project when the weight exceeds 132,275 lb (60 t). Note that any cargo, regardless of weight or density will require prior clearance for carriage by shipowner. Roll trailers are available for payloads up to 55 t and 60 t; heavy-duty trailers for up to 100 t and 180 t. Leased trailers, including drop frames, well trailers and extendables, are available on a one-trip basis from the shipowner. Roll and heavy-duty trailers are for pier-to-pier cargo only but leased trailers may move over the road with permits if required. Securing is achieved by chains, steel banding, wire and bottlescrews (turnbuckles) as necessary. Shipowner does not supply tarpaulins.	Maximum dimensions for a consignment loaded on a 20 ft bolster are: L 20 ft (6.10 m) × W 8 ft (2.43 m) × H 8 ft 6 in. (2.59 m). Payload maximum is 44,000 lb (20 t). Cargo may be loaded on a 20 ft (6.10 m) bolster or on 40 ft (12.19 m) flatbed trailer. In some cases the cargo may be blockstowed on the ro/ro decks of the ship. Equipment may be loaded or discharged at the shipper's or consignee's factory, or at the ocean terminal. For inland transport of door-to-door cargo on a 20 ft (6.10 m) bolster or a 40 ft (12.19 m) flatbed trailer, container rules apply. Web lashing, Signode steel banding, tarpaulins and shrink-wrapping are used to secure the cargo. Tarpaulins are normally supplied by the trucker or shipper.

5 Elimination of intermediate handling at terminal transfer points, i.e. ports, enables substantial labour savings to be realized, which in industrialized countries with high incomes *per capita* can realize considerable attractive financial savings.
6 Less packing needs for containerized shipments. In some cases, particularly with specialized containers, e.g. refrigerated tanks (liquid or powder), no packing is required. This produces substantial cost savings in international transport.
7 The elimination of intermediate handling coupled with the other advantages of containerized shipments, permits the cargo to arrive in a better condition when compared with conventional cargo shipments.
8 Because of the advantages of containerization, rates are likely to remain more competitive when compared with the former conventional tonnage ('tween-deck) shipments. A significant reason is that containerization is in the main a capital-intensive transport system compared with conventional liner systems, and has rationalized ports of call coupled with more intensive ship use.
9 Transits are much quicker compared with conventional cargo shipments. This is achieved through a combination of faster vessels, the rationalization of ports of call and substantially quicker cargo handling. An example is the UK–Australia service where the round voyage time has been reduced from the 20 weeks taken by conventional services some years ago to the current five weeks (approximately) taken by container vessels.
10 Faster transits and the advantages under items (7) and (8) encourage trade development and permit quicker payment of export invoices.
11 Containerization has permitted fleet rationalization. On average one container vessel – usually of much increased capacity and faster speed – has displaced up to eight 'tween-deck vessels on deep-sea services. This development has been facilitated by the rationalization of ports of call and the development of the 'hub and spoke' container ship feeder system.
12 Container vessels attain much improved utilization and generally are very much more productive than 'tween-deck tonnage.
13 Faster transits, usually coupled with more reliable schedules, and ultimately increased service frequency, are encouraging importers to hold reduced stocks/spares. This produces savings in warehouse accommodation needs, lessens risk of obsolescent stock, and reduces importers' working capital.
14 Containerization produces quicker transits and encourages rationalization of ports of call. This in many trades is stimulating trade expansion through much improved service standards. It will result in increased service frequency, which will aid trade development.
15 Provision of through documentation (consignment note) – bill of lading.
16 Provision of a through rate. This covers both maritime and surface transport cost. This factor and (15) aid marketing of the container concept.

17 More reliable transits – particularly disciplined controlled transit arrangements.

18 New markets have emerged through container development and advantages.

19 Maritime containerization is a capital-intensive project and is beyond the financial limit of many shipowners.

20 Not all merchandise can be conveniently containerized. However, as new maritime containers are introduced the percentage of this traffic falls annually.

21 Maritime containerization has greatly facilitated the development of consolidated or break-bulk consignments. This particularly favours the small exporter unable to fill one container load, his need being consolidated through use of a container land base.

22 Containerization thrives on use of IT, especially in container control/ tracking, customer billing, container stowage in the vessel, documentation processing, etc.

23 The international maritime container network expands annually as ports/ berths and their infrastructure are modernized. This involves the development of the dry port such as Ipoh, the development of new container berths; the relocation of container berths to accommodate larger vessels such as in the ports of Bangkok and Klang; the development of air-freight and land bridges, the development of the hub and spoke system and the new generation of container ships.

24 Containerization is a capital-intensive project beyond the financial ability of many shipowners. Many container services are operated by members of old conference groupings funding a new consortium. The finance required is huge, for a specialized ship(s) has to be built for at least three sets of containers for each ship. With regard to the latter, ownership has tended to be held by container hire operators, by industrial companies and by shipowning consortia. In all three sectors there has been much leasing of containers, operational control resting with the lessors. Further expense is incurred at the chosen terminals, where the authority bears the cost of providing specialized cranes, trailers, van carriers, etc., as well as strengthening quays and creating stacking space.

25 The container is a high capacity carrying unit, and in consequence, exporters with limited trade are unable to fill the container to capacity, and thereby take full advantage of an economical through rate, for example from exporters' factory premises to importers' warehouses. This situation has been overcome by the provision of container bases situated in industrial areas or port environs, where less than container load traffic (LCL) is stowed (stuffed) into a container with other compatible traffic with a similar destination/area.

26 In some trades a tiny percentage of traffic is incapable of being containerized, such as certain livestock. In this case the shipowner provides specialized non-container facilities on the vessel, a facility which inflates

the capital cost of the project, and sometimes results in poor utilization of the facility on the return passage.

27 The stratification of some trades varies considerably by time of year and direction. For example, a trade may have a preponderance of perishable cargo in one direction eight months of the year, whilst in the reverse direction the cargo may be consumer goods. This situation has to be reconciled in an acceptable container type(s) for use in both directions. In some trades, as a result of imbalance, extensive repositioning of containers is required. Another example is to have cargo in one direction with a low stowage factor, whilst in the reverse direction it is a high stowage factor. Such problems, although appearing difficult, have been overcome through the co-operation of all interested parties, particularly shippers/shipowners. Technological development, such as food storage/ processing, etc., has eased shipowners' problems considerably and has tended to level out peak seasonal nature of traffic in some trades.

28 The container-owning company, which may be a consortium of ship-owners, or container operator has a complex task in ensuring full utilization of such equipment. Most shipowner consortia monitor and control their inventory of containers by using IT. The task is an international one and involves many parties to ensure strict control of the container when in their hands. Some method of container control is essential to ensure good utilization of the equipment to maximize revenue.

29 In some countries restrictions exist regarding the inland movement, particularly by road, of certain containers exceeding a certain dimension/ weight. These have restrained full development of the larger container, which has yet to appear in many markets. Restrictions by canal/rail are virtually non-existent in many countries, although by rail there may be some constraints on the use of high cube containers to 9 ft 6 in. (2.90 m).

30 Overall, a total quality service adds value to the ports/countries served.

Containerization is responsible for the growth in world industrial and consumer markets. It has brought great economic and social changes to many countries, especially less developed countries, newly industrialized countries and developing/emerging countries. Overall its efficiency, as manifest in multi-modalism of which the major leg is sea transport, is important to the continuing development of world trade. It has stimulated the growth of logistics in world markets. Countries not in the global container network seriously disadvantage their economic and social development.

16.9 Container bases

The function of a container base is to consolidate break-bulk cargoes (i.e. less than full container load consignments) into full container loads. The container base may be under the management of a consortium of ship container operators, a container operator(s) engaged in the freight-forwarding business, a consortium comprising freight forwarders, road hauliers, etc., and others engaged in such business, or a local port authority. It can be situated in the port itself, the port environs, or an industrial area which supports the facility by generating adequate quantities of containerized import/export traffic. The container base is served by road; larger bases often have rail facilities.

The role of the container base can be summarized as: to be a convenient point to assemble LCL cargo; to provide export packing and handling services for FCL and out-of-gauge cargo; to provide inland customs clearance local to customers' business premises; to provide totally secure storage and packing for empty and loaded containers together with cleaning and repair services; and to offer office accommodation for container operators, freight forwarders and other maritime service companies.

The object of a container base is to consolidate break-bulk cargoes destined for the same area/country into full container loads to provide a service in that area, particularly for the smaller importer/exporter. Consequently, the process of stuffing (loading) and unstuffing (unloading) containers is performed at a container base. Many of the larger container bases are inland clearance depots offering customs clearance facilities for import and export cargoes.

The major advantages of the container base are to provide a service to the importer/exporter situated in the base's hinterland and to relieve the port authority of local customs clearance of import/export cargoes. This latter advantage tends to reduce the problems of port congestion, i.e. containers awaiting clearance due to non-availability of documents, and enables the throughput of the container berth to be maximized. It speeds transit because no inordinate delay is usually experienced at the port, which in turn encourages the development of international trade. The number of container bases increases as container trades expand.

Development of the intermodal transportation network is likely to grow to include sea and air. Combination of these two transport methods offers an economical alternative, average journey times being cut by approximately 75% when compared with sea freight. Transport costs are reduced by up to 50% compared with pure air freight. Examples are listed in Table 16.9. A recent development in the development of the sea/air, and sea/land bridge is the Kingdom of Saudi Arabia Ports Authority.

Table 16.9 Sea versus air transport costs: example routes

By sea		By air	
From	*To*	*From*	*To*
Hong Kong	Sharjah	Sharjah	Frankfurt
Osaka	Vancouver	Vancouver	Frankfurt
Fukuoka	Vladivostok	Vladivostok	Leningrad
Valparaiso	Recife	Recife	Frankfurt
Caracas	Miami	Miami	Frankfurt

The air waybill and bill of lading documents are used. To aid faster development, compatible containers are provided which go directly from the ship into the aircraft, without the goods needing to be loaded. Boeing Jumbo air freighters, with a payload of up to 103 tons, and capable of conveying pallets and containers, are used. A number of other sea/air routes exist between the Middle East and North America, with the air transit commencing from the North American east coast ports.

16.10 International Convention for Safe Containers 1972 (CSC)

The International Convention for Safe Containers (CSC) was adopted in 1972 and entry into force in 1977. It has two objectives. One is to maintain a high level of safety of human life in the transport and handling of containers, by providing generally acceptable test procedures and related strength requirements. The other is to facilitate international transport of containers by providing uniform international safety regulations, equally applicable to all modes of surface transport. In this way, proliferation of divergent national safety regulations is avoided.

Convention requirements apply to the great majority of freight containers used internationally, an exception being to those designed specially for carriage by air. Because not all containers, van or reusable packing boxes were affected, the scope of the Convention is limited to containers of a prescribed minimum size with corner fittings – devices which permit handling, security or stacking. The Convention includes two Annexes: (a) Annex I includes regulations for testing, inspection, approval and maintenance of containers, and (b) Annex II covers structural safety requirements and tests, including details of test procedures.

Annex I sets out procedures whereby containers used in international transport must be safety-approved by an administration of a contracting state or by an organization acting on its behalf, such as a classification society.

The CSC has been subjected to four amendments as detailed below:

- *1981 amendments.* Adoption: 2 April 1981, entry into force: 1 December 1981 (tacit acceptance). The amendments provided transitional arrangements for plating of containers (which had to be completed by 1 January 1985), and for the marking of the date of the container's next examination by 1 January 1987.
- *1983 amendments.* Adoption: 13 June 1983, entry into force: 1 January 1984 (tacit acceptance). The amendments extended the interval between re-examination to 30 months and allowed a choice of container re-examination procedures between the original periodic examination scheme or a new continuous examination programme.
- *1991 amendments.* Adoption: 17 May 1991, entry into force: 1 January 1993 (tacit acceptance). The amendments concerned Annexes I and II of

the Convention. They included the addition of a new Chapter V to Annex I concerning regulations for the approval of modified containers.

- *1993 amendments*. Adoption: 4 November 1993 (by the IMO Assembly), entry into force: 12 months after being accepted by two-thirds of contracting parties. Status: seven acceptances had been received by 2004 (44 acceptances are needed for the amendments to enter into force). The amendments concern the information contained on the CSC approval plate and also amend some of the test loads and testing procedures required by the Convention.

All containers require the Australian Quarantine Certification (AQIS) for the container floor when operating Australasian trade. Most containers today are built to HM Customs TIR, UIC, Australian Floor, CSC and Lloyd's or other classification society approval.

17 Seaports

17.1 The role of seaports

The seaport is the gateway to trade, and governments and international agencies are focusing more attention on the development of their maritime terminals, particularly in efficiency, technology and strategic geographical location. The seaport links into a transport chain providing door-to-door service. Customs examination is undertaken at the consignor/consignee premises, or at the nearby container freight station/dry port/freight village/free trade zone. Today, the modern port is a thriving trading centre, as in Rotterdam, Dubai and Hamburg. These factors are accelerating change in seaports:

(a) Port privatization is growing, as governments globally contract out the ownership and management of their ports, particularly those dealing with containers. Privatization is associated with greater port efficiency, facilitated by IT, substantial investment in new construction and berth provision, and a target-driven management culture. Governments view the development of trade as key to their nation's wealth through improved social and economic standards and related investment. Associated legal issues relating to privatization of ports include these questions: Does the state have the authority to grant a concession? Can foreign-controlled companies own ports? Will the new operator be the port authority and, if so, will it have the necessary powers to control safety, access, dredging, pilotage and environment matters? Will the new operator be granted any incentives, such as tax breaks, foreign dividend repatriation? Will licences and/or permits be required and who will be responsible for obtaining them? What is the policy regarding existing and future employees? Political questions include: Who will set tariffs, establish berthing policy and decide the right to charge foreign currency? Will the state provide adequate facilities for access? Will foreign operators be discriminated against?
(b) The growth of trade from India, Brazil, China and Russia is driving port modernization. Over 75% of India's international trade by value and 95% by volume is carried by sea. Low port productivity and poor transport logistics serving the hinterland have resulted in 11% of landed cost being

nearly double the global average. Slow cargo turn-round times contribute to this low percentage. To redress this situation, the Indian government in 2005 approved a US$174.4 million project to expand facilities at the port of Jawaharlal Nehru, near Mumbai, western India. The two-phase project will increase the berth draught from 12.5 m to 15 m and provide a fifth container terminal. The overall annual capacity of the five terminals will rise from 2.5 million TEU to 7 million TEU. The third container berth was completed in 2006 and added 1.3 TEU million capacity. The fourth terminal commenced operation in 2010 and involved the construction of a 700 m quay line. A further 1,000 m container line will be completed in 2014 and increase capacity to 1.5 million TEU. An additional container terminal is being built – again involving foreign capital and operation – at Kandala port. As a result India's container capacity may rise from 6 million TEU to 15.2 million TEU by 2012.

Seven Chinese container ports feature in the top 20 container terminals. In China the construction of the 3 million TEU capacity of Yang Shan Ports continued in 2006 to provide spare capacity for the predicted traffic growth in the Yangtze river delta to cope with the strong growth in iron ore and coking coal shipments from Australia to serve the steel mills of China; an investment programme is under way in the Australian ports. Dalrymple port will increase its coal capacity to 80 million tonnes and iron ore to 80 million tonnes. Newcastle, Port Waratah, the world's largest coal port, plans to raise annual capacity from 89 million tonnes to 120 million tonnes.

(c) Containerization is a growth market with larger vessels of 10,000 TEU capacity, double the capacity recorded in 1988. This growth has had a profound impact on port container investment and accelerated the switch from bulk cargo shipment of reefer and fruit carriers to containers. Port capacity in Egypt increased with the commissioning of the Suez Canal Container Terminal in October 2004 with an annual capacity of 500,000 TEUs. In 2004 the Maasvlakte 2 berth plan for long-term development of Rotterdam is now well underway and should increase port land by 1,000 ha and port capacity by 100 million tons. In 2002 the port of Rotterdam installed three container cranes in the southern side of the Delta terminal, each having an outreach of 67.5 m, making them suitable for loading and unloading ships 22 containers wide. The lifting height is 40 m, with a maximum lifting capacity of 77 tons. Around 50% of Rotterdam European Combined Terminal is automated. In Antwerp a large container terminal was opened at Deurganckdok in 2005 and the port handled 6.06 million TEU in 2004.

(d) Logistics is driving port expansion, primarily of railborne services. Examples include the Darwin–Adelaide rail link, opened in 2003; double stack container trains commenced operation in 2004 between Shanghai and Beijing; and the ports of Rotterdam, Dunkerque, Antwerp, and Le Havre continue to develop international barge operations served by the extensive network of rivers and canals, particularly the river Rhine. This expansion applies to containers as well as bulk dry and wet commodities, including LNG specialized tonnage. The largest inland waterway port in Europe is located at Duisburg, some 200 km inland. Another established canal route is Le Havre to Gennevilliers.

(e) Liquefied natural gas is a market growing 8% annually. Currently the world fleet is 170 ships with 100 on order. Shipment was expected to rise from 10 million tonnes to 77 million tonnes in 2009. There are new terminals at US Louisiana and Rotterdam, the latter covering a 60 ha site which will become the most important port for LNG in north-west Europe. The larger tankers are capable of holding 250,000 m^3 of LNG. LNG carriers require either a berth in a conventional port or a sophisticated offshore installation where they can be attached to a pipe network.

(f) Many shipping economists think that as container tonnage size continues to increase above 10,000 TEU and beyond the range of ports of call will decline. In answer to this possibility mega tonnage shipowners may well select mega container parks which can generate the trade volume to fill the larger tonnage and may rely on more feeder services to serve the hub port. Hub ports require a wide range of frequent services, especially feeder services.

(g) The port of Dubai is an example of outstanding growth since the 1970s. In the mid 1970s Jebel Ali in Dubai in the United Arab Emirates (UAE) consisted of little except desert and the seashore. The completion of phase I of the Port of Jebel Ali expansion raised port capacity from 4 million TEU to 5.7 million TEU. The investment of US$237 million includes dredging the access channel to a depth of 17 m, widening it to 325 m and constructing five additional berths equipped with 14 post-Panamax gantry cranes. Dubai port has been transformed by new roads, distribution centres and industrial plant, all gathered round one of the world's busiest ports. It is the sixth largest container port in the world and in 2004 handled 6.42 million TEU. In the UAE there are 11 seaports and 6 airports, all with satellite links to 230 countries. Supporting this activity are Free Zones embracing the Hamriyoh water berths for petrochemical bulk handling and general cargo berths. The flag ship ports are Jebel Ali and Port Rashid. Jebel Ali has become the transhipment point for goods serving many other points in the Gulf and ports on the Indian subcontinent. The ports of Dubai have become a major global hub for the Gulf region, thriving from free zones attracting global investors and entrepreneurs.

(h) The Port of Singapore (PSA) (Table 17.1) remains a leading world port and primarily a transhipment hub port in the region. The PSA International Singapore state-owned and operated port has received continuous investment in facilities and IT in all areas of its business. The range of special expertise includes: bunkering; cargo and damage reports; cargo and shipbroking; container agency; commercial diving services (under-water repair); crew managers – member of IMEC; crew manning agents;

Table 17.1 Top 20 container terminals and their throughput, 2009, 2010 and 2011 (in TEUs and % change)

Port name	2009	2010	Preliminary figures for 2011	% change 2010–09	% change 2011–10
Shanghai	25,002,000	29,069,000	31,700,000	16.27	9.05
Singapore	25,866,400	28,431,100	29,937,700	9.92	5.30
Hong Kong	21,040,096	23,699,242	24,404,000	12.64	2.97
Shenzhen	18,250,100	22,509,700	22,569,800	23.34	0.27
Busan	11,954,861	14,194,334	16,184,706	18.73	14.02
Ningbo	10,502,800	13,144,000	14,686,200	25.15	11.73
Guangzhou	11,190,000	12,550,000	14,400,000	12.15	14.74
Qingdao	10,260,000	12,012,000	13,020,000	17.08	8.39
Dubai	11,124,082	11,600,000	13,000,000	4.28	12.07
Rotterdam	9,743,290	11,145,804	11,900,000	14.39	6.77
Tianjin	8,700,000	10,080,000	11,500,000	15.86	14.09
Kaohsiung	8,581,273	9,181,211	9,636,289	6.99	4.96
Port Klang	7,309,779	8,871,745	9,377,434	21.37	5.70
Hamburg	7,007,704	7,900,000	9,021,800	12.73	14.20
Antwerp	7,309,639	8,468,475	8,664,243	15.85	2.31
Los Angeles	6,748,994	7,831,902	7,940,511	16.05	1.39
Tanjung Pelepas	6,016,452	6,530,000	7,500,000	8.54	14.85
Xiamen	4,680,355	5,820,000	6,460,700	24.35	11.01
Dalian	4,552,000	5,242,000	6,400,000	15.16	22.09
Long Beach	5,067,597	6,263,399	6,061,085	23.60	–3.23
Total top 20	**220,907,422**	**254,543,912**	**274,364468**	**15.23**	**7.79**

Sources: UNCTAD secretariat and *Containerisation International Online* (May 2012).

Note: In this list Singapore does not include the port of Jurong.

Reproduced with the kind permission of the UNCTAD secretariat.

cruise liner agency; cruise liner operations management/transit/turn-round; flag registration; freight forwarding services; hub accounting and documentation services; Malacca Singapore Straits Advisory Services; off-port limit services; tanker and LNG agency; tramp and bulk agency; transhipment operations; P&I representative; project logistics transportation; ship repairs and dry dock supervision; warehousing and storage; and seamen's travel services.

(i) Innovation is a key factor in global port management. Recent examples of innovation are the ports of Hong Kong and Singapore which use sophisticated IT programs to help load and unload ships efficiently. To cope with their very high traffic volumes (Table 17.1), these ports have quayside cranes which can operate two cranes simultaneously. Operative over the stacks of containers, Singapore Pasir Panjang terminal has cranes able to stack containers nine-high. The cranes' productivity is higher than that of traditional cranes, because they are worked remotely by an operator who oversees several rather than one.

(j) The growth of the trading centre port concept embraces the free trade zone, the inland clearance depot, the freight village, container freight stations, Distriparks. This kind of port permits imported cargo to be assembled/processed/manufactured and re-exported or distributed locally. A good example is Rotterdam.

(k) The enlargement of the EU has brought increased trade to new member states. An example is Poland, which has constructed that country's largest container terminal, DCT Gdansk. It has an annual capacity of 500,000 TEU with one berth able to handle 160,000 TEU of ro/ro traffic. The port can handle the biggest vessels in the Baltic. Its hinterland serves Warsaw and the south of Poland. A new motorway serves the port, which has open sea access and ice-free operation. Poland's current leading container terminal is Baltic Container Terminal at Gdynia, which reports estimate had a throughput of over 400,000 TEU in 2012. Global ports operator Hutchison is investing in Gdynia.

(l) Transhipment is generating new port development. This is a key factor in port selection by the shipowner/shipper, with particular emphasis on port productivity and dedicated cargo transhipment services, as found in Port Said and the ports at either end of the Panama Canal.

(m) The privatization of ports is a growth market. A number of companies, e.g. PSA, DP World and Hutchison, which bring good commercial practice to the privatized port by bringing in investment and other features of the modern seaport, such as IT and fresh styles of management. Private investors are particularly interested in container terminals and their logistics. Prior to privatization many seaports were government/state-owned and lacked investment and suffered from poor management. Many governments now realize that ports are the gateway to their country's trade and, knowing that world seaborne trade doubles every 12–15 years, have become aware of the need to develop an efficient trade network offering to the shipper lower distribution cost, lower inventory, better cost control, shippers more competitive, new market opportunities, better return on capital through higher throughput of the berth and development of a multimodal port infrastructure.

(n) Compliance with the IMO, MARPOL, ISPS Code and EU standards.

(o) The ongoing development of the VTMS.

The development of ports globally is likely to continue, especially in less developed and developing countries – many involving global port concessionaries. Improved professional port management significantly contributes to ship and port productivity, which for the modern container port is automization, technology and up to date IT.

17.2 Correlation between 20 leading terminals and service operators

Table 17.1 shows UNCTAD statistics for the top 20 ports for world container traffic in the period 2009–2011. In 2011 these 20 terminals accounted for 52% of world container throughput, and all 20 reported traffic increases. In Europe, increases were Rotterdam 6.7% and Hamburg 14.2%. In the Far East, increases at Shanghai were 9%, Singapore 5.3% and Hong Kong 3%. Dubai in the Middle East increased by 12.07%, though the USA experienced slower growth, with Los Angeles 1.4% and Long Beach 3.2%. Note that the top six container ports are all in the Far East.

Table 17.2, which identifies the 20 leading liner operators, shows an increase of 10% in 2011, compared with the previous year. Reports suggest that the largest carriers, Maersk, MSC and CMA CGM, represented 30% of the world's total container carrying capacity. The biggest gain came from MOL, who showed an increase of 23%. The years since 2011 have seen more capacity-sharing arrangements by shipping lines that could rearrange the formation of Table 17.2. It is likely that other co-operative ventures will follow in the next few years as the latest generation of container tonnage above 10,000 TEU is launched.

A summary of factors contributing to the dominance and growth of the top 20 container terminals follows.

(a) Economies of scale through larger ships and bigger shipping companies.
(b) IT and other forms of up-to-date technology represent a high capital and operation cost commitment, which can be recouped in investment terms through volume business and economies of scale.
(c) Mega container operators rely heavily on the mega container terminal operators which have the synergy and capital resources to harmonize the latest port technology with the latest mega container tonnage.
(d) The market share of the leading 20 container ports and container shipowners will likely increase. Both are in a capital-intensive industry and require volume business to sustain their considerable investment, which in turn has created tendency towards mergers between container shipowners. The shipper continues to demand more 'value added' benefit both from the shipowner and port operator.
(e) Port management is now high-tech and requires proficient management. It can be argued that there is now a global management system. An example is Dubai DP World, which has 20 ports around the world. This produces economies of scale in many areas of its business, including in its procurement and cross-fertilization of experience and facilities relative to one port compared with another in different countries while having a common product (the container) and client (the shipper). The management strategy is to acquire/develop hub ports so that containers may pass through a central hub from which ships pick them up at smaller ports for

Table 17.2 The 20 leading service operators of container ships, 1 January 2012 (number of ships and total shipboard capacity deployed, in TEUs)

Ranking (TEU)	Operator	Country/territory	Number of vessels	Average vessel size	TEU	Share of world total, TEU (%)	Cumulated share, TEU (%)	Growth in TEU over 2011 (%)
1	Maersk Line	Denmark	453	4,646	2,104,825	11.8	11.8	15.6
2	MSC	Switzerland	432	4,688	2,025,179	11.3	23.1	14.9
3	CMA CGM Group	France	290	4,004	1,161,141	6.5	29.5	8.5
4	APL	Singapore	144	4,168	600,168	3.4	32.9	1.4
5	COSCO	China	145	4,304	624,055	3.5	36.4	10.3
6	Evergreen Line	China, Taiwan Province of	159	3,590	570,843	3.2	39.6	-3.9
7	Hapag-Lloyd Group	Germany	145	4,476	648,976	3.6	43.2	15.8
8	CSCL	China	124	4,493	557,168	3.1	46.3	20.9
9	Hanjin	Korea, Republic of	101	4,927	497,641	2.8	49.1	11.2
10	MOL	Japan	107	4,194	448,727	2.5	51.6	23.6
11	OOCL	China, Hong Kong SAR	88	4,516	397,433	2.2	53.8	6.1
12	Zim	Israel	82	3,708	304,074	1.7	55.5	8.0
13	HMM	Korea, Republic of	70	4,497	314,770	1.8	57.3	10.4
14	NYK	Japan	93	4,129	383,964	2.1	59.4	8.8
15	Yang Ming	China, Taiwan Province of	84	4,089	343,476	1.9	61.3	6.4
16	Hamburg Sud	Germany	99	3,728	369,057	2.1	63.4	10.0
17	K Line	Japan	79	4,336	342,572	1.9	65.3	-1.6
18	CSAV	Chile	85	4,095	348,035	1.9	67.2	-9.1
19	PIL	Singapore	104	2,279	236,978	1.3	68.6	-0.5
20	Wan Hai Lines Limited	China, Taiwan Province of	89	2,080	185,146	1.0	69.6	8.8
Total top 20 carriers			**2,973**	**3,979**	**12,464,228**	**69.6**	**69.6**	**10.0**
Others			7,093	768	5,445,054	30.3	30.4	10.7
World container ship fleet			**10,066**	**1,678**	**17,909,282**	**100.0**	**100.0**	**10.2**

Source: Reproduced with the kind permission of the UNCTAD Secretariat.

a variety of destinations: the hub and spoke system. Three other leading global port operators are APM, part of the Maersk shipping group, Hutchison Ports of Hong Kong and Singapore PSA.

(f)   The ongoing development of a logistic port infrastructure.

17.3 Container port automation

Port automation in container port operation now looks to dominate as fast rising container volumes and larger ships push nearly every operator towards greater technical sophistication. Container automation involves extra investment costs of building the facilities, an expense justified only where high labour costs, limited land supply and co-operative unions make them a sound investment.

An automated container berth is found at the port of Hamburg, Altenwerder berth. The crane operators unload the containers with their grabbing equipment. The boxes are then picked up by an automated crane and swung on to driverless trucks, which glide into position when needed. The containers are lifted and stacked, handled entirely by machine, until loaded on to the lorry or railway wagon to take them away. The container terminal is an example of how some operators drive down costs and drive up consistency by using computers and robots. Fast-rising container volumes and larger ships are pushing nearly every operator towards greater technical complexity.

17.4 The growth of Chinese dominance in international trade

The growth of Chinese dominance in international trade is likely to continue on three fronts: market share, growth in high-tech container ports and the continuing growth of the Chinese fleet.

The China Shipping Container Lines (CSCL) had 15 vessels in 1997 and by 2011 this number had increased to 144 owned or chartered ships. A total of eight 9,500 TEU container ships were launched in 2006/7. The example given shows Asia/Europe trade operational costs of a 9,000 TEU is 600 USD/TEU compared with 780/850 TEU for a 6,000 TEU. The CSCL's aim is to become a global carrier that provides a complete network of services around the world, better service and better cost control.

17.5 Floating terminals

Development of port infrastructure has sometimes been unable to keep pace with the need for increased shipment sizes and faster and more efficient cargo-handling operations. There is a need to develop floating stevedoring facilities to overcome existing port inadequacies, particularly to improve the world's dry bulk commodity fleet. In recent decades the standard size of Panamax bulk carrier has increased from 50,000–60,000 dwt to 80,000 dwt and Capesize vessels from 100,000–130,000 dwt to 170,000 dwt. This trend is likely to continue because increased carrier size reduces the unit cost of transport and building cost per dwt. Larger vessels require deeper draughts at the loading and discharge ports. Smaller vessels serve shallow-water ports, while geared vessels are largely utilized in ports with inadequate or limited port infrastructure. India, Indonesia and China have experienced low draught-restricted ports and as a consequence have incurred high ocean freight charges. In terms of dredging costs, environmental issues and maintenance of the channel or berth to the required depth the floating terminal provides a cost-effective alternative to the shore-based facility. Relatively 'low value' commodities, such as coal, iron ore and bauxite, represent the major part of the seaborne dry bulk trade. The freight component represents a substantial portion of the landed cost of these commodities. Any savings made immediately translate into significant gross value savings.

Stevedoring involves operations relating to loading (shore to ship) and discharging of cargo (ship to shore) in the course of import and export trades. The stevedoring service mainly consists of supplying equipment, facilities and labour for cargo handling operations to support basic shore-based facilities whilst the vessel is in the port or berthed alongside a quay.

The floating terminal provides a cost-effective alternative to upgrading or constructing shore-based facilities and can open new sea gateways in this critical logistical link in the international industrial supply chain.

Floating terminals extend to a wide range of products. Floating car parks in Gothenburg Port, Sweden, are a low draught/low air draught floating facility of two to four storeys high and which houses 300–500 cars. It is designed to classification rules and provides a solution to the parking problems of ports and crowded cities with a waterfront. Auto-mooring meets the demands of ferry operators for shorter turn-round times in port and lower labour costs. To avoid handling mooring ropes it is remotely operated from shore side or ship. Floating terminals suitable for shuttle services provide smooth and safe access for foot passengers, stores and other light cargoes. Link spans and shore ramps handle traffic between shore and ship, allowing ro/ro ferries to berth at quays otherwise unsuitable because of a ferry's size or shape, or for berths to be created where there have never been quays. Shore ramps, permanent or mobile, provide direct access to all ro/ro decks.

Link spans form a bridge between the quay and vessel, and are in various sizes and are regarded as shore to ship facilities. The following functions and advantages feature in link spans: guidance and energy absorption during the vessel's docking; balanced deadweight imposing low weight on the vessel and low energy consumption during operation; fast operation independent of tidal variations; integrated passenger gangways; integrated auto-mooring; integrated semi-automatic bunkering manifold; and integrated separate lane for provisions handling. Overall, the entire docking procedure is remotely controlled by telemetry from the vessel.

A concentration of floating grab cranes exists in Rotterdam, Amsterdam, Antwerp and the Mississippi. The ideal operational environment is a sheltered dockside terminal with associated handling and storage facilities. Most raw materials are directly transhipped from barge to ship, or vice versa, by means of floating cranes. A cheaper and more flexible alternative to floating cranes has been the construction of dedicated shore-based loading or unloading facilities. Transfer vessels, floating terminals, and catamaran type or floating transfer stations are some of the recent developments to solve the logistic bottlenecks often associated with the floating grab cranes.

The world's largest floating coal terminal, the Coe Clerici flagship *Bulk Wayuù*, loads an average of 150 vessels per year – approximately 7 million tonnes of coal – in the Maracaibo Lake in Venezuela. It loads 700,000 tonnes of coal monthly. The coal arrives in barges from the mine-loading site and is directly transferred to the oceangoing bulk by the *Bulk Wayuù*. The coal transfer operation is carried out at a daily average rate of 30,000 tonnes requiring four heavy duty cranes and three mobile shiploaders. A floating coal terminal has the same advantages as a shore-based facility but has lower costs and has negligible environmental impact.

The floating terminal provides storage, sampling blending and weighing of the raw commodity. The availability of buffer stock minimizes exposure to possible demurrage claims, where receiving industrial ports are affected by draught restriction: an example of a way of overcoming this limitation is the transfer vessel *Bulk Gulf* employed in the Arabia Gulf. Because of insufficient draught at the jetty, Gulf Industrial Investment Company had to import iron ore for its palletization plant in Bahrain in either Panamax or partially laden Capesize vessels. The utilization of smaller vessels resulted in high freight cost or dead freight charges. Today, iron ore is received in the largest Capesize vessels fully laden, which is lightened by the *Bulk Gulf* some 40 nautical miles from the coast at a daily rate exceeding 3,500 tonnes. Once lightened by about 6,500 tonnes, both the lightened vessel and the *Bulk Gulf* proceed to the receiving jetty, where the lightened iron ore is self-discharged directly into the shore – receiving hopper Klaveness's transfer vessel. Bakra is carrying out similar operations in Saudi Arabia.

Logistics and industrial supply chain management are changing cargo transhipment. An example is the handling of dry bulk materials using logistics offshore solutions and the floating transfer station (FTS) developed by Coe Clerici Logistics. This station represents the next generation of floating cranes and combines the flexibility of the floating crane with the utility of a floating terminal. With conveyors the cycle time of the cranes is noticeably reduced making cargo discharging more efficient. The FTS has inbuilt flexibility and is used for the transhipment of raw materials, steel products or containers. It is self-propelled for coastal trade and incorporates buffer storage and was developed to achieve balance between clients' operational requirements and minimizing the overall cost of transhipment and shipping.

The main improvements of the FTS include: it is less sensitive to adverse weather conditions due to its greater platform stability and better sea-keeping capability; there is no additional stockpile created on a floating crane so that transhipment operations are prevented during mooring/unmooring and waiting for the feeder barge, while the FTS avails itself of buffer storage and continues to work during such periods; the cargo-handling facility for dry bulk consists of a combination of grab cranes, hopper and conveyor belts, minimizing spillage and dust emission during material transfer operations; faster loading and discharging rate and increased throughput are achieved consequent on the shorter grab cycle to reach the hopper; the prospect of the FTS being fitted with mechanical sampling for material size and quality assessment and being self-propelled and having a buffer storage, the utilization rate of the FTS can be maximized using the spare idle time to transport the commodity. The FTS concept is operational at Bourgas in the Black Sea, Piombino in Tuscany (Italy), Mumbai on the west coast of India and a new operation in the Mediterranean.

Advantages of the floating terminal over shore-based infrastructure include: the floating terminal can be positioned at the closest possible site to a mine or to end user, reducing transportation cost to the minimum; investment cost of a floating facility is much lower when compared to dedicated shore berth facilities; the project implementation time for a floating facility is between work, dredging or land acquisition and as a consequence statutory permits/ governmental approval are more accessible; substantial investment is required to build and equip port infrastructure, whereas for a floating terminal only the service cost is paid; and the effects of potential business disruption risk, such as a change in government policies and laws, reduction of the level of imports or exports, *force majeure* events, etc., are reduced by a mobile floating terminal. The ability to relocate the facility and secure alternative employment limits the operation's exposure to unforeseen business disruptions.

The Bulk Irony development Tuscany operation since 2003 has yielded annual freight savings of US$2.5 million, realized by lightening the fully laden Panamax bulk carriers carrying coal and iron ore by 12,000 tonnes in less than half a day. This operation takes place close to the island of Elba. The Panamax vessel then proceeds to the Lucchini Group steelmill jetty at Piombino port, which has port draught availability of 11.8 m. The operation complies with the requirements of MARPOL and the IMO standards and EU requirements.

Benefits of floating stevedoring outlets are that they: supplement existing ports' resources requiring expansion and capacity enhancement in order to increase cargo throughput; overcome port congestion; provide an interim solution in order to assist the economic viability of a shore-based facility; overcome the physical restrictions on ports, such as draught and vessel size limitation, lack of space and modern facilities; and provide a more commercially viable alternative to a shore-based facility when the trade volume does not justify investment in a shore-based facility or the trade is short lived, as happens for mines with limited reserves.

17.6 Factors influencing the shipowner's choice of seaport

The strategy on which the shipowner determines the choice of seaport is increasingly complex. The strategy is assessed according to an overall logistics plan that considers cost, transit time and the value added benefits arising from using a particular seaport. No international consignment is assessed solely on a port-to-port basis, but is now based on the whole journey from point of origin to destination of which the sea leg forms a part. There is increasing innovation in international distribution, especially through the development of land bridge and sea/air bridge concepts. The shipper is constantly seeking rising standards and exercises greater influence over the shipowner than before, mainly by demanding continuing improvement in service quality. The international distribution structure is being continuously improved to meet this objective and is bringing markets closer together in transit time and in comparative cost. There must be synergy between the shippers' needs/aspirations and the service provided by the shipowner.

These are factors influencing the shipowner's choice of seaport:

(a) Ship specification determines the range of ports a vessel may call on her schedule. This includes draught, beam, length, capacity and the facilities ashore required to handle the cargo or passengers.

(b) Location of the port. A seaport situated on a shipping lane has distinct advantages by being on a trade route thereby requiring no detour, to gain access to/from the port, in shorter voyage time. Strategic geographical location is a key factor for container tonnage: the transhipment and feeder services' availability and their frequency. Examples are ports of Dubai, Rotterdam, Singapore and Colombo

(c) The level of traffic available from the port, including both import and export cargoes. This factor covers existing and potential levels of traffic and analysis of the traffic handled, which may be from transhipment, free trade zone, rail, road, inland waterway, etc. Rotterdam and Singapore are major trading and transhipment ports. The concept of the free trade zone (FTZ) is a major criterion in port selection. Over 950 FTZs exist worldwide. Sites are usually located in the port environs and are free of customs examination and duty until leaving the area. These facilities enable companies to import products/components for manufacture, assembly, processing, labelling and distribution to neighbouring markets or despatch to more distant markets, crossing international boundaries by sea, air, canal or overland. Examples are Rotterdam, Hamburg and Dubai.

(d) The profitability the shipowner will generate from the port. The shipowner usually favours the port with the greatest potential. Shipowners hope to rationalize their ports of call and develop the 'hub and spoke' system, the spoke being the feeder service to the hub. Examples include the ports of Dubai, Colombo, Singapore, Rotterdam, Hamburg and, long-term, Mumbai.

(e) The operating costs: port and cargo/passenger dues, berth charges, victualling, hire of handling equipment, pilotage, towage and passenger and cargo handling costs.

(f) Numerous efficiency factors exist when undertaking a comparison of ports. These include: port tariffs and local taxes; tonnage handled per gang hour and the cost; the number of TEUs handled per hour, segregating the dispute records; stacking area for containers and storage capacity for bulk cargoes and liquid cargoes, such as tank farms; and exchange-rate issues of whether a tariff is based on local currency or an exchange currency, e.g. the US dollar.

(g) Competition is a major factor involved in all the aspects (a) to (p) and requires analysis and evaluation to anticipate short- and long-term prospects and prepare for developments.

(h) Peripheral resources within the port and their pricing. These include bunkering, victualling, ship repair facilities, container cleansing, servicing and repair facilities, medical facilities, maintenance of cargo handling equipment, security resources, tanker cleaning, etc.; and availability and cost of freight forwarders, hauliers, port agents, customs, shipbrokers, ship agents, liner cargo agents, etc. An example is Singapore.

(i) The quality of port management: its calibre and the strategy and policies adopted and the degree of understanding between port users and the management. Continuous liaison between the trade and port management is essential to provide the necessary flexibility when dealing with problems. Port privatization and concessionaries are adding a new dimension to professional port management.

(j) Many ports remain unionized and the discerning ship operator examines industrial relations records and trends. Disruption to port operations adversely impacts on planning schedules, places at risk the shipper's loyalty to the service and increases costs to the shipowner.

(k) The degree of technology employed in the port's operation. This includes all areas of the business, such as berth planning, operation and allocation; the processing of cargo documentation; billing; cargo-handling operation; and communications. Examples include the ports of Hamburg, Singapore and Dubai.

(l) Allied to (k) is the computerized port operation. Most ports of the world have this facility. Many are called traffic management schemes enabling ships to enter and leave the seaport under an IT radar network. These schemes substantially improve ship safety and enable continuous access to and from the port in all weathers, including dense fog. A modern traffic scheme exists in the port of Rotterdam.

(m) The quality of facilities serving the port is a major consideration, particularly with multi-modalism, with its need for rail, road and inland waterway systems. Dunkerque and Rotterdam are connected to extensive inland waterway systems, and dedicated services are provided to integrate these systems with the shipping schedules. In Port Klang an inland rail depot is being provided. Such services are increasing globally. In other ports the land bridge has been developed. West and east coast North American ports link by container rail services to the sea leg from the Far East to Europe. In Dubai and Singapore a maritime/air service is provided from Japan/Far East to Frankfurt and the United States. This involves a sea leg to Singapore or Dubai, from where the containerized cargo is air freighted to Frankfurt and/or the United States.

Another area is the trading port such as Singapore and Rotterdam. Goods are received and processed/assembled and subsequently sold and distributed. The area is usually a free trade zone and may be described as a Distripark, as in Rotterdam.

(n) Innovation is a key factor in successful port management. It applies to all areas of the business, such as floating terminals and container port automation.

(o) Compliance with MARPOL–IMO–ISPS codes and EU legislation.

(p) The value added benefit offered to the shipowner/shipper: the benefit to the shipper/shipowner from using a particular port, which may have potential for market growth, better infrastructure, greater profitability, less competition, or a combination of these factors.

17.7 Relationship between ships and ports

The role of seaports is changing rapidly worldwide. More major ports are becoming trading centres with free trade zones. Port development is being driven by market research, and port authorities and shipowners are changing their working methods to meet changing market conditions. Governments are opting out of port management/state authority and encouraging port privatization/concessionaires. Their objects are to develop/attract highly professional port management and substantially improve foreign capital investment, raise port productivity and stimulate trade, thereby raising the economic and social development of a country's resources through port modernization. Ports are fast becoming trading and distribution centres that exploit the economics of well-configured facilities of road/rail/inland waterways, on which they rely. A good example is Rotterdam, regarded by many shippers/shipowners as the gateway to Europe. It relies heavily on rail and inland waterway networks, with some 70% of its business categorized as transhipment traffic. An increasing volume of its business passes through the Distriparks.

As a result of their cost-effective global networks shipowners are bringing markets closer together through quicker voyage times and faster transhipment. Less cargo is customs cleared at the port, the trend being either to place it into a free trade zone for processing or to assemble it in an industrial area. It is against this background that progressive ports grow by providing the infrastructure to meet market opportunities. Growth requires much planning and flexibility in operation.

Many seaports have sophisticated IT networks enabling shipowners/agents and vessels to evaluate and communicate details of cargo transhipment and stowage before a vessel arrives.

Port authorities work closely with the shipowners and trades. Market trends and changes in the international distribution of trade are analysed. More countries no longer ship indigenous products but add value to them, increasing product value and providing more freshly skilled local employment. An example is Malaysia, which used to export timber to Europe for furniture manufacture. Today, that country adds value to the product and manufactures furniture for Ikea and despatches the finished furniture range in flat-packed condition to Europe. The distribution structure changes to meet the higher valued cargo and often attracts more disciplined schedules and higher quality service than before. Emerging markets in the subcontinent and Far East fall into this category.

Seaport operations no longer are labour intensive by relying on casual workers for much of its stevedoring. Today, they all have high levels of skill and are more marketing focused and flexible in work practice and attitude. Port privatization and concessionaries are changing the structure of port operation from a labour intensive industry to a high-tech activity by embracing a limited number of technically qualified personnel operating/maintaining a wide range of high-tech equipment. This change needs a continuous training programme to support it. All activities of the business are evaluated to improve cargo throughput, raise efficiency and develop the business.

International transit is no longer a seaport-to-seaport operation. The entrepreneur views the international distribution network in its entirety and not as individual transport modes each with their own characteristics. Seaport authorities and shipowners are but two of the many components in the distribution network. Both play an important role in co-ordinating development of the overall network. The more integrated the overall transit becomes the more attractive to the market and cost-effective the operation, whether by sea/rail/sea, or by sea/air/road, becomes. IT enables cargo to be tracked throughout its transit.

Governments and international agencies play an important role in port development. Governments regard ports as the gateway to trade, and the efficiency and profile of their ports are critical in attracting business and in remaining competitive. Continuous utilization of assets ensures return on funding of capital investments.

The interface between the ship and seaport is dependent on the compatibility between vessels and the port infrastructure on a cost-effective basis and on management teams with shared ideals, levels of professionalism and objectives. The shipowner and port operator have market-driven objectives, and focus on training, continuous investment, and high-technology.

It is significant that Dubai and Singapore are primary trading centres in their regions. They are regarded as 'one-stop ports', because shipowners rely on feeder services to generate cargo. Dubai is strategically placed at the crossroads of Asia, Europe and Africa. Singapore is the trading hub of the Far East market. Manufacturing and trading companies around the world increasingly recognize that efficient production and marketing must match an equally efficient system for shipping goods from factory to customer. This is why Singapore and Dubai are the distribution hubs of their regions.

The development of sea/air transfers at Dubai and Singapore arises from a range of established air freight consolidators serving the airports, offering daily services to a range of destinations. Cargo transfer from ship's deck to aircraft take-off takes less than five hours, involving the minimum of customs formalities, e.g. only one customs document for the entire transhipment. Cargo handling facilities and services are continuous. The sea/air connection is fast, cost saving and a reliable mode of transhipment. Repacking services are provided for goods in transit. Substantial savings can be made in many subsidiary costs of sea freight, warehouse fees, handling, wharfage, haulage costs and insurance. The transit time of transhipment cargo is guaranteed and insured against delay.

Singapore's port is served by 700 shipping lines and linked to 300 ports worldwide. The airport has 52 airlines serving 110 cities in 54 countries. Dubai's international airport is served by 53 airlines serving over 100 destinations. Its new cargo complex is one of the world's most modern. The seaport is essentially a transhipment point served by over 100 shipping lines, with over 60% of import cargo destined for re-export; it handles over 20.6 million TEUs annually.

17.8 Port state control

The Port State Authority has been introduced to raise ship management standards and comply with the ISM code. The organization/authority covers inspection and targets ships failing to comply with the ISM Code and the Maritime Labour Convention in course of introduction. The port state control checks that visiting foreign ships comply with international conventions on standards of safety, pollution prevention and crew conditions. Inspection is usually undertaken by the port state control maritime government, which has a maritime agency employing qualified maritime personnel, such as marine surveyor, marine superintendent, etc., who carry out ship inspections, examine all records, and check that all certificates/documents are valid. Inspection extends to the crew and compliance with the STCW code. The code of practice is found in the Paris Memorandum of Understanding on Port State Control.

17.9 Port of Rotterdam Authority

The port of Rotterdam in the Netherlands is situated in the heart of the European market of 450 million consumers. With a wide range of logistical and industrial facilities it has excellent hinterland connections and enjoys ongoing investment. The port has the following features: (a) customer friendly; (b) geographically strategically located; (c) operational 24 hours per day, 7 days per week; (d) located directly in the deep waters of the North Sea; (e) optimum access at all times, even for the largest vessels; (f) over 500 liner services to 1,000 ports worldwide; (g) quick turn-round time; (h) excellent nautical safety record; (i) six competitive hinterland modalities – road, rail, barge, pipelines, air and short sea/feeder (hub and spoke system) and central hub for Europe for cargo from Far East and the Americas; (j) situated on the estuary of the rivers Rhine and Meuse, major European waterway networks serving Germany, Belgium, France, Switzerland and Austria; (k) regular services to 200 European ports; (l) extensive connections to the European rail network expanding from liberalization of European rail transport – an example, the Betuwe route, a dedicated freight railway line between Rotterdam and Germany; (m) centre of European distribution; (n) comprehensive range of facilities for handling and storage; (o) market leader in seaport ICT; and (p) leading oil and chemical clusters/centres.

The port operates over 500 scheduled sailings per week and the standard water depth is 75 ft. The port handles dry bulk, liquid bulk, (petro)chemicals, containers, roll on/roll off, break bulk, distribution and has a wide range of related industries including agri-products, recycling, shipbuilding, bunkering and ship repairs. Facilities include a soya bean and palm oil refinery centre. The port operates a comprehensive range of logistic services for the handling of cars, fruit and fruit juices, food, steel, forest products, project cargo and other general cargo.

Distribution is a key attraction to port users. Companies may use one of the many logistics service providers or opt to establish their own operations. The port has modern and extensive tank parks for all types of liquid bulk and state-of-the-art distribution facilities for general cargo. The port has three large-scale business parks for distribution that are solely dedicated to containerized cargo. These are called Distriparks and focus on both logistic service providers and businesses that want to establish their own European Distribution Centre (EDC). The modern industrial parks provide the necessary space for ware-housing and 'value adding' logistics, such as repackaging, labelling, assembly and quality control. The strategic location of the Distriparks, directly next to the container terminals, allows companies swiftly to obtain cargo for disposal. All modes of transport are in the direct vicinity. Each Distripark has its own characteristics. Distripark Eemhaven accommodates logistic service providers. Distripark Botlek offers specialized facilities for the storage and distribution of chemicals while Distripark Maasvlakte is the centre for large-scale pan-European distribution.

Rotterdam operates a unique Vessel Traffic Management Information System. The elaborate network of traffic control centres and radar stations enables ships to be monitored continuously from 60 km from the coastline to the port area. The Harbour Co-ordinating Centre (HCC) is responsible for the central co-ordination of shipping traffic. For dangerous and hazardous substances, shipping traffic reports to the HCC. The port complies fully with the IMO–ISPS code.

The port investment plan embraces the reclamation of 2,000 ha for a new industrial site. 'Maasvlakte 2' should create land for future development. Currently the port and industrial areas cover more than 10,000 ha, of which 5,000 ha have been allocated to business sites. IT is essential to the management of cargo passing through the port. The Port of Rotterdam Authority, customs and the port business community have together developed a port-wide community system that aims to offer all parties in the port the possibility to quickly, efficiently and accurately exchange IT data to optimize logistics and raise levels of customer service.

18 Multi-modalism

Global supply chain management and international logistics

Multi-modalism is the operation of a door-to-door/warehouse-to-warehouse service for the shipper and involves two or more forms of transport. The merchandise is conveyed in the same unitized form for the entire transit. This operation may also be described as inter-modalism.

A variety of forms of multi-modalism exists:

(a) Containerization – FCL/LCL/road/sea/rail.
(b) Land bridge via trailer/truck – road/sea/road.
(c) Land bridge via pallet/IATA container – road/sea/air/road.
(d) Trailer/truck – road/sea/road.
(e) Swapbody – road/rail/sea/road.

18.1 Factors in favour of multi-modalism

The international distribution network is becoming increasingly integrated, with multi-modalism playing a major role. The traditional seaport-to-seaport or airport-to-airport operation is no longer viable in today's competitive global market. The international entrepreneur, for example, designs a product in country A, assembles it in country B and sources its component units from countries C, D and E. It is an extensive IT-driven logistics operation that combines the activities of carriers, suppliers/manufacturers and the consignor and consignee. Its efficiency directly bears on its scale and market penetration. It is capital intensive, with a high level of utilization that helps fund the capital expenditure necessary. It is a global operation, subject to no time barriers or trade barriers that might impair its development. The more extensive the global multi-modal network, the greater the acceleration of world trade growth. Multi-modal facilities offer low-cost global distribution which, coupled with fast transit in dedicated services, brings markets closer together and bridges the gap between rich and poor nations. It particularly aids poorer nations to compete in world markets by having a low-cost labour force responsive to technical training and which therefore produces added value to the indigenous commodities they produce. The total product concept is being applied to global transport.

The key to the operation of multi-modalism is the non-vessel operating carrier (NVOC) or non-vessel operating common carrier (NVOCC). This vessel allows a container (FCL or LCL) movement or trailer transit. Carriers issue bills of lading for the carriage of goods on ships they neither own nor operate. The carrier is usually a freight forwarder issuing a 'house' bill of lading for a container or trailer movement, or, if the trailer movement is in the UK/Continental trade, a CMR consignment note. For example, a freight forwarder offers a groupage service using a nominated shipping line and infrastructure. The freight forwarder offers his own tariff for the service but buys from the shipping line at a box rate. NVOCC allows shipping companies to concentrate on ship management and the freight forwarder to use his expertise in marketing and cargo consolidation. This type of operation is particularly evident in the Far East, US, African and European trades. Good facilities enable effective operation.

All forms of multi-modalism involve a dedicated service, usually under non-vessel operating common carrier (NVOCC) or non-vessel operating carrier (NVOC) arrangements.

These factors outline why shippers favour multi-modalism:

(a) The service is reliable, frequent and competitively priced. Goods arrive within a scheduled programme involving various transport modes and carriers operating in different countries.

(b) In many companies it features as a global network either as a supply or retail chain. The former may comprise an assembly/process plant serving a local market whilst the latter involves the retailer buying the product in an overseas market. The retailer may be a shop, manufacturer, consumer, etc.

(c) Many companies operate their global schedules on the 'just in time' basis, requiring dedicated and integrated schedules within the shipper's warehouses and distribution arrangements. Multi-modalism is ideal for this system. Many companies regard it as a distribution arm of their business. IT strongly encourages multi-modalism as a global distribution system.

(d) The service is tailor-made for the trade/commodities it serves with its high-tech purpose-built equipment. This service provides adequate protection to the goods and arrival of the product in an excellent condition. The product may be refrigerated, fragile cargo or high-tech electrical goods.

(e) It has a high profile which is a good marketing ploy in the promotion of a company's business.

(f) Companies are looking for offshore manufacturing and sourcing outlets for their components and bulk cargo needs. Countries with an established multi-modal global network are especially well placed in such a selection process.

(g) The documentation requirements are minimal with the combined transport bill of lading involving one through rate and a common code of conditions.

(h) More companies are focusing on international distribution as an important element of their international business. Such companies identify two profit centres: the manufacture/supply of the product, and the channel of distribution from the supply point to the overseas destination.

(i) Companies using the multi-modal network as a supply chain are sensitive to transit times and their capital tied up in transit. Quicker transit times bring closer together the sourcing and assembly plants situated in different countries, thus reducing the amount of capital tied up in transport, which in turn reduces the company's requirements for working capital, a critical factor with the multinational enterprise.

(j) A key factor is the level of facilities provided by the NVOCC at the terminal warehouse. Many have purpose-built sorting facilities for specialist cargoes, as found in Distriparks and Districentres. The ports of Singapore, Rotterdam and Dubai are leaders in the trading port concept, offering Districentres, Distriparks and, in Rotterdam, European Distribution Centres are linked to a range of multi-modal outlets.

18.2 Rationale for the development of multi-modalism

Multi-modalism is closely aligned to containerization. It is a transit system extending beyond the port-to-port journey to land transport and facilities. Multi-modalism involves the integration of all transport modes requiring co-ordination of all carriers to provide a dedicated through-transit service. Maritime containers feature strongly in multi-modal operations. Shippers look to the carrier to provide the optimum route for their buyers at a competitive tariff and acceptable through-transit time. Emphasis is placed on technology, finance, market development, quality control, cargo tracking, paperless trading information systems, simplified documentation and a common code of carrier's liability.

Factors in the development of multi-modalism are these:

(a) Air/rail/sea/canal/ports operators are work closely together to remain competitive and to facilitate trade development. Examples include the sea/air bridge from Singapore and Dubai and the sea/rail land bridge in North America.

(b) Governments are taking more interest in the development of their nation's economies by encouraging a global trade strategy and providing the facilities to realise this objective. China is expanding its trade and has seven seaports among the leading 20 ports handling containers. India is also following this strategy, as is the UAE port in becoming the hub port of the Gulf region.

(c) The development of Distriparks, Districentres and free trade zones continues to grow.

(d) The documentation involving the carrier's liability and code of practice relative to multi-modalism is observed through the auspices of the International Chamber of Commerce and other international bodies.

(e) World markets are rapidly changing and the Far East is the fastest growing market. Facilities are continuously being improved at Singapore in an established industrial zone. Many companies use multi-modalism in their global distribution systems.

(f) Containerization technology continues to improve. The market is shifting from being product-driven to being consumer-led; the shipper is now the dominant factor in container design and development. GE SeaCo are market leaders in designing innovative containers to meet shippers' needs in a fast-changing logistically driven market. Examples are the general purpose container range – (a) pallet wide 20 × 2.4 × 8 ft 6 in.; (b) high cube pallet wide 20 × 2.4 × 9 ft 6 in.; (c) pallet wide 40 × 2.4 × 8 ft 6 in.; (d) high cube pallet wide 40 × 2.4 × 9 ft 6 in.; (e) high cube pallet wide 4.5 × 2.4 × 9 ft 6 in.; and (f) bulk pallet wide high cube pallet wide 20 × 2.4 × 9 ft 6 in. The high cube container fleet now totals 350,000 TEU, mostly in the transPacific and Caribbean trade, a high cube container being ideal for high cube and low weight ratio products. Palletization is popular as a cargo unit distributor and GE SeaCo has developed the Sea Cell container, whose use favours multi-modalism.

(g) Most mega container operators have customized logistics departments to advise their clients on providing the most cost-efficient method of distribution and optimal routes.

(h) The enlargement of the EU has resulted in a harmonized customs union which is a single market with no trade barriers to the entrepreneur. The EU favours a multinational transport network. The same obtains in the North American Free Trade Area (NAFTA), covering Canada, Mexico and the United States. Such trading areas, to favour multi-modalism, remove international boundaries as impediments to market-driven distribution centres operating the 'hub and spoke' system.

(i) Fast-moving consumer goods markets, such as those for foodstuffs and consumer products require sophisticated distribution networks. These involve efficient logistics operations, as found in the 'hub and spoke' system. Good logistics speed transit times, reduce inventory costs in terms of stock, provide a service to the consumer and mean quicker movement through the supply chain to the consumer. Cost-effectiveness is the key stimulant for multi-modalism.

(j) EDI and IT have revolutionized distribution logistics. It knows no international boundaries or time zones and provides ultimate control over performance monitoring of the goods. It can route and segregate cargoes.

Technology will have a major role in the continuing expansion of the multi-modal network. It is a major facilitator of world trade development.

18.3 Features of multi-modalism

Analysis of multi-modalism reveals that the objectives of the discriminating shipowner seeking to move unitized cargo are: to attain a high level of utilization of shipboard capacity; and to get a good return on capital employed to produce adequate profit. This profit can fund tonnage replacement featuring the latest technology. Formulation and execution of the multi-modal service requires all involved to work well with management. The main features of multi-modalism are these:

(a) It thrives on EDI and IT in a global network linking the shipper (exporter/ importer) and carrier at all stages of the transit.
(b) It provides a dedicated service, each operator/carrier committed to the schedule.
(c) It operates under NVOCC or NVOC arrangements.
(d) It develops and co-ordinates the best features of the individual transport modes to the advantage of the shipper.
(e) There is good utilization of multi-modal facilities which permits competitive door-to-door/warehouse-to-warehouse through-rates to be offered, thus exploiting economies of scale and yielding a favourable return on investment in transport.
(f) It encourages shippers to pre-book shipments' cubic capacity months in advance. This aids good planning and the tracking down availability of multi-modal resources. IT allows continuous dialogue between the shipper and carrier.
(g) An increasing number of operators provide logistics departments customized to clients' needs. This customization encourages closer co-operation between the shipper and operator, and ensures commitment to the market by user and provider of the multi-modal network.
(h) Good utilization of the structures encourages investment by the carrier and the shipper (exporter/importer). It generates a spirit of partnership and mutual understanding between the shipper and carrier.
(i) Multi-modalism is market-led. It brings buyer and seller closer and enables international business to flow unimpeded in a spirit of understanding and common ideals. The multi-modal system is an extension of the factory supply chain and features in manufacturers' plans for their international businesses. Continuous monitoring raises levels of efficiency and further exploits the levels of competitiveness, with advantages for exporter and importer. Monitoring occurs for packaging, transit times, documentation, stowage, EDI, IT and transport capacity utilization.
(j) Multi-modal services are competitive because they offer through-rates door to door/warehouse to warehouse. This process enables the shipper to monitor his international distribution costs and compare alternative route options on a value added basis. The container operator's function is to offer a complete package of services suited to the individual needs of customers. These services include storage of goods in bonded and free warehouses, stock administration, order processing, assembly, modification, packing, national and international distribution and customs documents.

(k) The International Chamber of Commerce and other international bodies permit a common code of liability and processing of documents. This has generated the confidence in which multi-modalism operates. Examples include the combined transport bill of lading, Incoterms 2010 – FCA, CPT, CIP, DDU, DDP – and ICC UCP No. 600, covering payment by documentary credits.

(l) Multi-modalism has generated a new climate in global international distribution. The market is at the centre of its operations so that a closer partnership obtains between the carrier and shipper. One area of especial concern is to maintain schedules and further improve them to reduce the time capital/goods are in transit and to speed up the distribution network. These moves will improve added value and provide greater profit and better service to the importer. This last point pertains to foodstuff and goods of a high-tech, low weight ratio. Today the shipper looks continuously to improve and develop/penetrate new markets; carriers are responding positively.

(m) Multi-modalism is giving new impetus to the development of seaports and airports. Port authorities worldwide are developing port enclaves through Districentres and free trade zones. They are also initiating and encouraging the port operators on whom they rely to develop and improve existing multi-modal networks and port facilities. Examples of such developments may be found in the ports of Singapore, Dubai, Klang and Rotterdam. Port authorities are co-ordinating activities and developing strategies on an unprecedented scale, particularly with regard to transhipment cargo and sea/air markets. Shipowners are commissioning larger container vessels in response to the growth of the one-stop port operation; they operate the hub and spoke system to improve overall transit time and gain increased efficiency. Table 18.1 provides examples of sea/air operations.

(n) Associated with (m) is the changing pattern of international distribution. It is less port to port and more multi-modalism, relieving port congestion and enabling development of ICD/dry ports, free trade zones and local import and export control customs arrangements. The creation of a new vision and enthusiasm at all levels in the supply chain, to develop and improve value added benefit, has motivated the exporter and importer using the network system.

(o) Market research is essential to any improvement. This requires continuous marketing of the network, including commodity specification, variation in tonnage flow relative to origin and destination, transit time, etc.

(p) Multi-modalism favours both large and small shipper operations as well as the full load or consolidated consignment.

(q) Multi-modalism develops new markets, improves product/commodity quality, raises loadability, reduces transit times, reduces packing and aids the growth of high-tech fast-moving consumer markets. It brings cultures and the international business world closer together in their objectives and ideology.

Table 18.1 Transit times (days)

Trade routes	Seaport	Markets	Sea	Tran-ship-ment	Air	Overall transit time
Japan–Europe	Singapore		8	2	1	11
South Korea–Europe	Singapore		9	2	1	12
Taiwan–Europe	Singapore	UK	5	2	1	8
Hong Kong–Europe	Singapore	France	4	2	1	7
Korea–Europe	Dubai	Belgium	17	2	1	20
Taiwan–Europe	Dubai	Italy	15	2	1	18
Hong Kong–Europe	Dubai	Germany	12	2	1	15
Singapore–Europe	Dubai	Switzerland	10	2	1	13
Mumbai–Europe	Dubai	Spain	7	2	1	10
Chennai–Europe	Dubai		9	2	1	12
Karachi–Europe	Dubai		7	2	1	10

There is no doubt that multi-modalism contributes to the changing pattern of international trade. It opens up countries with low labour costs to the industrialized Westernized markets of great buying power. Such industrialized high labour cost countries are increasingly reliant for the development of their global manufacturing business on production in low-cost markets and then employing multi-modalism to distribute their goods cost-effectively to high GDP markets. The shipper/manufacturer/supplier/exporter/importer has a new perspective on international distribution by formulating high-profile logistics departments responsible for global distribution operations. Multi-modalism is generating a globalized market place.

18.4 Multi-modalism strategy

The strategy to adopt with regard to multi-modalism is essentially market led and high-tech. Market growth provides the cash flow to fund the continuing investment. As the system develops, economies of scale reduce development costs, as experienced when IT was introduced. Qualified experienced personnel with complete commitment and a clear vision of the market's needs help assure multi-modalism's future.

Matters requiring special attention are these:

(a) Shippers and operators must study trading patterns to identify and develop new opportunities for multi-modalism. Existing systems must be evaluated and improved in line with changing trading patterns. Markets must be studied to discern opportunities. The lead time to introduce improvements must be short and fully co-ordinated with everyone concerned.
(b) Trading blocs such as ASEAN, the EU and NAFTA need to review the structure of their internal and external market multi-modal systems.

Countries with good multi-modal facilities have advantages when growing their external markets and improving their systems. The more closely trading blocs work together, the greater the benefits in market growth and distribution arrangements. The total distribution product requires a spirit of understanding to prevail among all parties involved.

(c) The markets of the Pacific Rim are a fast-growing and fast changing sector; they require particular attention for agents to benefit from the opportunities offered.

(d) The subcontinent, especially India, South Africa and China are also developing markets with many opportunities. Multi-modalism greatly facilitates the development of their global container networks.

(e) The role of swapbodies is fast developing, especially in European markets involving road/sea/rail. The implications of the value added benefit of the Channel Tunnel must also be considered.

(f) The airport and seaport – especially the latter – are key players in the development of multi-modalism. There is a need to develop inter-modal strategies and a strong interface with all concerned. Vision, flexibility and pragmatism are required at all levels of the businesses.

(g) Multi-modalism supports the 'just in time' strategy.

(h) Major shippers, particularly the multinationals, are companies with great investment resources and high-calibre personnel. They are leading the development of multi-modalism in many markets. However, the smaller shipper, who may be a subcontractor, is also benefiting from such developments.

During the next decades the multi-modal network will continue to expand globally, along with industrial and social economic development.

18.5 Global supply chain management and international logistics

Associated with multi-modalism is logistics. Shippers look increasingly at the total production and value added chain: in consequence shippers also look more closely at the logistics part of their business. The shipper, then, is no longer solely concerned with point-to-point operations, such as airport to airport or seaport to seaport, but is concerned with the total product along the whole length of the value added chain. This concern is closely associated with 'just in time' management techniques.

The aim of logistics is to get the right product at the right place at the right time. It is about the planning, organization, control and execution of the flow of goods from purchasing through production and distribution to the final customer and so satisfy the requirements of the market. In international distribution terms this is the process of warehousing, transporting and distributing goods and cargo, and the positioning of containers and/or equipment. It is an integrated and high-quality package of services which emphasize care of the cargo and provision of the most efficient co-ordination and management of the transport process. It comprises transport, forwarding, storage and distribution, and is adapted to the specific requirements of the product, the supplier and his buyers: it is a total package covering all links in the logistic chain, even though the different components can also be offered individually. It provides on a global basis production, warehousing, distribution and transport for shippers.

Maersk Line is a market leader in logistic services and provides a total transport service package suited to individual manufacturers and their customers' needs. Examples include high value consumer goods of wines and chemicals. Shippers are increasing their demand for supply chain visibility and especially connectivity with the parties involved. The current trend is towards global buying in the retail business and global selling of chemicals and high value consumer goods. Shippers require more extensive supply chain management services in addition to basic container shipping. Maersk Line (which merged with P&O Nedlloyd Logistics) is involved in managing the international supply train to supermarkets. Chemicals are progressively sold from stock holdings closer to the destination, rather than an order that has long delivery times. New concepts have been developed for some of the major petrochemical companies, including virtual warehousing and pipeline visibility.

P&O Nedlloyd operates a complete logistics system termed P&O Nedlloyd Flowmaster (Figure 18.1), which manages the flow of goods and information. It has these seven elements:

(a) *Merchandise,* in principle anything from computers to clothing and from wood products to chemicals.
(b) *Equipment,* embracing ships, aircraft, trucks and Districentres.
(c) *Loading units,* ranging from the management, loading and repair of containers, trailers and swapbodies to the manufacture of boxes and crates for vulnerable cargo.
(d) *Personnel:* specialists who use their experience to devise a solution to logistics problems.
(e) *Payment,* usually via IT.
(f) *Documents:* all the paperwork and file space necessary to comply with all formalities.
(g) *Information,* provided on paper, telephone or by IT covering, for example, location of goods and arrival time at a port or other facility.

P&O Nedlloyd had a sophisticated information system which is essential to the build-up of its networks and integrated transport. It can determine the most suitable place for a distribution centre, taking into account internal and external factors, such as road congestion, facilities and regional market developments.

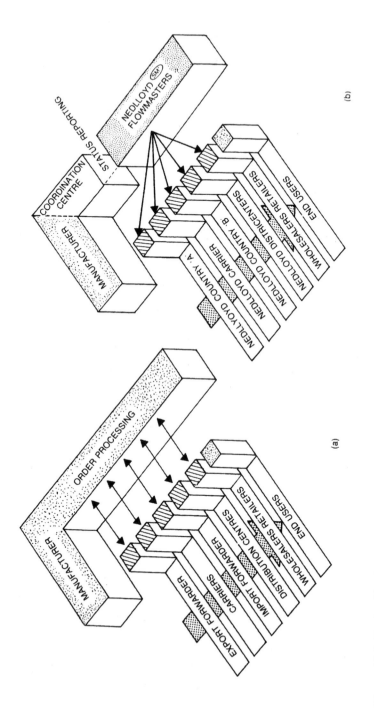

Figure 18.1 The Nedlloyd Flowmaster logistics system (a) how it usually is, (b) how it could be.

Source: Reproduced by kind permission of Nedlloyd.

The development of logistics networks has emerged as a result of these reasons:

(a) Companies increasingly concentrate on their 'core activities' of production and sales.
(b) Companies are tending to decentralize their production overseas.
(c) Product life cycle is shortening so that fast and flexible distribution is essential.

Companies are contracting out elements in distribution, such as physical transport and storage. Distribution can be more efficient and cheaper by employing a total transport company such as P&O Nedlloyd: the client knows that his cargo is supervised by one agency at all times door to door.

The example P&O Nedlloyd Flowmaster system is a total transport package suited to individual manufacturers and their customers' needs. The manufacturer despatches his products to a strategically located Districentre, which is in reality a warehouse. At this stage P&O Nedlloyd the operator assumes management and control of the operation. The benefits include:

(a) Customer services are designed and delivered to each client's individual needs.
(b) Fully integrated services are provided, i.e. distribution logistics are co-ordinated with procurement and production logistics.
(c) One-stop shopping is available for logistics services, most or all services being co-ordinated at one Districentre.
(d) Improved reliability means the client is better able to keep promises made to customers.
(e) Broader market research is available for clients using an established distribution system.
(f) There are shorter lead times for clients seeking to streamline their reaction times in the market place.
(g) Increased flexibility means that a client's market opportunities are not limited by distribution constraints.
(h) Lower logistics costs are possible with economies of scale.
(i) Manufacturers and their clients alike seek a higher satisfaction profile.
(j) Value added benefits are derived from such services.

When P&O Nedlloyd merged with the Maersk Line in 2006 it increased its global influence and expertise in global logistics and in international supply chain management. Logistics is a growth market of great complexity. It is aligned to supply chain management. It is widely used today by shippers large and small. The global logistics operator focuses on four key areas: (a) supply chain management – vendor management, information, communication – key benefits are reduced inventory levels; (b) delivery and customs clearance – inventory management, order picking, quality control, and security; (c) distribution management – quality control, consolidation and delivery and information; and (d) import logistics and outbound distribution – supply chain management, information and consolidation. The key results are hands-on control of delivery schedules and reduced shipment costs from the consolidation and integration of inwards and outwards distribution. The global logistic supply pipeline has nine basic elements from: (a) procurement of the order; (b) manufacturing of the product; (c) quality control; (d) handling/packaging; (e) despatch by sea/air; (f) delivery to logistic delivery centre; (g) handling/sorting; (h) delivery to the store; and (i) to the end consumer. Through all the phases IT enables complete transparency of all operations to all parties. The Districentres and Distriparks in the port of Rotterdam are important components in the logistics market. They are a main European gateway using multi-modalism. Major freight forwarders are logistic operators and work with containerized shipping companies. Readers are strongly recommended to read Alan Branch's book *Global Supply Chain Management and International Logistics* (Routledge, Abingdon, 2009).

19 The international consignment

A study of shipping needs to examine international consignment, suitability of transport modes, delivery trade terms of sale, and export documentation.

19.1 Factors to consider when evaluating suitability of transport mode(s) for an international consignment

These factors must be considered when evaluating suitability of transport mode(s) for an international consignment:

(a) Nature of the commodity, its dimensions/weight and whether any special facilities are required during transit. For example, livestock require special facilities; garments require a high cube container, unitized cargo requires pallets in a Sea Cell container, meat requires refrigerated accommodation.

(b) The nature and quantity of packaging and its costs. Air freight, flowers, medical supplies, containerization and through international multi-modalism road/rail services require less packaging.

(c) The extent to which the consignment aids cargo handling. For example, palletized cargo facilitates handling by forklift truck, while lightweight cartons are suited to containers. Awkwardly shaped packages may require special facilities and/or handling arrangements, and may be subject to a freight surcharge.

(d) Any statutory obligations imposed relative to the transit. Certain products need special facilities to be transported and in terminals. These restrict route/service and choice of transport mode. For example, the movement of meat/offal, etc. requires special facilities by the operator to ship it and inspection facilities at the import terminal. Statutory obligations can influence choice of packaging, as found for example in the Australian trade in its use of straw and case wood.

(e) Dangerous cargo. Regulations are stringent regarding its packaging, stowage, and mixture with other cargoes during stowage. These can restrict service/routing schedules.

(f) Terms of export contract. For example, they may stipulate that goods must be consigned to a national or specified shipping line/airline operator to save currency. This policy in shipping is called flag discrimination.

(g) Suitability of available transport services. For example, air freighters have limited capacity/weight/dimensions; weight restrictions may apply at a particular berth/shipping service, etc.

(h) The transit time and related urgency of consignment.

(i) The overall transport cost and evaluation of alternatives. Transport cost is an important item, and includes: rate; evaluation of transit time; cost of packaging; and convenience/reliability of services. Frequent service means less storage in warehouse; reduces risk of obsolescence of product; requires less working capital through less stockpiling, etc.; facilitates smoother production flow; and helps to produce better customer relations. Service, quality, risk of pilferage/ damage and the condition of goods on arrival are also relevant.

(j) Quantity of cargo available and period over which shipment is to be made. It is desirable to undertake a transport distribution analysis of the options available to decide which is the most favourable.

(k) Proximity and convenience, transport cost of the consignors/consignees, promises relative to the seaport/airport, and the local facilities available.

(l) The shipping routes available, their cost, other costs, range of facilities, quality of resources, general availability, overall efficiency and convenience of operation.

(m) Distribution services used by the exporter's competitors, and the strengths and weaknesses of the competition.

(n) Likely changes in the foreseeable future, such as provision of modern tonnage.

(o) The value added benefit derived by the shipper resulting from the service used. This can be evaluated in financial and perceived benefit terms. Value added is becoming increasingly important as companies focus attention on international distribution strategies and especially on logistics evaluation. Global logistics and international supply chain management influence choice of transport mode and carrier.

19.2 Delivery trade terms of sale and the export contract

The basis of the price quotation depends on correct interpretation of the delivery trade terms of sale and determine the following:

(a) The charges paid by the buyer and seller.

(b) Where delivery takes place in order to complete the export contract.

(c) When the property and risk pass from the seller to the buyer. The following examples are relevant:
   (i)   cash against documents – on payment;
   (ii) documents against payment – on payment;
   (iii) open account – payment by importer usually on receipt of merchandise;

    (iv)   documents against acceptance – on acceptance;
    (v)   letter of credit – on acceptance of documents by bank.

These financial aspects are vital in determining the delivery trade terms of sale.

   Here is information in a typical export contract in UK, though requirements can differ by individual country. The following may be found in an export sales contract, or a commercial export invoice:

(a) Seller's name and address.
(b) Buyer's name and address.
(c) Confirmation that the document constitutes a contract of the goods sold to an addressee and that he has bought according to the terms and conditions laid down.
(d) Number and quantity of goods precisely and fully described to avoid later misunderstanding or dispute. Details of batches, etc. and how they reconcile goods description with custom tariff specification.
(e) Price – in UK often quoted in sterling unless otherwise required. This may be US dollars or the buyer's currency. To counter inflation, particularly with long-term contracts, an escalation clause is usually included to reduce risk of sterling fluctuations. The tendency is to invoice in foreign currencies.
(f) Terms of delivery, e.g. CIP Kuala Lumpur, CIF Lagos, FOB Felixstowe, EXW Luton.
(g) Terms of payment, e.g. letter of credit, sight draft.
(h) Delivery date/shipment date or period.
(i) Methods of shipment FCL or LCL, e.g. container routing, ro/ro-trailer, air freight.
(j) Method of packing.
(k) Insurance – cover note terms.
(l) Import or export licence details or other instructions, such as certificate of origin, ATA carnet, etc.
(m) Shipping/freight/documentary requirements and/or details as found on the export cargo shipping instructions. Case marking instruction.
(n) Contract conditions, e.g. sale, delivery, performance (quality) of goods, arbitration, pre-shipment inspection (SGS), etc.
(o) Signature – copy for buyer to return signed to seller.

The Incoterms2010 are observed in 90% of world trade. The terms are included in most contracts for trade and provide guidance to all parties and individuals involved in the trade agreement or process. The 11 Incoterm rules are in two classes: rules for any mode or modes of transport, and rules for sea and inland waterway transport.

   The following is a brief commentary on the Incoterms, which use 'it' when referring to a person:

Incoterms2010 rules for any mode or modes of transport

EXW Ex Works

'Ex Works' means that the seller delivers when it places the goods at the disposal of the buyer at the seller's premises or at another named place (e.g. works, factory, warehouse, etc.). The seller does not need to load the goods on any collecting vehicle, nor does it need to clear the goods for export, where such clearance is applicable.

FCA Free Carrier

'Free Carrier' means that the seller delivers the goods to the carrier or another person nominated by the buyer at the seller's premises or another named place. The parties are well advised to specify as clearly as possible the point within the named place of delivery, as the risk passes to the buyer at that point.

CPT Carriage Paid To

'Carriage Paid To' means that the seller delivers the goods to the carrier or another person nominated by the seller at an agreed place (if any such place is agreed between parties) and that the seller must contract for and pay the costs of carriage necessary to bring the goods to the named place of destination.

CIP Carriage And Insurance Paid To

'Carriage and Insurance Paid to' means that the seller delivers the goods to the carrier or another person nominated by the seller at an agreed place (if any such place is agreed between parties) and that the seller must contract for and pay the costs of carriage necessary to bring the goods to the named place of destination. 'The seller also contracts for insurance cover against the buyer's risk of loss of or damage to the goods during the carriage. The buyer should note that under CIP the seller is required to obtain insurance only on minimum cover. Should the buyer wish to have more insurance protection, it will need either to agree as much expressly with the seller or to make its own extra insurance arrangements.'

DAT Delivered At Terminal

'Delivered at Terminal' means that the seller delivers when the goods, once unloaded from the arriving means of transport, are placed at the disposal of the buyer at a named terminal at the named port or place of destination. 'Terminal' includes a place, whether covered or not, such as a quay, warehouse, container yard or road, rail or air cargo terminal. The seller bears all risks involved in bringing the goods to and unloading them at the terminal at the named port or place of destination.

DAP Delivered At Place

'Delivered at Place' means that the seller delivers when the goods are placed at the disposal of the buyer on the arriving means of transport ready for unloading at the named place of destination. The seller bears all risks involved in bringing the goods to the named place.

DDP Delivered Duty Paid

'Delivered Duty Paid' means that the seller delivers the goods when the goods are placed at the disposal of the buyer, cleared for import on the arriving means of transport ready for unloading at the named place of destination. The seller bears all the costs and risks involved in bringing the goods to the place of destination and has an obligation to clear the goods not only for export but also for import, to pay any duty for both export and import and to carry out all customs formalities.

Incoterms2010 rules for sea and inland waterway transport

FAS Free Alongside Ship

'Free Alongside Ship' means that the seller delivers when the goods are placed alongside the vessel (e.g. on a quay or a barge) nominated by the buyer at the named port of shipment. The risk of loss of or damage to the goods passes when the goods are alongside the ship, and the buyer bears all costs from that moment onwards.

FOB Free On Board

'Free On Board' means that the seller delivers the goods on board the vessel nominated by the buyer at the named port of shipment or procures the goods already so delivered. The risk of loss or of damage to the goods passes when the goods are on board the vessel, and the buyer bears all costs from that moment onwards.

CFR Cost and Freight

'Cost and Freight' means that the seller delivers the goods on board the vessel or procures the goods already so delivered. The risk of loss of or damage to the goods passes when the goods are on board the vessel. The seller must contract for and pay the costs and freight necessary to bring the goods to the named port of destination.

CIF Cost, Insurance and Freight

'Cost, Insurance and Freight' means that the seller delivers the goods on board the vessel or procures the goods already so delivered. The risk of loss of or damage to the goods passes when the goods are on board the vessel. The seller must contract for and pay the costs and freight necessary to bring the goods to the named port of destination. 'The seller also contracts for insurance cover against the buyer's risk of loss of or damage to the goods during the carriage. The buyer should note that under CIF the seller is required to obtain insurance only on minimum cover. Should the buyer wish to have more insurance protection, it will need either to agree as much expressly with the seller or to make its own extra insurance arrangements.'

(Source: International Chamber of Commerce. The editor of *Branch's Elements of Shipping* acknowledges with appreciation ICC permission to reproduce the extracts of the Incoterms2010 given above. Readers are encouraged to purchase Incoterms2010, available from the ICC business bookstore at www.iccbooks.com, to gain full understanding of the rules.)

Incoterms2010 reflect the changes and development of international distribution during recent years, especially the development of combined transport, logistics and associated documentation, together with advances in EDI and IT. The liner cargo containerized market strongly favours the Incoterms2010 associated with combined transport.

Current practice is that, when the seller/exporter undertakes the main carriage arrangements, the operation is treated as a profit centre: the exporter is able to make some profit.

Other trade terms are these:

(a) *Loco.* This term includes in the price of goods cost of packaging and conveyance to the place named.
(b) *Turnkey.* This term arises where the export sales contract provides for the seller (exporter) to supply the goods and to launch/introduce them in the area defined by the importer. It involves the exporter providing the facility and setting it up on the site. This is common with large-scale engineering projects, where the seller is responsible for the entire operation through from construction to full operation. It is particularly common in the Emirate States, the former states of the Eastern bloc and in consortiums.

19.3 Receipt of export order

Efficient export management is required to process an export order. Six areas need especial attention: cash flow, administration, payment, insurance, risk areas and total cost. The following check points must be scrutinized when dealing with price list tendering. This should be done before dealing with the export order acceptance. These check points emphasize the importance of ensuring that all special costs are included which may enter into an export order as well a disciplined timescale to execute the order and ensure the goods arrive on time without damage:

(a) Adequately clear – technical and not commercial – description of goods using the Harmonized Commodity Description and Coding System (H/S).
(b) Goods specification – use metric.
(c) Quantities offered/available with delivery details including address and required arrival date.
(d) Price:
  (i)   amounts or per unit;
  (ii) currency;
  (iii) delivery terms which may involve part shipments over a scheduled period and/or transhipment – EXW, FCA, CPT, DAF – multi-modalism.
(e) Terms of payment, including provision for currency rate variation.
(f) Terms of delivery, ex stock, forward, etc. – relevant estimate.
(g) Transportation mode(s), e.g. container, air freight, sea freight, road haulier.
(h) Cargo insurance and perhaps credit insurance.
(i) Packaging and packing together with marking of the goods.
(j) Offer by pro-forma invoice.
(k) Identity of goods, country of origin and shipment.
(l) Specific documentation needs such as export licence, certificate of origin, preshipment certificate, etc.
(m) Tender bond to be followed by performance bond.

Prior to receipt of the indent/order a customer may need a pro-forma invoice, which is essential before a customer can open a bank credit in the supplier's favour. On receipt of the indent or order from the overseas client, the export marketing manager will check the specification and price in the order with the quotation together with its period of validity. Care must be taken to ensure the client is not trying to take advantage of an out-of-date quotation. For example, where the quotation was FOB, the export marketing manager must note whether the customer wishes the supplier to arrange for freight and insurance on his behalf. The method of payment will be noted and checked with quotation terms. For example, where payment is to be made under a documentary credit, the documents the banks require must be carefully noted. The required delivery date will be particularly noted; if the delivery date is given and the client has been obliged to obtain an import licence for the particular consignment, the date of expiry must be noted. Most exporters will deal only with overseas buyers able to negotiate using IT.

Given below is a receipt of order checklist:

(a) *Goods*
    (i)   quality;
    (ii) quantity;
    (iii) description.
(b) *Payment*
    (i)   price;
    (ii) method, i.e. letter of credit, open account, or documents against payment or acceptance;
    (iii) timescale;
    (iv) currency variation provision.
(c) *Shipment*
    (i)   mode of transport/route/transhipment and whether buyer requests any specific carrier;
    (ii) any constraints, i.e. packing/weighing/dimensions/statutory and route restrictions;
    (iii) timescale enforcing despatch and arrival date;
    (iv) any marks, i.e. special marking on cases/cartons to identify them.
(d) *Additional requirements*
    (i)   insurance;
    (ii) preshipment inspection;
    (iii) documentation such as certificate of origin;
    (iv) specific packing – see item (c)(ii);
    (v)   commissions or discount;
    (vi) details of agent handling buyer's order and likely specific request.
(e) *Comparison with quotation*

A pro-forma invoice is a document similar to a sales invoice except that it is headed 'pro-forma'. It is not a record of sales effected but a representation of a sales invoice issued prior to the sale. The pro-forma invoice contains all relevant details, e.g. full description of goods, packing specification, price of goods with period of validity, cost of cases, and where relevant cost of freight and insurance. It is particularly used for quotations to customers and for submission to various authorities. Terms of payment are always shown but it may not be possible to give shipping marks until a firm order is received. When used as a quotation the pro-forma invoice constitutes a binding offer of the goods covered by it, and the price and conditions shown. The pro-forma invoice is mainly associated with LDCs and countries with exchange control regulations requiring central government/bank approval to confirm monies will be available to fund the goods to be imported.

As soon as the exporter receives the letter of credit, he should check it against his pro-forma invoice to ensure both documents agree with each other. Usually, the contract will be in a more detailed form than the letter of credit, but it is important the exporter should be able to prepare his documents complying with both the contract and the credit. The exporters must be fully aware of the terms and provisions of UCP 600. For general guidance this checklist should be followed by an exporter:

1 The terms of the letter of credit which may be revocable or irrevocable.
2 The name and address of the exporter (beneficiary).
3 The amount of the credit which may be in sterling or a foreign currency.
4 The name and address of the importer (accreditor).
5 The name of the party on whom the bills of exchange are to be drawn, and whether they are to be at sight or of a particular tenor.
6 The terms of the contract and shipment (i.e. whether EXW, FCA, CIF, CPT, CIP, and so on).
7 A brief description of the goods covered by the credit. Too much detail may create errors which can cause delay.
8 Precise instructions as to the documents against which payment is to be made.
9 Details of shipment including whether any transhipment is allowed, data on the latest shipment date and details of port of departure and destination should be recorded.
10 Whether the credit is available for one or more shipments.
11 The expiry date.

It is important to check the reverse side of the letter of credit and any attachments to it that may influence the credit as to further additional terms. Ideally both the seller (exporter) and the buyer (importer) should endeavour to make the credit terms as simple as practicable.

When the seller (exporter) is uncertain of just how much of the credit he will draw, arrangements should be made with the buyer (importer) to have the value of the documentary letter of credit prefixed by the word 'about'. This will permit up to a 10% margin over or under the amount specified. The word 'about' preceding the quantity of goods also allows a 10% margin in the quantity to be shipped. Alternatively the documentary letter of credit may specify a 'tolerance' – such as 7.5% to 5% more or less – by which the seller (exporter) should be guided.

Documentation will usually involve the 'clean' on-board combined transport multi-modal bill of lading. For international rail movements the CIM consignment note is required; for international road haulage transit this is the CMR consignment note.

Multi-modalism means it is essential the shipper pre-books the consignment throughout the transit from warehouse to warehouse via a dedicated service. The booking is generally processed by major shippers to the first carrier, and involves booking cargo space for the entire transit, e.g. by rail/ship/rail, and for any supply of a specialist container type. Pre-planning for international distribution helps ensure delivery dates are met.

19.4 Progress of export order and checklist

In the processing of an export consignment there are up to four contracts to execute. These include the export sales contract, the contract of carriage, the financial contract and the contract of cargo insurance. All these have to be considered while processing the export consignment.

To ensure the complex procedure of preparing the goods, packing, forwarding, shipping, insurance, customs clearance, invoice and collecting payment do not go wrong, it is suggested a checklist or progress sheet be prepared for each export order. A suggested version follows, though there are various ways of processing a given export order:

1 Manufacturer receives, in export sales office, initial export enquiry.
2 Costing department calculates approximate total weight/volume of the finished packed goods.
3 Details of weight/measurement of goods submitted to shipping department to obtain insurance/freight rates to destination delivery point. This involves obtaining quotations from freight forwarders and checking out documentation required such as export licence, certificate of origin, etc.
4 Costing department completes non-transport calculations.
5 Credit controller obtains satisfactory status report on potential customer.
6 Insurance/freight quotation submitted to costing department to formulate overall quotation.
7 Formal quotation prepared including currency, terms of delivery (Incoterms2010) and required terms of payment. If, for example, it is CPT, CIP, it includes price of goods and related transportation. Many exporters regard the two elements as two separate profit centres and place a mark up on each and formulate them into one overall quotation.
8 Quotation sent to prospective overseas buyer. It includes a validity clause.
9 E-mail or fax sent asking the buyer to expedite the reply.
10 Purchase order (offer) received.
11 Export sales office checks out stock availability/manufacturing lead time/delivery schedules.
12 Export sales office rechecks credit status report. Any change from item (5).
13 Agree to accept order only if customer will pay by confirmed letter of credit.
14 Export sales office raises order acknowledgement (acceptance) to establish sales contract.
15 Export sales office despatches acknowledgement to buyer. Note that if the seller is not being paid by letter of credit, pass to item (23).
16 Await receipt of letter of credit if item (13) applies.
17 Letter of credit received.
18 Export sales office check out whether all the conditions can be met.
19 Export sales office request amendment/extension to letter of credit.
20 Export sales office awaits amendment/extension to letter of credit.

21 Export sales office receives amendment/extension to letter of credit and checks that all the conditions have now been met.

22 Export sales office confirms all the conditions have now been met and despatches acknowledgement to the buyer.

23 Export sales office issues authority for the goods to be manufactured and packed. The task of monitoring progress of manufacture of goods/packaging is handled by the Logistics Shipping Department which maintains close liaison with the Production Department to ensure the despatch date is achieved within the timescale defined in the letter of credit/export or import licence/cargo space booked on carrier's flight/sailing/trailer.

24 Logistics Shipping Department establishes total weight/measurement of packed goods and has the completed order checked out.

25 Logistics Shipping Department raises shipping documents and export cargo shipping instructions (ECSI) noting any letter of credit conditions including any pre-shipment inspection obligations such as SGS.

26 Pre-shipment inspection completed (if applicable) and clean report of findings issued. Goods despatched to airport/seaport/inland clearance depot, etc., in accordance with the terms of sale Incoterms and freight forwarder's/buyer's/buyer's agent's instructions. Documents to be provided include BL/AWB/CMR consignment note/packing list/export licence/certificate of origin/certificate of insurance/commercial invoice, etc. The range and nature of the documents will vary by commodity/terms of sale/destination country. The seller provides these. The task of processing cargo through customs is likely to be undertaken by the freight forwarder, unless the seller has the goods cleared under a local export control arrangement, in which case the seller handles all the export documentation and customs clearance arrangements.

27 Await shipping documents.

28 Shipping documents received confirming goods despatched on specified flight/sailing/trailer – buyer informed.

29 Documents checked by Logistics Shipping Department – any errors found and corrected documents requested.

30 Receive corrected documents.

31 Logistics Shipping Department collates documents and letter of credit.

32 Seller raises bill of exchange signed by a director.

33 Logistics Shipping Department checks all documents against letter of credit.

34 Logistics Shipping Department presents all documents to the bank within agreed timescale.

35 Seller awaits payment or acceptance of the bill of exchange.

36 Seller receives funds from the bank. If the funds are not in the seller's currency (e.g. sterling), the exporter should sell at spot or place against for which finance should have been arranged under (15).

37 Legal requirements followed through such as VAT.

The above arrangements vary by circumstances and most companies use IT in their export consignment processing. Critical areas of variation are in the terms of payment, the method of carriage and the customs arrangements. Remember: the seller is responsible for providing the buyer with all the requisite documents to enable the goods to be processed/imported through customs in the destination country. The seller must check these. The overriding factors are: adherence to the timescale to ensure the goods arrive on the agreed date; and ensuring that all documents are in order to enable the consignment to arrive in a quality condition.

Most companies worldwide use IT when processing their export consignments. Export Master is a long established integrated export and management and administration system. These are the important documents involved:

(a) *Consular invoice.* A consular invoice may have to be prepared where the goods are consigned to countries enforcing *ad valorem* import duties (*ad valorem* tax is levied in proportion to the estimated value of the goods). Such invoices have to be certified by the consul of the country to which the goods are consigned either at the place from which the goods are despatched, which is usual, or at the port/airport/ICD of departure.

(b) *Export invoice.* The exporter completes an export invoice which embodies the date, name of the consignee, quantity and description of the goods, marks and measurements of packages, cost of the goods, packing, carriage, freight, postage, insurance premiums, etc. The actual form of invoice varies with the method of price quotation.

(c) *The invoice.* The invoice is a document rendered by one person to another in regard of goods which have been sold. The invoice is not necessarily a contract of sale. It may form a contract of sale if it is in writing containing all the material terms. On the other hand it may not be a complete memorandum of the contract of sale and therefore evidence may be given to vary the contract which is inferred from it.

(d) *Certificate of origin.* Certificates of origin specify the nature of quantity/value of the goods, etc, together with their place of manufacture. Some countries require such a document, often to simplify their customs duties. Additionally they are needed when merchandise is imported to a country that allows preferential duties on British goods, owing to trade agreements.

(e) *Contract of affreightment.* This is found in the bill of lading/CIM/CMR documentation.

(f) *Marine insurance policy/certificate.* This acknowledges that the cargo value as declared has been insured for the maritime transit.

(g) *Charter party.* This involves hire/charter of a ship.

(h) *Letter of credit.* This document enables the beneficiary to obtain payment of funds from the issuer, or from an agent if the insurer complies with certain conditions laid down in the credit. This document may be a commercial credit. It may be issued to finance international trade involving shipments of goods between countries, or non-commercial or personal credits for the use of individuals, e.g. consular letters of credit issued to tourists and holidaymakers. The commercial credit may be a bank credit, i.e. drawn on an issuing bank undertaking due payment, or non-bank credit, which although issued through a bank does not carry any bank undertaking. The letter of credit may either be revocable or irrevocable.

(i) *Mate's receipt.* Sometimes issued in lieu of a bill of lading to confirm cargo has been placed on board a ship pending issue of bill of lading.

(j) *Dock receipt.* Sometimes issued by the port authority to confirm receipt of cargo on the quay/warehouse pending shipment.

(k) *Letters of hypothecation.* Banker's documents outlining conditions under which the international transaction will be executed on the exporter's behalf, who will have given certain pledges to his banker.

(l) *Packing list.* A document providing a list of the contents of a package/consignment(s).

(m) *ATA carnet.* An international customs document to cover the temporary export of certain goods (commercial samples and exhibits for international trade fairs abroad and professional equipment) to countries party to the ATA Convention and cover reimport of such goods.

(n) *Pre-shipment inspection certificates.* An increasing number of shippers and various organizations/authorities/governments in countries throughout the world insist that the goods are inspected for quality, the quantity being exported and the price(s) proposed and market price(s), and the exchange rate at the time of shipment. The organizations undertaking such work – which can extend to transhipment en route – are the Société Générale de Surveillance (SGS) and classification societies.

(o) *Certificate of shipment.* The FIATA forwarder's certificate of receipt (RCR) and forwarding certificate of transport (FCT) are becoming increasingly accepted in the shipping trade as the recognizable documents confirming receipt of the goods. These documents are usually issued under FCA Free Carrier Incoterms involving multi-modal transport operations. Alternatively, they may be EXW (ex works). In such situations the freight forwarder would be acting as principal or road carrier.

(p) *Performance certificates.* This customs requirement involves GSP, EUR 1.

Usually there are three restraints requiring to be dealt with before goods can be released to customers by the shipowner or his agent as detailed below:

(i) Clearance by customs or any other relevant statutory body, including the port health authority or Department for Environment, Food and Rural Affairs.

(ii) Surrender of an original bill of lading correctly endorsed, unless a waybill has been issued.

(iii) Payment of outstanding charges including freight, customs duty and VAT.

In countries and ports where the consignment is delivered into and shipped out of a 'freeport' some of the above requirements may not be applicable. Shipowners issue an arrival notification form (ANF) to the party receiving the goods advising of goods coming forward for delivery. This ensures smooth delivery and enables the recipient to pre-plan all the necessary arrangements, such as customs clearance documentation, collection, duty payment, etc.

19.5 Business-to-Business (B2B) and Business-to-Consumer (B2C) customers

During recent years, greatly facilitated by IT (and e-commerce), there has been an enormous increase in Business-to-Business (B2B) and Business to Consumer (B2C). To the exporter, they are an efficient means to develop an international portfolio; they particularly eliminate the intermediary, with significant cost savings, and accelerate decision-making. They strongly encourage a logistic and IT focused approach to business. They favour both the MNIs and SEMs and generate business using IT.

The Business to Business IT (e-commerce) market is well established. It enables the international sales teams to concentrate on selling, which requires face-to-face meeting, and the administration on sales using IT. It is a low cost method of exporting and avoids provision of multiple copies of catalogues. B2B emerges from good relationships between exporter and importer.

The Business-to-Consumer is distinguished from B2B by the nature of the customer and how that customer uses the product. In business marketing international customers are organizations such as businesses, government bodies, and institutions such as hospitals. The Business-to-Consumer market is increasingly dominated by IT sales, such as of cars and accessories, home appliances and accessories, books, financial services, tourism, transport and food products. It is of increasing importance in the EU market and OECD countries.

B2B and B2C, to thrive, require a well maintained website. In reality, most organisations employ an IT manager to cope with the evolving technology, and have a website supervised by well trained and proficient personnel who can handle global enquiries whatever the time locally. The website in the language of the buyer focuses on individual markets. It is often prudent for a business to have a local contact in distant markets, e.g. an agent/distributor/ franchisee who can demonstrate the product to the importer.

Consumer and business markets differ in their nature, market demand, import behaviour, exporter/importer relationships, buying power, and market environmental influences, such as legal, technical, cultural, political, exchange control and economic. The country/company credit rating should be checked prior to conducting any business. Readers wishing to know more about the technique of exporting and importing are recommended to read these two books: Alan Branch, *Export Practice and Management*, 5th edn (2007), www.thomsonlearning.co.uk/branch5; Alan Branch, *International Purchasing and Management* (2001), www.thomsonlearning.co.uk.

20 Information technology and electronic data interchange

20.1 Introduction

Information technology (IT) now dominates communications worldwide. IT is especially dominant in global trade in service and product manufacturing industries, in the processing of the export consignment, the international banking payment systems and global distribution including the terminal, carriers, customs, cargo status, stowage, data bank, planning, etc. IT's relentless progress recognizes no languages, cultures or time zone barriers. IT has shrunk the world, bringing markets closer together.

Shipping and trade are at the forefront of these changes, shipping having a central role in the development of global trade. The more sophisticated the maritime network in terms of efficiency and value added network (VAN), the greater is acceleration in trade development. Shipping is particularly important to the global container network. Shipping cannot develop in isolation because it is part of the international network of business. IT enables all constituents of international business to communicate in a user-friendly, harmonious and completely integrated manner to produce dedicated services and procedures.

The effect of the rapid advances in IT on competition in the changing international market place and the way in which businesses are run is inarguable. One of the best examples is provided by the European Union.

A main factor justifying the need for a European single market and for effective economic integration of millions of people and many nations has been the estimated cost to industry of a fragmented market. This cost was £160 billion a few years ago and was made up of: expensive national customs-related procedures; billions of pounds of losses due to the inefficiencies created by varying product standards, especially in the electronics and telecommunications industries; and high administrative costs incurred throughout the whole trading chain, especially by small companies, discouraging them from seeking trans-border business. An EU survey concluded that differing national standards and regulations are the principal barriers to EU trade. There is now pressure to develop international standards, especially in communications, IT and product data. Companies can now treat the EU as a single market, an acceptance stimulated by paperless trading, IT and transnational logistics.

One example of EU commitment to IT is the launch of the Galileo programme. It involves an array of 30 satellites covering the entire planet, with local ground transmitters to provide universal services available to all users in any location including sheltered areas (tunnels, underground car parks, etc.). The Galileo programme has been operational since 2008 and is managed by the European Space Agency. It provides the EU with a system of global cover over which it has full control and which meets its accuracy, reliability and security requirements. It has a tool essential to its transport development policy. For example, Galileo allows instant trace of goods carried on the railway network, facilitating a 'just in time' policy. Galileo permits accurate positioning of ships carrying dangerous cargoes and provides maritime authorities with the means to ensure safe navigation, particularly in areas of high traffic density, such as the Ushant TSS. Galileo has revolutionized transport facilitating logistic development and professional management.

The same pressures driving European integration are behind the development of other regional trading areas, notably the North America Free Trade Area (NAFTA). Others under development include Asia – the Association of South East Asian Nations (ASEAN), the Asia Pacific Economic Co-operation (APEC) forum objective to create a grand goal of free trade in the Pacific by 2020, and SAFTA, featuring seven countries including India, Pakistan and Sri Lanka; Africa – the Economic Community of West African States (ECOWAS); the Caribbean – the Caribbean Community and Common Market (CARICOM). South America, Africa and Australasia are following. The objective for all of them is to generate a powerful regional economic base and to strengthen their competitive position. IT, a global high-tech distribution network and efficient working practices are important.

Complex products are rarely designed, manufactured and maintained at a single location or by a single company. Cross-border collaborative product development and global economic integration are increasingly necessary for major companies if they are to remain competitive. This is particularly evident in the European Union and Far East, especially India and China. Seaports such as Singapore and Rotterdam have developed the Distripark concept to assemble, process and distribute companies' products to serve local markets and develop a regional network.

Worldwide governmental commitment and co-operation are essential if the rapid advances in IT are to create new markets, eliminate trade barriers and improve procedures and working practices. International agreement is required to develop global procedures and standards, as well as to reduce non-tariff barriers and accelerate trade flows. WTO and Incoterms already recognize this. Inevitably affecting national economies is the ability of major industries to choose different parts of the world in which to manufacture, assemble and trade in their products.

Electronic commerce follows on from worldwide use of IT in business. Traders worldwide have to compete in a global environment in which the availability of technology and IT means that organizations will increasingly trade with other IT users and systems, both of which have to be open and be based on international standards.

Electronic commerce (e-commerce) represents a paradigm shift in the way in which business operates. A further example is 'concurrent engineering', the process whereby individual components of a particular product can be manufactured simultaneously in different locations and often in different countries all as part of a single process. This requires organizations to use a common digital base in real time for the design, development, manufacture, distribution and servicing of products. It is termed CAL – Continuous Acquisition and Life Cycle Support – and IT is crucial to these developments. There is now the 'virtual enterprise' whereby organizations integrate their whole business process, including all independent component companies and services, and so create a single trading entity. The key to the success of this operation of out-sourcing component units globally is the development of multi-modalism, global logistics, international supply chain management and the role of IT in international distribution.

IT allows 'the application-to-application exchange of computer-held information in a structural format via a telecommunications network'. This means that data passes from one computer into another computer without printing or manual manipulation. It requires structured data – normally in a neutral data standard – to allow further processing. It permits paperless trading without boundaries or time zones. This is demonstrated by Bolero.

World trade is changing into an increasingly global supply chain. Many companies source components in one part of the world, assemble them in another and sell them in yet another. This pattern of trade has radically changed world trading because of IT.

The development of an effective integrated global supply chain, including all the processes involved in the trade and payment cycle, has to be carefully planned, predicted and controlled. Traditional management was too slow, error prone and inflexible for a global supply chain to operate competitively. This may be demonstrated by the fact that 11–14 participants may have been involved in any single export/import process: banks, exporter, forwarder, customs, port, carrier, port, customs, forwarder, importer.

Planning and co-ordinating the movement of goods and the flow of payment through such a complex system to a predictable level of certainty was almost impossible. IT brings discipline and control to trading.

IT benefits three areas: strategic, operational and opportunity. These include the overall functioning of the business and affect the company's business. They include a faster trading cycle, 'just in time' manufacturing, terms of trade dictated by bargaining power, and a need to respond to highly competitive market entrants. It embraces B2B and B2C. Today we live in a global world of trade underpinned by IT.

The roles that Bolero, INMARSAT, shipping companies and port authorities are playing in the development of EDI, together with Export Master – a software house specializing in the international trade sector, particularly in the area of processing the international consignment – are now examined.

20.2 Bolero

Bolero is an IT open system that makes all trade communications easier by using IT. Bolero operates through four areas: (a) the rule book – legal framework; (b) digital signatures/certificate of authority; (c) standardized documents; and (d) neutral ownership. To the business involved in international trade, Bolero allows its users to undertake the following five areas: (a) exchange standardized commercial, financial and official documents in a legally binding and secure format; (b) usually standard documentation; (c) integrate back office data systems; (d) improve supply chain efficiency; and (e) use the open nature of the system to trade in a multi-bank environment.

Bolero is likely to become the international standard for Business-to-Business (B2B) e-commerce because the world's largest banks and major logistics companies support it. It is also used by a large number of multinational trading businesses.

Bolero has made the international trade industry IT-literate. Exporters/importers need to understand the preference for paperless trade, processes including CMI electronic bills of lading, Incoterms, Uniform Customs and Practice for Documentary Credits – ICC guidelines on best practice.

International trade was fraught with financial, logistic and time inefficiencies. Created by the world's logistics and banking communities, Bolero.net is eliminating inefficiencies by moving world trade to the Internet, allowing documents and data to be exchanged 'on line' between all parties in the supply chain. Most of the world's top 10 banks now use Bolero.net, as do major trading houses such as Mitsui and Marubeni and carriers such as Kline, Cosco and Evergreen.

The Bolero.net messaging system is operated by SWIFT. This utilizes the latest encryption technology, which validates messages. Rigorous registration procedures act as the gatekeeper for prospective users of Bolero.net. Bolero XML is a validated, global, cross industry XML standards solution that allows all parties of a supply chain to seamlessly 'talk' to each other by automating their information exchange.

The backbone of the Bolero system is the Core Messaging Platform, which enables users to exchange electronic trade documents via the Internet. The system is secure and underpinned by a unique legal structure. It is maintained by a third party. All messages between users are validated, acknowledged and notifications are provided as requested. Additional messages determine whether the recipient accepts or refuses the stated offer. Bolero.net is committed to maintaining an open, non-proprietary system, working with a range of third party partners to develop specific 'Bolero.net enabled' interface products and 'Bolero.net qualified' consultancy services for the community. The benefits of Bolero.net include: improved time efficiency; better administrative procedures; improved security systems; improved co-ordination across information systems; improved customer services; better inventory control; consistent legal framework process; and document improvement and fraud reduction. The benefits of Bolero.net extend to legal, technical, marketing, production and servicing departments of business.

20.3 International Maritime Satellite Organization (INMARSAT)

The International Maritime Satellite Organization (INMARSAT) is an internationally owned co-operative providing mobile communications worldwide. Established in 1979 to serve the maritime industry, INMARSAT is now the sole provider of mobile global satellite communications for commercial, distress and safety applications, at sea, in the air and on land. It is based in London, and has 75 member countries. Readers are urged to visit the INMARSAT website for latest information. INMARSAT is renowned for its innovative, reliable and cost-effective communication solutions to the maritime industry for many years. INMARSAT works closely with industry, providing communication solutions that are now indispensable to on-board operations.

In response to an ever-increasing need for data-driven, cost-effective and secure communications at sea, INMARSAT has developed a unique new service family – INMARSAT Fleet – providing fully integrated satellite com-munication services incorporating voice and data applications.

The first INMARSAT fleet service, Fleet F77, provides the high quality and speed of a full 64 kbit/s Mobile ISDN service, as well as the flexibility of the INMARSAT Mobile Packet Data service, where users are charged for the amount of information sent and received rather than the time for which they are connected. This combination provides cost-effective, almost total global communications, with immediate and secure access to business critical information, image transfer and video communications – whenever it is needed. INMARSAT Fleet F77 is also equipped to meet the latest distress and safety specifications of the Global Maritime Distress and Safety System (GMDSS). Through four-stage voice pre-emption and prioritization, INMARSAT Fleet F77 supports the accreditation of vessels' systems and ensures high priority distress and safety needs are met as follows:

(a) *Proven reliability*. INMARSAT has provided effective communication to maritime industry for many years. Via INMARSAT customers have access to proven technology and outstanding service.
(b) *Choice and flexibility*. INMARSAT offers solutions that meet the specific needs of maritime industry, allowing end-users to create communications that suit individual requirements.

(c) *Cost-effective.* Customers can choose the most cost-effective communications channel, be it Mobile ISDN or the Mobile Packet Data service – allowing 'always on' working.

(d) *High speed.* A mobile office at sea, INMARSAT offers fast online and intranet access, image transfer and video communications at high speed.

(e) *Global coverage.* Coverage of all ocean areas is available to maritime users.

(f) *Enhanced safety.* Voice prioritization and pre-emption ensure that all distress and safety needs are prioritized and dealt with effectively.

(g) *Ease of installation.* INMARSAT offers ease of installation through new, lightweight antenna technologies and light, compact below-decks equipment, offering comprehensive connection options.

(h) *Compatibility.* INMARSAT is accessed through a satcoms unit, compatible with standard applications and systems, allowing users to carry out business as usual virtually wherever they are. It operates using industry standard Mobile IP and ISDN user interfaces. A wide variety of standard applications are also available, extending the availability of commonly used, off-the-shelf software to the ship at sea.

INMARSAT Fleet in action

(a) *E-mail.* Via INMARSAT Fleet, users gain reliable, quick and easy access to e-mail whenever and virtually wherever it is needed. New e-mail services are offered by variety of providers.

(b) *Secure on-line access.* Reliable and secure access to online information or the corporate intranet has become an everyday communications need. INMARSAT makes this a reality for those at sea, seamlessly integrating corporate IT networks and facilitating access to secure information resources through Internet protocol (IP). Using INMARSAT's Mobile Packet Data service, an online connection can be maintained with no charging applicable, until traffic is passed to or from the vessel.

(c) *E-commerce.* Through its built-in IP connectivity, INMARSAT offers the maritime industry fast, flexible and secure access to 24 hour trading throughout the world via the maritime e-commerce sector.

(d) *Video and digital image communications.* Access to video-conferencing and digital imagery via INMARSAT Fleet ensures that cruise and leisure vessels have the communications facilities to meet increased passenger requirements for online, fast and high availability communications.

(e) *Distress and safety communication.* INMARSAT provides voice prioritization and pre-emption, an essential service allowing the interruption and clearing of routine calls and lower priority communication to give way to voice communication, addressing high priority distress and safety needs.

(f) *Secure communications.* Confidential data communication requires secure transmission. INMARSAT ensures that the maritime industry is confident in the security of information transferred.

(g) *Voice communication*. Through INMARSAT Fleet's integral voice service, users throughout all sectors of the maritime industry and the world's ocean regions are provided with immediate and clear digital voice communications. SIM card call operation offers great flexibility for social calling and multiple users. Study Figure 20.1 and below.

(h) *Service flexibility*. Mobile ISDN and Mobile Packet Data Service: two key data services are available via INMARSAT. Selecting the more appropriate of the two will depend on what is to be sent and what it is that is to be received. The Mobile ISDN service is perhaps best used when transmitting large files or when high transmission speed is important. The Mobile Packet Data service can be more efficient for applications that are interactive, such as e-mail, Web or intranet access.

(i) *Mobile ISDN*. Video-conferencing, large file transfer, store and forward video, photo transmission, high quality audio, secure voice and data.

(j) *Mobile Packet Data Service*. Navigational data updates, interactive e-mail, database queries, e-commerce, IP/corporate LAN access, intranet access, vessel telemetry transmission.

INMARSAT's unique ability to provide an integrated service with worldwide coverage extends 'business as usual' on a global basis in the maritime industry.

Above and below deck equipment

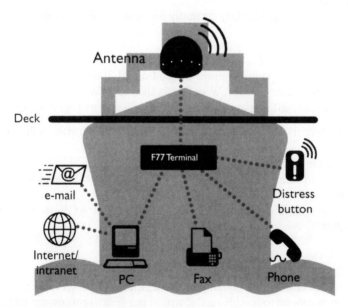

Figure 20.1 Above and below deck equipment.

Source: By courtesy of INMARSAT Ltd.

Through the integration of IT and mobile satellite communications, INMARSAT Fleet provides flexible, immediate access to a range of business.

INMARSAT 1–3 to 1–4 migration and coverage enhancement

INMARSAT spot beam services benefit from recent significant coverage enhancements. These are automatic and do not require terminal update. Figure 20.2 gives an example outline of the migration and subsequent coverage enhancements of specified maritime digital services (Fleet F77,128 kbps, F55, F33 and mini-M) from the INMARSAT–3 (1–3) to INMARSAT–4 (1–4) generation satellites, as from 2005. The timings given below are subject to change depending upon: (a) launch timing and (b) success of launch and In Orbit Testing (IOT) of F1 and F2.

Status of 1–4, Flight 1 (1–4 F1)

1–4 F1 successfully launched on 11 March 2005.
1–4 F1 will be located at 64° E covering the IOR.
1–4 F1 will carry all maritime digital services using its regional beams.

Approximately 10 weeks after launch, existing 1–3 traffic will switch to 1–4 F1.
1–4 F1 carrying operational maritime traffic estimated Q2,2005.
For a period of one month the 1–3 will be co-located with 1–4 F1 (as back-up).
Enhanced coverage availability currently planned in IOR from end of Q2 2005.

Status of 1–4, Flight 2 (1–4 F2)

1–4 is scheduled for launch before the end of Q4,2005 (exact date TBC).
1–4 F2 will be located at 53° W covering the AOR-W.
1–4 F2 will carry all maritime digital services using its regional beams.

Approximately 10 weeks after launch, existing 1–3 traffic will switch to 1–4 F2.
1–4 F2 carrying operational maritime traffic Q4,2005.
For a period of one month the 1–3 at 54° W will be co-located with 1–4 F2 (as back-up).
Enhanced coverage availability currently planned in AOR-W from end of Q4,2005.

Coverage impact (IOR and AOR-W)

Under 1–4 F1 and F2 the coverage enhancement of the services in the right hand column proved to be substantial within the ocean regions served by these satellites. This provided a significant increase in coverage and flexibility to existing maritime end users. As each 1–4 entered service, a revised bulletin

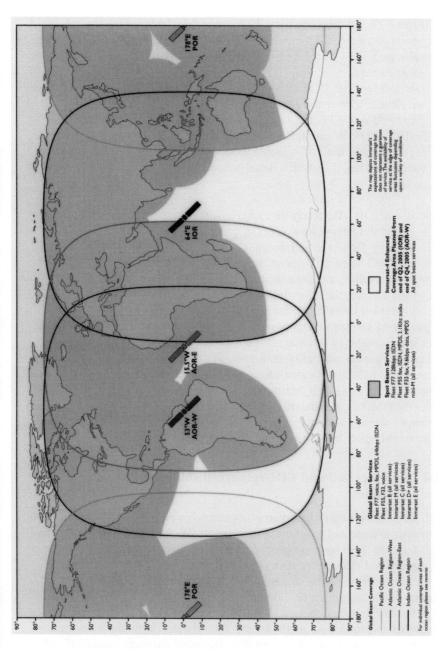

Global Beam Coverage

—— Pacific Ocean Region
—— Atlantic Ocean Region–West
—— Atlantic Ocean Region–East
—— Indian Ocean Region

For individual coverage areas of each
ocean region please see reverse

Global Beam Services
Fleet: F77 voice, fax, MPDS, 64kbps ISDN
Fleet F55, F33, voice
Inmarsat B (all services)
Inmarsat M (all services)
Inmarsat C (all services)
Inmarsat D+ (all services)
Inmarsat E (all services)

▨ **Spot Beam Services**
Fleet F77 128kbps ISDN
Fleet F55 fax, ISDN, MPDS, 3.1Khz audio
Fleet F33 fax, 9.6kbps data, MPDS
mini-M (all services)

☐ **Inmarsat-4 Enhanced**
Coverage Area Planned from
end of Q2, 2005 (IOR) and
end of Q4, 2005 (AOR-W)
All spot beam services

The map depicts Inmarsat's
expectations of coverage but
does not represent a guarantee
of service. The availability of
service at the edge of coverage
areas fluctuates depending
upon a variety of conditions.

Figure 20.2 Coverage of maritime digital services with planned INMARSAT–4 enhancements.

Source: By courtesy of INMARSAT Ltd.

board was uploaded to the NCS to redefine the coverage of the respective MES type.

- *Fleet F77*. 128 kbps on Fleet F77 is now available within the enhanced coverage area, but initially ran in existing 1–3 spot beam coverage areas, prior to 1–4 F1 and F2 launch and subsequent transition and coverage enhancement.
- *GMDSS Services*. INMARSAT B, C, E and Fleet F77 service and coverage are already global and remain unaffected.
- *Fleet F55 and F33*. The current spot beam coverage is now enhanced in both the AOR-W and IOR, effectively giving total coverage in these ocean regions, using the 1–4 regional beams, to allow data and fax communications within this area. Global voice telephony remains as currently defined.

AOR-W and IOR, effectively give total coverage in these ocean regions, using the 1–4 regional beams for voice, fax and data communication.

To benefit from the enhanced coverage offered by 1–4 F1 and F2 (IOR/AOR-W) terminals operating in these ocean regions re-point to the appropriate satellite, i.e. ensuring that they are logged on to IOR or AOR-W.

1–4 and F2 carry the following maritime services: INMARSAT B, C, D/D+, E, mini-M, M, Fleet F77, F55, F33.

Quality of service was improved under 1–4, compared to 1–3 operation, especially at edges of coverage.

Recognizing the efficiency and reliability of the INMARSAT system, the International Maritime Organization (IMO) made satellite communications a cornerstone of its Global Maritime Distress and Safety System (GMDSS). Under the GMDSS, a Standard A or Standard C ship earth station now satisfies regulatory communications requirements for ships operating in almost all parts of the world, apart from the extreme polar regions.

20.4 Computerized and EDI-resourced shipping companies

With the development of the Internet, e-commerce brought a new era of global international trade and maritime managements. With its global interactive and swift features from business procedure to management concept, the Internet has rapidly and thoroughly changed every aspect of modern commerce.

An examination of the strategic objective of a mega shipowner COSCO, relating the development of e-commerce, can help establish on the basis of IT a flexible e-transport and e-logistics system. This system comprises comprehensive transport methods and co-ordinates with the environment. This IT-based business model is capable of meeting the requirements of global customers because it takes an integrated marketing and sales system as its business platform, the restructuring of logistics, information flow and business process as its management platform, and customer satisfaction as its enterprise cultural platform.

The first objective using IT is to satisfy customers' changing demands around the global to develop COSCO's e-commerce. Global transnational corporations require carriers to provide services on a worldwide basis. Increasing globalization of outsourcing and commerce, entails manufacturers making increasing demands on global supply chains. Hence, with such characteristics as globalization, individuality and real-time response, the Internet is quickly attracting clientele to the Web for the Web's appearance of a virtual digital forum. Along with the development of e-commerce, customers/shipper demand is changing from physical transaction to virtual/digital transaction, i.e. obtaining what they want through online transactions. Shippers require a combination of the Web and the real-time circumstances of the supply chain, its management and integration based on customers' requirements. IT has changed customers'/shippers' behaviour and the diversity of their needs in the global market enabling the customer to control the international shipping market by using the Web. The shipper/customer co-operates with the shipowner/carrier continuously, making the starting point of COSCO's development of IT communications global customer demand and effective responses to it.

The second fundamental strategy is to provide a global marketing system as a business platform for COSCO's development of e-commerce. This involved in the early days of IT communications in trade changing from a line-oriented business to a global carrier, a process embracing the co-ordination of resources, such as personnel, equipment, information/market research/ market intelligence and networks globally to form a global marketing system. E-commerce brings enterprises closer to customers/shippers. COSCO's e-commerce system is a global on-line reflection of its marketing and sales system continuously reflecting and monitoring market demands and identifying new customers. This embraces customer profile and behavioural patterns essential in planning supply chain/container capacity needs.

The third aspect is the realignment of logistics information flow and business process as a management platform. Logistics manages/plans all transport modes in the customer's supply chain, all the time aware of a product's value added benefit to the consumer. Information flow solves the problem of information transfer between the main bodies in supply chains. Business methods inside an enterprise merge with mutual understanding of logistics and information flow. COSCO's e-commerce management platform is a combination of logistics, information flow and business process in a scientific, national and economical way that links production and consumption: it is a valuable planning resource and a further benefit to the shipper of logistic management. To accomplish this requires high-specification hardware and software technology and collation of data provided by the logistic supplier from the market place, including service quality and cost based on customers' demands. By analysing the two kinds of information, a transaction is made on the basis of supply–demand. There is a natural connection between shipping, other logistic suppliers, and customers in which the global carrier has innate advantages in the development of electronic logistics. The key advantage arises when a global network is taken as a base and unites suppliers in each link of customers' supply chains. This unity of effort establishes a virtual logistics networks for customers.

The fourth element is a one-stop service. Online service is directly integrated with the customers' intranet to link it with their e-commerce and provide service for them. This embraces the global marketing networks and all consignment formalities for the export consignment. It also features cargo tracking and customs for both export and import consignments. It embraces the throughput transit.

The fifth factor is COSCO's global information system as the technology basis for the development of COSCO's e-commerce. To set up a comprehensive e-commerce system, a prerequisite is to provide a complete IT system to support enterprise, financial, trade and legal activities without resort to paper.

The sixth factor is customer satisfaction. The objective of e-commerce is to develop harmony and understanding with customers through communication. E-commerce continues to develop in scope in all sectors of the maritime business. Examples of online capabilities available on the Internet to shippers, from major transport companies to maritime carriers, include these: (a) payment; (b) cargo notification; (c) shippers posting their requirements for tonnage, rates, delivery times and other conditions; (d) shippers' viewing rates and information on capacity, rates, routing, delivery times and other conditions; (e) carriers posting their available capacity, rates, routes, delivery times and other conditions; (f) carriers responding to loads offered by shippers at carriers' posted rates; (g) printing and receiving bills of lading; (h) cargo booking and confirmation; (i) carriers and shippers making on-line contracts based on mutually agreed offers; (j) tracking movements of shipments along the transport chain; and (k) shippers responding to offers of capacity, delivery time and rates set by carriers.

The maritime e-community provides information and communication technology (ICT) services, ranging from safety guidelines to new sites and e-business ventures (see Figure 20.1) dealing with procurement, crewing and chartering. These services respond to the social and trading needs of the shipping community and steer the industry to a point where information 'on board the vessels' is crucial for efficient management of shipping operations.

The growing need for IT is driven by increased demand for safety (ISM code) and operational reporting, and has led to a requirement that data is accurate, relevant, timely, and benefits the company commercially.

Land earth station operators (LESOs) compete in a tight market and their services are declining because the cost of satellite communications is getting cheaper. INMARSAT is a pioneer in global mobile satellite communication. This maritime mobile ISDN and mobile packet data service combines the high quality and speed of a mobile ISD service with the world's first global, high speed maritime mobile packet data service via satellite. Its functions include e-mail delivery, securing Internet and intranet access and voice and two fax services. It is a veritable mobile office at sea.

The INMARSAT fleet family features three solutions that are designed to meet the requirements of specific maritime sectors and is optimized for operation over the current satellites. It provides 'value added solutions' to the maritime industry, and these are:

(a) With decreasing communication cost and high speed, it will be more cost-effective to deploy software systems 'on board' vessels.
(b) ASP – type solutions or web-enabled systems normally deployed on the net are essential tools in maritime businesses: information sharing, on demand access, openness and flexibility all sharpen current business practices and relationships.
(c) Effective use of the Internet enhances aspects of daily business transactions.

The Internet is the prime method of communication in the maritime industry. The unprecedented volume of e-activity has made the maritime industry focus on the development of inter-operability standards to minimize the danger of creating islands of information, or the stifling of innovation because of locking-in a company's information, which happens when companies do not use universal interchange formats. The provision of common standards eliminates misinterpretation of terms/language and reduces the risk of the core message being misunderstood. The maritime industry is experiencing greater transparency because of continuous research undertaken by the Maritime E-commerce Association (MECA) and Marine Transaction Services (MTS). The SFI coding system structure, developed by Norges Skips Forsknings Institute of Norway, is a *de facto* international classification standard of high quality providing functional subdivision of technical and financial information.

IT makes a substantial contribution to a more efficient shipping business. Rapid convergence of technologies, the ever increasing ship–shore communications, and promising data exchange standards create new opportunities.

20.5 Customs; e-commerce

Electronic transmission is evident in Customs because it speeds cargo clearance and generates greater efficiency and paperless trading. The UK has been a leading industrial nation in the development and operation of e-commerce in relation to export and import customs declarations/procedures and associated customs activities, such as Excise, IPR, OPR, etc. Systems have been developed with the WCO and EU to promote the freedom of movement of goods with discipline.

The core of HM Customs is CHIEF, from which were developed NES, CFSP and NCTS. Manual systems have been almost eliminated and exporters/importers/agents/seaports/airports/carriers operate online with Customs. CHIEF began in 1992, followed by NES/CFSP/NCTS in 2000/02. As IT develops, trade facilitation and globalization expand, though there is concern that fraudulent e-commerce needs new and effective measures of detection and prohibition.

Trade must have adequate computer resources to handle Customs e-commerce. Companies must possess adequate IT software to maximize the benefits of electronic communication/documentation, in Customs and in processing export/import consignments.

Change in Customs regulations/control, transmitted into e-commerce, is particularly noticeable in logistics.

20.6 Computerized Export Processing: Exportmaster

Software and the export shipping process

The use of IT to manage and facilitate commercial documentation and administration is standard practice in most business departments. In export shipping, however, many companies have only recently become aware of the opportunities for automation that IT presents.

Commercial and shipping documentation is undertaken either by the exporting manufacturer/trader or by the forwarder or, more often, by a combination of both. The term 'forwarder' in this connection could encompass a carrier, a shipping and forwarding agent, an export management company or a third party logistics provider (3PL) who has undertaken export administration on behalf of a principal.

In some cases company IT systems used by the exporter make no specific provision for export requirements. Consequently export documentation tends to be produced 'off-line' by using word-processor documents and spreadsheets, with templates providing short cuts through text-entry processes. When those companies that prepare documents on a typewriter or submit them hand-written these disadvantages occur:

1   Data has to be keyed first into the company's processing system and then into the export documents. It may also need to be rekeyed or copied-and-pasted between individual documents. Rekeying is a time-consuming and wasteful process.
2   Wherever rekeying or re-entering takes place, opportunities for error abound. Errors can cause problems at ports of arrival, rejection of letters of credit and financial discrepancies.
3   Documents produced from multiple systems and in unformalized environments such as word-processing inevitably lack a consistent format and professional appearance. This has undesirable implications for the exporter's image.

4   The information contained in the documents is not available for reporting or calculation purposes. It is text only.
5   The process includes no structure to ensure that the correct documents are produced or related activities carried out. Fulfilment of a shipment becomes dependent upon individuals remembering to perform activities.

Specialized export software systems

Various software products are available with which to produce commercial and shipping documentation for export. These range from programs providing little more than manually keying-in data into an on-screen form to a highly automated system with rules and procedures and specialized shipping-related data maintenance facilities. The example used in this chapter falls into the latter category. 'Exportmaster' software, developed by Exportmaster Systems, is used by manufacturers, traders, retailers and by suppliers of forwarding, logistics and financial export services. The two versions relevant to shipping operations are Exportmaster ShipShape, which deals primarily with documentation, and Exportmaster Professional, which includes costing, pricing and quotation facilities.

The purposes of export software implementation

When exporters undertake a move to an automated export system at their own, their forwarder's or their agent's premises, then these purposes apply:

1   To speed up the shipping process and move the goods more quickly.
2   To eliminate rekeying and other repetitive activity.
3   To reduce the likelihood of errors.
4   To present a more professional image.
5   To be able to extract management information.
6   To reduce dependence upon the presence or knowledge of individuals.
7   To improve customer service through status control and avoidance of shipping problems.

The forwarder or other third party offering IT documentation and administrative services to the exporter may be doing so in the knowledge that, by going beyond the provision of a service for moving the goods and by offering these benefits to their principal, they are adding value to their service and therefore justifying their charges.

Figure 20.3 illustrates the main functions likely to be required of an export system with regard to shipping documentation and operations.

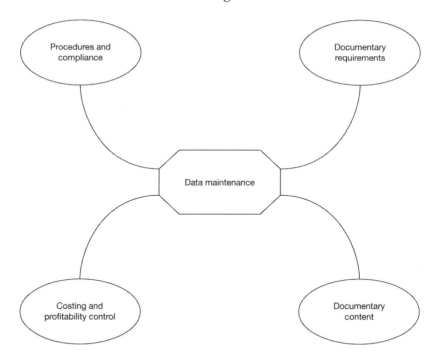

Figure 20.3 Export shipping system functionality.

Components of the export system

Forms

Most export documents require the completion of forms (see Figure 20.4). Traditionally these were supplied as pre-printed stationery; IT sometimes allows the user fill in these pre-printed versions. Exportmaster, however, is equipped with a digitized range of standard forms, including the SITPRO/UN-approved set, which it can reproduce on plain paper as it completes them. Only when the issuing authority insists on its use should pre-printed stationery be employed. Whether computer-generated or pre-printed, the forms with their contents can be viewed on-screen before printing. This allows them to be checked and adjusted more easily.

Documents

Within the export system the word *document* means more than it does elsewhere. Not to be confused with the *form* it is but one component of the document. *Document* can mean the piece of paper or its equivalent that comes from printing or other production process; but the word may also refer to the *document design*. The *document design* is a configuration of text, data, layout,

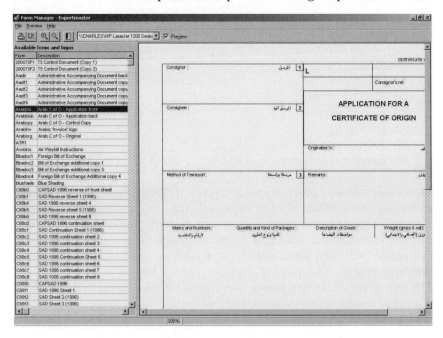

Figure 20.4 A form being displayed in Exportmaster's forms library.

rules and conditions that generates the desired outcome, which may be printed, stored or electronically transmitted. The most important properties controlled by a *document design* are these:

1 The size and orientation (portrait/landscape) of the document.
2 The number of copies normally required.
3 Whether any printing is required on the reverse of the sheet.
4 Items of *fixed text*. Fixed text is text that will always be the same on a document, regardless of which shipment is being processed. *Example: 'Total Value'.*
5 Items of *data*. These are items that are specific to a particular shipment and that will therefore vary from shipment to shipment. *Example: 'Shipped under Import Licence 579234'.*
6 The *positions* in which fixed text and data items are to appear.
7 The *fonts* and *style attributes* for the fixed text and data items.
8 The *order* in which line items (product lines) are to be *sorted*. For example, line items are sometimes sorted into tariff code order.
9 Whether the line items are to be *sub-totalled* and at what level, e.g. commodity code, country of origin or product group.
10 Whether anything is to be included in or excluded from a particular sheet in a *multi-part set*.

11 Whether any *scripted conditional rule* is to be applied and in what circumstances. For example, a document might include a special clause only when a particular product appeared amongst the line items on a shipment.
12 The *default method of output* for the document, which might be:
    (a) Printing on paper.
    (b) E-mailing.
    (c) Faxing.
    (d) Storing as a PDF file.
    (e) Electronic transmission (UneDocs, e-Biz-XML, etc.).

Most export software provides the basic set of SITPRO/UN-aligned documents and forms, while others offer an expanded range incorporating forms issued by other organizations, such as port and customs authorities, banks and carriers. Exportmaster includes a document design module with which users can create their own documents from scratch or make adaptations of the standard versions. The range of documents is not limited to standard forms. The way in which documentation is prepared can be adapted to the needs of individual customers and countries of destination.

Export-specific data

Corporate systems handling manufacturing, order processing, accounting and finance do not always hold the sort of data needed to complete a typical set of export documents. In order to avoid manual entry of all missing items against each shipment, the export system should hold the export-specific data against customers, territories and products in a way that it is automatically available to shipments while they are being set up or downloaded.

Standing data may be stored in Exportmaster under these categories:

1 Territories.
2 Customers.
3 Products.
4 Customs commodity codes.
5 Hazard classifications.
6 Countries of origin.
7 Expenses (including freight, insurance and shipping rates).

The more data is held as standard in these databases, the less a user needs to intervene when dealing with individual shipments.

Procedures

Rules and procedures are created within the system to suit customers or groups of customers (see Figure 20.5). These incorporate activities to be performed

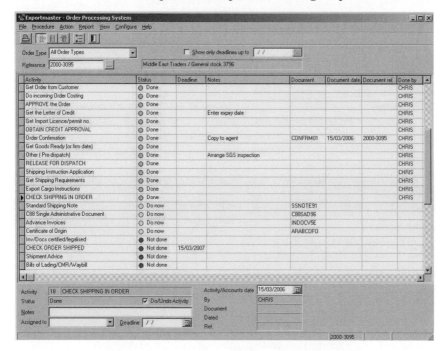

Figure 20.5 Exportmaster's procedural system in use for a shipment.

(e.g. legalization, arranging an inspection or obtaining an import licence or letter of credit) and documents to be produced. Double-clicking on a line updates the status of the line to *'Done'* and records the date and identity of the user. If the line calls for a document, production of that document is automatically triggered. Activities can be date-deadlined and action reports generated. At any stage in the life of a shipment the screen shows what has been done, what needs to be done immediately, and what remains to be done.

Costings

Costing templates allow costings to be prepared for shipments on a 'before and after' basis. This enables anticipated costs and margins to be compared with 'actuals'. Unlike a spreadsheet, a costing can draw data dynamically from the shipment itself and from the standing databases. Because it is part of an integrated system, its results are available for use in management reports, which allows identification of true nett profit after all export expenses, down to the level of individual products per customer or destination.

A shipment costing can deal with terms from 'Ex works' to 'Delivered duty paid', while product-pricing costings can include on-costs in detail, including the consumer price on a supermarket shelf in the country of destination.

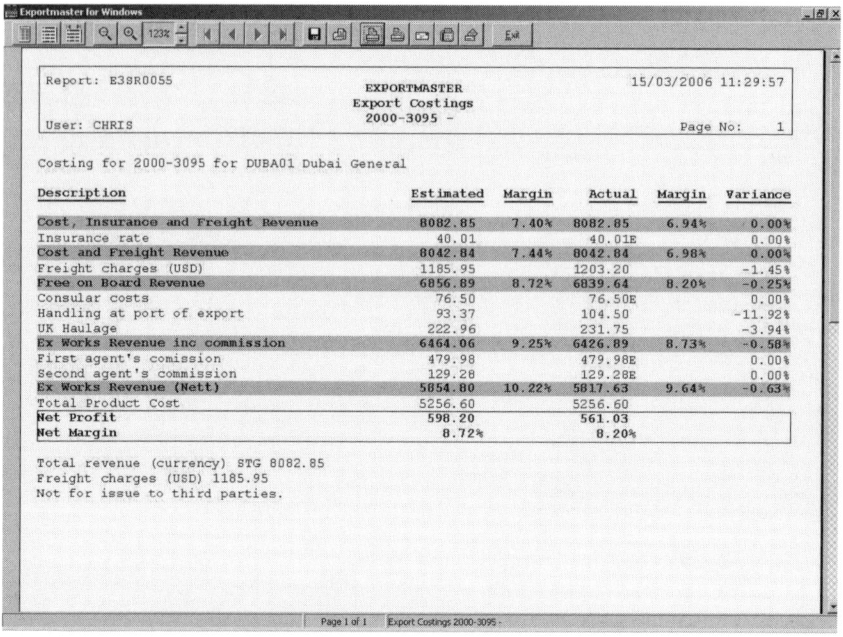

Description	Estimated	Margin	Actual	Margin	Variance
Cost, Insurance and Freight Revenue	8082.85	7.40%	8082.85	6.94%	0.00%
Insurance rate	40.01		40.01E		0.00%
Cost and Freight Revenue	8042.84	7.44%	8042.84	6.98%	0.00%
Freight charges (USD)	1185.95		1203.20		-1.45%
Free on Board Revenue	6856.89	8.72%	6839.64	8.20%	-0.25%
Consular costs	76.50		76.50E		0.00%
Handling at port of export	93.37		104.50		-11.92%
UK Haulage	222.96		231.75		-3.94%
Ex Works Revenue inc commission	6464.06	9.25%	6426.89	8.73%	-0.58%
First agent's comission	479.98		479.98E		0.00%
Second agent's commission	129.28		129.28E		0.00%
Ex Works Revenue (Nett)	5854.80	10.22%	5817.63	9.64%	-0.63%
Total Product Cost	5256.60		5256.60		
Net Profit	598.20		561.03		
Net Margin	8.72%		8.20%		

Figure 20.6 An Exportmaster costing, showing a CIF transaction.

Management information

One of the problems in the early days of e-commerce was that no historical data was generated in an extractable format. What was stored was merely text. Nowadays, IT offers an integrated export software system containing structured data for both current and historical transactions, all of which can be retrieved and interrogated. This is because IT memory has increased exponentially in recent years (see Figure 20.6).

An example of a current-activity-report definition might be: show the quantity, revenue and volume (for storage calculation purposes) of all shipments for Saudi Arabia which are scheduled for shipment between 1 November and 30 November and which have not yet been shipped.

An example of a historical report definition could be: list the quantity, revenue and profit (value and percentage) of worldwide sales for the year to date at the levels of territory, customer and individual product and compare the figures with those of the previous year, expressing the difference as a percentage.

The export software shipping process

Figure 20.7 illustrates a typical process employing the Exportmaster system. Not all functions shown will be relevant to all shippers. Users need employ only those modules appropriate to their particular situation.

Data capture

The term *data capture* refers to the acquisition of transaction-related data by the system, probably by one of the following methods:

1   Manual entry by the user.
2   Electronic download of data across a network from a corporate processing system.
3   Reading a computer file that has been supplied by a third party service provider.
4   Reading a spreadsheet in an agreed format e-mailed by a principal or third party.

Regardless of the method used, relevant export-specific standing data already stored in Exportmaster will be automatically merged with the newly entered data, without the need for rekeying by the user. Other data-related functions can occur automatically during or after the data capture process, including the generation of consolidated 'customs items' by tariff code or of 'hazard items' consolidated by classification for dangerous goods documentation.

Data manipulation

However comprehensively the standing data in the system is maintained, there is always some item that may require user intervention. Some examples are these:

1   Information not normally available when the shipment is created, e.g. Name of vessel, Berth of loading, Flight number, etc.
2   Requirements of an unusual, non-standard shipment.
3   Requirements of a letter of credit demanding a particular wording.
4   Last-minute alterations to a despatch.

An advantage of an integrated data-driven system is that, once an alteration has been made (for example, a change in product description to comply with a letter of credit), that alteration will be automatically reflected in all documents for the transaction making use of the affected data.

Data manipulation can be made through data-screens (Figure 20.8) or through the medium of a selected document (Figure 20.9). Editing via a document has the advantage that it is absolutely clear where a particular piece

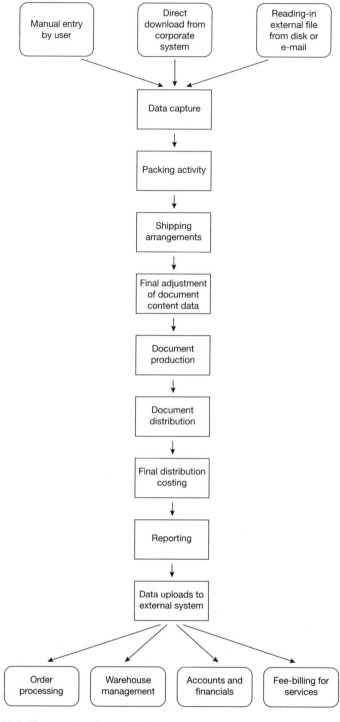

Figure 20.7 The export software shipping process.

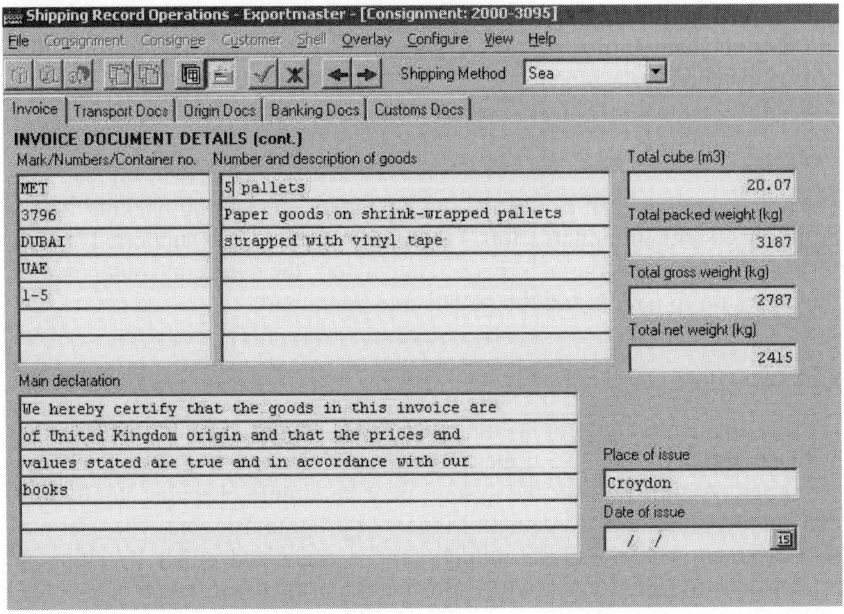

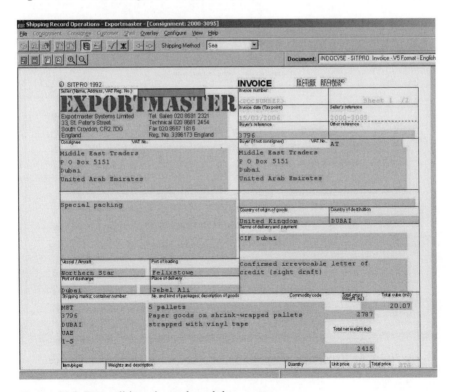

Figure 20.8 Data editing via a data field screen.

Figure 20.9 Data editing via a selected document.

of data will appear on the document in question. The disadvantage is that only the data relevant to that particular document is visible. Full information is obtained via the data-screens.

Packing

Packing operations can be carried out on-screen, permitting packing lists to be produced with minimum effort. Multiple-level packing is supported, so that, for example, products might be packed into inners, the inners into outer cartons, the outers on to pallets and the pallets into containers.

Following procedures

If the status control system is employed, the user steps through the activities as illustrated in Figure 20.5. Lines requiring action are colour-coded and state *'Do now'*. Action lines in the system may be simple checklist items, lines that control other lines, document triggers or program triggers. The user may also produce *Action Reports*, which can be organized either by shipment reference or by activity. Action reports can be printed out, faxed or e-mailed and their contents can be determined by deadline date if necessary (see Figure 20.10).

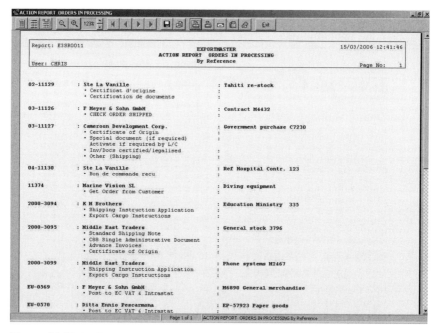

Figure 20.10 An Exportmaster Action Report, grouped by shipment reference.

Document production and distribution (procedural or on-demand)

For most users action lines trigger documents in the procedural system. However, documents can be produced at any time on demand without reference to that system. The user chooses *Direct print*, selects a shipment, and the document required for that document to be printed.

Documents may be printed (locally or remotely over a network), faxed, e-mailed or stored in PDF format. With the use of scripting they can be transformed into other formats (EDI or XML for instance) for electronic transmission to other systems. Electronic transmission is now the norm rather than the exception. An example is the replacement of the C88 (SAD) paper document by electronic submissions to the UK customs authorities under the New Export System (NES).

Document types

Because users can design their own documents, there is effectively no limitation to the type of document that the system can produce, subject usually only to the page-size limitations of the printers used. The types of document most frequently produced by Exportmaster include:

1 Invoices (commercial and consular) and their derivatives.
2 Packing lists.
3 Shipping notes, instructions and advice and other despatch documents.
4 Certificates of origin.
5 Movement certificates.
6 Transport documents.
7 Insurance documents.
8 Bank collection documents.
9 Shipping marks and other labels.
10 Letters (standard and semi-standard) usually relating to other documents.
11 Customs declarations.
12 Hazardous goods declarations.
13 Customized certificates of quality assurance, conformity, etc.

Costings

Most exporters undertake a consignment profitability costing to ensure that the costs incurred are consistent with anticipated profit margins on the transaction (see Figure 20.6). Where a third party is handling the process, the preparation of costings may not be considered appropriate.

EU VAT and Intrastat reporting

Exporters shipping significant quantities of goods to member countries of the EU are required to submit regular Intrastat statistical reports and associated

VAT declarations (the EC Sales List). Exportmaster can be configured to generate and validate these reports as a by-product of the normal documentation process. The reports can be produced in printed form or as electronic files for transmission to the customs authorities via e-mail or an EDI network.

Historical reporting

Export principals can undertake historical reporting on export transactions, but it is rarely needed for third party service providers.

Links to parallel activities

It is often the case at the end of the process that data is uploaded to another system in order to enable further activity. For example, an exporter's invoices might be uploaded to an accounts system, or a forwarder might pass the transaction across to a fee billing system.

The benefits of using an integrated export system with the greatest amount of automation that is practically achievable are becoming self-evident. Regardless of those benefits, the adoption of dedicated export-specific software systems is growing as exporters keep pace with IT developments in order to remain competitive. Export shipping personnel are now obliged to be familiar with IT and its software because IT is now the standard method of operation.

21 Ship management

21.1 Introduction

Ship management is a shore based and ship board day-to-day safe operation of a vessel to ensure compliance of the ship's regulations and being customer cost effective. This entails compliance with safety, environmental protection and security. It is management of an asset, 'the ship', and operation of cost + compliance + revenue production.

Ship management has grown considerably in scope in recent years. The most important companies in the world are: V-ships, Columbia Ship Management, Barber International, ASP Ship Management and Orient Ship Management, the largest of which is V Ships, managing a fleet of over 650 vessels, an international company with 44 offices located in 26 countries employing 1,100 office staff and 22,500 sea staff. V Ships has, in addition to its core ship management activities, a broad range of maritime operations, including crewing, leisure, financial, consulting, commercial and agency services.

There are three main ship management models:

(a) *Traditional*. This embraces a fully integrated in-house management by the ship owner.
(b) *Outsourcing*. Often termed third party ship management, this focuses on a full or crew contracted out management whereby technical, crewing, accounting, risk, safety-embracing environmental protection, quality and security functions are performed by a specialist supplier – a ship management company which could nominate a ship manager.
(c) *Hybrid*. Partial outsourcing of selected functions, including joint venture type relationships and bench marking.

Third party ship management represents an estimated 35% of the shipping industry and is growing annually. Shipowners are becoming increasingly confident of third party operators and the quality of service they offer. They are regarded as professional seafarers and managers equipped with good quality ship and shore operational skills. Factors driving the expansion of third party ship management are these:

(a) A commitment by shipowners to embrace the concept of international quality assurance. Costs can sometimes be reduced by outsourcing crewing and technical/commercial ship management.
(b) Increased awareness and emphasis on education, training and welfare of maritime personnel.
(c) Implementation of innovative technology in operations, which brings in transparency and new competence requirements.
(d) The efficiency gained from using the experience and knowledge capital of the ship management company.

Further factors driving third party ship management include: the introduction of new legislation, the 1990 Oil Pollution Act (OPA 90) and the ISM code, the revised standards of STCW 2010; and the double hull tanker provision and the port state control. ISMA and BIMCO recognize the importance of the ship manager, and the latter organization has introduced the standard ship management agreements, Shipman 98 and Crewman A and B. In 2006 and 2010 the IMO decided to undertake a major strategic review of the STCW code to devise new international regulation of ship construction. This review focused on four objectives: (a) broad, over-arching safety, environmental and/or security standards that ships are required to meet during their lifecycle; (b) the required level to be achieved by the requirements applied by class societies and other recognized bodies, administrations and the IMO; (c) clear, demonstrable, verifiable, long-standing, implementable and achievable, irrespective of ship design and technology; and (d) a code specific and not open to differing interpretations. These measures should have a noticeable influence on ship management.

The growth of ship management and logistics has been dramatic. There is much interaction between the maritime marketing plan and fleet operation/management. The liner cargo network extends beyond the port to embrace overland transport focusing on the supply chain. The old liner conference system dealt with a port to port operation. Today, multinational enterprises representing over 60% of world trade operate a logistic function that operates to move goods in an efficient flow. Many mega container firms operate shipping company-owned logistics divisions, enabling the buyer to entrust all the purchasing/ordering/packaging/distribution/control to one company cost effectively in accordance with the buyer's specification. IT dominates all areas of ship management, ashore and shipboard, includings surveys, maintenance schedules, sailings, crew manning, stores, voyage planning, voyage estimates, bunkering, port charges, budgetary management and profitability. Vessel operational and navigational management is high-tech and can be entrusted to the Master and the crew. Ship management changed dramatically with the introduction of the ISM code, the ISPS provisions, port state control, International Maritime Labour Convention, the growth of third party ship management and maritime legislation through the IMO. It is complex, but in effect is management of the fleet. Broadly, it falls into six divisions – marketing, fleet management, technical, financial, purchasing, investment and legal disciplines: many work together.

21.2 Marketing aspects of ship management

Marketing is the process of identifying a market and responding to it. It is a management function. The shipowner's business and marketing plan objective is to maximize nett revenue to the service compatible with the environment in which the trade operates. This includes competition, operational alliances, flag discrimination, liner conference terms and government legislation.

The shipping company provides a product/service on an international basis and responds to environmental opportunities and threats in the overseas markets served, each with different configurations and behaviours. The ship operator decides in which market segment they wish to participate and the position that the company desires in the market place, with regard to the culture of the management, the resources available, the market forecast and overall level of profitability. To be successful in an international market the ship operator must develop competitive products. Any decision is preferably market research driven, based on market forecast, and likely to foster good client-operator relationships.

Marketing management should be customer focused, identifying and meeting client needs to add value to the business, intending to beat the competition in the market. It may be fast ferry, LNG, oil tanker, container, ro/ro, ore carrier or PCTC. There should be dialogue between the marketeer/the ship operator to provide the best possible service to the product and the shipper using the service, which may mean importer, exporter, or other decision-maker, such as an agent. To achieve this objective, marketing management focuses on four areas: analysis, planning, implementation and control.

International marketing embraces: economic indicators (exchange rates, GNP, GDP, taxation levels); government and political strategies and attitudes adopted by government featuring shipping issues and protectionism in any form; competition, cultural and demographic issues, technology, particularly whether a country is low-tech or high-tech; legal and ethical constraints; ecology and resource limitations, and profile of the company in international trade and shipping company culture.

International marketing reflects continuous industrial growth, vast technological advances and changing economic forces. The effective international shipowner recognizes that customer/shipper needs for services and cost competitiveness have top priority in an international marketing strategy. Shipowners acknowledge that traditional divisions separating administration in the shipping industry are now largely irrelevant. Shippers no longer seek a variety of modal services, but demand single source, integrated logistic services, as found in NVOCC/NVOC/logistic operators which proficiently solve logistic problems in global supply chains.

The cruise passenger rate is based on a daily tariff according to type of accommodation provided and duration of the cruise. Much additional income comes from retail outlets on the ship, such as a restaurant, bar, shop and leisure facilities. Additional income comes from port-centred excursions.

Income in the ferry business is based on passenger tariffs, car length, and, for a multi-purpose ferry, the road haulage unit. Revenue accrues from a range of shipboard facilities. Ship management skills in a multi-ferry business include varying car deck capacity in line with the market demand of motorist and road haulage vehicles. On a cruise vessel and multi-purpose/fast ferry business market research techniques are used to identify passenger needs/preferences.

The bulk cargo markets – dry and wet – are dominated by chartered tonnage. Ship managers formulate fixtures when market conditions are most favourable and rely on IT resources relative to freight indices to set the optimum rate.

For freight the tariff should be based on cost plus an element of profit. The latter is not always possible because of market fluctuations. The container market deals with an imbalance of trade involving the repositioning of empty containers and allocation of slots within an operating alliance.

The shipowner, particularly one engaged in liner-type services, should prepare an annual marketing plan covering these items:

(a) The marketing objectives of the trade/service.
(b) The nature of the service during the next 12 months, giving details of ship disposition, sailing schedules, ports of call, etc.
(c) The market profile the shipping route will serve and the nature of the traffic sought.
(d) The tariffs and particularly any special concessions to attract new business and develop existing flows through possibly more favourable rebate/discounts.
(e) Any new features on the service, particularly new tonnage, additional ports of call, improved transit, better customs clearance arrangements, simpler documentation, more attractive tariffs.
(f) Budgeted forecast of carryings on the route in the next 12 months by tonnage, segregated into various commodity classifications and country of origin.
(g) Any significant developments on the route foreseen in the next 12 months and how the service will benefit. For example, a new industrial complex may be opening up in a country which could generate much additional business to the route.
(h) Details of any promotional campaigns to sustain existing business and also obtain additional traffic.
(i) Technique to be used to measure route performance particularly carryings at regular intervals throughout the 12 months. This may involve regular monthly meetings with sales personnel to discuss results attained and sales strategy, particularly any new promotions.

(j) Details of the sales targets for each sales sector.
(k) The plan should stress the competitive advantages the route has over other services, and the salient points the salesforce should stress.
(l) The plan should be flexible in its approach to take account of any changed situation which may emerge in the next 12 months.
(m) It should be devised to produce a profitable service through the strategy on tariffs: selling must be towards this sole objective. Its aim is to increase market share on a profitable basis, particularly of those commodities which are viable or capable of becoming viable.

The marketing plan's aim should be to provide adequate traffic to produce a profitable service. This should reflect other objectives for the forthcoming year, in terms of actual forecast carryings and the manner in which the traffic is to be secured.

21.3 Fleet management

Management of the fleet is important to a shipping company because of its focus on financial marketing and customers. It involves the following criteria, which are influenced in particular by ship classification, flag state authority; by the market(s) in which the ships operate; and by the commodities carried.

(a) The first objective is for the board of directors to define the business plan and for the fleet manager to respond, working within the legal framework of the maritime industry and its associates. Ship safety remains paramount at all times.
(b) The plan should reflect the board's objectives. These must be market and budget driven and have the full commitment of, and be accountable to, all participants.
(c) Fleet capacity resources must be matched to the market forecast and be reflected in the budget and sailing programme. Maximum resources must be available at peak periods. Increased capacity in terms of ton miles can be realized through quicker speeds.
(d) The plan must be costed and relate to the cargo mix revenue on each voyage or maritime leg to ensure the budgeted profit is achieved.
(e) The sailing programme must focus on port charges, bunker facilities, shipyard location, port technology, port navigation resources, optimum speed compatible with cost, competition, cargo mix revenue, production, cargo transhipment cost, port infrastructure, turn-round time, stores and catering availability and so on. BIMCO and port authorities have Internet facilities offering access to databases.
(f) Total quality management compliance, featuring DNV SEP and similar schemes, ISMA standards, ISM code and ISO 9002.
(g) Bunkering, ship repairs, and ship surveys should be undertaken at strategically located ports and shipyards. To be cost effective, these

involve staged payments on survey programmes and cause minimum disruption to the sailing programme.

(h) Crew management like the ship survey programme is a critical cost item in fleet management. Offshore crews such as Filipino are currently cheaper than European.

(i) Ports of call selection is critical. Many factors are involved, especially revenue production and profitability.

(j) Port cost and disbursements and insurance all need constant review to ensure the shipowner obtains a favourable deal.

(k) Pilotage, tonnage dues and towage costs vary between ports. Masters with a pilotage exemption certificate can assist in reducing such costs. Towage dues may be reduced when modern tonnage has transverse propulsion units.

(l) Provision of properly trained and certificated officers and crew.

(m) Compliance with the ISM code's principles of Quality Assurance for safety and environment protection.

(n) Supply of stores and spares, and placing of insurance.

(o) Guidance and/or instructions on ship maintenance, repairs, operational and commercial activities of the ship.

(p) Full use is made of IT resources, including most recent shore and shipboard software for ship maintenance and survey.

(q) Maintain a close and continuous liaison with the national registry and classification society to ensure effective operations, such as harmonized surveys and programmed shipboard workload of preventative maintenance.

(r) Voyage planning – a key area, especially in the chartering market.

(s) Need to keep in touch with the markets continuously, especially those involving competitors and innovators.

(t) The business plan sets out clear financial objectives for the fleet. This may involve leasing vessels, or chartering rather than outright ownership, to reduce cost and take advantage of any tax concessions.

(u) Port captaincy is an important role and requires continuous monitoring.

(v) The fleet manager works closely with the marketing/logistics department to ensure the fleet attains optimum performance at all times. Forward planning is essential and full use should be made of IT throughout the company and its maritime activities. Continuous dialogue and minimization of the effects of imbalance in trade flows are paramount, as is the need to have the minimum number of ballast trips.

(w) Full use is made of the IT for communications and procurement.

(x) Regular meetings are held to monitor performance against budget.

(y) The ship's Master and crew participate in planning and execution. Many shipping companies ensure the ship's Master, chief officer and chief engineer remain permanently assigned to a particular vessel and so become accountable for the vessel's efficiency performance. Crew overtime is minimized and within budget. Satellite communication is maintained with the crew.

(z) The merits of 'flagging out' should be examined where high crew costs are incurred.

The fleet manager's role varies by type of vessel/nature of the trade and the degree of outsourcing/third party ship management.

21.4 Technical aspects of ship management

The maintenance and provision of ships form a significant cost in the shipowner's annual budget. The aim is to provide a fleet which is compatible and economical to market requirements at the lowest possible cost, having regard to safety, statutory obligations and service standards. The following points are relevant:

(a) Surveys to be conducted outside peak traffic period and of minimum duration compatible with market and economic circumstances.

(b) As much work as practicable prior to survey to be done during the time the vessel is in traffic as is compatible with cost and other factors.

(c) Examine the merits of using classification societies and technical services, such as those available from Lloyd's Register.

(d) Vessels should be designed to keep maintenance expenditure to a minimum, as should crew cost by using modern navigational aids and shipboard labour-saving devices.

(e) A number of options exist with regard to ship surveys and these should be carefully and continuously reviewed. These include voyage survey, continuous survey, BIS notation involving 'built for in water survey', and planned maintenance systems. Planned maintenance systems are popular in harmonized ship survey programmes. Surveys include sighting survey, special periodical survey – hull and equipment, continuous survey – machinery, bottom survey; tailshaft survey, auxiliary boiler survey, EO class – four yearly survey, EO annual survey, loadline annual inspection, annual general survey, and safety radio certificate.

(f) The development of shipboard management techniques should be explored (see *Maritime Economics: Management and Marketing,* Chapter 14).

(g) Competitive tendering should be adopted with regard to ship surveys. Areas requiring particular attention in the decision to award the tender to the successful shipyard include: timescale of work contracted, quality of work, industrial relations record, steaming time to and from the shipyard, payment schedule and any prolonged credit payment system, relations with the yard, currency used and the shipyard's experience in handling the type of vessel involved.

(h) Overall the technical aspects of ship management cover a range of engineering and technical support services. Full use must be made of IT in the application and monitoring of technical services.

Table 21.1 Monitoring parameters in fleet management

ROB	Safety	Critical	Performance	Personnel	Repair	Master
Fuel	ISM Code	Cargo gear	Machinery	Sign on	Critical	Vendor
Diesel	Certificates	Machinery	Cargo gear	Sign off	Non-	Agents
Lubricants	Survey	Load line		Confidential	critical	P&I
Critical	SOLAS	Navigation			Docking	clubs
spares	Stability	Communica-				Port
	IOPP	tion				details
		Holds/tanks				Shipyard
						Shipping
						Manager
						Checklist

The technical superintendent responsible for the operation of the vessels must keep track of the following: ROB (remaining on board full) requirements, safety, critical situations and performance. Table 21.1 identifies variation in fleet management parameters, from ship to ship and trade.

21.5 Financial aspects of ship management

An important factor in successful ship management is adequate financial control to ensure optimum use of the shipping company's resources. To achieve this there must be disciplined budgetary control covering revenue and expenditure budgets on a service, ship, profit centre, divisional or other convenient basis.

Budget control must be formulated with the agreement of those managing revenue production, marketing and services. It concerns passengers, freight, accompanied cars, catering income, chartering income and miscellaneous receipts. In the case of expenditure it will include ship maintenance, port dues, crew cost, fuel, port agents' charges, agents' passenger/freight commission, ship insurance, etc. The budget must be reviewed continuously to reflect variations in expenditure and revenue. Full use must be made of IT. Budgets should be produced for capital investment programmes and cash forecasts.

Most Masters are now involved in budgetary control. The Master and his chief engineer are responsible for expenditure and revenue budgets formulated on an annual basis and which take account of cargo to be conveyed and ship operating costs, including fuel, crew, maintenance, port charges, etc. This type of budgetary control is likely to become more common and is dealt with more fully in Chapter 15 of Alan Branch's *Maritime Economics: Management and Marketing*.

The object of budgetary control is to ensure maximum profitability of service/ships and is important in ship management. Large shipping companies usually produce one- and five-year budget business plans, giving indicators of future prospects for company finances and any defects in commercial/operating/investment policy. It should cover the following points:

(a) The shipping company's investment plans in the next five years.
(b) Traffic forecasts in the next five years by trade route and the predicted financial results by service annually.
(c) A brief commentary on each service for results in the next five years and significant features likely to arise, such as new ships, more competition, new pooling agreements under liner conference terms, expansion of flag discrimination, market developments, etc.
(d) International events which could prejudice the company's five-year developments. These may include further development of third world countries' fleets, more infiltration by former Eastern bloc countries into cross trades, or the expansion of national fleets enjoying operating subsidies or some other form of state aid. These developments could reduce a shipping company's market share and result in a reduced fleet and withdrawn services.
(e) Statutory developments which may result in the need for more training of sea-going personnel, the provision of improved fire prevention equipment, or more severe survey requirements for older vessels.
(f) Future plans of the company, particularly for new services, rationalization of ports of call, reorganization of the company structure with more decentralization, etc.
(g) Investment needs in the next five years and how these are to be financed. These may use the company's existing financial resources, obtaining government aid, selling older ships, the realization of redundant estate assets, e.g. the sale of a disused office block, using loan capital, etc.
(h) Assessment of how the major competitors will develop in the next five years, and how the shipping company will combat the situation.
(i) Political events must be assessed, e.g. the development of free trade areas and the expansion of existing ones.
(j) International trade forecast for the next five years and how the shipping company may feature in such developments. For example, liner trades on some routes may expand while movement of crude oil may be stabilized.
(k) Any possible takeover of another shipping company or ancillary activity, e.g. shipbroking, freight forwarding, ports, etc.
(l) Budgetary control should focus on the cash flow forecast and related financial planning to ensure the company develops viably. Budgetary control includes complex financial activities, such as tax-based leasing, which is a force in debt factoring. Financial analysis produces, with appropriate cash flow projections, an assessment of the liabilities outstanding on a ship.

The business plan should explain what the shipping company intends to do during the next five years.

For shipowners outsourcing the vessel operating budget the business plan may feature six key areas: manning – wages, travel, victualling (35%–50%); insurance – H&M, P&I, other (10%–20%); stores – deck and engine, rentals, fresh water, etc. (7%–12%); lubricants – cylinder, crankcase, etc. (4%–8%);

R&M – spares, dry dock, maintenance, survey, etc. (20%–30%); and administration – management fees, registration, communications (5%–8%). Financial reporting of the operating budget embraces these areas: (a) draft – approved budget (owner signs off); (b) owner provides one-twelfth of agreed funds at beginning of each month; (c) third party ship manager maintains vessels' accounts (actual and committed expenditure); (d) monthly and quarterly reporting to owner; (e) analysis and explanation of variances; (f) payments effected electronically from the vessel's bank account; and (g) owners can access and interrogate financial records.

21.6 Purchasing aspects of ship management

Third party ship management offers competitive purchasing through the volume business provided to the vendor. It embraces a range of maritime industry products, including bunkering, victualling, ship stores, lubricants, spares, surveys/maintenance.

The ship management company focuses on volume contracts when dealing with shipyards and bunkering stations and ship chandlers. It can secure discounted rates and on favourable credit terms, which can prove attractive to the small family-size shipping company as well as the mega operator in a competitive market. Alan Branch's *International Purchasing and Management* may be helpful to readers wishing to produce a coherent international purchasing plan.

21.7 Investment aspects of ship management

Ship investment is important to ship management. International trade is a speculative business and is subject to political fluctuations. For example, the development of the Far East mercantile fleets, the expansion of flag discrimination practices and flagging out have all had a profound effect on trade. It may take two to three years to construct a vessel from shipping company proposal to build through to launch. The ship will have an economic operational life of 12 to 15 years, depending on type and use. Shipping is not an attractive proposition to investors because it produces modest returns on capital invested.

Capital investment may be for building new tonnage, converting existing tonnage or buying second-hand tonnage. The following factors must be borne in mind as criteria for investment decision-making:

(a) The actual market prospects of the trade or route both in the short term and the long term.
(b) An analysis of the existing tonnage.
(c) Account must be taken of existing competition and likely future developments.
(d) Any political factors relevant to investment in ships.

(e) The availability of capital is critical, because many shipowners have difficulty in raising capital without resorting to credit or subsidy facilities.

(f) The method of financing may be through loan capital from the banks or government sources; leasing; through raising capital on the stock exchange by the issue of share capital; by utilizing existing funds through a combination of liquid assets and short-term investment; or the sale of displaced ships or other company assets, such as an office block. It is usually a mixture of these.

(g) The economics of the new tonnage involves the evaluation of direct costs, such as fuel, crew, maintenance and port charges, and indirect costs, such as depreciation, loan cost, etc. This kind of expenditure must be related to revenue production.

(h) New ships can attract tax relief in the form of depreciation and other fiscal benefits.

(i) An assessment should be made of return on investment. A return on new investment of at least between 20% and 25% should be sought.

(j) The commercial factors should be closely examined, particularly with regard to maintaining the existing market share on the route and securing/attracting new profitable business to the trade.

(k) An assessment must be made of the available shipyard capacity and time-scale of the project.

(l) The investment memorandum should conclude by outlining the financial merits of the investment in new tonnage investment, etc., and the financial effect on the shipping company if no investment is made and/or resorting to chartering, buying second-hand tonnage, leasing or converting existing tonnage.

Ship investment is a risk activity and is speculative, reflecting the uncertainty of international trade and the unpredictability of future changes throughout the 12–15 year life span of the ships. The investment objective must be to maintain and develop existing market shares and develop new markets to sustain and exploit investment profitability (see also *Maritime Economics: Management Marketing,* Chapter 4).

21.8 Ship management legal disciplines

Recent years have seen more legislation introduced concerning the shipping industry than almost any other period in its history. Existing legislation, such as the 1990 Oil Pollution Act, the ISM and ISPS codes and STCW, most likely will be followed by new legislation in Europe and elsewhere. The IMO 2006 review of STCW and ship construction is an example.

For the owner or ship manager who uses a third party manning agent and who is not large enough to require that the agent provides him with a dedicated pool of sea staff, STCW 1995 and Manila amendments 2010 could present major problems as will subsequent conventions. The vessel operator is responsible for ensuring that convention requirements are met to the satisfaction of port state control.

An opportunity, however, is presented to the ship manager with a large pool of sea staff (or access to one) and who is prepared to enter into a manning-only agreement. This manager should be in a position to provide a properly qualified and dedicated crew well versed in the requirements of the ISM code and which satisfies port state inspection. Legislation provides challenges and opportunities for ship managers, who must take cognizance of the ISPS code.

21.9 ISM Code

The International Ship Management Code of the International Maritime Organization operative in 1998 represents the first licensing scheme without which shipping companies and their ships cannot operate. Mandatory from 2002 it supersedes the guidelines on management for safe operation and for the prevention of pollution adopted by the IMO assembly in 1991. Details are given below of the IMO citation. Chapter IX, 'The management of the safe operation of ships', makes mandatory the ISM Code, which requires a safety management system to be established by the shipowner or any person who has assumed responsibility for the ship (the 'Company'). The chapter was adopted in May 1994 and entered into force on 1 July 1998.

The aims of the ISM Code are to ensure safety at sea, the prevention of human injury or loss of life and the avoidance of damage to the environment – in particular the marine environment – and property. The functional requirements for a safety management system to realize these mandatory objectives are these: (a) a safety and environmental policy; (b) instructions and procedures to ensure safe operation of ships and protection of the environment; (c) defined levels of authority and lines of communication between and amongst shore and shipboard personnel; (d) procedures for reporting accidents and nonconformities within the provision of the ISM Code; (e) emergency response procedures; and (f) procedures for internal audits and management reviews.

Each shipowning company has to establish a safety and environment protection policy, complemented and maintained by all staff ashore and on board ship. To ensure the safe operation of the vessel, companies must appoint a shore-based designated person as a link between ship and shore management. This person must have direct access to the highest level of management while effectively communicating with seagoing personnel. The ISM Code does not relegate a Master's responsibility but rather endorses and enhances a Master's authority.

The code lays down assessment procedures for a company's safety management systems, company fleet and as required in shore-based offices. Each ship in a company fleet, as well as the company shore-based management systems, requires separate certification. These assessment procedures are to be followed when either the shipboard systems or shore-based systems or both are to be assessed for certification, which is usually by an accredited ship classification society, such as Lloyd's Register of Shipping. This involves the Safety Management Certificate, which is valid for five years and subject to periodical verification and additional verification (if required) in accordance with regulation 6 of Chapter IX of the convention, the Safety Management system as found to comply with the requirements of the ISM Code.

The Safety Management Certificate confirms these: (a) an appropriate management system has been defined by the company for dealing with safety and pollution prevention on board; (b) the system is understood and implemented by those responsible for the various functions; (c) as far as periodic assessments can determine, the key actions indicated in the system are being carried out; (d) and the records are available to demonstrate the effective implementation of the system. The scheme does not in any way replace class surveys of any kind. The document of compliance is issued by an accredited ship classification society to certify that the safety management system of the specified shipping company has been audited in full compliance with the ISM Code relative to the shipping company vessels, relative to the safe operation of the ship and for pollution prevention.

Readers wishing to study this topic further should read Alan Branch's *Shipping and Air Freight Documentation for Importers and Exporters.*

21.10 Risk management in the modern shipping industry

Shipping has always been a risk business and, like other industries, it is responding to increased scrutiny, increased competition and squeezing of profit margins. Companies now focus on the core business and are outsourcing tasks outside their expertise because they know that success comes from in-depth knowledge and constant monitoring of the market. Shipping companies wish to know their risk and so develop risk management programmes using IT to control and monitor market movements and gain overview of market exposure and its influence on financial outcomes.

Tough competition and high exposure in the market have increased the shipping business risks without any amelioration through higher profit margins and greater potential to carry the risks. The primary market risks shipping companies face are freight rates, foreign exchange rates, usually against the US dollar, oil prices (bunker prices) and interest rates (shipowners). The volatility of these four market risks in shipping confirms that the greatest risk in shipping is oil bunker prices.

In shipping taking no risk means it is impossible to make any profit. Shipping companies are good traders in their core business – the shipping and freight market – the area shipping companies should expose themselves to. Risks that should be avoided and hedged are exposure outside the core business and exposure that causes uncontrollable volatility in earnings.

The advantages of risk management embrace stable earnings, financial gains and comparative advantages. By controlling costs through budget management, and focusing on and optimizing the earnings of the core business, management of risk can realize long-term stability in earnings. Further financial gain arises because financial institutions value company risk below that of other enterprises. Such benefits influence how much the company can borrow, reducing the cost of capital (interest) and reducing the size of equity reserve requirements. A positive cash flow in a shipping company generates market confidence to shippers and to investors – shareholders and banks.

The disadvantages of risk management focus on when the company decides to establish a hedge (i.e. a pooled investment facility perhaps run by the company), circumstances arise to make assumptions or to take a point of reference from the budget. Such assumptions or budgets may be wrong, making the hedge either unnecessary or established at too high a price. A sudden change in exposure to the markets may force the shipping company to terminate the hedge, which sometimes may yield a profit though sometimes a loss. To be successful at bunker hedging, the shipping company needs disciplined dealing with the market. Some strategists believe risk management is the fixing of prices at the lowest possible level, but this is incomplete. If the prices locked-in are not counter-balanced by favourable market exposure, the shipowner probably ends up having to explain the speculation and anticipate unpleasant final accounts. It is prudent to choose an associate, offering a partnership to someone in the bunker business who can provide the shipping company with reliable specialist information for taking correct decisions.

To counter currency and bunker price volatility, shipping companies can opt for the BAF and CAF mechanism. Adopting a risk management strategy can turn volatility into opportunities and so achieve earnings growth and stability.

21.11 Case study: Vector Maritime Systems (www.vectormaritime.com)

This section deals with a leading third party ship management company, Vector Maritime Systems. The company offers easy to use methods to provide answers to comprehensive maritime business situations. Administration, traditionally paper-based, is now fully automated using IT to collect all information in auditable form. This is a summary of the seven modules involved:

(a) *Maintenance* is based on a system that manages planned maintenance, defect monitoring, repairs, work specification, dry-docking and follow up. It is designed to cover the need of modern marine engineers, superintendents and naval architects to control the requirements of business and legislation.
(b) *Finance*. This covers all the financial needs of a maritime company. Beyond the standard maritime multi-currency, multi-company accounting

functions, it includes a sophisticated budget management system, cash-flow management and an advanced cost accounting module that links with all operational modules in vector management.

(c) *Operations*. The operations system is designed to meet the needs of a ship operator, managing all activities regarding voyage definition, detailed follow-up, including chart-based fleet tracking and freight collection. It may optionally integrate with the Vector Chartering Management for voyage estimation and charter party details as well as other Vector management system modules. Positional and performance information (actual, planned and historical) is recorded and is available for viewing on an electronic chart. A number of electronic charts formats (bitmaps and vector from different hydrographic offices) are supported, such as ARCS, NOA, BSB. This is achieved by utilizing Euronav's OEM software and allows automated 'best fit' and zoom capability. However, in the Vector management system implementation, it is used with positional and performance plotting and can offer unique management information that provide ship managers with fast access to other modules, such as crew lists, crew records or requisitions status, etc.

(d) *Purchasing*. This is formulated on a workflow-based purchasing system for the shipping industry. The system is modular, allowing it to synchronize with a variety of budgets, enabling incremental build-up to a complete and comprehensive system. The system supports the purchasing department in procurement of spare parts, supplies, service, lubricants, bunkers, etc. It covers the entire cycle based on the company's own workflow rules, from requisition to evaluation, enquiry, quotation, input, comparison, ordering, delivery, invoice registration (including web invoicing) and invoice checking. The office and ship are integrated with seamless work flow, giving full synchronization of up-to-date requisition status, delivery notification and late delivery alarms. The system automatically updates data libraries (spares, supplies, etc.).

(e) *ISM*. This is developed specifically for the shipping industry to fulfil the SMS requirements of the ISM Code. It simplifies the storage updating and tracking of all documentation required by the ISM Code. The ISM Manager: integrates office and shipboard systems; supports the creation, update and approval of controlled documents and the automatic distribution to ships; records incident and accident occurrences together with course analysis; fully implements the SMS from ship reporting through to back office analysis – includes the Vector Workflow Engine that allows efficient handling of disparities, monitoring from initial logging to corrective action and verification; and includes additional modules for auditing, drills and checklists.

(f) *Manning*. The crewing module is a flexible crew management system designed to address the needs of modern crewing departments. It covers all aspects of seagoing personnel of a maritime company, including staff selection, crew planning and career development. It offers optional appraisal and performance modules, with follow-up training and external and internal training results for each employee. The workflow method allows efficient and auditable crew monitoring by using procedures that span the agencies of all involved parties (head office, manning office, external manning agent, ships, etc.).

(g) *Knowledge*. The Vector knowledge manager permits the ship management company to manage the 'unstructured' information (messages and documents) and correlate it with the structured information from the operational systems (Maintenance, Purchasing, ISM, etc.). It is a combination of advanced office-based messaging system and document management system.

22 Political aspects

22.1 Flag discrimination

Study of elements of shipping must include political aspects: flag discrimination, flags of convenience and subsidies.

Flag discrimination comprises the various acts and pressures exerted by governments to direct cargoes to ships of their own flag, regardless of commercial considerations normally governing routing of cargoes. It also applies to directing their port authorities to offer favourable rates and bunker charges to their national flag vessels.

Powers against flag discrimination in its various forms are incorporated in the Merchant Shipping Act 1974 – Part III of which enables the UK government to take counter-action against foreign governments where UK shipping or trade interests are affected, or where they are required to meet Britain's international obligations. Orders can be made to obtain information, to regulate the carriage of goods, to levy charges on ships, to refuse admittance of ships to UK ports, and to approve or disapprove agreements. The Merchant Shipping Act 1988 provided the UK government with powers of retaliation against unfair trading practices by overseas competitors.

Flag discrimination impedes competition within the shipping industry, because it can divert trade to less efficient carriers and obscure the real cost of the service. The more important methods by which it may be exercised are these:

(a) *Import licences.* A number of countries, including Chile, Brazil, Gabon, Malaysia, Peru, Sudan and India, have used granting of import licences to ensure carriage of cargo in ships of their own national flag.
(b) *Discriminatory customs and other dues.* Preferential rates of customs and other dues are used to influence cargoes into ships of the national flag. Discriminatory charges in harbour, lighthouse pilotage and tonnage dues, consular fees and taxes on freight revenue are other means of favouring the national flag.
(c) *Administrative pressures.* Although in many countries there may be no statutory provisions reserving cargoes to ships of the national flag, the same result is achieved by some administrative pressure.

(d) *Direct legislative control.* This is the most damaging form of flag discrimination. In the early 1990s countries such as Argentina, Brazil, Chile, Ecuador, Peru, Turkey, Uruguay, Venezuela and Egypt resorted to some forms of direct legislative control.

(e) *Exchange control.* The manipulation of 'exchange control' offers ways of making shipment in national vessels either obligatory or so commercially attractive that it has the same effect.

(f) *Bilateral trade treaties.* In all, over thirty countries have entered into bilateral trade treaties, which include shipping clauses reserving either the whole of the trade between the two countries, or as much of it as possible, to the ships of the two flags.

Many South American and developing countries build fleets for prestige purposes, and to reduce the drain on their foreign exchange practise flag discrimination. Their shipping is usually subsidized in several ways as follows:

(a) Up to 50% of all goods passing through their ports must be carried in their own ships.

(b) A small concession in customs charges to reduce transport costs when charging full conference rates.

(c) A customs surcharge on goods carried by foreign ships.

Additionally other countries practise flag discrimination as follows:

(a) All chartered tonnage is reserved for the national flag.

(b) All coastal services are reserved for the national flag.

(c) A freight allocation agency is set up favouring the national flag and fixing rates.

(d) There are higher bunker charges for foreign tonnage.

Flag discrimination is a serious problem facing the industry, but because it takes so many forms and is inspired by diverse motives there is no straightforward remedy. Compromise and expediency offer no long-term solution. Determined and concerted action by governments is required throughout the world. WTO and EU continue to strive to reduce the practice of flag discrimination.

22.2 Flags of convenience

Shipping companies, like any other undertakings, are subject to income and profits taxes of the state where they operate. Level of tax is important to the shipowner. This problem is aggravated for the shipping industry by the enormous cost of replacement, a cost which continues to rise as building costs increase. Shipowners in any maritime country are disadvantaged when competing with tax-free or almost tax-free national merchant fleets under flags of convenience – or open registries, as they are now termed. Two countries featuring prominently in this practice are Liberia and Panama.

In 2012, 35 countries or territories accounted for 94% of the total world tonnage (Table 22.1). As an example, Greece has the largest fleet ownership in deadweight tonnage, representing 16.1% of the total world tonnage, followed by Japan at 15.4%. The two countries' combined tonnage represents 31.5% of the total world tonnage. The table shows that the top five countries with the largest owned fleets in 2012 were Greece, Japan, Germany, China and the Republic of Korea. What the table further shows is that the majority of the owned fleets from these countries in 2012 were under a foreign or different flag.

Table 22.2 shows that in 2012 Panama, Liberia, Marshall Islands, Hong Kong (China) and Singapore were the five largest registries. The column 'percent of tonnage owned by foreigners' shows that each of these operates as an open registry. Each open registry showed growth between 2011 and 2012, demonstrating an increase in the use of open registries, the top five accounting for 54.75% of world tonnage.

Numerous classification societies means the criteria by which a shipowner chooses a society are complex. Many countries specify which classification society to use. One criterion acknowledges that the prime responsibility for safe and pollution-free operation of a ship lies with its owner, operator and flag state. When a shipowner enters the specified classification society he must comply with its regulations and operate in accordance with three international requirements:

(a) *Structural integrity.* The classification society has the task of ensuring that ship maintenance and surveys are undertaken. This technical work, in accord with the regulations, is entrusted to the society by the state.
(b) *Safety equipment.* Every society must have the competence to undertake an annual audit of every ship on its registry to ensure safety equipment is fully operational and in accordance with international conditions.
(c) *Personnel qualifications.* All shipboard personnel must have the appropriate experience/competence and documentary evidence of qualifications relating to ship manning levels.

The guidelines by which a shipowner will select a classification society selection are these:

(a) The administration should have a comprehensive body of laws and regulations to implement the requisite international standards.
(b) The flag state should have a recognized system of casualty investigation and undertake investigations promptly and thoroughly.
(c) There should be a corporate law identifying the link between the ship and flag state.

Table 22.1 The 35 countries and territories with the largest owned fleets, as of 1 January 2012ᵃ (dwt)

Country or territory of ownershipᵇ	Number of vessels			Deadweight tonnage				
	National flagᶜ	Foreign flag	Total	National flagᶜ	Foreign flag	Total	Foreign flag as a % of total	Estimated market share 1 January 2012
Greece	738	2,583	3,321	64,921,486	159,130,395	224,051,881	71.02	16.10
Japan	717	3,243	3,960	20,452,832	197,210,070	217,662,902	90.60	15.64
Germany	422	3,567	3,989	17,296,198	108,330,510	125,626,708	86.23	9.03
China	2,060	1,569	3,629	51,716,318	72,285,422	124,001,740	58.29	8.91
Korea, Republic of	740	496	1,236	17,102,300	39,083,270	56,185,570	69.56	4.04
United States	741	1,314	2,055	7,162,685	47,460,048	54,622,733	86.89	3.92
China, Hong Kong SAR	470	383	853	28,884,470	16,601,518	45,485,988	36.50	3.27
Norway	851	1,141	1,992	15,772,288	27,327,579	43,099,867	63.41	3.10
Denmark	394	649	1,043	13,463,727	26,527,607	39,991,334	66.33	2.87
China, Taiwan Province of	102	601	703	4,076,815	34,968,474	39,045,289	89.56	2.81
Singapore	712	398	1,110	22,082,648	16,480,079	38,562,727	42.74	2.77
Bermuda	17	251	268	2,297,441	27,698,605	29,996,046	92.34	2.16
Italy	608	226	834	18,113,984	6,874,748	24,988,732	27.51	1.80
Turkey	527	647	1,174	8,554,745	14,925,883	23,480,628	63.57	1.69
Canada	205	251	456	2,489,989	19,360,007	21,849,996	88.60	1.57
India	455	105	560	15,276,544	6,086,410	21,362,954	28.49	1.53
Russian Federation	1,336	451	1,787	5,410,608	14,957,599	20,368,207	73.44	1.46
United Kingdom	230	480	710	2,034,570	16,395,185	18,429,755	88.96	1.32
Belgium	97	180	277	6,319,103	8,202,208	14,521,311	56.48	1.04
Malaysia	432	107	539	9,710,922	4,734,174	14,445,096	32.77	1.04
Brazil	113	59	172	2,279,733	11,481,795	13,761,528	83.43	0.99
Saudi Arabia	75	117	192	1,852,378	10,887,737	12,740,115	85.46	0.92

Country								
Netherlands	576	386	962	4,901,301	6,799,943	11,701,244	58.11	0.84
Indonesia	951	91	1,042	9,300,711	2,292,255	11,592,966	19.77	0.83
Iran	67	71	138	829,704	10,634,685	11,464,389	92.76	0.82
France	188	297	485	3,430,417	7,740,496	11,170,913	69.29	0.80
United Arab Emirates	65	365	430	609,032	8,187,103	8,796,135	93.08	0.63
Cyprus	62	152	214	2,044,256	5,092,849	7,137,105	71.36	0.51
Viet Nam	477	79	556	4,706,563	1,988,446	6,695,009	29.70	0.48
Kuwait	44	42	86	3,956,910	2,735,309	6,692,219	40.87	0.4
Sweden	99	208	307	1,070,563	5,325,853	6,396,416	83.26	0.46
Isle of Man	6	38	44	226,810	6,131,401	6,358,211	96.43	0.46
Thailand	277	67	344	3,610,570	1,542,980	5,153,550	29.94	0.37
Switzerland	39	142	181	1,189,376	3,700,886	4,890,262	75.68	0.35
Qatar	48	37	85	881,688	3,745,663	4,627,351	80.95	0.33
Total top 35 economies	14,941	20,793	35,734	374,029,685	952,927,192	1,326,956,877	71.81	95.34
Other owners	2,172	1,816	3,988	22,491,261	42,344,181	64,835,442	65.31	4.66
Total of known economy of ownership	17,113	22,609	39,722	396,520,946	995,271,373	1,391,792,319	71.51	100.00
Others, unknown economy of ownership			7,179			126,317,184		
World total			46,901			1,518,109,503		

Source: Compiled by the UNCTAD secretariat, on the basis of data supplied by *IHS Fairplay.*

Notes

[a] Vessels of 1000 GT and above, ranked by deadweight tonnage – excluding the United States Reserve Fleet and the United States and Canadian Great Lakes fleets (which have a combined tonnage of 5.3 million dwt).

[b] The country of ownership indicates where the true controlling interest (that is, the parent company) of the fleet is located. In several cases, determining this has required making certain judgements. Thus, for example, Greece is shown as the country of ownership for vessels owned by a Greek national with representative offices in New York, London and Piraeus, although the owner may be domiciled in the United States.

[c] Includes vessels flying the national flag but registered in second registries such as the Danish International Ship Register (DIS), the Norwegian International Ship Register (NIS) or the French International Ship Register (FIS).

Table 22.2 The 35 flags of registration with the largest registered deadweight tonnage (ranked by deadweight tonnage), as of 1 January 2012[a]

Flag of registrations	Number of vessels	Deadweight tonnage, in thousands dwt	Average vessel size, dwt	Share of world total, dwt (%)	Cumulated share, dwt (%)	Tonnage registered for foreign owners in thousands dwt	% of tonnage owned by foreigners	Dwt growth 2012/11 (%)
Panama	8,127	328,210	40,385	21.39	21.39	328,112	99.97	7.25
Liberia	3,030	189,911	62,677	12.38	33.77	189,911	100.00	14.24
Marshall Islands	1,876	122,857	65,489	8.01	41.78	122,857	100.00	24.40
China, Hong Kong SAR	1,935	116,806	60,365	7.61	49.40	87,907	75.26	27.33
Singapore	2,877	82,084	28,531	5.35	54.75	59,910	72.99	21.99
Greece	1,386	72,558	52,351	4.73	59.48	7,520	10.36	1.59
Malta	1,815	71,287	39,277	4.65	64.12	71,241	99.94	16.30
Bahamas	1,409	69,105	49,046	4.50	68.63	68,620	99.30	2.43
China	4,148	58,195	14,030	3.79	72.42	5,983	10.28	10.34
Cyprus	1,022	32,986	32,276	2.15	74.57	30,940	93.80	2.06
Japan	5,619	23,572	4,195	1.54	76.11	398	1.69	6.18
Isle Of Man	410	22,542	54,980	1.47	77.58	22,315	98.99	16.06
Italy	1,667	21,763	13,055	1.42	79.00	3,523	16.19	11.95
Republic of Korea	2,916	19,157	6,570	1.25	80.25	1,460	7.62	-4.95
United Kingdom	1,662	18,664	11,230	1.22	81.46	16,615	89.02	9.80
Norway (NIS)	535	17,896	33,450	1.17	82.63	3,248	18.15	-0.94
Germany	868	17,482	20,141	1.14	83.77	123	0.70	-0.48

India	1,443	16,141	11,186	1.05	84.82	668	4.14	5.65
Antigua and Barbuda	1,322	14,402	10,894	0.94	85.76	14,402	100.00	3.67
Denmark (DIS)	534	13,846	25,929	0.90	86.66	372	2.69	-3.20
Indonesia	6,332	13,512	2,134	0.88	87.54	3,483	25.78	11.63
United States	6,461	11,997	1,857	0.78	88.32	4,585	38.22	-5.25
Bermuda	164	11,598	70,722	0.76	89.08	9,301	80.19	6.80
Malaysia	1,449	10,895	7,519	0.71	89.79	990	9.09	1.58
Turkey	1,360	9,535	7,011	0.62	90.41	710	7.45	9.03
Netherlands	1,382	8,279	5,991	0.54	90.95	3,338	40.31	17.67
France (FIS)	161	7,973	49,521	0.52	91.47	4,980	62.47	1.17
Russian Federation	3,362	7,413	2,205	0.48	91.95	1,632	22.01	0.18
Philippines	1,995	6,694	3,355	0.44	92.39	5,834	87.16	-3.63
Belgium	235	6,663	28,352	0.43	92.83	326	4.90	-2.02
Viet Nam	1,525	6,072	3,982	0.40	93.22	845	13.92	2.94
Saint Vincent and the Grenadines	857	5,636	6,577	0.37	93.59	5,636	100.00	-15.89
China, Taiwan Province of	906	4,328	4,777	0.28	93.87	147	3.40	0.43
Thailand	850	4,249	4,999	0.28	94.15	398	9.36	-6.90
Kuwait	206	3,976	19,301	0.26	94.41	1	0.02	32.27
Total top 35 flags of registration	71,846	1,448,285	20,158	94.41	94.41	1,082,977		10.65
World total	104,305	1,534,019	14,707	100.00	100.00	1,133,417		9.91

Source: Compiled by the UNCTAD secretariat, on the basis of data supplied by *IHS Fairplay*. Reproduced with the kind permission of the UNCTAD Secretariat.

Notes: [a] Seagoing propelled merchant ships of 100 GT and above; ranked by deadweight tonnage.

(d) The flag state should require that every ship on its register has a 'decision-maker' available to the registry 24 hours per day.
(e) There should be provided a publicly available register of ships.
(f) The flag state should be a signatory to the principal international conventions essential to maritime safety and protection of the environment.
(g) There should be staff available who are competent to answer enquiries from owners and operators.
(h) It should have the ability to issue seamen's identity books.
(i) There should be available a current list of all ships registered in its flag.
(j) The flag state should be committed to ensuring it does not register a ship from another registry without a deletion certificate from the previous register.
(k) The flag state should provide the IMO with annual details of all personnel injury records, casualties and pollution incidents occurring on or to its ships.

The subject is also comprehensively examined in Chapter 8, the IACS and Lloyd's Register.

There has been a dramatic decline in the numbers and size of vessels registered with the mainland or domestic registers of traditional maritime nations. Not many decades ago major maritime states like Britain, Norway and Germany had fleets on their domestic registers large enough to rank them among the world's biggest flags. None is now in the top ten.

A major attraction in 'flagging out' tonnage lies in the reduced manning scales/levels required and in the tax allowances against new and second-hand tonnage. These two factors – reduced manning cost/scales and taxation benefits/allowances – yield cost savings in manning levels and encourage new tonnage provision. These factors exert global pressure on shipowners to develop trade worldwide, increase market share and provide competitive tariffs.

The practice of flagging out from national registries to open registries has been growing but this may change when national governments offer more favourable terms to encourage shipowners to register with their national flag. This ploy includes: tax relief on ship investment/depreciation; more favourable social security/insurance/taxations for seafarers; improved training benefits; and tonnage tax relief.

22.3 Subsidies

Subsidies distort the competitive structure of shipping and increase the cost of world shipping services. This is because they permit the use of less efficient vessels and which are sometimes more expensive than is warranted economically. However, it is difficult to see how a country like the United States can operate ships without subsidies, since the labour costs there are much higher than in other countries. In a world where international specialization was fully used and where no questions of national security were posed, shipowning would be undertaken only by those countries most fitted by their cost structures and efficiency to operate ships. Details of the types of subsidy are these:

(a) Building subsidies may be a percentage of the total building cost or a fixed sum of the ship construction cost. It is usually applied on certain conditions, particularly as a means of sustaining the shipyard industry in the maritime country rather than allow the vessel to be built in a foreign yard at perhaps a lower cost and to a quicker timescale. This is relevant to state-owned fleets and can be seen as part of the nation's economy and as an aid to trade development.

In non-state-owned fleets, building subsidies are available in similar terms or with no constraints so that a subsidy may be given to a vessel built in a foreign yard. It must be recognized that not all maritime nations, particularly third world countries, have their own shipyards, although this may become less common as their industrialization develops. Few shipowners have the funds to provide new tonnage and rarely can find more than one-third from the shipping company's own financial resources, the rest being provided from government and/or financial institutions.

(b) Shipyard subsidies tend to arise in a period of depression in the international shipbuilding industry. Governments may subsidize the shipyard for new construction and for repair work irrespective of whether the vessels are of foreign registration or of the particular maritime nation involved.

(c) A further subsidy is to offer interest-free or low interest loans to the shipowners for new tonnage. This may be subject to various conditions, such as the ship's being built in the maritime country shipyard. Furthermore, it may be sponsored under a 'scrap and build' policy whereby, for example, three vessels in excess of 15 years old are scrapped and two new ones provided in their place. A similar condition could arise in subsidies for building.

(d) An operating subsidy arises when the shipping company is either granted a specified sum to make good the loss incurred each year or an operating grant. The latter is usually provided annually over a specified period.

(e) A subvention arises when a shipping company provides a service essential to the economic and social well-being of a community.

(f) Subsidies also arise in the form of fleet insurance funded by the state, as can be found with some former Eastern bloc tonnage. It also extends to crew subsidization, such as state-financed social security/insurance contributions.

Features of subsidies and their policies are these:

1   Subsidy enables the maritime government to save hard currency. If the cargo is conveyed in a foreign registered ship it would involve a hard

currency out-payment. Likewise, the subsidized shipping company carries cargo for other countries and may operate in a cross-trade operation. This earns invisible exports for the maritime country.

2   Subsidy inflates the world shipping fleet capacity beyond the level trade can support. In some trades it destroys the commercial freedom of the seas. This is apparent when two competing companies seek the same traffic flow, one of which is subsidized and the other is not. The former can usually undercut the latter in the knowledge that if he incurs a loss on the traffic, the government will still subsidize the service.

3   Subsidy encourages uneconomic ship operation because there is no incentive in some conditions to reduce costs in the knowledge the state will make good the loss and the service will not be withdrawn.

4   Subsidy intensifies the notion of nationalism, fleets being built up for commercial reasons and for prestige and strategic considerations. It saves hard currency and encourages flag discrimination in many countries.

5   Subsidy interferes in financial evaluation when assessing the economics of a shipping service. For example, if a service is losing some £4 million annually and its invisible export contribution is £5 million, the state could decide that retention of the service is justified. Moreover, if the service were closed and it would cost some £6 million annually in hard currency for foreign carriers to convey such cargo for the maritime country, it would be justified to retain the service and subsidize it.

6   Countries having high wage scales find it increasingly difficult to compete with fleets with low wage scales relative to crew cost. Attempts have been made by industrial maritime nations to reduce their crew complement, with some measure of success. These nations, to sustain their relatively high cost fleet, often provide some form of subsidy and foster flag discrimination.

7   Subsidy does not usually encourage efficiency, for in some cases there is no incentive to keep ship operating costs to a low level safe in the knowledge that the state will fund it.

The practice of operating subsidized fleets is increasing, particularly in developing countries anxious to save hard currency by conveying their own trade. Credit remains crucial in any shipbuilding project negotiation. Banks now offer loans for new tonnage over a longer period. Governments in many countries are endeavouring to sustain their national shipyards by offering generous credit facilities. In many countries this involves substantial subsidies to national and to foreign buyers. Linking national shipyards and shipping companies is support for the former which is passed on to the latter. Government support effectively reduces the cost of capital to shipping companies and takes many forms, some examples being these:

(a)   Direct investment grants to shipping companies for new and/or second-hand ships. These are available in Korea and Taiwan. Grants to shipyards may assist shipowners.

(b) Soft loans, with low interest rates, or moratoria financed by governments. Within the EU, finance terms more favourable than OECD terms count against the limit of aid to shipbuilding set under the EU Sixth Directive on shipbuilding.

(c) The tax position of shipping companies when the government provides for accelerated depreciation allowances, low or zero corporation tax, and availability of tax-free reserves. The actual value of depreciation allowances and tax-free reserves depend on the rate of corporation tax – the higher the tax rate the greater the benefit to the company. These benefits exist in some form in many EU and Nordic nations, in Japan and in other countries.

(d) The favourable tax treatment of individuals and partnerships investing in shipping.

These are the points raised at the 1990 meeting of the OECD Maritime Transport Committee, consisting of eight countries. The Committee concluded it would not be practical or acceptable to phase out subsidies to shipping. The OECD cited these reasons for continuing with subsidies:

(a) to ensure the maintenance of a national flag or nationally owned fleet for security or strategic purposes;

(b) to maintain employment of national seafarers in order to secure maritime know-how and a pool of personnel in case of need;

(c) to maintain a relatively free shipping market and preserve the freedom of shippers' choice;

(d) to make available shipping services to remote communities in the country's territory which are otherwise not commercially viable;

(e) to assist their operators in competing with other fleets who are in a favourable economic position due to non-commercial advantages granted by another state or to particular characteristics of their national economics;

(f) to increase the contribution of shipping to the balance of payments;

(g) to modernize their fleets, make them more competitive or to ease structural adjustment.

It is likely that the degree of fleet subsidies and protection will increase in the decades to come, especially among nations developing their national fleet.

22.4 Contribution of shipping to invisible exports

As an invisible export shipping revenue can contribute substantially to the balance of payments of major shipowning countries. The contribution may arise in these two ways:

(a) A large volume of the country's trade may be carried in its own ships, so that foreign exchange is not required to pay freight on imports. Conversely, foreign exchange is earned where freight on exports carried in the country's ships is paid by the importing country.

(b) Where a country's ships carry passengers and freight between other countries, substantial amounts of foreign exchange may be earned.

APPENDIX
Shipping terms and abbreviations

Act of God   An act that could not have been prevented by any amount of human care and forethought.

ADR   European agreement on the international carriage of dangerous goods by road.

Affreightment   A contract for the carriage of goods by sea for shipment expressed in charter party or bill of lading.

Agent   One who represents a principal, or buys or sells for another.

ANF   Arrival notification form – advice to consignee of goods coming forward.

APT   Afterpeak tank.

Arbitration   Method of settling disputes which is usually binding on the parties concerned.

BAF   Bunker adjustment factor. Freight adjustment factor to reflect current cost of bunkers.

Balance of trade   Financial statement of balance of a country's visible trade exports and imports.

bdi   Both days included.

BIFA   British International Freight Association.

Bilateralism   Trade between two countries.

BK   Bar keel.

Bond   Guarantee to customs of specified amount of duty to be paid.

Box   Colloquial name for a container.

Break-bulk cargo   Goods shipped loose in the vessel's hold and not in a container.

Breaking bulk   Commencing discharge.

Bulk unitization   Means to consolidate multiple packages or items into a single-load device.

BV   Bureau Veritas – French ship classification society.

CABAF   Currency and bunker adjustment factor – a combination of CAF and BAF.

CAD   Cash against documents.

CAF   Currency adjustment factor – freight adjustment factor to reflect currency exchange fluctuations.

Cargo manifest   Inventory of cargo shipped.

CB   Container base.

CCC   Customs clearance certificate.

C&D   Collected and delivered.

CFS   Container freight station. Place for packing and unpacking LCL consignments.

CHIEF   Customs Handling of Import and Export Freight.

CIF   Cost, insurance and freight.

Closing date   Latest date cargo accepted for shipment by (liner) shipowner for specified sailing.

CMI   Comité Maritime International – an international committee of maritime lawyers.

C/N   Consignment note.

C/O   Certificate of origin or cash with order.

COD   Cash on delivery.

Collector's office   Customs accommodation where declaration(s) (entries) are scrutinized and amounts payable collected.

Consignee   Name of agent, company or person receiving consignment.

Consignor   Name of agent, company or person sending consignment (the shipper).

COP   Custom of port.

COT   Customer's own transport. Customer collects from/delivers to CFS/CY (container yard) or other specified point.

C/P   Charter party.

cpd   Charterers pay dues.

CPT   Carriage paid to. A combined transport Incoterm.

CSC   Container Safety Convention.

CTD   Combined transport document.

CTL   Constructive total loss.

CWE   Cleared without examination. Cleared customs without inspection.

D/A   Deposit account.

DAF   Delivery at frontier. An Incoterm applicable to all modes of transport.

DDO   Despatch money payable discharging only.

DDU   Delivered duty unpaid. An Incoterm applicable to all modes of transport.

Demurrage   Charge raised for detaining cargo/FCL container/trailer/ship for longer period than prescribed.

DES   Delivered ex-ship. A conventional port-to-port Incoterm of sale.

Despatch   Money paid by shipowner to charterer for earlier loading or discharging of cargo as scheduled in charter party.

DGN   Dangerous goods note.

DLO   Despatch money payable loading only.

D1/2D   Despatch money payable at half demurrage rate.

D/O   Delivery order.

D/P   Documents against payment.

Dunnage   Wood, mats, etc. used to facilitate stowage of cargo.

Dutiable cargo   Cargo which attracts some form of duty, that is Customs and Excise or VAT.

ECSI   Export cargo shipping instruction – shipping instructions from shipper to carrier.

EDI   Electronic data interchange. The transfer of structured data from one computer system to another.

Embarkation   Process of passengers joining a ship.

ETA   Estimated time of arrival.

ETD   Estimated time of departure.

Exchange rate   Price of one currency in terms of another.

Export licence   Government-issued document authorizing export of restricted goods.

Faa   Free of all average.

FAS   Free alongside ship. A conventional/port-to-port only Incoterm of sale.

FCA   Free carrier (named places). Combined transport Incoterm.

FCL   Full container load.

Feeder vessel   A short sea vessel used to fetch and carry goods and containers to and from deep-sea vessels operating on basis of hub and spoke concept.

FFI   For further instructions.

FIO   Free in and out. Cargo is loaded and discharged at no cost to the shipowner.

Fixture   Conclusion of shipbroker's negotiations to charter a ship.

FO   Free overside.

Forwarder's bill of lading   A bill of lading issued by a freight forwarder.

Forwarder's receipt   A document issued by a freight forwarder which provides evidence of receipt of the goods.

FOW   First open water.

Freight   Amount payable for the carriage of goods or a description of the goods conveyed.

Freight ton   Tonnage on which freight is charged.

Fwd   Forward.

Heterogeneous cargo   Variety of cargoes.

High stowage factor   Cargo which has a high bulk to low weight relationship, e.g. hay.

IATA   International Air Transport Association.

ICD   Inland clearance depot.

IMO   International Maritime Organization.

Indemnity   Compensation for loss/damage or injury.

Inland clearance depot   Customs cargo clearance depot.

IT   Information technology.

Laydays   Period allotted in charter party for loading/discharging cargo.

L/C   Letter of credit – document in which the terms of a documentary credit transaction is set out.

LL   Load line.

LMC   Lloyd's machinery certification.

LNG   Liquefied natural gas (type of vessel).

Loading broker   Person who acts on behalf of liner company at a port.

LPG   Liquid petroleum gas.

Lump sum freight   Remuneration paid to shipowner for charter of a ship, or portion of it, irrespective of quantity of cargo loaded.

Manifest   List of goods/passengers on a vessel/aircraft/truck.

M'dise   Merchandise.

Measurement ton   A cubic metre.

MMO   Multi-modal operator.

MSA   Merchant Shipping Act.

MV   Motor vessel.

Negotiable bill of lading   One capable of being negotiated by transfer or endorsement.

Notify Party   Party to whom arrival notification form is sent.

NVOC   Non-vessel-owning/operating carrier.

OBO   Oil bulk ore carriers – multi-purpose bulk carriers.

OEC   Overpaid entry certificate.

O/H   Overheight. A container or trailer with goods protruding above the unit profile.

OSD   Open shelter deck.

Overvalued currency   Currency whose rate of exchange is persistently below the parity rate.

PC   Passenger certificate.

Per pro   On behalf of.

P/L   Partial loss.

Pre-entered   Process of lodging with customs appropriate documentation for scrutiny prior to cargo customs clearance and shipment.

PTL   Partial total loss.

Receiving date   Date from which cargo is accepted for shipment for specified sailing.

Reefer   Refrigerated.

Removal note   Confirms goods clear of customs.

Ro/ro   Roll on/roll off – a vehicular ferry service.

SAD   Single administrative document.

SHInc   Sundays and holidays included.

Shipper   The person tendering the goods for carriage.

Shut out   Cargo refused shipment because it arrived after closing date.

Slot   Space on board a vessel occupied by a container or sailing schedule allocation.

SSN   Standard Shipping Note.

Stuffing/stripping   The action of packing/unpacking a container.

TC   Time charter.

TEU   Twenty ft equivalent unit – container measurement, i.e. 1 × 40 ft = 2 TEU; 1 × 20 ft = 1 TEU.

T/L   Total loss.
TLO   Total loss only.
ULCC   Ultra-large crude carrier.
ULD   Unit load device.
UN   United Nations.
UNCTAD   United Nations Conference on Trade and Development.
Undervalued currency   Currency whose rate of exchange is persistently
    above the parity.
Unit loads   Containerized or palletized traffic.
VLCC   Very large crude carrier.
WTO   World Trade Organization.
WWDSHEX   Weather working days Sundays and holidays excepted. A
    charter party term.

Readers are also urged to study the *Dictionary of Shipping International
Business Trade Terms and Abbreviations* (5th edn 2005, with 18,000 entries)
by Alan Branch, published by Witherbys (www.witherbys.com).

Recommended reading

Alan Branch (2009), *Global Supply Chain Management and International Logistics*, Routledge, Abingdon.

Alan Branch (1998), *Shipping and Air Freight Documentation for Importers and Exporters and Associate Terms* (2nd edition), Witherby, Livingston.

BIMCO annual review, BIMCO Informatique A/S.

BIMCO publications, BIMCO Informatique A/S, Denmark, https://www.bimco.org.

IMO newsletters, International Maritime Organization, London.

International Chamber of Commerce publications, Paris, http://store.iccwbo.org/.

Suez Canal Authority annual report, http://www.suezcanal.gov.eg/.

UNCTAD annual maritime transport review, United Nations Conference on Trade and Development, Trade Logistics Branch, Division on Technology and Logistics, Geneva.

WTO annual international trade statistics, http://onlinebookshop.wto.org/shop/article_details.asp?Id_Article=814&lang=EN.

Index

Page references to Figures or Tables will be in *italics*.

ores, cargo 249
Organization for Economic Co-operation and Development (OECD) 170–1
Organization for Petroleum Exporting Countries (OPEC) 171–2
OSD (open shelter deck) 478
outsourcing 447
Outward Processing Relief 106
overpaid entry certificate (OEC) 478
overvalued currency 478
ownership of vessels 292

P&O Nedlloyd (PONL) 345
packing types 260–3
palletization 257
Panama Canal 32, 43, 209
Panamax tanker 62, 63, 64
paper roll tippling clamp, fork-lift trucks 254
papers, ship *see* certificates and documents
parcel tankers 63
partial loss (P/L) 478
partial total loss (PTL) 478
passenger certificate (PC) 478
passenger fares, theory 182–3
Passenger Shipping Association (PSA) 172–3
Passenger Shipping Association Retail Agents (PSARA) 172
Passenger Ship Safety Certificate 34
passenger vessels 13, 73; special trade, certificates carried by 114–15
payload function 25
PC (passenger certificate) 478
PCC (Processing under Customs Control) 106
PCTC (Pure Car and Truck Carrier) 78
Permit to Operate High-Speed Craft Certificate 119
per pro (on behalf of) 478
personnel director 282
PFSP (Port Facility Security Plans) 214, 215
P/L (partial loss) 478
planned maintenance system 39–40
platform flats 357
platform supply vessels 74, 76

political aspects 463–74; flag discrimination 463–4; flags of convenience 464–70; subsidies 470–3
pollution: Conventions 150; noxious liquid chemical substances, ships carrying 117–18; oil *see* oil pollution documentation; prevention 147–8
Port Facility Security Plans (PFSP) 214, 215
Port of Singapore (PSA) 379–80, 391, 392
ports 377–90; automation 384; Chinese dominance in international trade, growth 384; correlation between 20 leading terminals and service operators 382, *383*, 384; custom of port (COP) 476; discharging 313; floating terminals 27, 384–5; International Ship and Port Facility Security Code (ISPS Code) 32, 93, 94–5, 213–17; loading 312–13; Port of Rotterdam Authority, Netherlands 123, 125, 392–4; Port State Control 26, 213–17, 392; privatization 377, 381; role 377–81; security 213–17; shipowners' choice, factors influencing 388–90; and ships 390–2; turn-around times 349
Port State Authority 392
power jacks 258
pre-entered process 478
PREMARPOL tankers 59
pre-shipment declaration, standard 104
Prestige, sinking of (2002) 59
Pride of Kent (P&O passenger ferry ship) *74*, 203
Procedures and Arrangements Manual (P&A) 117
Processing under Customs Control (PCC) 106
product carriers 45, 63
product/chemical carriers 76, 78
prohibitions and restrictions, export controls 102
project forwarding 300
propeller shaft 11
propulsion types, future trends 20–2
pro-rata freight 197
protest, ship's 120–1